TABLE OF CONTENTS

VISUAL QUICKSTART GUIDE

DREAMWEAVER 4

FOR WINDOWS AND MACINTOSH

J. Tarin Towers

Peachpit Press

Visual QuickStart Guide
Dreamweaver 4 for Windows and Macintosh
J. Tarin Towers

Peachpit Press

1249 Eighth Street
Berkeley, CA 94710
510/524-2178
800/283-9444
510/524-2221 (fax)
Find us on the World Wide Web at: http://www.peachpit.com

Published by Peachpit Press in association with Macromedia Press
Peachpit Press is a division of Addison Wesley Longman

Editors: Cary Norsworthy, Rebecca Gulick, Becky Morgan
Production Coordinators: Lisa Brazieal, Kate Reber
Copyeditor: Dave Awl
Compositor: Christi Payne, Book Arts
Indexer: Karin Arrigoni, Write Away
Cover Design: The Visual Group

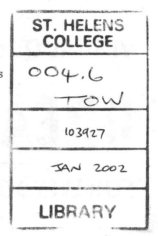
Notice of rights

Notice of liability

Trademarks

ISBN 0-201-73430-3

9 8 7 6 5 4 3 2 1

♻ Printed on recycled paper
Printed and bound in the United States of America

Acknowledgements

I'd like to thank everyone who helped me with this book: Cary Norsworthy, my editor and reluctant dictator, for attempting to keep me and the book in line; Becky Morgan and Rebecca Gulick, for tending to each chapter like the ornery child it was; Dave Awl, for being a magnificent copyeditor and ocelot tender; Sasha Magee, who contributed to Chapters 16 and 19; Paul LaFarge, who contributed to Chapters 14 and 15; Marjorie Baer and Nancy Ruenzel for their diligence and patience; Lisa Brazieal, Christi Payne, and Kate Reber, for gluing the electrons onto the pages and producing the excellent relative linking art; David Van Ness, for the initial 1.2 design; Wendy Sharp, Peachpit's Macromedia Press contact; Eric Ott, Scott Unterberg, and Alisse Berger at Macromedia, for helping me get the stuff I needed; Julie Hallstrom, Macromedia's eagle-eyed tech reviewer; Christian Cosas, Amy Franceschini, Derek Powazek, Jamie Zawinski, Dave Eggers, Zhenia Timmerman, Bitch Magazine, and ye olde Cocktail designers, for lending me their art; the good folks behind the scenes at Macromedia, for writing an even better product; and many, many faithful readers who sent in comments, suggestions, compliments, questions, and encouragement.

I'd also like to thank my family, for putting up with galley reviews in their basement again, and Katie Degentesh and Garrick Lee, for cheerleading. And large, fuzzy thank-you's to Brian Matheson, Sean Porter, jwz, Scott Kildall, all my friends who are geeks, and all my friends who aren't.

Chapter 15: **Filling Out Forms** **377**

Chapter 16: **Behavior Modification** **405**

INTRODUCTION

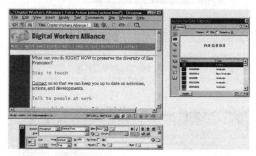

Figure 1 Here's Dreamweaver's Document window, where you edit your pages. Below it is the Property inspector, for editing all sorts of attributes, and the Assets panel, for tracking and reusing objects.

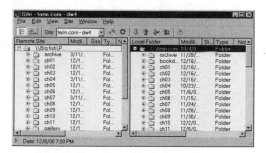

Figure 2 The Site window lets you manage your files locally and on your Web site.

Welcome to the Dreamweaver 4 for Windows and Macintosh: Visual QuickStart Guide! Dreamweaver (**Figures 1** and **2**) is exciting software: it's simple to use and it's one of the very best WYSIWYG (What You See Is What You Get) Web-page editing tools ever to come down the pike.

Dreamweaver isn't just another visual HTML tool. It does do what all the best editors do: creates tables, edits frames, and switches easily from page view to HTML view.

But Dreamweaver goes way beyond the other editors to allow you to create Dynamic HTML (DHTML) gadgets and pages. Dreamweaver fully supports Cascading Style Sheets (CSS), as well as layers and JavaScript behaviors. It even includes its own DHTML animation tool: Timelines. And a full-fledged FTP client, complete with visual site maps, is built right in.

What's New?

Dreamweaver 4 introduces several new features that simplify page production and site management.

If you've used this book for past versions of Dreamweaver, you'll notice things have moved around a bit. This book includes one new chapter. *Workflow & Collaboration,* Chapter 21, discusses the improved features in design notes and file check-in, as well as how to integrate the Site window with some common content management systems. Dreamweaver's other new features include the following:

New toolbar (Chapter 1): Right on the Document window (**Figure 3**), you now have shortcuts for managing files, previewing your pages, and debugging code. This is part of Dreamweaver's new look—Macromedia has standardized many panels and shortcuts across its different software programs, which include Fireworks and Flash.

The Assets panel (Chapter 2): tracks all the images (**Figure 4**), movies, colors, and links from one central location, regardless of which folder they're in on your local site. The Assets panel is also the new management tool in templates and libraries, detailed in Chapter 18.

O'Reilly Code Reference (Chapter 4): If you're interested in learning HTML, you can now look up tags in a special reference panel.

Figure 3 The new toolbar on the Document window includes handy shortcut menus.

Figure 4 The new Assets panel helps you keep track of objects, colors, and URLs, as well as templates and library items.

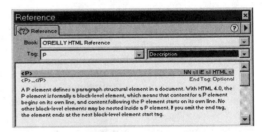

Figure 5 The O'Reilly Code Reference offers help for those learning to code.

WHAT'S NEW?

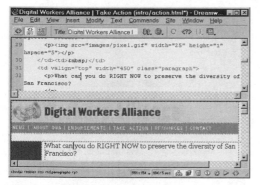

Figure 6 You can now view both design and code in the Document window in Split view.

Figure 7 Using this simple new dialog box, you can create Flash objects without leaving Dreamweaver.

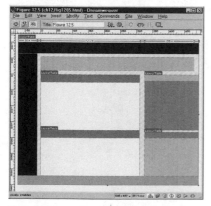

Figure 8 Draw your tables on the page in the new Layout Mode.

Improved Text and Code Editing (Chapter 4, and throughout the book): You can now see your code in the Code inspector, you can switch to Code view in the Document window, or you can view both at once with Split view (**Figure 6**). Also new, you can edit XML, JSP, CSS and other files in Dreamweaver. The Code inspector also features live syntax coloring, so that your code colors itself while you type it.

Flash Buttons and Flash Text (Chapter 7): Flash can be hard to learn, but now you can create simple Flash rollovers either in button form or as simple Flash text objects, all without leaving Dreamweaver (**Figure 7**).

Improved Style Sheet Management (Chapter 11): Style sheets have always been pretty easy to create in Dreamweaver—but it hasn't always been easy to save your styles into external style sheets, or to keep track of where your styles are while you're working on a page. Dreamweaver now makes it easy to create an external style sheet from the get-go and apply it to other pages in a snap.

Table Layout Mode (Chapter 12): Dreamweaver now lets you *draw* layouts using tables and table cells (**Figure 8**). You draw boxes to hold content on your page, and then it fills in an entire page layout based on your design. You can also set autostretch columns, so that your design always fits 100 percent of the browser window. It now inserts spacer gifs, if you like.

WHAT'S NEW?

JavaScript Debugger (Chapter 16): If you're working on design and scripts at the same time, you can debug your work right from the Document window using a standard debugger that includes breakpoints and code navigation.

Improved Templates (Chapter 18): Templates and template pages are now easier to create and navigate. The highlighting for editable regions is much easier to understand.

Keyboard Shortcut Manager (Chapter 19): You no longer even have to open a file, nor do you have to guess which shortcuts are free, in order to edit them. Using a simple dialog box, you can save several different sets of shortcuts (**Figure 9**).

Improved Design Notes (Chapter 21): Boy, have design notes grown up since Dreamweaver 3! Now, they're not only easier to find and open, you can track them by creating file view columns for different attributes in the Site window (**Figure 10**). You can also find all design notes that contain specific information by running a site report.

Content Management Integration (Chapter 21): If your site uses WebDav or Visual Source Safe to manage files, you can hitch up the Sites window to either system.

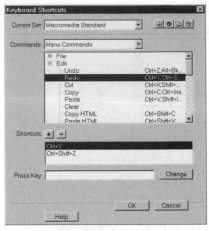

Figure 9 Change keyboard shortcuts without even opening a text file.

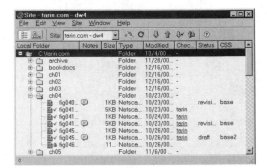

Figure 10 You can track design notes using their new icons, as well as by creating your own columns in the Site window, like the Status and CSS columns pictured here.

QuickStart Conventions

If you've read any other Visual QuickStart Guide, you know that this book is made up of two main components: numbered lists that take you step by step through the things you want learn, and illustrations that show you what the heck I'm talking about.

I explain what needs to be explained, but I don't pontificate about the acceleration of information technology or wax dramatic about proprietary tags.

✔ Tips

- In every chapter, you'll find tips like these that point out something extra handy.

- Code in the book is set off in code font.

- Sometimes you can find extra tidbits of info in the figure captions, too.

Who Should Use This Book?

No matter what your level of Web experience, you can use Dreamweaver and this book. I'm assuming you've used some sort of page-creation tool before, even if it's just a text editor. You should use this book if you're:

- An absolute beginner who wants an editor that writes great HTML.

- A graphic designer who's used to using document editors like Director, PageMaker, or Photoshop, but who isn't as proficient with HTML.

- An HTML expert who likes to hand code but wants automation of simple tasks.

- Frightened of Dynamic HTML.

- Someone who needs to learn Dreamweaver quickly.

QUICKSTART CONVENTIONS

What's in this Book

Here's a quick rundown of what I cover in this book.

Getting Started

In the first four chapters I introduce you to the Dreamweaver interface, setting up local file management, creating a basic page, and learning HTML. If you never want to look at any HTML when you use Dreamweaver, you don't have to; on the other hand, if you want to learn HTML, there's no better way than by creating a page and looking at the code you just made. Chapter 2 walks you through setting up a local site, which is the first thing you should do so that all of Dreamweaver's site management, linking, and updating tools will work for you. Chapter 3 includes a walk-through of how to set up a basic page. Chapter 4 discusses Dreamweaver's code editing tools.

Links and Media

It's simple to insert images, sound files, Flash, and other media using Dreamweaver. Basically, all media on Web pages is inserted using links, and you'll find out about those in here, too. Chapter 6 describes linking in more detail than you thought possible. Chapter 5 includes everything you need to know about inserting images, and Appendix A, on the Web site for this book, describes how to make client-side image maps with the image map editor. Chapter 7 includes multimedia basics, including Flash, rollovers, and navigation bars.

Text and Typography

Chapters 8 through 11 talk about text and all the things you can do with it. Text is the meat of most pages, and we'll go into detail about how to format it, how paragraphs and block formatting work, and how to make useful things like lists and headlines. Chapter 10 discusses how to create reusable HTML styles to speed up text formatting. Chapter 11 covers Cascading Style Sheets, which also allow you to reuse your formatting—but CSS formatting is infinitely updateable, across any number of pages.

Browser Wars

FYI, this is a sidebar. You'll often find advanced, technical, or interesting additions to the how-to lists in sidebars like these throughout the book.

Netscape Navigator and Microsoft Internet Explorer (IE) have a few display differences that may affect your pages subtly. The best way to design for both browsers is to test your pages on both browsers and to compromise where you see differences. Fonts may appear slightly larger in IE (as pictured in Chapter 11). Margins may appear off in IE (or off in Netscape, if you prefer Explorer's way). Table and layer placement are mostly the same, but they're based on slightly different browser margins, so you need to check your work. And there are some differences in how style sheets are processed, the most common of which are covered in Chapter 11.

Netscape released Netscape 6 while I was writing this book. It differs in a few places from Netscape 4.x—mostly by supporting former Internet Explorer-only features. Just as Explorer supported more and more Netscape-only features in each subsequent release, Netscape is picking up some W3C specifications that formerly only Explorer supported. These newly supported attributes appear mainly in style sheets (Chapter 11), layers (Chapter 14), and behaviors (Chapter 16), and I mention, where relevant, what Netscape 4.x doesn't support and what Netscape 6 does.

Netscape 6 isn't as stable as it could be in terms of displaying tables and layers. The first thing you should try when addressing strange placement problems is the Netscape Resize Fix (Commands > Add Netscape Resize Fix), which is covered in Chapter 12. Netscape 6 is a stickler for correct code, more than earlier versions of Navigator.

Appendix C on the Web site for this book goes into more detail about browser compatibility issues, including designing for older and text-only browsers.

Page Layout

Chapters 12 through 14 are what most folks consider the "intermediate" range in HTML. Chapter 12 is tables, 13 is frames, and 14 is layers. Chapter 12 discusses both the standard and layout views for creating tables. Chapter 13 makes it easy to use a complex layout with frames. And Chapter 14 introduces layers, which are part of dynamic HTML. All these layout tools are much easier to construct in Dreamweaver than by hand-coding.

Interactivity

The Web is about interaction, from simple guestbooks to complicated user interfaces that change the page based on preferences. Chapter 15 introduces forms, the basic way to collect user input on everything from shopping sites to online quizzes. Chapter 16 covers behaviors, a Chinese food menu way of putting together JavaScript actions—choose one from column A and one from column B. Chapter 17 discusses Timelines, Dreamweaver's DHTML animation tool.

Exploiting Dreamweaver

Dreamweaver comes out of the box ready to go and easy to use, but you can add your own reusable widgets and modify the existing interface without doing any sort of programming. Chapter 18 discusses three ways of automating common tasks in Dreamweaver: libraries, templates, and history. Libraries let you reuse common page elements across an entire site. You can also create versatile templates with read-only design features, and you can update the design of pages based on these templates just by updating the template file. The History panel tracks all your actions while you're editing, so that you can have more control over what you can undo or redo. You can even save or record common, useful actions as commands so that you can reuse them from the Commands menu.

But Wait, There's More on the Web Site!

The companion Web site for this book contains lots and lots of links to developers' pages, handy shareware tools, and example sites, and because the page is on the Web, you don't have to type in a bunch of URLs. You'll also find online appendixes covering the image map editor, HTML preferences, and browser compatibility.

Visit http://www.peachpit.com/vqs/dreamweaver and let me know what you think of the book and the Web site by e-mailing dreamweaver@tarin.com.

Chapter 19 is all about customizing the Dreamweaver interface. You can add objects to the Objects panel and even create your own categories on it. You can also rearrange the menus on the Document or Site window. And if you're picky about keyboard shortcuts for your common tasks, you can not only more easily manage those, you can save several different sets of keyboard commands.

Putting It Online

Chapter 20 is all about site management with Dreamweaver's Site window, a full-fledged FTP client. You can upload and download files easily. You an also track links across your entire site and have Dreamweaver fix them for you. You can use the Site Map to visually examine and add links.

Chapter 21 is about working in groups with Dreamweaver. You can use different checkout names to keep track of who's working on which file. And design notes allow you to save data about Web pages and media files, such as due dates, template versions, or file status.

HTML is HTML

Like the song, HTML remains the same, whether you construct it on a Mac or PC. Even better, Dreamweaver's Roundtrip HTML feature ensures that HTML you create outside the program will retain its formatting—although obvious errors, like unclosed tags, will be fixed.

The PC version of Dreamweaver comes with HomeSite, and the Mac version comes with BBEdit. You can set up either program to work with any HTML editor you like, however. See Appendix D, on the companion Web site for this book, to find out how to set up these editors and how Dreamweaver will treat your HTML.

Special to Mac Users

I wrote this book on a PC, but I had a Mac on the same desk. And just as with Dreamweaver 3, Dreamweaver wrote the program with a code base entirely specific to each platform. Much of the program is written in cross-platform languages like JavaScript, XML, and HTML, and the Mac version of Dreamweaver was written for the Mac, not written for Windows and ported over.

The differences between the Mac and Windows versions are negligible, as you can see in **Figures 11** and **12**.

There are some basic platform differences that will cause the screen shots to look slightly different. Windows windows (ha ha) have a menu bar affixed to each and every window; the Mac menu bar is always at the top of the screen, and it changes based on the program you choose from the Application menu (the one in the upper left of the Mac screen, next to the clock).

Windows windows close by clicking on the close box on the upper right, whereas close boxes on the Mac are on the upper left. Occasionally, buttons will have different names. For instance, in some dialog boxes, the button says Browse in Windows and Choose on the Mac. They're always close enough.

Keyboard conventions

When I refer to key commands, I put the Windows command first and the Mac command in parentheses, like this: Press Ctrl+L (Command+L)

I use this format for some other differences, too, like system fonts:

The source code uses the Courier New (Courier) font face.

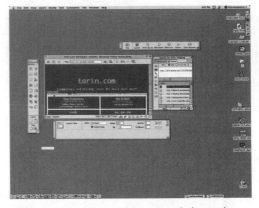

Figure 11 Dreamweaver's Document window and some of its floating windows, as seen on the Mac.

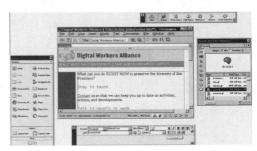

Figure 12 Dreamweaver's Document window and some of its floating windows, as seen on a PC. Not many differences other than the title bar and menu bar.

Figure 13 If you're a Windows user, right-click on an object to pop up a contextual menu. If you're a Mac user, just click on the object while holding down the Control key. The pop-up menu will appear in a second or two.

Mouse conventions

Some Mac mice have more than one button; some don't. For that matter, some folks don't really use mice at all, they have those touch-pad and stylus thingies. That said, I do refer to right-clicking a lot. On a Windows machine, when you click the right rather than the left mouse button, a contextual pop-up menu appears (**Figure 13**).

Pop-up menus, or context menus, are available on all Mac systems that can run Dreamweaver 4. To make a pop-up menu appear on a Mac system 8.x or later, Control+click on the object. Options available from pop-up menus are always available as menu bar options, too, so you'll never miss functionality in Dreamweaver even if you don't right-click.

And now... on to the book!

GETTING STARTED

Objects panel   Launcher   Document
                                     window

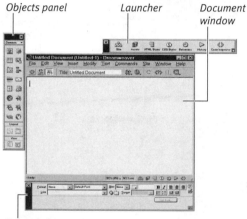

Property inspector

Figure 1.1 Here's the Dreamweaver work environment, complete with the floating windows you'll see on startup.

When you start Dreamweaver for the first time, you'll see a main window, called the Document window, and several floating panels (**Figure 1.1**).

You'll use the Document window and its trusty fleet of panels for everything from typography to animation. Dreamweaver can make your work life easier, no matter whether you're creating a simple home page or a large and complex site. If you've used Dreamweaver before, the first difference you'll notice is the new toolbar, which gives you quick options for twiddling with your code and managing your files.

The main components of Dreamweaver that I'll introduce in this chapter are the Launcher, the Site window, the Document window, the HTML Code inspector, the Objects panel, and the Property inspector.

Dreamweaver Tools

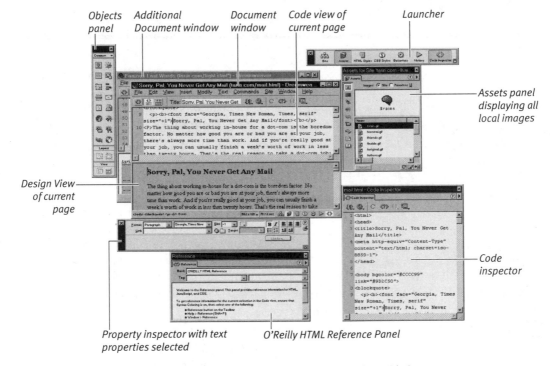

Objects panel   Additional Document window   Document window   Code view of current page   Launcher

Assets panel displaying all local images

Design View of current page

Code inspector

Property inspector with text properties selected   O'Reilly HTML Reference Panel

Figure 1.2 Here's the Dreamweaver environment, complete with the two new tools in Dreamweaver 4: The Assets panel and the Code Reference Panel.

Figure 1.3 You can open any of Dreamweaver's windows, panels, and inspectors from the Document window's Window menu.

The Dreamweaver Environment

Oddly, all those windows that are available from the Window menu aren't necessarily called windows (**Figure 1.3**). These are the panels and inspectors that make up Dreamweaver. Some of them are so useful you'll have them open all the time; others are specialized, and you can put them away when you're not using them.

A *window* is a stand-alone screen element that will show up on the Windows status bar (the Mac doesn't display windows separately in the Applications menu). The Document window is one example of a window. Another example is the Site window (**Figure 1.4**), which we'll explore in Chapter 2 when we set up a local site.

You can have multiple Document windows open; the filename for each will appear at the bottom of the Window menu (**Figure 1.5**).

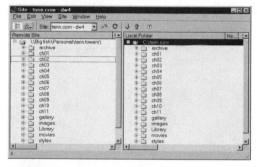

Figure 1.4 The Site window allows you to manage local and remote Web sites, including HTML pages and media objects.

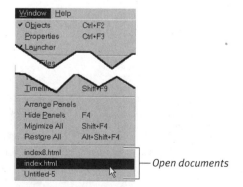

— *Open documents*

Figure 1.5 When you're working with multiple documents, each will appear in its own Document window. Each of these will be accessible from the Window menu.

Panels and inspectors

The miniature, floating windows that you use to edit various elements of your Web pages are called either *inspectors* or *panels*. These are similar to the tools you may have used in other multimedia creation programs, such as Photoshop, Fireworks, PageMaker, or Flash. You can control your workspace by moving any of these floating panels, or by closing them to get rid of them altogether.

✔ Tips

- To view or hide any window, panel, or inspector, select its name from the Window menu.

- Keyboard shortcuts for each panel are listed in the Window menu.

- Read the sidebar *Stacking Panels,* later in this chapter, to find out how to save screen space.

Panels vs. Inspectors

In general, an *inspector* changes its appearance and options based on the current selection, whereas a *panel* controls elements, such as styles or library items, that are available to the entire current site. Not that it's a huge distinction, but you may wonder why a window is called one thing or the other.

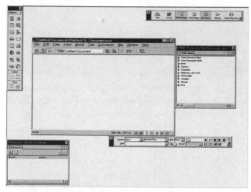

Figure 1.6 Dreamweaver remembers panel positions; if this is where your panels are when you exit the program, this is where they'll be when you open Dreamweaver again the next time.

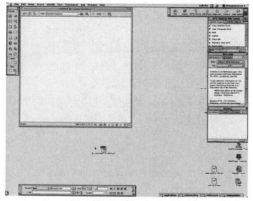

Figure 1.7 To have Dreamweaver clean up your workspace, select Arrange Panels from the Window menu bar.

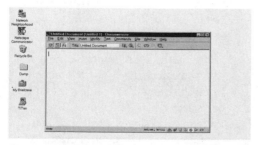

Figure 1.8 To hide all panels for an uncluttered view of your workspace, press F4. Because Dreamweaver remembers where everything was (and which panels were open), you can press F4 again to bring it all back.

Arranging Your Workspace

Dreamweaver's floating windows are contextual—for example, you don't need to have the Frames inspector open unless you're working with frames at the moment. You don't need to keep everything open, only the stuff you're working with.

To close any panel:

◆ Just click on the X in the upper-right corner (Windows). On a Mac, click on the close box in the upper-left corner.

✔ Tips

■ New in Dreamweaver 4, panels will snap together at the edges so you can dock a panel to the side of the Document window. Try dragging an open panel to the side of the window, and watch it snap into place.

■ Dreamweaver will remember where your panels are when you exit. When you reopen Dreamweaver, only the panels you had open will appear, and they'll be where you left them (**Figure 1.6**).

■ To move the floating panels back to their original, default positions, select Window > Arrange Panels from the Document window menu bar (**Figure 1.7**). You can also do this if you've accidentally dragged a panel off-screen.

■ To hide all floating panels, press F4, or select Window > Hide Panels from the Document window menu bar (**Figure 1.8**).

■ Windows users: You can minimize all Dreamweaver components by pressing Shift+F4, and restore them by pressing Alt+Shift+F4.

The Launcher

The Launcher (**Figure 1.9**) provides an easy, one-click way to open some auxiliary tools in Dreamweaver. Click on the Launcher button, and the window or panel will open. Click on the same button, and the window will close.

Site

The Site window (Chapters 2, 20 and 21) is the tool you use both to organize your files in a local site on your hard drive and to put those files up on your remote Web site.

HTML Styles

The HTML Styles panel (Chapter 10) lets you create text styles in plain HTML, similar to text styles in programs like Word or Quark.

CSS Styles

The CSS Styles panel helps you keep track of any custom style sheets you add to a page or site. Style sheets are explained in Chapter 11.

Behaviors

The Behaviors panel (Chapter 16) is used to set up JavaScript actions.

History

The History panel keeps track of each action that you perform in Dreamweaver. It's discussed later in this chapter, as well as in Chapter 18.

Code Inspector

Clicking on the Code Inspector button opens the Code inspector, which is discussed later in this chapter. We'll be using the Code inspector throughout this book.

Direction button

Code Inspector button is selected

Figure 1.9 Click on one of the Launcher buttons to pop open the associated window. Note how the Code Inspector button looks "pushed in."

Launcher Tips

- Click on the Direction button to change the orientation of the Launcher.

- If you close the Launcher and wish to open it again, select Window > Launcher from the Document window menu bar.

- Even when the Launcher window is closed, a mini version of the Launcher will be visible in the bottom-right corner of the Document window, as seen in Figures 1.6 and 1.8.

- When a Dreamweaver window is open, its Launcher button will look like it's "pushed in" (**Figure 1.9**).

- In the Launcher bar in the Document window status bar, any active features will be "lit up."

- If you don't want the Launcher to appear in the status bar for some reason, you can change this preference. From the Document window menu bar, select Edit > Preferences. The Preferences dialog box will appear. In the Category list box, select Status Bar. In the Status Bar panel of the dialog box, deselect the checkbox marked Show Mini-Launcher in Status Bar. You can always reselect it later.

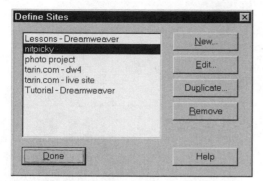

Figure 1.10 You can set up different sites for different projects.

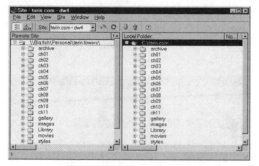

Figure 1.11 The Site window lets you work with local and remote files at the same time.

Planning Your Site

Links between pages in your Web site will work best if you set up a local site.

A Web site is just a collection of files and folders on a computer that's connected to the Internet. When these files are on your local computer, they're called a local site. When they're on a Web server, they're called a remote site. If you set up your files locally in the same way as they'll appear online—using the same folder names and keeping things in the same places—everything will be easy to track.

You can keep different projects in different local sites (**Figure 1.10**). Start out with a main folder (also called the root folder), and put other folders for that site inside it. I create specific folders for images, movies, and sound files, as well as style sheets.

You must set up a local site in order to use the Library, the Assets panel, and Templates.

The Site window

The Site window (**Figure 1.11**) is Dreamweaver's tool for tracking local and remote site files. When you start creating a site, you should go to Chapter 2, so that you can set up your local site.

The Site window also makes it easy for you to put your files up on the Web, in the remote site. Chapter 20 tells you all you need to know about getting your stuff online.

The Site map

The Site map (**Figure 1.12**) is a visual depiction of how your files are interrelated. You can see broken links and draw paths between files.

The Link Checker

The Link Checker (**Figure 1.13**) can look for broken links and can change any link in your site when you move or update a file.

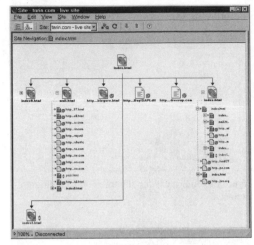

Figure 1.12 The Site Map view of your site shows you where links go in a visual format.

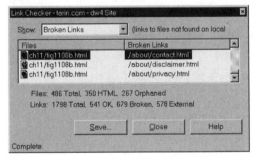

Figure 1.13 You can check all the links between files in your site with the Link Checker.

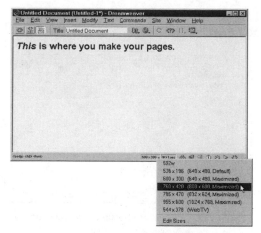

Figure 1.14 Click the arrow on the window size indicator to select a common, preset window size.

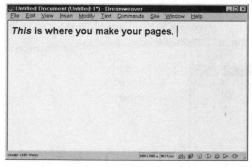

Figure 1.15 You can make the toolbar go away if you want more screen space.

The Document Window

The Document window (shown in detail on the next page in **Figure 1.17**) is the main center of activity in Dreamweaver.

At the top: The *title bar* displays the filename and the title of the current Web page. All of Dreamweaver's commands are available from the Document window *menu bar*. The new *toolbar* offers shortcut menus and different page views. (See next page.)

In the middle: The *body* of the HTML document is displayed in the main viewing area of the Document window. Because Dreamweaver is a WYSIWYG (What You See Is What You Get) HTML tool, the Document window approximates what you'll see in a Web browser window.

At the bottom: The *status bar* indicates three things about the current document:

◆ The *tag selector* displays all the HTML tags surrounding your current selection.

◆ The *window size indicator* displays the current size of the Document window so you can flip between common window sizes. The numbers will change if you resize the document window; you can select a preset window size by clicking the down arrow to display a pop-up menu (**Figure 1.14**).

◆ The *download stats area* displays the total size, in K (kilobytes), of the current page, and the amount of time it would take to download over a 28.8 Kbps modem.

The Launcher bar, also in the status bar, is described in the section called *The Launcher.*

To hide the toolbar:

◆ From the Document window menu bar, select View > Toolbar.

The toolbar disappears (**Figure 1.15**).

✔ Tip

- You can resize the Document window as you would any other window: by clicking on the lower-right corner and dragging to make the window larger or smaller. I show the Document window in many different sizes throughout this book, depending on the kind of content I'm discussing at the time. As you can see in **Figures 1.16** and **1.17**, the Mac and Windows versions of Dreamweaver are nearly identical.

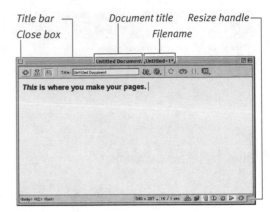

Title bar   Document title   Resize handle

Close box   Filename

Figure 1.16 Dreamweaver's Document window for the Mac.

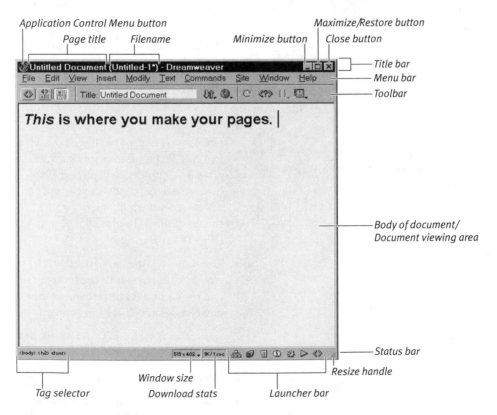

Application Control Menu button   Maximize/Restore button

Page title   Filename   Minimize button   Close button

Title bar

Menu bar

Toolbar

This is where you make your pages.

Body of document/ Document viewing area

Status bar

Resize handle

Tag selector   Window size   Download stats   Launcher bar

Figure 1.17 The Document window is where you compose your pages. This is the Windows version.

The New Toolbar

The toolbar, new in Dreamweaver 4 (**Figure 1.18**), offers quick access to common tasks.

Code view

Split view

Design view   *Page title*

File Management   *Refresh*   *Code navigation*

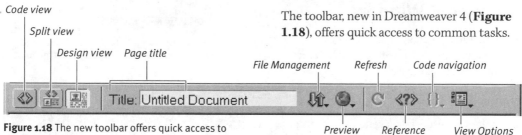

Preview   *Reference*   *View Options*

Figure 1.18 The new toolbar offers quick access to common tasks.

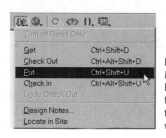

Figure 1.19 The File Management menu lets you upload files directly from the Document window.

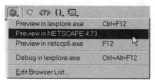

Figure 1.20 You can choose a browser quickly using the Preview menu.

Figure 1.21 The View Options menu lets you turn visual aids off and on, among other things.

Figure 1.22 In Code view or in the Code inspector, the View Options menu offers HTML options.

Switching Views The new view options allow you to look at just the WYSIWYG (or Design) view, to see Code and Design views at the same time, or to see just code without opening the Code inspector. See *Looking at Code* on page 14 and Chapter 4 for more.

Page Title Edit the title of your page without opening the Page Properties dialog box. See Chapter 3 for more on page properties.

File Management The File Management menu (**Figure 1.19**) lets you put files on the Web or get the most recent version from your remote site. See Chapter 20.

Preview Preview/Debug in the browser menu (**Figure 1.20**) offers a list of browsers in which to view your page. See Chapter 3.

Refresh The Refresh Design View button updates your page when you're working on the code in Dreamweaver or another editor.

Reference The Reference button pops open the definition of the current tag in the Reference panel. See Chapter 4.

Code Navigation The Code Navigation menu lets you set a breakpoint for debugging JavaScript. See Chapter 16.

View Options The View Options menu (**Figure 1.21**) offers toggles for turning on borders and other elements, as well as the grid and the ruler. In Code view, this menu offers HTML viewing options (**Figure 1.22**).

Measuring in the Document Window

You can add a ruler and a grid to the Document window to help you with sizing and placing elements.

Using the rulers

The rulers are especially useful for resizing tables, layers, and images.

To view the rulers:

◆ From the Document window menu bar, select View > Rulers > Show. You can also select this from the View Options menu on the toolbar (**Figure 1.23**).

The rulers will appear (**Figure 1.24**).

To change ruler units:

◆ From the Document window menu bar, select View > Rulers > and then choose Pixels, Inches, or Centimeters. The ruler measurements will change.

By default, the rulers' zero points, or starting points for measurements, start at the top left corner. You can change this, if you want, so that it's at the corner of a table or layer.

To change the zero point:

◆ Click on the zero point (**Figure 1.25**), and drag it into the window. When the point is where you want it to be, let go of the mouse button.

Now, when you look at the rulers, the measurements will reflect the new zero point. If you change your mind, you can reset the zero point to its original position (View > Rulers > Reset Origin).

Using the grid

The grid proves its usefulness when you're placing elements by dragging them on the page.

Figure 1.23 Select Rulers from the Options menu.

The zero point   *Measurements in pixels*

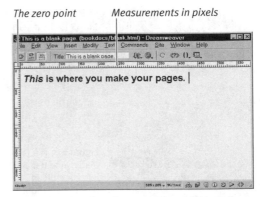

Figure 1.24 View the rulers to see how big your ideas are. Pixels are the default ruler unit.

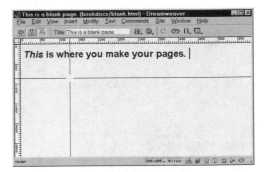

Figure 1.25 Click on the zero point and drag it to a new location to change the ruler origins.

Gridlines lined up at 50 pixels

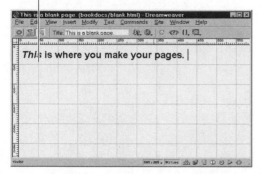

Figure 1.26 To get even more precise measurements, turn on the grid.

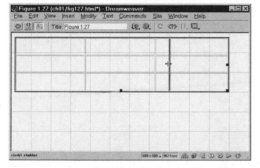

Figure 1.27 When I drag the table border, it snaps to the grid. I can change the grid increments using the Grid Settings dialog box.

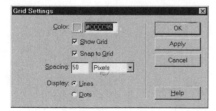

Figure 1.28 Control the grid by changing the Grid settings.

✔ Tip

■ Rulers and grids are most useful for positioning tables and layers, discussed in Chapters 12 and 14. Both elements can provide visual guidelines for sizing and laying out content.

To view the grid:

◆ From the Document window menu bar, select View > Grid > Show Grid.

The grid will appear (**Figure 1.26**). You can make draggable items snap to the grid lines. That means that when you drag a layout cell (Chapter 12) or a layer (Chapter 14), its borders will snap to the grid lines like a weak magnet.

To turn on the "snapping" option:

1. Show the grid, if you haven't.

2. From the Document window menu bar, select View > Grid > Snap To.

Now table borders and layers that you drag in the Document window will snap to the grid (**Figure 1.27**).

To change grid settings:

1. From the Document window menu bar, select View > Grid > Edit Grid. The Grid Settings dialog box will open (**Figure 1.28**).

2. To change the color of the grid lines, click on the color box, and the color picker will appear. Click on a color to choose it.

3. The Show Grid checkbox turns the grid on. The Snap to Grid option turns on snapping. You can have snapping turned on and the grid hidden at the same time.

4. To change the spacing of the grid lines, type a number in the Spacing text box, and choose a unit from the Spacing drop-down menu: Pixels, Inches, or Centimeters.

5. To display dotted rather than solid lines, click on the Dots radio button.

6. To view your changes before you return to the Document window, click on Apply.

7. To accept the changes, click on OK. The Grid Settings dialog box will close, and you'll return to the Document window.

Looking at Code

The Code inspector (formerly the HTML inspector, **Figure 1.29**) shows the HTML code for the current page. You can also view HTML code in Code view (see *The New Toolbar,* earlier in this chapter). Dreamweaver always adds the code shown in Figure 1.29 to a new page.

To open or close the Code inspector:

◆ From the Document window menu bar, select Window > Code Inspector.

or

Click on the Code Inspector button on the Launcher.

or

Press F10.

In any case, the Code inspector will appear.

Any changes that you make to the code in the Code inspector will appear in the Document window when you click in that window or close the Code inspector, and any changes that you make in the Document window will be automatically updated in the Code inspector.

✔ Tip

■ Click on the View Options menu on the toolbar to turn on Word Wrap or Line Numbers. These options are fully described in Chapter 4.

Panel tab   View Options menu button

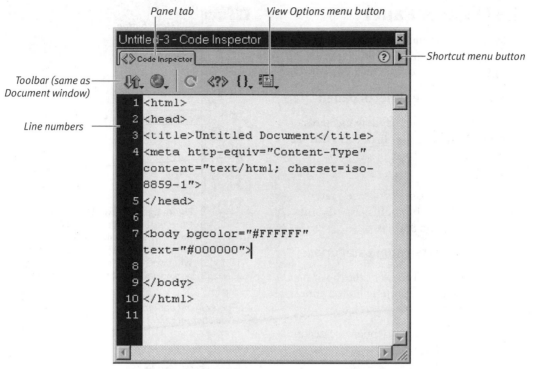

Toolbar (same as
Document window)

Line numbers

Shortcut menu button

Figure 1.29 The Code inspector allows you to view and edit code for the pages in the Document window.

LOOKING AT CODE

About HTML

Chapter 4 presents an introduction to working with HTML. Although you never, ever have to look at the code if you don't want to, you can learn a lot about HTML by working in the Document window and then checking what the code is doing in the Code inspector or the Code view.

Unlike many Web page apps, Dreamweaver doesn't use made-up tags, nor does it rewrite your painstaking code. It does offer tools to help you clean up bad code or fix common errors, and it even synchronizes with other editors.

Chapter 4 discusses these tools, as well as the Quick Tag editor, which allows you to change or insert single tags without leaving the Document window. It also describes how you can set Dreamweaver's preferences for rewriting and formatting your code.

The Objects Panel

The Objects panel (**Figure 1.30**) offers short-cut buttons for inserting common page elements.

To view or hide the Objects panel:

◆ From the Document window menu bar, select Window > Objects or press Ctrl+F2 (Command+F2). The Objects panel will appear.

The Objects panel consists of seven categories: Characters, Common, Forms, Frames, Head, Invisibles, and Special.

To change Objects panel categories:

1. Click on the menu arrow at the top of the Objects panel. A pop-up menu will appear (**Figure 1.31**).

2. From the pop-up menu, choose a category. The Objects panel will display the set you picked.

To insert an object:

1. With both the current page and the Objects panel in view, click on the icon for the object you wish to insert.

   If Dreamweaver needs more information to insert the object, a dialog box will appear.

2. Fill out the dialog box, if necessary, and then click on OK.

   The object will appear in the Document window.

To select and modify an object:

◆ You can select most objects by highlighting them or clicking on them. The Property inspector will display an object's properties once you've selected it.

   For specifics, refer to the chapter in which the type of object in question is discussed.

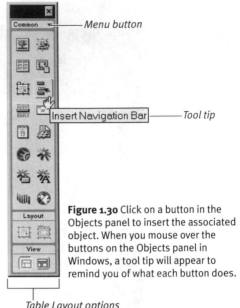

Figure 1.30 Click on a button in the Objects panel to insert the associated object. When you mouse over the buttons on the Objects panel in Windows, a tool tip will appear to remind you of what each button does.

Menu button

Tool tip

Table Layout options (see Chapter 12)

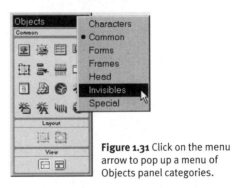

Figure 1.31 Click on the menu arrow to pop up a menu of Objects panel categories.

Figure 1.32 Objects available from the Insert menu. Submenus include Interactive Images, Media, Frames, Form Objects, Invisible Tags, Head Tags, and Special Characters.

Figure 1.33 Special Characters—helps you insert special symbols without memorizing their HTML code .

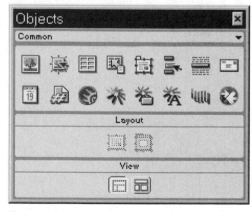

Figure 1.34 Common elements

Dreamweaver Objects

All of the objects available from the Objects panel are also accessible from the Insert menu (**Figure 1.32**). The submenus in the Objects panel are Characters, Common, Forms, Frames, Head, Invisibles, and Special.

The **Characters** category (**Figure 1.33**) includes special text symbols such as copyright marks and Euro signs (Chapter 8), as well as the line break and the nonbreaking space (Chapter 9).

Common elements (**Figure 1.34**) include (from left to right):

◆ Images (Chapter 5)

◆ Rollover Images (Chapters 5 and 16)

◆ Tables (Chapter 12)

◆ Tabular Data (Chapter 12)

◆ Layers (Chapter 14)

◆ Navigation Bars (Chapter 7)

◆ Horizontal Rules (Chapter 9)

◆ Line Breaks (Chapters 3 and 9)

◆ E-mail Links (Chapter 6)

◆ Date (Chapter 3)

◆ Server-Side Includes (Chapter 17)

◆ Fireworks HTML (Chapter 5)

◆ Flash Movies, Flash Buttons, and Flash Text (Chapter 7)

◆ Shockwave Director Elements (Chapter 7)

DREAMWEAVER OBJECTS

Form elements (Figure 1.35) appear on pages that feature interactive forms, which are discussed in Chapter 15. **Frame elements (Figure 1.36)** are actually prefab frames layouts and are described in Chapter 13. **Head elements (Figure 1.37)** are discussed on the Web site for this book.

Invisible elements (Figure 1.38) are:

◆ Named Anchors (Chapter 6)

◆ Comments (Chapter 4)

◆ Scripts (Chapter 16)

Special elements (Figure 1.39) are:

◆ Applets (Chapter 7)

◆ Plug-ins (Chapter 7)

◆ ActiveX Controls (Chapter 7)

✔ Tips

■ You can create custom objects and even add categories to the Objects panel. See Chapter 19 to find out how.

■ You can view text in addition to (**Figure 1.39**) or instead of (**Figure 1.37**) images on the Objects Panel. View the Preferences dialog box (Edit > Preferences), and click on General. From the Objects Panel drop-down menu, select the option you want, and click on OK to apply your changes.

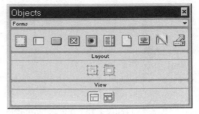

Figure 1.35 The Form elements category of the Objects panel lets you drop forms and form fields onto your pages.

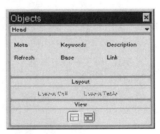

Figure 1.36 Frame elements

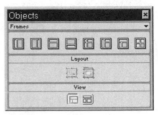

Figure 1.37 Head elements

Figure 1.38 Invisible elements

Figure 1.39 Special elements—helps you to add some types of media content

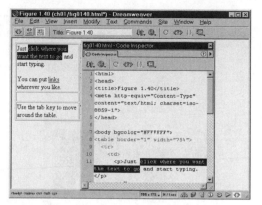

Figure 1.40 The Document window and the Code inspector offer parallel selection: highlight code in one window, and it will also be selected in the other.

Selecting Objects and Code

Selecting objects in the Document window is similar to selecting them in any other program:

◆ To select a word, double-click on it.

◆ To select a line of text, click to the left of it to highlight it, or press Shift+Arrow to select a few characters at a time.

◆ To select an image, click on it.

◆ To select a table, right-click on it (Control+ click on the Mac), and from the pop-up menu that appears, choose Table > Select Table.

When an item is selected, you can cut, copy, delete, or paste over it. You can also modify it with the Property inspector.

If you select an item in the Document window and then open the Code inspector or Code view, the item will remain selected in the Code inspector, which is really handy for finding things in particular table cells or on pages with a lot of content (**Figure 1.40**).

Similarly, if you select some code in the Code inspector and then return to the Document window, the objects you selected will appear highlighted there.

To select code:

1. To select all the code and content that appears between a particular set of tags, first click on a word or image that's formatted by the tag, in either the Code or Document window.

2. Click on the appropriate tag in the tag selector that appears in the Document window's status bar (**Figure 1.41**).

For instance, to select an entire paragraph, you can click on a word within it and then click on the <p> tag on the tag selector. This makes selecting any tags, such as links <a>, tables <table>, and the entire body of a page <body> easier.

✔ Tip

■ You can also select a line of code in the Code inspector by clicking on one of the line numbers in the left margin.

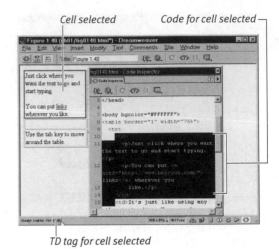

Cell selected   Code for cell selected

TD tag for cell selected

Figure 1.41 Click on one of the tags in the tag selector in the Document window's status bar to select the tag and everything it encloses. The tag I selected was <td>, a table cell.

Apply button   Expander arrow

Figure 1.42 The Property inspector changes appearance depending on what item is selected. This figure shows image properties.

Apply button   Expander arrow

Figure 1.43 Click on the expander arrow, and the Property inspector will expand to show more options. This figure shows table properties.

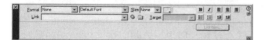

Figure 1.44 Text properties are the ones you'll see most often.

✔ Tips

- All Property inspectors except text have an Apply button (**Figures 1.42** and **1.43**). It's basically a metaphor; you can click anywhere on the Property inspector to apply your changes.

- You can also display the Property inspector by double-clicking on some objects.

The Property Inspector

You'll use the Property inspector more than any other floating window, because it lets you work with the specific attributes of almost every object you can put on your page. It displays text properties most often, and it changes appearance depending on what object you have selected.

To display the Property inspector:

1. From the Document window menu bar, select Modify > Selection Properties or Window > Properties, or press Ctrl+F3 (Command+F3). The Property inspector will appear (**Figure 1.42**).

2. To display the entire Property inspector, click on the expander arrow in the bottom-right corner of the Property inspector (**Figure 1.43**).

   If no object is selected, the Property inspector will display text properties (**Figure 1.44**).

To modify object properties:

1. Select the object you wish to modify.

2. Display the Property inspector, if it isn't already onscreen.

3. Based on your choices: Click on formatting buttons, make menu selections from the drop-down menus, type numbers or names in the text boxes, and select checkboxes or radio buttons.

4. Some of your choices will be applied immediately; to make sure properties are applied to the selection, click on the Apply button (shown in **Figures 1.42** and **1.43**).

Invisible Elements

Dreamweaver's Document window approximates what you'd see in a Web browser window; it tries to replicate the way a browser would interpret HTML.

One exception to this is invisible elements. These elements would not be visible to a Web browser, but you may have occasion to display them in order to select, edit, or move them.

To view invisible elements:

◆ From the Document window menu bar, select View > Visual Aids > Invisible Elements.

   Any invisible elements on the current page will show up in the form of little icons (**Figure 1.45**).

To change invisible element preferences:

1. From the Document window menu bar, select Edit > Preferences. The Preferences dialog box will appear.

2. In the Category box at the left of the Preferences dialog box, click on Invisible Elements. The Invisible Elements panel of the dialog box will appear (**Figure 1.46**).

3. The Invisible Elements panel of the dialog box displays all the invisible elements that will become visible when you select View > Invisible Elements.

   Each invisible element has a corresponding checkbox. Line breaks are deselected by default.

4. To deselect any element, click on its checkbox to remove the checkmark.

   To select any element without a checkmark, click on its checkbox to add one.

5. When you're finished, click on OK to close the Preferences dialog box.

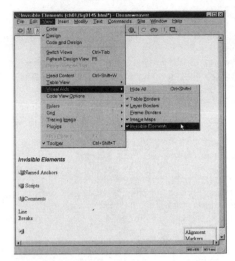

Figure 1.45 When you view invisible elements, you may see all kinds of little icons that weren't visible before.

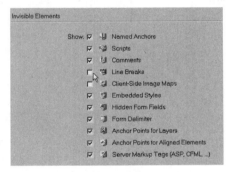

Figure 1.46 You can choose not to view certain invisible elements when you want to see some, but not all, of them. The Invisible Elements panel of the Preferences dialog box is shown in close-up so you can read it.

✔ Tips

■ Each of these invisible elements is discussed in the chapter that covers the topic to which it's related.

■ **Figure 1.46** is also a handy reference for what the symbols stand for.

■ Click on an invisible element icon to examine it with the Property inspector.

Figure 1.47 From the Edit menu, you can see what your last action was, so you can Repeat it or Undo it.

About History

Dreamweaver stores the actions that you perform in a History file, similar to how a Web browser stores the sites you visit.

Dreamweaver now supports multiple levels of Undo. For example, suppose you accidentally backspace to delete a table, and then you paste an image on the page. A single undo would un-paste the image. A second undo brings back the table.

To undo an action:

◆ Press Ctrl+Z (Command+Z)

 or

 From the Document window menu bar, select Edit > Undo [Action Name] (**Figure 1.47**).

You can also repeat your last action.

To repeat an action:

◆ Press Ctrl+Y (Command+Y)

 or

 From the Document window menu bar, select Edit > Redo [Action Name] (**Figure 1.47**).

You can also repeat any action you have performed while Dreamweaver is open.

To use the History panel:

1. From the Document window menu bar, select Window > History. The History panel will appear (**Figure 1.48**).

2. In the History panel is a list of actions you have performed. Click on an action, and then click on Replay to repeat the action.

You can also combine and even save actions. The History panel is described in more detail in Chapter 18.

Figure 1.48 The History panel contains a list of the previous actions you performed during this session of Dreamweaver (until you Quit). You can repeat any one of them by selecting it and then clicking Replay.

Drag to space here

Click and grab here

Figure 1.49 To stack panels, click on the name tab of a panel and drag it onto another. In this case, I'm dragging the HTML Styles panel onto the History panel.

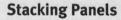

Stacking Panels

You can stack any of Dreamweaver's panels except the Property inspector on top of one another to save screen space. In **Figure 1.48,** the History panel is stacked with several other panels.

To stack a panel, click on its tab, drag on top of another panel (**Figure 1.49**), and let go. Names (or symbols, if space is tight) for the panels will appear as tabs that you can click on to change from one panel to the next.

To unstack a panel, click on its tab and drag it off the stack.

SETTING UP A LOCAL SITE

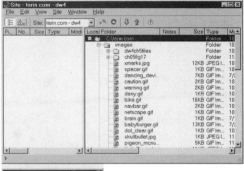

Figure 2.1 The Site window operates as a local site management and site planning tool, as well as an FTP client. This is the local site view. In Chapter 20, I'll discuss the Remote Site view and the Site Map view. The other window pictured here is the Assets panel.

What you probably want to do with this book is jump to the fun parts and start making Web pages. You can skip this chapter and make Web pages willy-nilly, but if you do, you'll miss out on some of the best time-saving tools that come with Dreamweaver.

This chapter describes how to set up Dream-weaver so that it helps you manage a set of pages as a *local site*. A local site is a collection of pages on your computer that are destined to be part of a site on the Internet. You should set up your pages locally in the same folders they'll be in on the Web.

Sometimes half the battle of creating a Web site is figuring out where all the files are. If they're scattered all over your hard drive, you need to locate them, check all the links and image locations, upload the files, and then check all the links again.

Dreamweaver's file management tools (**Figure 2.1**) don't preclude having to check your links, but they do make it easier to administer things, especially if you keep your pages and folders in the same order they'll be on your site.

The Site window and the Assets panel are the tools we'll learn about in this chapter. The Site window helps you set up your local Web site files. The Assets panel helps you keep track of images and other site resources.

About the Site Window

Dreamweaver's Site window (**Figure 2.2**) is both a file-management tool and a full-fledged FTP client that helps you put your site online.

✔ Tips

■ All the column headings are also buttons; click on any one of them to sort the directory contents by that criterion.

■ You can drag the borders between the column buttons to adjust the column width.

■ You can add, remove, and rearrange the column headings. See Chapter 21 to find out how.

Site pull-down menu

Refresh button

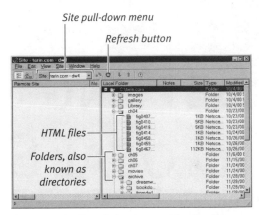

Figure 2.2 The Site window is a combination file-management tool and FTP client.

HTML files

Folders, also known as directories

What's Where

This short chapter will teach you how to set up a local site—or several. First, you'll get acquainted with the Site window. Then, you'll designate a folder on your computer as the central folder, or *site root folder*. You'll find out how to add, edit, and delete sites. And we'll look at some tips for file management in the Site window.

After that, we'll find out how to track images, colors, URLs, and movies using the Assets panel. You can create Favorites lists and nicknames for your most-used elements. Library items and Templates are discussed in Chapter 18.

Chapter 20 describes everything you need to know about link management, including checking links, from a single page to an entire site. You need to set up a local site as described in this chapter as a prerequisite for using the fancy link tools described in Chapters 6 and 20.

Chapter 20 covers preparing your site for prime time and then putting it up on the Internet. You'll learn to use the Site window as an FTP tool to download and upload files. Chapter 20 also describes site management tools such as the Site Map and the Link Checker.

Chapter 21, new to this edition, covers collaborative tools such as file check-in, Design Notes, and sharing files between sites and between users.

You'll find more tips on site management on the Web site for this book, including how to use <head> tags to your advantage.

Figure 2.3 Click on the Site button on the Launcher.

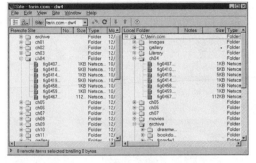

Figure 2.4 Here, I'm showing remote files in the Site window as well as local files. The remote stuff is covered in Chapter 20. First, though, you need to set up a local site to hold all your files so that you can get Dreamweaver to keep track of your links.

The Site Window

In the Site window, you designate a folder, or *directory,* on your computer or local network as a local site.

This folder becomes the *site root folder*—which means that it's the central folder that contains all the files and folders in your site.

Ideally, you set up this folder to contain all the folders and files that will appear on your Web site—in the same order. That is, if your homage to Grandma will be in the Grandma folder on the Web, it should be in the Grandma folder on your local site, too.

Dreamweaver uses the location of the site root folder to code relative links, including the paths for images. (Relative links, which are described more fully in Chapter 6, are efficient shortcuts to pages within the same Web site.)

Managing files in local and remote sites takes place in the Site window (**Figure 2.2**).

To view the Site window:

◆ From the Document window menu bar, select Window > Site Files.

   or

   Press F8.

   or

   Click on the Site button on the Launcher or Launcher bar (**Figure 2.3**).

Either way, the Site window will appear (**Figure 2.4**). When you first view the Site window, it will be empty. Before you can begin working with a local site, you must set one up on your computer.

Setting Up a Local Site

You need to designate a local site to use the site tools. You need to set this up in Dreamweaver even if you've designated this folder in your head, in another program.

You can base a local site on the contents of an existing Web site, or you can set up a local site before any version of it exists at all. Before you do either, you need to pick a root directory (a home folder) for your local site.

To designate a new local site root:

1. From the Document window menu bar, select Site > Define Sites.

   or

   From the Site window's local site drop-down menu, select Define Sites. Either way, the Define Sites dialog box will appear (**Figure 2.5**), including two sample sites. I've included my own sites here.

2. Click on New to open the Site Definition dialog box (**Figure 2.6**).

3. Click on the folder icon next to the Local Root Folder text field. The Choose Local Folder dialog box will appear (**Figures 2.7** and **2.8**).

4. You can select an existing folder or create a new one:

   ◆ To select an existing folder, click on its icon, and then click on Select (Windows) or Open (Mac) to close the Choose Local Folder dialog box and return to the Site Definition dialog box.

   ◆ To create a new folder, click on the New Folder button and type a name for the new folder. Double-click on its icon to select it and return to the Site Definition window.

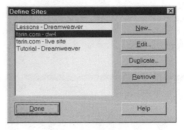

Figure 2.5 The Define Sites dialog box lets you manage multiple local and remote sites.

Figure 2.6 Set up local sites and connection information in the Site Definition dialog box.

Figure 2.7 Use the Choose Local Folder dialog box to select a folder to serve as the main directory, or site root folder, for your new local site.

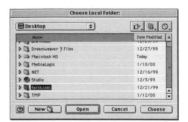

Figure 2.8 The Mac view of the Choose Local Folder dialog box. Click on Choose instead of Select.

SETTING UP A LOCAL SITE

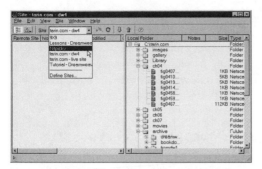

Figure 2.9 I have several different local sites set up for different projects in progress.

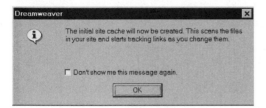

Figure 2.10 After you click on OK in the Site Definition dialog box, this dialog box (or another, similar one) will appear, confirming whether you'd like to create the cache.

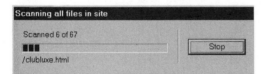

Figure 2.11 While the cache is being created, a dialog box will appear informing you of Dreamweaver's progress.

- When you create a site and click on OK in the Site Definition dialog box, a dialog box will tell you that the cache will be created (**Figure 2.10**). Creating the cache will take a few seconds (**Figure 2.11**).

- Remember that everything having to do with a remote site, including how to put your pages on the Web, is discussed in Chapter 20. Chapter 20 also describes how site maps work. Design notes are covered in Chapter 21.

5. In the Site Definition dialog box, type a site name in the Site Name text box.

6. Click on OK to close the dialog box.

The rest of the options in the Site Definition dialog box are explained in Chapter 20, *Managing Your Web Sites,* and Chapter 21, *Workflow & Collaboration.*

✔ Tips

- A new local site may or may not have any documents in it when you create it. You can create a local site based on an existing folder that's chock full of docs, or you can create a blank folder and download part or all of an existing site into it.

- Or, you can create a blank folder for a site that doesn't have any docs at all yet— because you're going to create them. I recommend setting up a local site at the point you begin using Dreamweaver, even if you haven't created a single page yet.

- You can create as many local sites as you want. I have different local sites for different parts of my main remote site (**Figure 2.9**).

- Dreamweaver can create an index, called a cache, of your local site, which allows it to perform faster searches when you find or replace text (see Chapter 8). The cache also remembers when you link one file to another on your local site. You can then update a link site-wide when you move or rename a file (see *To rename a file*, later in this chapter; the process is described in further detail in Chapter 20). To create a local cache in which Dreamweaver stores information about the local site root, relative links, and filenames, simply leave the Enable Cache checkbox checked in the Site Definition dialog box. You must enable the cache to use the Assets panel.

It's All Relative

You may have noticed that Dreamweaver is picky about coding relative paths (a.k.a. relative links or relative URLs). When you insert an image or a link to a local file on a page in Dreamweaver, a dialog box appears notifying you that the link will use a `file://` path until you save the page. When you do so, Dreamweaver converts these `file://` paths into the same relative paths that will be used online.

When you create a local site in Dreamweaver, it codes site-root relative paths based on the directory structure of the local sites. Take this example: Your local site root is `C:\HTML`. The current page is in `C:\HTML\Bubba`, and your images folder for the project is `C:\HTML\Images\Current`. When you save the page, Dreamweaver will make a relative link like this one:

```
<img src="/Images/Current/Bubba.gif">
```

Using local sites in Dreamweaver is easier than hand-coding relative links.

I designate each project folder on my computer as a separate local site. Then, when I put the files online, the links remain intact.

You can choose to have Dreamweaver update all relative links when you perform a Save As, rename a page, or move a page into a different folder. You set this option in the Preferences dialog box. Press Ctrl+U (Command+U) to view the Preferences dialog box, and click on General to bring that panel to the front. From the Update Links drop-down menu, select Prompt, Always, or Never, and then click on OK to close the Preferences dialog box. See Chapter 6 for more about relative links.

To speed Dreamweaver in storing and updating the paths for relative links and filenames, make sure the Cache checkbox in the Site Definition dialog box is checked.

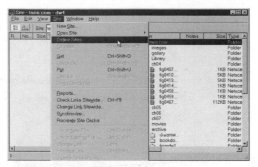

Figure 2.12 Select Define Sites from the Site window menu bar (or the Document window menu bar).

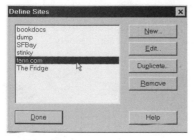

Figure 2.13 This drop-down menu allows you to switch from local site to local site; it also offers the quickest way to open the Define Sites dialog box.

Figure 2.14 In the Define Sites dialog box, select the name of the site you want to edit.

Figure 2.15 Do you really want to delete this site? If so, click on Yes. No files will be deleted, but the site will be removed from Dreamweaver's list of local sites.

Editing and Deleting Local Sites

You can edit the information about a local site, or delete one that you're no longer using.

To edit a local site:

1. From the Document window menu bar or the Site window menu bar, select Define Sites (**Figure 2.12**).

   or

   In the Site window, select Define Sites from the [site name] drop-down menu (**Figure 2.13**).

   Either way, the Define Sites dialog box will appear.

2. In the dialog box, select the name of the site you want to edit (**Figure 2.14**).

3. Click on Edit. The Site Definition dialog box will appear.

4. Make any necessary changes to the local site information in the Site Definition dialog box.

5. When you're done, click on OK to return to the Site window.

To delete a site:

1. Follow steps 1 and 2, above, to display the site information for the site you want to delete.

2. Click on Remove. A dialog box will appear, asking if you really want to do that (**Figure 2.15**). Click on Yes.

   Dreamweaver will remove the site from the listing of its local sites in the Site window, but it will not delete any files or folders from any remote or local site.

Site Window Tips and Shortcuts

You can perform a lot of common Dreamweaver file tasks with a couple of clicks.

To open a file:

1. In the Site window, view the local or remote site the file resides in.

2. Double-click on it. The file will open in the Document window (**Figure 2.16**).

To preview a file:

1. In the Site window, view the local or remote site the file resides in.

2. Right-click (Control+click) on the file. From the pop-up menu that appears (**Figure 2.17**), choose Preview in Browser > [Name].

   or

   From the menu bar, select File > Preview in Browser > [Browser name]. The file will open in the selected browser.

To create a new folder:

1. In the Site window, click where you want the new directory (folder) to appear.

2. From the Site window menu bar, select File > New Folder (on the Mac: Site > Site Files View > New Folder). A new folder will appear.

3. Type a name for the folder, hit Enter (Return), and you're done (**Figure 2.18**).

To delete a file or folder:

1. Right-click (Control+click) on the file or folder you want to delete.

2. From the pop-up menu that appears (**Figure 2.17**), choose Delete. A dialog box will appear to confirm your choice; click on OK to delete the file.

Figure 2.16 Double-click on a file icon in the Site window, and the page will open in the Document window.

Figure 2.17 The pop-up menu for files in the Site window offers lots of handy shortcuts. Windows users: Just right-click on a file or folder. Mac users: Control+click to pop up the menu.

Figure 2.18 Creating a new folder in the Site window. Note that this is the Mac view of the Site window; it's pretty much the same as the one for Windows.

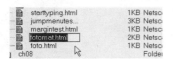

Figure 2.19 When a box appears around the filename, you can type the new filename.

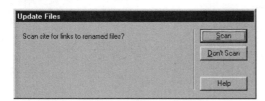

Figure 2.20 Once Dreamweaver knows about your links, either through a cache or by scanning the site, the Update Files dialog box will appear, and it will tell you which pages link to the renamed or moved page.

Figure 2.21 If you haven't created a cache for your site, this dialog box will appear and ask you whether you wish to scan for links to a renamed or moved file.

To rename a file or folder:

1. Right-click (Control+click) on the file, and from the pop-up menu that appears, select Rename. A box will appear around the filename (**Figures 2.18** and **2.19**).

2. Type the new filename and press Enter (Return). A dialog box will appear while Dreamweaver scans for links to this file. If it finds any affected files, the Update Files dialog box will appear, asking if you want to update links in that set of files (**Figure 2.20**).

   You may instead get a dialog box that asks you whether you wish to scan for files (**Figure 2.21**). If this dialog box appears, click on Scan to look for affected pages.

3. Click Update, and Dreamweaver will change links in any files that link to the page you renamed.

✔ Tip

- There are also menu options for each of these shortcuts. Open, Preview, Check Target Browsers, Delete, New Folder, and many other options are available under the File menu on the Site window menu bar. On the Macintosh, the menu command for some options is Site > Site Files View > [...].

Moving Files

You can also use the Site window like a file manager to move files around.

To move files from folder to folder:

1. View the file(s) you want to move by double-clicking the folder that contains them. To select multiple files, hold down Ctrl (Command) while clicking. To select contiguous files, hold down Shift while clicking.

2. Click on the selected file(s) or folder(s), hold down the mouse button, and drag them to a new location. See steps 2 and 3 under *To rename a file or folder* at the top of the previous page to find out about updating links to renamed or moved files.

To toggle between local sites:

◆ In the Site window, select the name of the site you want to display from the Site drop-down menu. The Site window will display the files and folders of the site you selected.

✔ Tips

■ Folders on local and remote sites that contain files will be indicated by a symbol next to the folder. To display the contents of the folder, double-click on the folder icon (**Figure 2.22**), or click on the symbol, which is a + sign if you are using Windows, or an arrow symbol on the Mac.

■ If you are connected to a remote site when you switch sites in the Site window, Dreamweaver will automatically disconnect you from the remote site, even if the two local sites are on the same server. Just reconnect to establish contact with the server again. See Chapter 20 to find out how to set up remote site information and connect to a server.

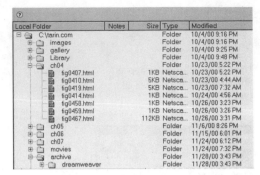

Figure 2.22 Folders with hidden contents have a plus sign to the left of them. Folders with their contents displayed have the files indented under them. To open or close a folder, double-click on it. The Mac uses blue arrows instead of plus signs.

Asset categories

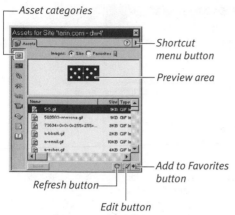

Shortcut menu button

Preview area

Add to Favorites button

Refresh button

Edit button

Figure 2.23 The Assets panel keeps track of images, movies, URLs, color swatches, and other files in your local site.

Figure 2.24 Click on the Assets button on the Launcher.

Figure 2.25 Dreamweaver comes with two example sites pre-installed. If you're bereft of images and you want to play around with assets, you can use these sites to figure out the Assets panel.

Managing Assets

The Assets panel keeps track of several kinds of media, allowing you to find and preview any image or movie in your site, no matter what folder it's in.

About the Assets panel

You must create a local site and enable the site cache in order for the Assets panel to display anything (**Figure 2.23**). Dreamweaver keeps track of Assets as a separate set for each site.

To view the Assets panel:

◆ From the Document window menu bar, select Window > Assets.

or

On the Launcher or Launcher bar, click on the Assets button (**Figure 2.24**)

or

Press F11.

In any case, the Assets panel will appear.

To view the Assets for a different local site:

◆ From the Document window menu bar, select Site > Open Site > [Site Name].

The Site window will appear, displaying files for that local site. When you return to the Document window or open the Assets panel, the panel will display assets in the site you just opened (**Figure 2.25**).

✔ Tip

■ If you don't have many files but you want to play with the Assets panel now, open one of the pre-installed sites (Lessons–Dreamweaver or Tutorial–Dreamweaver).

Kinds of Assets

The Assets panel keeps track of the following types of files.

Images

Any JPEG, GIF, or PNG image files stored in your local site.

Colors

All colors, including background, link, and text colors, used in local site pages (**Figure 2.26**).

Figure 2.26 All colors in your local site are stored as swatches in the Assets panel, whether they're Web safe or not, and whether they're hex codes or alphanumeric names.

URLs

All external, or absolute, URLs used on HTML pages. These include `http://` and `https://` URLs, as well as `mailto:` addresses and Gopher, FTP, and `file://` paths (**Figure 2.27**).

Flash

Any Flash movies, Flash buttons, and Flash text objects in your local site (**Figure 2.28**). Flash movies should be saved as `.SWF` files; `.FLA` files are source files and aren't displayed.

Figure 2.27 All absolute URLs in your local site are stored in the Assets panel, including FTP and mailto links.

Shockwave

Any Shockwave movies, games, and the like stored in your local site.

Movies

Any QuickTime or MPEG movie files stored in your local site.

Scripts

External, not inline, JavaScript or VBScript files that are stored locally as independent files.

Templates and Library items

Figure 2.28 The Assets panel keeps track of all your Flash movies, buttons, and text objects.

These are special, reusable HTML files in Dreamweaver and are described in Chapter 18.

Figure 2.29 If your Assets panel is empty, Dreamweaver may need to refresh its memory about your site.

Figure 2.30 Click on the Refresh button to make Dreamweaver re-read the site cache.

Figure 2.31 This dialog box will appear for just a second if you click on Refresh, or for a little longer if you have to rebuild the site cache.

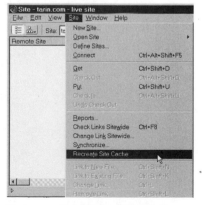

Figure 2.32 Rebuild the site cache if Dreamweaver can't find your assets.

How Assets Work

When you create a local site, Dreamweaver tracks all its files and builds a *site cache*, or index, of these files. Dreamweaver keeps track of the relative links between files in your local site, as well as minding the locations of all the items described on the previous page.

If the Assets panel is empty:

◆ On the Assets panel (**Figure 2.29**), click the Refresh button (**Figure 2.30**).

Dreamweaver will re-read the site cache (**Figure 2.31**) and index your assets. In a moment or two, the Assets panel will display your assets (assuming you have some).

Keep in mind that if you don't have any Flash objects, for example, then the Assets panel can't display them.

If you add or delete an asset and the panel doesn't change:

1. Open the Site window (Window > Site Files).

2. From the Site window menu bar, select Site > Recreate Site Cache (**Figure 2.32**).

   or

   Hold down the Ctrl (Command) key while clicking on the Assets panel's Refresh button.

   Dreamweaver will rebuild the site cache (**Figure 2.31**), which may take some time on large sites. (It has to index all those links.)

If this doesn't work, try quitting and restarting Dreamweaver, and rebuild the site cache again if necessary.

Using the Assets Panel

The Assets panel displays vital statistics about assets, including previews. For more about previewing, see *Previewing and Inserting Assets* on page 40.

To view assets:

◆ To view a category, click on its button on the Assets panel (**Figure 2.33**).

◆ To view site files (all assets for a category), click on the Site radio button (**Figure 2.34**). To view Favorites (see *Using Favorites and Nicknames,* later in this chapter), click on the Favorites radio button. The Favorites list will be empty until you add items to it.

Figure 2.33 Click on a category button in the Assets panel to view that kind of asset.

Figure 2.34 Click on the Site radio button to view all the assets in your site, or Favorites to view only those files you've designated as such.

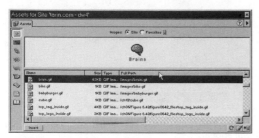

Figure 2.35 You can sort images by file type, size, and name. You can also sort them by path, as I did with this image, which also sorts by the folder the image is in.

Figure 2.36 Here, I've sorted colors into Websafe and non-Websafe. Within each group, or all together if you click the Value column heading, they'll be arranged by value. That often means that similar colors are grouped together. Named colors are also grouped together. Finally, I'm clicking and dragging the column between the category borders.

Figure 2.37 I've sorted links by protocol type. I've also shortened the preview area; you can enlarge it if you're dealing with images or movies.

To sort assets:

1. View the category you want to sort.

2. Click on one of the column headings to sort by that heading (**Figure 2.35**).

For example, you can sort images by file type to separate GIFs from JPEGs (**Figure 2.35**); you can sort colors by the Type column (**Figure 2.36**); and you can sort links into HTTP, mailto, and FTP (**Figure 2.37**).

✔ Tips

■ You can drag the borders between column headings to resize the columns if you want to make a particular column more readable (**Figure 2.36**). You can resize the Assets panel, too, as I have here.

■ To resize the preview area, drag the border between it and the Assets list box (**Figure 2.37**). See the next page for more about previews.

Previewing and Inserting Assets

The Assets panel lets you preview items before inserting them.

To preview an asset:

◆ Select the asset in the Asset panel.

   If the asset is an image, a preview will appear (**Figure 2.38**).

   If the asset is a color, the tone will appear in the list box, and the preview area will display the Hex and RGB codes for the color (**Figure 2.39**).

   If the asset is a URL, the preview area will display the full path (**Figure 2.40**).

   If the asset is a Flash, Shockwave, or other movie, a placeholder will appear in the preview area (**Figure 2.41**). Click the green Play arrow to play the movie. You may need to mouse over some objects for them to play. Click the red Stop button to stop the movie once you've played it.

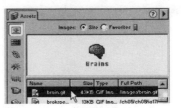

Figure 2.38 A preview of the image will appear.

Figure 2.39 The hex and RGB codes for the image will appear, and you'll see the color in use as text. See Chapter 3 for more on color codes.

Figure 2.40 The preview area shows the full URL.

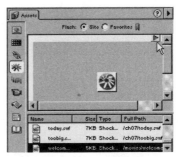

Figure 2.41 If your Flash object is made by Dreamweaver (Flash text or Flash button), it'll appear as in Figure 2.38. Otherwise, you'll get a placeholder and a Play button.

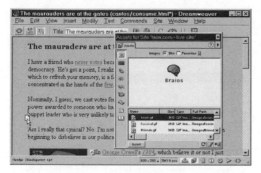

Figure 2.42 Here, I'm dragging the image onto the page.

To insert an asset:

1. Select the asset.

2. If the asset is an image, movie, or script, you can drag it into the Document window (**Figure 2.42**), or click on the Insert button at the bottom of the panel to drop it onto your page at the insertion point.

   If the asset is a link or color, select some text in the Document window. Then select the asset and click on the Apply button at the bottom of the panel.

   If the asset is a link and you drag it into the Document window, the full path will be displayed, and you can edit this text.

   If the asset is a color and you drag it into the Document window, the next text you type will appear in that color.

Using Favorites and Nicknames

If you have 4,000 images in your site, a list of all those files might be more unwieldy than just using the Site window to find things. However, you can create a list of Favorites for each category (excepting Library items and Templates) so you can track your most-used assets separately.

To add an asset to Favorites:

1. Select the asset in the Assets panel.

2. Click on the Add to Favorites button (**Figure 2.43**). A dialog box may appear telling you that you have to view Favorites in order to see them (um, okay).

The asset will be added to your list of Favorites (**Figure 2.44**).

To view Favorites:

1. In the Assets panel, click on the category you want to manage.

2. Click on the Favorites radio button (**Figure 2.45**).

The Favorites list will appear (**Figure 2.44**).

To create a folder for Favorites:

1. View a Favorites category (see above).

2. On the Assets panel, click on the New Favorites Folder button (**Figure 2.46**).

3. In the space that appears, type a name for the folder (**Figure 2.47**) and press Enter (Return).

4. Now you can select assets and drag them into the folder (**Figure 2.48**). To select several assets, hold down Ctrl (Command) while you click, or Shift for consecutive items:

Figure 2.43 Click on the Add to Favorites button.

Figure 2.44 Only those assets you designate as Favorites will appear in the Favorites list.

Figure 2.45 Click on the Favorites radio button.

Figure 2.46 Click on the New Favorites Folder button.

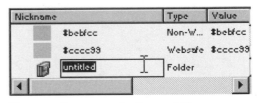

Figure 2.47 Type a name for the new folder.

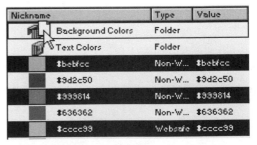

Figure 2.48 Select assets and drag them into the folder. Hold down Ctrl (Command) or Shift to select nonadjacent or consecutive assets.

Figure 2.49 When you view Favorites for images or movies, the full filename is truncated.

Figure 2.50 Click on the Remove From Favorites button.

Figure 2.51 Here, I've got three folders holding all my favorite colors.

Figure 2.52 From the pop-up menu that appears, select Edit Nickname.

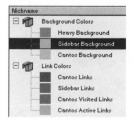

Figure 2.53 I've nick-named all my colors so I know what's what.

To remove a Favorite:

1. View Favorites for a category in the Assets panel, as described on the last page (**Figure 2.49**)

2. Select the item to remove.

3. Click on the Remove From Favorites button (**Figure 2.50**).

The asset will be removed from the Favorites list, but it will still appear in the Site list. If you remove an entire Favorites folder, you will remove all the assets within it from the list.

Nicknaming assets

You can create nicknames for frequently used assets in addition to putting them in the Favorites list—but you can nickname them only after you add them to Favorites.

To nickname a Favorite:

1. View Favorites for a category in the Assets panel, as described on the last page (**Figure 2.51**).

2. Select the Favorite you want to nickname.

3. Right-click (Control+click) the favorite and, from the pop-up menu that appears (**Figure 2.52**), select Edit Nickname.

4. When the box appears around the name, type a nickname and press Enter (Return).

This won't change the filename—the nickname is used only in the Favorites list (**Figure 2.53**).

Editing and Sharing Assets

You can edit directly assets from the Assets panel. You can also share assets between sites.

Editing assets

Editing images and movies in the Assets panel consists of opening them in an external editor. To find out how to set up an external editor, see *Image Editor Integration*, in Chapter 5.

To edit an image or movie:

1. Select the asset in the Assets panel.

2. Click on the Edit button (**Figure 2.54**).

3. The asset will open in the external editor. Be sure to save your changes. If the new asset doesn't reload in the Document window, select View > Refresh Design View, or press F5.

To edit a color or URL:

1. Add the asset to your Favorites, as described in *Using Favorites and Nicknames*. You can edit only colors and URLs that are stored as Favorites.

2. Select the Favorites radio button, and select the asset.

3. If the asset is a URL, click on Edit, and the Edit URL dialog box will appear (**Figure 2.55**). You can then edit both the URL path and the nickname for the asset. If you give a URL a nickname, that text will appear if you drag the URL into the Document window.

   If the asset is a color, click on Edit, and the color picker will appear (**Figure 2.56**). You can choose a new color. For more on using the color picker, see Chapter 3.

Figure 2.54 Click on the Edit button. The asset will open in an editor, unless it's a color or URL.

Figure 2.55 Edit a URL's path or nickname (default text) using the Edit URL dialog box.

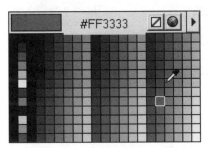

Figure 2.56 You can change any color in your Favorites. For example, if you have a color nicknamed Body Text and you change the color you use for your pages, change the color associated with the nickname.

Creating New Colors

Any time you use a color on your site, it will be added to the Assets panel. If you want to create a color *before* you use it, you can. (For instance, if you're given a list of site colors by the designer.)

Click within the Favorites folder, if you have one. (If not, see *Using Favorites and Nicknames* in this chapter for help setting one up.) Then, click on the Shortcut menu button and select New Color. The color picker will appear. Select your color, and it'll appear in the Favorites folder, where you can nickname it.

Figure 2.57 Right-click (Control+click) on an asset, or click on the Shortcut menu button, and select Copy To Site > [Site Name].

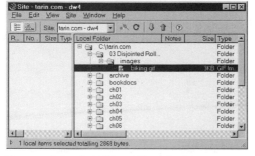

Figure 2.58 I copied biking.gif from the Dreamweaver Lessons site into my site, and it copied all the surrounding folders as well. I'm free to move the image and delete the folders, of course.

Figure 2.59 Right-click (Control+click) on an asset, or click on the Shortcut menu button, and select Locate in Site.

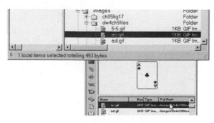

Figure 2.60 Dreamweaver found my image, right where I'd left it.

Sharing assets

If you have an asset you want to use in more than one site, you must place it in both sites.

To copy an asset to a different site:

1. Select the asset in the Assets panel.

2. Click on the Shortcut menu button, and in the menu that appears (**Figure 2.57**), select Copy to Site > [Site Name].

3. The asset will be copied to the Favorites list for its category in the other site.

    If the asset is a color or URL, it will be stored in Favorites.

    If the asset is an image, script, or movie, the file will also be copied.

After you copy an asset file, you may be curious to know where Dreamweaver put it (**Figure 2.58**). It generally creates a copy of the folder or folders from the first site into the second site. For example, if the file poppy.gif is stored in flowers/images/poppy.gif, the folder flowers, as well as the folder images, will be copied in addition to the file.

To locate an asset in a site:

1. Open the site that contains the asset (Site > Open Site > [Site Name]).

2. In the Assets panel, select the asset.

3. Click on the Shortcut menu button, and when the menu appears (**Figure 2.59**), select Locate in Site.

The Site window will open, if it isn't open already, and the asset will be selected (**Figure 2.60**). You can feel free to move the asset and to delete any extra folders Dreamweaver created. When Dreamweaver updates the site cache, it'll find the asset again.

BASIC
WEB PAGES

Figure 3.1 The McSweeney's Web site (www.mcsweeneys.net) uses mostly text, but it still looks snappy.

Figure 3.2 Klaud Design (www.klaud.com) is the home of designer Zhenia Timerman.

In the first chapter, we got acquainted with the Dreamweaver interface. This chapter describes how to use the Document window to create and save Web pages (**Figures 3.1–3.2**).

To start with, I'll walk you through creating a simple Web page that uses tables, links, images, and text. We'll also learn how to adjust the properties of a page, including the title and the page background.

In this chapter, we'll learn how to:

◆ Open a page

◆ Create a new page

◆ Add content to a page

◆ Set the page title

◆ Adjust the page properties

◆ Save your work

◆ Save a copy of your page

◆ Preview the page in a browser

◆ Print the page from the browser

◆ Close the file

This chapter also describes how to select and use colors in Dreamweaver. I'll refer to this material throughout the book.

Creating and Opening HTML Files

When you start Dreamweaver, a new, blank page will appear in the Document window.

To create a new file:

◆ From the Document window menu bar, select File > New, or press Ctrl+N (Command+N).

A new, blank document will appear.

Opening files

If you have previously created HTML files that you want to update, you can open them with Dreamweaver. Dreamweaver won't change your code, but it may alert you of errors such as redundant or unclosed tags (see Chapter 4).

When you open a file in Dreamweaver, it will appear in a new Document window.

To open a file:

1. From the Document window menu bar, select File > Open. The Open dialog box will appear (**Figures 3.3** and **3.4**).

2. If the file extension is not .htm or .html (you're opening a .cgi or .asp file, for instance), select All Types from the Files of Type list box. (On the Mac, select All Documents from the Show drop-down menu. See **Figure 3.4**.)

Browse through the files and folders on your computer, and select a file you want to open.

3. Click on Open. The file will appear in a new Document window.

✔ Tip

■ You can open the last four files you viewed with Dreamweaver by selecting them from the File menu (**Figure 3.5**).

Figure 3.3 Use the Open dialog box to select a file on your computer to open in the Document window. By default, the Open dialog box first looks in the last folder that you opened.

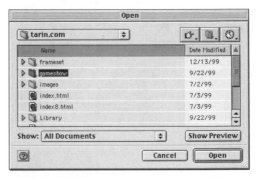

Figure 3.4 The Open dialog box looks a little different on the Mac, but it works the same way.

Figure 3.5 Open the last four files that you've edited in Dreamweaver by selecting their names from the File menu.

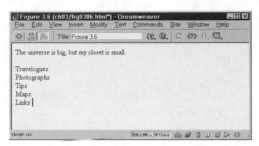

Figure 3.6 Type or paste whatever text you like in the Document window. After the first line, I pressed Enter (Return) to create a paragraph break; the breaks between the next five lines are line breaks.

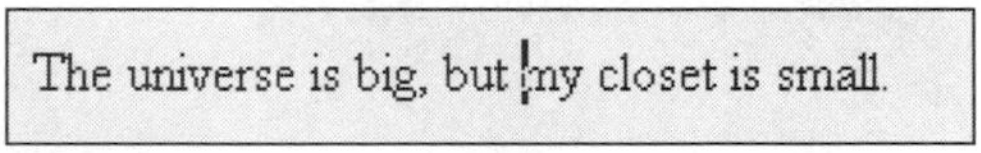

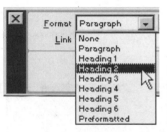

Figure 3.7 Click within the line you want to make into a heading.

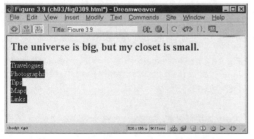

Figure 3.8 Select a heading size from the Property inspector.

Figure 3.9 Now my text has become a heading, and I've selected some lines to make bold.

Creating Content

When you open Dreamweaver, the Document window creates a new, blank page. You can start from this tabula rasa to create your own Web page.

To place text:

1. Just start typing!

2. Press Enter (Return) to make a paragraph break, or press Shift+Enter (Shift+Return) to make a line break (**Figure 3.6**).

You can also copy and paste text from another program and paste it into the Document window.

To create a heading:

1. Select the text you want to make into a heading by clicking within that paragraph (**Figure 3.7**).

2. From the Property inspector's Format drop-down menu, select a heading from 1 (largest) to 7 (smallest) (**Figure 3.8**).

   The heading will become bold and its size will change (**Figure 3.9**).

To make text bold or italic:

1. Select the text you want to modify.

2. Click on the Bold or Italic button on the Property inspector.

   The text will change appearance (**Figure 3.10**).

✔ Tips

■ Dreamweaver offers common commands, such as copy, cut, paste, and undo, in the Edit menu (**Figure 3.11**).

■ For more about formatting text in Dreamweaver, see Chapter 8, *Fonts and Characters,* and Chapter 9, *Paragraphs and Block Formatting.*

Laying out a page with tables

On my example page, I'm going to insert a table. Tables are covered in Chapter 12. Once you insert a table, you can insert, paste, or drag content into its cells.

To insert a table:

1. From the Document window menu bar, select Insert > Table. The Insert Table dialog box will appear (**Figure 3.12**).

2. Type the number of columns and rows you want to appear in your table. For our example, I'm going to use three columns and two rows.

3. Specify the width of your table by typing a number in the Width text box, and selecting either pixels or percent from the drop-down menu. To use the table as a page layout, I'm going to specify the width as 100 percent (of the browser window).

4. Click on OK. The Insert Table dialog box will close, and the table will appear on your page (**Figure 3.13**).

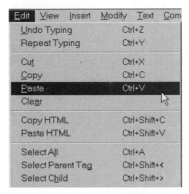

Figure 3.10 I've made the selected text bold.

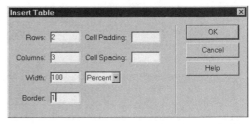

Figure 3.11 You can use Dreamweaver as a text editor, too. The Edit menu offers common commands.

Figure 3.12 These are the settings I've selected for the Insert Table dialog box to create the table shown in **Figure 3.13**.

Figure 3.13 A basic table. To use it as a page layout, set its width to 100 percent.

Figure 3.14 You can set a table height by dragging the bottom border down. The table will also expand if you place content into it.

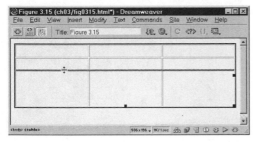

Figure 3.15 You can drag the border between rows to create a smaller top row. See **Figure 3.17** to see what I've done with this.

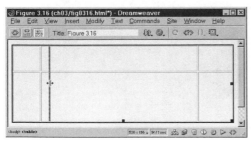

Figure 3.16 You can drag the border between columns before or after you put content in them.

To change the layout:

1. Mouse over a border between two cells or around the outside of the table, and the pointer will turn into a double-headed arrow you can use to drag the borders.

2. To change the height of the table (**Figure 3.14**), drag the bottom border.

   To change the height of the two horizontal rows, drag the border (**Figure 3.15**).

3. To change the width of the columns, drag their borders (**Figure 3.16**). You can readjust them at any time.

✔ Tip

■ You can draw complex table layouts using Layout View (Chapter 7) or drawing layers and converting to tables (Chapter 14).

Adding images and media

Images and media files are not embedded in a page; rather, the Web page contains inline links and spacing information so the browser knows where to go get the files and how to display them. In Dreamweaver, you simply place the file where you want it to go on the page, and it writes the linking code.

To place an image:

1. Click to place the insertion point where you want the image to appear. I'm going to click within a table cell (**Figure 3.17**).

2. From the Document window menu bar, select Insert > Image. The Select Image Source dialog box will appear (**Figure 3.18**).

   Browse through the files and folders on your computer and select the image file. The image pathname will appear in the URL text box.

3. Click on Select. The Select Image Source dialog box will close, and the image will appear on the page (**Figure 3.19**).

To find out more about images and image properties, see Chapter 5, *Working with Images*. Inserting media objects is very similar, and I cover that subject in Chapter 7.

Figure 3.17 Here's my page in progress. I've combined the cells in the top row (see Chapter 12), and I'm going to place an image in the left-hand cell.

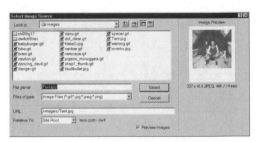

Figure 3.18 Insert an image onto your page by selecting its image file in the Select Image Source dialog box. This is the Windows version; the Mac view is shown in **Figure 3.30**.

Figure 3.19 After I inserted the image, the table resized to accommodate it. I can resize either the image, the table, or both.

Figure 3.20 Highlight the text you want to make into a link.

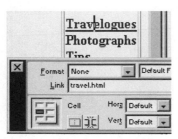

Figure 3.21 Type the link in the Property inspector's Link text box, or click on Browse to choose a file. Either way, the text will become linked and the link will be displayed in the Property inspector. The tag for a link is *<a>*.

To make a link:

1. Highlight the object (text or image) that you want to make into a link (**Figure 3.20**).

2. In the Link text box on the Property inspector, either click Browse, and select a file from your local site; or, type or paste the URL of an Internet link.

3. Press Enter (Return), and the object will become linked (**Figure 3.21**).

For more about links, see Chapter 6, *Working with Links.*

Page Properties

Page properties are elements that apply to an entire page, rather than a single object on the page. Visual properties include the page's title, a background color or image, and the text and link colors. Other page properties include the document encoding and the site folders, if any.

To change the page title:

1. In the Document window toolbar, click within the Page Title text box.

2. Type a new title and press Enter (Return) (**Figure 3.22**).

Choose a good title for your page, something more descriptive than "My Home Page." Many search engines use the words in the page title to index pages.

✔ Tips

- The page title is stored in the document's <head> tag.

- Unlike some other page creation tools, Dreamweaver doesn't prompt you to give your pages a title—in fact, it titles all your pages "Untitled Document" until you change the Page Properties.

- The title you give your page will be displayed in the Web browser's title bar (**Figure 3.23**).

- In Chapter 21, I'll show you how to use site reports to find all untitled pages in your site.

Figure 3.22 Type your page title in the Page Title text box.

Tips for Time Travelers - Netscape 6

Figure 3.23 The title you choose for your Web page will be displayed in the Web browser's title bar.

Text from Other Sources

When you paste text from another program, such as an e-mail or word-processing program, it may lose all its formatting, including paragraph breaks. (If you paste text copied from a Web browser or HTML mail program, it should retain its paragraph formatting.)

One way to prevent loss of formatting is to use a word-processing program to save the text as HTML, and then open the file in Dreamweaver. Many word processors, including AppleWorks, Microsoft Word, Nisus Writer, and Corel WordPerfect, include HTML conversion extensions (try File > Save as HTML, or consult the program's help files).

Although these programs write atrocious HTML in some cases, they're just fine for coding paragraph and line breaks.

Another good shortcut is Microsoft Excel's Save as HTML feature, which saves spreadsheets as not-too-terrible HTML tables.

No matter what other program you use to create an HTML file, you can easily clean up the big boo-boos by selecting Commands > Clean Up HTML (or Clean Up Word HTML for MS Word files) and selecting which common mistakes you want to correct. Chapter 4 describes Roundtrip HTML in more detail.

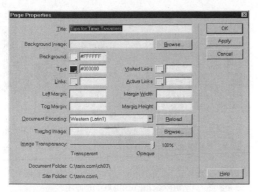

Figure 3.24 The Page Properties dialog box allows you to set options that apply to an entire page.

Other Page Properties

Other page properties are stored in the Page Properties dialog box.

To view page properties:

◆ From the Document window menu bar, select Modify > Page Properties or press Ctrl+J (Command+J). The Page Properties dialog box will appear (**Figure 3.24**).

About Document Encoding

If you're composing Web pages in a language that uses a non-Western (non-Latin) alphabet, you probably browse the Web using Document encoding for that language. Web pages in alphabets such as Chinese, Cyrillic, Finnish, Greek, Japanese, Korean, and some Eastern European languages use special text encoding to display fonts that can interpret and display the characters that language uses.

To set the encoding for your page so that Web browsers can load the proper set of fonts, select your language from the Document Encoding drop-down menu in the Page Properties dialog box.

To find out how to change the encoding for the entire program, see Chapter 4.

Modifying the Page Color and Background

By default, Dreamweaver will set the background color of your page as plain white and the text color as black. You can choose a different background color, or use a background image instead.

Background and text colors

You can conceivably use any color as the background color. Keep in mind that you may need to change the text colors as well, so that the text will show up readably (**Figure 3.25**).

To set the background and text colors:

1. Open the Page Properties dialog box by pressing Ctrl+J (Command+J).

2. In the Background text box, type the hex code for the color you wish to use.

   or

   Click on the Background color box. The color picker will appear (**Figure 3.26**). Click on a color with the eyedropper to select it; the color can be any color in the picker or on your desktop (**Figure 3.27**).

   The other color options are described later, in the section, *Colors and Web Pages*.

3. Repeat step 2 for the Text color and the Link colors, if you wish.

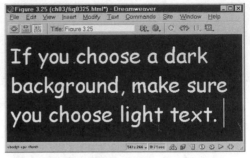

Figure 3.25 Make sure your text color is visible and readable on your background color.

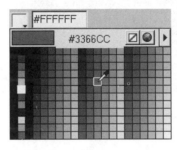

Figure 3.26 The color picker opens when you click on any color button within a dialog box or on the Property inspector.

Visible desktop (all colors are potential selections)   Background color box

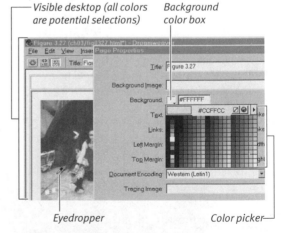

Eyedropper   Color picker

Figure 3.27 Here, I'm selecting a color from my photograph to serve as the background color. Any color I click on with the eyedropper, anywhere on my desktop, can serve as a color choice.

Figure 3.28 Here's my page, with a background color chosen from the photograph on it. I've also changed the link colors.

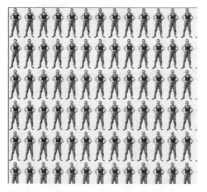

Figure 3.29 A tiled background image. The tiny image repeats from left to right and then down the page.

4. In any case, when the code for each color appears in its text box, click on Apply to preview the color on your page; or click on OK to apply the colors and close the dialog box (**Figure 3.28**).

✔ Tips

■ More details about how link colors work are available in Chapter 6.

■ You can find out how to make selected text a different color in Chapters 8 and 11.

Setting a background image

Most browsers created after Netscape Navigator 2 support background images. A background image can consist of one large image, but more frequently, it's a smaller image that the browser window tiles so that it repeats in a contiguous pattern across and down the browser window (**Figure 3.29**).

✔ Tip

■ Take care when using background images. You've seen pages where the background took primacy over the content, rendering the text unreadable and the other images gratuitous. Be subtle, or use table backgrounds to provide blank space for your text (see Chapter 12).

Converting Other Color Numbers into Hex

Colors in HTML are signified by a six-digit code called a hex code. Colors are also definable by a three-number sequence of hue, saturation, and value, or by another three-number sequence: the red-green-blue, or RGB, ratio. There are boxes for these numbers in the Color dialog box (see **Figures 3.24** and **3.50**).

You can get the RGB sequence of a particular color from an image editor, like Photoshop or Paint Shop Pro, and then duplicate the color by typing the correct numbers into the right boxes in the Color dialog box. Then, of course, you should jot down that hex code for further reference. (You can copy RGB numbers into an image editor, too, if you want to duplicate a background color in an image for some reason.)

To set a background image:

1. Open the Page Properties dialog box by selecting Modify > Page Properties from the Document window menu bar.

2. Click on the Browse (Choose) button next to the Background Image field. The Select Image Source dialog box will appear (**Figure 3.30**). This is similar to the Open dialog box.

3. Browse through the files and folders on your computer until you find the GIF or JPEG image that you want to use. Click on the file icon so that the image's pathname appears in the URL text box.

4. Click on Select (Open) to close this dialog box and return to the Page Properties dialog box, where the image pathname appears in the Background Image text box.

5. Click on OK to close the Page Properties dialog box and return to the Document window, where your background image will appear (**Figure 3.31**).

✔ Tip

- You can set both a background image and a background color. The image will override the color in most cases, and the color will show up in browsers that support background colors but not background images.

  To find out about Tracing Images, see Chapter 14. To find out about setting backgrounds for tables, see Chapter 12.

Figure 3.30 The Select Image Source dialog box, like an Open dialog box, lets you browse through your computer's files to select an image. The Image Preview at the right displays the image's dimensions, file size, and download time. Click on Show Preview to view it or Hide Preview to hide it. This is the Mac version; the Windows view was shown in **Figure 3.18**.

Figure 3.31 Here, I've added a subtle background image to my page. I've also modified the central table cell so it uses a solid background color, to ensure readability. See Chapter 12 for details.

Figure 3.32 Type a filename for your Web page in the File name text box, then click on Save to save it.

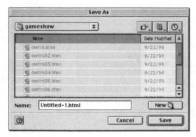

Figure 3.33 The Mac view of the Save As dialog box.

Dial the Right Extension

By default, PCs will save HTML files with the .htm extension, and Macs will save them with the .html extension. If you want to use a different extension, change the preferences. From the Document window menu bar, select Edit > Preferences, and select the General category. In the Add Extension When Saving text box, type your preferred file extension, whether it's html, cgi, or asp. You'll need to specify any exceptions to this extension by typing the full filename, such as dork.html, when you save a file.

The two most common extensions are .html and .htm. Why use one over the other? I prefer .html. The extension .htm is a throwback to when many PCs (as opposed to Macs or Unix machines) could only read eight-letter filenames with three-letter extensions. Now that that's no longer true, I prefer to standardize with .html.

Saving Your Work

If you're creating more than just an afternoon's entertainment, you'll want to save the work you do to the Web pages you make.

To save the current page:

1. From the Document window menu bar, select File > Save, or press Ctrl+S (Command+S). The Save As dialog box will appear (**Figures 3.32** and **3.33**).

2. Make sure you select the correct folder in which you want to store the file.

3. Type a name for your file in the File name text box. The name should not include any spaces, but you can use underscores (as in main_page.html).

4. Click on Save. The Save As dialog box will close, and you'll return to the Document window.

To save all open files:

1. From the Document window menu bar, select File > Save All.

2. All the named files that have been changed since the last time you saved will be saved now.

3. A Save As dialog box will appear for any open files that have not been named and saved.

Saving a Copy of a File

If you want to use a page as a template for another, similar page, you can save a copy of the page with a different filename. Guidelines for using Dreamweaver templates and creating custom templates are in Chapter 18.

To save a copy of a page:

1. Open the page in the Document window, if it's not there already.

2. From the Document window menu bar, select File > Save As. The Save As dialog box will appear (**Figure 3.34**).

3. Type a new filename for the new page in the File name text box.

4. Click on Save. The Save As dialog box will close and return you to the Document window.

The Document window will now display the copy of the file, as indicated by the filename in the Document window's title bar.

To close a page:

◆ Click on the close box, or select File > Close from the window's menu bar.

Occasionally, you may open a page, make a few changes, and realize that something has gone horribly wrong. Or you may be fooling around with a document you have no intention of saving. In those instances, you can close without saving the changes.

To close without saving:

1. From the Document window menu bar, select File > Close. A dialog box will appear asking you if you want to save your changes (**Figure 3.35**).

2. Click on No. The dialog box will close, and a new, blank document will appear in the Document window.

Figure 3.34 You use the same Save As dialog box to save a copy of a file as you do to save it in the first place. In this figure, we're saving the file mill.html as mill2.html, so we'll have two versions of the same file.

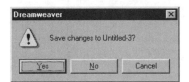

Figure 3.35 To close a file (such as a template, for example) without saving the changes, click on No when this dialog box appears.

Dreamweaver Templates vs. Copying Files

You may be used to creating a Web page and then saving copies of it over and over in order to create many pages based on the design of the first.

Dreamweaver has a built-in template feature, described in Chapter 18. Dream Templates, as they're called, have their pros and cons. In those templates, you need to designate areas of the page that can be changed. Everything else on the page is fixed, and only those marked areas are editable. These regions may also be used in conjunction with XML.

This is a great idea for locking pages and giving basic data entry work to temps or interns (or marketing). On the other hand, sometimes it's just easier to do it the old-fashioned way and skip the fancy stuff.

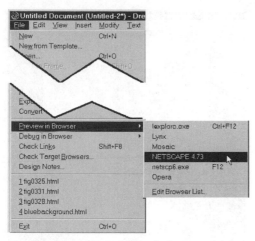

Figure 3.36 Select File > Preview in Browser and then select a browser. Find out how to add browsers to your list on the Web site for this book.

Preview button

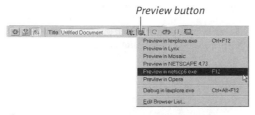

Figure 3.37 Select a browser from the Preview menu.

Figure 3.38 Preview your page, at any stage of its progress, in a browser so you can see what it really looks like. In the Document window, visual aids such as table borders are still visible, whereas they are invisible in the browser (unless you specified a border).

Previewing in a Browser

Although Dreamweaver is pretty much WYSIWYG, there are some tags it doesn't support. Also, Dreamweaver's representation of HTML is like a cross between how Explorer and Netscape display pages. To find out how your page looks in a particular browser, you need to actually use that browser to view your page.

To view your page in a browser:

1. With the page you want to preview open in the Document window or the Code inspector, select File > Preview in Browser > Browser Name from the menu bar (**Figure 3.36**); or from the Preview menu on the toolbar (**Figure 3.37**); or press F12.

   ◆ If the browser isn't open yet, Dreamweaver will launch it and load the current page (**Figure 3.38**).

   ◆ If the browser is already open, Dreamweaver will load the current page into a new window (Explorer, Netscape 6) or into the last-used window (Navigator).

2. To make changes, return to the Document window by using the Taskbar (the Applications menu on the Mac).

✔ Tips

■ Dreamweaver creates a temp file that it uses as the browser preview file. Pressing Reload or Refresh in the browser window may not show the most current version of the file. Instead, you'll need to repeat the steps for previewing.

■ For more details on previewing, and to find out how to edit the browser preview list, refer to the book's Web site.

■ You can also open a saved file on your hard drive in the browser window. Choose File > Open Page from the browser's menu bar.

Printing from the Browser Window

Dreamweaver's Document window does not include a Print command. You can, however, print a file after you preview it in the browser window.

To print a file:

1. Preview the file in the browser window as described in the previous section.

2. From the Web browser's menu bar, select File > Print. The Print dialog box will appear.

3. Verify the number of copies, the destination printer, and the pages to print in the Print dialog box.

4. Click on OK. The browser will send the document to the printer.

You can return to Dreamweaver by using the Windows Taskbar (the Applications menu on a Mac).

Figure 3.39 Navigator 4's Print Preview feature lets you see what you're getting before you send it to the printer. Good thing, because white text won't print on white paper (this page has a dark background when viewed in the browser, which you can choose not to print). You can change printing options in your browser. See the sidebar below.

Fancy-Schmancy Printing Options

Both Netscape Navigator and Microsoft Internet Explorer offer some convenient printing options. Navigator 4.x (Windows only) offers the File > Print Preview command (**Figure 3.39**). Navigator's Page Setup dialog box (File > Page Setup) offers options for printing backgrounds, black text (instead of printing a background in order to show text), and headers. (On the Mac, open the Page Setup dialog box and select Browser from the Options drop-down menu.) Internet Explorer's Print dialog box (File > Print) lets you choose frame printing options. You can also print a table of all the links on a given page, or print each page linked from that page.

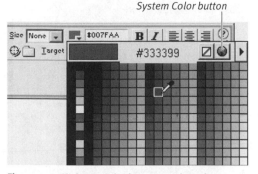

System Color button

Figure 3.40 Click any Color button, such as the Background color box in the Page Properties dialog box, or the text color button on the Property inspector, and the color picker will appear—then just click on a color to select it. That includes colors not only in the picker but anywhere on your desktop.

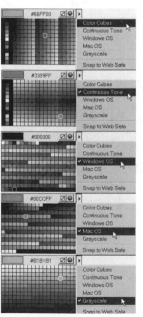

Figure 3.41 Different views of the color picker: Color Cubes, Continuous Tone, Windows OS, Mac OS, Grayscale. Obviously, these all look grayscale in a black-and-white book. Color Cubes and Continuous Tone are Websafe palettes; see the sidebar *Browser-Safe Colors* for more.

Colors and Web Pages

In Web pages, each color you can use is represented by a hexadecimal code, a six-digit number that represents a particular color.

There are many different color selections you can make for your Web pages, including background color, text color, link color, active link color, and visited link color. You can also choose colors for text selections, image borders, table backgrounds, table borders, frame borders, layers, and more.

This isn't even counting any colors that appear in images you add to your pages.

In general, it's a good idea to keep a fixed color scheme in mind while planning your pages. It's an even better idea to plan text and background colors with readability in mind; if you clash yellow text with an orange background, it may look striking, but no one will stick around to read a page that gives them a headache.

Choosing Color

You can choose from millions of colors or only Websafe ones using the System color picker, which you can get to by clicking on the Color Wheel button on the color picker (**Figure 3.40**). Mac and Windows versions of the dialog box are quite different; we'll look at both in detail. Additionally, you can click on the menu button to array the colors in different patterns (**Figure 3.41**). The first two are Websafe; the latter three aren't. See the sidebar *Browser-Safe Colors*, later in this chapter, for more.

Colors and Windows

Windows users have a single, difficult dialog box to deal with, whereas Mac users get seven different user-friendly options for choosing color. Sorry, folks, that's the way it is.

To use the System color picker (Windows):

1. Open the color picker (**Figure 3.42**) by clicking on any color button

2. On the color picker, click on the Color wheel button. The Color dialog box will appear (**Figure 3.43**).

3. You can choose one of the preselected colors by clicking on it, or you can select a slot for a custom color by first clicking on one of the Custom Colors boxes at the left of the dialog box.

4. Click on a hue (color) in the large colors box, and then click on a shade (lighter or darker) in the narrow panel to the right of that. The combination of your clicks will be displayed in the Color|Solid box.

5. To select this color, click on the Add to Custom Colors button. Your color will appear in the box you selected in Step 3.

6. Click on OK to close the Color dialog box. The hex code for the color you chose will appear in the Color text box.

✔ Tip

- You can also type the name of a color, such as red or silver, in a color text box.

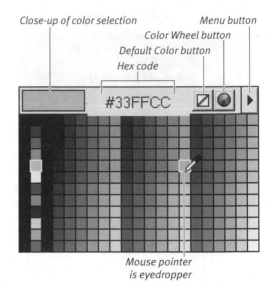

Close-up of color selection *Menu button*
Color Wheel button
Default Color button
Hex code

Mouse pointer is eyedropper

Figure 3.42 Click on the Color Wheel button on the color picker to open the System color picker.

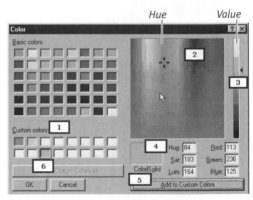

Hue *Value*

Figure 3.43 The Color dialog box. (1) Select a predefined color, or select an empty Custom Colors box. (2) Select a hue and (3) a shade. (4) click on the Color|Solid box and (5) click on Add to Custom Colors. (6) Click on the color if it isn't selected, and then click on OK.

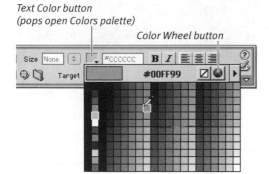

*Text Color button
(pops open Colors palette)*

Color Wheel button

Figure 3.44 Click on the Color Wheel button on the color picker to open the Color dialog box.

Colors for the Mac

The standard System color picker for the Mac looks somewhat different. It offers several different tools for selecting colors: CMYK Picker, Crayon Picker, HLS Picker, HSV Picker, HTML Picker, and RGB Picker. You can use any of these tools by clicking on it in the list box at the left of the dialog box.

You open the Mac Color dialog box the same way you do the Windows one: On the color picker, click on the color box (**Figure 3.44**).

Color-Pickin' Tips

◆ When you open the color picker (**Figure 3.42**), the mouse pointer turns into an eyedropper that you can use to select a color inside or outside the color picker.

◆ If you have the color picker open and decide that you'd rather not change the color just now, click on the Default Color button to return the color value to default, or press Esc to close with no change.

◆ Read the sidebar called *Browser-Safe Colors*, later in this chapter, to find out more.

Using the Crayon Picker

The easiest color picker to use is the Crayon Picker (**Figure 3.45**). You can choose from preselected colors, all Websafe.

To use the Crayon Picker:

◆ Click on a crayon in the box. The color that you choose will appear in the New color swatch, and its cutesy name will appear in the Name area.

✔ Tip

■ The crayons are all Websafe colors. If you select a non-Websafe color with another picker, a name such as "Carnation-ish" will appear (**Figure 3.46**), indicating an inexact match to the closest Websafe color.

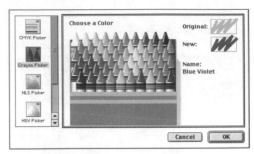

Figure 3.45 The Crayon picker, in the Color dialog box for the Mac. Click on a crayon to choose a color.

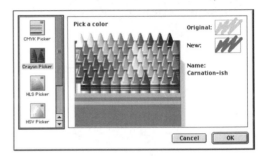

Figure 3.46 If you choose a non-Websafe color when using the Crayon Picker, the name will end in -ish.

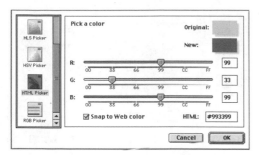

Figure 3.47 The HTML Picker, in the Color dialog box for the Mac. These colors are Websafe unless you turn off the Snap to Web color checkbox.

The HTML Picker

You can select a color in any picker and make it a Websafe color with the HTML Picker.

To use the HTML Picker:

1. When you click on the HTML Picker button, the HTML Picker will appear (**Figure 3.47**) and convert any prior color selection into a Websafe color.

2. To change colors within the Websafe continuum, click on the Hex pairs (00, 33, and so on) on the R, G, or B color sliders. (RGB stands for red, green, and blue.) The hex code will appear in the HTML text box.

✔ Tip

■ To select a non-Websafe color, deselect the Web color checkbox, and use the sliders to select whatever color you like.

Browser-Safe Colors

You may have heard something about browser-safe color schemes. There are 216 colors that both Netscape and Microsoft browsers on both Windows and Macintosh platforms use, and these colors are called "browser safe." The colors in the browser-safe area all contain a 00, 33, 66, 99, CC, or FF pair in their hex code. Windows colors are generally slightly darker, whereas Macintosh colors are more accurate and are described as lighter and brighter. If you have access to both Windows and Macintosh machines on the same desk, compare nearly any page and you'll be surprised at the differences in many colors.

The color picker that you'll see when you click on any color selection button (**Figure 3.40**), in a dialog box or in the Property inspector, is comprised of these browser-safe colors, some of which repeat in the palette's 252 squares. If you're planning your page around browser-safe colors, the color picker is a good place to start.

Additionally, you'll notice that the pointer for the color picker is an eyedropper rather than a regular pointer. You can use the eyedropper to select any color you can see inside the Dreamweaver window, including colors in images.

From the options menu on the color picker, you can toggle on and off the Snap to Web Safe option. If you choose a non-Websafe color, such as one within a photograph or within one of the non-Websafe panels, Dreamweaver will convert it to a Websafe color if this option is on. That means if you need an exact match, you should turn this snapping off.

About HSV, RGB, and CYMK

The standard color picker that's similar to the Windows Color dialog box is the HSV Picker (**Figure 3.48**). HSV stands for hue, saturation, and value. For those of you unversed in color theory, a hue is a specific named color, such as blue or red; the saturation is the difference between a given tone and the nearest gray; and the value is the relative lightness (tint) or darkness (shade) of the color.

To use the HSV Picker:

1. Click on a color in the color wheel. Your selection will be displayed in the New color box. That sets the hue and saturation.

2. Adjust the slider bar to make the color lighter (towards 100) or darker (towards 0). That's the value.

3. You can fine-tune any of the values by typing a number in its text box.

The HSL Picker (**Figure 3.49**) works the same way; the letters stand for hue, saturation, and lightness.

RGB and CMYK are two ways of measuring color by its components. RGB is used commonly for digital images, while CMYK is used for four-color printing. RGB is red-green-blue; those are the primary components of white in visible light, like on a computer screen (as opposed to paint, where we think of the primaries as red, blue, and yellow). The CMYK scale is cyan, magenta, yellow, and black; these are the primary colors for ink, and most color graphics are printed using layers of these colors.

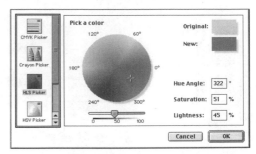

Figure 3.48 The HSV (Hue Saturation Value) Picker, in the Color dialog box for the Mac.

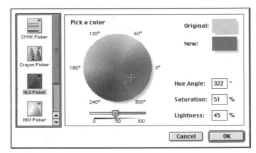

Figure 3.49 The HSL Picker (Hue, Saturation Lightness), in the Color dialog box for the Mac, is quite similar to the HSV picker.

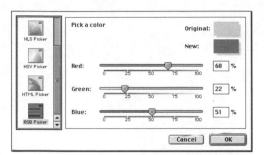

Figure 3.50 The RGB Picker (again in the Mac Color dialog box) uses the Red-Green-Blue values of visible light.

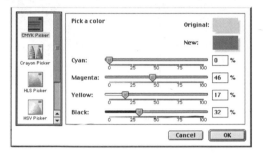

Figure 3.51 The CMYK (Cyan, Magenta, Yellow, and Black) Picker resembles the RGB picker; both are Mac color tools. Printers' inks use these four colors.

In both RGB (**Figure 3.50**) and CMYK (**Figure 3.51**), all colors can be represented by how much of each primary color they contain. You'll mostly want to use these pickers if you have the color values already—from Photoshop or Fireworks, for example.

In any case, you can type values in a color's text box or use the sliders to increase or decrease the amount of each primary color.

EDITING HTML

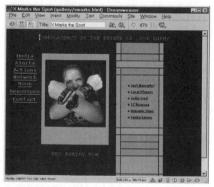

Figure 4.1 When you create a page in Design view in the Document window, you can drag and drop, insert and edit, without having to know a thing about HTML.

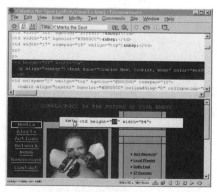

Figure 4.2 Tools such as the split view, which shows Design and Code views, and the Quick Tag editor, which hones in on specific tags to edit, can expedite any hand-coding you do.

HTML is the primary language of the Web. A few years ago, you couldn't create any pages without knowing how to write simple HTML code. With Dreamweaver, you can work in the Document window (**Figure 4.1**) to create page layouts and content without ever having to learn the actual code behind your creations. If you're interested in seeing what Dreamweaver does while you're inserting objects or if you like to hand code, you'll find abundant tools to help you do—or learn—the job quickly and well (**Figure 4.2**).

The letters *HTML* stand for HyperText Markup Language. *Hypertext* is oldschool speak for "pages that have words that link to things." Now, of course, images and multimedia files can also act as links, and the list of things on the other end of the link has expanded to include any and all digital files.

What, then, is a *markup language*? If you've ever seen proofreader's marks (**Figure 4.3**), that's the basic idea. Each mark indicates what the text should look like in final production.

About HTML

HTML evolved from a language called SGML (Standard Generalized Markup Language). In ye olden days of digital book and CD-ROM production, an editor used little pieces of SGML code called tags to mark, say, where the italics in a sentence started and stopped. Microsoft Word uses similar tags in its language RTF (Rich Text Format) to indicate the formatting the user creates with buttons and menus.

A tag generally has two parts: an opening and a closing (**Figure 4.4**). The stuff in between any pair of tags is what the tags modify, whether that's text, images, or other tags. Tags generally operate in pairs, like quotation marks and parentheses do, and they can be overlapped, or nested, just like multiple sets of quotation marks (**Figure 4.5**).

For instance, you may have a sentence with a link in it. All the text, including the link, may be included in a paragraph tag. The paragraph may be in a table cell, which is in a table row, which is in a table (**Figure 4.6**). The table, and everything else on the page, is included in the basic tag structure of a page, which tells the Web browser that this is a bona fide Web page and where to go from there.

The browser reads all the tags on a page and then draws the page, filling in the contents and shaping the text based on what the tags have to say.

HTML is an easy language to learn because the tags it uses are self-explanatory for the most part (see **Table 4.1**). P is for paragraph, B is for bold, I is for italic, IMG means image, and so on. Not all the tags are that transparent, but if you follow along in the Code inspector as you modify your page, you can pick up quite a bit.

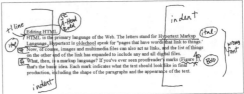

Figure 4.3 Marking up a page with HTML is just like marking up a page by hand with proofreader's marks.

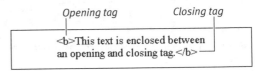

Figure 4.4 This text is enclosed by the two halves of a tag. The tag in this case is the <b> tag, which marks text as bold.

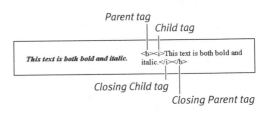

Figure 4.5 Notice that the tags envelop the text in order. The opening <i> tag is closest to the text, as is the closing </i> tag. The <b> tag envelops the <i> tag in the same way, and is called the parent tag for that reason.

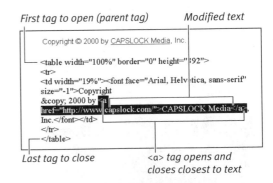

Figure 4.6 The highlighted tag is the <a> tag, which makes a link. The <a> tag includes an attribute, href, which means that it's a Web link, and a value (in quotation marks), which is the address of the Web site.

Head contents   Page title

Page contents start with body tag

Figure 4.7 Viewing the source of a Web page reveals the code behind it. From your browser's menu bar, select View > Page Source (or its equivalent command). To save the page for use in Dreamweaver, from the page source's menu bar, select File > Save As.

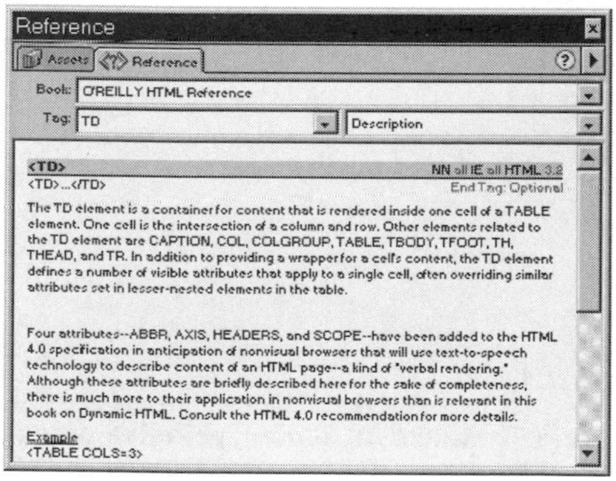

Figure 4.8 The Code Reference allows you to select a tag or attribute and then find out more about how it works.

Learning HTML

The best way to learn about Web pages is to view the source of pages on the Web that you like. You can save the page and open it in Dreamweaver to learn more. From your browser's menu bar, select View > Source, and you'll get a text window that shows you what's going on behind the scenes (**Figure 4.7**).

New in Dreamweaver 4 is the Code Reference (**Figure 4.8**), which allows you to select a tag and then read up on what it does. See *Using the Code Reference*, later in this chapter.

In most chapters of this book, I discuss specific tags and attributes and how they work (**Tables 4.1 and 4.2**). In order to feel comfortable working directly with the code, you need to stop thinking of HTML as a programming language. It's really not. It's more of an electronic shorthand for Post-It notes and highlighter pens.

In this chapter, I'll continue to introduce the basic principles of HTML. You'll find out how to edit pages in the Code inspector or Code view (**Figure 4.9**), as well as in the Quick Tag editor. You'll be able to format the HTML code to your taste using the Options menu. You'll also find out how to clean up HTML mistakes made by software or humans.

Appendix D on the Web site for this book offers copious details about HTML preferences and about using external HTML editors in conjunction with Dreamweaver.

Table 4.1 introduces some common tags we'll be seeing over the course of the book. **Table 4.2** shows you what an attribute is— it's like an adverb that modifies the action of the tag.

Table 4.1

Common HTML tags

Tag	Name	Use	Always Closed?
<HTML>	HTML	Document	Y
<HEAD>	Head	Document	Y
<TITLE>	Page Title	Document	Y
<BODY>*	Body	Document	Y
<H1>, <H2>...<H7>	Headings	Text Block	Y
<P>	Paragraph	Text Block	N
<BLOCKQUOTE>	Blockquote	Text Block	Y
<CENTER>	Center	Text Block	Y
<PRE>	Preformatted Text	Text Block	Y
 	Line Break	Text	N
<I>	Italic	Text	Y
<B>	Bold	Text	Y
<TT>	Teletype	Text	Y
<FONT>*	Font	Text	Y
<UL>	Bulleted List	List	Y
<OL>	Numbered List	List	Y
<LI>	List Item	List	N
<DL>	Definition List	List	Y
<DD>, <DT>	Definition Items	List	Y
<A>*	Anchor	Links	Y
<IMG>*	Image	Image Paths	N
<TABLE>*	Table	Table	Y
<TR>	Table Row	Table	Y
<TD>	Table Cell	Table	Y
<FORM>*	Form	Form	Y
<INPUT>*	Form Field	Form	N
<SELECT>*	Form Menu	Form	Y

*Indicates Tags that usually take attributes

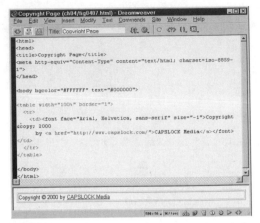

Figure 4.9 The table and its contents from **Figure 4.6** are shown here in the context of the code for an entire page. The first tag on a Web page is <html> and the closing tag is </html>. All visible contents are enclosed within the <body> tag. The <head> tag, at the top of every Web page, contains defining information for the page, such as the language it's in and the title of the page.

Table 4.2

Tags That Take Attributes, with Examples

Tag	Example
<A>	<a HREF="http://www.nasa.gov"> Mars-2, Earth-0</a>
<BODY>	<BODY bgcolor="#FFFFFF" link="#FF3300" vlink="#CC99CC" alink="#0000FF">Your entire visible page goes here.</BODY>
<IMG>	<IMG SRC="/images/doggie.gif">
<FONT>	<FONT FACE="Courier, Courier New" COLOR="red" SIZE="+2">This text will appear in Courier, in red, and two sizes larger than normal text.</FONT>
<TABLE>	<TABLE width="100%" border="1" align="center" cellpadding="10" cellspacing="5"><TR><TD>There must be rows and cells within opening and closing table tags.</TR></TD></TABLE>

Roundtrip HTML

Dreamweaver was designed for use by both codephobes and codephiles. If you never want to see a line of code in your life, you don't have to.

On the other hand, if you know how to tweak HTML to make it work for you, you've probably experienced the frustration of opening a page in a WYSIWYG editor and having it munged to bits by the purportedly helpful code engine of a program like FrontPage.

Dreamweaver writes valid code in the first place, and it uses no proprietary tags other than the JavaScript it writes (see Chapter 16). On the other hand, if you want to use mildly illegal code (such as wrapping a single <font> tag around an entire page instead of each paragraph), Dreamweaver can be coaxed into letting that slide.

Dreamweaver will not remove proprietary tags. Some made-up tags may be valid XML template markup created for a database application (see Chapters 18 and 19). If you write HTML improperly in the Code inspector, however, Dreamweaver will mark tags that are unclosed, missing quotation marks, or badly overlapped. Error highlighting is on automatically in Design view; you can turn it on in Code view by selecting Highlight Invalid HTML from the Options menu. (**Figure 4.10**). Click on the yellow mark in either window to read a brief description of the error in the Property inspector.

Dreamweaver does have corrective features, which you can modify or turn off (see *Cleaning Up HTML*, later in this chapter). And you can use Dreamweaver simultaneously with an external editor. This group of features together makes up what Macromedia calls Roundtrip HTML. More tips for Roundtrip HTML are included on the book's Web site, in Appendix B. Making Dreamweaver work with external editors is covered in Appendix D, also on the Web site.

Unclosed or extra <center> tag   Extra closing <b> tag

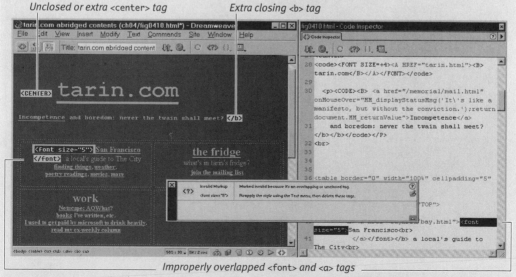

Improperly overlapped <font> and <a> tags

Figure 4.10 If you forget to close a tag, or if you overlap two tags improperly, Dreamweaver will mark the bad tags in yellow in both the Code inspector and the Document window, with descriptions available from the Property inspector.

Working with Code

The Code inspector (**Figure 4.11**) (formerly the HTML inspector) lets you both view and edit the HTML code for a page. The Code inspector displays the code that tells the page how to display in a Web browser or in the Document window.

To view the Code inspector:

◆ From the Document window menu bar, select Window > Code Inspector.

or

Press F10.

or

Click on the Launcher or Launcher bar's Show Code Inspector button (**Figure 4.12**).

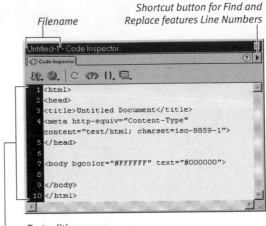

Filename

Shortcut button for Find and Replace features Line Numbers

Text editing space

Figure 4.11 The Code inspector is Dreamweaver's built-in HTML code editor.

Code inspector button (Launcher bar)

Code inspector button (Launcher)

Figure 4.12 Click on the Code inspector button on the Launcher or Launcher bar to view the Code inspector.

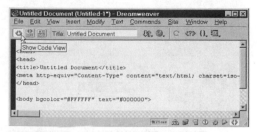

Figure 4.13 To view HTML code in the Document window, click on the Show Code View button on the toolbar.

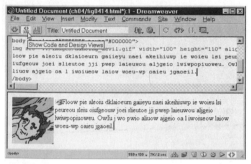

Figure 4.14 To view both Code and Design views in the Document window, click on the Show Code and Design Views button on the toolbar.

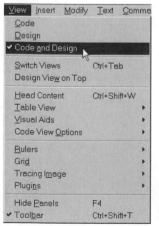

About Code View and Split View

New in Dreamweaver 4, Code View and Split View let you view the HTML code for your page directly in the Document window. The Code View has the same features and functions as the Code inspector, including line numbers and word wrap. The regular Document window WYSIWYG view is called Design View. To view just the code, click on the Code View button (**Figure 4.13**). To view the code and the Design View in a frames-like split window, click on the Split View button (**Figure 4.14**).

✔ Tip

- You can also change views by selecting Code, Design, or Code and Design from the View menu (**Figure 4.15**) or by pressing Ctrl+T.

Figure 4.15 The View menu offers the same choices for viewing the page or the code in the Document window. You can also keep the Design view on top of other windows.

About selections

As I described in Chapter 1, any selections you make in the Document window will also be made in the Code inspector (**Figure 4.16**), and vice versa. This of course applies to the Code View as well.

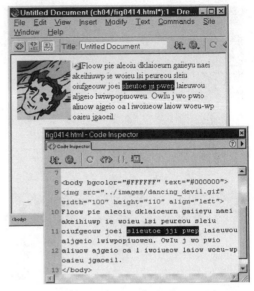

Figure 4.16 When I select text in the Document window, the Code inspector also highlights the selection.

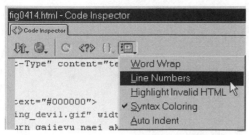

Figure 4.17 The View Options menu for formatting HTML appears on the Code inspector and Code view toolbars.

Wrap option unchecked

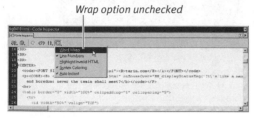

Figure 4.18 I unchecked the Wrap option. Even with the Code inspector, really, really wide, long lines of code scroll offscreen horizontally. Word wrapping is applied to this page in **Figure 4.19**.

Figure 4.19 When text is wrapped, long lines of code, such as lines 15 and 21 here, may wrap over onto unnumbered lines.

Code Options

The Code Inspector toolbar includes a View Options menu (**Figure 4.17**). The options include Word Wrap, for viewing long lines of code; Line Numbers, for quickly locating a line of code; Highlight Invalid HTML, which marks up bad syntax; Syntax Coloring, for marking types of tags with different colors; and Auto Indent, for formatting chunks of code with indenting. Let's look at each option in turn.

About Word Wrap

In the Code inspector, you can turn on Word Wrap so that the text wraps to the window width. This is *soft wrapping*—no line breaks are inserted. You can toggle wrapping on and off by selecting Word Wrap from the View Options menu. Unwrapped code is shown in **Figure 4.18**, and Word Wrap is turned on in **Figure 4.19**. For more on wrapping preferences, see *Setting HTML Preferences,* later in this chapter.

About line numbers

When you turn on line numbering, each line of code is numbered in the Code inspector. A line of code may wrap over into an unnumbered line (**Figure 4.19**). Line numbers can be useful for discussing pages with your colleagues, as in, "Hey, Steph, the table I'm having trouble with starts on line 47." Line numbers—sans wrapping—should be the same in Dreamweaver as in line editors such as vi.

✔ Tip

■ To select an entire line of code, wrapped or unwrapped, click on its line number. Line 15 is selected in **Figure 4.19**.

About Syntax Coloring

You can turn on syntax coloring so that specific tags are instantly marked by particular colors as soon as you insert an object or type some code (**Figure 4.20**). These colors appear only in Dreamweaver—they won't show up in a browser or text editor. You must turn on Syntax Coloring in the Code Inspector's View Options menu in order for Dreamweaver's Reference feature to work properly (see *Using the Code Reference*, later in this chapter). You can toggle coloring on and off by selecting Syntax Coloring from the View Options menu. To pick the colors for a tag or family of tags, see *Setting HTML Preferences*, later in this chapter.

About Auto Indent

As you add code in Dreamweaver, either by creating in the Document window or by hand-coding in Code View, Dreamweaver can automatically indent blocks of code. For example, you probably want your code for the rows and cells in a table to appear indented so that you can spot them easily when checking out the code (**Figure 4.21**). You can toggle auto-indenting on and off by selecting Auto Indent from the Options menu.

✔ Tip

■ You can set indent for only tables or only framesets, or for particular tags. To decide the space per indent or to select which tags get indented automatically, see *Setting HTML Preferences*, later in this chapter.

Figure 4.20 Although it's hard to see in black and white, the tags for the table cells, the paragraphs, and the links are all marked with different colors in Code view.

Figure 4.21 The tags within this table are indented so that you can find table rows <tr> and table cells <td> easily.

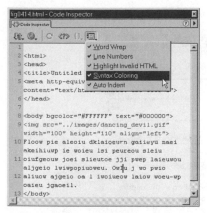

Figure 4.22 Turn on Syntax Coloring from the View Options menu to make the Code Reference's context-sensitive feature work.

Reference button

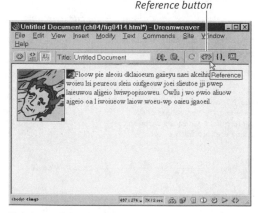

Figure 4.23 Select an object or a tag, and then click on the Reference button to read about the associated code.

Using the Code Reference

Dreamweaver now offers tag-by-tag help in the form of a context-sensitive Reference panel. If you want to know what a tag does, you can select it and open the Reference to read a description and some basic rules.

The text in the Reference panel comes from O'Reilly textbooks, which are reliable and well-written.

To use the Reference while working:

1. You must turn on syntax coloring in order for the Reference to recognize a tag. In Document window Code view or in the Code inspector, select Syntax Coloring from the View Options menu (**Figure 4.22**).

2. Click within your document (any view) on a tag or modified object that you want to learn more about.

3. Click the Reference button. (**Figure 4.23**). The Reference panel will appear (**Figure 4.24**).

To browse the Reference:

1. In the Reference panel, select one of the three topics from the Book drop-down menu: HTML, CSS, or JavaScript.

2. Select an HTML tag, CSS attribute, or JavaScript object from the drop-down menu on the left.

3. To read about additional attributes of HTML tags or JavaScript objects, select an attribute from the Description drop-down menu on the right.

Tag name

Browser version compatibility

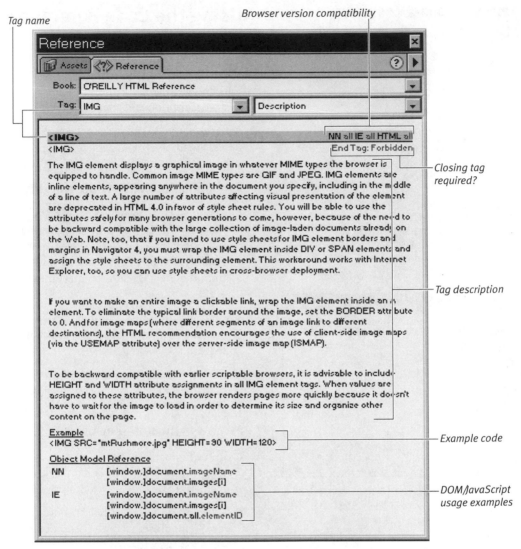

Closing tag required?

Tag description

Example code

DOM/JavaScript usage examples

Figure 4.24 The Reference panel provides handy information about most HTML tags and attributes.

Figure 4.25 The Quick Tag editor. Pretty unassuming looking, yes?

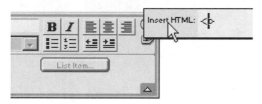

Figure 4.26 Click on the Quick Tag editor button on the Property inspector to pop open the editor.

Figure 4.27 Click on the gray selection handle to drag the editor away from the Property inspector.

Figure 4.28 You can drag the editor wherever you like.

Using the Quick Tag Editor

Describing how to use the Quick Tag editor is much harder than actually using it. The QT editor, as I'll call it, allows you to insert or edit HTML code one chunk at a time in the Document window, without even having to open the Code inspector or Code View.

It's true that there are instances when you may find it easier to simply type the code you want in the Code inspector. But if you're learning HTML as you go, the QT editor offers shortcuts and safeguards that virtually guarantee clean code, even if you've never written a line of HTML.

The QT editor (**Figure 4.25**) offers several different modes in which you can fine-tune your HTML. Which mode you work in depends on what item(s) you select (text, tag, object, and so on) before you open the editor.

No matter what selection you make, though, you open the QT editor in one of two ways.

To open the QT editor:

◆ Click on the QT editor button on the Property inspector (**Figure 4.26**).

or

Press Ctrl+T (Command+T).

You'll see a typing area, and the words Edit Tag, Insert HTML, or Wrap Tag. Those are the names of the edit modes.

To close the QT editor:

◆ Simply press Enter (Return).

To move the QT editor:

1. Click on its selection handle; that's the gray part of the editor (**Figure 4.27**).

2. Drag it wherever you like (**Figure 4.28**).

Working in Wrap Tag mode

Wrap Tag mode (**Figure 4.29**) allows you to select an object or some text and then wrap a tag around it. For instance, if you select some unformatted text and then enter the <center> tag in the QT editor, the tag will open at the beginning of your selection and close at the end of it, and your text will be centered.

✔ Tips

- In Wrap Tag mode, you can enter only one tag at a time.

- The editor opens in Wrap Tag mode if you select text or an object rather than an HTML tag.

Working in Insert HTML mode

Insert HTML mode allows you to insert as much HTML as you want at the insertion point. You can insert multiple tags if you like.

✔ Tips

- Insert HTML mode is the default Quick Tag editor mode if you haven't selected a specific object or tag (**Figure 4.30**).

- If you insert only an opening tag with Insert HTML mode, the closing tags will be inserted for you if they're required. You can move them afterward, if you like.

Figure 4.29 The Quick Tag editor in Wrap Tag mode. Use this mode to insert a tag around some text or another object.

Figure 4.30 The Quick Tag editor in Insert HTML mode. Use this mode to insert more than one tag, or some code that doesn't directly modify text or an object on your page.

Figure 4.31 The Quick Tag editor in Edit Tag mode. Use this mode to edit existing code.

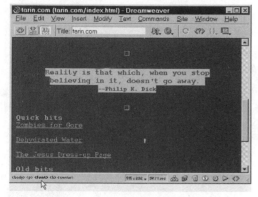

Figure 4.32 Click on a tag in the tag selector to highlight the entire tag and its contents. Right-click (Control+click) on a tag in the tag selector to pop up a menu of editing options.

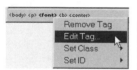

Figure 4.33 Right-click (Control+click) on a tag in the tag selector for more options.

Working in Edit Tag mode

To edit an existing tag, you'll use Edit Tag mode (**Figure 4.31**). You can change the tag itself; or add, delete, or change its attributes.

✔ Tips

- If you select the contents of a tag, but not an entire tag, the QT editor will second-guess you and select the whole thing.

- The best way to select an entire tag is by clicking on it in the tag selector in the lower-left corner of the Document window (**Figure 4.32**). You can also right-click (Control+click) on a tag there for more options (**Figure 4.33**).

To insert a tag using the QT editor:

1. In the Document window, select the text or object to which you want to apply a tag in Wrap Tag mode (**Figure 4.34**).

or

To work in Insert HTML mode, click where you want to insert the code.

2. Open the Quick Tag editor by clicking on the Quick Tag editor button, or by pressing Ctrl+T (Command+T).

If the QT editor does not open in your preferred mode, press Ctrl+T (Command+T) again, until the QT editor shows the mode you desire.

3. After a second or two, the Tag Hints menu will appear (**Figure 4.35**).

Select a tag from the menu by double-clicking it or pressing Enter (Return).

or

Type a few characters of your tag, and the menu will scroll to the closest tag alphabetically, so you can select it.

or

If you wish to type code directly, instead of choosing it from the menu, click within the brackets to dismiss the Tag Hints menu.

4. Either way, when the tag you like appears in the brackets in the QT editor, you can do one of two things.

To insert the tag as is, press Enter (Return).

To add attributes to the tag, type a space. After the space, the Tag Hints menu will appear again (**Figure 4.36**).

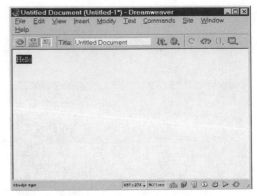

Figure 4.34 Select the text or object you want to wrap a tag around using Wrap Tag mode, or just click in the Document window to use Insert HTML mode.

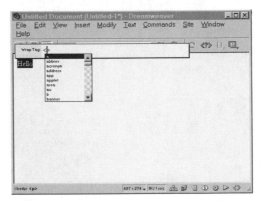

Figure 4.35 If you pause while typing, the Tag Hints menu will appear.

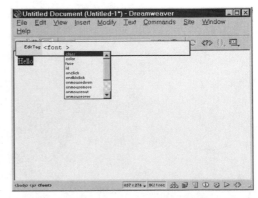

Figure 4.36 Type a space after the tag name to add an attribute, and the Tag Hints menu, which lists the available attributes for that tag, will appear.

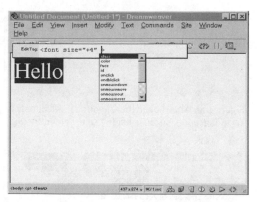

Figure 4.37 You can continue to add attributes by typing a space after each one.

Figure 4.38 I did not add the closing </font> tag, but Dreamweaver did it for me. Dreamweaver watches your syntax in both Wrap Tag and Insert HTML mode.

Figure 4.39 I selected just part of the text that's surrounded by a <font> tag.

5. Follow steps 3–4 for each attribute you wish to put in the tag (**Figure 4.37**).

6. When you're finished, press Enter (Return) to close the QT editor and apply the code to the selection. Dreamweaver will close any tags you opened (**Figure 4.38**).

To edit a tag using the QT editor:

1. In the Document window, select the tag you wish to edit. (Click the text or object, and then click the appropriate tag in the tag selector). If you don't select an entire tag (**Figure 4.39**), Dreamweaver will select the whole tag, and possibly its parent tag.

continued on next page

USING THE QUICK TAG EDITOR

2. Open the Quick Tag editor (**Figure 4.40**) by clicking on the QT editor button, or by pressing Ctrl+T (Command+T).

3. If the QT editor does not open in Edit Tag mode, press Ctrl+T (Command+T) once or twice more (**Figure 4.41**).

4. You can edit the tag itself, or any attribute of the tag. To scroll through the attributes of the tag, press Tab (**Figure 4.42**); to move backward, press Shift+Tab.

5. With the tag name or an attribute name selected, you can type over it to change it. If you pause while typing, the Tag Hints menu will appear (**Figure 4.43**).

6. Select a tag from the menu by double-clicking it or pressing Enter (Return).

or

If you wish to type code directly instead of choosing it from the menu, click within the brackets or press Esc to dismiss the Tag Hints menu.

7. To add attributes to the tag, type a space. After the space, the Hints menu will appear again, listing available attributes for the tag, or available values for the attribute.

8. When you're finished, press Enter (Return) to close the QT editor and apply the code to the selection (**Figure 4.44**).

✔ Tip

■ If you Tab or Shift+Tab after you've edited an attribute, your changes will be applied to the tag immediately. You can pause changes until you close the QT editor. To set this and other preferences, see Appendix D on the Web site for this book.

Figure 4.40 When I open the QT editor, it will appear in Wrap Tag mode, because I didn't select an entire tag.

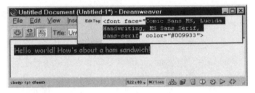

Figure 4.41 When I switch to Edit Tag mode by pressing Ctrl+T (Command+T), the Editor will select the entire tag's worth of text.

Figure 4.42 Press Tab to hop from one attribute to the next within the tag and the editor.

Figure 4.43 After you press Tab, your edits, if any, will be applied to the tag. If you pause while editing, the Tag Hints menu may reappear.

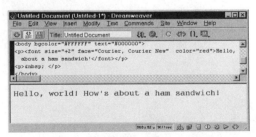

Figure 4.44 Now I'm all done. In Split view, you can see that I changed two of three <font> tag attributes.

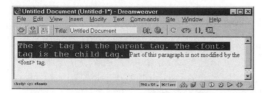

Figure 4.45 You can see in the tag selector that of the two tags modifying the text, the parent tag, the `<p>` tag in this case, has been selected.

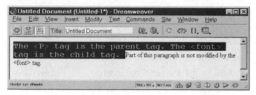

Figure 4.46 With the `<p>` tag selected, I pressed Ctrl+Shift+>, and the child tag (the `<font>` tag) was selected. This can come in very handy when trying to select links, list items, and blockquotes, as well as font modifications.

Figure 4.47 Right-click (Control+click) on the tag in the status bar, and select Remove Tag from the menu that appears.

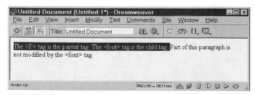

Figure 4.48 The `<font>` tag that I right-clicked on in Figure 4.47 was removed.

Selecting Parent and Child Tags

While you're editing tags, you may find it difficult to select a tag for whatever reason. You can toggle from the tag you've selected with the QT editor to its immediate surrounding tag, called the parent tag, or to the immediate tag it envelops, called the child tag. This works whether you're working in the QT editor or just in the Document window.

To select the parent tag:

◆ Press Ctrl+Shift+< (Less Than); on the Mac, it's Command+Shift+< (Less Than).

or

From the menu bar, select Edit > Select Parent Tag (**Figure 4.45**).

To select the child tag:

◆ Press Ctrl+Shift+> (Greater Than); on the Mac, it's Command+Shift+> (Greater Than).

or

From the menu bar, select Edit > Select Child Tag (**Figure 4.46**). If there is no child tag inside the selected tag, the tag will simply remain selected.

Removing a tag

You can also delete tags from within the Document window. Dreamweaver watches your back and won't let you remove some tags; for instance, the `<body>` tag is required.

To remove a tag:

1. Click on the object or text affected by the offending tag.

2. Right-click (Control+click) on the tag in the tag selector in the lower-left corner of the Document window (**Figure 4.47**).

3. From the pop-up menu that appears, select Remove Tag. The tag will be deleted (**Figure 4.48**).

About the Hints Menu

The Hints menu will appear after a few seconds when you open the tag selector. It's a regular old drop-down menu. To select a tag, scroll through the menu using the scrollbars or arrow keys, or type a few letters of the tag, and the menu will scroll down alphabetically. For example, type cen, and the menu will scroll to center. To enter a selection, press Enter (Return), or double-click the entry.

If you pause for a few seconds while editing or entering a tag or an attribute, the Hints menu will come back. The Hints menu will also appear for attributes of a tag if you type a space after the tag.

If you select the name of an attribute, available standard values for that attribute will appear. For example, the tag <td> (table cell) offers several attributes, including align. If you select the align attribute, the Hints menu will offer left, center, and right as available values. On the other hand, another attribute of the <td> tag is bgcolor. If you select that attribute, every code for every color will not appear. You'll have to type the hex code yourself, or save your changes and then select the color using the Property inspector.

To make the Hints menu go away, click the QT editor, press Esc, or just keep typing. If the Hints menu doesn't appear when you want it to, I'm afraid you'll have to close the QT editor and try it again, or just type the tag or attribute.

The Tag Hints menu contents are in a file called TagAttributeList.txt, inside Dreamweaver's Configuration folder. You can add tags, attributes, or values to this file, or you can delete esoteric tags you don't use. Make a backup of this file before you edit it.

To set preferences, see Appendix D on the book's Web site.

Figure 4.49 On the Invisibles category of the Objects panel, click on the Comment button.

Figure 4.50 Leave a message for yourself or for future producers of the page by using the Insert Comment dialog box. Dreamweaver enters the special opening and closing comment brackets for you.

```
Untitled-1 - Code Inspector

8  <p>Doot de doot doo doot de doot
   doody doot doo</p>
9
10 <!--Last updated when oil was
   alive. -->
11 </body>
```

Figure 4.51 The comment appears in the Code inspector, but not in the Document window.

Inserting Comments

Comments are invisible notes you want to leave for yourself in the code—they won't show up in the browser window, but anyone can see these comments in the source code. You might want to add a reminder of when you created the file, when you last updated it, or who made the last revision.

You can also use comments to demarcate sections of a document, such as where a table begins and ends, or what part of the document constitutes the footer and copyright notice.

Comments look like this:

```
<!-- You can't see me -->
```

To add a comment:

1. In either Code or Design View in the Document window, click to place the insertion point in the area where you want the comment to appear.

2. From the Document window menu bar, select Insert > Invisible Tags > Comment.
   or
   On the Objects panel (Invisibles category), click on the Comment button (**Figure 4.49**).

3. The Insert Comment dialog box will appear (**Figure 4.50**).

4. Type the text you want to include in the comment in the Comment text box.

5. Click on OK to close the dialog box.

If you have invisible element viewing turned on (View > Invisible Elements), you'll see the comment icon. 🖺.

Otherwise, you can look at the comment in the Code inspector (**Figure 4.51**).

continued on next page

✔ Tips

- You can view or edit the comments later on by selecting the Comment icon and viewing the Property inspector (**Figure 4.52**) or the Quick Tag editor (**Figure 4.53**).
- To add comments to a file without storing them in the file itself and making them public, see *Using Design Notes* in Chapter 21. You can also add comments to non-HTML files this way.

Comment
Last updated when oil was alive.

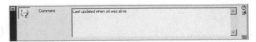

Figure 4.52 You can view or edit your comment in the Property inspector by clicking on the Comment icon in the Document window.

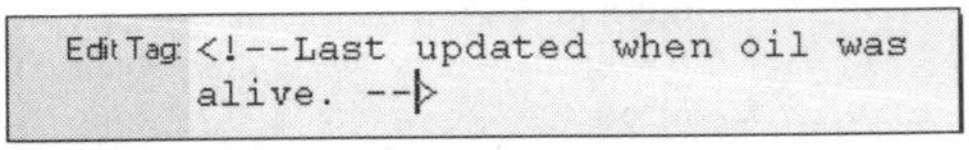
Edit Tag: <!--Last updated when oil was alive. -->

Figure 4.53 You can view or edit your comment in the QT editor by clicking on the Comment icon and pressing Ctrl+T (Command+T).

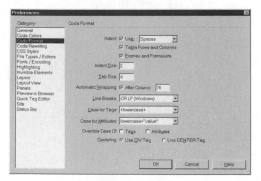

Figure 4.54 The Code Format panel of the Preferences dialog box lets you get nitpicky about how your code is constructed.

Setting HTML Preferences

If you work somewhere that has a house HTML style guide, it's probably specific about things like indenting (or not), tag case (upper or lower), and how text is wrapped. In production groups, the interaction of individual coders' pages with the entire site and with vi and CVS (two tools used in Unix environments) has a lot to do with these standards. Even if you work for yourself, setting up house rules for consistency is a good idea.

✔ Tip

- More HTML preferences (including Code Color preferences, Quick Tag editor preferences, and External Editor preferences) are discussed in Appendix D on the Web site for this book. HTML Cleanup preferences are discussed later in this chapter.

To change Code Format preferences:

1. From the Document window menu bar, select Edit > Preferences. The Preferences dialog box will appear.

2. In the Category box at the left of the dialog box, click on Code Format. That panel of the dialog box will appear (**Figure 4.54**).

3. To turn off indenting altogether, uncheck the Indent checkbox.

4. To use Spaces or Tabs for indent, select that option from the Use drop-down menu.

   For more on indenting, see the sidebar, *HTML Code Format Details*, on page 96.

continued on next page

5. You can have Dreamweaver automatically wrap text in the Code inspector by checking the Automatic Wrapping checkbox.

   For more on wrapping, see *HTML Format Details*.

6. To set the format for line breaks, select Windows, Macintosh, or Unix from the Line Breaks drop-down menu.

   For more on line breaks, see the sidebar, *HTML Format Details*.

7. To set the case for tags, select lowercase or UPPERCASE from the Case for Tags drop-down menu. For more on tag case, see the sidebar, *HTML Format Details*.

8. To set the default tag for centering text, click the Use DIV Tag or Use CENTER Tag radio button. To go oldschool, use CENTER. The DIV tag is a new-ish version of the paragraph tag. These tags are described in detail in Chapters 6 and 14.

9. When you're all set, click on OK to save your changes and close the Preferences dialog box.

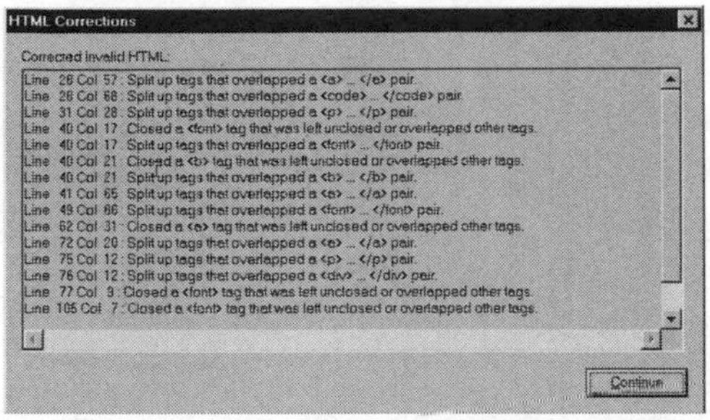

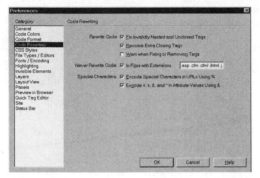

Figure 4.55 When you open a file with errors in it, you can get a prompt like this one that tells you what's being fixed. This is the file that I trashed in **Figure 4.10**.

Figure 4.56 The Code Rewriting panel of the Preferences dialog box. The Warn When Fixing or Removing Tags checkbox is turned off by default; check it if you want to see the prompt in **Figure 4.55**.

✔ **Tip**

■ For assistance in modifying the other attributes, see Appendix D on the Web site for this book.

Cleaning Up HTML

For the most part, Dreamweaver writes passable, clean code. If you modify the code, Dreamweaver usually avoids changing it back. On the other hand, some applications (most notably Microsoft products) write hideous code that begs intervention from the UN.

Dreamweaver offers several handy shortcuts for cleaning up gnarly code. You may have handwritten the code half-smashed on No-Doz and Jolt cola, or an intern may have demonstrated his or her lack of brilliance all over your site, or you may have produced pages in a lackluster editor.

Dreamweaver even makes some common errors that are easily fixed. There are three ways to clean up your code: opening a file, using the Clean Up HTML command, and using the Clean Up Word HTML command.

What Dreamweaver does on opening a file

Dreamweaver makes certain revisions to a page when it's first opened. To get a prompt when these changes occur (**Figure 4.55**), or to turn off some of the automatic corrections, you can modify the preferences. If you're a beginning coder, it's best to leave most of these options as is.

To modify the auto-cleanup prefs:

1. From the Document window menu bar, select Edit > Preferences. The Preferences dialog box will appear.

2. In the Category list at the left, select Code Rewriting. That panel of the dialog box will appear (**Figure 4.56**).

3. To see a prompt when Dreamweaver modifies your code, check the Warn When Fixing or Removing Tags checkbox.

HTML Code Format Details

Good code is nitpicky, right? This sidebar describes some of the nitpickier details and rationales for indenting, wrapping, line breaks, and tag case. Use this sidebar in conjunction with the steps in the preceding sections.

◆ **Indenting:** By default, Dreamweaver indents certain elements of HTML—the rows and cells in a table, for example. Not indenting may save some download time on very large pages.

To set an indent size (the default is two spaces or two tabs), type a number in the Indent text box. To set the tab size, because tabs in HTML are spaces, type a number in the Tab text box.

Some production teams indent in tables or on frameset pages even if they don't do so anywhere else. (It makes working with nested tables and framesets easier.) To turn on indenting specifically for Table Rows and Columns or Frames and Framesets, check the appropriate box.

◆ **Wrapping:** To wrap within the Code inspector window automatically, check the Automatic Wrapping checkbox. To turn off autowrapping, uncheck it. (You can wrap individual pages differently by using the Options menu in the Code inspector or Code View.)

The default column width for text-based programs like vi and Telnet is usually 76 or 80 columns (a column in this context is the number of monospace characters across a window). To set a different width, type it in the After Column text box.

◆ **Line Breaks:** Line breaks are done differently on different platforms. Because line breaks are actually characters, a line-break character may show up in Unix, for example, if a Mac or Windows line break is inserted. If you work with pages that will be checked in to a document management system like CVS, be sure to check with your house style guide or an engineer to verify your choices here.

◆ **Tag Case:** Some folks are especially picky about whether tags and attributes are written in UPPERCASE or lowercase.

To set the case for attributes (the case can be the same or different from tag case), select lowercase or UPPERCASE from the Case for Attributes drop-down menu.

(Attribute values are always lowercase, as in `<TD ALIGN="center">`.)

You can have Dreamweaver override the tag and attribute case for documents that were produced in other applications or before you edited preferences.

To change the HTML case of older documents opened in Dreamweaver, check the Tags and/or Attributes checkbox in the Override Case Of line. Handily enough, the Clean Up HTML command (described in the next section) will set the proper tag case for your documents.

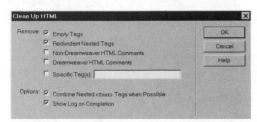

Figure 4.57 Choose which elements to clean up in the Clean Up HTML dialog box.

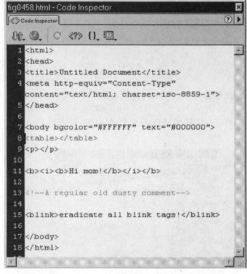

Figure 4.58 This "page" is really just a catalog of errors to be fixed.

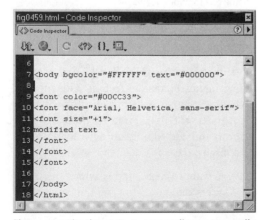

Figure 4.59 The three <font> tags on line 14 can easily be combined into a single <font> tag using the Clean Up HTML command.

Performing additional clean-up

Aside from Dreamweaver's automatic cleanup functions, you can have it perform more specific code-massaging at any point.

To clean up HTML code:

1. From the Document window menu bar, select Commands > Clean Up HTML. The Clean Up HTML dialog box will appear (**Figure 4.57**).

2. Dreamweaver lets you remove the following boo-boos (**Figure 4.58**):
   ◆ Empty Tags (Lines 8 and 9)
   ◆ Redundant Nested Tags (Line 11)
   ◆ Non-Dreamweaver HTML Comments (regular comments not inserted by the program; Line 13)
   ◆ Dreamweaver HTML Comments (This option removes comments Dreamweaver inserts with scripts and the like).
   ◆ Specific Tags (any specified tag; Line 15). You must type the tag in the text box. Type tags without brackets, and separate multiple tags with commas. For example: blink, u, tt).

   Check the box beside the garbage you want to be removed (**Figure 4.57**).

3. Even Dreamweaver is guilty of redundancy when coding <font> tags (**Figure 4.59**). To combine all redundant font tags, check the Combine Nested <font> Tags When Possible checkbox.

4. To see for yourself the errors Dreamweaver catches, check the Show Log on Completion checkbox.

continued on next page

5. Ready? Click on OK. Dreamweaver will scan the page for the selected errors, and if you chose to display a log, it will return a list of what it fixed (**Figure 4.60**).

Cleaning Up Word HTML

Many text documents, for better or worse, are prepared in Microsoft Word at one stage or another in the production process. Word (95, 97, 98, 00) offers a timesaving Save As HTML feature that puts in paragraphs, line breaks, links, and most text formatting. But it does it so badly!

Fortunately, the errors Word makes when converting pages to HTML are *consistently* bad. The Dreamweaver team figured out the error patterns and wrote a widget to fix most of them.

To clean up Word HTML:

1. In the Document window, open the page you saved as HTML using Word.

2. From the Document window menu bar, select Commands > Clean Up Word HTML.

Dreamweaver will read the document info to determine which version of Word was responsible for the damage. If it can't detect this information, a warning will appear (**Figure 4.61**). Your document may not have been prepared in Word; you might want to run it through twice.

In any case, the Clean Up Word HTML dialog box will appear, perhaps after you click on OK to dismiss the dialog (**Figure 4.62, Figure 4.63** and **Figure 4.64**).

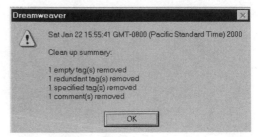

Figure 4.60 After cleaning up the stuff in **Figure 4.58**, this dialog box shows what was done.

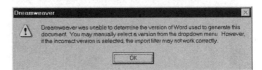

Figure 4.61 This dialog box will appear if you use Clean Up Word HTML to fix a file that wasn't created in Word, or that was created with an ancient version.

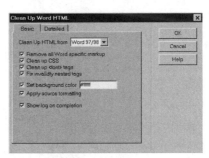

Figure 4.62 The Clean Up Word HTML dialog box for Word 97/98.

Nesting Instincts

Valid, by-the-spec HTML asks that `<font>` tags be nested inside `<p>` tags. This means that each paragraph contains its own font formatting. This can take up quite a bit of room and add significant download time to large pages.

If you want to cheat on this, which the browsers allow, then turn off the Fix Invalidly Nested and Unclosed Tags option. Then, you can use a single `<font>` tag to modify as many blocks of text as you desire.

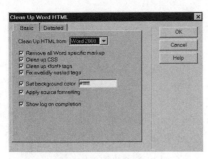

Figure 4.63 The Clean Up Word HTML dialog box for Word 2000.

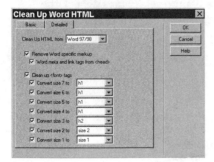

Figure 4.64 The Detailed panel of the Clean Up Word HTML dialog box for Word 97/98.

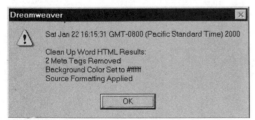

Figure 4.65 This dialog box is a log of the changes that were made using the Clean Up Word HTML command.

3. If Dreamweaver detects the version of Word used to save the HTML, it will appear in the Clean Up HTML From drop-down menu. If not, select your version. (For Word 95, select Word 97/98). You may get a warning that the version is different from what Dreamweaver detected.

4. The following options are available for fixing. For more details about Word-specific markup, see the sidebar, *Detailed Word Markup.*

   ◆ Remove Word specific markup (tags that aren't standard HTML tags)

   ◆ Clean Up CSS (fixes modifications made using Cascading Style Sheets)

   ◆ Clean Up <font> tags (consolidates redundant text formatting)

   ◆ Fix Invalidly Nested Tags (rearranges tags nested in nonstandard order)

   ◆ Set Background Color. (Type the hex code in the text box. #ffffff is white. If you don't know the hex code, skip this one and apply the background color later.)

   ◆ Apply Source Formatting. (Makes modifications to the indenting, line breaks, and case selections. See *Setting HTML Preferences*, earlier in this chapter.)

5. To see a dialog box describing the fixes Dreamweaver made, make sure the Show Log on Completion checkbox is marked.

6. Ready? Click on OK. Dreamweaver will make the selected revisions and display a log if you asked it to do so (**Figure 4.65**).

CLEANING UP HTML

Detailed Word Markup

Word makes some singular, usually unnecessary additions to standard HTML code when you save a Word file as HTML. If any of this proprietary code is something you want to address on your own, you can ask Dreamweaver not to remove it.

In the Clean Up HTML dialog box, click on the Detailed tab. That panel will come to the front (**Figure 4.64** and **Figure 4.66**).

In all versions of Word, the program applies its own <meta> and <link> tags in the head of the document. If these are useless to you, check the Word Meta and Link Tags from <head> checkbox (**Figure 4.67**).

◆ Word 97/98: Word 97 and 98 make peculiar choices when it comes to font sizes. To convert Word's font size choices to your own, click the checkbox for the font size, and then select a heading size or font size from the associated drop-down menu. For example, a wise choice would be to assign size 3 text to the default size in Dreamweaver. If you want to keep Word's size assignment, select Don't Change.

◆ Word 2000: Word is getting ahead of itself in using XML, or in other words, it includes proprietary code for perfectly vanilla HTML functions. It also makes a few more boo-boos.

To remove XML from the opening <html> document tag, check that box.

To remove other Word HTML markup (in the form of proprietary tags), check the Word XML Markup checkbox.

To remove pseudo-code, check the <![if …]><![endif]> Conditional Tags and Their Contents checkbox.

To remove both empty paragraphs and extra margins, check that box.

These details can be modified at any point during your cleanup.

Figure 4.67 Word inserted these META and XML tags; the two META NAME tags will be removed, as will all the extraneous XML markup. These tags may be useful for importing documents; if so, uncheck the XML checkbox.

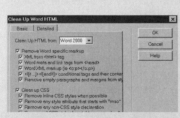

Figure 4.66 The Detailed panel of the Clean Up Word HTML dialog box for Word 2000.

WORKING WITH IMAGES

Figure 5.1 The splash page for Christian Cosas's personal home page uses a simple image against a plain background. Both the image and the text link point to the site's table of contents, shown in **Figure 5.2**.

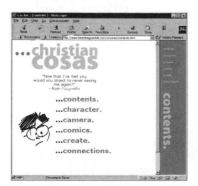

Figure 5.2 The site includes linked images—the words are all image files. With 11 images on the page including the background, the whole page weighs in at only 27K.

Most basic Web pages are composed of a combination of text, links, and images. Used to be, if you found an image online, you had to download it, get offline, and then open the image in a viewing program. That all seems like ancient history these days.

Now that images are easy to use, some Web pages use them at the expense of their visitors' taste and time. **Figures 5.1** and **5.2** show Christian Cosas's site, which makes excellent use of images.

How do you use images well? By making them an integral part of the design of the page, and not by adding them willy-nilly. We've all seen pages with dancing chili peppers sitting beside headlines for no apparent reason—not so good.

In this chapter, we'll find out how to place an image, how to resize it, and how to add a border. We'll discuss image file formats and image alignment, as well as how to make images work with slow connections. And we'll find out about integrating external editors—including Fireworks—with Dreamweaver, so that you can easily edit images while you're making pages.

✔ Tips

- To find out about using background images, refer to Chapter 3.

- For instructions on making an image map, see Appendix A on the Web site.

Placing an Image

There are several ways to place images using Dreamweaver.

To place an image:

1. With the desired page open in the Document window, click at the place on the page where you'd like the image to appear.

2. From the Document window menu bar, select Insert > Image (**Figure 5.3**).

   or

   Click on the Image button in the (**Figure 5.4**).

   or

   Press Ctrl+Alt+I (Command+Option+I). Regardless of the method, the Select Image Source dialog box will appear (**Figures 5.5** and **5.6**).

3. If you know the location of the image on the Web or on your computer, type it in the URL text box.

   or

   Browse through the files and folders on your computer until you find the image file. Click on the image file's icon or file name, so that its name appears in the File name text box.

4. Click on OK to close the Insert Image dialog box. The image will appear at the insertion point in the Document window.

✔ Tip

- If you haven't yet saved your page, a dialog box will appear telling you about file pathnames. Click on OK to close this dialog box. Ideally, you should select images from your local site, or you can copy them there. If you haven't yet set up a local site, see Chapter 2. Pathnames are described further in Chapter 6.

Figure 5.3 Select Insert > Image from the Document window menu bar.

Figure 5.4 Click on the Image button in the Objects panel.

Figure 5.5 The Select Image Source dialog box is similar to the familiar Open dialog box. If you click on a filename, a preview of the image is displayed.

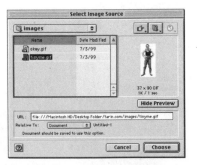

Figure 5.6 The Select Image Source dialog box on the Mac. Click the Show/Hide Preview button to show or hide the image preview.

Figure 5.7 The Assets panel can catalog all the images in your local site, no matter what folder they're in. Each local site will display different assets.

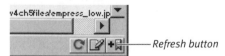
— Refresh button

Figure 5.8 To update the list of images in your site, click the Refresh button.

Inserting Images with the Assets Panel

Dreamweaver 4's new tool for managing images and other media objects is called the Assets panel (**Figure 5.7**). I introduced you to the Assets panel in Chapter 3, which is where you'll find a full description of how this handy tool works, including how to catalog Favorites. Right now, I'll show you how to insert a simple image with the Assets panel.

✔ Tip

- In order for the Assets panel to catalog your images, you must create a local site with a site cache. This is discussed in Chapter 2.

To place an image asset:

1. Open the local site in which your images are located by selecting Site > Open Site > Site Name from the Document window menu bar.

2. Open the Assets panel by selecting Window > Assets from the Document window menu bar. The Assets panel will appear (**Figure 5.7**).

3. Click on the Images button at the left to display your images. You may need to refresh the view of the images cataloged in your site by clicking the Refresh button (**Figure 5.8**).

Definitions

A splash page (**Figure 5.1**) is what you call an opening screen that leads in to the rest of a site. Not essential, the splash page should be simple, load quickly, and show you what the point of a site is. A home page, on the other hand (**Figure 5.2**), generally serves as a table of contents for the main sections of a site.

4. To view a preview of any image in the Assets panel, click on its name. A preview will appear (**Figure 5.9**).

5. To place a selected image, simply drag it onto the page (**Figure 5.10**), from either the list box or the image preview panel. You can also click the Insert button to place the selected image.

Figure 5.9 Click on the name of any image listed in the Assets panel to see a preview of the image.

Drag image onto page

Select image

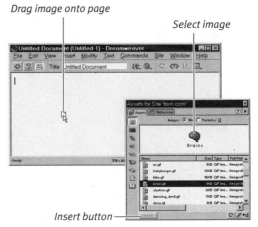

Insert button

Figure 5.10 Click on the Insert button to insert the selected image, or simply drag it onto the page where you want it to appear.

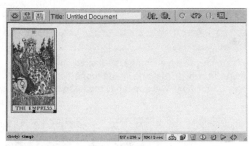

Figure 5.11 When you select an image, boxes called handles will appear in the lower-right corner of the image.

Figure 5.12 The Property inspector, displaying properties for the currently selected image. Note that the Apply button is a tiny thumbnail of the selected image.

Figure 5.13 When multiple images are selected, they appear highlighted in gray, and handles are not visible.

Selecting an Image

When you insert an image using Dreamweaver, it will remain selected, but you'll need to select an image any time you want to work with it.

When you select an image with Dreamweaver, boxes called *handles* will appear in the lower-right corner of the image (**Figure 5.11**), which you can use to resize the image. Also, a preview of the image will appear in the Property inspector (**Figure 5.12**). This image preview acts as the Apply button for image properties.

To select/deselect an image:

◆ To select an image, just click on it.

◆ To deselect an image, click in any other part of the Document window.

◆ To select multiple images, hold down the Shift key while you click on each image (**Figure 5.13**), or drag the cursor over multiple images.

✔ Tips

■ When an image is selected, you can copy, cut, delete, or paste over it, just as you do with text in a word processor. All of these commands are available from the Document window's Edit menu.

■ Double-click on an image to make the Select Image Source dialog box appear.

■ If you want to replace one image with a different image, drag the Src Point to File icon to a different image file in the Site window. See Chapters 6 and 20 for more about linking in the Site window.

The Property Inspector

As with most objects in Dreamweaver, the Property inspector (**Figure 5.14**) displays properties specific to images when an image is selected.

To use the Property inspector:

1. Display the Property inspector, if it isn't already visible, by selecting Modify > Selection Properties from the Document window menu bar.

2. Select the image whose properties you'd like to investigate. The Property inspector will display properties for that image with a thumbnail of the image appearing as the Apply button.

3. To display all the image properties that the inspector has to offer, click on the expander arrow in the bottom-right corner of the inspector (**Figure 5.15**).

✔ Tip

■ You can also display the Property inspector by double-clicking the image. If the Select Image Source dialog box appears, click on Cancel.

Expander arrow ⌐

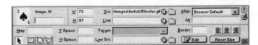

Figure 5.14 When an image is selected, the Property inspector will display the image properties. A thumbnail of the image will appear as the Apply button.

Figure 5.15 Click on the Expander arrow in the bottom-right corner of the Property inspector (look at the pointer in **Figure 5.14**) to display the full set of Image properties.

What *Not* to Do

Images can add information to a page, or you can use a Web page as a vehicle to display important images such as artwork, product illustrations, or portraits. Images can also be put to good use for buttons and logos (as in **Figures 5.1** and **5.2**, where the links and titles are all images rather than HTML text). On the other hand, images aren't essential to good page design, and extraneous images can make a page downright impossible to look at. **Figure 5.16** shows a page that uses images capably to add information to the page. The page in **Figure 5.17** could do without any of the images on it.

Figure 5.16 The Web site for Maximag.com uses images for buttons and logos, and the page has a solid design. Note how the image buttons are all the same size and use the same basic look as the titles.

Figure 5.17 Avoid graphics with no obvious purpose, informational, aesthetic, or otherwise. Note the extraneous bullets, the gangs of horizontal rules, the icons whose backgrounds clash with the page background, the mismatched navigation buttons, and the icky "under construction" signs.

THE PROPERTY INSPECTOR

Image Formats

Most Web browsers display two image formats: CompuServe GIF (known as simply GIF) and JPEG (also called JPG). Dreamweaver also supports a relatively new image format called PNG.

If you've got digitized images that you want to use in your pages, but they're in a format other than GIF, JPEG, or PNG, you need to use an image-editing program to convert them to the proper format before you can put them on your page. (Generally, you can do this by selecting File > Save As or File > Export from the image editor's menu bar.)

JPEG & GIF: What's the Diff?

The JPEG format (**Figure 5.18**) was designed for digitized color photographs. JPEGs can support millions of colors, and they're best used when that's what you need. JPEGs are what's called a "lossy" format: the more you compress them, the more information they lose (in the sense of number of colors, which can lead to decreases in the sharpness of the image).

The GIF format (**Figure 5.19**) was invented by CompuServe so that folks on their online service could exchange graphics quickly and easily. GIFs support up to 256 colors (any 256, not a predetermined set). GIFs are the best choice for images with large areas of flat color, most nonphotographic images, and some black-and-white or grayscale photographs, as well as many black-and-white graphics.

✔ Tip

- Animated GIFs in the GIF89a format will display in Dreamweaver, although the animation won't play in the Document window. To watch the animation, preview the page with the graphic on it in your Web browser. For information about creating animated GIFs, see the book's Web site.

Figure 5.18 This image illustrates the best use of the JPEG format. It's a color photograph with lots of different colors, varying levels of contrast, and high-resolution details.

Figure 5.19 The images in this little collage are all GIFs. They have in common a limited palette, large areas that are the same color, and very little fine detail. The lower-right image is an animated gif.

How Do You Say CHEEZ?

Like a lot of computer lingo, there's some question as to the pronunciation of image file names. Although no one says gee-eye-eff, people can't agree on whether it's pronounced *gif*, like gift, or *Jif*, like the peanut butter. (I personally prefer the gif(t) pronunciation.) The other terms are easier. JPEG is pronounced *jay-peg*, like a hyphenated name. And PNG is pronounced *ping*, as in pong.

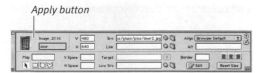

Apply button

Figure 5.20 Name your image by typing a name in the image text box and clicking on the Apply button.

Figure 5.21 Right-click (or Control+click on the Mac) to pop up a menu of options for editing and working with image files.

PNG Pong

PNG is a new image format developed by some designers who were frustrated by the limitations of the GIF format and the lossiness of JPEG. Additionally, the GIF format is owned by CompuServe, who requires software that produces GIFs to license the GIF patent.

The PNG development group would like PNG eventually to replace the GIF as a patent-free, lossless image format with dozens of new features. But right now, only a handful of browsers can display it at all. Versions of Navigator or Explorer later than 4 should be able to display the PNG format. Additionally, users of Navigator 2 or later can download a plug-in to enable PNG viewing. You can find out all about PNG at http://www.libpng.org/pub/png/.

Image Properties

Once the image is on the page, there are several properties you can adjust. These include appearance properties (dimensions and border), layout properties (alignment, Vspace, and Hspace), and page loading properties (Alt tags and low source).

You can also provide a name for any of your images. This name doesn't show up on screen, but it can be useful if you're planning on working directly with the code, and it's essential for using images in JavaScript or VBscript code.

To name an image:

1. Select the image by clicking on it.

2. In the Property inspector, type a name for your image (all lowercase, no spaces or funky characters) in the Image text box (**Figure 5.20**).

3. Press Enter (Return) or click on the Apply button.

   The image will now be named in the code.

✔ Tip

■ When you right-click (Control+click) on an image in Dreamweaver, a contextual menu appears that offers many options for working with the selected image (**Figure 5.21**). You can adjust different image properties, including the Low Source image and the Alt Tag (under *Image Loading Properties,* later in this chapter). You can also edit the image tag, open the image with an editor, set Design Notes for the image (see Chapter 21), or work with an attached Template (see Chapter 18).

Appearance Properties

In Dreamweaver, the default for displaying images is to display them without any border, but you can add a border if you'd like.

To add an image border:

1. Select the image to which you'd like to add a border (**Figure 5.22**). The Property inspector will display the image properties.

2. If necessary, expand the Property inspector by clicking on the Expander arrow in the lower-right corner.

3. In the Property inspector, type a number in pixels in the Border text box (**Figure 5.23**).

4. Press Enter (Return), or click on the Apply button. The border will be displayed around the image in the Document window (**Figure 5.24**).

The default border color is black, unless you link the image, in which case the image border will take on the link color (see Chapter 6). You can also drag to select an image and then use the <FONT> tag to set a border color. See Chapter 8 to find out about font colors.

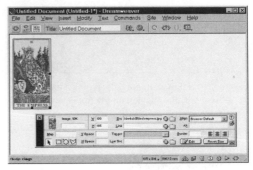

Figure 5.22 Select the image to display image properties in the Property inspector.

Figure 5.23 Type a number, in pixels, in the Border text box.

Figure 5.24 Click on the Apply button, and the border will appear around the image. From the left, I used no border, a five-pixel border, a 10-pixel border, and a 50-pixel border.

Transparent GIFs

All GIFs are rectangular, but some are more rectangular than others. You can use an image editing program to create a GIF89 or GIF89a, which support transparency and interlacing (see the sidebar *Image Size*, later in this chapter). Everything that's a certain color (or colors) in the image will disappear. The trick to making this work to your advantage on a Web page is making the transparency color the same color as your page's background (or vice versa). For obvious reasons, the easiest colors to match are white and black. (To find out how to match the page's background color to an image's RGB color, see Chapter 3.)

Figure 5.25 Type the new measurement in the W or H text box.

Figure 5.26 When the original image dimensions have been changed, the new measurements are displayed in boldface.

Figure 5.27 After I changed the width to two inches (and after Dreamweaver converted it to 192 pixels), the image appeared as shown.

Drag to Resize

You can drag to resize an image using the three selection handles shown in **Figure 5.22**, and Dreamweaver will enter the new H and W values in the Property inspector. To constrain the image to its original scale, hold down the Shift key while you drag.

Otherwise, if you type the numbers in the box in the Property inspector, the proportions of the image won't be constrained, and you may end up with a funny-looking image like the one in **Figure 5.27**. You can turn on the Grid (see Chapter 1) if you want to drag images to fit certain dimensions in pixels, inches, or centimeters.

When you first place an image with Dreamweaver, it will have the original dimensions it was given when it was created. It's easy to reassign a new height and width to an image to make it fit into the layout of your page.

To change image dimensions:

1. Select the image you'd like to resize. The Property inspector will display the Image dimensions in pixels in the W(idth) and H(eight) text boxes.

2. In either text box, you can type a new measurement in any of the following units: pixels, centimeters (cm), inches (in), millimeters (mm), picas (pc), or points (pt).

   For instance, to change the image width to 2 inches, you'd type 2in (no space between measurement and unit) in the W text box (**Figure 5.25**).

3. Press Enter (Return), or click on the Apply button. The Property inspector will convert your measurements to pixels, if necessary, and the new measurement will be displayed in boldface in the text box (**Figure 5.26**).

The Document window will display the image in its new measurement(s) (**Figure 5.27**).

continued on next page

✔ Tips

- To return the image to its original dimensions, click on the text box label (the letter W or H), or right-click (Ctrl+click) on the image, and select Reset Size to return the image to its original size.

- If the browser knows the image dimensions when it loads the page, the page will finish loading faster, because the browser will pre-draw a space of the right size for the image.

- Changing an image's dimensions with Dreamweaver does not change the file size of the image.

- Shrinking an image usually doesn't affect the resolution, but enlarging it may make it look grainy.

- Although Dreamweaver may re-render the image beautifully, the user's browser may not, and image quality could suffer.

Image Size

When you look at image properties in the Property inspector, one thing you'll see is the image's size. This is a handy shortcut—otherwise, you'd have to use your operating system's file management system to see the file size of the image.

Why do you want to know the file size of your images? Because the smaller your image is—in kilobytes (K), not screen size—the faster it will load. Nothing kills interest in a Web site faster than a horrendous download time, and each image on your page increases that time, so it's wise to keep image size low.

You can see the total file size for your entire page, as well as an estimate of how long it will take to load, in the document window status bar.

What can you do to make images load faster?

- ◆ Always specify the dimensions of your image. Browsers will read this information and draw a space for the image, so that the rest of the page can load while it's waiting for the image data to come through.

- ◆ Provide a low-res version of high-resolution and other fat images. (See *To use a low-source image*, earlier in this chapter.)

- ◆ Use fewer colors. There are few good reasons to use millions of colors in run-of-the-mill graphics.

- ◆ Use GIFs for everything but color photographs and extremely high-color graphics.

- ◆ Provide thumbnails. If you're putting art or photographs on the Web, and you really need to use million-color JPEGs, put each large image on a separate page, and provide links to them through tiny, linked thumbnail images (image linking is described in Chapter 6).

- ◆ Use interlaced GIFs. This image format will load in chunks. Once all the chunks are loaded, the image will come together.

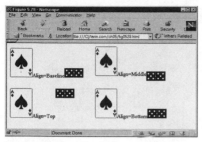

Figure 5.28 Each alignment option was applied to the domino graphic (not the ace). Depending on the option, the domino is either aligned with the largest object in the same paragraph (the ace) or with the text.

Figure 5.29 These options are similar to the ones in **Figure 5.28**. See the sidebar for how these minute distinctions work.

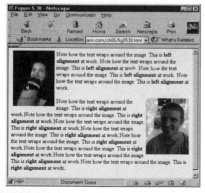

Figure 5.30 Here are the most useful alignment options: Left and Right. Note how the text wraps around the image in both cases; the left alignment applies to the second chunk of text that wraps around the right-aligned image, as well. Left and Right alignment always keeps the image at the specified margin of the page (or the table cell).

Layout Properties

Image alignment is slightly more complicated than text alignment. There are 10 options for image alignment; those options are detailed in the sidebar on this page and demonstrated in **Figures 5.28–5.30**.

To adjust image alignment:

1. Select the image whose alignment you want to adjust.

2. In the Property inspector, click on the Alignment drop-down box and select one of the alignment options displayed in Figures 5.28–5.30.

As soon as you select an option, the image will move. Some options visibly differ from others only when combined with other objects.

✔ Tip

■ To center an image on the page, select the image and select Text > Alignment > Center from the Document window menu bar.

LAYOUT PROPERTIES

Notes on Alignment Options

◆ The Browser Default alignment is usually *Baseline*.

◆ The Baseline option aligns the bottom of the image with the baseline of the text or the nearest object. A text baseline is the imaginary line the text sits on.

◆ The Bottom option aligns the image's bottom with the bottom of the largest nearby object, and Top aligns the top of the image with the top of the object.

◆ Middle aligns the middle of the image with the text baseline.

◆ Text Top aligns the image's top with the tallest character in the nearest line of text.

◆ Absolute Bottom aligns the bottom of the image with the lowest descender in the nearest line of text (the letter g, in **Figure 5.29**).

◆ Absolute Middle aligns the middle of the image with the middle of the text.

◆ The Left and Right options align the image with the respective margin, wrapping the nearby text so that the image stays at the margin.

Figure 5.31 By default, Dreamweaver places a space between each image placed in a row. In the second row of images, I removed the spaces to place the images even closer together.

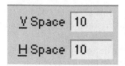

Figure 5.32 In the Vspace and/or Hspace text box, type the amount of space, in pixels, that you want to surround your image.

Figure 5.33 I added 10 pixels of both Vspace and Hspace to the image on the right. I dragged to highlight both the image and the space around it.

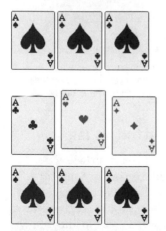

Figure 5.34 The center image, the ace of hearts, has 10 pixels of Vspace and Hspace surrounding it. Notice how the Vspace affects the entire paragraph (or row): The images above and below it are the same distance from the entire row, even though only one of the images has Vspace added to it.

An image can bump right up against text or other images, as seen in **Figure 5.31**. (By default, Dreamweaver places a space between each image.) If you want your image to have some breathing room, you can put some invisible space around the image. Vspace is vertical space, above and below the image. Hspace is horizontal space, to the left and right of the image.

To adjust Vspace & Hspace:

1. Click on the image to which you want to add some space.

2. In the Property inspector, type a number, in pixels, in the Vspace or Hspace text box (**Figure 5.32**).

3. Press Enter (Return) or click on the Apply button. You'll see the rectangle of highlighting around the image increase in size when you drag to select it (**Figure 5.33**).

Most likely, you'll want to experiment with the amount of Vspace and Hspace you need on your pages. In **Figure 5.34**, the image at the center has 10 pixels of Vspace and Hspace surrounding it.

Page Loading Properties

Not everyone who surfs the Web does so with image capabilities. Some users who have graphical browsers turn off image auto-loading, whereas others browse with a text-only browser. Visually impaired users may use text-to-speech browsers that read the page to them; and finally, mobile users may access the Web on a tiny, text-only screen, or by having their phone service read the page aloud. The only way these users will know the content of your images is if you provide a text alternative, called an Alt tag.

To use an image Alt tag:

1. Select the image for which you want to provide an Alt tag.

2. In the Property inspector, type a description in the Alt text box (**Figure 5.35**).

3. Press Enter (Return), or click on the Apply button.

Users who view your page without image-viewing capability will be able to read the text description to find out whether they want to view or download the image (**Figure 5.36**).

✔ Tips

- Users of many graphical browsers will see the Alt text displayed as a tool tip when they mouse over the image (**Figure 5.37**).

- Unlike a regular HTML entity, the Alt tag can be in plain English with capital and lowercase letters, spaces, and punctuation; and it can be much longer than the tiny box on the Property inspector implies.

- See Chapter 21 to find out how to create a site report that lists all the images on a page, or in your site, that do not include Alt tags.

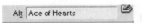

Figure 5.35 Type the alternate text description in the Alt text box.

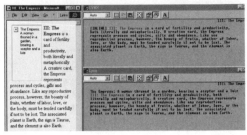

Figure 5.36 In the browser window at the left, IE has auto-image loading turned off. Instead of the broken image icon, the user sees the text description, and can decide whether to load the image. At the right are two windows from Lynx, the most popular text-only browser. The upper window shows the page without an Alt tag—all you see is [INLINE] to indicate an image. The other Lynx window displays the Alt tag.

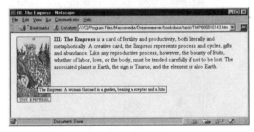

Figure 5.37 Alt tags come in handy even when browsing with images; when you mouse over the image in Navigator 4, you can read the Alt tag.

Beyond the Alt Tag

If you're using an image map (see Appendix A), a button bar, or some other navigational tool that relies on images as links, make sure you supply a text equivalent so that users who aren't loading images can still browse your site. Appendix C on the Web site discusses making a plain-text version of your site, and other ways to accommodate users who don't or can't see images when browsing the Web.

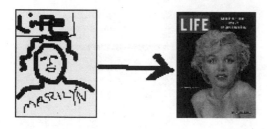

1K---21K

Figure 5.38 The image on the right, which is the image I want to use on my page, is a 21K full-color JPEG. The image on the left, which took me about 10 seconds to make in a paint program, is a 1K black-and-white GIF. The low-source image will load immediately while the browser downloads the larger image. That way, no one has to feel like they're waiting. (Generally, a black-and-white or fewer-color version of the same image is used, but there isn't a good way to show this in print.)

Loading...

Figure 5.39 Another way to use the low source image is to create a simple animated gif that blinks on and off and says "Loading...". I once thought that this was a scripted icon that actually knew whether the image was loading or not, but it's just a very clever use of the low-source image.

Low Src

Figure 5.40 Type the location of the image in the Low Src text box; click on the Browse icon to open the Select Image Source dialog box; or drag the Point to File icon to an image in the Sites window.

If your image is larger than 30K, it will take more than a few seconds to load. One option to take the pain out of waiting is to provide a low-source, or low-res, image that will load more quickly. It will be replaced by the regular image once it finishes loading. **Figures 5.38** and **5.39** demonstrate this effect.

To use a low-source image:

1. Use your image editor to create a smaller, faster-loading image, such as a black-and-white or grayscale version of the image.

2. Select the large image for which you created the low-source version in step 1.

3. In the Property inspector's Low Source text box (**Figure 5.40**), type the location of the image, and press Enter (Return).

   or

   Click on the Browse icon, and use the Select Image Source dialog box to browse through the files and folders on your computer. When you locate the image, click on its name, and then click on Open to close the dialog box and return to the Dreamweaver window.

Your selection will not be visible in the Document window. You can try the effect if you preview the page in your browser, although it will be much faster on your desktop than downloading the image from the Internet.

✔ Tips

- When you upload your page to the Web server, be sure to send both versions of the image with the page.

- You can drag the Low Src Point to File icon to the low-source image in the Site window. See Chapter 20 for details.

- For an image from Fireworks, the Low Src option might not appear. Right-click (Control+click) on the image and select Low Source from the menu.

Image Editor Integration

If you want to edit an image while you're working with it, it's a snap. Dreamweaver has full image editor integration, and you can set Dreamweaver to work with your favorite editor, whether it's Fireworks, Paint Shop Pro, or Photoshop. When you click on Edit, the image will open in the editor, and then when you return to Dreamweaver, your saved changes will reload automatically.

✔ Tip

- If you have installed Fireworks, Dreamweaver should already be set up to work with its sister program.

To select an image editor:

1. Open the Preferences dialog box by pressing Ctrl+U (Command+U).

2. Click on File Types/Editors to show that panel (**Figure 5.41**).

3. In the Extensions list box, select an image extension (.gif, .png, or .jpg, which is listed as .jpg .jpe .jpeg).

4. Click on the + button above the Editors list box. The Select External Editor dialog box will appear. (**Figure 5.42**).

5. Locate the program file for the image editor (on Windows, it will end in .exe).

6. Click on Open to select the program file.

7. Repeat steps 3-6 to select more than one image editor.

8. Click on OK to save your changes and close the Preferences dialog box.

Step 3: Extensions List box   *Step 4: Click + button to add an editor*

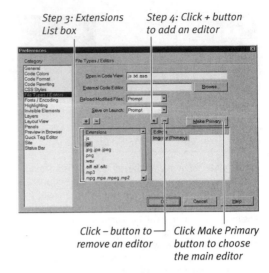

Click – button to remove an editor   *Click Make Primary button to choose the main editor*

Figure 5.41 You can set your preferences to work with any image editor so that you can modify images while you're placing them on your pages using Dreamweaver.

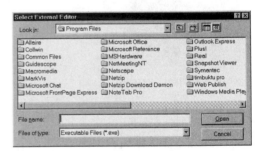

Figure 5.42 Using this dialog box—it's just like an Open dialog box—select the program file for your image editor.

More Image Editing Hints

When you want to edit an image, just select it in the Document window and then click on Edit in the expanded Property inspector (**Figure 5.43**). The image will be updated when you return to Dreamweaver.

You can choose more than one image editor to work with. For example, you might use Fireworks for most things, but you might also want to use Debabelizer or GIF Converter to work on specific attributes, like optimization or animation.

If you choose more than one editor, you can make one the primary editor by selecting its name in the Editors list box and clicking on Make Primary. The Primary program will open when you click on the Edit button on the Property inspector.

If you have specified several different image editors, you can right-click (Control+click) on the image and then from the menu that appears, select Edit With > *Editor Name*.

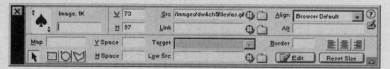

Figure 5.43 Click on the Edit button to open the selected image in your editor of choice.

WORKING WITH LINKS

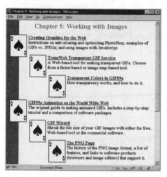

Figure 6.1 This page uses images, a background image, tables, and style sheets, but the real content is in the links. Even if I added background music, Shockwave, files, frames, and a flaming logo, the links would still be the meat here.

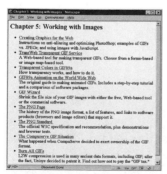

Figure 6.2 This is the same page as shown in **Figure 6.1,** with all the extras removed. The content remains the same—you can get there from here with nothing but links.

A *hyperlink*, or simply a *link,* is a pointer from one page or file to another. The page that contains the link is called the *referring page*, and the destination of the click is called the *target* of the link. One could easily argue that links, more than fancy typographical or image capabilities, differentiate the Web (**Figures 6.1** and **6.2**) from any of its electronic file-transfer predecessors, including FTP, gopher, and Archie. Although the bells and whistles of the showier pages are what impress the easily impressed and cause the browser market to boom, the fact is that the most important element in the Hypertext Transfer Protocol—that *http* at the beginning of Web URLs—is the word hypertext.

With regular old HTML, you can link your pages to other documents within your own site or anywhere in the world. I say "documents" because you can link to images, multimedia files, and downloadable programs, as well as other Web pages.

In this chapter you'll find out how to make a link, how relative links work, and how to make an e-mail link. You'll be able to link images as well as text. You'll find out how to use the Site window to point to the page you want to link to. And you'll find out about using named anchors to link to specific locations on a page.

Kinds of Links

Before you start putting links on your Web pages, you should be aware of the different kinds of pathnames you can use to link to another document on the Internet (**Figure 6.3**). There are four different kinds of links you can use:

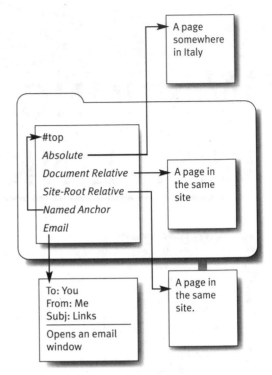

◆ **Absolute pathnames**
(`http://www.tarin.com/BayArea/ baynav.html`) point to a location on the Internet outside the site where the current page is located. In the pathname `http://www.tarin.com/BayArea/baynav. html`, the document `baynav.html` is located within the `BayArea/` directory, which is within the root site `www.tarin.com/`.

◆ **Document-relative pathnames**
(`home.html`, `../baynav.html`) point from the current page to another document within the same site, using dots and slashes to tell the browser when it needs to look in another directory to find the page. You can link from one document to another without using the full URL, and Dreamweaver will keep track of what those dots and slashes mean—and it can also make sure your links are correct when you update your site, as long as you make your changes in Dreamweaver.

Figure 6.3 For the visual thinkers in the house, a representation of where links go.

A Basic Link

The HTML code for a link looks like this:
`<A HREF="file.html">linked text</A>`
The A stands for anchor, the original name for links. HREF means Hypertext Reference.

- **Site-root-relative pathnames**
  (/baynav.html) also point from the current document to another document that's within the same site. Instead of using dots and slashes to indicate moving from folder to folder, the Web browser starts at the home directory and looks for the page from there. If you're constructing a large site in which pages might be moved around outside of Dreamweaver, site-root relative links will still be correct even if the page is moved.

- **Named anchors** link to a point within a page; either from point to point on a single page, or from one page to a specific location on another page. See *Linking to a Section of a Page*, later in this chapter.

Pick Your Links Carefully

Why use relative links? Why not just include the entire http://ramalamading-dong every time? There are a few basic reasons: One, because Dreamweaver can keep track of your relative links for you and make sure they're correct. Two, because you save time, space, and file size—and minimize the chance of errors—by not spelling out the entire address every time. Three, if you keep a copy of your Web site in more than one location or if you relocate it to a different domain or server, you want the links to be correct whether the visitor is looking at your page on www.dingdong.com or www.bopshebop.org, and with relative links, you don't need to re-code each page.

More About Relative Links

Everyone knows that a Web address looks like this:

```
http://www.site.com/page.html
```

On the other hand, if you're linking to pages within the same site, you don't need to include the entire, absolute URL in your link. If you use a relative link, the browser will look for the page within the same site. Then, your link might look like this in the code:

```
page.html or /page.html
```

Which is which? The first example is a *document-relative link* from one page to another page in the same folder (**Figure 6.4**). You can also use document-relative links to link pages in different folders together.

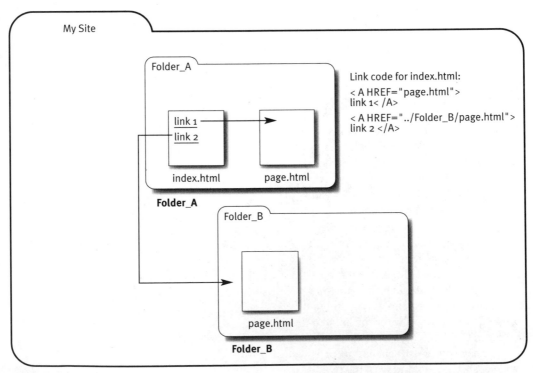

Figure 6.4 Document-relative links can be (A) between pages in the same folder or (B) between pages in different folders within the same site.

The second example is *a site-root relative link* from a page anywhere in the site to a page that's in the main folder of a site (**Figure 6.5**). You can also use site-root relative links to link to pages or images anywhere in your site.

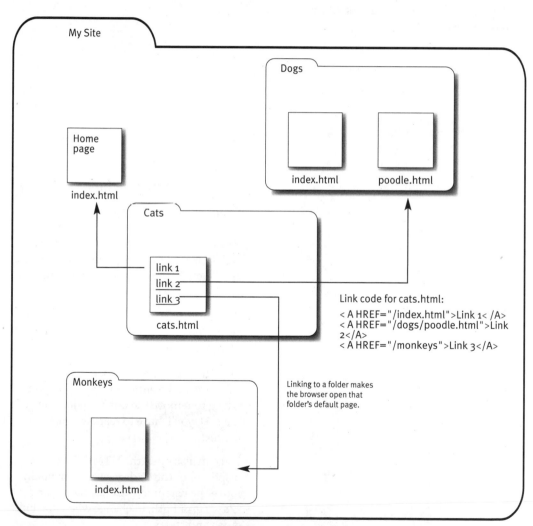

Figure 6.5 Site-root relative links can be (A) between any page and the home page; (B) between any page and a page in a different folder; or (B) between a page and a folder.

In either case, Dreamweaver will do the coding for you—all you have to do is specify which kind of link to use (**Figure 6.6**). Still confused? Here are some pointers:

◆ If the whole concept stumps you, stick with document-relative links.

◆ To link to pages in the same folder, always use document-relative links.

◆ If you're making a large site in which pages might move around a lot, use site-root relative links.

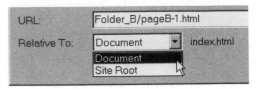

Figure 6.6 In the Select File dialog box, choose whether you want the link to be Site-root or Document relative. See **Figures 6.11** and **6.12** to see the entire dialog box.

Removing Links

To unlink, delink, or remove a link, highlight the text or image that's currently linked. Then, in the Property inspector, highlight the URL in the Link text box, and delete it. Press Enter (Return), and poof! No more link.

You can also select the link and, from the Document window menu bar, select Modify > Remove link.

In both cases, be aware that Dreamweaver will remove the entire <a> tag—so if you're trying to remove the link from just part of the text, you'll have to reapply it again to the rest.

You can also open the HTML Code inspector or the Code view and manually move the beginning <a> tag, the closing </a> tag, or both, to change where the link stops and starts.

◆ When you want to make a navigation bar without having to change the links on every different page, use site-root relative links (**Figure 6.7**). This is particularly useful for Library items (see Chapter 18).

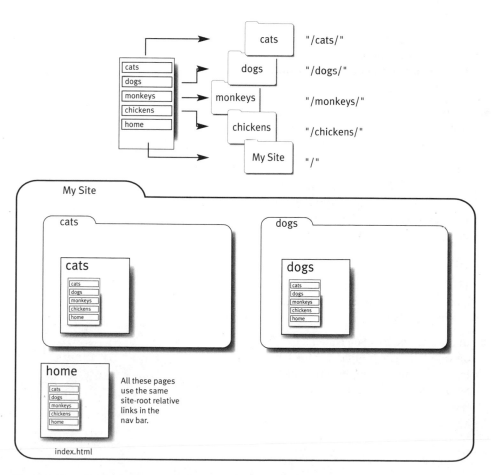

Figure 6.7 A navigation bar is a good place to use site-root relative links.

Making Links

Making links with Dreamweaver is easier than eating pie. You don't even have to remember any keystrokes or use any dialog boxes—just use the ever-handy Property inspector to put your links in there.

To link to a page on the Internet using a full URL, follow these steps. To link to a page within your site, see the next page.

To make a text link:

1. With your page open in the Document window, highlight the text you want to make into a link (**Figure 6.8**).

2. If necessary, display the Property inspector by selecting Modify > Selection Properties from the Document window menu bar.

3. In the Link text box, type (or paste) the location of the document to which you want to link (**Figure 6.9**).

4. Press Enter (Return).
   Your text will now be linked, indicated in your document window by underlining and a change of color for the text you selected (**Figure 6.10**).

✔ Tips

- The Link text box is also a drop-down menu. Click on it to choose from a list of recently used links.

- In the Site window, you can link to a file on your local site by dragging the Point to File icon onto a file in the Site window. See *Pointing to a File,* later in this chapter.

Link text box   Browse button

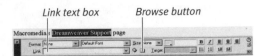

Figure 6.8 Highlight the text you want to make into a link.

Figure 6.9 In the Property inspector's Link text box, type or paste the URL of the document you're linking to.

Figure 6.10 Press Enter (Return), and the text you selected will become a link.

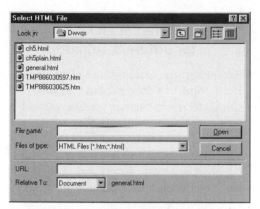

Figure 6.11 The Select HTML File dialog box functions like the Open dialog boxes you're used to by now.

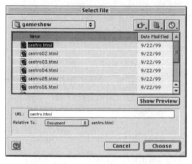

Figure 6.12 The Select HTML File dialog box on the Macintosh.

Figure 6.13 From the pull-down menu, select either Document, to make the link relative to the current page, or Site Root, to make the link relative to a central location on your Web site.

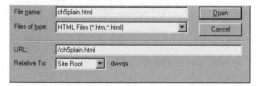

Figure 6.14 When you're all done, you should see a filename in the File name text box and the path to that file in the URL text box.

Making Relative Links

To have Dreamweaver manage relative links, or links between pages in your site, you must create a local site on your hard drive (explained in Chapter 2).

You can select a page in your local site by selecting a file or by pointing to it.

To select a local file to link to:

1. Save the page you're working on by selecting File > Save from the Document window menu bar. If this is the first time you're saving the page, the Save As dialog box will appear. Make sure you're saving the file in the correct directory (folder), and type a filename in the File name text box. Click on Save to close the Save As dialog box and save the file.

2. Select the text you want to make into a link (as shown back in **Figure 6.8**).

3. In the Property inspector, click on the Browse button 🗀.

   The Select HTML File dialog box appears (**Figures 6.11** and **6.12**).

4. From the Relative To pull-down menu, select either Document or Site Root (**Figure 6.13**). If you're not sure which to choose, choose Document.

5. Browse through the files and folders on your computer until you locate the document to which you want to link. Click on the file's icon so that its name shows up in the File name text box. The URL text box will display the link path (**Figure 6.14**).

6. Click on Open to choose the file.

The Select HTML File dialog box will close, returning you to the Document window. You'll see your link underlined and the path displayed in the Property inspector.

✔ Tip

■ If you're linking to a page in the same folder as the one you're working on, you can simply type the filename in the Property inspector's Link text box; for example, `contents.html`.

Different Links for Different Things

Except in those cases where you're using a relative link to a document in the same site as the referring page, you always need to specify the protocol type for the link. Even though some browsers can locate sites that lack the http:// when typed into the browser's location field, most browsers won't recognize links without a protocol type being specified.

Besides http, there are several other kinds of protocols you may use; mailto and ftp are the two most common after http.

`ftp://`	File Transfer Protocol
`mailto:`	An Internet e-mail address; launches a mail composition window in some browsers
`gopher://`	Gopher hypertext index
`shttp://`	Secure Hypertext Transfer Protocol, used by secure commerce servers supporting the protocol
`news:`	A Usenet or other network news resource group or discussion group; often launches a newsgroup browser
`telnet:`	Remote access to a Telnet server; often launches a Telnet client
`wais://`	Wide Area Internet Search

In general, if the protocol type is left off a coded URL, the browser will look for a local file rather than an Internet URL.

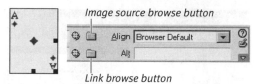

Image source browse button

Link browse button

Figure 6.15 Select the image you want to make into a link.

Figure 6.16 Type or paste the URL in the Property inspector, or click on the Browse button to choose a file.

Figure 6.17 After you specify the link in your Property inspector, you can add a border to your image, if you like.

Border width text box

Figure 6.18 To add a border to the image's link, specify a border width of 1 or higher in the Property inspector. Dreamweaver adds a border of 0 by default to prevent unwanted borders from being added—if 0 isn't specified, a linked image will have a border of 1 in most browsers. The border color will be the same as the standard link color.

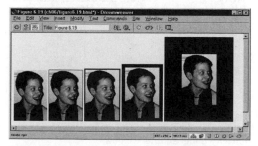

Figure 6.19 Here, the image has, from the left, no border; a 1-pixel border; a 3-pixel border; a 5-pixel border; and a 10-pixel border. The last image has a 50-pixel border.

Image Links

You can make an image into a link, too. Buttons and navigation arrows are obvious examples, but you can make any image point to anything on the Web.

To make an image link:

1. With your page open in the Document window, select the image you want to make into a link by clicking on it (**Figure 6.15**).

2. If necessary, display the Property inspector (Window > Properties).

3. In the Link text box, type (or paste) the location of the document to which you want to link (**Figure 6.16**).

   or

   Click on the Link browse button 📁 and select the local file to which you want to link. See *Making Relative Links* if you need help with the details.

   Make sure you click on the Link browse button, instead of the similar button next to the Image Src text box above it, which will ask you to choose an image.

4. Press Enter (Return), or click on the Apply button.

   Your image will be linked, and you can add a link border to it (**Figure 6.17**).

To add a border:

1. Select the image by clicking on it.

2. In the expanded Property inspector, type a number in the Border text box (**Figure 6.18**). Try numbers such as 1, 2, and 5.

3. Press Enter (Return), or click on the Apply button, and the border will appear (**Figure 6.19**).

IMAGE LINKS

Pointing to a File

Dreamweaver's Site window is a tool for managing your files on both your computer and your remote Web server. The remote stuff is covered in Chapter 20. In terms of linking, though, there's an extremely handy visual tool you can use to make links by drawing a line from your page to the file you want to link to.

If you haven't yet set up a local site, please do so following the instructions in Chapter 2.

To point to a file in the Site window:

1. Save the page you're working on.

2. Open the Site window by selecting Window > Site Files from the Document window menu bar (**Figure 6.20**).

3. Figure out where the file you want to link to is located, expanding folders as necessary (**Figure 6.21**).

4. Select the text or image you want to make into a link.

5. On the Property inspector, click on the Point to File icon (**Figure 6.22**), and hold down the mouse button while you drag the arrow to the file in the Site window (**Figure 6.23**).

   Your link will become underlined, and the path of the link will appear in the Property inspector's Link text box.

✔ Tips

■ You can also change the source of an image or media file by dragging the Point to File icon to a different image or media file in the Site window.

■ If you don't select anything to serve as the link before you drag the icon over, the title of the page or its file name will appear on your page as the link text.

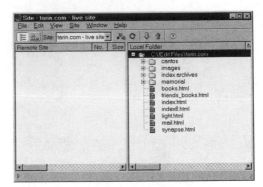

Figure 6.20 The Site window displays the files in your local site. You can create a relative link from a page in your site to any other file in your site.

Figure 6.21 Expand folders as necessary until you find the file you want to link to.

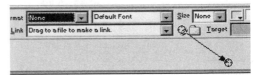

Figure 6.22 After you select the object you want to make into a link, click on the Point to File icon on the Property inspector.

Figure 6.23 Drag the icon onto the file you want to link to. The Site window will automatically float to the top if it's under another window.

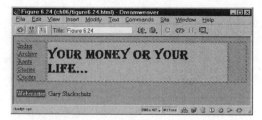

Figure 6.24 Highlight the text you want to become an e-mail link.

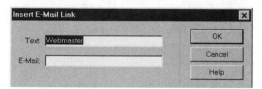

Figure 6.25 Use the Insert E-mail Link text box to enter your text and your e-mail address.

Figure 6.26 Include the full address in the format name@domain.suffix. Do not include the "mailto" protocol or any HTML.

Linking to an E-mail Address

If you want your fans to be able to contact you, the best way is to provide a link to your e-mail address. E-mail links look like this:

```
<AHREF="mailto:dreamweaver@tarin.com">
send mail</A>
```

You can insert them using a dialog box or the Property inspector.

To insert an e-mail link (auto):

1. Highlight the text you want to make into an e-mail link, or just click the insertion point at the place where you want the link to appear (**Figure 6.24**).

2. From the Document window menu bar, select Insert > E-mail Link. The Insert E-mail Link dialog box will appear (**Figure 6.25**).

   If you highlighted text to serve as a link in step 1, that text will appear in the Text text box. You may edit it or leave it as is, or you can type new text.

3. Type the full e-mail address in the E-mail text box (**Figure 6.26**).

4. Click on OK to close the Insert E-mail Link dialog box and insert your e-mail link.

To make an e-mail link (manual):

1. Highlight the text or image you want to make into an e-mail link (**Figure 6.27**).

2. In the Property inspector Link text box, type mailto:address@domain.com, substituting the proper, full e-mail address for *address@domain.com* (**Figure 6.28**).

3. Press Enter (Return).

   Your text or image will be linked (**Figure 6.29**).

✔ Tips

■ When your visitor clicks on an e-mail link in the browser window, the browser will generally pop open a mail window. You may also want to provide the address in plain text so that people using different software can get the e-mail address easily.

■ Keep in mind that spam sniffers, the robots that go around collecting e-mail addresses, do so by reading mailto: links. You may want to use an alternate email address, or create one on your domain that can filter out the spam.

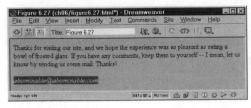

Figure 6.27 Highlight the text you want to turn into an e-mail link.

Figure 6.28 Type the full address in the Property inspector, and type mailto: in front of it, without a space.

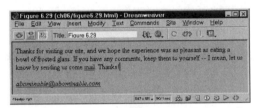

Figure 6.29 E-mail links look just like any other links: They're underlined and link-colored. I also used italics here. Note that I linked both the word "mail" and the e-mail address, as well as spelling it out for people without mail programs hooked up to their Web browsers.

Figure 6.30 Name your anchor with the Insert Named Anchor dialog box. I'd rather name an anchor at this location "aced" than "ace_of_diamonds," because it's easier to spell, type, and remember.

Linking to a Section of a Page

When you link to a specific location on a Web page, it's referred to as using a *named anchor*. A named anchor consists of two parts: a *named entity* at the point on an HTML page where you want your visitor to land, and a *link* to that anchor. Whereas regular old links point to an entire document, named anchors link to a *place on* a document. Very long documents should be broken into separate pages, but there can be cases where you want a clickable table of contents (or something similar) that will direct visitors to an area of a page instead of the top of it. You can also place a link to take users from the bottom of a page to the top (see **Figure 6.36**, page 140).

First, you need to name the part of the page you want to link to. You can name a piece of text, an image, or a headline, for instance.

To name a spot on the page:

1. Open the document in which you want to insert a named anchor, or destination, and click to place the insertion point at the place where you want it, or highlight an entity to name (such as a piece of text or an image).

2. From the Document window menu bar, select Insert > Invisible Tags > Named Anchor.

   The Insert Named Anchor dialog box will appear (**Figure 6.30**).

3. Type a name for your anchor in the Anchor Name text box. This name should be a single lowercase word or number, for simplicity's sake.

continued on next page

LINKING TO A SECTION OF A PAGE

What's in a URL?

Your typical Web URL might look like this: `http://www.peachpit.com/`, but then again, it might look like this:

`http://www.macromedia.com/support/dreamweaver/whatsnew/`

or like this:

`http://husky.northern-hs.ga.k12.md.us/`

What's all that stuff mean, anyway?

The `http:` is the name of the protocol, which in the case of a Web site is the Hypertext Transfer Protocol. (See the sidebar *Different Links for Different Things,* earlier in this chapter, for a description of each kind.)

The slashes (and those are forward slashes, not backslashes) indicate something else.

Everything between the first two slashes and the next slash is called the *domain name.*

The `www`, or whatever is the first "word" in a URL following the slashes, is the name of the Web server. Most folks these days use `www` because it's easy to remember.

The `.com` or `.gov` is called the *top-level domain,* which is administrated by InterNIC.

In the three-part URLs you see most often, such as `www.peachpit.com`, or `thomas.loc.gov`, the word between the `www.` and the `.com` is commonly called the domain name; it is referred to as the *second level domain* by

administrators and the InterNIC. It's the part you buy, if you want to register, say, `macromedia.com`.

In the third example above, there is a several-level hierarchy to the domain name. If you read the URL from back to front, the `.us` is the US domain used by state governments and such. The `.md` is the Maryland sub-domain; the `.k12` is the educational sub-domain of Maryland; and the `.ga` is the county subdomain of the educational system. The `.northern-hs` is the individual high school, and `husky` is the name of the Web server itself.

In the second example, the domain name itself is uncomplicated, and the rest of the URL, `support/dreamweaver/whatsnew/`, indicates three levels of directories within the Web server—which after all is just a computer like any other. Think of it like subfolders on your computer: `C:\Program Files\Macromedia\Dreamweaver`, for instance.

If the URL ends in a filename, as in `http://www.tarin.com/fridge.html`, that means that the fridge.html is the document itself that you're requesting. If the URL ends in a slash, it means that you're getting the *default file* for that directory. In most cases, `http://www.dhtmlzone.com/index.html` and `http://www.dhtmlzone.com/` are the same file.

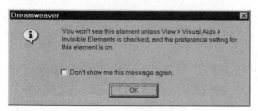

Figure 6.31 This dialog box appears when you insert an invisible element with invisible element viewing turned off.

Anchor element marker

Figure 6.32 The little blip next to the image is the Anchor icon (it has a little anchor on it). You can view or hide these invisible element icons as needed by selecting View > Visual Aids > Invisible Elements From the Document window menu bar.

Figure 6.33 Click on an invisible element icon, and the Property inspector will display information about it.

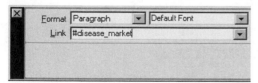

Figure 6.34 Select the text or image you want to link to the named anchor.

Figure 6.35 Type the name of the anchor in the Link text box, preceded by the # sign.

4. Click on OK to close the Insert Named Anchor dialog box and return to the Document window.

A dialog box may appear (**Figure 6.31**) that tells you what I'm about to tell you right now: You won't see any visible evidence of your anchor unless invisible element viewing is turned on.

To view invisible elements:

◆ From the Document window menu bar, select View > Visual Aids > Invisible Elements.

Any invisible elements on your pages will appear, in the form of icons (**Figure 6.32**). To figure out what an invisible element is or does, click on its icon, and the Property inspector will display properties for that element (**Figure 6.33**).

To link to a named anchor:

1. In the Document window, select the text or image you want to use as a link (**Figure 6.34**).

2. In the Property inspector, type the pound sign (#) in the Link text box.

3. With no space between the pound sign and the name of the anchor, type the anchor name in the Link text box. For instance, if your anchor name is top, you'd type #top in the Link text box (**Figure 6.35**).

4. Press Enter (Return), and your text or image will become linked to the named anchor.

continued on next page

✔ Tips

■ The page in **Figure 6.36** includes a table of contents at the top of the page. Even though the document is broken up into separate files, each link points to a specific part of each page (right above the section head). A link to the table of contents is included at the end of each section.

■ To link to an anchor on the same page, the Link text box only needs to include the # and the name of the link, as in #fred.

■ To link to an anchor on a page in the same directory, the link would be something like people.html#fred.

■ To link to an anchor on a page elsewhere on the Web, the link would be something like http://www.homer.com/donut.htm#mmm.

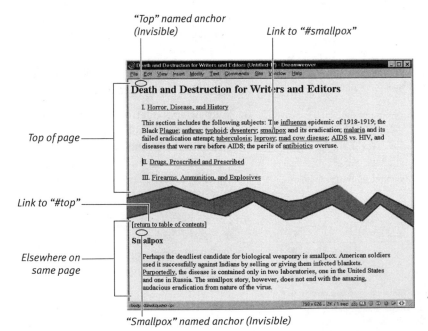

"Top" named anchor (Invisible)

Link to "#smallpox"

Top of page

Link to "#top"

Elsewhere on same page

"Smallpox" named anchor (Invisible)

Figure 6.36 This page is an example of a document that uses named anchors. I've hidden the toolbar in this view (View > Toolbar).

Figure 6.37 I used a target=_blank setting to make a link in the first browser window (back) open in a second browser window. Use this setting sparingly; it can get annoying if over-applied.

Figure 6.38 When you use the target=_blank attribute, clicking on a link on one page spawns a new browser window that then loads the link.

Opening Links in a New Window

A linked page opens by default in the same browser window as the previous page. If you want your link to open in a separate window, then you have to assign it a target, which is an attribute of the anchor tag that tells the browser in what space it should open the link in question.

The main use of targets is in frames-based sites, which use targets to determine in which frame to open a link. This aspect of targets is thoroughly explained in Chapter 13. However, you may want links to external sites to open in a separate browser window to keep visitors on your site.

To set a target for a new window:

1. Create a link as explained in Making Links, earlier in this chapter.

2. If necessary, expand the Property inspector by clicking on the expander arrow in the lower-right corner.

3. From the Target pull-down menu, choose _blank (**Figure 6.37**).

   Choosing _blank will make a brand-new browser window open and load the target of the link (**Figure 6.38**).

   If you choose _top, the link will open in the same window as the current page. (This target is more useful for frames and isn't needed to make links behave, but it's useful if you set a base target, as described in Chapter 13.)

Aiming Targets

There are two kinds of targets that you might want to use in non-frames pages.

- ◆ `target=_blank` makes the link open in a new, blank browser window.

- ◆ `target=_top` makes the link replace the content of the current window. By default, your linked pages will open this way.

The other kinds of targets apply only to frames. If you're making a page that you plan on using in a frames-based site, refer to Chapter 13, which also includes instructions on how to set a base target for an entire page.

✔ Tip

- ■ Some HTML editors automatically insert the `target=""` attribute into the code. This is harmless; it simply reiterates that the link will open in the default or base target location. You can also remove this code with impunity in the Code inspector.

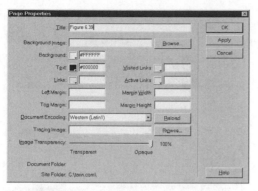

Figure 6.39 You can modify Link, Alink, and Vlink colors with the Page Properties dialog box.

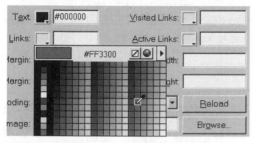

Figure 6.40 Click on the color box, and when the color picker appears, click on a color to select it.

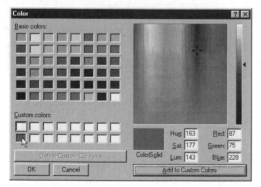

Figure 6.41 For tips on using this dialog box and the equivalent Color dialog box for the Mac, see Chapter 3.

Changing Link Colors

Link colors are part of what's known as page properties—the set of options that are applied to an entire page, rather than to an object on that page. The other page properties are covered in Chapter 3.

To change a page's link colors:

1. With the page open in the Document window, select Modify > Page Properties from the menu bar. The Page Properties dialog box will appear (**Figure 6.39**).

2. The text boxes marked Links, Visited Links, and Active Links control those colors for the current page. (See the sidebar *Link, Alink, and Vlink* for details about those options.) Type (or paste) the hex code for the desired color in the appropriate text box.

   or

   Click on the color box beside the appropriate text box. The color picker will appear (**Figure 6.40**). Click on a color to select it.

   or

   For details on choosing a color from your desktop or on using the Color dialog box for the PC (**Figure 6.41**) or the Mac, see Chapter 3.

3. After you choose a color, the hex code for that color will appear in the Page Properties dialog box. Click on OK to close the dialog box and return to the Dreamweaver window, or keep the dialog box open and modify the other link color options.

Smart Linking Strategies

Links exist so visitors will click on them. Although there's no single right way to make a link, keep these tips in mind so that your links will make people want to click (**Figures 6.42** and **6.43**).

◆ Link on a meaningful word or phrase that gives the user some idea of where they're headed.

  Right: Visit our <u>renewable energy resource page</u> to find out more.

  Wrong: <u>Click here</u> to find out more about renewable energy.

◆ When you link to something other than an HTML page, such as a sound or multimedia file, warn the user what's coming, and how big the file is.

  Right: <u>Combustion</u> (AU File, 153K)

  Wrong: <u>My Friend Larry</u> (This is wrong if it points to a 500K MIDI file with no warning.)

◆ If you're linking words within a sentence, stop the link before the punctuation, and don't underline spaces unnecessarily.

  Right: I grew up in <u>Texas</u>, <u>Michigan</u>, and <u>Sri Lanka</u>.

  Wrong: The best red wines come from <u>France, Italy, Germany, and California</u>, in that order.

◆ Making links into non sequiturs (such as the word <u>cheese</u> pointing to a Kung Fu movie site) can work well for irreverent sites but isn't as effective when you want someone to visit a particular page on purpose.

◆ If you rely on images (particularly button bars or image maps) as navigational tools, be sure to provide text equivalents of the same links.

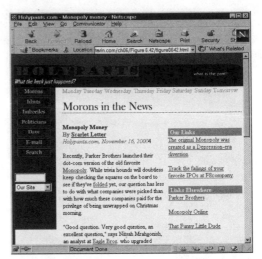

Figure 6.42 This page illustrates good link usage — there are links in the body of the story as well as in the navigation areas, and punctuation is excluded from the link underlining.

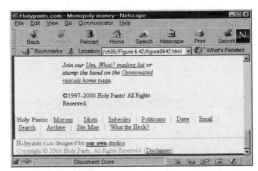

Figure 6.43 At the bottom of the same page in **Figure 6.42**, text equivalents of all the button links are provided.

◆ Come up with house rules about link length and structure, and stick to them.

◆ Use readable link colors. Make sure the text is visible on top of any background colors or images you use.

Common Top-Level Domains

.com	Commercial entity	.in	India
.edu	Educational entity	.it	Italy
.gov	U.S. Government	.jp	Japan
.mil	U.S. Military	.kr	South Korea
.net	Network provider	.mx	Mexico
.org	Nonprofit organization	.my	Malaysia
.au	Australia	.nl	Netherlands
.ca	Canada	.no	Norway
.ch	Switzerland	.nz	New Zealand
.cn	China	.se	Sweden
.de	Germany	.sg	Singapore
.dk	Denmark	.tw	Taiwan
.es	Spain	.uk	United Kingdom
.fi	Finland	.us	United States
.fr	France	.za	South Africa
.ie	Ireland		

Link, Alink, and Vlink

There are three kinds of Link colors: Link, Alink (Active Link), and Vlink (Visited Link). The link color is what users see when they haven't yet visited the target of the link. The Alink color is what they see while they're in the act of clicking on a link, and the Vlink color is the color the link assumes when the user has already visited the target page. (The last several days, weeks, or months of visits are recorded in the browser's History file, which is how the browser knows which links to assign the Vlink color.) If you don't choose colors for these options, the browser default colors will be used instead. In most cases, make sure that you have two different colors for Link and Vlink, so that users can tell what parts of your site they've already visited.

SMART LINKING STRATEGIES

INSERTING AND PLAYING MEDIA

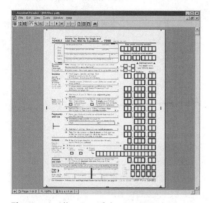

Figure 7.1 All sorts of documents, in every format, can be accessed over the Web.

Figure 7.2 Plug-ins such as Shockwave turned the Web into a multimedia experience. Without Shockwave, online gaming wouldn't be nearly as cool. And I wouldn't be able to abduct aliens at http://www.shockwave.com.

Before Mosaic, any file that wasn't text or HTML had to be downloaded and saved to open later with a separate application. All media, including images, were "save and play"—you couldn't view anything inline, and no one had so much as thought of streaming media.

With Netscape Navigator 1.1, you could automatically launch a helper application to play a downloaded file, and audio and Adobe Acrobat started becoming part of the life of the Web (**Figure 7.1**).

Navigator 2 went a step further and forever changed the face of the Web. Plug-ins could play or view darned near any type of file you could think of. Now, not only could you view Shockwave movies inline (**Figure 7.2**), but music could also be embedded invisibly into Web pages. Java, VRML, and other rich media soon followed.

Dreamweaver makes it easy to insert the code for these multimedia objects onto your pages.

In fact, inserting most media objects is just like inserting an image. (See Chapter 5, if you haven't yet worked with images.) Just like when you insert an image, what you're really doing is inserting the URL for the media object. When you do that, a placeholder for the object appears in the document window. After that, you can apply additional properties, including dimensions, Vspace and Hspace, and page-loading helpers (Alt tags and low-res images).

In this chapter , we'll take a look at how to make images interactive using rollovers and navigation bars. Then, we'll explore how to link to media, using sound files as our example. We'll move on to Netscape plug-ins, including Shockwave and Flash. In Dreamweaver 4, you can even create simple Flash text objects and buttons without leaving the Document window. We'll also address the basics of putting Java and ActiveX on your pages.

✔ Tips

- You can insert any of these objects using the Common category of the Objects panel (Window > Objects) and you can modify them using the Property inspector (Window > Properties or Modify > Selection Properties). I'm just refreshing your memory, in case you'd forgotten.

- New in Dreamweaver 4 is the Assets panel, which can keep track of not only images (see *Inserting Images with the Assets Panel* in Chapter 5), but Flash, Shockwave, and other movies in your local site. To find out more about working with Assets, see Chapter 3.

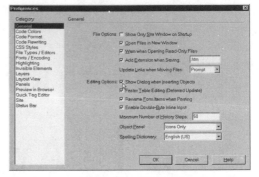

Figure 7.3 Deselect the Show Dialog When Inserting Objects checkbox to skip the Insert dialog boxes and have Dreamweaver insert a media placeholder right away.

- You can insert a placeholder for most media instead of choosing a file right away—which is handy if you're creating the page before the file is ready. From the Document window menu bar, select Edit > Preferences. In the General panel of the Preferences dialog box (**Figure 7.3**), deselect the Show Dialog when Inserting Objects checkbox. Then click OK to close the dialog box and save your changes.

- You can set up external editors for working with media objects in Dreamweaver. See *Image Editor Integration,* in Chapter 5, and follow the instructions for the proper file type (instead of image files, select a different file type).

Figure 7.4 One common use of image rollovers is a set of buttons that "light up" when they're moused over. Dreamweaver's Launcher, Launcher bar, and Objects panel use image rollovers to make buttons appear "pushed in" or "lit up."

Figure 7.5 You can use any sort of images in a rollover, as long as they're the same size.

Image Rollovers

Image rollovers let you seemingly stack two images on top of one another so that when you perform an action in the browser such as mousing over an image, another image appears. This is how button "highlighting" (**Figure 7.4**) and other, similar image tricks happen.

In technical terms, an image rollover is a JavaScript action that lets you swap the source of one image with another image file, so that when a user event happens, the browser loads the second image (**Figure 7.5**). To find out more about how JavaScript and Dreamweaver Behaviors work, see Chapter 16.

In Dreamweaver, a simple image rollover makes three things happen on your page: The images preload when the Web page loads, so that the rollovers are ready to go; second, when the user mouses over the specified image, a different image file is displayed; and finally, when the user mouses away from the image, the original image is restored.

The two images need to be the same size, or the second image will be smooshed into the first one's shape.

For the best results, you must save your page before you begin.

To set up a Rollover Image:

1. Click on the Rollover Image button on the Objects panel [image].

   or

   From the Document window menu bar, select Insert > Interactive Images > Rollover Image. The Insert Rollover Image dialog box will appear (**Figure 7.6**).

2. Select the source of the Original Image and the Rollover Image by typing the filenames in the respective text boxes, or clicking Browse to use the Original Source dialog box to select a local image.

3. You can edit the image name in the Image Name text box. Use a memorable, all-lowercase name.

4. Will your image link to another Web page? If so, type the URL in the When Clicked, Go To URL text box. Or click on Browse to select a page from your local site.

5. Click on OK to close the Insert Image Rollover dialog box and return to the Document window.

6. Preview your page in a JavaScript-capable browser to test the rollover effect.

✔ Tips

- The Preload Images option will be checked by default—leave it checked. There's no good reason *not* to preload images, because it eliminates wait time that would otherwise be caused by having to download the replacement image only when it's requested.

- For more about links, see Chapter 6. For more about how rollovers work, see Chapter 16.

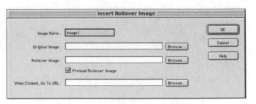

Figure 7.6 The Rollover Image dialog box lets you swap one image for another without even learning behaviors.

Holy Rollovers

In Dreamweaver 1.0, you needed to create three JavaScript Behaviors in order to make a successful image rollover. In Dreamweaver 3 and 4, you can use a single dialog box. That's great.

To find out how to make more-complicated image rollovers, see Chapter 16. You can use behaviors to have user events other than mouseovers (such as clicks or keypresses) make the images change source; you can have an event for one image trigger a source change for a different image or multiple images; you can make it so that mousing out doesn't require the source to swap back; or you can have the mouseout cause an entirely different image to appear.

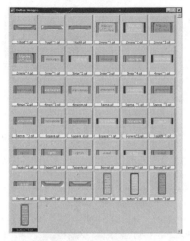

Figure 7.7 This is my collection of future button images, displayed in an image catalog program.

Figure 7.8 These are all the button images, displayed as navbars.

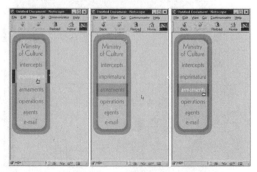

Figure 7.9 The three browser windows depict the three button states: Over, Down, Over While Down.

Using Navigation Bars

If you want to create a navigation bar (also called *navbar* or *button bar*) to guide people through your site, Dreamweaver can simplify the process. Otherwise, you'd have to write a complex rollover for each button in the navigation bar. Using Dreamweaver, you just fill in the blanks.

A button can have as many as four looks in a Dreamweaver navigation bar: Up, or initial; Over, or "lit up" (when the user mouses over the button); Down, or "pushed in" (when the user clicks on the button); and Over While Down (when the user mouses over the button while it's "pushed in"). You need have only one set of images to create a navigation bar, but you must create a separate image file for each state of each button on the bar. **Figures 7.7** and **7.8** show the four sets of images that will be used as buttons in the four different states. **Figure 7.9** shows the buttons in action.

✔ Tips

- This chapter assumes you're starting from scratch with a batch of images, but you can expedite things if you use Macromedia Fireworks to create your buttons. You can use the Button Editor to export the buttons, along with prewritten HTML and JavaScript. Then you can edit the pages in Dreamweaver. In the Save As or Export dialog box of Fireworks, select Dreamweaver 4 from the Style drop-down menu in the HTML area of the dialog box.

- See Chapter 16 for tips on editing navbars by using Behaviors.

To make sure your links work properly, all your images should be stored in your local site (see Chapter 2), and the page should be saved before you begin.

To insert a navigation bar:

1. On the Objects panel, click on the Insert Navigation Bar button ![icon].

   or

   From the Document window menu bar, select Insert > Interactive Images > Navigation bar.

   Either way, the Insert Navigation Bar dialog box will appear (**Figure 7.10**).

2. In the Up Image text box, type the filename of the image you wish to use; or, click on Browse, and use the Select Image Source dialog box (**Figures 7.11** and **7.12**) to select the image from a folder in your local site.

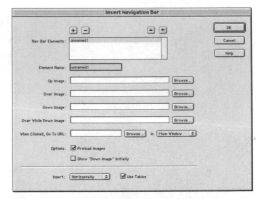

Figure 7.10 The Insert Navigation Bar dialog box.

Figure 7.11 The Select Image Source dialog box. With the preview turned on, you can make sure your button states look as they're supposed to.

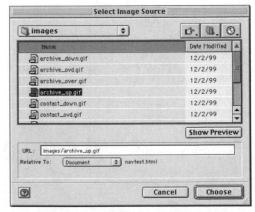

Figure 7.12 The Select Image Source dialog box for the Mac. Click Show Preview to see a thumbnail of the selected image.

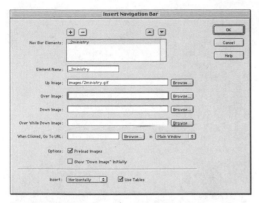

Figure 7.13 After you select the Up image, Dreamweaver inserts the button name in the Name text box.

Figure 7.14 On this navigation bar, the Ministry of Culture page will load with the Ministry button already selected, or down.

Figure 7.15 Navigation bars can be horizontal, too.

3. After you select the first image, Dreamweaver will insert a name for the button in the Element Name text box (**Figure 7.13**). You may edit this name if you wish.

4. Repeat step 2 for any additional positions for your button: Up, Down, and Over While Down.

5. If this button should be in the down state when the page loads (**Figure 7.14**), check the Show "Down Image" Initially checkbox. An asterisk will appear by the name of the selected over-while-down image.

   Usage example: You're putting a button bar on the Archive page; one of your buttons says "Archive," and you want the button to be pushed in when the user visits this page. You'd then change this option by showing the appropriate buttons pushed in to highlight each section.

6. In the When Clicked, Go To URL text box, type the URL for your link; or, if the link is a page on your site, click Browse and use the Select HTML file dialog box to select the page and set the local path.

7. To insert another button, click on the + button. Then, follow steps 1-6 to specify images and links.

8. The navigation bar can display across the page or down the page. Select Vertically (**Figure 7.14**) or Horizontally (**Figure 7.15**) from the Insert drop-down menu.

9. To use tables to make your navigation bar stay in shape, select that checkbox. You can edit this table later; see Chapter 12.

10. To rearrange the order of the buttons, select a button name and then use the up and down arrow buttons to move the button through the list.

11. If you're not using dynamically served images, leave the Preload Images checkbox checked, so that the Web browser can fetch all the images for all the button states while the page is loading (instead of having to go get them when the user mouses over them).

12. When you're finished, click on OK to close the Insert Navigation Bar dialog box and return to the Document window. Your navigation bar will be displayed (**Figure 7.16**).

13. After the navbar is on your page, you must preview it in a browser to test it (**Figure 7.17**). From the Document window menu bar, select File > Preview in Browser > [Browser Name], or Press F12.

✔ Tips

■ See Chapter 3 for more about previewing.

■ To find out how to modify the table Dreamweaver inserts with your navbar, see Chapter 12; in particular, the section *Row Heights and Column Widths* may help.

■ To find out about adding the navbar to the Library so you can reuse it, see Chapter 18.

■ Make sure, when you put this page on the Web, that you upload all the images along with the page (see *About Dependent Files,* in Chapter 20). I'd recommend uploading a test page with the navbar on it, so you can check all the image locations, before you try to use it on a live page.

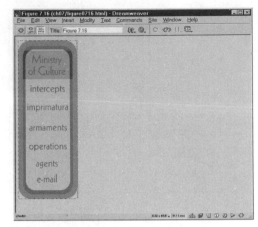

Figure 7.16 The navigation bar appears in the Document window. You can see the table border, barely, around the buttons.

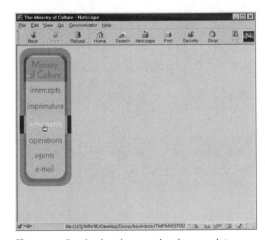

Figure 7.17 Previewing the page in a browser lets you test all the rollover effects.

Figure 7.18 Modifying a navigation bar uses practically the same dialog box as the one for adding it.

To modify your navbar:

1. From the Document window menu bar, select Modify > Navigation bar. The Modify Navigation bar dialog box will appear (**Figure 7.18**).

2. Make any necessary changes as described in the preceding section. For example, you may need to add or change a URL; you might want to select a different image to start in the Down position; or you may want to rearrange the order in which your images appear.

3. When you're done, click on OK to close the Modify Navigation Bar dialog box and insert your updated navigation bar.

✔ Tips

■ You can create more complex rollovers for your navbar with Behaviors, as described in Chapter 16.

■ Also using Behaviors, you can have different actions cause different button states to appear. See the sidebar *Set Navbar Image* in Chapter 16.

USING NAVIGATION BARS

Using Sound Files

Sound files come in more flavors than ice cream (see the sidebar, *Sound File Types*). Not all browsers support all sound files, but any browser that supports plug-ins or ActiveX (Navigator or Explorer versions 2 or later) should be able to play most sound files. Navigator 3 or later's pre-installed LiveAudio plug-in plays nearly every common sound file type.

There are two ways to add a sound file to your page. One way is to link to the sound file, so that the user downloads and plays it when clicking on the link. The other way is to embed the sound file so that it begins to load when the page loads, and a plug-in will play it automatically when the sound file finishes loading.

A sound link is like any other link. See Chapter 6 for more about how links work.

To link to a sound file:

1. In the Document window, select the text or image that you want to make into the link.

2. In the Property inspector, type the pathname for the sound file in the Link text box (**Figure 7.19**).

   or

   Click on the Browse icon (it looks like a folder), and use the Select File dialog box to choose a sound file from your computer (**Figure 7.20**). Be sure to select All Files (*.*) from the Files of type drop-down menu.

Figure 7.19 Type the location of the sound file in the Property inspector's Link text box.

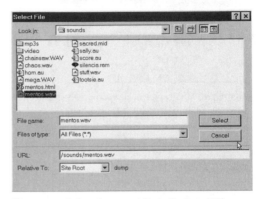

Figure 7.20 Select the sound file in the Insert File dialog box.

Figure 7.21 WinAmp is one kind of helper app that plays sound files.

3. Press Enter (Return). The selection will be linked to the sound file.

   When users click on the link, they'll download the sound file (**Figure 7.21**).

   When the user clicks on the link on your page, one of three things will happen:

   ◆ An external program, or "Helper App," will launch to play the sound file (**Figure 7.21**); or

   ◆ The browser will play it using its own capabilities or those of a plug-in; or

   ◆ If the browser doesn't support or recognize the file type, an error will occur. Sometimes a dialog box will open that says "Unrecognized file type," and sometimes the browser will open the file as if it were text.

The Sound of Downloads

When linking to sound files, it's a good idea to let your users know what they're in for. Unless the sound is very small, it's good practice to indicate the file type and file size of sound files so that users know whether to download them. For instance, some older Mac browsers don't support .WAV files, and some older PC browsers don't support .AIFF files. And any user on a 14.4 kbps modem wants advance notice before they start downloading a 100K+ sound file.

A line like this near the link should do the trick:

They Killed Kenny! (10K .WAV)

or even better:

They Killed Kenny! (10K .WAV, 9K .AIFF)

Embedding sound files

Embedding a sound file is similar to linking to an image. You can add the <embed> tag by inserting the sound file as plug-in content, or you can add the code by hand.

To embed a sound file:

1. Open the document you want to attach the sound file to in the Document window.

2. Click to place the insertion point at the place in the document where you want the sound controller to appear. For invisible sound files, you can place the file anywhere, although at the top or bottom of the document is usually more convenient.

3. View the HTML source for the page in the Code inspector by selecting Window > HTML from the Document window menu bar (or by pressing F10).

4. For a sound file with no controls showing, type the following line of code:

   ```
   <embed src="sounds/yoursound.wav"
   autoplay="TRUE" hidden="TRUE">
   </embed>
   ```

   Where sounds/yoursound.wav is the pathname of the sound file.

5. Save your changes to the page (**Figures 7.22** and **7.23**).

6. Preview the page in a browser to make sure it works.

Figure 7.22 The code for a standard, non-visible Netscape controller (top), and for a standard visible controller.

Figure 7.23 This is the same page we saw in **Figure 7.22**. Note that the hidden controller is marked with a standard placeholder, and the visible one is given the specified dimensions.

✔ Tips

- You can embed a sound file with or without the use of the plug-in dialog box. Because Dreamweaver's Insert > Media > Plug-in feature doesn't include all the stuff you need for embedding sounds in a page, I'm going to discuss embedded sound and plug-ins as if they were two different entities.

- You can also link to or embed movie files, or you can insert them as plug-ins. You can keep track of movies (such as RealVideo or QuickTime) using the Assets panel.

Explorer's <bgsound> Tag

Versions of Internet Explorer before 4.0 do not support embedded sound files. Explorer uses a proprietary tag called <bgsound>. You can use the <embed> and <bgsound> tags on the same page.

A <bgsound> tag goes in the body of the document and looks like this:

```
<bgsound src="sounds/mysound.wav"
loop="infinite" autoplay="true"
volume=0>
```

The loop parameter can be either infinite or a number. Volume can be 0 (full) to −10,000 (lowest). There are no user controls to display with the <bgsound> tag.

Sound File Parameters

If you want your visitors to enjoy your embedded sound, they'll need to have the correct plug-in on their computer, which is no sweat if they're using a browser that supports such things. If you want to use a dialog box to insert these parameters (rather than typing them into the code), see *Extra Parameters,* later in this chapter.

Here's the skinny on some of the different parameters you can employ with sound files that use the <embed> tag:

◆ **src="" (required)**

The source of the file.

◆ **name=""**

Name the embedded file if you want to call it from a script. If you use the name value, you must also include the master-sound attribute (no value).

◆ **controls=console|smallconsole| true|false**

(Required for visible controllers.)

◆ **hidden=true|false**

Determines whether the controller is visible.

◆ **autoplay=true|false**

Determines whether the sound begins playing as soon as it loads.

◆ **volume=0%–100%**

Percent of system volume used.

◆ **loop=true|false|n**

Determines whether the sound will loop continuously. A setting of loop=3 would make the file loop three times.

Sound File Types

`.AIFF`: Macintosh Audio format.

`.AU`: Sun Audio format.

`.DCR`: Shockwave audio (also used for Shockwave movies). Requires Shockwave plug-in.

`.LA`, `.LAM`, `.LMA`: Netscape streaming audio. Handled automatically by Netscape 4 and higher.

`.MID`, `.MIDI`: MIDI electronic music format. Requires plug-in in Netscape 2.0.

`.MOD`, `.RMF`: Beatnik audio format. Requires Beatnik plug-in. (Note: once Beatnik is installed, it will also handle `.AIFF`, `.AU`, `.MID`, and `.WAV` by default.)

`.MOV`: QuickTime audio (also used for QuickTime movies). Requires QuickTime plug-in.

`.MPG`: MPEG, or MP3 files, which provide CD-quality sound. Requires an audio plug-in such as RealPlayer or QuickTime or a helper app such as WinAmp.

`.RAM`, `.RPM`: RealAudio (also used for RealVideo). Requires RealAudio or RealPlayer plug-in.

`.WAV`: Windows Audio.

Figure 7.24 The standard Netscape LiveAudio sound controller, embedded in a page. LiveAudio plays .AIFF, .AU, .MID, and .WAV files, among others.

Figure 7.25 The same controller in Explorer. Note that it ignores the given dimensions.

◆ **height** and **width**

(Required for visible controllers.)

Determines the height and width of the controller. For console: height=60 width=144. For smallconsole: height=15 width=144.

When you adjust the height and width of an embedded controller, its placeholder changes shape in the Document window.

◆ **align="LEFT|RIGHT|TOP|BOTTOM"**

Defines alignment for visible controllers.

◆ **HSPACE="n" VSPACE="n"**

Sets space around visible controllers.

◆ **type="MimeType"**

Use for listing the mime type of a plug-in.

A standard audio controller (**Figures 7.24** and **7.25**) would have the following settings:

```
<embed src="sounds/yoursound.wav"
height="60" width="144"
controls="CONSOLE" autostart="FALSE"
loop="FALSE"></embed>
```

✔ Tips

■ If the source for the sound file isn't correct, the console will not show up in Navigator.

■ Quotation marks are not essential for anything but SRC, but proper HTML prefers them.

■ It's a good idea to include on the page the URLs of the plug-in and your favorite browser.

Noembed

If you want to provide a description of a sound or other plug-in for browsers without plug-in capability, use the NOEMBED tag:

```
<noembed>
```

```
This page contains content available only with the DorkBlast plug-in and a plug-in capable browser.
```

```
</noembed>
```

Netscape Plug-ins

Netscape plug-ins work in Netscape 2 or later and in Internet Explorer version 5 or later. Many plug-ins can be set either to run inline or to launch a helper app. They can also be set to play different qualities of content depending on the computer or modem speed. The RealPlayer is a good example of both of these traits.

There are some ActiveX equivalents to Netscape plug-ins; see *ActiveX,* later in this chapter, and the documentation for the specific plug-in.

To insert a Netscape plug-in:

1. In the Document window, click to place the insertion point at the place on the page where you want the plug-in to appear.

2. From the Document window menu bar, select Insert > Media > Plugin.

   or

   Click on the Insert Plug-in button on the Special panel of the Objects panel 🐾.

3. Either way, the Select File dialog box will appear (**Figure 7.26**). When you locate the file, click on Open.

4. When the pathname of the plug-in appears in the File Name text box, click on OK. The dialog box will close and a plug-in placeholder will appear in the Document window 🔲.

✔ Tip

■ You can use the Behavior called Check Plug-in to determine whether a visitor has a particular plug-in installed. See Chapter 16 for more details.

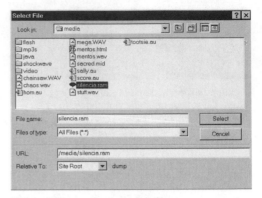

Figure 7.26 Browse for the plug-in files on your computer. Remember that you're looking for the media file to be played, not the plug-in component (DLL) that plays it.

Playing Plug-ins in Dreamweaver

Dreamweaver now supports some plug-ins, which means you can play them inline in the Document window. You must have the plug-in installed in Netscape's (or Dreamweaver's) plug-ins folder for Dreamweaver to be able to play the plug-in.

There are two ways to play a plug-in with Dreamweaver. First, on the Property inspector for a selected plug-in, there's a Play button with a green arrow. Press this button to play the selected object. The button will turn into a red Stop button, the use of which you can guess.

Alternatively, you can select View > Plug-ins > Play (and Stop). You can also select View > Plugins > Play All (or Stop All) for pages that have multiple plug-ins.

Your mileage may vary. A couple notes: Don't do this with ActiveX. The Play button's there, but Macromedia doesn't recommend doing so. I had problems getting Dreamweaver to play even a simple .WAV file. The support for playing Flash and Shockwave files has improved, though, and you can do this easily with Flash buttons and Flash text.

Figure 7.27 The Property inspector, displaying plug-in properties.

Plug-in Properties

Properties you can set for Netscape plug-ins include the following:

Name the plug-in by typing a name for it in the text box.

Set dimensions for the plug-in by typing the W(idth) and H(eight) in the associated text boxes.

Change the Source by typing it in the Src text box. Click on the Folder icon to browse for the file on your computer.

If a user doesn't have the plug-in installed, they can be directed to an installation page. Type the URL for this page in the Plg URL text box.

Set the alignment of the plug-in on the page by selecting an alignment from the Align drop-down menu. These alignment options are the same as for images. (I discuss image alignment in Chapter 5.)

To provide an alternate image for browsers without plug-in capabilities, type the Image source in the Alt text box. Click on the Folder icon to browse for the image on your computer.

V space and H space denote an amount of space around the plug-in. Border describes a visible border around the plug-in. (I discuss these options further with regard to images in Chapter 5.) The units for these options are in pixels. Type a number without units in the appropriate text box.

After you insert the placeholder, you can set additional properties for the plug-in. Note that most of these properties are quite similar to the image properties discussed in Chapter 5. See the sidebar *Plug-in Properties* for details.

To set Plug-in properties:

1. Select the Plug-in placeholder in the Document window. The Property inspector will display Plug-in properties (**Figure 7.27**).

2. Change any properties in the Property inspector, and click on the Apply button.

3. To set extra parameters, click on the Parameters button. (See *Extra Parameters,* later in this chapter.)

✔ Tips

■ If you change the source for the plug-in by clicking on the folder icon, you'll need to select the appropriate file type, or All Files, from the Files of Type drop-down menu.

■ Most properties for other media types are quite similar to the properties for plug-ins. Additional properties for items such as Java, Shockwave, Flash, and ActiveX are discussed in Appendix G on the Web site for this book, *Media Properties.*

NETSCAPE PLUG-INS

Shockwave and Flash

Shockwave and Flash Player are Netscape plug-ins, but you get more up-front ability to set their attributes by using the Insert > Media > Shockwave and Insert > Media > Flash tools. Director, Flash, and Dreamweaver are developed by Macromedia, after all, and integration of the three is one of Dreamweaver's big selling points.

To insert a Shockwave or Flash file:

1. In the Document window, click to place the insertion point at the place on the page where you want the Shockwave or Flash movie to appear.

2. From the Document window menu bar, select Insert > Media > Shockwave or Insert > Media > Flash.

   or

   Click on the Insert Shockwave or Insert Flash button on the Common panel of the Objects panel ⚙.

3. The Select Shockwave or Select Flash dialog box will appear (**Figure 7.28**). Locate the file on your computer. Click on Open when you find the file.

4. When the filename of the movie appears in the File name text box, click on OK. The dialog box will close and an icon will appear in the Document window ⚙.

✔ Tips

■ You can set additional properties for Shockwave (**Figure 7.29**) and Flash (**Figure 7.30**). They're quite similar to the plug-in properties discussed earlier in this chapter; for additional details, see Appendix G on the book's Web site.

■ Behaviors for detecting whether a browser has Shockwave or Flash installed and for inserting Shockwave or Flash controls are discussed in Chapter 16.

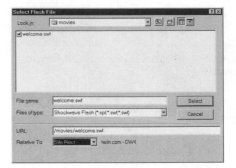

Figure 7.28 Choose a .DCR, .DIR, or .DXR file (Shockwave) or a .SWF, .SPL, or .SWT (Shockwave Flash Template) file from your computer.

Figure 7.29 The Property inspector, displaying Shockwave for Director properties.

Figure 7.30 The Property inspector, displaying Flash properties. Note that Flash has a few extra attributes.

Using Aftershock with Dreamweaver

Aftershock is an HTML tool used with Director and Flash to create HTML files using Shockwave. You can open files created with Aftershock and edit them in Dreamweaver. You can also select the relevant HTML and paste it into other Dreamweaver documents.

If you want to edit Aftershock object files that have been inserted into Dreamweaver HTML documents, view them in the Property inspector and click on Launch Aftershock. Edit the Aftershock file, close the program, and accept the This File has Been Edited dialog box. For more on using Dreamweaver with external editors, see the Tip earlier in this chapter.

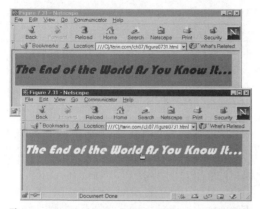

Figure 7.31 A Flash text object in Navigator, with and without the rollover.

Figure 7.32 A bank of Flash buttons. In the StarSpinner button style, the rollover effect makes the star get bigger and spin around.

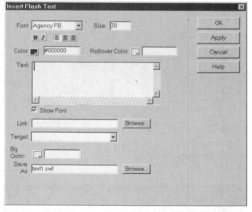

Figure 7.33 Create your Flash text elements using the Insert Flash Text dialog box.

Creating Flash Objects in Dreamweaver

Macromedia Flash is a versatile form of multimedia that uses incredibly compressed vector graphics to present interactive images and movies. The program, however, can be complicated to learn, and if you want to get your site up in a hurry, you might need to contract out the fancy stuff. For the simple Flash object, however, Dreamweaver 4 offers an easy-to-use tool for creating basic Flash text objects and buttons.

Both Flash text (**Figure 7.31**) and Flash buttons (**Figure 7.32**) can feature rollovers and can link to other pages. Keep in mind, however, that the user must have a Flash-capable browser to see your text at all.

About Flash text

Flash text objects are the fastest, easiest way to create a text image in the font you want, with an automatic rollover effect. You can't put a border around a Flash object.

To insert Flash text:

1. From the Document window menu bar, select Insert > Interactive Images > Flash Text.

   or

   On the Common category of the Objects panel, click on the Insert Flash Text button 🅰.

   Either way, the Insert Flash Text dialog box appears (**Figure 7.33**).

continued on next page

2. To select the folder the Flash file will be stored in, click on Browse. The Select File dialog box appears. Browse until you find the right folder. (Be sure to name your Flash file something memorable.)

   If you don't choose a folder before saving your Flash Text file, the file will be stored in the same folder as the current page. Dreamweaver requires that you use Document-relative rather than Site-root relative paths for these objects. See Chapter 6 for more on relative links.

3. Type the text you want to use in the Text text box.

   You can modify the way the text will appear in several ways (**Figures 7.34** and **7.35**):

   ◆ Choose a font from the Font drop-down menu. To preview the font face in the Text text box, leave the Show Font checkbox checked.

   ◆ Type the font size in the Size text box.

   ◆ To make the text bold or italic, select the text and click on the B or I button. Unfortunately, you can't select just part of the text; it must *all* be bold or italic.

   ◆ To set the alignment of the text within the rectangle, click on the left, right, or center alignment button.

   ◆ To choose a color for the text, you can type a hex code or click on the Color button and use the eyedropper to choose a color. For more on using colors, see Chapter 3.

   ◆ If you want the text color to change when the user mouses over the button, choose a rollover color that's different from the text color (**Figure 7.36**).

   ◆ To set a background color other than white, choose a background color using the Bg Color button. In **Figure 7.31**, I used a different background color than the page's background; in **Figure 7.36**, they're the same.

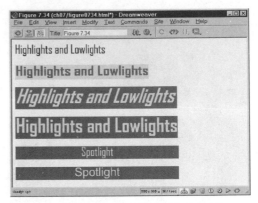

Figure 7.34 I created several similar Flash text items. The second image is the same size as the first, with Bold text and different colors. The middle two images use a large font size. The bottom two images show alignment—but I couldn't find any appreciable difference in the alignment settings.

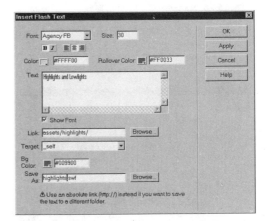

Figure 7.35 These are the settings I used for the fourth item in **Figure 7.34**.

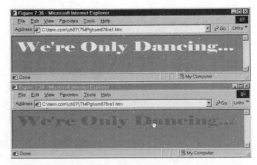

Figure 7.36 The text changes color when the user mouses over it.

Figure 7.37 I made changes to my text in the dialog box and clicked on Apply to preview them before I returned to the Document window.

Figure 7.38 You can change the background color, the dimensions, the alignment, and the Vspace and Hspace of your Flash text object in the Property inspector.

Figure 7.39 You have three scaling options for your Flash text.

Figure 7.40 The first image on this page has not been resized. The second three images have been resized, and, from top to bottom, their Scaling attributes are Show All, Exact Fit (which stretches the text), and No Border (which scales the text out of the box). The bottom two images are scaled to 100 percent of the window, and again are scaled as Show All and Exact Fit.

◆ If the text should link to another page, type the link in the Link text box, or click on Browse and choose a file from your local site.

4. If your site uses frames and you need to set a target for the link, select it from the Target text box (see Chapter 13). You can also set other targets based on the windows in your site (see Chapter 16).

5. To preview the way your text looks, click on Apply. You can make changes before you continue (**Figure 7.37**).

6. Click OK to close the dialog box and save your changes.

✔ Tips

■ You can use any font you like for the text without having to worry about the user's font set (see Chapter 8). The font is stored in the Flash file rather than on the page.

■ To edit your Flash text, double-click on it, and the Insert Flash Text dialog box will reappear.

■ You can change the background color of your Flash text in the Property inspector (**Figure 7.38**).

■ To change the way the Flash text fits within the borders of the object, you can change the Scale in the Property inspector (**Figures 7.39** and **7.40**). Default (Show All) makes all the text fit in the box without distorting the font. Exact fit stretches the text to fit the dimensions of the box. No border may make the text run outside the box.

■ You can set alignment and Vspace and Hspace in the Property inspector as you would for an image. See Chapter 5.

Using Flash Buttons

Flash buttons, like Flash text, are small files that can include text and links as well as rollover effects. Flash buttons are templates that offer preset styles and visual effects.

To create a Flash button:

1. From the Document window menu bar, select Insert > Interactive Images > Flash Button.

   or

   On the Common category of the Objects panel, click on the Insert Flash Button button 📷.

   Either way, the Insert Flash Button dialog box appears (**Figure 7.41**).

2. Browse through the list of available looks for your button. You can choose from various kinds of arrows and the like (**Figure 7.42**), or you can choose a button that has room for text (**Figure 7.43**).

3. To select the folder the Flash file will be stored in, click on Browse. The Select File dialog box will appear. Browse until you find the right folder. (Be sure to name your Flash file something memorable.)

   If you don't choose a folder before saving your Flash Button file, it will be stored in the same folder as the current page.

4. If you chose a button that has text, type the text in the Button Text text box. You may have to find out by trial and error whether your text is too long to fit on the button (**Figure 7.44**).

5. Choose a Font Face from the Font drop-down menu.

   The Font Size is often non-negotiable; if you enlarge the font, the words on the button may get cut off (**Figure 7.45**).

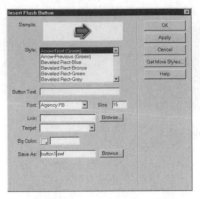

Figure 7.41 Choose the format and create your button in the Insert Flash Button dialog box.

Figure 7.42 Some of the buttons are text-free arrows and Play buttons. These buttons are the "Control" series.

Figure 7.43 You can choose from a variety of looks for text buttons. Of course, you'll probably want your buttons to say different things, and you'll probably want a set of them to look the same.

Figure 7.44 You've got a limited amount of space on a button, even if you enlarge it.

Figure 7.45 The top button is fine at size 12, but the bottom one's text is too big with a point size of 16.

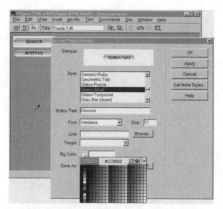

Figure 7.46 In the first visible button here, I didn't choose a background color, so it defaulted to white, which looks bad. On the second one, I chose the background color of the page. Click on the Background Color button, and click the eyedropper on the page background to choose that color.

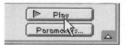

Figure 7.47 Select the button you want to test, and click on Play in the Property inspector. This works with Flash text, too.

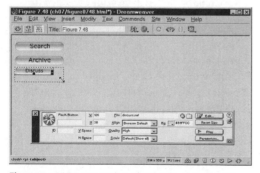

Figure 7.48 You can resize a button by dragging its handles or by typing new dimensions in the H and W text boxes on the Property inspector. To reset the size, click on Reset Size on the Property inspector.

6. Set the background color for your button; you can click the eyedropper on the background color of the page to choose that color (**Figure 7.46**).

7. Type the link for the button in the Link text box, or click on Browse and choose a file from your local site.

8. If your site uses frames or additional windows, and you need to set a target for the link, select it from the Target text box.

9. To preview the way your button looks, click on Apply. You can make changes before you continue.

10. Click OK to close the dialog box and save your changes.

✔ Tips

- To edit your Flash text or Flash button, double-click on it, and the Insert Flash Text (or Button) dialog box will reappear.

- To preview the rollover effects in the Document window, select the Flash object. In the Property inspector, click on Play (**Figure 7.47**). Now, when you mouse over the button, you'll see the rollover in play. When you're done, click on Stop.

- You can resize the Flash object as you would an image by selecting it and dragging its handles (**Figure 7.48**). The resizing will be done to scale; the text will grow to fit the new dimensions, but that doesn't mean that too-large text will fit on a button. See the tips under Flash Text for more on scaling.

- You can get additional button templates from Macromedia Exchange by clicking on Get More Styles in the Insert Flash Button dialog box. Your browser will open and take you to the Exchange, where you can download new button templates created by other users.

Duplicating Your Efforts

When you create a Flash button, you probably want to create a whole set of buttons that look and act the same. Each button will say something different, presumably, and will link to a different page.

Instead of going through the motions of selecting a button type and a background color and so on over and over, you can save your changes in a new file and then insert the new files onto your page.

1. Create a Flash button that has all the attributes you want to reuse.

2. Double-click on the button to display the Insert Flash Button dialog box.

3. Make appropriate changes in the Button Text text box and the Link text box.

4. Type a new filename for the button in the Save As text box.

5. Click on OK to save your changes in the new file.

Now, your new button will be displayed, but the old one will have disappeared. Don't worry. Go ahead and follow the steps above for each button in your set, taking care to provide a new filename for each one.

To insert your new buttons, open the Flash panel of the Assets panel (Window > Assets) or the appropriate folder in the Site window, and drag each button in turn into its place on the page. To stack a group of buttons vertically in a table cell or elsewhere, press Shift+Enter (Shift+Return) after each button to insert a line break.

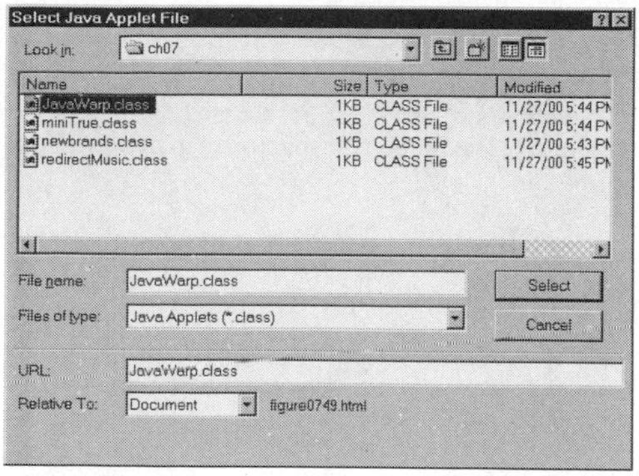

Figure 7.49 Select the class file from your computer. The file will probably have the `.CLASS` extension.

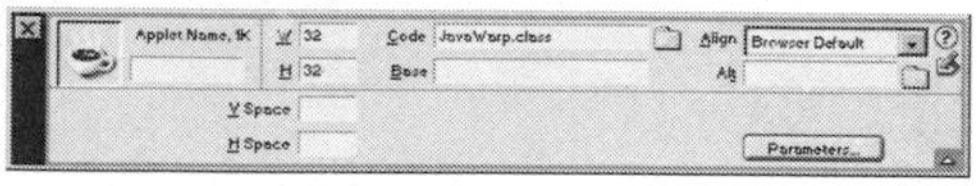

Figure 7.50 The Property inspector, displaying Applet properties.

Java Applets

Java is an object-oriented programming language based on C++ and developed by Sun Microsystems. The goal of Java is to be as cross-platform as possible. Currently, most Java applets (little applications) are run inline inside a Web browser, although stand-alone programs—and even operating systems—have been written for Java.

Java applets run on Netscape 2 or later for PCs, Netscape 2.2 or later for the Mac, and Internet Explorer 3 or later for either platform.

To insert a Java applet:

1. In the Document window, click to place the insertion point at the place on the page where you want the Java applet to appear.
2. From the Document window menu bar, select Insert > Media > Applet.

   or

   Click on the Insert Applet button on the Special category of the Objects panel.

   Either way, the Select Java Applet File dialog box will appear (**Figure 7.49**).
3. Locate the applet on your computer. When you locate the source file, click on Open.
4. When the pathname of the applet appears in the File name text box, click on OK. The dialog box will close and a placeholder will appear in the window.

✔ Tips

- Some applets will run on your computer; others must be on a Web server, depending on how many additional classes they require to run.
- You can set additional properties for Java applets (**Figure 7.50**). Many of them are similar to plug-in properties; for additional details, see Appendix G on the book's Web site.

ActiveX

ActiveX is a software architecture developed by Microsoft for use in Internet Explorer 3 or later. An ActiveX control can act like a plug-in and invisibly play multimedia content, or it can act like Java or JavaScript and serve as a miniature program that runs inside the Internet Explorer Web browser.

There is a plug-in for Netscape 4 that plays some ActiveX controls, but support is not built into the program and the plug-in should not be counted on to work. Dreamweaver tries to be as cross-platform as possible about this; you can insert an ActiveX control and specify the Netscape plug-in equivalent, and Dreamweaver will write code for both programs simultaneously.

To insert an ActiveX control:

1. In the Document window, click to place the insertion point at the place on the page where you want the ActiveX control to appear.

2. From the Document window menu bar, select Insert > Media > ActiveX.

   or

   Click on the Insert ActiveX button on the Special category of the Objects panel 📷 .

   Either way, an ActiveX placeholder will appear in the Document window at the insertion point 📷 .

3. Click on the placeholder to display ActiveX attributes in the Property inspector (**Figure 7.51**). Fill in the Class ID and other required properties (refer to the documentation for the control if you need help).

Figure 7.51 The Property inspector, displaying ActiveX properties.

✔ Tips

- You can use JavaScript to have the browser go to one URL if the browser is ActiveX capable and to a different URL if it's not. See the section in Chapter 16 called *Check Plug-in,* and use the ActiveX checkbox.

- Macromedia recommends that you refer to the documentation for the ActiveX control to determine the requisite IDs and parameters needed.

- You can set additional properties for ActiveX controls. Many of them are similar to plug-in properties; for additional details about ActiveX properties, see Appendix G on the companion Web site for this book.

- Frequently used Class IDs are stored in the Property inspector. To delete one permanently, click on the Minus (–) button on the Property inspector for ActiveX.

ACTIVEX

Figure 7.52 Add any extra attributes for your multimedia files in the Parameters dialog box.

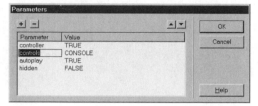

Figure 7.53 These are the parameters for an embedded sound file. I sometimes find it more expedient to type the parameters in the HTML inspector and then proof them in the Parameters dialog box.

Reordering and Removing Parameters

You can change the operation order of parameters by clicking on the name of the parameter in question and clicking on the up or down arrow buttons to move the parameter through the list. You can also delete a parameter:

1. Follow steps 1 and 2 in the list on this page to open the Parameters dialog box.

2. Click on the name of the parameter you want to delete.

3. Click on the Minus button. The parameter will be deleted.

Extra Parameters

Some multimedia objects require other parameters for optimal performance. These parameters may be indicated in the documentation for the language or program you're using. Of course, if it's an applet or object you wrote yourself, you'll know all about it already. (See the sections on sound for details about embedded sound parameters.)

To set additional object parameters:

1. In the Document window, select the placeholder for the object. The Property inspector will display the object's properties.

2. On the Property inspector, click on the Parameters button. The Parameters dialog box appears (**Figure 7.52**).

3. Click on the Plus (+) button. The Parameter text field becomes available.

4. Type the name of the parameter in the Parameter text field (such as loop).

5. Press the Tab key. The Value text field becomes available.

6. Type the value of the parameter in the Value text field (such as TRUE).

7. Repeat steps 3–6 for any additional parameters.

8. When you're all set, click on OK to close the dialog box, and return to the Document window.

Figure 7.53 shows the Parameters dialog box displaying parameters for an embedded sound file.

FONTS AND CHARACTERS

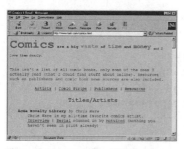

Figure 8.1 You can use different sizes, colors, and text styles on a single Web page, or even in a single paragraph.

What's Where

This chapter covers font sizes, font faces, text styles, font colors, special characters, finding and replacing text, and spell checking. Comments are covered in Chapter 9.

Chapter 9 covers all the basics of laying out blocks of text: paragraphs versus line breaks, headings, preformatted text, numbered lists, bulleted lists, definition lists, paragraph alignment, divisions, indent and outdent, nonbreaking spaces, and horizontal rules.

Chapter 10 deals with saving formatting as an HTML Style, and Chapter 11 will teach you all about CSS Styles, or Cascading Style Sheets.

Text comes in all shapes, sizes, and colors—or at least it can do so on Web pages (**Figure 8.1**). In this chapter, we'll go over the most basic ways of working with text, including cutting and pasting. Then, we'll find out how to accomplish rudimentary typographical changes: font size, font face, and font color. We'll also look at various text styles, from bold and italic to code fonts.

We'll also find out how to insert special characters like accented letters and copyright marks.

And we'll see how you can use Dreamweaver's word-processing tools, such as find-and-replace and spell check, to keep your Web pages clean and shiny.

Basically, this chapter covers changes that you can make on the character level—that is, to individual words or groups of words. There's a lot more you can do with text, of course—see the sidebar on this page.

Placing Text

There are several ways to put text on your pages with Dreamweaver (**Figure 8.2**).

To put text on your page:

◆ Just start typing in the Document window!

or

Select some text from another program or window, copy the text to the clipboard (usually by pressing Ctrl+C (Command+C)), return to the Dreamweaver window, and paste it there by pressing Ctrl+V (Command+V).

or

Convert a text file or word-processed document to HTML, and then open it with Dreamweaver.

Once you have text on your Web page, you can treat it like you do in any other text editor. You can highlight the text and then copy, cut, delete, or paste over it. Use these commands:

◆ Copy: Ctrl+C (Command+C)

◆ Cut: Ctrl+X (Command+X)

◆ Paste: Ctrl+V (Command+V)

◆ Clear: Delete/Backspace

✔ Tips

■ If you copy text from another source and paste it into the Document window, it may not retain any formatting you've given it—including paragraph breaks. See Chapter 9 for information on using preformatted text.

■ You can copy and paste formatted text. To copy the text with its HTML formatting, select Edit > Copy HTML. To paste the formatted text in the Document window, select Edit > Paste. To paste the HTML code itself, select Edit > Paste HTML.

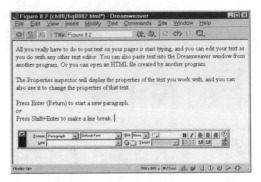

Figure 8.2 You can use the Dreamweaver Document window to type and edit text as you do with any other text editor.

Mom, What's Deprecated?

Custom style sheets are so nifty that they're making obsolete a lot of the physical font manipulations people have been so happy about for a while—most of the stuff in this chapter. The <font> tag, for instance, is eventually going to die quietly, along with its attributes—a process called deprecation (meaning the tags are being phased out of the HTML standard).

On the other hand, this won't be a quick or easy death. Tons of people still use Navigator and Explorer 3 and 4, and all those folks still look at pages that use the <font> tag. And people who use versions of Navigator earlier than 4, and versions of Explorer earlier than 3, can't see all the wonderful things that style sheets can do. The audience that uses older browsers may be shrinking, but it's not gone.

If you want to design for a wide audience, you need to be able to use these deprecated tags for the older generation browsers, and find out how to get along without them in the newest incarnations. Although the deprecated tags may eventually be phased out, they won't die until no one on earth is surfing with an out-of-date browser: not a likely prospect, unless the earth loses all electrical power tomorrow.

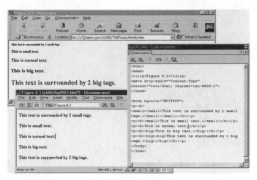

Figure 8.3 The big and small tags can be used for relative size changes. Note that the size changes show up in the browser window, but not in Dreamweaver's Document window.

Changing Font Size

There are several ways to indicate font size in HTML. Using style sheets (see Chapter 11), you can set a font size in points, like you do in word-processing and page-layout programs.

Without style sheets, however, you set font sizes relative to a base size. This base size is not something you can fix exactly, because every user has the option of customizing the basic font size in their browser program to whatever size they choose. The font sizes that you set will be relative to this basic font size, which is usually 12 or 14 points.

There are two separate scales you can use to determine size: the "absolute" scale (1–7), which is still relative to the user's preferences; and the relative-to-base-font scale (-3 to +4). Some folks also prefer using the very relative <big> and <small> tags.

Figure 8.3 demonstrates the use of the <big> and <small> tags. Using these tags isn't an HTML convention directly supported by Dreamweaver, but it works in browsers that support the tags.

To use these tags, simply nest your text within them:

```
<big>this is big text</big> <small>this
is small text</small>
```

If you're not comfortable adding code to your pages by hand, you may want to go back and read Chapter 4.

Language Encoding

Not everyone makes Web pages in the English language, and Dreamweaver addresses that. Western encoding is what most European languages use, and you can also set the encoding as Japanese, Traditional Chinese, Simplified Chinese, Korean, Central European, Cyrillic, Greek, Icelandic for the Mac, or any other non-Western encoding set you have installed. To do this, open the Preferences dialog box by pressing Ctrl+U (Command+U), and then click on Fonts/Encoding to bring that panel to the front of the dialog box. Choose your language group from the Default Encoding drop-down menu, and click on the language in the Font Settings list box to choose a font group. In order to use non-Western encoding, you need to have the appropriate fonts installed; Asian languages in particular require a system that supports double-byte encoding.

You can also set encoding for a single page in the Page Properties dialog box (Modify > Page Properties).

Absolute Font Sizes

Absolute font sizes are based on the default text size of 3, which in most browsers is about 12 points. When you set an absolute size, you're not setting a point size, but rather telling the Web browser to display bigger fonts (size 4–7, which would be 14–24 points, based on a 12-point default) or small fonts (size 1–2, which would be 9–10 points).

Keep in mind, too, that the various browsers, platforms, and screen resolutions display point sizes relative to how they draw fonts in the first place.

To use the absolute scale:

1. Select the text that you want to resize.

2. From the Document window menu bar, choose Text > Size 🔖 and then choose a number between 1 and 7 (**Figure 8.4**).

   or

   In the Property inspector, click on the Size drop-down menu, and choose a number between 1 and 7 (**Figure 8.5**). You can also simply type the number in the Size text box.

In any case, the size of your text will change (**Figure 8.6**).

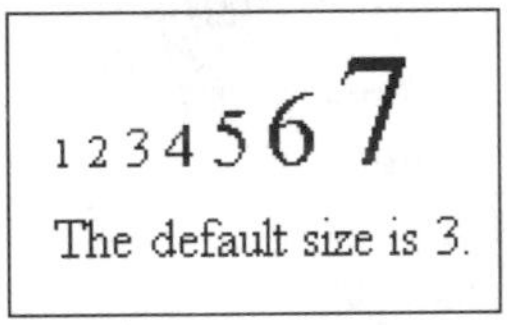

✔ Tips

- If you choose size 3, you likely won't see any change in size, because size 3 is the default font size unless you specify otherwise.

- If you change font size and then change your mind, select the offending text, and then select Default from the Text > Size menu.

- When changing font size, you can click within the text and select an existing <font> tag in the tag selector to ensure that you apply the formatting to the entire tag.

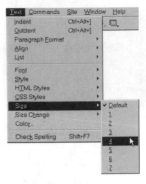

Figure 8.4 To adjust text size on the absolute scale, select Text > Size > *N* (where *N* is the absolute text size you want) from the Document window menu bar.

Figure 8.5 You can also choose a text size from the Property inspector's Size drop-down menu.

$123456\,7$

The default size is 3.

Figure 8.6 The absolute scale of text starts with the size 1 as the smallest available size and moves up to a maximum font size of 7.

- To change the size of all the text on a page, select Edit > Select All (Ctrl+A/Command+A) from the Document window menu bar. Then follow the steps described earlier. Or, you can change the base font size, as described in *Setting a Base Font Size,* later in this chapter.

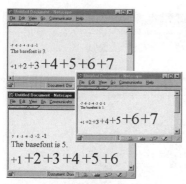

Figure 8.7 In these three examples, the base font size is 3, 1, and 5 (moving clockwise). Notice how none of the examples exceeds the maximum absolute size of 7 or the minimum absolute size of 1 (**Figure 8.6**).

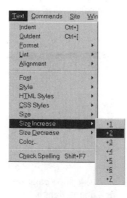

Figure 8.8 To increase relative font size, select Text > Size Change > *N* (where *N* is the absolute text size you want).

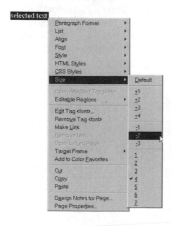

Figure 8.9 The context menu for selected text includes a great big text size menu. Just right-click the text (Control+click on the Mac).

Relative Font Sizes

Relative font sizes let you add or subtract from the user's font size to make the text, no matter what, appear larger or smaller. The sizes are in relation to a base font size of 3, unless you change that size, as described in the next section. The effects of relative font sizes are displayed in **Figure 8.7**. Relative font sizes are the best choice if you want your page to look basically the same to everyone—that is, if you want all your sizes to be on the same scale.

To use relative font sizes:

Select the text you want to resize.

◆ To choose from a menu of common relative sizes, select Text > Size Change from the menu bar, and then choose a number from +1 to +4 or −1 to −3 (**Figure 8.8**).

◆ To either increase or decrease size, select a number from the Size drop-down menu on the Property inspector (**Figure 8.5**).

◆ To see a menu of all font sizes, select the text and then right-click (Control+click) on it, and then from the pop-up menu, select Size (**Figure 8.9**).

You'll see the size change immediately, but if you set a base font size, it won't show up properly until you preview the page in a browser.

✔ Tips

■ You can also type a font size, whether it's absolute or relative, in the Property inspector or the Quick Tag editor.

■ The Property inspector's Size drop-down menu doubles as a text box.

■ As there are only seven gradations of font size in total, the actual deportment of the font will vary depending on the base font size. In other words, if your base font size is 5, and you increase it by +7, the size still won't get any bigger than 7 (**Figure 8.7**).

Setting a Base Font Size

You can set a base font size other than 3 for your page, in which case all differing font sizes will be set relative to this new size.

To set the base font size:

1. Open the Code inspector for your page by selecting Window > Code Inspector from the Document window menu bar (or by pressing F10).

2. At the top of the document, locate the <body> tag.

3. Directly after the <body> tag, but before any other text, type the following line of code:

   ```
   <basefont size="n">
   ```

   where *n* is a number between 1 and 7. Your code would look something like this:

   ```
   <body>
   ```

   ```
   <basefont size="4">
   ```

   although there may be other stuff inside the <body> tag (**Figure 8.10**).

4. Press Ctrl+S (Command+S) to save the changes to the code.

5. Close the Code inspector by pressing F10.

Because Dreamweaver doesn't directly support the <basefont> tag, you won't see any size changes in the Dreamweaver window. However, any size changes you make will be based on the base font number you specified, rather than on the default base font size of 3. (You didn't go to all that trouble to set a base font of 3, did you?) You'll see the change to the base font size when you preview the page in your Web browser (File > Preview in Browser), as shown in **Figure 8.11**. See Chapter 3 for details on previewing.

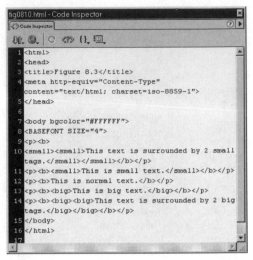

Figure 8.10 Here's the code for the page. You can see the <body> tag at line 7, and the inserted <basefont> tag at line 8.

Figure 8.11 The page on the left is the same page we looked at in **Figure 8.3**. The page on the right is the same document, with the <basefont> code added. Note that the "normal" sized text is a size bigger, because I set the base font size to 4. Resetting the base font size works with the relative sizes I discuss in this chapter as well.

Figure 8.12 In many browsers, the <strong> tag displays as bold and the <em> tag displays as italic. In Lynx, a text-only browser, all four tags are given the same emphasis. Other browsers, such as text-to-speech browsers or cell phone browsers, may interpret the <strong> and <em> tags differently.

■ Text styles as discussed in this section are also different from HTML styles, discussed in Chapter 10. HTML styles and CSS both allow you to create a set of attributes and combine a text style, such as bold, with another text attribute, such as color or font face. HTML styles, however, use the <font> tag rather than style sheets, and they can't be automatically updated.

Using Text Styles

You're probably used to using text styles, such as bold, italic, and underline, in your word-processing program or page-layout tool. You can use these styles in HTML, too, to add emphasis or visual contrast to pieces of text.

There are two kinds of styles in HTML: physical and logical. Physical styles tell the text exactly how to look, whereas logical styles suggest an attribute and let the browser decide how to interpret it. For example, <b> (bold) is a physical style. On the other hand, <strong> (strong emphasis) is a logical style. Although most graphical browsers display the <strong> tag as bold text, other software may treat it differently. Text-to-speech browsers, for instance, may read <strong> text with verbal emphasis.

Figure 8.12 contrasts the bold and strong tags, as well as the italic and emphasis tags.

✔ Tips

■ Text styles are not the same as style sheets. Text styles are specific tags that affect how text is interpreted on screen. They have not been deprecated along with the <font> tag, because there's more call to make them available to single words and not groups of layout elements. (See the sidebar, *Mom, What's Deprecated,* earlier in this chapter.) Style sheets, as explained in Chapter 11, offer even more text attributes than regular text styles, but not all browsers have style-sheet-processing capabilities.

Physical Text Styles

The most common physical text styles in most documents are bold and italic. You can also underline text (see Tips, below).

To make text bold:

1. In the Document window, select the text you'd like to make bold.

2. In the Property inspector, click on the Bold button **B**. The text will become bold.

To italicize text:

1. In the Document window, select the text you'd like to make italic.

2. In the Property inspector, click on the Italic button *I*. The text will become italic.

To underline text:

1. In the Document window, select the text you'd like to appear underlined.

2. From the Document window menu bar, choose Text > Style > Underline. The text will become underlined.

✔ Tips

- If you prefer menu commands to the Property inspector, you can choose Bold and Italic from the Text > Style menu instead.

- The key commands for bold and italic are Ctrl+B (Command+B) and Ctrl+I (Command+I), respectively.

- Try to avoid underlining text that is not linked, unless the context demands it. When users see underlined text, they often assume it's a link to something.

- To remove a text style, reapply it by repeating the key command, reselecting the menu command, or clicking again on the style button.

More Physical Text Styles

Physical text styles (other than the ones on the previous page) are demonstrated in **Table 8.1**. Strikethrough and teletype are supported by Dreamweaver, and you can apply them by using the Text > Style menu.

Table 8.1

Physical Text Styles

STYLE	APPEARANCE	CODE EXAMPLE
Strikethrough	~~strikes out text~~	`<strike>strikes out text</strike>`
Superscript	$E=MC^2$	`E=MC<sup>2</sup>`
Subscript	H_2O	`H<sub>2</sub>0`
Typewriter or teletype	old fashioned monospace font	`<tt>old fashioned monospace font</tt>`

Logical Text Styles

The logical styles that Dreamweaver supports are shown in **Figure 8.13** as displayed by most browsers. If you have a special concern as to how they're used in a specific browser, such as an email program or a handheld device, you'll need to load the page into that browser.

To use a logical style:

1. In the Document window, select the text whose style you'd like to change.

2. From the Document window menu bar, select Text > Style and then choose an item from the list. The text will change appearance to reflect your choice.

✔ Tip

- To use a style that Dreamweaver doesn't support, apply the style to the code. See Chapter 4 if you need help with HTML.

Style Name	Tag	Uses
Emphasis	<em>	indicates importance
Strong Emphasis	<strong>	indicates strong importance
Code	<code>	programming code and scientific equations
Variable	<var>	in tutorials, marks placeholders for user-defined text
Sample	<samp>	samples of code output
Keyboard	<kbd>	in tutorials, indicates text the user should input
Citation	<cite>	a citation or reference
Definition	<dfn>	marks the first use of a keyword in educational texts

Figure 8.13 This figure illustrates how the logical text styles supported by Dreamweaver are displayed in most browsers. There are many other such styles; these are merely some of the most common. To mark up text with any of these styles, select Text > Style > *N* (where *N* is the style you wish to use) from the Dreamweaver menu bar.

Old Style and Old Style Light

Some text styles are hardly used anymore, and you might wonder what they were ever used for in the first place. You'll find many of these tags if you browse through the list in the Quick Tag editor or the Reference panel (both are described in Chapter 4).

When the computer scientists at CERN invented the protocols now known as the Web, the Internet was used largely by scientists working for the government or universities. The Web Tim Berners-Lee envisioned was an updateable library of papers, theories, data findings, and discussion. That helps explain why tags such as <acronym>, <citation>, <code>, <keyboard>, <sample>, and <variable> appeared in the definition of the HTML Language, now under the care of the W3C (The World Wide Web Consortium). Some of the more common tags are illustrated in **Figure 8.13**. The <acronym> tag does not change the appearance of text, but the code looks like this:

```
The <acronym title="World Wide Web Consortium">W3C</acronym> is located in
Switzerland.
```

As with many of these tags, the <acronym> tag is used rarely; it's included in the Quick Tag editor Hints menu, but not in the menu bar. It would be convenient for indexers if all uses of acronyms carried the tag with the title attribute defined; however, its use isn't widespread enough to be practical. Of course, there's probably a research lab somewhere that loves it for in-house cataloguing. If you're out there, let me know.

Changing Font Face

Unless you specify a font face, any text on your pages will appear in the user's browser window in their browser's default font face. Most users probably have Times New Roman (Times) as their default proportional font, although some may have changed it.

When specifying font faces on a Web page, keep in mind that not every user has every font installed—far from it. Additionally, fonts that come from the same typeface family can be named several different things (such as Arial, Helvetica, and Univers), or the same font may be named different things on different platforms (Times New Roman on Windows is nearly the same as Times and New York on the Mac).

To get around trying to guess who has what font, you can use one of Dreamweaver's preset combinations, which include fonts nearly everyone owns. You can also create your own *font group* or *font combination* that offers the Web browser several choices. The browser will check to see if the first suggested font is installed, and then the second, and so on. If none of the recommended display fonts are available, the text will be displayed in the user's default browser font—not the end of the world.

✔ Tips

■ When changing font face, you can click within the text and select an existing <font> tag in the tag selector to ensure that you apply the formatting to the entire tag and that you don't add any additional, redundant <font> tags. So, if you've applied a size, you should apply the face settings to the same tag.

■ If Dreamweaver does create redundant <font> tags, use the clean-up feature to combine them. Select Commands > Clean up HTML from the document window menu bar. See Chapter 4 for more details on cleaning up your code.

■ Dreamweaver's preset font combinations consist of system fonts that are found on nearly every computer sold in the last five years. If you want users to be able to see a special font if they have it installed, be sure to back up that font with a similar-looking, more-common font.

■ For logos and other collateral that absolutely, positively *needs* to be in the right font face, you'll have to use images. You can also create Flash text objects right in Dreamweaver and use whatever fonts you have installed in those pieces of text. Everything you need to know about inserting images is in Chapter 5, and Flash and Flash text are described in Chapter 7.

Creating a Font Group

Dreamweaver offers several preset font combinations, shown in **Figure 8.14**. You can also define your own font combinations.

To create a font group:

1. From the Document window menu bar, select Text > Font > Edit Font List.

   or

   In the Property inspector (**Figure 8.15**), choose Edit Font List from the Font Face drop-down menu.

   In either case, the Font List dialog box will appear (**Figure 8.16**).

2. Dreamweaver's existing font combinations will appear in the Font List text box. All system fonts installed on your computer will appear in the Available Fonts list box.

3. Locate your first-choice font in the Available Fonts list box and click on it.

4. Click on the Left Arrow button, and the font's name will appear in the Chosen Fonts list box (**Figure 8.17**).

5. Repeat steps 3 and 4 for all the font faces you want to appear in this particular font combination.

6. To add the name of a font you don't own, type it in the text box below the Available Fonts list box. For example, you may have Bookman on your Mac, but if you want to make Bookman Old Style your second choice and you don't have it, you need to type it here.

Arial, Helvetica, sans serif

Times New Roman, Times, serif

Courier New, Courier, mono

Georgia, Times New Roman, Times, serif

Verdana, Arial, Helvetica, sans serif

Figure 8.14 These are the preset font combinations available in Dreamweaver. You can include any number of fonts in a font combination; the browser will try each one in turn, from left to right. Serif, Sans Serif, and Mono are not fonts, but types of fonts. See the sidebar, *I Shot the Serif,* earlier in this chapter.

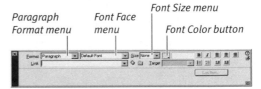

Figure 8.15 The Property inspector allows you to set the font face for text, among other things.

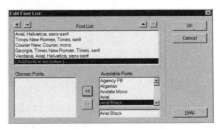

Figure 8.16 The Font List dialog box lets you define font combinations using any font on your computer.

Figure 8.17 Choose the font from the Available Fonts list box, then click on the Left Arrow button to move it to the Chosen Fonts list box.

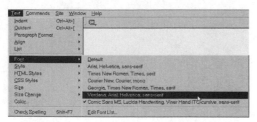

Figure 8.18 I've added a font combination to the Font Face drop-down menu. You can select Edit Font List from the same menu to add more fonts.

I Shot the Serif

Serifs are those curly things some fonts use at the ends of strokes in letters. They have their origins in ancient times when stonecutters had to make a terminating stroke in a letter in order to remove the chisel from the stone.

A sans serif font, then, is a font without any serifs. As illustrated in **Figure 8.14**, sans serif fonts look different than serif fonts.

Mono refers to a monospace, or a fixed-width font. In a fixed-width font, each letter occupies the same amount of space. E-mail and Telnet programs use these.

A proportional font is designed so that each character takes up only as much space as it needs. Letter combinations such as fi and th are fitted together.

Proportional fonts are used for body text on most Web pages, whereas fixed-width fonts are used for the text typed into forms and for several text styles, such as teletype, code, and citation. Preformatted text (Chapter 9) also uses a fixed-width font.

Courier New (Courier), used in **Figure 8.14**, is the most popular fixed-width font. Some browsers, however, allow their users to change their proportional and fixed-width fonts so that the choices don't necessarily correspond to their character.

7. To remove a font you chose, click on the Right Arrow button.

8. When you've chosen the right combination of fonts, click on the + button to add the font combination to the Font List list box.

9. When you're all done, click on OK to close the dialog box and return to the Document window. Your new font combination will be available in the Text > Font menu and in the Property inspector's Font Face drop-down list (**Figure 8.18**).

✔ Tips

- There's no preview available in the Font List dialog box, and Dreamweaver doesn't allow you to display an individual font without adding it to the Font List. Therefore, it's advisable to view your font faces in another program (such as Word or PageMaker) so that you know what you're getting.

- You can change the order in which the font combinations appear in the list. Open the Edit Font List dialog box, and in the Font List list box, click on a font combination you'd like to move up or down in the list of fonts. Then click on the Up or Down Arrow buttons. When you're done, click on OK to close the Font List dialog box.

To set the face for selected text:

1. With the document open in the browser window, highlight the text for which you wish to change the font.

2. From the Document window menu bar, choose Text > Font and then choose a font group from the list (**Figure 8.19**).

   or

   In the Property inspector, choose a font face group from the Font Face drop-down menu (**Figure 8.20**).

The selected text will change to the first installed font face on the list.

✔ Tip

- To remove any font face specifications, select the text for which you've changed the font face, and then change the font face settings to Default Font, using either the Text > Font menu or the Property inspector.

To set the face for an entire page:

1. With the document open in the browser window, select Edit > Select All from the Document window menu bar.

2. From the Document window menu bar, select Text > Font and then choose a font group from the list (**Figure 8.19**).

   or

   In the Property inspector, choose a font face group from the Font Face drop-down menu (**Figure 8.20**).

All the text on the page will change to the first installed font face on the list, unless it's formatted using a tag, such as <code>.

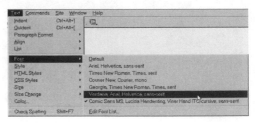

Figure 8.19 From the Document window menu bar, select Text > Font and then choose a font combination from the menu bar. Any font combinations you added with the Font List dialog box will appear in this menu.

Figure 8.20 You can choose a font combination from the Property inspector's Font Face drop-down menu.

Base Font Face

You can set the base font for a page, too, by adding the FACE attribute to the <basefont> tag. Follow the instructions in the section, *Setting a Base Font Size*, and to the base font tag, add the attribute FACE ="Name", where "Name" is the name of the font you want to specify. Your code will look something like this:

```
<basefont size="4" FACE="Arial">
```

Older versions of Explorer and some "third-party" browsers don't support this attribute; the worst that can happen is that the page's font face will still be the browser default.

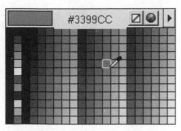

Figure 8.21 Click on the font color box, and then select a color by clicking on a color choice in the color picker. Note how the pointer becomes an eyedropper.

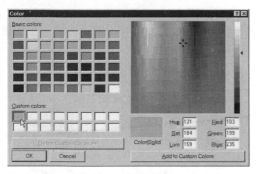

Figure 8.22 The Color dialog box offers a wider range of color choices. As described in Chapter 3, the Mac Color dialog box is somewhat different than this one, for the PC.

Changing Font Color

You learned how to set the text color for an entire page in Chapter 3. You can also set a different font color for specific pieces of text.

To change font color:

1. With your page open in the Document window, select the text you want the color change to affect.

2. In the Property inspector, type (or paste) the hex code for the color in the Color text box and press Enter (Return).

   or

   Click on the Colors button beside the Color text box. The Colors palette will appear (**Figure 8.21**). Click on a color to select it.

   or

   Click on the color box in the color picker ▦. The Color dialog box will appear (**Figure 8.22**). Click on a hue and shade to choose a color, and click on OK to close the Color dialog box and return to the Page Properties dialog box. (For more details on using the Color dialog box, refer to Chapter 3.)

No matter the method you use, the color of the text will change to reflect your choice.

continued on next page

CHANGING FONT COLOR

✔ Tips

- When you click on the color box on the Property inspector, the cursor turns into an eyedropper. You can then click the eyedropper on any text or background color on the page or elsewhere on the desktop, and the selected text will change to that color.

- To remove a font color you've set, select the text in question and then delete the hex code from the Font Color text box in the Property inspector.

- To jump directly to the Color dialog box, select Text > Color from the Document window menu bar.

Color Recycling

Hex codes are defined in Chapter 3; in short, it's sufficient to say they have six (hex) digits and they use the hexadecimal, or 16-digit method, of counting (which is why they use letters and numbers).

To use the same color on another piece of text:

1. Select the hex code (including the # sign) from the Property inspector's Color text box and copy it to the clipboard by pressing Ctrl+C (Command+C).

2. Select the next piece of text for which you want to change the color.

3. Paste the hex code into the Property inspector's Color text box, by pressing Ctrl+V (Command+V).

4. Press Enter (Return) and your text will change to that other color.

Of course, you can also use the eyedropper to choose the color if it's already on your page.

Special Characters

HTML is a language based on plain English text (also called ASCII), in which the characters you see on your keyboard are also the standard characters in the language. There are many other characters, however, that you may need to use on your pages. Special codes, called escape sequences, are used to reproduce these characters. The code for a copyright mark looks like this:

©

Dreamweaver now supports inserting these characters using a dialog box similar to Keycaps on the Mac or to Word's Insert Symbol feature.

Those Wacky Characters

A few characters that aren't included in Dreamweaver's set of characters are the ampersand and the left and right angle brackets (greater-than and less-than signs). They require special codes because they are essential characters in HTML code that don't normally get printed in body text. Dreamweaver doesn't include these tags in its list of special characters because you can type them directly in the Document window. Dreamweaver recognizes what you want and supplies the code for them in the background. If you're curious, those codes are:

                    &   &amp;

                    <   &lt;

                    >   &gt;

Another good tip about characters: the code for an accented e, or é, is é —self explanatory, it means "an e with an acute accent." You can work from here: A capital e with an acute accent is É, and an i with an acute accent is í. Same goes for ñ, ü, and ò. (Try them and see.)

On the Web site for this book, I've included links to pages that list *all* the special character codes.

Using the History panel described in Chapter 18, you can repeat a character without having to use the menu or dialog box. Also discussed in Chapter 18 is the Library, which is a good place to store updateable pieces of your site that get repeated from page to page, such as copyright notices.

SPECIAL CHARACTERS

To insert a special character:

1. In the Document window, click within the text at the point where you want the special character to appear.

2. From the Document window menu bar, select Insert > Special Characters.

   If the character you want appears in the menu (**Figure 8.23**), select it. The character will appear in the Document window.

   or

   If the character you want doesn't appear in the menu, select Other. The Insert Other Character dialog box will appear (**Figure 8.24**).

3. When you see the character you want to use, click on it, and its escape sequence will appear in the Insert text box.

4. Click on OK to close the Insert Other Character dialog box and place the character on your page.

To insert special characters using the Objects panel:

1. In the Document window, click within the text at the point where you want the special character to appear.

2. Click the menu button at the top of the Objects panel, and from the menu that appears, select Characters. The Objects panel will display the Special Characters category (**Figure 8.25**).

3. To insert a character, just click on it, or drag it onto the page. For more options, click on "Other," and see steps 3 and 4 in the previous list of instructions.

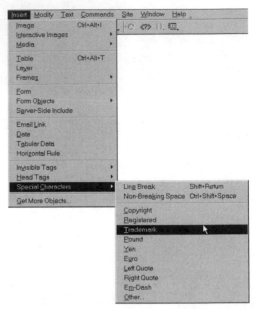

Figure 8.23 These are the characters available from the Insert > Special Characters menu.

Figure 8.24 To insert a character other than the ones in the menu, choose Other from the Insert > Special Characters menu, and this dialog box will appear.

Figure 8.25 Using the Special Characters category of the Objects panel, you can add a special character to your text with a single click. To make the buttons easier to read, I set my Object panel to display both Icons and Text. You can do this in the General panel of the Preferences dialog box (Edit > Preferences).

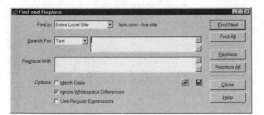

Figure 8.26 Type the text you want to find in the Search For text box.

Find and Replace

Dreamweaver can search your document and locate a particular piece of text. It can also replace one text string (a bunch of characters, whether they're code or words) with another.

To find a piece of text in the current page:

1. With the current page open in the Document window, choose Edit > Find and Replace from the Document window menu bar, or press Ctrl+F (Command+F). The Find and Replace dialog box will appear (**Figure 8.26**).

   For details on searching more than one page at a time, see the sidebar, next page.

2. Type what you're looking for in the text box. This can be a whole word, a phrase, or part of a word.

3. To look for a particular case pattern (upper or lower), place a check mark in the Match Case checkbox.

4. To look for text and ignore spacing differences (i.e., to find both "tophat" and "top hat"), place a check mark in the Ignore Whitespace Differences checkbox.

5. Click on Find Next. If Dreamweaver finds what you're looking for, it will highlight the text in question on the current page (although you may have to move the Find dialog box to see it).

6. Click on Close to close the Find dialog box.

FIND AND REPLACE

✔ Tips

■ If Dreamweaver can't find the text in question, a dialog box will appear telling you it didn't find the search item.

■ To find the same item again (even on a different page), select Edit > Find Again from the Document window menu bar, or press F3.

■ You can also use the Find command in the Code inspector. Right-click on some space in (Control+click) the Code inspector to get the command from a pop-up menu.

■ Click on Find All in the Find and Replace dialog box to pop up a list box containing all instances of your query (**Figure 8.27**).

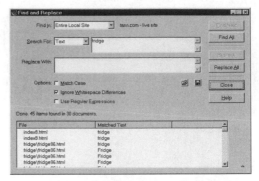

Figure 8.27 I chose Current Site from the Find In drop-down menu, and then clicked Find All, The dialog box expanded to show me a list of every instance of my search string. I can double-click any entry to open it.

FIND AND REPLACE

Seek and Ye Shall Find

Dreamweaver includes some exhaustive search features for the current page, a local directory, or an entire local site. You can also use regular expressions and load or save searches.

To search an entire local site, a page from that site must be open. (See Chapter 2 for more.) Select **Entire Local Site** from the Find In menu to search the folders that makes up your site. To search within a few files in your site, select **Selected Files in Site**, open the Site window, and hold down Ctrl or Command while clicking. Then go back to the Find dialog box.

To search a local directory, select **Folder** from the Find In menu. Type the name of the directory in the text box, or click the folder icon to browse. You can also choose what type of text to find by choosing one of these options from the Search For drop-down menu:

◆ **Text** Regular old text.

◆ **Code Inspector** Searches text and tags.

◆ **HTML Tags** HTML tags and attributes, ignoring text not in tags.

◆ **Text (Advanced)** Defines a search for text within or outside tags. Additional menus include one that lets you choose "inside tag" or "not inside tag," and a menu to choose tags. Click on + to add additional search options for attributes.

◆ **Regular Expressions** Special text descriptors that let you refine a search. To enable regular expressions, click on that checkbox. To find out more about Regular Expressions, see this book's Web site.

You can save a search query by clicking on the Disk icon. To load it later, click on the Folder icon and choose the file.

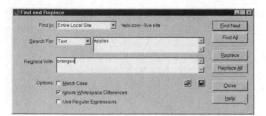

Figure 8.28 Type the text you want to find In the Search For text box, and the text you want to replace it with in the Replace With text box.

✔ Tips

- For advanced search tips, see the previous page.

- Keep in mind that automatically replacing all instances of text can create problems. Imagine replacing all instances of "cat" with "dog" and ending up with a site full of words like "dogegory" and "Aldograz."

To replace one piece of text with another:

1. From the Document window menu bar, select Edit > Find and Replace, or press Ctrl+H (Command+H). The Find and Replace dialog box will appear (**Figure 8.28**).

2. Type the text you want to destroy in the Search For text box.

3. Type the text you want to replace it with in the Replace With text box.

4. If you want to restrict the search to a specific case pattern (upper or lower), place a check mark in the Match case checkbox.

5. To look for text and ignore spacing differences (i.e., to find both "tophat" and "top hat"), place a check mark in the Ignore Whitespace Differences checkbox.

6. To supervise the search, click on Find Next, and when Dreamweaver finds an instance of the Find text string (the words or tags in the Find text box), it will highlight it in the document window. Then, you can click on Replace to supplant it with the text in the Replace text box.

   or

   To have Dreamweaver automatically replace all Find What text with the Replace With text, click on Replace All. A dialog box will appear informing you about how many replacements were made.

7. When you're all done, click on Close to return to the Document window.

Checking Your Spelling

One nice thing about using a WYSIWYG editor to do HTML is that you can check the spelling on your pages without the spell checker constantly stopping to ask you about tags or URLs. You can check the spelling of an individual selection or an entire page.

To check the spelling of a page:

1. With the page in question open in the Document window, click to place the insertion point at the beginning of the page (or the place at which you'd like to begin the spell check). You can also select a single word you're unsure about.

2. From the Document window menu bar, select Text > Check Spelling, or press Shift+F7. The Check Spelling dialog box will appear (**Figure 8.29**).

3. When Dreamweaver finds the first questionable word, that word will appear in the Word Not Found in Dictionary text box. You have several options here:

   ◆ If the word is spelled correctly, click on Ignore.

   ◆ If the word is spelled correctly, and you think it might appear more than once on your page, click on Ignore All.

   ◆ If the word is misspelled, and the correct spelling appears in the Suggestions list box, click on the correct word, and then click on Change.

   ◆ If you think the word may be misspelled more than once, click on the correct word in the Suggestions list box, and then click on Change All.

   ◆ You can also manually correct the word by typing the correction in the Change To text box and then clicking on Change.

   ◆ Make this choice for each word the spell check questions.

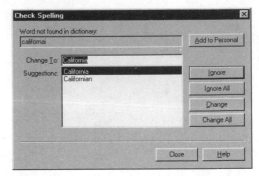

Figure 8.29 The Check Spelling dialog box allows you to ignore the unrecognized word, add it to your personal dictionary, or change it, either by typing it into the Change To text box or by choosing a word from the Suggestions list box.

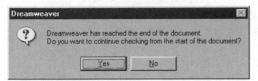

Figure 8.30 If you are checking the spelling of a single word or sentence, click on No. If you started the spell check partway through the document and you want to check the whole document, click on Yes.

Figure 8.31 When the spell check is complete, you'll be told how many errors were found. Unfortunately, this includes words you added to your personal dictionary or ignored.

4. When the spell check reaches the end of the page, Dreamweaver may ask you if you want to check the beginning of the document (**Figure 8.30**). It's usually a good idea to click on Yes.

5. When the spell check is complete (including cases where there are no spelling errors), a dialog box will appear telling you so (**Figure 8.31**). Click on OK to close this dialog box and return to the Document window.

✔ Tips

■ If a word is spelled correctly but is not in the dictionary, such as unusual proper names (Ronkowski or Gravity7), slang, abbreviations, or lingo, you can add it to the custom dictionary. Click on the Add to Personal button in the Check Spelling dialog box. The word will be added to your personal dictionary, and future spell checks will not question this word. Keep in mind, though, that you may also have to add variations on the word, such as plurals (gorrillafishes) or possessives (Dorkface's).

■ To spell check a single word or phrase, highlight the text in question, and then start the spell check as described in Step 1. If you want to skip the rest of the page, when the dialog box appears asking you if you want to check the rest of the document (shown in **Figure 8.30**), click on No, and the spell check will go away.

PARAGRAPHS AND BLOCK FORMATTING

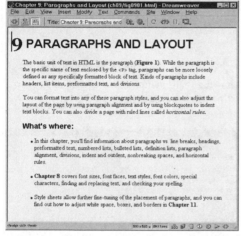

Figure 9.1 I formatted an HTML version of this page in Dreamweaver by applying paragraph breaks, two kinds of headings, blockquotes, and a bulleted list. I also used the Arial font face for the headings, and applied the bold and <tt> styles in a few places. If I had wanted to replicate the layout of this page (including columns), I would have used tables.

The basic unit of text is the paragraph, although in HTML the paragraph is a specific tag. Paragraphs in HTML are blocks of text enclosed by the <p> tag (**Figure 9.1**), but paragraphs can also be more loosely defined as any specifically formatted block of text. Paragraph types include headers, list items, preformatted text, and divisions.

You can format text into any of these paragraph styles, and you can adjust the layout of the page by using paragraph alignment and by using blockquotes to indent text blocks. You can also divide a page with ruled lines called *horizontal rules*.

What's Where

In this chapter, you'll find information about paragraphs versus line breaks, headings, preformatted text, numbered lists, bulleted lists, definition lists, paragraph alignment, divisions, indents and outdents, nonbreaking spaces, and horizontal rules.

Chapter 8 covers font sizes, font faces, text styles, font colors, special characters, finding and replacing text, and checking your spelling.

Style sheets allow further fine-tuning of the placement of paragraphs; you can find out how to adjust white space, boxes, and borders in Chapter 11.

Paragraphs vs. Line Breaks

Your elementary school English teacher probably told you that a paragraph contains a minimum of three sentences, and that longer paragraphs include a topic sentence. In HTML, the paragraph is simply a unit of text enclosed by <p> tags, and each paragraph is automatically separated from other paragraphs by a blank line. **Figure 9.2** shows a page that consists of four paragraphs.

To make a paragraph:

1. In the Document window, type the text that will constitute the first paragraph. The text will wrap automatically.

2. At the end of the paragraph, press Enter (Return).

The line will be broken, and a line of blank space will be inserted between the paragraph and the insertion point (**Figure 9.3**).

To apply paragraph style to existing text:

1. Click within the block of text to which you want to apply paragraph tags.
   or
   Select several blocks of text by highlighting them.

2. In the Property inspector, select Paragraph from the Format drop-down menu (**Figure 9.4**).

The paragraph style will be applied to the text. See *Paragraph Properties,* on page 200, to find out what this entails.

✔ Tip

■ You can also place the insertion point within an existing block of text and press Enter (Return) to insert a paragraph break.

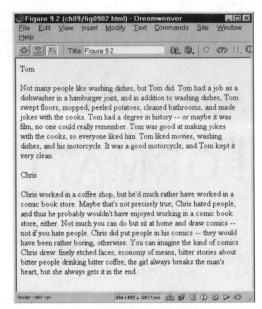

Figure 9.2 There are four paragraphs on this page: The single-word lines are paragraphs, too.

Figure 9.3 The text will wrap in the Document window—and in the browser window, as well—until you insert a paragraph break. When you press Enter (Return), the insertion point will skip a line of blank space and then start a new paragraph. Technically, there are three paragraphs on this page.

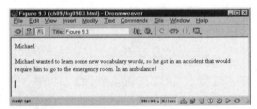

Figure 9.4 To easily surround text with paragraph tags, select the text and then choose Paragraph from the Property inspector's Format drop-down menu.

Figure 9.5 The only way to break a line without adding white space, as you would in a poem, is to use a line break rather than a paragraph break. Press Shift+Enter (Shift+Return).

Insert Line Break button

Figure 9.6 Click on the Insert Line Break button to insert a line break at the insertion point; or, drag the button onto the page.

If you want to break the line without inserting a line of blank space, you can use a line break.

To make a line break:

1. In the Document window, type the text in the first paragraph. The text will wrap automatically.

2. At the end of the line you want to break, press Shift+Enter (Shift+Return).

The line will break, and the insertion point will begin at the next line (**Figure 9.5**).

You can also insert a line break using the Characters panel of the Objects panel (**Figure 9.6**). You can then click the Insert Line Break button or drag the button to the page.

✔ Tip

■ You can achieve the same effect by selecting Insert > Special Characters > Line Break from the Document window menu bar.

Paragraph Properties

The tag for a paragraph is <p>. In the old days of hand-coding HTML, people often didn't close paragraphs with a </p> tag—technically, the <p> tag doesn't need a closing tag. However, the most recent HTML specifications prefer that you surround a paragraph with <p> and </p> tags, as Dreamweaver does.

Until the introduction of style sheets, this wasn't an issue anyone worried about; however, style sheets allow you to change the properties of an enclosed tag, and defining the <p> tag's properties only does any good if you close your paragraphs with the </p> tag.

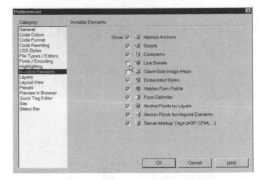

Figure 9.7 The Invisible Elements panel of the Preferences dialog box allows you to select which objects have visible markers when you view invisible elements.

What's My Line Break?

The tag for a line break is <br>. The <br> tag is one of a few tags that doesn't need to be closed. You close your paragraphs with the </p> tag

Line breaks are invisible on screen. By default, they aren't even visible with invisible-element viewing turned on (View > Invisible Elements). To view <br> tags as invisible entities, you'll need to change your preferences.

1. From the Document window menu bar, select Edit > Preferences. The Preferences dialog box will appear.

2. In the Category list box, click on Invisible Elements. That panel of the dialog box will become visible (**Figure 9.7**).

3. Check the box next to Line Breaks.

4. Click on OK to update your preferences and close the dialog box.

Now line breaks will show up in the Document window as symbols ▣. You'll be able to select them to view their properties or edit them in Edit Tag Mode using the Quick Tag editor. For information about line break properties, see the Web site for this book.

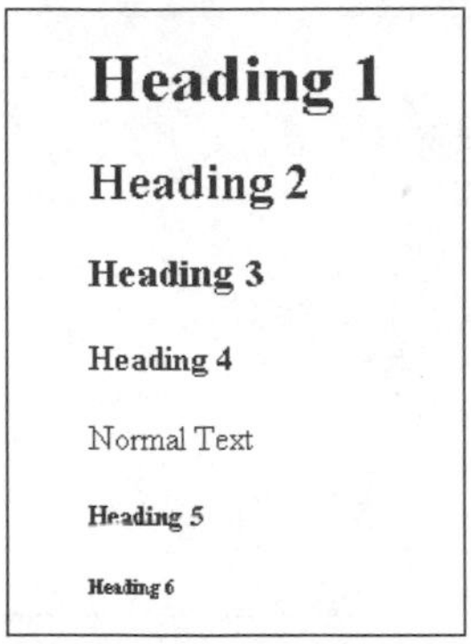

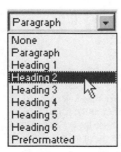

Figure 9.8 There are six levels of headings, from 1 (largest) to 6 (smallest). Heading 4 is the same size as the default font size.

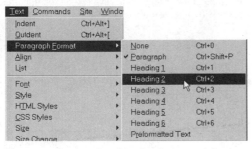

Figure 9.9 Choose a heading size, from 1 to 6, from the Text > Paragraph Format menu.

Figure 9.10 You can also set headings using the Property inspector's Format drop-down menu.

Creating Headings

Think of headings (also called headers) as being the same as headlines in a newspaper. They're generally larger than the body text of an article and bold. A heading is a block-type tag; that is, a line of white space precedes and follows a heading, just like other kinds of paragraphs.

There are six sizes, or levels, of headings (**Figure 9.8**). Heading 1 is the largest, and Heading 6 is often smaller than default body text.

To format a heading:

1. Click within the line or block of text you want to make into a heading.

2. From the Document window menu bar, select Text > Paragraph Format > and from the menu that appears (**Figure 9.9**), select a heading (size 1–6).

   or

   On the Property inspector, select a heading (size 1–6) from the Format drop-down menu (**Figure 9.10**).

The text will become a heading: That is, there will likely be a size change; the text will become bold; and a blank line will be inserted after the heading (**Figure 9.11**).

Figure 9.11 There are two paragraphs on this page; the first is in Heading 2 format, and the second is in Paragraph format.

Using Preformatted Text

In general, when you paste text into the Document window, it doesn't retain any of its formatting. This includes line breaks, paragraph breaks, spacing, tabs, text-formatted tables, and the like.

If you have formatted text in another program and you wish it to retain its shape, you can insert it into the page's HTML as preformatted text. None of the other conventions of HTML will govern this text; for instance, in HTML, only one typed space will be displayed, even if you type 50 in a row. In preformatted text, any shaping of the text done with spaces or line breaks will be preserved.

Figure 9.12 shows a piece of ASCII art preserved with preformatted text, and **Figure 9.13** shows the same characters without the preformatted text format applied.

It's generally easier to set up the preformatted style before you paste in the text.

To place preformatted text:

1. In the Document window, click to place the insertion point where you want the preformatted text to begin.

2. From the Document window menu bar, select Text > Paragraph Format > Preformatted Text.

   or

   On the Property inspector, select Preformatted Text from the Format drop-down menu (**Figure 9.14**).

3. Now you can paste in the text from the other program and it will retain that program's formatting.

✔ Tip

■ You can also apply the preformatted style to text already on a page, or type the work directly into Dreamweaver.

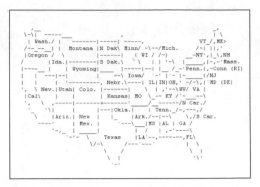

Figure 9.12 Someone worked very hard formatting this map of the United States in a text editor. (Pictures made with plain text are called *ASCII art*.)

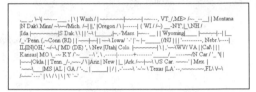

Figure 9.13 If you don't preserve the preformatted text, the picture looks like a jumble of characters.

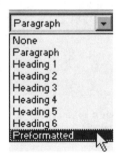

Figure 9.14 Select Preformatted from the Property inspector's Format drop-down menu.

Div and Span

There are two other kinds of text blocks that you might run across: <div> and <span>. The <div> tag stands for division, and it's used to mark blocks of text that (generally) span more than one paragraph. You can't end the division within a paragraph, because the </div> closing tag automatically breaks the paragraph. The <span> tag, on the other hand, can be used to mark up an area of text within a single block of text, such as within a paragraph or blockquote.

These two tags are mostly used in conjunction with style sheets, but I'm pointing them out here because of their properties of breaking paragraphs (or not). In the sidebar called *Terms of Alignment* (later in this chapter), we'll look more closely at the alignment properties of the <div> and <span> tags.

Preformatted Face

By default, the font used in preformatted text is the default monospace font, generally Courier or Courier New. The reason for this, as explained in Chapter 8, is that each character in a monospace font is the same width, which means that you can more easily control formatting of ASCII art or poetry (**Figure 9.15**).

You can change the font face, however, in addition to designating it as preformatted. Follow the steps in Chapter 8, in *Changing Font Face*, to change the face of the preformatted text. Or you can refer to Chapter 11 to find out how to change the attributes of the <PRE> tag.

Figure 9.15 If you apply a non-monospace font to preformatted text, you'll get a different effect, because each character (including spaces) is not the same width.

Formatting Lists

Dreamweaver directly supports two kinds of lists: numbered lists, also called ordered lists; and bulleted lists, also called unordered lists. There is an additional kind of list, called a definition list, that is partially supported by Dreamweaver.

Numbered Lists

The tag for a numbered list is <ol>. Each list item uses the <li> tag.

To make a numbered list:

1. In the Dreamweaver window, type (or paste) the items you'd like to make into a numbered list, omitting the numbers (**Figure 9.16**).

2. Select the list items.

3. From the Document window menu bar, select Text > List > Ordered List.
   or
   On the Property inspector, click on the Ordered List button ▤.

The list will become numbered (**Figure 9.17**).

To add an item to a numbered list:

1. To add an item to the end of a list, click to place the insertion point at the end of the last numbered line, and press Enter (Return). A new number will appear at the end of the list.

2. To add an item to the middle of the list, click to place the insertion point at the end of one of the lines, and press Enter (Return). A new number will appear in the middle of the list (**Figure 9.18**).

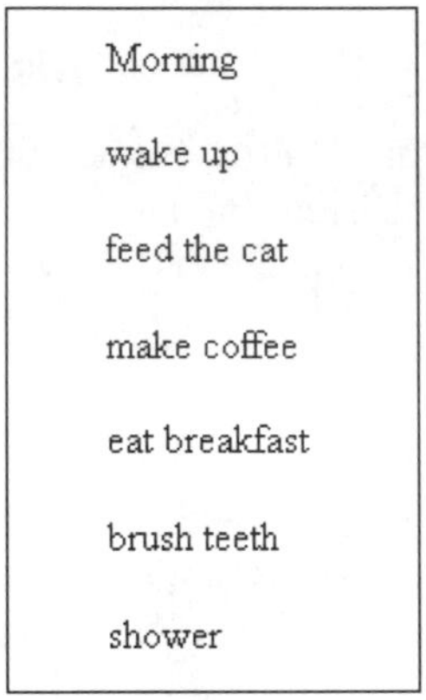

Morning

wake up

feed the cat

make coffee

eat breakfast

brush teeth

shower

Figure 9.16 Type the items you want to make into a list.

Morning

1. wake up
2. feed the cat
3. make coffee
4. eat breakfast
5. brush teeth
6. shower

Figure 9.17 After the Ordered List style is applied, the list items will be numbered and indented from the left margin. A paragraph break is automatically applied before and after the list.

Morning

1. wake up
2. feed the cat
3. make coffee
4.
5. eat breakfast
6. brush teeth
7. shower

Figure 9.18 If you add or remove items from the list, it will automatically renumber itself.

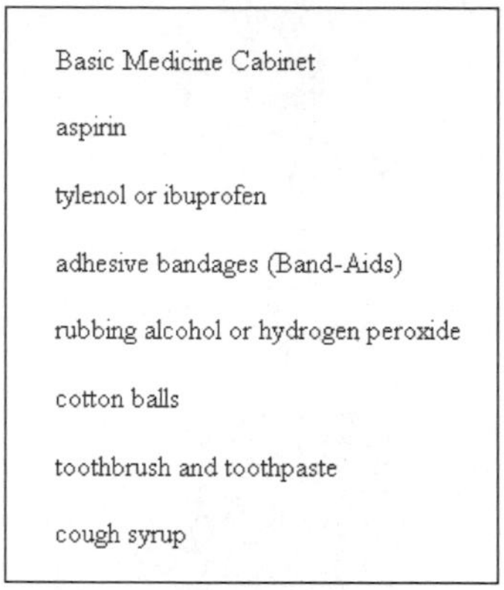

Basic Medicine Cabinet

aspirin

tylenol or ibuprofen

adhesive bandages (Band-Aids)

rubbing alcohol or hydrogen peroxide

cotton balls

toothbrush and toothpaste

cough syrup

Figure 9.19 Type the items you want to appear in the list, one to a line.

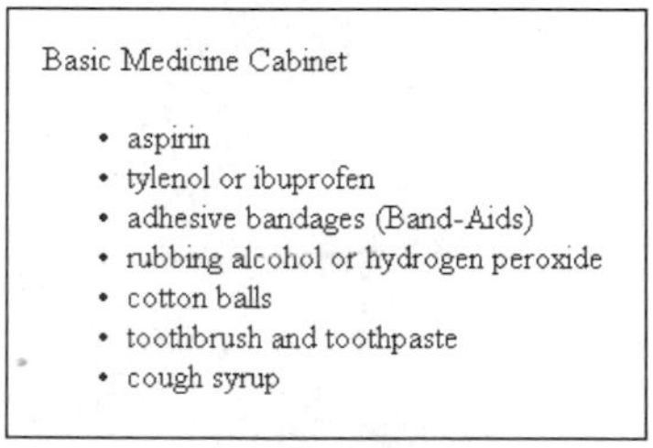

Basic Medicine Cabinet

- aspirin
- tylenol or ibuprofen
- adhesive bandages (Band-Aids)
- rubbing alcohol or hydrogen peroxide
- cotton balls
- toothbrush and toothpaste
- cough syrup

Figure 9.20 After you select the Unordered List format, the list items will be single-spaced and indented, and bullets will be added.

To remove an item from a numbered list:

1. Select the item to be removed, and press Delete (Backspace). The text will disappear.

2. Press Delete (Backspace) again, and the numbered line will be removed.

The list will renumber itself to reflect any additions or subtractions from the list.

Bulleted Lists

An unordered list is also called a bulleted list. As you might imagine, the list is outlined with bullets instead of numbers. The tag for a numbered list is <ul>. Each list item uses the <li> tag.

To make a bulleted list:

1. In the Dreamweaver window, type (or paste) the items you'd like to make into a bulleted list, omitting any asterisks or other bullet placeholders (**Figure 9.19**).

2. Select the list items.

3. From the Document window menu bar, select Text > List > Unordered List.

   or

   On the Property inspector, click on the Unordered List button ▤.

The list will become bulleted, single-spaced, and indented (**Figure 9.20**).

continued on next page

FORMATTING LISTS

Additional List Properties

Some additional list properties are available in Dreamweaver. See Appendix E on the Web site for this book for details on how to use them.

✔ Tips

- To convert a list back to paragraph style, reapply the style (select it from the menu bar or deselect the list button on the Property inspector).

- If some extraneous text before or after the list gets added to the list, select the offending line of text and click on the corresponding list button to deselect it.

- You can also select Text > List > None from the Document window menu bar to clear list attributes from selected text.

- Lists can only be bulleted or numbered, not both (thank goodness). To convert a list from bulleted to numbered (or vice versa), select the list and then apply the other list format.

- By default, a paragraph break will be inserted both before and after the list. Press Enter (Return) twice to end the list.

- The items in the list will be single-spaced by default. To add a line of blank space between the list items, press Shift+Enter (Shift+Return) twice after each list item.

- Other list options are available using style sheets; see Chapter 11.

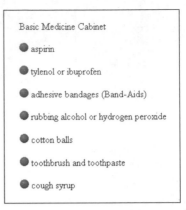

Figure 9.21 You can use tiny images on each line instead of making a bulleted list.

Images as Bullets

You may have seen a page that appears to use small images as bullets (**Figure 9.21**). This is not, in fact, a bulleted list. Each image is placed on a line (you can copy and paste them with Dreamweaver), and then the lines can be optionally indented. (See *Indenting Text*, later in this chapter).

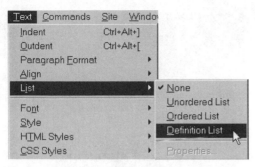

Figure 9.22 Type the terms and definitions, one to a line, in the Document window.

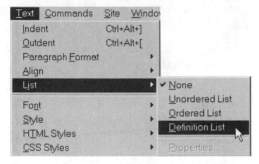

Figure 9.23 From the Document window menu bar, select Text > List > Definition List.

Figure 9.24 The list will be formatted so that every other item is a term or a definition. You can add other formatting and line breaks later.

Definition Lists

A third kind of list, called a definition list <dl>, is also supported by Dreamweaver. In a definition list, there are two kinds of list items: a definition term <dt>, and a definition <dd>.

As you'd find in a glossary, the definition is indented under the definition term. The items in a definition list don't have to be definitions; you can use the definition list style anywhere you want this sort of formatting.

To make a definition list:

1. Type the definition terms and the definitions in the Document window (**Figure 9.22**). Press Enter (Return) after each term and definition, and omit any indentations.

2. Select the list items. From the Document window menu bar, select Text > List > Definition List (**Figure 9.23**).

The list will be formatted so that every other item is a term and a definition (**Figure 9.24**).

✔ Tips

- If you're having trouble getting Dreamweaver to format the list properly, try selecting the text for each definition or term in the HTML inspector. Make sure you select all opening and closing tags (including <p> and </p> tags).

- If you want to format the definition list yourself, surround each definition term with <dt> and </dt>, and every definition with <dd> and </dd>.

- You can include more than one definition per definition term.

- You can cheat on indents by creating a definition list with just <dt> tags. This is an alternative way to indent blocks of text, because each is indented only from the left margin, not from both margins (as opposed to blockquotes).

Aligning Paragraphs

As is the case with word-processing programs, you can align part or all of a page of text with the left margin, the right margin, or the center of the page (**Figure 9.25**).

To change the alignment of text:

1. Select the text whose alignment you wish to change. This can be a single paragraph, a heading, a list, or an entire page.

2. From the Document window menu bar, select Text > Align > and then Left, Right, or Center.

   or

   On the Property inspector, click on the Left, Right, or Center alignment button .

The text will become aligned according to the option you selected.

✔ Tips

■ When you're working with images, or with tables, there are more than three alignment options available. Refer to Chapter 5 or to Chapter 12 for more on these alignment options.

■ Dreamweaver uses the <div> tag for center alignment. If you prefer the <center> tag, or if you have reason to believe your audience has a large pre-3.0 browser contingent, you can set Dreamweaver's preferences to use it for centering text and images. Or, you can stick with the more CSS-compatible <div align=center> tag. View preferences (Edit > Preferences), and select the Code Format category. In that section of the dialog box, at the bottom, click on the radio button for either <div> or <center> as the default centering tag.

Figure 9.25 You can align text to the left margin, the center of the page, or the right margin.

Terms of Alignment

Depending on what kind of text you're aligning—and how much—Dreamweaver may use different code. All default (unspecified) alignment is to the left margin.

The <center> tag can be used to center any element between the opening tag and the closing </center> tag.

Headers are aligned by using the align attribute within the <Hn> tag. For instance: <H2 align=center>.

A similar attribute exists for paragraphs, although it's being deprecated (removed from the HTML standard). Dreamweaver, however, uses this code: <p align=right> The align attribute will end with the closing </p> tag.

For more than one line of text, Dreamweaver tends to use the <div> tag to define all the text with non-left alignment. For instance: <div align=center>centered text</div>.

As mentioned earlier in the chapter, the </div> tag creates a paragraph break. Centering applies to an entire division or paragraph; this includes line breaks within the <p> or <div>.

To align part of a paragraph or division, you can use the <span> tag to surround a few lines of text within a <p> or <div>:

```
<span align=right> one
line<br></span>
```

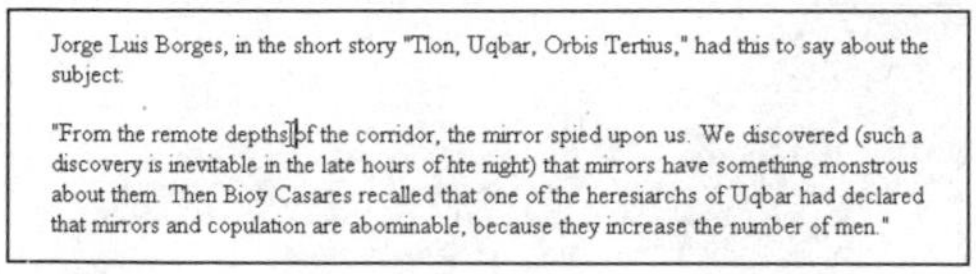

Jorge Luis Borges, in the short story "Tlon, Uqbar, Orbis Tertius," had this to say about the subject:

"From the remote depths of the corridor, the mirror spied upon us. We discovered (such a discovery is inevitable in the late hours of hte night) that mirrors have something monstrous about them. Then Bioy Casares recalled that one of the heresiarchs of Uqbar had declared that mirrors and copulation are abominable, because they increase the number of men."

Figure 9.26 Click within the paragraph you want to indent.

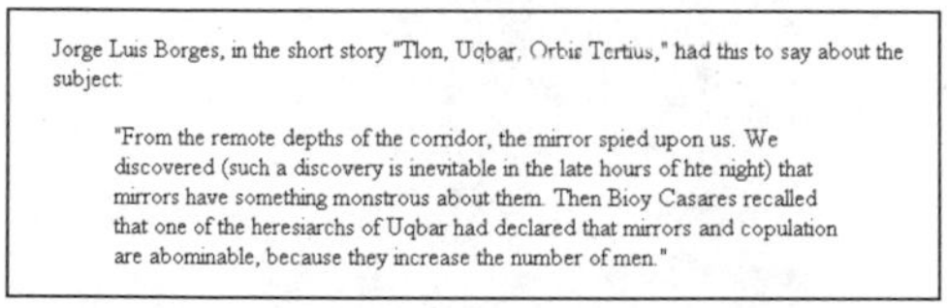

Jorge Luis Borges, in the short story "Tlon, Uqbar, Orbis Tertius," had this to say about the subject:

"From the remote depths of the corridor, the mirror spied upon us. We discovered (such a discovery is inevitable in the late hours of hte night) that mirrors have something monstrous about them. Then Bioy Casares recalled that one of the heresiarchs of Uqbar had declared that mirrors and copulation are abominable, because they increase the number of men."

Figure 9.27 Dreamweaver indents text by applying the <blockquote> tag.

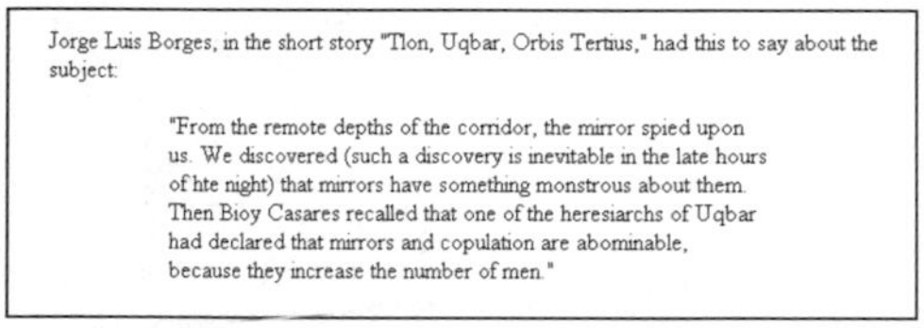

Jorge Luis Borges, in the short story "Tlon, Uqbar, Orbis Tertius," had this to say about the subject:

"From the remote depths of the corridor, the mirror spied upon us. We discovered (such a discovery is inevitable in the late hours of hte night) that mirrors have something monstrous about them. Then Bioy Casares recalled that one of the heresiarchs of Uqbar had declared that mirrors and copulation are abominable, because they increase the number of men."

Figure 9.28 You can indent the paragraph more than one level; by doing so here, it becomes more apparent that blockquotes are indented from both margins.

Indenting Text

There are no tabs in regular HTML; the kind of five-space paragraph indent used in other types of desktop publishing is generally replaced by setting off each paragraph by a line of white space.

You can, however, indent an entire block of text. One way to accomplish this is by using definition lists (see *Formatting Lists,* earlier in this chapter). Or use the <blockquote> tag, which is what Dreamweaver does.

To indent a block of text:

1. In the Dreamweaver window, click within the paragraph you wish to indent; to select more than one paragraph, highlight the text you want to indent (**Figure 9.26**).

2. From the Document window menu bar, select Text > Indent.

   or

   On the Property inspector, click on the Indent button ⊞.

Either way, the text will become indented (**Figure 9.27**).

✔ Tips

- You can repeat Step 2 for multiple indent levels (**Figure 9.28**).

- The <blockquote> tag indents text from both margins; to indent text from one margin only, use a definition list (see *Formatting Lists,* earlier in this chapter).

- You can also create an artificial indent by using nonbreaking spaces (see *The Nonbreaking Space,* later in this chapter).

- Tables are another way to create margins. See Chapter 12.

- Paragraph indents are available by using style sheets; see Chapter 11.

Removing indents

If you change your mind, you can remove one or more indent levels. Dreamweaver calls this "outdenting."

To remove a level of indent:

1. In the Dreamweaver window, click within the paragraph from which you wish to remove a level of indent; to select more than one paragraph, highlight the text.

2. From the Document window menu bar, select Text > Outdent.

   or

   On the Property inspector, click on the Outdent button ⬛.

Either way, one level of indent will be removed (**Figure 9.29**).

✔ Tip

■ You can repeat step 2 until the text is at the margin, if you like.

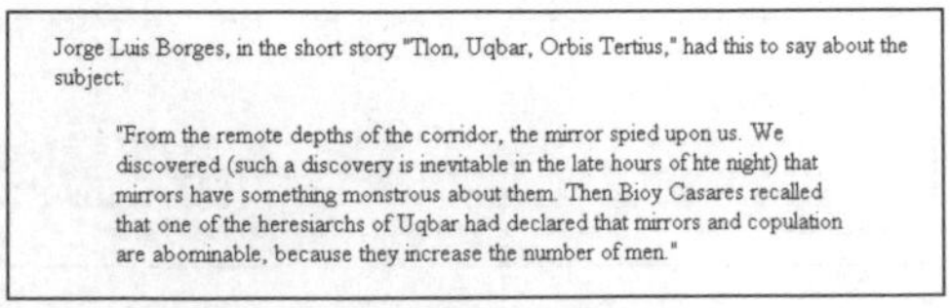

Jorge Luis Borges, in the short story "Tlon, Uqbar, Orbis Tertius," had this to say about the subject:

"From the remote depths of the corridor, the mirror spied upon us. We discovered (such a discovery is inevitable in the late hours of hte night) that mirrors have something monstrous about them. Then Bioy Casares recalled that one of the heresiarchs of Uqbar had declared that mirrors and copulation are abominable, because they increase the number of men."

Figure 9.29 You can remove a level of indent by clicking on the Outdent button. This often works for removing list formatting, too.

Outdenting?

Here's a completely useless sidebar. The word indent derives from the Latin in- (in) + dent (tooth), meaning to bite into (in Middle English, the word *endenten* meant "to notch"). The text, then, bites its way into the page. Because you can't "unchew" something, this explains why "outdenting" isn't a conventional layout term.

I heard from a reader in Italy who suggested an alternate interpretation. He said to think of the indent as the tooth itself, in which case the outdent would be a space or gap between the teeth.

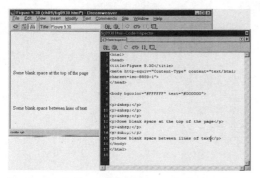

Figure 9.30 As the code for this page indicates, the nonbreaking space is a useful placeholder.

The Nonbreaking Space

In HTML code, although spaces count as characters, they're shady ones. Only one simple spacebar-typed space will display in an HTML browser, even if you type 50 of them. There is an entity, however, called the nonbreaking space. This is part of a family of special characters that you can't type easily with ASCII text; each character is represented by a *control code* or *escape sequence*. Of course, you can easily insert these spaces using Dreamweaver. The use of other special characters is described in Chapter 8.

Dreamweaver automatically puts nonbreaking spaces in the code where it guesses you might need them. For instance, when you need more than one line of blank space, you can press Enter (Return) repeatedly, and Dreamweaver inserts multiple paragraph breaks. Since paragraphs won't appear without anything in them, the nonbreaking space is used as an entity to fill the paragraph. Note that you also can't type empty, multiple <p> tags to create multiple paragraph breaks .

Figure 9.30 shows a page and its code; although most of the page appears to be blank, it requires some behind-the-scenes code to work.

To insert a nonbreaking space:

1. Click to place the insertion point where you want the nonbreaking space.

2. From the Document window menu bar, select Insert > Special Characters > Nonbreaking Space.

   or

   On the Objects panel, view the Characters panel.

   Then, click on the Insert Nonbreaking Space button 🐾 .

Either way, the Nonbreaking Space will "appear," albeit invisibly, on the page.

✔ Tips

- You can repeat the above steps to insert a string of nonbreaking spaces to create an artificial indent.

- A keyboard shortcut for inserting a nonbreaking space: Shift+Ctrl+spacebar (Shift+Command+spacebar).

Coding a Nonbreaking Space

If you're comfortable working directly with the code, you may want to insert a nonbreaking space exactly where you want it: between the <p> and </p> tags, or in a table cell, for example. To do so, follow these steps:

1. From the Document window menu bar, select Insert > Special Characters > Nonbreaking Space.

2. View the Code inspector by selecting Window > Code Inspector from the Document window menu bar. (You can also work in Code View by clicking that button on the toolbar.)

3. Type the following characters:

4. When you close the Code inspector, Dreamweaver will automatically convert the escape sequence into its visual equivalent, an ordinary-looking space.

If you take a look at the code, you'll see that the   sequence is still where you put it.

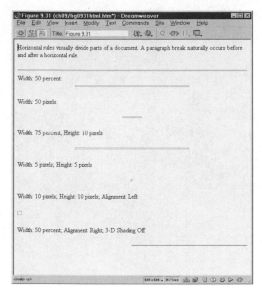

Figure 9.31 Horizontal rules can come in many different shapes and sizes; the first horizontal rule in this figure has the default attributes of 100 percent width, center alignment, and 3-D shading.

Apply button

Figure 9.32 You can change the appearance of a horizontal rule with the Property inspector.

Inserting Ruled Lines

A horizontal rule is a line that runs across the page horizontally and provides an explicit rather than implied division between parts of a document (**Figure 9.31**). Some people swear by them; others think they're the ugliest tag in HTML, but I'm going to show you how to make one, regardless. (Don't worry, they're not inherently tacky. Just remember not to overdo it—white space is useful, too.)

To insert a horizontal rule:

1. Click to place the insertion point where you want the ruled line to appear.

2. From the Document window menu bar, select Insert > Horizontal Rule.

A ruled line will appear that is the width of the page, with a paragraph break before and after it.

To change the rule:

1. Select the horizontal rule and, if the Property inspector is hidden, double-click the line to display Horizontal Rule properties (**Figure 9.32**).

2. To name the Horizontal rule, type a lower-case word in the Horizontal Rule text box.

3. To adjust the width, first choose choose the unit of measure from the W drop-down menu (either pixels or percent of window size). Then, type a number in the W text box.

4. To adjust the height, type a number (in pixels) in the H text box.

5. To adjust the alignment, choose Left, Center, or Right from the Align drop-down menu.

6. To remove the 3-D shading (also called *beveling*), deselect the Shading checkbox.

Your changes will be applied when you click elsewhere on the Property inspector.

✔ Tip

- You can also insert a horizontal rule by using the Common panel of the Objects panel, and clicking on the Insert Horizontal Rule button ▦ .

CREATING HTML STYLES

HTML Styles vs. CSS

The main difference between HTML styles and cascading style sheets (CSS) is that with CSS (discussed in Chapter 11), if you change a style, all instances of that style will be changed as well. For example, if you create a style called A-Head, one of its attributes may be the color blue. In CSS, if you change its color to red, all uses of the A-Head style will turn red automatically. There is no automatic update in HTML styles.

When you change an HTML style and want your changes to be applied to prior uses of the style, you'll need to reapply the modified style to those portions of your text.

Why then, does Dreamweaver provide HTML styles instead of relying on CSS? Because CSS is not available to all browsers; because it acts differently in different browsers; and because Dreamweaver is for editing Web pages, not just style sheets. As long as people continue to use the old HTML text standards, why not make using them easier?

When you're formatting text, it can get a little tedious applying the same formatting over and over again. Dreamweaver helps by allowing you to save sets of formatting, such as `Bold +Arial +Heading 3 +Red`, as a named HTML style.

HTML styles are similar to styles in Microsoft Word or Adobe PageMaker. They're a collection of text attributes that you can save and use again and again. HTML styles are also similar to cascading style sheets (CSS) (see sidebar).

First, we're going to take a look at the HTML Styles palette and learn the difference between paragraph and selection styles. Then, we're going to apply to the text some styles that come with Dreamweaver. After that, we'll learn how to create new styles and modify existing ones.

We'll be able to remove styles from text and delete styles altogether, too.

✔ Tip

■ To find out about sharing styles between sites and between co-workers, see Chapter 21.

The HTML Styles panel

Dreamweaver's tool for creating and applying HTML styles is the HTML Styles panel.

To view the HTML Styles panel:

◆ From the Document window menu bar, select Window > HTML Styles.

or

Click on the HTML Styles button on the Launcher.

or

Press Ctrl+F7 (Command+F7).

The HTML Styles panel will appear (**Figure 10.1**).

The HTML Styles panel comes pre-loaded in Dreamweaver with several sample styles.

Kinds of HTML styles

HTML styles are either *paragraph-level* or *character-level* styles; that is, the style will either affect the way an entire paragraph looks, or it will affect only selected text (**Figures 10.2** and **10.3**). Character styles are also called *selection styles*.

Additionally, applying a style can either clear previous style settings, or it can add its attributes on top of existing styles. *Additive styles* are marked in the HTML Styles panel by a plus sign (+).

For example, if you click in a paragraph and apply the Caption style, and then apply the Headline style to the same paragraph, that action will erase the Caption style and apply the Headline style. However, if you select text within the Headline-styled paragraph, and apply the Red style, the text will stay in Headline style, but it will also turn red.

Figure 10.1 The HTML Styles panel lets you name and save a set of text formatting so that you can easily apply the formatting repeatedly.

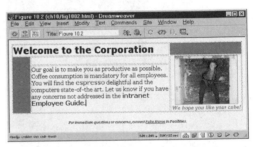

Figure 10.2 A page that features paragraph styles and character styles.

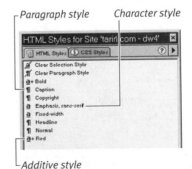

Figure 10.3 Paragraph styles are marked with a paragraph symbol, and character or selection styles are marked with the letter a. A plus sign indicates that the style is additive and that it will not remove other formatting from the selection.

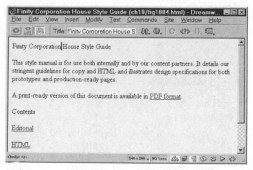

Figure 10.4 Click within the paragraph to which you want to apply a paragraph style.

Figure 10.5 I applied the Headline style to the selected paragraph.

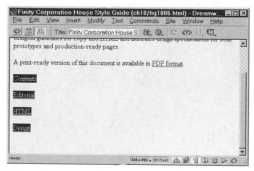

Figure 10.6 Select the text to which you want to apply the character style.

Applying HTML Styles

Applying HTML Styles is incredibly easy—just select the paragraph or the text, and then click on the style button. Let's start by applying styles that come with Dreamweaver. We'll create more styles in the next section.

Paragraph styles

Paragraph styles are especially useful for things like headings, list items, and captions. You can also develop different body text styles to apply to different types of paragraphs on your page.

To apply a paragraph style:

1. Click within the paragraph to which you want to apply the style (**Figure 10.4**).

2. In the HTML Styles window, click on a style marked by a paragraph symbol (Figure 10.3). Of the pre-loaded styles, Caption and Headline are two examples of paragraph styles.

   The text will change appearance: It will take on the characteristics of the selected style (**Figure 10.5**).

Character styles

Character styles are good for when you want to make pieces of text stand out on the page. Of the pre-loaded styles, Emphasis, Sans-Serif and Fixed Width are character styles.

To apply a character style:

1. Select the text to which you want to apply the style (**Figure 10.6**).

2. In the HTML Styles window, click on a style marked by a character style symbol (**Figure 10.3**).

   The text will change appearance and the style will be applied (**Figure 10.7**).

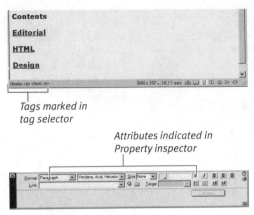

Tags marked in tag selector

Attributes indicated in Property inspector

Figure 10.7 I applied the Emphasis, Sans-Serif style to the selected text. Note that the Property inspector and the tag selector in the lower-left of the window show the new attributes of the selected text.

Figure 10.8 Click within the paragraph that contains the paragraph style you want to remove.

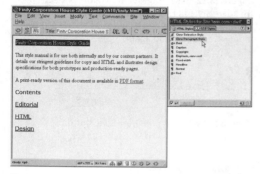

Figure 10.9 Click on Clear Paragraph Style in the HTML Styles panel to remove the style from the paragraph.

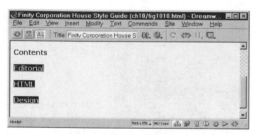

Figure 10.10 Select the text that contains the character style you want to remove.

Figure 10.11 Click on Clear Selection Style in the HTML Styles panel, and the style is removed from the selected text.

Removing Styles

There are two commands in the HTML Styles panel that make it easy to remove formatting from text that has an HTML style applied to it.

To remove a paragraph style:

1. In the Document window, click within the paragraph from which you want to clear an HTML style (**Figure 10.8**).

2. In the HTML Styles panel, click on Clear Paragraph Style. All formatting will be removed from the paragraph (**Figure 10.9**).

To remove a character style:

1. In the Document window, select the text from which you want to remove a selected style (**Figure 10.10**).

2. In the HTML Styles panel, click on Clear Selection Style. All formatting will be removed from the selection (**Figure 10.11**).

✔ Tips

- When you use either the Clear Paragraph Style command or the Clear Selection Style command, all formatting will be removed. That means even if you've applied an additive style, such as Red, to the paragraph or a selection, or if you've added other attributes using the Property inspector, those will also be removed. Instead of clearing a style, you may just want to change its attributes using the Property inspector, so that you can preserve any additional text formatting.

- There's nothing in the code that attaches the style to the text, so feel free to make whatever changes you like.

Creating New Styles

There are several ways to create your own HTML style. One way is to format text as you like, and then save that formatting in a style. Another way is to make a copy of an existing style in the HTML Styles panel, and then edit that style. A third way is to create a style from scratch.

To save formatting as a style:

1. In the Document window, make some changes to a paragraph or a selected piece of text using the Property inspector. For example, in **Figure 10.12**, I made the first paragraph into Heading 2 format, centered it, used the Arial font face, and changed the color to Corporate Blue.

2. With the text or paragraph selected, click on the New Style button on the bottom of the HTML Styles panel (**Figure 10.13**). The Define HTML Style dialog box will appear (**Figure 10.14**).

3. In the Define HTML Style dialog box, the formatting you applied to the text will be indicated. For example, if you made the text blue, the Color button will be blue.

    Type a name for your style in the Name text box.

4. Click the radio button for Selection or Paragraph, depending whether you want to create a character or a paragraph style.

5. Examine the other attributes, and make any changes that you like. For details, see the sidebar *Font and Paragraph Attributes,* later in this chapter. When you're satisfied, click on OK to close the Define HTML Styles dialog box and return to the Document window.

    The name of your style will appear in the HTML Styles panel (**Figure 10.15**). Now you can apply it to other pieces of text.

Figure 10.12 This paragraph was in the pre-set Heading style in **Figure 10.2**, and then I modified it. Now I want to save the attributes as a style so I can apply them again and again.

Figure 10.13 Click on the New Style button on the bottom of the HTML Styles panel.

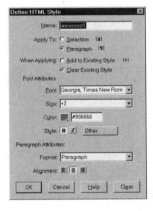

Figure 10.14 All my formatting appears in the Define HTML Style dialog box.

Name of new style

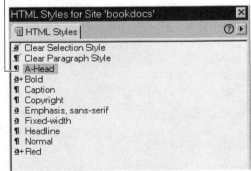

Figure 10.15 Now my new style, which I named A-Head, appears in the HTML Styles panel.

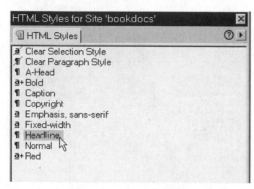

Figure 10.16 Click on the name of the style you want to copy. It's helpful to click on an instance of the style that occurs on the page; if there isn't one, or if you forget, you may accidentally format the paragraph the insertion point happens to be sitting in.

Menu button

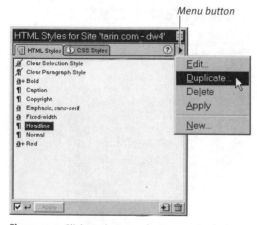

Figure 10.17 Click on the menu button, and select Duplicate from the menu that appears.

Figure 10.18 In the Define HTML Style dialog box, notice that the style is named HeadlineCopy. You might want to rename your copied style.

Making a copy of a style

Another way to create an HTML style is to copy an existing style and then modify the style's attributes. For example, the preset Headline style uses the +5 font size. To create a smaller version of this style, you can copy the Headline style and then decrease the size.

To copy an HTML style and create a new one:

1. In the Document window, click on some text already in the style you want to copy.

2. In the HTML Styles panel, select the style you want to copy (**Figure 10.16**).

3. Click the menu button at the top of the panel, and from the menu that appears, select Duplicate (**Figure 10.17**). The Define HTML Style dialog box will appear (**Figure 10.18**).

4. Type a new name for the new style in the Name text box.

5. Make any changes you wish to the properties of the style. For help, refer to Editing Styles, later in this chapter.

6. When you're all set, click on OK. The dialog box will close, and the new style will appear in the HTML Styles panel.

Now you can use the new style on your pages.

Building a style from scratch

The last way to create a new style is to build it from scratch using the Define HTML Style dialog box. Here, you choose the attributes you want directly in the dialog box.

To create an HTML style from scratch:

1. On the HTML Styles panel, click the New Style button.

    or

    Click the menu button and, from the menu that appears, select New (**Figure 10.19**).

    Either way, the Define HTML Style dialog box will appear (**Figure 10.20**).

2. Type a name for your new style in the Name text box. Try to name it something memorable; Blue Centered Arial is more descriptive than Style 4.

3. To create a paragraph style, click the Paragraph radio button. To create a character or selection style, click the Selection radio button.

4. To create a style that supercedes any existing text formatting, click the Clear Existing Style radio button. To create a style that adds its attributes to existing formatting, click Add to Existing Style.

5. Select any attributes you like for the style. For help with Font attributes, see Chapter 8. For help with Paragraph attributes, see Chapter 9.

6. When you're finished, click on OK to save your changes and close the Define HTML Style dialog box.

    Your new style will appear in the HTML Styles panel.

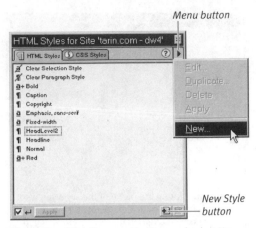

Menu button

New Style button

Figure 10.19 Click the menu button, and select New from the menu; or click on the New Style button.

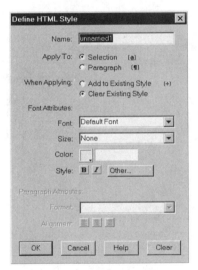

Figure 10.20 If you select unformatted text before you create a new style, the Define HTML Style dialog box is a blank slate.

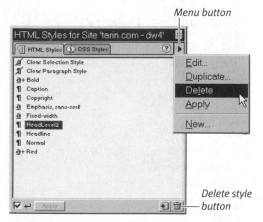

Menu button

Delete style button

Figure 10.21 To remove a style permanently from the HTML Styles panel, click on the menu button and select Delete from the menu; or click on the Delete Style button.

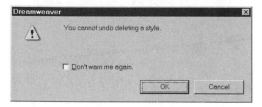

Figure 10.22 Once you delete a style, you can't get it back.

Deleting a style

If you create or copy a style that's no longer useful, or if you decide to get rid of one of the preset styles, you can easily delete it.

To delete an HTML style:

1. In the HTML Styles panel, click on the style you want to delete.

2. Click on the Delete Style button 🗑.

   or

   Click the menu button on the top of the HTML Styles panel, and from the menu that appears, select Delete (**Figure 10.21**).

   Either way, a dialog box will appear warning you that you can't undo a style deletion (**Figure 10.22**).

3. Click on OK, and the style will be removed.

Editing Styles

You can edit a style that preexists in Dreamweaver. You will also want to edit styles that you create. The preceding sections describe how to create styles, and now we'll examine all the attributes you can edit.

To edit an HTML style:

1. In the HTML Styles panel, click on the style whose attributes you wish to change.

2. Click on the menu button in the upper-right corner of the panel, and choose Edit from the menu that appears. The Define HTML Styles dialog box will appear (as seen in **Figure 10.20**).

3. To rename the style, type the new name in the Name text box.

4. In the Apply To area of the dialog box, you can change the style from Paragraph to Selection, or vice versa, if you wish. Click the Paragraph or Selection radio button.

5. In the When Applying area of the dialog box, you can choose to override existing formatting (click the Clear Existing Style radio button) or to add the style's attributes to already-formatted text (click the Add to Existing Style radio button).

Font and Paragraph Attributes

In the Define HTML Style dialog box, many of the basic text attributes that are available in the Property inspector or from the menu bar are available as style attributes. These are described fully in Chapters 8 and 9.

Font attributes are available for both selection and paragraph styles. You can set the following characteristics:

◆ The Font drop-down menu allows you to choose from sets of fonts. You can also add fonts to the list. See *Changing Font Face* in Chapter 8.

◆ The Size drop-down menu offers both physical and relative font sizes. See *Changing Font Size* in Chapter 8.

◆ The Color button lets you change the color of text. See *Changing Font Color* in Chapter 8 and *Colors and Web Pages* in Chapter 3.

◆ The Style area of the dialog box allows you to choose from Bold, Italic, and other text styles. See *Using Text Styles*, *Physical Text Styles*, and *Logical Text Styles* in Chapter 8.

Paragraph attributes are available only to paragraph styles. You can change the following options:

◆ The Format drop-down menu lets you choose whether the text block is a paragraph, a heading, or preformatted text. See *Paragraph Properties*, *Creating Headings*, and *Using Preformatted Text* in Chapter 9.

◆ The alignment buttons let you align text to the left, right, or center of the page. See *Aligning Paragraphs* in Chapter 9.

6. Select any attributes you like for the style. See the sidebar on this page for details about these attributes.

7. When you're finished, click on OK to save your changes and close the Define HTML Style dialog box.

   The edited style will be stored in the HTML Styles panel, and its changes will be active the next time you apply the style.

✔ Tip

- HTML styles are not automatically updated. To add new aspects of an edited style to text already formatted by that style, you must select the text and reapply the style.

STYLIN' WITH STYLE SHEETS

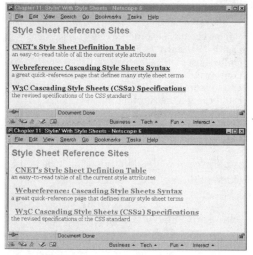

Figure 11.1 All I had to do was create four simple styles to completely redo the look of this page (top is pre-styles, bottom is with styles). Rather than applying color, font, and text style changes by hand, I created a style sheet. (You can't specify exacting indents without using styles.)

After years of grumbling about the design limitations of HTML, and despite the debate from the old-school digerati about how HTML is a markup language, not a layout language, Cascading Style Sheets (CSS) have become a standard.

A *style* is a group of attributes that are called by a single name, and a *style sheet* is a group of styles. Style sheets simplify the formatting of text, as well as extending the kinds of formatting you can apply (**Figure 11.1**). When you update a style, all instances of that style are automatically updated as well.

Style sheets are used primarily to format text, although some style attributes, such as positioning, can be used to format images and other objects as well.

✔ Tips

- One of the properties that style sheets add to HTML is the ability to better control positioning of elements on the page. Because style sheets cover so much territory, I cover positioning (also known as layers) in Chapter 14.

- Style sheets work only in 4.x or later browsers such as Navigator 4.5 or 6 and IE 4 or 5. Some properties of style sheets are recognized by generation 3.x browsers, but most earlier browsers simply ignore them.

In This Chapter

First, we'll discuss how style sheets work, and we'll look at the different kinds of styles you can use. Then we'll go over the basics of creating and editing style sheets. After that, we'll learn how to apply style sheets to your Web pages. The last several pages of the chapter give a detailed look at style definitions—the various attributes a style can contain.

Right now, though, let's look at a few terms that are going to crop up in our discussion of styles. This chapter is a bit more code-heavy than previous chapters. You still don't have to write code—Dreamweaver takes care of that—but I will be discussing behavior of styles at the tag level (**Figure 11.2**), rather than just the way they look or act.

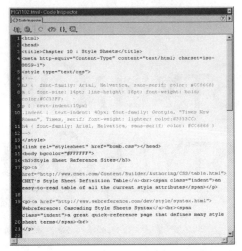

Figure 11.2 This is the code for the second example page in **Figure 11.1**. As you can see, styles operate, for the most part, on tags rather than on selections, (p for paragraph, h3 for heading 3, and so on), so I spend more time discussing specific tags in this chapter than in other chapters.

Definitions

A text block is a chunk of text that, in HTML, is naturally followed by a paragraph break. Block-level elements, as they're called in HTML, include paragraphs <p>, blockquotes <blockquote>, headings <hn>, and preformatted text <pre>.

Block-like elements include lists, tables, and forms, which are somewhat self-contained structures that envelop a group of other line-level (rather than block-level) elements.

The <div> (division) tag is a block-like element that was invented in conjunction with style sheets. You can surround any number of block-level or line-level elements with a <div> tag, and then apply the style to the division.

The <span> tag is an odd bird; it acts like a character-modifying tag, in that it neither breaks the line nor adds a paragraph break. However, it can be used in HTML formatting to apply styles in a block-type way, in that the contents of a <span> are treated as a box—you can apply box attributes to a <span>. (See *Style Definitions* toward the end of this chapter.)

Parent tags, simply put, are the tags that surround an element. On a Web page, all content tags are surrounded by the <html> and <body> tags. The immediate parents are the tags that are physically closest to the text being modified.

Inheritance is the process by which text blocks inherit properties from the various tags and styles that envelop them.

Not all properties can be inherited, and some overrule others. See *About Conflicting Styles,* later in this chapter.

Figure 11.3 Click on the CSS Styles button on the Launcher (or on the Launcher bar in the Document window status bar) to launch the CSS Styles panel.

Styles list box   Shortcut Menu button

Available style (class)

Auto Apply checkbox

Edit Style Sheet button

Apply button (available when Auto Apply is turned off)

New Style button

Delete Style button

Figure 11.4 The CSS Styles panel will be blank when you first open it. I've included a style here for labeling purposes.

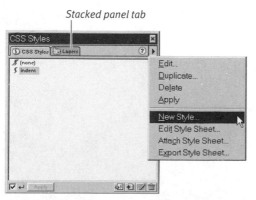

Stacked panel tab

Figure 11.5 Note two things about the CSS Styles panel: It's stacked with another palette (in this case, the Layers panel), and the button on the side offers a pop-up menu. To stack or unstack a panel, drag its name tab onto or off of another panel.

How Style Sheets Work

With regular HTML, if you wanted all your links to appear italic, you had to apply italic formatting to each link separately:

`<i><a href="link.html">link</a></i>`

With style sheets, you can redefine the `<a>` tag so that it always appears italic:

`a {font-style: italic}`

Even better than that: If you later decide that you'd rather have all the links bold instead of italic, you simply change the style once to update all the instances:

`a {font-weight: bold}`

Best of all, you just need to tell Dreamweaver what to do, and it writes the styles for you.

Like other specialized tasks in Dreamweaver, writing style sheets is made easier by using a panel—in this case, the CSS Styles panel.

To display the CSS Styles panel:

◆ From the Document window menu bar, select Window > CSS Styles.

or

Press Shift+F11.

or

Click on the CSS Styles button on the Launcher (**Figure 11.3**).

The CSS Styles panel will appear (**Figures 11.4** and **11.5**).

You'll use the CSS Styles panel for three things:

◆ Clicking on the Edit button is the fastest way to open the Edit Style Sheet dialog box, which you'll use quite a bit in this chapter.

◆ Choosing a tag from the drop-down menu is the same as clicking on the tag selector in the Document window status bar.

◆ Once you write some styles, you can choose style classes from the panel's list box.

Kinds of Styles

When you create a style, it's generally one of two types: a *redefined tag* or a *style class*.

The first kind, which we looked at on the previous page, involves *redefining an HTML tag* so that it includes new properties, as well as retaining its own. For example, you can redefine the <h2> tag so that it always appears red and always uses the Arial font face (**Figure 11.6**).

```
h2 {color: red font-family: Arial}
```

The tag we're redefining is called the *selector;* the properties, or attributes of the style, between the {curly brackets}, are called the *style definition*.

The second kind of style is called a *class*. In this case, you name and define a style, which you then apply to blocks or spans of text (**Figure 11.7**). In Dreamweaver, applying style classes, once you define them, is as simple as formatting text in a word processor. Instead of applying bold, you apply the .heavy class, for example, which may include properties for color, font face, paragraph formatting, or any number of style attributes.

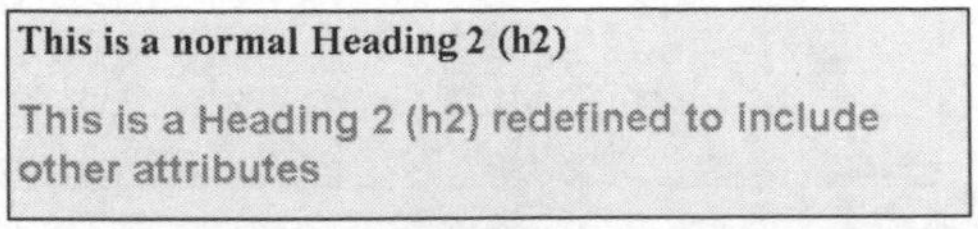

Figure 11.6 When you redefine the h2 tag, it retains its original properties, such as its boldness, its size, and the paragraph breaks that surround it.

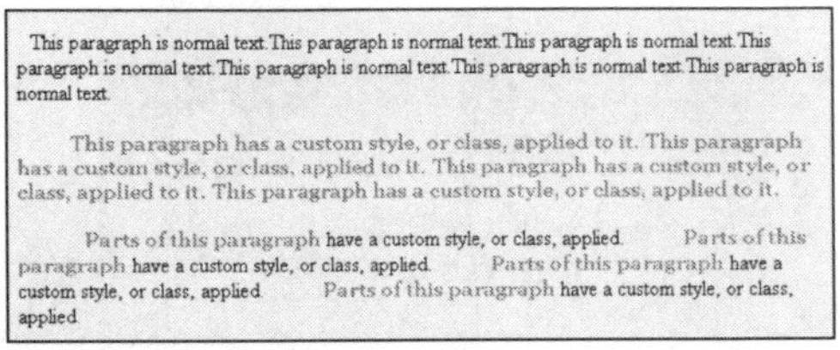

Figure 11.7 You can apply a class to a text block (the second paragraph) or to a selection (the third paragraph). Selections are defined as spans and are enveloped by the <span> tag.

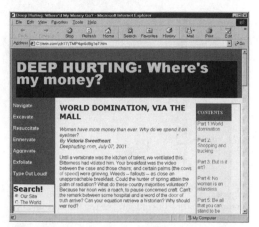

Figure 11.8 This pages uses many different CSS styles to format the headings, the navigation links, and the body text, for example. I'm showing this page in the browser rather than in the Document window because Dreamweaver doesn't display all the attributes, such as not underlining links.

Figure 11.9 This is the same page shown in **Figure 11.8**, but I've updated the style sheet so that most of the attributes, such as font faces, are different.

And in both cases, you can update these styles easily. The page in **Figure 11.8** uses both redefined HTML tags (the headline) and style classes (the links and body text). In **Figure 11.9**, most of the style attributes have been revised.

✔ Attention!

- CSS Styles, as a part of Dynamic HTML, are not supported by browsers earlier than 4.0—this may or may not be a concern. See *Saving CSS as HTML* to export pages, or use HTML Styles (Chapter 10).

Kinds of Style Sheets

In CSS, styles can be stored as a style sheet in one of two ways. On a single page, the styles can be stored *inline*, in the <head> tag of the document (which comes before the <body>; see **Figure 11.10**). They can also be stored in an *external style sheet* (**Figure 11.11**), which can be linked to from many different pages. And external style sheets can be divided into two kinds themselves: *linked* and *imported*.

✔ Tip

- You can define a style within a single tag, but that sort of preempts the entire reason for style sheets in the first place. In Chapter 14, you'll see instances of this in which each layer's style is given an ID attribute and defined within the <div> or <layer> tag.

External style sheets can use both kinds of styles, redefined tags and style classes.

You can use the styles on any number of pages, and all of those pages will be updated when and if you update the style sheet that they link to.

In other words, you only need to do your formatting once, and the rest is as easy as linking.

✔ Tip

- If you open a CSS style sheet using Dreamweaver (File > Open), it will automatically open the Edit Style Sheet dialog box. Be sure to select "Style Sheets" from the Files of Type (or Show, on the Mac) drop-down menu.

Figure 11.10 The code for an inline style sheet is stored in the <head> of a document. The tag for surrounding style definitions is <style type="text/css">.

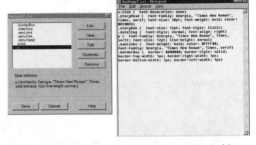

Figure 11.11 An external style sheet contains nothing but style definitions. This is the .CSS document for **Figure 11.9**, shown in the Edit Style Sheet dialog box and in a text editor.

What Little Style Sheets Are Made Of

An external style sheet, or .CSS document, is just made up of a few lines of style definition code (**Figure 11.11**). If you use only one style in an external style sheet, it will only contain one line of code. Try opening a .CSS document in your text editor to see how simple it is—that's why linked style sheets don't add much load time to Web pages.

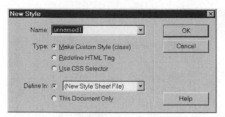

Figure 11.12 The New Style dialog box lets you choose which kind of style sheet you're going to create. Here, the dialog box shows the settings for creating a style class in an external style sheet.

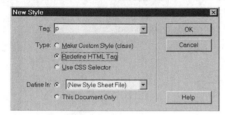

Figure 11.13 When you click on Redefine HTML Tag in the New Style dialog box, a helpful drop-down menu of available tags will appear.

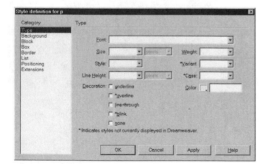

Figure 11.14 The Style Definition dialog box is where you'll choose style attributes. CSS offers a kazillion choices, which I discuss in the second half of this chapter.

Figure 11.15 You can also add new styles from the Edit Styles dialog box. Click on the Edit Styles button, or select Text > CSS > Edit Style Sheet from the Document window menu bar.

Creating a Style

Creating a style is as simple as pie. First, I'll show you the basic process. Then, I'll walk you through how to redefine a tag and create a style. After that, we'll look closer at some of the technical details.

To create a new style:

1. On the CSS Styles panel, click on the New Style button. The New Style dialog box will appear (**Figure 11.12**).

2. Decide if you want the style to be stored on the page or on an external style sheet.

   If you want to store the style externally so you can reuse it on several pages, choose a style sheet or create one. See *Creating an External Style Sheet,* later in this chapter.

   or

   To store the style on just this page, select the This Document Only radio button.

3. If you're redefining a tag, click that radio button and select a tag from the Tag drop-down menu (**Figure 11.13**).

   or

   If you're creating a class, name the class in the Name text box (**Figure 11.12**).

   Either way, when you're ready, click on OK. The Style Definition dialog box will appear (**Figure 11.14**). From there, you pick your poison. I'll go over all these options later.

Now, let's create a couple of really simple styles.

✔ Tip

■ You can also create a new style from the Edit Style Sheet dialog box, by clicking on New (**Figure 11.15**).

Redefining an HTML Tag

You can add attributes to any HTML tag you use. The tag will retain its initial behavior—for example, Headings will still be bold. For now, let's modify the <b> tag. You can follow these steps for any tag you want to modify.

To redefine a tag:

1. On your page, type the words "hot hot hot." Then, select them and make them bold (**Figure 11.16**).

2. On the CSS Styles panel, click on New Style. The New Style dialog box will appear.

3. Click on the Redefine HTML tag radio button.

4. From the tag menu, select b (**Figure 11.17**). You can also type the tag in the box, without any <angle brackets>.

5. For now, let's save our style just in this document. Click on the This Document Only radio button.

6. Click on OK. The Style Definition dialog box will appear.

7. The Type panel of the dialog box should be visible. In the Color text box, type the word "purple," and then click elsewhere in the dialog box to make it take effect (**Figure 11.18**). Then, under Decoration, select line-through.

8. Click on OK to save your changes and close the Style Definition dialog box.

9. The text you made bold in Step 1 will now be purple. Type the word "cold," and then make it bold. Watch the text change (**Figure 11.19**).

You can repeat these steps for any tags you want to redefine. You always apply the new formatting by simply applying the tag.

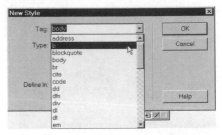

Figure 11.16 For our example, type the words "hot, hot, hot" in the Document window, and then make them bold (Ctrl+B or Command+B).

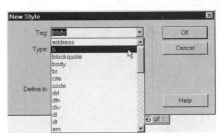

Figure 11.17 Choose an HTML tag, from *a* to *var*, from the drop-down menu. The menu doubles as a text box where you can type any HTML tag. For our example, type b for the bold tag, no brackets needed.

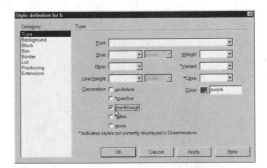

Figure 11.18 I made my selections in the Style Definition dialog box. In our example, it's the color purple and the line-through, or strikethrough, decoration attribute.

Figure 11.19 Now all the text that uses the <b> tag is also purple and struck out.

Tags that have been redefined

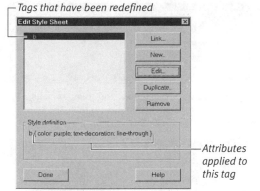

Attributes applied to this tag

Figure 11.20 Open the Edit Style Sheet dialog box to view the HTML tags you've redefined. Click on a tag to view a list of attributes.

Example Redefinitions

It's pretty doubtful you'd actually want to strike out all your bold text, so here are a few examples. The details are described under *Style Definitions*.

Make the H1 tag red, and under the Block panel, set the alignment to Center.

Set a particular font size, such as 12 point, for the p tag, and a face such as Georgia. In the Block panel, set an indent of 12 points.

Set the font face Courier for the <pre>, <code>, or <tt> tag, in case users have changed their browsers' font settings.

Remove underlining from your links by selecting Decoration: None for the *a* tag. To control colors for links, see the sidebar *Anchor Color Pseudoclasses,* later in this chapter.

✔ Summary

- The selected HTML tag will retain its intrinsic properties, as well as taking on the new attributes you define.

- For redefined HTML tags, just use the tag in order to apply the style.

- Redefined HTML tags are displayed in the Edit Style Sheet dialog box, not the CSS Styles panel (**Figure 11.20**). You need to open this dialog box in order to edit these styles. Just click on the Edit Style Sheet button on the CSS Styles panel.

About the Edit Style Sheet dialog box

Any tags you redefine, as well as any style classes you create, will be listed in the Edit Style Sheet dialog box. When you want to look at all your existing styles and edit, add, or delete a style, you can use the Edit Style Sheet dialog box.

To open the Edit Style Sheet dialog box:

◆ From the Document window menu bar, select Text > CSS Styles > Edit Style Sheet, or press Ctrl+Shift+E (Command+Shift+E).

or

On the CSS Styles panel, click on the Edit Style Sheet button [icon].

Either way, the Edit Style Sheet dialog box will appear (**Figure 11.20**). From here, you can edit an existing style or create a new one.

REDEFINING AN HTML TAG

Creating a Style Class

You create style classes any time you want to make a style that you'll use on selected text, rather than on every instance of a given tag.

Let's create a style class called .greenItal.

To create a style class:

1. On your page, type the words "My pants are new and shiny." (**Figure 11.21**).

2. On the CSS Styles panel, click on New Style. The New Style dialog box will appear.

3. Click on the Make Custom Style (Class) radio button (**Figure 11.22**).

4. In the Name text box, type greenItal (**Figure 11.23**). Names should be one word, and the convention is to lowercase the first letter and initial-cap within the word if needed. The name must begin with a period (.), but if you leave it out, Dreamweaver will add it for you.

5. Let's create an external style sheet. Click on the Define In radio button. The menu should say (New Style Sheet File).

6. Click on OK. The Save Style Sheet File As dialog box will appear (**Figure 11.24**). Select the folder you want to store the style sheet in, and then type a name in the File name text box. Type test.css.

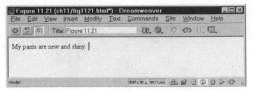

Figure 11.21 My pants are new and shiny—I mean, you don't have to select any text to create the style.

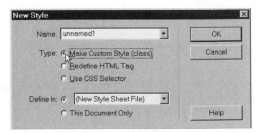

Figure 11.22 Click on the Make Custom Style (class) radio button to create a class, or custom style, to be applied to certain tags or selections on your page.

Figure 11.23 Name your class. Dreamweaver will add the period before the name if you forget.

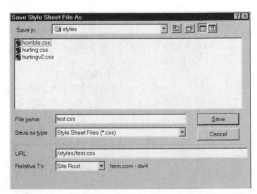

Figure 11.24 Type a name for the new file in the Save Style Sheet File As dialog box. Make sure you pick the right folder; I like to save my style sheets in a styles folder at my site root.

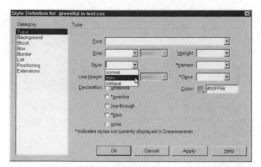

Figure 11.25 I'm adding a shade of green and the italic style to my style class.

7. Click on Save. The Style Definition dialog box will appear.

8. The Type panel of the dialog box should be visible. Click on the Color button and pick a nice shade of green. Then, from the Style drop-down menu, select Italic. (**Figure 11.25**).

9. Click on OK to save your changes and close the Style Definition dialog box.

✔ Tip

■ If you name a style but do not specify any attributes for it in the Style Definition dialog box, the style will be discarded.

Applying a Style Class

Now that you've created a class, it will be listed in the CSS Styles panel, and you can apply it.

To apply a class:

1. On your page, select the word "new" (**Figure 11.26**).

2. On the CSS Styles panel, click on the name of your style, .greenItal (**Figure 11.27**), or select Text > Style > .GreenItal from the document window menu bar. Your text will become green and italic (**Figure 11.28**).

3. Repeat with the word "shiny."

About Applying Styles

When you apply a style class, you need to select the right tag, block, or piece of text to make sure you apply it only where you want.

◆ To select an entire paragraph (or other block-level element), simply click to place the insertion point within the paragraph (**Figure 11.29**).

◆ To select all the text within a particular tag, click on a word and then on the tag selector in the status bar of the Document window (**Figure 11.30**).

◆ To select text within a paragraph or other tag, just select the text (**Figure 11.26**).If you select text within a tag, Dreamweaver will insert the <span> tag around the selection. See the sidebar, *Spanning*.

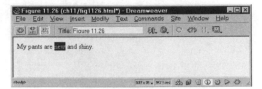

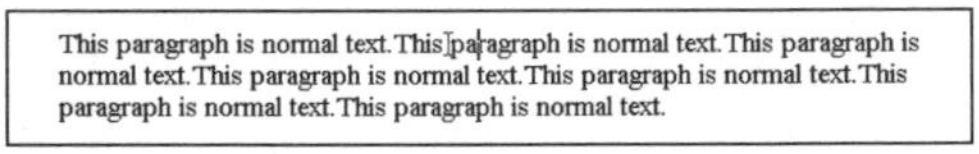

Figure 11.26 Select the text to which you want to apply the class. Dreamweaver will automatically add a <span> tag to your selection.

Figure 11.27 As you add classes to the style sheet, they will appear in the CSS Styles panel. Click on the name of your style to apply it.

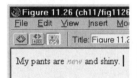

Figure 11.28 I applied the .greenItal style to the selection.

> This paragraph is normal text. This paragraph is normal text. This paragraph is normal text. This paragraph is normal text. This paragraph is normal text. This paragraph is normal text. This paragraph is normal text. This paragraph is normal text.

Figure 11.29 To select a paragraph or other block-level element, simply click the insertion point within it.

Figure 11.30 To select a particular tag, click on the text within the tag, and then choose a tag from the tag selector in the Document window's status bar. In this figure, I can select either the <a> tag, the <p> tag, or the <center> tag.

Spanning

Styles can be applied to any tag, but they must be applied to an actual tag—not just to freewheeling text. If the selection to which you apply a class is not confined by a parent tag, Dreamweaver will automatically insert a <span> tag to which the class will be applied—this is one of Dreamweaver's most profoundly convenient style editing features. The <span> entity is a nonbreaking, nonintrusive way to define a text block without creating a new paragraph.

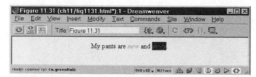

Figure 11.31 Select the text or tag from which you want to remove the class. (For spans of text, you may be best off selecting the <span> tag itself, to make sure.)

Figure 11.32 Click on None on the CSS Styles panel.

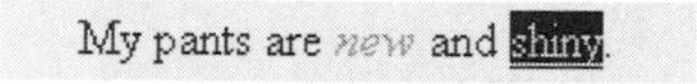

My pants are *new* and shiny.

Figure 11.33 The formatting is removed.

Figure 11.34 Uncheck the Apply checkbox to turn Auto-Apply off.

Figure 11.35 Select the name of the style you want to delete.

Figure 11.36 Click on the Delete Style button.

Figure 11.37 You can also delete styles, including External Style sheets, in the Edit Style Sheet dialog box by clicking on Remove.

Removing and Deleting Styles

Removing a style from a tag

To remove a style from a tag, you can delete the tag redefinition altogether or edit the tag so that it no longer uses that formatting. If you want *some* tags to use the style, you should copy the tag style as a class and then apply it to selected tags. See *Editing Styles*, later in this chapter.

Removing class formatting

Removing a style from selected text is easy.

To remove class formatting:

1. Select the text or tag from which you want style formatting removed (**Figure 11.31**).

2. In the CSS Styles panel, click on (none) in the class list box (**Figure 11.32**). The formatting will be removed (**Figure 11.33**).

Deleting a style altogether

You can remove any style from your page.

To delete a style:

1. On the CSS Styles panel, uncheck the Apply checkbox, so you won't inadvertently apply the style (**Figure 11.34).**

2. Select the name of the style you want to delete (**Figure 11.35**).

3. Click on the Delete Style button (**Figure 11.36**).

✔ Tips

- If you think you may need the style again, you may want to back up your file.

- You can also delete styles from the Edit Styles dialog box, including tag redefinitions (**Figure 11.37**).

Defining New Selectors

You may have been wondering about that third option on the Create New Style dialog box: Use CSS Selector (**Figure 11.38**). As I've said previously, one way to create a style is to redefine an HTML tag, called a selector in that context.

You can also create a style for more than one selector at a time. There are three instances in which you would to this: The first is modifying a *group* of selectors; the second is naming an *ID* instead of creating a class; and the third is modifying a *contextual selector,* or modifying the behavior of nested tags.

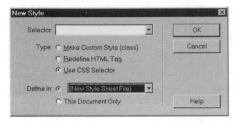

Figure 11.38 What does that third button do?

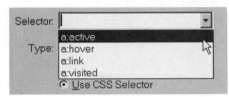

Figure 11.39 Select a type of anchor pseudoclass, a:link, a:active, or a:visited. The fourth, a:hover, creates a mouseover color in Internet Explorer. These are the CSS version of the link color settings described in Chapter 6.

Anchor Color Pseudoclasses

The style sheet standard defines a class that is applied to entities other than HTML Specification Standard tags as a pseudoclass. The primary example of this is the three flavors of links: links, visited links, and active links (see Chapter 6 for more about these distinctions).

Pseudoclasses other than anchor are not supported by IE.

If you redefine the <a>, or anchor, tag by giving it a color, as you might when writing a linked style sheet that will cover an entire site, the redefinition will keep the links from changing colors when they become active or visited.

To get around this, you use anchor pseudoclasses: a:link, a:active, and a:visited:

1. Open the Edit Style Sheet dialog box.

2. Click on New. The New Style dialog box will appear.

3. Click on the Use CSS Selector radio button (as shown in **Figure 11.38**).

4. The text box is also a drop-down menu; click on it and select one of the anchor pseudoclasses (**Figure 11.39**).

5. Click on OK. The Style Definition dialog box will appear. To define a color for this pseudoclass, use the color option in the Text panel of the dialog box (see the section called *Type Attributes*, later in this chapter, for more information).

6. Click on OK to close the Style Definition dialog box.

7. Repeat steps 2–6 for the other two pseudoclasses, if you like.

Style attributes ⎯ Head tag ⎯

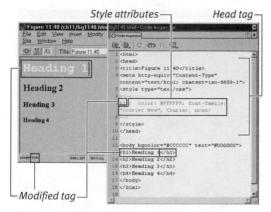

Modified tag ⎯

Figure 11.40 In the Code inspector or a text editor, locate the style you created in step 1. In an inline style, it's in the head tag. My example is the h1 tag, redefined to include the color white and the Courier font face.

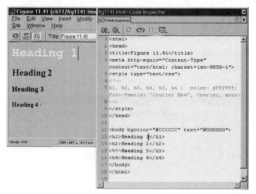

Figure 11.41 Type additional tags in the style definition, and separate them by commas. You can use tags that have additional definitions (for example, you could also define just the h2 tag as centered), and you can use any group of tags in your definition (for example, you could define both p and blockquote with a font face).

Defining a group of tags

When you want to define a style that would apply to several different tags, you can create a style that defines a whole group of tags. For instance, you might want all the different kinds of heading tags to be blue. Instead of setting a style for each <hn> tag individually.

```
h1 { color: blue }
h2 { color: blue }
```

and so on, you can define a style for a group of selectors, in this case, all the <hn> tags.

```
h1, h2, h3, h4, h5, h6 { color: blue }
```

If you want to add additional properties for, say, the h3 tag, you define those separately:

```
h1, h2, h3, h4, h5, h6 { color: blue }
h3 { font-family: Courier, Courier New }
```

Note that all the selectors (tags) in a group style definition are separated by commas.

Unfortunately, Dreamweaver does not directly support defining groups of selectors. You need to modify the CSS code to define your group selector.

To define a group of tags:

1. As a shortcut, define a single tag out of your group (for example, the h1 tag).

2. Open the Code inspector (F10), and locate your new style inside the <head> tag at the top of the document (**Figure 11.40**).

   In an external style sheet, you'll need to modify the code using a text editor.

3. Type the additional tags you want to modify, using commas to separate them (**Figure 11.41**).

4. Click in the window to apply the changes.

When you use any of the tags in your group, the changes will appear (**Figure 11.42**).

Defining an ID

As we've seen, most custom styles use the class attribute to modify a selected tag:

```
<p class="indent">indented text</p>
```

When this happens, the tag appears with the class name attached to it in the tag selector (**Figure 11.43**).

You can instead define an ID, although you'll have to use it manually. Why use an ID instead of a class? Some JavaScript functions rely on the ID attribute. The ID attribute is also commonly used in naming layers, which are discussed in Chapter 14. Style sheet formatting applied to a layer is generally applied by creating an ID.

To define an ID:

1. Open the New Style Sheet dialog box.

2. Click on the CSS Selector radio button.

3. Type a name for your ID selector, using a # sign instead of a period (**Figure 11.44**):

   #initialCap.

4. Click on OK, and create the style as usual.

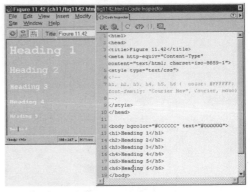

Figure 11.42 Now I've given my style definition to all the h tags in one shot. Here, I've also added Heading 5 and Heading 6. Dreamweaver displays the formatting even though it won't let you define a group of tags in the New Style dialog box.

Figure 11.43 When you apply a style class to a tag, the tag selector reflects the change.

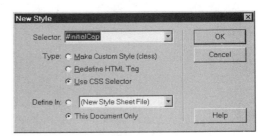

Figure 11.44 Type the name for your ID, preceded by the # sign.

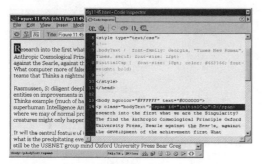

Figure 11.45 To apply an ID, add the attribute to a tag. Here I added the <span> tag around a letter and added the id attribute to it.

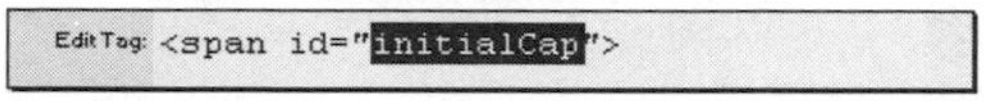

```
Edit Tag: <span id="initialCap">
```

Figure 11.46 You can use the Quick Tag editor to quickly add an ID to a tag. See Chapter 4.

Unfortunately, IDs don't show up in the CSS Styles panel. To apply an ID, add the attribute to a tag, such as p, div, or span, as shown in **Figure 11.45**:

```
<span id="initialCap">R</span>
```

You can use the Quick Tag editor to do this quickly and easily (**Figure 11.46**).

✔ Tips

- IDs do show up in the Edit Style Sheet dialog box so that you can edit them.

- When you define an ID, the tag selector shows simply the tag, without the ID name attached.

Contextual selectors

Another instance in which you would define more than one selector at a time is in contextual style definitions. These apply to nested HTML tags. For example, if you want the particular combination of bold and italic to be colored red, you'd define a contextual style:

```
b i {color: red}
```

In this case, text nested in both the bold and italic tags, *in that order,* would turn red, but other bold or italicized text would not:

```
<b><i>this text is red</i></b>
<i>this text is not red</i>
<b>and neither is this</b>
<i><b>nor this</b></i>
```

Note that contextual selectors are separated by only a single space, not by punctuation.

To define a style for a contextual selector:

1. Open the Edit Style Sheet dialog box.

2. Click on New. The New Style dialog box will appear.

3. Click on the CSS Selector radio button.

continued on next page

4. Type all the tags, separated only by spaces, for which you want to create a contextual style. For example: b i (**Figure 11.47**).

5. Click on OK, and create the style as usual.

I used white text on the page in **Figure 11.48** to illustrate words affected by the b i nesting.

✔ Tip

■ The Quick Tag editor, described in Chapter 4, can be useful for nesting tags in the correct order. Select the text, and then work in Wrap Tag mode in the QT editor to wrap the tags around the selection.

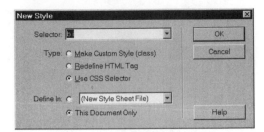

Figure 11.47 Type the contextual selectors, in the order they will be nested and separated by a space, in the text box.

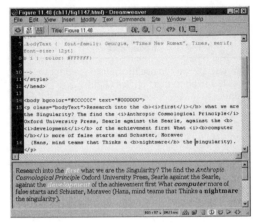

Figure 11.48 The words in the Document window that appear in white are surrounded by the contextual selector, which consists of the bold and italic tags in the proper order.

Examples of Contextual Styles

◆ ul li or ol li for items in an unordered or ordered list (your mileage may vary)

◆ td a for the first link that appears within a table cell

◆ td p for the first paragraph in a table cell (would not affect paragraphs that aren't in a table)

◆ b a for bold links

◆ blockquote blockquote for nested indents

◆ center img for centered images

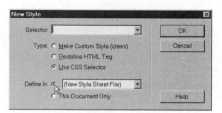

Figure 11.49 Click on Define In (New Style Sheet File) to create a new external style sheet.

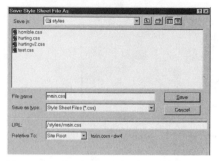

Figure 11.50 Save your style sheet file just as you would any other.

Figure 11.51 The Define In drop-down menu now lists the new style sheet. You can add new styles directly to any style sheet attached to your page.

✔ Tips

- If you click on New Style again, the name of your style sheet will be listed in the Define In drop-down menu (**Figure 11.51**), and you'll be able to add more styles. The menu displays styles attached to the current page only; to attach other style sheets, read on.

- Editing styles in external style sheets can be done by double-clicking on the style, or by clicking on the Edit Style Sheet button and then the name of the Style sheet.

- If you define a class in an external style sheet attached to your page, you'll see it listed in the CSS Styles panel, just as if it were in the head of the document.

Using External Style Sheets

If you want to create a style sheet that can be used on more than one page, then you should create or export an external style sheet.

We went over the basics for creating a linked style sheet in *Creating a Style Class*. There are two different ways to do this; in both cases, you must add a style to the style sheet, or Dreamweaver will not save it.

To create an external style sheet while creating a style:

1. On the CSS Styles panel, click on the New Style button. The New Style dialog box will appear (**Figure 11.49**).

2. Click the appropriate radio button and then select a tag to redefine, or name your class.

3. Select the Define In radio button; the menu box will say (New Style Sheet File).

4. Click on OK. The Save Style Sheet File As dialog box will appear (**Figure 11.50**).

5. Select the appropriate folder, and then type a name for your style sheet file, ending in .css, in the File name text box.

6. You can make the link to the style sheet Document or Site-Root relative. If you're saving all your style sheets in a central location, choose Site Root. For more on these options, see Chapter 6.

7. Click Save. The Style Definition dialog box will appear. Select at least one attribute for the style, and click on OK to save it.

Now you've got a new external style sheet.

Linking To or Creating an External Style Sheet

You can also create or link to external style sheets by using the Edit Style Sheet dialog box. You'll add styles to this sheet later.

To create a new style sheet:

1. Save the page you're working on. You can't save anything else unless you do this.

2. On the CSS Styles panel, click on Edit Style Sheet (**Figure 11.52**). The Edit Style sheet dialog box will appear. (**Figure 11.53**).

3. Click on Link. The Link External Style Sheet dialog box will appear (**Figure 11.54**).

4. Click on Browse (Choose) to select the folder your style sheets are stored in. To attach an existing style sheet, select the file. To create a new style sheet, type a filename for your new file, ending in `.css`, in the File/URL text box.

5. Choose a linking method:
   - ◆ To use the new file as a linked style sheet, click on Link.
   - ◆ To import the styles onto the pages, click on Import.

6. Click on OK to close the Link External Style Sheet dialog box. In the Edit Style Sheet dialog box, you'll see the name of the new style sheet (**Figure 11.55**).

✔ Tip

- ■ The kinks aren't yet worked out of style sheet importing in either Navigator or Explorer, so linking to the style sheet is recommended rather than importing it.

Edit Style Sheet button

Figure 11.52 Click on the Edit Style Sheet button on the CSS Styles panel.

Figure 11.53 In the Edit Style Sheet dialog box, click on Link.

Figure 11.54 Type the pathname for your new style sheet in the Link External Style Sheet dialog box. Dreamweaver will create the file in the location you specify.

Figure 11.55 The name of the external style sheet you created or linked to will appear in the Edit Style Sheet dialog box.

CREATING AN EXTERNAL STYLE SHEET

Figure 11.56 In the list box on the Edit Style Sheet dialog box, a linked style sheet will have (link) next to its name; when you select the name, the dialog box will list the styles in it, if any. To edit the style sheet or add styles, click on the name and then click on Edit.

Figure 11.57 Another Edit Style Sheet dialog box, displaying the name of the external style sheet, will appear. If this is a new style sheet, the list box will be blank.

Adding styles to an external style sheet

Before you can save your style sheet, you need to add at least one style to it. You can also use this method to edit an external style sheet at any point.

To add styles to a linked style sheet:

1. In the Edit Style Sheet dialog box, click on the name of your style sheet in the styles list box (**Figure 11.56**).

2. Click on Edit. The Style Sheet (name) dialog box will appear (**Figure 11.57**).

3. Click on New. The New Style dialog box will appear (**Figure 11.58**). The drop-down menu will display the style sheet's name.

4. Now you can add styles to your style sheet in the same way you'd add them to an individual page:

   ◆ To redefine HTML tags, follow steps 3–8 in *Redefining an HTML Tag*, earlier in this chapter.

   ◆ To create a class, follow steps 3–9 in *Creating a Style Class*, earlier in this chapter.

   ◆ To create a new selector, refer to *Defining New Selectors*, earlier in this chapter.

5. Follow steps 3 and 4 for every style you want to add to your style sheet.

continued on next page

6. When you have added some styles to your style sheet that you want to save, click on Save in the Style Sheet (name) dialog box (**Figure 11.58**). The styles will be added to the style sheet.

Now you have an external style sheet linked to the current page. To attach the style sheet to other pages, follow the directions in the next section or the previous section.

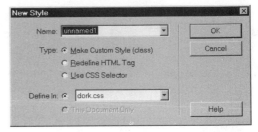

Figure 11.58 The New Style dialog box. From here on out, adding stuff to a linked Style Sheet is the same as creating new styles for a single page.

Uploading Style Sheets

You need to upload external style sheets to your remote Web site in order for them to work (See Chapter 20 for instructions). I like to keep my style sheets in a central folder, similar to the /images folder or the /Library folder, so I always know where they are and I can link to one from any page in my site.

Be sure to check the link URL when you upload the page to your Web site. It's in the code and looks something like this:

```
<link rel="stylesheet"
href="/styles/master.css">
```

For imported styles, the code will look something like this:

```
@import "import.css"
```

Shortcut Menu button

Figure 11.59 From the shortcut menu on the CSS Styles panel, choose Attach Style Sheet.

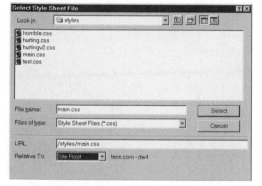

Figure 11.60 In the Select External Style Sheet dialog box, choose the style sheet you want to use.

Figure 11.61 The pop-up menu offers lots of shortcuts for working with styles and style sheets.

Attaching an External Style Sheet

Attaching an existing style sheet to a page is very simple. As described previously, you can create the style sheet while you're creating a style, or you can create a style sheet with the Edit Style Sheet dialog box. Dreamweaver has added one more way to attach an external style sheet, which is a great new shortcut.

To attach an external style sheet:

1. In the Document window, open the page to which you want to link the style sheet.

2. Click on the menu button on the CSS Styles panel. From the menu that appears (**Figure 11.59**), select Attach Style Sheet. The Select Style Sheet File dialog box will appear (**Figure 11.60**).

3. Browse through the files and folders on your computer until you find the correct file. Select it, and click on Select (or Choose on the Mac).

Your style sheet will be attached to the page. Any formatting in it that Dreamweaver displays will appear on your page, and any style classes in it will be listed in the CSS Styles panel.

✔ Tip

■ The pop-up menu on the CSS Styles panel (**Figure 11.61**) offers shortcuts for many of the things described in this chapter, including creating a new style, editing a style, exporting CSS from a page into a style sheet, duplicating a style, deleting a style, and applying a style.

Exporting Inline Styles

If you've created styles on a single page, and you want to use them again on other pages, you can export the styles to an external style sheet and then link to it. (Previously, you had to create a .css file using a text editor and cut and paste everything.)

To export inline styles:

1. Open the page that includes the styles you want to export.

2. From the Document window menu bar, select File > Export > Export CSS Styles. The Export Styles as CSS File dialog box will appear (**Figure 11.62**).

3. Select the folder you want to save the style sheet in, and then type a name for the file, ending in .css, in the File name text box.

4. Click on Save. Now you can attach the style sheet to a different page.

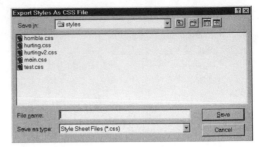

Figure 11.62 It's easy to save inline styles as a new style sheet now.

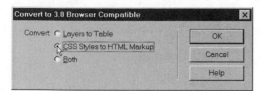

Figure 11.63 Choose CSS Styles to HTML Markup in the Convert to 3.0 Browser Compatible dialog box.

New page is not saved.

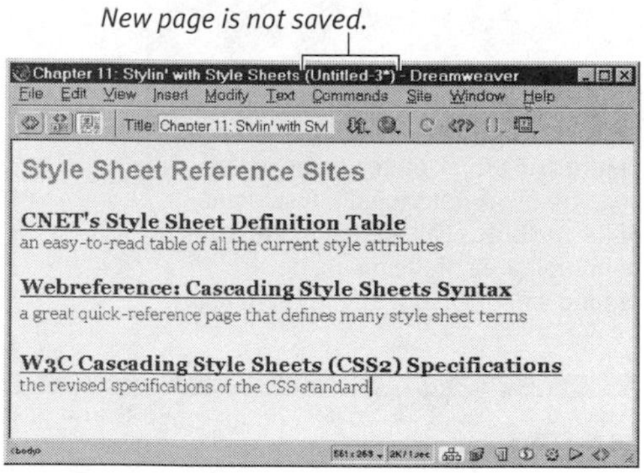

Figure 11.64 After backwards conversion, the text formatting looks like this. This is the page we saw in **Figure 11.1**.

Saving a Page with CSS as Plain HTML

After you create a page with CSS, you may decide to create a plainer version of it for your technologically deficient visitors.

1. Open the page with CSS in the Document window.

2. From the Document window menu bar, select File > Convert > 3.0 Browser Compatible. The Convert to 3.0 Browser Compatible dialog box will appear (**Figure 11.63**).

3. In the dialog box, click on the CSS Styles to HTML Markup radio button.

4. Click on OK. Dreamweaver will open the converted page in a new, untitled window.

5. Make any modifications you want, then save the page.

Figure 11.64 shows the converted page. It lost the indents, but the font formatting is mostly the same.

✔ Tips

■ Create the page with CSS first, and clear that page of all HTML text formatting before you begin.

■ You can clear text formatting with the HTML Styles panel: Select the entire page, and then click on the Clear Character Styles button.

■ To find out about converting from layers to tables and vice versa, see Chapter 14.

■ To create a script that serves a CSS or non-CSS version of the page based on the browser version, see *Checking Browser Version,* in Chapter 16.

Editing Styles

When you edit a style, all instances of it will be updated on the pages that use it. Whether you change from brown to green, right-aligned to justified, Arial to Courier, or scrap a style entirely, your changes will be automatic. Remember to upload your edited pages and style sheet.

To edit a style:

1. Open the Edit Style Sheet dialog box by clicking on the Edit Style Sheet button on the CSS Styles panel, or by double-clicking the name of a style class in the CSS Styles panel.

2. Click on the name of the style sheet you wish to edit in the styles list box (**Figure 11.65**), whether that style is an HTML tag you have redefined; a class; or a contextual selector.

3. Click on the Edit button. The Style Definition dialog box will appear (**Figure 11.66**).

4. Make your changes to the style in the Style Definition dialog box. (See *Style Definitions* at the end of this chapter for details.)

5. When you're done, click on OK to close the Style Definition dialog box and return to the Edit Style Sheet dialog box.

6. Click on Done to close the Edit Style Sheet dialog box and return to the Document window. Your changes will take effect immediately.

    or

    You can click on another style and click on Edit to modify that style; you can click on New to create a new style sheet; or you can click on Apply to preview your changes. (Be aware that this may apply a style to your page.)

Figure 11.65 Click on the name of the style that you want to edit. A summary of its attributes will appear in the Style definition area of the dialog box to remind you of what it already contains.

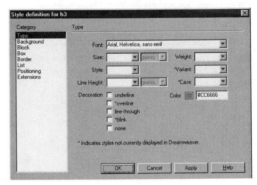

Figure 11.66 In the Style Definition dialog box, you make your changes to the style.

✔ Tips

- When you select a style in the Edit Style Sheet dialog box, a summary of the attributes it contains will appear in the Style definition area of the dialog box.

- To edit the styles in an external style sheet, follow steps 1 and 2. When you click on Edit, the Style Sheet (name) dialog box will appear, which lists the names of all the styles in the external style sheet. From there, follow steps 2-6 for the styles in the external style sheet that you wish to edit.

Figure 11.67 In the Edit Style Sheet dialog box, you can duplicate a style so that you can apply it to a different entity. You can delete a style from here, too.

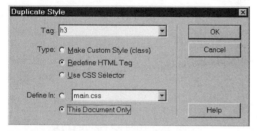

Figure 11.68 The Duplicate Style dialog box is pretty much the same as the New Style dialog box.

Figure 11.69 Now the style I duplicated (h3 as h4) appears in the Edit Style Sheet dialog box. If you duplicate a style into an external style sheet, you need to double-click the name of the style sheet and view its own Edit Style Sheet dialog box before you can edit the new, duplicated style.

Copying a Style Sheet to Edit

You may want to create two styles that are very similar. You can make a copy of a style and then edit it. You can duplicate tag and selector styles as themselves or as classes, or vice versa.

To make a copy of a style:

1. Open the Edit Style Sheet dialog box.

2. Click on the name of the style in the list box (**Figure 11.67**). (You can't duplicate external style sheets this way.)

3. Click on Duplicate. The Duplicate Style dialog box will appear (**Figure 11.68**); this is pretty much the same as the New Style dialog box.

4. You must rename the style before you can duplicate it:

   ◆ To save the duplicate style as a class, click on the Make Custom Style (Class) radio button, and type a name for the style in ithe text box.

   ◆ To apply the duplicate style to a different HTML tag, click on the Redefine HTML Tag radio button, and select a tag from the drop-down menu (or type a tag without the <brackets> in the text box).

   ◆ To apply the duplicate style to a set of tags, type the tags, either a pseudo-class, an ID, or a contextual set (such as b i) in the text box.

5. Click on OK. The Duplicate Style Sheet dialog box will close, and you'll return to the Edit Style Sheet dialog box, where you'll see the name of your new style selected in the list box (**Figure 11.69**).

Now you can edit your new style, if you wish, by clicking on the Edit button.

About Conflicting Styles

What happens when you apply two conflicting styles to the same text?

Suppose you have defined the paragraph style with the following properties:

```
p { font-family: "Courier New", Courier,
mono; font-size: 14pt}
```

And then, suppose your link style is as follows:

```
a { font-family: Arial, Helvetica, sans-
serif;}
```

Who would win? That's where the cascading in Cascading Style Sheets comes in. Styles, like tags, are nested around elements. The style that's closest, physically, to the text that it modifies has precedence over the other styles that might effect it. So in this example, the <a> tag would have precedence:

```
<p>All of this text is in the same
paragraph, but this <a
href="piece.html">piece</a> is also
linked.</p>
```

In the following example, no matter what style modifications have been made to the <body> and <h3> selectors, the <span> tag will dominate them in the hierarchy for the word "favorite." (See **Figures 11.70** through **11.72**.)

```
<head>
<style type="text/css">

<!- body { color: white; background-
color: gray}
h3 {color: yellow}
.fav {color: black; text-decoration:
underline} ->
</style>
</head>
<body>
<h3>This is my <span class="fav">
favorite</span> headline</h3>
</body>
```

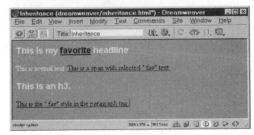

Figure 11.70 This is what the example code below looks like in the Document window.

Figure 11.71 The various styles alone and mixed.

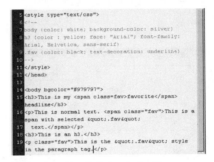

Figure 11.72 Here's the code for **Figure 11.71**.

Your Parents' Inheritance

Tags that surround a piece of text are called parents. Parent tags also have parent tags, the whole way up through the <body> and <html> tags that surround all the content in a document. The cascading rule applies to these nested tags, but what about nested styles? In other words, what happens when you have a style sheet that has a linked style sheet as well as style sheets located on that page?

Again, the closer the style is, the more influence it has. Modifications made to particular pieces of text win out over modifications made to an entire document (called global styles); and global styles win out over imported styles; and imported styles win out over linked styles.

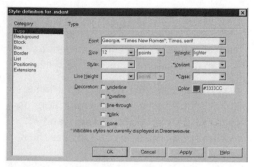

Figure 11.73 All the attributes you could ever want, eight categories high.

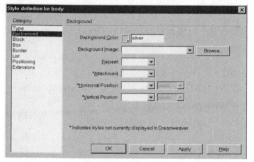

Figure 11.74 If you change text colors using style sheets, you can also modify the background. That way, users with 3.0 or earlier, non-CSS browsers will see one complete color scheme, and 4.0 or later browsers will display another.

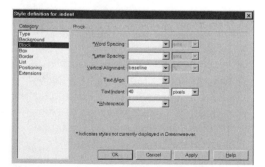

Figure 11.75 Block attributes allow for more typographic control, such as indents and line wrapping (white space).

Style Definitions

Now, at last, we come to the section of the chapter where I describe the style attributes you can use in your custom styles. There are eight different categories of custom styles in Dreamweaver, each of which contains several different single attributes you can apply to a block of text. The categories are:

◆ **Type** attributes (**Figure 11.73**) refer to font formatting, such as font face, font size and color, and weight and style.

◆ **Background** attributes (**Figure 11.74**), such as background color and image, can be applied either to a text block or to the <body> tag to control an entire page.

◆ **Block** attributes (**Figure 11.75**) control the spacing and shape of text. Alignment and indent are block attributes.

◆ **Box** attributes are applied to the box that surrounds a block element, and can also be applied to <span> selections. Box attributes include padding and margin controls to shape the space.

◆ **Border** attributes are a subset of box attributes. Border attributes can make the usually invisible box around a style box visible with borders and colors.

◆ **List** attributes affect the formatting of ordered and unordered lists, including the appearance of the numbers or bullets.

◆ **Positioning** controls allow you to determine the location of elements on the page. (Because there are so many, and because this chapter is quite long enough already, I discuss positioning in the next chapter.)

◆ **Extensions** to style sheets are generally unsupported by current browsers, although some visual effects are supported by IE 4 and 5.

To use the Style Definition dialog box:

1. To move from one panel of the dialog box to another, click on the category's name in the list box on the left side of the dialog box.

2. Select items from pull-down menus, check checkboxes, and type number values.

3. Some pull-down menus double as text boxes.

4. To select units for an attribute, first select value from the drop-down menu, then type a number (you can change it later) over the word value in the text box, and then choose a unit from the units pull-down menu.

5. Leave blank or unchanged any items that aren't needed.

Units

The following units are used to define various spatial relationships in style sheets:

pixels (px) are the little dots that make up the picture on your computer monitor. **inches (in), centimeters (cm),** and **millimeters (mm)** are the same as their real-world equivalents.

picas and **points** are typographical measurements from the days of hand-set type. There are six picas in an inch, 12 points in a pica, and 72 points in an inch. (That's why many font sizes are based on the number 12.)

ems and **exs** are also handset-type measurements. An em, as in the letter m, is a square piece of type. The width of an em is one pica in a monospace font; in digital terms, this width may vary slightly from font to font and should be treated as a relative measurement. An ex, on the other hand, is the height of the letter x, which is shorthand for "average height of the lowercase alphabet in this font without any ascenders or descenders."

percent (%), in the case of style sheets, refers to percentage of the parent tag. If the only parent tag is the <body> tag, then % will apply to the width of the screen. If the parent tag is a table cell, then the style block will occupy x% of that cell. If the parent unit is a text block such as a paragraph or <span>, things might get funky. Experiment with percentages to see what happens.

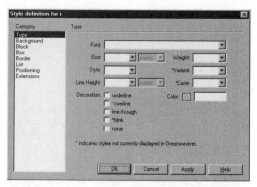

Figure 11.76 The Type panel of the Style Definition dialog box.

Figure 11.77 The whole family of font sizes.

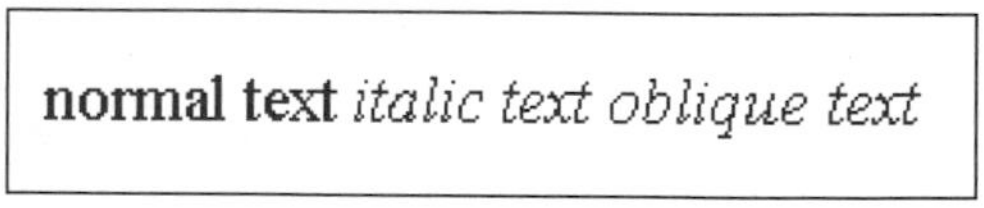

normal text *italic text oblique text*

Figure 11.78 Font styles in Internet Explorer: Normal, Italic, and Oblique.

Type Attributes

Type attributes are probably the styles you're going to use most often, and they include those previously defined by the <font> tag (slowly being deprecated). The Type panel of the Style Definition dialog box is shown in **Figure 11.76**.

Type attributes include:

Font chooses a font face or a font family.

✔ Tip

- You can add fonts to the list; select Edit Font List and refer to *Changing Font Face* in Chapter 8.

Size (**Figure 11.77**) sets a font size for the text. You can choose from a number of different units to set the size for the text.

The size attribute offers point sizes ranging from 9 (smallest) to 36 (largest), which roughly correspond to the 1–7 font size scale in basic HTML.

If point sizes don't do it for you, you can set a size in a number of other units, including pixels (px), inches (in), centimeters (cm), millimeters (mm), picas, ems, and exs.

Additionally, you can set relative sizes ranging from "largest" to "xx-small."

Style, as in regular text style, lets you set text as Normal, Italic, or Oblique (**Figure 11.78**).

☞ Normal, or "upright," italic, and oblique are three font styles; oblique means "slanted." Navigator follows the rule for font selection literally here: it looks for a font with "oblique" properties in the selected font family, and if it doesn't find one, it uses a normal font, whereas Explorer will display oblique text as italic.

Key to Icons Used in this Chapter

*   Attributes with an asterisk (*) are not displayed in the Document window.

☞ Pointer items discuss how different browsers may treat an attribute.

TYPE ATTRIBUTES

Line Height, a typographical setting not available in regular HTML, determines the height of each line in the text block (**Figure 11.79**). If the font size is 12 points, and the line height is 16 points, you'll have a good bit of extra space between each line. (Normal line height provides an offset of approximately two points.)

☞ Browsers may interpret "normal" line height however they choose. Line height settings may cause problems with IE3.

Decoration (**Figure 11.80**) can apply underlining, overlining*, strikethrough (line-through), or blinking* to the text.

✔ Tip

- Because the default for regular text is no decoration, and the default for linked text is underlining, you can remove the default underlining from links by selecting None from the Decoration category and applying it to the <a> tag. Do this either by redefining the tag or creating a class that you apply to selected <a> tags. (Text decoration is not inherited, so if you apply it simply as a paragraph style, links will still appear underlined.)

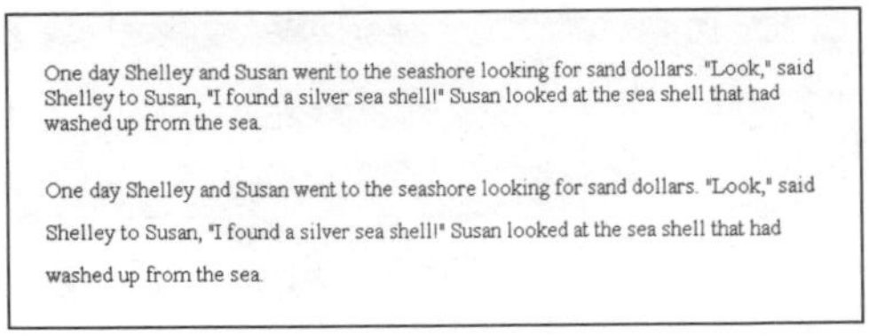

One day Shelley and Susan went to the seashore looking for sand dollars. "Look," said Shelley to Susan, "I found a silver sea shell!" Susan looked at the sea shell that had washed up from the sea.
One day Shelley and Susan went to the seashore looking for sand dollars. "Look," said Shelley to Susan, "I found a silver sea shell!" Susan looked at the sea shell that had washed up from the sea.

Figure 11.79 Line height as interpreted by Navigator 4.5. The top paragraph has no line height set. The second paragraph has a line height of 24 points (to a font size of 14 points).

Untitled Document - Microsoft Internet Explorer
No Decoration (Even links can be displayed without decoration)
Underlined text Overlined text Strikethrough text
Done
My Computer
No Decoration (Even links can be displayed without decoration)
Underlined text Overlined text Strikethrough text
Document: Done

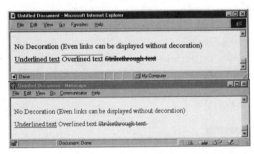

Figure 11.80 Text decoration, as displayed by Internet Explorer (above) and Netscape Navigator (below). Note that Navigator 4.5 does not display overline; Netscape 6 does.

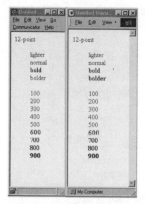

Figure 11.81 Weight variations, at 14 points. Neither browser does much with lighter weights, and Navigator 4.x also handles "bolder" unpredictably. You can see the typographical differences between Navigator and Explorer here; Netscape 6 acts the same as 4.x regarding font-weight.

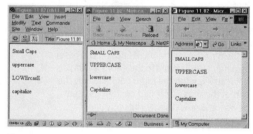

Figure 11.82 Here's Dreamweaver not displaying the font variant Small Caps, and Navigator 6 and Explorer 5 doing variations on it. Both browsers support the text case settings now—note how the text in the Document window is wrong, and the browsers correct it with instructions from the style sheet.

Weight (**Figure 11.81**) is the same as boldness `<b>`, or `<strong>`. You can apply a relative weight (lighter, normal, bold, bolder), or a numerical weight from 100–900 . The weight of normal text is generally 400, whereas boldface text has a weight of about 700.

☞ The only font **Variant*** (**Figure 11.82**) currently supported by Dreamweaver is SMALL CAPS. Explorer 5 and Netscape 6 display small caps.

☞ **Case*** (**Figure 11.82**) allows you to apply all-lowercase, all-uppercase, or title case (The First Letter In Each Word) to a text block. This would come in especially handy for setting headers or captions.

Color, of course, acts the same as `<font color=n>`.

✔ Tip

■ To find out about selecting colors, see *Colors and Web Pages* and *Modifying the Page Background* in Chapter 3.

Background Attributes

Background attributes allow you to place a background color or image behind a text block. They will be superimposed over any other background color or image on the page. The Background panel of the Style Definition dialog box is shown in **Figure 11.83**.

✔ Tips

- To set the background color or image for a page, see *Modifying the Page Background* in Chapter 3.

- To set the background color or image for a table, see *Coloring Tables* in Chapter 12.

- To use style sheets to apply a background color or image to an entire page, apply the style to the <body> tag.

Background attributes include:

☞ **Background color** and **background image** can be applied to an entire page or to a text block (**Figure 11.84**). If both are used, the text block background will be superimposed over the page background (**Figure 11.85**).

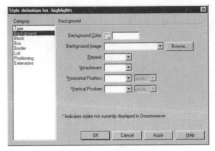

Figure 11.83 You can define properties of a background color or image for either a text block or the page body using the Background panel of the Style Definition dialog box.

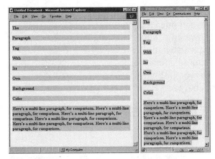

Figure 11.84 I redefined the paragraph tag to have its own background color. Explorer 5 (on the left) makes paragraphs occupy 100 percent of the parent tag (the page body, in this case) by default, and colors in the entire width. Navigator 4.5 (on the right) colors in only the part of the paragraph that contains content. Netscape 6 now displays backgrounds for paragraphs like Explorer does.

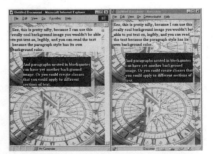

Figure 11.85 If you use a background color (first paragraph) or background image (second paragraph) for a text block, it will be superimposed over the page background. Note how the blockquote style (second paragraph) is rectangular in both Explorer (left) and Navigator (right).

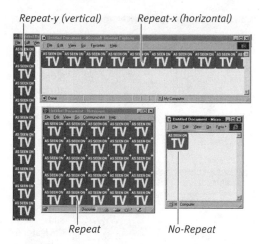

Repeat-y (vertical)   Repeat-x (horizontal)

Repeat   No-Repeat

Figure 11.86 The four flavors of background repeat.

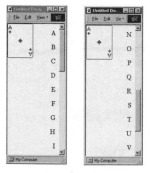

Figure 11.87 A demonstration of the fixed attachment background attribute (also called a watermark) in IE. The image of the ace is set to not repeat. Normally, a tiny background image like this one would scroll off the screen. With fixed attachment set, the ace stays in place while you scroll through the text at right.

The rest of the attributes all apply to a background image.

Repeat (**Figure 11.86**) determines whether the background image is tiled, and if so, how. If the image is displayed in an element that is smaller than the image dimensions, the image will be cropped to fit the element's dimensions.

*No-repeat** prevents the image from tiling.

Repeat tiles the image as it would be tiled in a page background image: from left to right in columns proceeding down the page.

*Repeat-x** displays a horizontal "band" of images; the image is tiled in one row across the page.

*Repeat-y** displays vertical "band" of images; the image is tiled in one column down the page.

Attachment* means the relative attachment of the background image to the page, in particular for full-page background images. Normally, when you scroll through a page, the background image moves, and so does the content—this is both default and scroll. The fixed attachment attribute fixes the background image in place, so that when you scroll through a page, the content "moves," and the background image "stands still" (**Figure 11.87**).

☞ Currently, IE4 supports the fixed option, but Navigator 4.5 and 6 both treat fixed as scroll.

Horizontal position and **vertical position** mark the position of the background image, relative to the element. If you want a small background image centered on the page or in a table or table cell, set both settings to Center. You can also set a pixel value from the left and top of the page. See Chapter 14 for more about positioning.

BACKGROUND ATTRIBUTES

Block Attributes

Block attributes apply typographical constraints to the alignment and spacing of words and characters within the selected element. The Block panel of the Style Definition dialog box is shown in **Figure 11.88**.

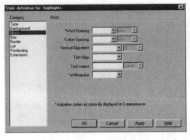

Figure 11.88 The Block attributes panel of the Style Definition dialog box.

Block attributes include:

Word spacing* is used to adjust the space between words, and **Letter spacing*** is used to adjust the space between characters.

Units available for using word and letter spacing include "normal" (no units), pixels, inches (in), centimeters (cm), millimeters (mm), picas, ems, and exs.

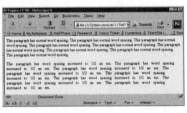

Figure 11.89 Explorer 5 and Navigator 6 both process letter spacing.

☞ 4.x doesn't support letter spacing, but IE and Netscape 6 do (**Figure 11.89**).

☞ The only browser that currently supports word spacing is Netscape 6 (**Figure 11.90**).

☞ You can specify either positive or negative values, although not all browsers will support the latter.

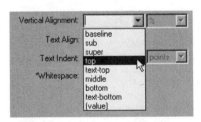

Figure 11.90 Only Netscape 6 supports word spacing.

☞ If property alignment is set to justify, this will most likely overrule word spacing, whereas letter spacing will override justification.

☞ The "normal" settings for word and letter spacing are left up to the individual browser.

Vertical alignment* (**Figures 11.91** and **11.92**) controls the vertical position of the selection. You may use these attributes most often to align text and images within a table cell (Chapter 12) or a layer (Chapter 14).

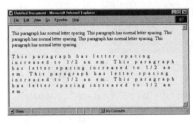

Figure 11.91 Vertical alignment attributes include subscript and superscript, as well as options similar to those used for images.

Figure 11.92 Vertical alignment options for text aligned with floating images.

BLOCK ATTRIBUTES

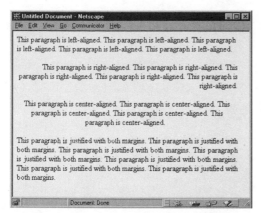

Figure 11.93 Text block alignment options, from top to bottom, are left, right, center, and justify. Note that the margin gutter is greater on the right than on the left; Navigator is leaving room for a scrollbar. (Explorer displays vertical scrollbars whether they're needed or not.)

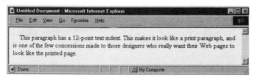

Figure 11.94 A paragraph with a 12-point indent.

Superscript (super) text is smaller text raised above the baseline text, as in E=mc^2. **Subscript (sub)** text dips below the baseline, as in H_2SO_4.

The other vertical alignment options are used with text and images in combination (**Figure 11.92**), or with two images aligned within a parent layer.

The **baseline** is the imaginary line that text sits on. (*Descenders*, as in the letters *j* and *g*, dip below the baseline, whereas *ascenders,* as in the letters *l* and *d*, rise above lowercase text.) Baseline alignment makes text vertically align to the baseline of nearby text, or the bottom of an image align to the text baseline.

Top, **middle**, and **bottom** are self-explanatory.

Text-top and **text-bottom** align an object with the tallest ascender in the text or the lowest descender in the text, respectively.

Text align sets alignment for the text within the margins of the page or the block unit. As in regular HTML, alignment options are left, right, and center, with the additional justify option (**Figure 11.93**).

Text indent* applies a tab-like indent to the first line of a block-type element (**Figure 11.94**).

*Dreamweaver displays indents unpredictably.

Units available for using indents include "normal" (no units), pixels, inches (in), centimeters (cm), millimeters (mm), picas, ems, and exs.

☞ You can use negative values to create a hanging indent, but not all browsers will support this.

continued on next page

✔ Tip

■ Indents are not inherited, which means that line breaks used within paragraphs can cause unpredictable indent behavior. You might experiment with applying a class with indent properties to spans within paragraphs, which is what I did to get the indents in **Figure 11.95**.

Whitespace* controls the use of spacing within the selection. Normal ignores extra spaces and text-based breaks; Pre treats the text as if it were enclosed in <pre> tags, conserving the use of spaces and text-based breaks; Nowrap, similar to the nowrap setting for table cells, allows the line to break only when a <br> tag is used. This last setting is useful particularly for layers and block elements with dimensions smaller than 100 percent of the page.

*Style definition
for <p> tag*

*Style definition
for indent class*

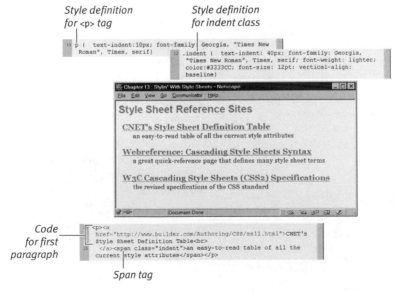

*Code
for first
paragraph*

Span tag

Figure 11.95 The indent property is not inherited, so tags within the block element—the <p> in this case—won't be indented unless you apply separate <span> formatting.

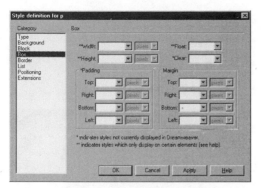

Figure 11.96 The Box attributes panel of the Style Definition dialog box allows you to define the dimensions of the imaginary box that surrounds text blocks.

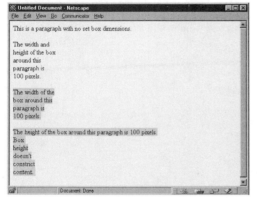

Figure 11.97 The box attributes of these paragraphs, from top to bottom: None, 100x100 pixels, 100 pixels across, and 100 pixels high. Horizontal measurements will break a line, but vertical measurements will not crop content. I used a background color on the bottom two paragraphs so you could see the dimensions more clearly.

Box Attributes

You can imagine all style modifications to HTML elements as being rectangular, or box-shaped. Box attributes, then, are styles applied to the (generally invisible) box that surrounds a block (or span) of text. The Box panel of the Style Definition dialog box is shown in **Figure 11.96**.

Box attributes include:

Height* and **Width*** of the box can be expressed in a number of units, including pixels, inches (in), centimeters (cm), millimeters (mm), picas, ems, and exs, and percentage of the parent unit (%). To use the default dimensions of the box, leave these spaces blank, or choose Auto. Dreamweaver handles box dimensions correctly only for images and layers.

Box width will break a line, but box height will not crop the content of the box to fit within the box (**Figure 11.97**).

Navigator respects box dimensions, but Explorer does not. Navigator 4.5 only displays boxes as true rectangles if borders are applied (see next section).

Float* places the entity at the left or right margin, effectively separating it from the regular flow of the page. Other elements will wrap around floating elements. Dreamweaver displays floating images correctly, but not other elements.

The **Clear*** setting determines the relationship of floating elements to the selected entity. A clear setting of both keeps objects from occupying the margins on either side of a selected entity. A clear setting of none allows floating entities to occupy either margin. Settings of left or right protect the respective margin. Dreamweaver only displays this attribute correctly when it is applied to images.

continued on next page

✔ Tip

- To apply the both setting, you need to type the word "both" (without the quotes) in the Clear text box, because it is not available from the drop-down menu.

Padding* is similar to cell padding used in tables. Padding is blank space between an object and its margin or visible border. Padding is set as a unit value in pixels, inches (in), centimeters (cm), millimeters (mm), picas, ems, and exs, and percentage of the parent unit (%).

✔ Tips

- To set percentage values for any attribute other than height, you need to type the % directly into the code.

- Padding is only visible when you use a visible border (see the next section, *Border Attributes*).

- You can specify padding for the top, bottom, left, and right independently.

Margins* (**Figure 11.98**) are the location of the border around the box (whether or not that border is visible). Margins are set as either auto, or as a number of units, including pixels, inches (in), centimeters (cm), millimeters (mm), picas, ems, and exs, and percentage of the parent element (%). Dreamweaver displays margins properly only when they are applied to block elements.

✔ Tips

- Setting top and bottom margins is a nice alternative to line spacing; you can subtly increase the spacing between paragraphs.

- You can set margins for the top, bottom, left, and right independently.

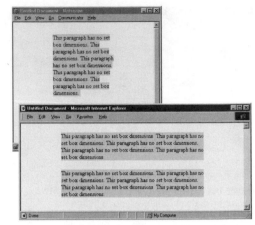

Figure 11.98 In this example, I added the following margins to the <p> tag: 100 pixels on the left and right, and 25 pixels at the top. I showed two different window sizes here (Navigator 4.5 is at the top) to show how window size affects left and right margins.

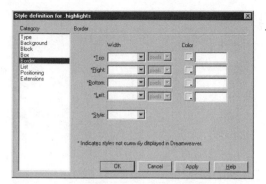

Figure 11.99 Border attributes allow you to make the border around the box visible.

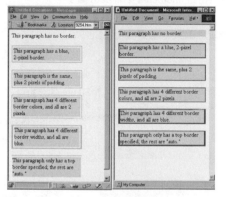

Figure 11.100 Border settings on Navigator 4.5 (L) and IE5 (R). I set a box width of 200 pixels, which Navigator requires and IE ignores. Border colors are treated differently by the two browsers.

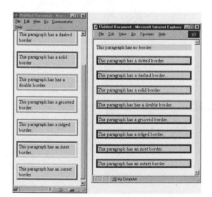

Figure 11.101 Border styles, displayed by Navigator 4.5 (L) and IE (R). Neither browser displays all border styles as described: "dotted" and "dashed" don't look like their names.

Border Attributes

Border attributes are a subset of box attributes, but in the interests of space and neatness, Dreamweaver displays them in their own panel in the Style Definition dialog box (**Figure 11.99**).

*Border elements are not displayed by Dreamweaver in the Document window.

Borders are composed of four entities: the **top**, **right**, **bottom**, and **left**.

You can set a **width** and a **color** for each entity (**Figure 11.100**). In addition to setting a value for border width, you can set a relative value such as thin, medium, or thick. The auto setting will display the browser's default border width (generally a pixel or two).

☞ Navigator 4.x will display different border widths, but not different border colors. In fact, it may handle them pretty strangely.

☞ Navigator 4.x will only display box borders if a box width is specified (you can specify 100 percent). Explorer ignores box widths.

☞ Navigator and Explorer deal with color combinations differently.

You can also choose from a number of **border styles** (**Figure 11.101**). You must set a border style (solid is a good choice) in order for borders to show up at all. Navigator 6 displays all border styles correctly.

✔ Tips

- Padding, a box property, starts doing its thing when you use visible borders.

- You can get interesting beveled effects by specifying borders for two of the four sides of the box and leaving the other two sides blank.

List Attributes

List attributes are applied to ordered (numbered) and unordered (bulleted) lists. The List panel of the Style Definition dialog box is shown in **Figure 11.102**.

* Dreamweaver does not display list attributes in the Document window.

The **Types*** of list attributes that apply to Ordered Lists (**Figure 11.103**) are decimals (1., 2., etc.) lower-roman (i., ii., etc.), upper-roman (I, II, etc.), lower-alpha (a., b., etc.), and upper-alpha (A., B., etc.).

For unordered lists, the **Types*** of bullets available include discs, circles, and squares (**Figure 11.104**).

You can also apply a **Bullet Image*** (**Figure 11.105**) to unordered lists, for which you supply an image URL.

☞ Navigator 4.x does not display bullet images.

The **Position*** of the list items applies to what the text will do when it wraps. Inside will indent all the text to the bullet point, whereas outside will wrap the text to the margin (**Figure 11.106**).

☞ Navigator 4.x does not display inside wrapping.

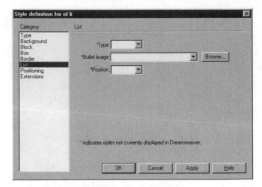

Figure 11.102 The List panel of the Style Definition dialog box lets you define the format of ordered (numbered) or unordered (bulleted) lists.

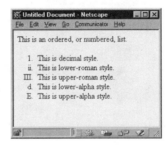

Figure 11.103 An ordered list, formatted with the five different types of ordered list styles.

Figure 11.104 An unordered list, formatted with the three different types of unordered list styles.

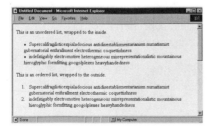

Figure 11.106 The first list is wrapped to the inside, and the second list is wrapped to the outside.

Figure 11.105 An unordered list, using bullet images.

LIST ATTRIBUTES

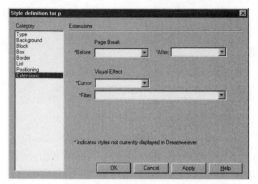

Figure 11.107 The Extensions panel offers extensions to the W3C style sheet specifications.

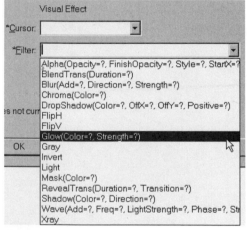

Figure 11.108 The visual effects filters are proprietary, unsupported gimmicks that work only in Internet Explorer.

Extensions

The attributes in the Extensions panel of the Style Definition dialog box (**Figure 11.107**) are not supported by most browsers.

The **Page Break** extension is a proposed style attribute that is not currently supported by any browser. This extension will allow you to recommend a page break before or after a given text block that would break the page when printing the document.

The **Cursor** extension is supported by IE 4 and 5. When the user mouses over a style callout, the cursor (pointer) changes into an icon other than the pointer.

The **Visual Effects Filters** are supposedly supported by IE 4 and 5. I had extremely mixed results using these filters, and I suggest you experiment with them rather than count on them. To apply a visual effects filter, choose it from the drop-down menu (**Figure 11.108**). You need to replace any question marks with values. I'm guessing that you use hex codes for colors; the units for the other values are anyone's guess, as these are not covered in the Dreamweaver manual or help files.

As with all things, in style sheets and in general Web design, experimentation is the key.

SETTING UP TABLES

Club Luxe February Schedule		
Date & Time	Band Name	Booking Contact
02/12 9 p.m.	Inspired	Karen
02/13 10 p.m.	Long Walk Home	Karen
02/14 8:30 p.m.	Poetry Night	Leonard
02/16 10 p.m.	The Hangnails	LuAnn
02/17 9 p.m.	Little Lost Dog	Karen
02/18 9 p.m.	Bonewart	LuAnn
02/20 TBA	Rumpled Stilt Walker	Karen
02/21 8:30 p.m.	Poetry Night	Leonard
02/23 9 p.m.	Cardboard Milk Truck	LuAnn
02/25 10 p.m.	Alonzo & the Rats	Karen
02/26 9 p.m.	Lesson Plan	Karen
02/27 10 p.m.	Karaoke From Mars	Karen
02/28 9 p.m.	Poetry Night	Leonard

Figure 12.1 HTML tables can be used to create all kinds of data tables.

Figure 12.2 With a little imagination, you can use tables to replicate nearly any layout you can make with page layout programs such as Quark or PageMaker.

Before table functionality was added to HTML, all images and text aligned on the left side of a Web page by default. Originally, tables were used to simplify presenting tabular data, such as scientific reports (**Figure 12.1**), but clever designers quickly realized that tables could also be used to increase their design options (**Figure 12.2**). You can create complex table layouts for entire-page designs.

Like the mailboxes that line the wall at the post office, each individual cubbyhole, called a *cell*, holds discrete information that doesn't ooze over into the other boxes. As you can see in **Figure 12.3** on the next page, tables are divided into rows, which cross the table horizontally, and columns, which span the table vertically.

Hand-coding a table is tiresome at best. In fact, tables are probably the most convenient feature of most WYSIWYG Web page creation programs, although many of these tools code tables rather sloppily—not so with Macromedia Dreamweaver.

Dreamweaver 4 offers a new feature called *Layout View* that lets you actually draw tables and table cells on a page, exactly where you want them to go. The program then fills in the rest of the columns and rows to space out the page. Once you have this basic layout, you can add, resize, and move around the elements on the page.

Setting Up Tables

Creating a table is a three-part process, although the second and third steps often take place simultaneously.

To create a table:

1. First, you insert the table onto your page.

2. Then, you modify the properties of the table and its cells. You can change the size, the layout, the spacing, the color scheme, and so on.

3. Finally, you insert content, such as text and images, into the table.

✔ Tips

- It helps to draw a sketch of your page before you get started (**Figure 12.4**) and then add or subtract elements as you proceed.

- You can do any of these things in Standard View or Layout View (**Figure 12.5**). Some actions, such as combining or splitting cells, you can do only in Standard View. Others, such as creating Autostretch columns, you can do only in Layout View. I'm going to discuss both in this chapter.

- Although virtually every current Web browser handles tables correctly, a few older browsers, and some nongraphic browsers, don't. See Appendix A on the Web site for tips on working with different kinds of browsers.

- You can also draw complex layouts using layers and then have Dreamweaver convert the page into tables. From the document window menu bar, select Modify > Convert > Layers to Tables. See Chapter 14 for more on layers.

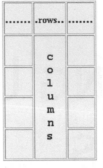

Figure 12.3 This table consists of three columns and five rows. The center column consists of only two cells, the larger of which was created by merging together four cells.

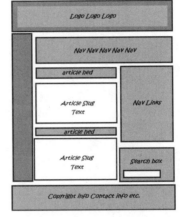

Figure 12.4 Draw a sketch of your table before you begin. You can use pencil and paper or a paint program.

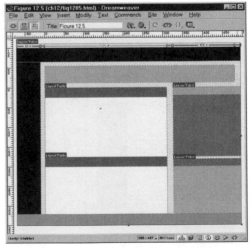

Figure 12.5 This is the finalized table layout based on the rough sketch in **Figure 12.4**. I drew the cells in Layout Mode; you can see I have four tables and several cells contained within one page-sized table.

Figure 12.6 In Layout View, each individual table has a tab marking it, and you must draw a cell in a specific spot in order to place content within it. The white areas are useable cells and the gray areas are undefined areas used to space out the rest of the table.

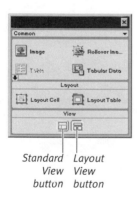

Standard   Layout
View   View
button   button

Figure 12.7 Click on the Layout View button. The other button returns you to Standard View.

About Layout Tables

Dreamweaver 4 introduces a new tool for drawing page layouts. You draw some boxes on a page, and then Dreamweaver fills in the HTML for an entire page design. These layouts are drawn using tables, which Dreamweaver calls *layout tables*.

✔ Tip

- Layout tables do not use different tags than regular tables; however, they do employ *spacer gifs,* which are invisible, one-pixel images that are used to force the spacing of tables. See *About Spacer Gifs,* later in this chapter.

Layout View and Standard View

To work with layout tables, Dreamweaver uses a different editing paradigm, called *Layout View* (**Figure 12.6**). You draw cells on the page the same way you draw text boxes in Quark or image slices in Fireworks.

To turn on layout view:

◆ On the Objects panel (Window > Objects), click on the Layout View button (**Figure 12.7**).

    or

    From the Document window menu bar, select View > Table View > Layout View.

Dreamweaver will show the page in Layout View. If there are no tables on your page, the Document window will look the same. If there are tables on your page, they'll appear with tabs like the ones in **Figure 12.6**.

continued on next page

✔ Tips

- The first time you select Layout View, a dialog box will appear (**Figure 12.8**) explaining what layout view is. To make this thing go away forever, click the Don't show me this message again checkbox.

- You can't insert a table the usual way (Insert > Table) in Layout View, and you can't draw a layout cell or layout table in Standard View. To tell which view you're in, look at the Objects panel, or view the menu command without selecting anything.

- To toggle those tabs on and off, select View > Table View > Show Layout Table Tabs.

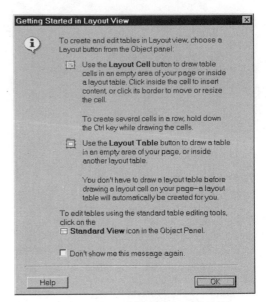

Figure 12.8 The purpose of this dialog box is to introduce you to Layout View. Check the box to make it go away.

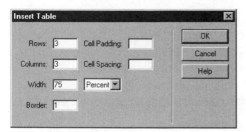

Figure 12.9 Set the initial size of your table in the Insert Table dialog box.

Figure 12.10 Here, I'm setting the table width to 100 percent of the browser window.

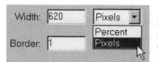

Figure 12.11 I'm setting the table width to an exact pixel width.

Figure 12.12 I inserted a new table with five rows and two columns. It takes up 75 percent of the window.

✔ Tips

- Even if you specify an exact width in pixels, your table may resize itself—it will stretch to fit the content you put in it. If you set a percentage width, the table will resize based on the width of the user's browser window.

- You can always go back later to add additional rows or columns or to make other adjustments to your table specifications. See *Adding Columns and Rows in Standard View*, later in this chapter.

Inserting a Table in Standard View

When you insert a table in this mode, you first choose a starting width and decide how many columns and rows you want to begin with.

To insert a table (Standard View):

1. Click to place the insertion point where you'd like the table to appear. This can be on a blank page or inside an existing table cell.

2. From the Document Window menu bar, select Insert > Table.

   or

   Click on the Table button on the Objects panel 𝄇.

   Either way, the Insert Table dialog box will appear (**Figure 12.9**).

3. Type the number of rows you want in your table in the Rows text box.

4. Type the number of columns you want in your table in the Columns text box.

5. Choose a width for your table in either Pixels or Percent.

   To set the table width to a percentage of the page width, select Percent from the Width drop-down menu and type a number in the Width text box (**Figure 12.10**).

   or

   To set an exact width, select Pixels from the Width drop-down menu and type a number in the text box (**Figure 12.11**). I'll discuss the other table options later in this chapter.

6. Click on OK to close the Insert Table dialog box. Your new table will appear (**Figure 12.12**).

Drawing a Layout

When you work with layout tables, keep the sketch of your page in mind (**Figure 12.4**).

There are two ways to go about drawing layouts: You can draw a layout cell first, or you can draw a layout table first and add cells to it.

Drawing a layout cell

First, we're going to draw a layout cell and watch Dreamweaver populate the rest of the table to complete a full-page layout.

To draw a layout cell:

1. Make sure you're working in Layout View.

2. On the Objects panel, click on the Draw Layout Cell button (**Figure 12.13**). The pointer will turn into crosshairs.

3. In the Document window, draw a rectangle that is big enough to hold your content (**Figure 12.14**).

When you let go of the mouse button, your cell will appear, and Dreamweaver will also draw more cells to complete a table. Cells can't float in space; they live in tables (**Figure 12.15**).

Drawing a layout table

You can also draw a layout table on the page and then populate it with cells.

To draw a layout table:

1. On the Objects panel, click on the Draw Layout Table button (**Figure 12.13**). The pointer will turn into crosshairs.

2. In the Document window, draw a rectangle on your page where you want a table to go (**Figure 12.16**).

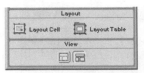

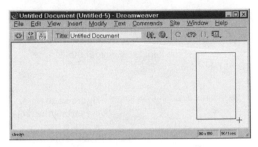

Figure 12.13 Click on the Draw Layout Cell or Draw Layout Table button on the Objects panel.

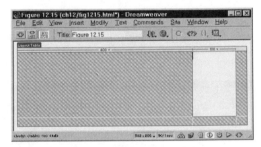

Figure 12.14 Draw a cell that's a container for content in your overall page design.

Figure 12.15 When you draw a layout cell, Dreamweaver fills in the content to make a full-page table layout.

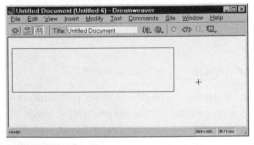

Figure 12.16 Draw a table on your page. Tables initially start at the left margin, but you don't need to put content there.

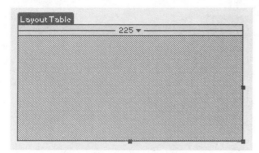

Figure 12.17 When you draw a blank layout table, it starts its life without any layout cells.

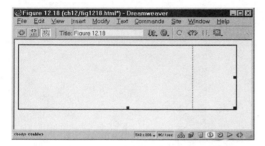

Figure 12.18 The page layout shown in **Figure 12.15** in Layout View doesn't actually exist as such in reality, also known as Standard View. You need to finish drawing any cells that you want to hold content and let Dreamweaver fill in the placeholders for layout areas without text or images.

New layout cell

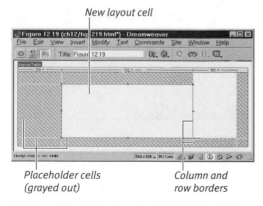

Placeholder cells (grayed out)   *Column and row borders*

Figure 12.19 I added a layout cell to the table. Note the borders that mark the other, unfilled cells that hold the table together.

When you let go of the mouse button, your table will appear—with nary a cell to be seen (**Figure 12.17**). You need to add them.

Adding cells to a layout table

Whether you start by drawing a layout cell or a layout table, you need to add cells to it to hold content. **Figure 12.18** shows what the table I drew in **Figure 12.15** looks like in standard view—in reality, there are only two cells I can populate with content, until I draw more cells.

✔ Tip

■ You cannot overlap layout cells.

To add a cell to a layout:

1. Start in Layout View with a table created by drawing a layout cell or a layout table.

2. On the Objects panel, click on the Layout Cell button. The pointer will turn into crosshairs.

3. Within the boundaries of the table, draw a rectangular container for your content.

Dreamweaver will create the cell and show column and row borders (**Figure 12.19**).

Drawing a table inside a table

You can nest a table within a table just by drawing it there (**Figure 12.20**).

Drawing a table around cells

You may want to draw a table around a set of contiguous cells. Click on Layout Table, and drag the cursor around the cells (**Figure 12.21**). You can even extend the table past the cells you included (**Figure 12.22**).

Drawing a sequence of cells

If you hold down the Control (Command) button while you draw, you can keep drawing cells instead of having to click on the button each time. The cursor will snap to any column or row borders so you can match heights and widths easily.

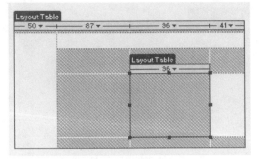

Figure 12.20 Nest a table within a table by drawing it on some blank space inside the larger table.

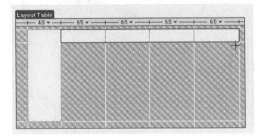

Figure 12.21 Click on Draw Layout Table, and then drag the cursor around the cells to enclose them in a table.

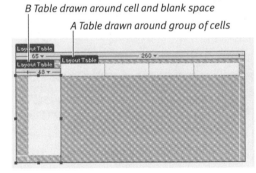

Figure 12.22 You can draw a table to enclose just a group of cells (A) or a cell and some blank space (B).

Name That Table

If you're planning on working with table code directly, it may help to know which table you're working on, particularly if you've inserted a table within a table. You can name your table, in which case the table code will say something like

```
<table name="main">
```

To name your table, first select it. Then, in the Property inspector, type a name in the Table Name text box , and press Enter (Return) or click on the Apply button. The table name will be inserted into the code.

Figure 12.23 When you click within a table, these tags appear in the tag selector. Click on a tag to select it. The tags are <table>, <tr> for table row, and <td> for table data, a.k.a. cell.

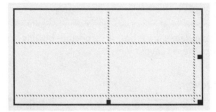

Figure 12.24 The entire table will be selected. In Standard View, a dark outline will appear around the table, and handles will appear in the lower-right corner of the table.

Table tab

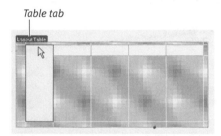

Figure 12.25 To select an item in Layout View, click on a folder's tab or the outside edge of any cell or table.

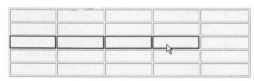

Figure 12.26 Click and drag to select all or part of a row. You can drag up to select a column.

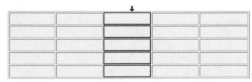

Figure 12.27 When the cursor becomes a black arrow, click to select a column or row.

Selecting Elements

To modify a table cell, column, or row, or a table itself, you need to select it.

To select a table in either view:

1. Click within the table.

2. Click on the <table> tag in the tag selector (**Figure 12.23**).

   or

   Click on the table's outside edge.

Either way, your table will be selected (**Figure 12.24**) and you can copy, cut, drag, or delete it.

To select a table in Standard View:

◆ From the Document window menu bar, select Modify > Table > Select Table.

   or

   Right-click (Control+click) on the table, and from the pop-up menu that appears, select Table > Select Table.

To select in Layout View:

1. Click within the table or cell.

2. Click on the item's outside edge or the table's tab (**Figure 12.25**).

Handles will appear around a selected layout table or layout cell, as we saw in **Figure 12.22**.

To select a column or row:

◆ In Standard View, hold down the mouse button and drag up to select a column or across to select a row (**Figure 12.26**).

   or

   When you mouse over the top or left table border, the cursor will turn into a black arrow (**Figure 12.27**). Then, you just click to select the entire column or row.

continued on next page

SELECTING ELEMENTS

✔ Tips

- **Figures 12.28** to **12.31** show the Properties inspector for tables and cells in both views.

- In Layout View, table borders are green, and cell borders are blue. Like the Property inspector and the tag inspector, this will tell you what you have selected.

- Occasionally, when you click on the `<td>` tag in the tag selector in Layout View, the Property inspector will instead bring up `<table>` properties. Click on the edge of the cell to select it.

- Hold down the Shift key while clicking to select or deselect multiple cells in Standard View. Hold down the Ctrl key and you can even select noncontiguous cells (**Figure 12.32**).

- You can toggle off table borders in Standard View while you're working by selecting View >Visual Aids > Table Borders. Then, you'll need to rely on the tag selector to select a table or cell surrounding your content.

- To delete a table in either view, select it and then press Delete. The table contents will also be deleted, unless you move the contents into another container or onto another page before you delete the table.

- When Dreamweaver creates cells (any cell in Standard Mode or layout cells in Layout Mode), it includes a character called a nonbreaking space, which looks like ` `. Many browsers will not draw space for tables that include no content; this invisible character is like a marker for the cell. (In some cases, an invisible image is used; see *About Spacer Gifs,* later on.)

- After you select a column or row in standard view, you can delete it by pressing Delete. You can also click within an area of the table and select Modify > Table > Delete Row (or Delete Column).

Figure 12.28 When the table is selected, the Property inspector will display Table properties. This is in Standard View.

Figure 12.29 Here's the Property inspector showing Table Properties in Layout View.

Apply button

Selected object's name (cell)

Figure 12.30 The Property inspector, displaying Table Cell properties in Standard View. You can identify the Property inspectors for each view by the appearance of the Apply button and the displayed name of the selected object.

Figure 12.31 The Property inspector, displaying Table Cell properties in Layout View. Mostly, the options are the same, but oddly, they're arranged quite differently.

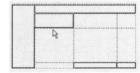

Figure 12.32 Hold down the Ctrl or Shift key to select multiple cells in Standard View. Then, you can modify a property such as background color or add a CSS style to all the selected cells.

SELECTING ELEMENTS

Figure 12.33 Select the table by clicking on its tag in the tag selector.

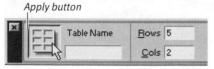

Apply button

Figure 12.34 Type a new number in the Rows and Cols text boxes. Click on the Apply button to add the new items.

Adding a Single Cell to a Table

If you want to add a row with only one cell in it to your page, you can edit the code. The blank space in the row will not be able to hold content unless you add more cells or increase the column span of the existing cell.

1. From the Document window menu bar, select Window > Code Inspector. The Code inspector will appear.

2. To add a cell at the end of a table, locate the closing table tag, </table>, and type the following line of code just before it: <tr><td> </td></tr>.

This adds a new row <tr> with only one cell in it <td> (**Figure 12.35**). Cells are not displayed unless they have something In them. The   entity adds invisible content to the cell so it will show up as a lay-out element. To increase the columnspan of the pictured cell, you'd add this code to the <td> tag:

colspan="2"

That would make the cell span two columns.

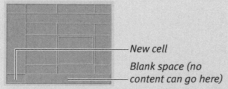

— *New cell*

Blank space (no
content can go here)

Figure 12.35 A single cell was added to this table. Note the blank space in the rest of the row.

Adding Columns and Rows in Standard View

You can add more columns or rows to your table. Later in this chapter, we'll resize columns and rows and split and merge cells in a table.

Adding cells to a table

There are several ways to add cells to a table. One quick way to change the dimensions of your table is by using the Property inspector.

To change the number of columns or rows:

1. Select the entire table by clicking on its outside border or by clicking within it and selecting <table> in the tag selector (**Figure 12.33**). The Property inspector will display table properties.

2. Type a new number of columns in the Cols text box, and a new number of rows in the Rows text box. (**Figure 12.34**).

Your table will change size as it adds or deletes columns and rows from its layout.

✔ Tip

■ If the cursor is in the last cell in the table, pressing Tab will add another row.

To delete a row or column:

1. Click to place the insertion point within the row or column you want to delete.

2. From the Document window menu bar, select Modify > Table > Delete Row (or Delete Column).

The row (or column) and all its contents will disappear.

Adding columns and rows

You can also easily insert a column or row in Standard View using the Modify menu.

To add columns or rows:

1. Click in a cell adjacent to where you want to add a column or row.

2. From the Document window menu bar, select Modify > Table > Insert Rows or Columns. The Insert Rows or Columns dialog box will appear **(Figure 12.36)**.

3. Click on the Rows radio button to add rows, or the Columns radio button to add columns.

4. In the Number of Rows (or Columns) text box, type the number of rows (or columns) you want to add.

5. Select the position of the new elements.

   ◆ Rows: To insert new rows above the selected cell, click on the Above the Selection radio button. To insert new rows below the selected cell, click on the Below the Selection radio button.

   ◆ Columns: To place the new columns to the left of the selected cell, click on the Before current Column radio button. To place the new columns to the right of the selected cell, click on the After current Column radio button.

6. Click on OK to close the dialog box and add the new rows or columns to your table.

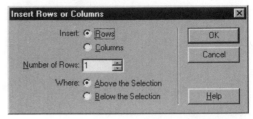

Figure 12.36 Use the Insert Rows or Columns dialog box to add columns and rows where you want them.

Figure 12.37 Click in the cell below where you want the new row to appear, or to the right of where you want the new column to appear.

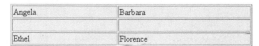

Figure 12.38 The new row will appear above the cell you selected.

Figure 12.39 Right-click (Control+click) on the table, and choose Table > Insert Column from the pop-up menu. You can also add a single row above the insertion point this way.

Figure 12.40 A new column will appear to the left of the column you selected.

To add a single row:

1. Click in a table cell below where you want the new row to appear (**Figure 12.37**).

2. From the Document window menu bar, select Modify > Table > Insert Row, or press Ctrl+M (Command+M). The new row will appear above the insertion point (**Figure 12.38**).

To add a single column:

1. Right-click (Control+click) on the column directly to the left of where you want the new column to appear (as in **Figure 12.37**).

2. From the pop-up menu, select Table > Insert Column (**Figure 12.39**).

A new column will appear to the left of the column you selected (**Figure 12.40**).

ADDING COLUMNS AND ROWS

Resizing Table Elements

When you add or remove elements from a table, it often resizes. You can also set the size of a table, a column, or a row.

You may have set a width for your table when you created it, but you can adjust the width of the table at any time. Table widths are set either in pixels or percent of screen width.

To set the table width (either view):

1. Select the table.

2. In the Property inspector:
   ◆ For Standard View, select either Pixels or Percent (%) from the W (Width) drop-down menu (**Figure 12.41**).
   ◆ For Layout View, select the Fixed radio button to set a pixel width, or Autostretch to set the width to 100 percent of the screen.

3. Type a number in the W (Width) text box (the Fixed text box, In Layout View) and press Enter (Return).

To resize a table by dragging (either view):

1. Select the table. Selection handles will appear around the table (**Figure 12.42**).

2. Drag the table to resize it (**Figure 12.43**). In Layout View, Dreamweaver will fill in space between the cells and the table; you can then resize the cells, if you want.

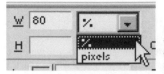

Figure 12.41 Type the width of the table in the W (Width) text box.

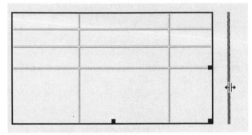

Figure 12.42 Grabbing a table by its selection handles in Standard View.

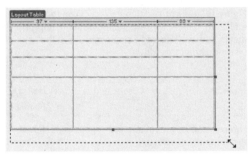

Figure 12.43 Resizing a layout table in Layout View by dragging. To make a table smaller, you may first need to clear heights and widths or resize cells.

You Ought to Be in Pixels

If you set a column's width in pixels, the text you type or paste into the cells in that column will wrap to fit in the column. However, if you place an image wider than the column in one of those cells, the column will still expand to fit the image.

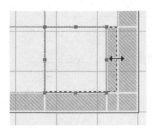

Figure 12.44 You can resize a cell by dragging it over unfilled space in the table. To enlarge one cell, you may first need to reduce the size of adjacent cells.

Figure 12.45 You can set exact height and width for columns, rows, and cells, as well as tables.

✔ Tips

■ You can also resize cells by dragging in Layout Mode (**Figure 12.44**).

■ You can also set an exact height or width for a column, row, or cell by selecting the column or row in Standard View, or the cell <td> in either view, and typing values in the Property inspector (**Figure 12.45**).

■ You can use Dreamweaver's grid for exact measurements when resizing your table and its cells (**Figure 12.44**). To turn on the grid, select View > Grid > Show from the Document window menu bar. For more about the grid, see Chapter 1.

RESIZING TABLE ELEMENTS

Mom & Pop's Row & Column Span

Selecting cells and then merging them or splitting them is the easiest way to change column span or row span; this is described in the upcoming section *Merging and Splitting Cells*. However, if you want to do it the old-fashioned way using old-fashioned terminology, you're welcome to. Note that you cannot split a single-span cell this way.

In the code, a cell generally occupies one column and one row, but if you combine two or more cells into one, it can span any number of columns using the colspan and rowspan attributes:

```
<td colspan="2" rowspan="2"> </td>
```

To increase (or decrease) row span:

1. Click to place the insertion point in the upper of the two cells you want to combine (or in the cell you want to split).

2. From the Document window menu bar, select Modify > Table > Increase Row Span (Decrease Row Span). The table cell will combine with the cell directly below it (split from the table cell it was previously combined with).

To increase (or decrease) column span:

1. Click to place the insertion point in the leftmost of the two cells you want to combine (or in the cell you want to split).

2. From the Document window menu bar, select Modify > Table > Increase Column Span (Decrease Column Span). The table cell will combine with the cell directly to the right of it (split from the table cell it was previously combined with).

Dragging Columns and Rows in Standard View

You can adjust column width or row height by simply clicking and dragging.

To drag column and row borders:

1. When you move the mouse over a border between cells, the pointer will turn into a double-headed arrow (**Figure 12.46**).

2. Click on the border and drag it to a new location (**Figure 12.47**). This will set the specifications for the dimensions of the table elements involved.

✔ Tips

- Although you *can* set row height, a row's height will expand to fit the content.

- As with column and row dimensions, cell height and widths are not an exact science; the size of the content and the quirks of the browser will vary your mileage. Using layout view to draw the table and standard view to set the details works well for me.

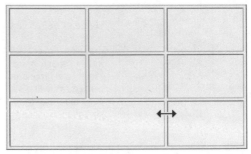

Figure 12.46 Mouse over the table border and the pointer will turn into a double-headed arrow.

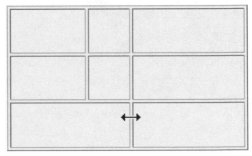

Figure 12.47 Use the double-headed arrow to drag the border to a new location.

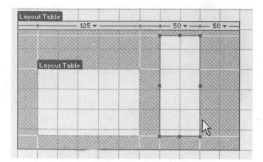

Figure 12.48 Select a layout cell so you can move it within the table.

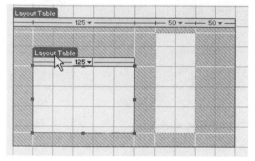

Figure 12.49 Select a nested layout table to move it within the parent table.

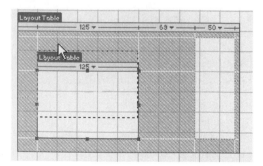

Figure 12.50 In this figure, I've moved the layout cell to the right and I'm in the process of moving the nested layout table up. When you drag a layout element, it will snap to the grid if snapping is turned on.

Moving a Layout Element

You can use the grid (View > Grid > Show) to help you place things. See Chapter 1 for details on adjusting the grid.

You cannot overlap any containers—cells can't overlap with each other, or tables, or vice versa. Before your table is hyperpopulated, though, you can move a cell or table anywhere you like. You can move a nested table within a table, but you can't place a table just anywhere on the page without using a layout table.

To move a container:

1. Select the layout cell or layout table by clicking on its outside edge so that handles appear (**Figures 12.48** and **12.49**).

2. Click and hold and drag the container to a new location in the table (**Figure 12.50**).

    or

    Use the arrow keys to move the container one pixel at a time. Hold down shift while using the arrow keys to move the container 10 pixels at a time.

About Width Settings in Layout View

Width settings in tables are generally expressed in pixels or in percent of the window size. In layout view, you can also set the width of a table or column to *autostretch;* that is, the table will always fill the browser window, no matter what size the window is (**Figure 12.51**). Autostretch columns are spaced proportionally to preserve your design.

Reading width settings

The width of each column in a selected table appears as the column header (**Figure 12.52**).

◆ If it's a pixel width, you'll see a whole number.

◆ If it's an autostretch width, you'll see a wavy line.

◆ If the content of the column is wider than the column's fixed width, you'll see two numbers in the column header.

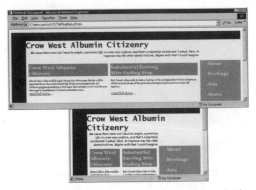

Figure 12.51 Here you see two browser windows both displaying the table at 100 percent width. The center column's width is set to Autostretch.

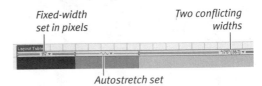

Figure 12.52 Column headers above the top cell in each table indicate the widths.

Stupid No-Wrap Tricks

Text in table cells usually wraps to fit the width of the cell. If you turn off text wrapping, the cell will expand to fit the text.

To set the no-wrap option, click within the cell (either view), or the column or row (standard view), and then select the No Wrap checkbox on the Property inspector.

To break a line in non-wrapped text, press Enter (Return) to start a new paragraph, or Shift+Enter (Shift+Return) for a line break. If you change the cell's contents so there is extra blank space in the unused cell, you can clear column widths to close up empty space. See *Getting Nitpicky About Widths,* later in this chapter.

Column Headers

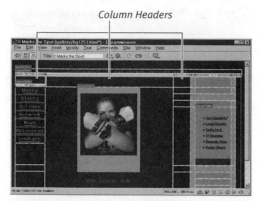

Figure 12.53 In this table, I set the largest column to autostretch. I don't want the navigation columns to expand, but the large one can do so without spoiling the look.

Figure 12.54 Here, the browser window shows you a much narrower view of the same table, and the column stretched (or rather, shrank) successfully.

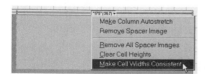

Figure 12.55 If your column has expanded to fit the content in it, you may want to reset the width to reflect reality.

Applying width settings

It's likely that in your table you'll want to set some columns to exact widths and some to autostretch (**Figures 12.53** and **12.54**).

Making widths consistent

If you see two numbers in a column heading, it means that the width that's currently displayed in the Document window, or the width of the content in the cell, conflicts with the width setting in the code for the table.

To make widths consistent:

1. Click on the column heading.

2. From the menu that appears, select Make Widths Consistent (**Figure 12.55**).

Now, only the actual column width will be specified.

Using Autostretch

Autostretch is a new feature in Layout View that makes a table fit to browser-window width.

To set autostretch for a column in Layout View:

1. Click on the tab of the layout table that contains your column. The column headings will appear.

2. Select the column you want to set to autostretch, and click on the column header button. From the menu that appears, select Make Column Autostretch (**Figure 12.56**).

If you haven't selected a spacer, you'll be asked to do so in the Choose Spacer Image dialog box (**Figure 12.57**).

To select a spacer gif:

- The Choose Spacer Image dialog box will appear if you haven't yet chosen a spacer. You're offered three choices:

  - To create a spacer gif, click on Create a spacer image file. The Save Spacer Image File As dialog box will appear. Choose the folder (such as /images), and type a filename for the image. Then, click on Save.

  - To use a spacer that's already in your site, click on Use an existing spacer image. The Select Spacer Image File dialog box will appear. Select your image, and click on Select (Choose).

  - To avoid spacers altogether, select Don't use spacer image for autostretch tables. Your mileage may vary—the autostretch properties will be based on fixed and percentage widths, and the table may not shrink to accommodate small browser windows.

Figure 12.56 Click on the column header of the most flexible cell in your layout, and select Make Column Autostretch from the menu.

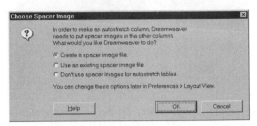

Figure 12.57 The first time you use autostretch, Dreamweaver will ask you to choose or create a spacer image.

Figure 12.58 Select Make Column Fixed Width from the column header menu.

About Spacer Gifs

A spacer image is a 1-pixel by 1-pixel transparent gif that is resized in order to stretch the width of a column. For example, to make a column stay 100 pixels wide, whether or not it includes content—and no matter how wide the browser window is—the image dimensions are set to 100x1.

If a column includes no content, neither a spacer nor a nonbreaking space, it basically won't exist as a layout element.

In order for autostretch to work, you may need spacer gifs to make the fixed-width columns stay fixed. Yes, it's cheating—but it works, so it's okay. You can reuse the same spacer gif each time you need one.

To find out how to reset the spacer you use, see *Spacer Preferences*, later in this chapter.

Getting Nitpicky About Widths

You can clear row heights and column widths to reflect new content in your table. Cells without content may shrink if you clear these values.

1. Select the table in either view.

2. From the Document window menu bar, select Modify > Table > Clear Cell Heights (or Clear Cell Widths).

   or

   In the Property inspector (**Figure 12.60**), click on the Clear Row Heights button or the Clear Column Widths button (Standard View).

   You can also convert all widths expressed in pixels to percents, or vice-versa. Afterwards, you can use the column headings in Layout View to reset some values, if you want.

To convert from percentages to pixels:

1. Select the table in either view.

2. In the Property inspector, click on the appropriate button (**Figure 12.60**).

   or

   From the Document window menu bar, select Modify > Table > Convert Widths to Pixels (or Percent).

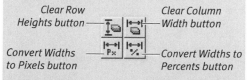

Clear Row Heights button *Clear Column Width button*

Convert Widths to Pixels button *Convert Widths to Percents button*

Figure 12.60 In either view, you can use the Property inspector to clear cell dimensions. In Standard View (pictured), you can convert the units of your widths.

Setting exact widths

If it's important that a column have an exact width (for instance, if it contains a navigational or layout element that's *purrfect*), then you should set that column's width.

To set an exact width:

1. Click on the tab of the layout table that contains your column. The column headings will appear.

2. At the top of the column for which you want to set the width, click on the column header button.

3. From the menu that appears, select Make Column Fixed Width (**Figure 12.58**).

Dreamweaver will set the width of the column to the content that appears in it. The number in pixels will appear in the column header.

You can also set a width by dragging; or you can use the Property inspector. Select the table or cell, and in the Property inspector's Fixed text box, type a number in pixels.

About height settings

Dreamweaver sets table and row heights in layout tables to fill out the page, based on the size of the Document window when you first draw the table. After you fill the table with content, you may want to clear these settings.

To clear row heights:

1. Click on the column header so that the menu appears (**Figure 12.59**).

2. From the menu, select Clear Cell Heights.

Rows without content may shrink.

Figure 12.59 Select Clear Cell Heights from the column header menu.

Merging and Splitting Cells

In standard view, you can combine two adjacent cells into a single, larger cell. You can also split a cell into one or more other cells.

To merge cells:

1. In Standard View, select two or more cells you want to combine (**Figure 12.61**).

2. On the Property inspector, click on the Merge Cells button .

The cells will be combined (**Figure 12.62**).

✔ Tips

- You can merge an entire column or row into one cell.

- If you change your mind, you can split the cell using the split cell button. Also see the sidebar *Mom & Pop's Row & Column Span.*

To split a cell:

1. In Standard View, click within the cell you wish to split (**Figure 12.63**).

2. From the Document window menu bar, select Modify > Table > Split Cell.
The Split Cell dialog box will appear (**Figure 12.64**).

3. Choose whether to split the cell into rows or columns by clicking on the appropriate radio button.

4. Type a Number of Rows (or Columns) in the text box.

5. Click on OK to close the dialog box and add the cells to the table (**Figure 12.65**).

Figure 12.61 Select the cells you want to combine.

Figure 12.62 Cells in two rows merge to create one large cell that spans two rows.

Figure 12.63 Select the cell you want to split. It may already span more than one row or it may be a single, unadulterated cell.

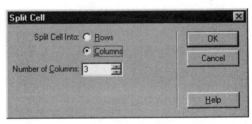

Figure 12.64 In the Split Cell dialog box, specify how many columns or rows to split the cell into.

Figure 12.65 The cell divides into three rows.

MERGING AND SPLITTING CELLS

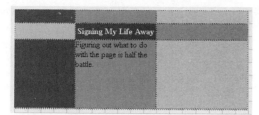

Figure 12.66 You can type and format text in a table just as you would on a blank page. See the upcoming sections on alignment and spacing to find out how to format this content.

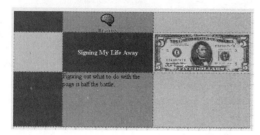

Figure 12.67 The top image made the row taller after I inserted it, and the five-dollar bill stretched both its column and the entire table. See the previous sections on making cell widths consistent and clearing row heights and column widths to find out about formatting table dimensions.

Adding Content to a Table

Now that you've got your table right where you want it, you need to put stuff in it.

To add text to your table, just click in the cell where you want your text to go, and start typing and formatting (**Figure 12.66**). The table and its cells may expand to accommodate the content (**Figure 12.67**).

✔ Tips

- You can move from cell to cell in a table by pressing the Tab key. Shift+Tab moves the cursor backwards.

- You can drag images and text into table cells from elsewhere on the page. Highlight the text or image, and then click on it and drag it into its new home.

- You can create a table within a table in both Standard and Layout Views.

Table header cells

You can format a table header cell to mark the purpose of your table. The tag is <th>.

To use a header cell:

1. Select the cell, row, or column that you'd like to format as a header cell (**Figure 12.68**).

2. In the Property inspector (**Figure 12.69**), select the Header checkbox.

3. The text in the selected cell will be centered and boldfaced. (**Figure 12.70**).

✔ Tip

■ The appearance of table header cells may vary slightly from browser to browser, but the concept is the same: They stand out from the rest of the table.

Number of Days in Each Month	
January	31
February	28 (29)
March	31
April	30
May	31
June	30
July	31
August	31
September	30
October	31
November	30
December	31

Figure 12.68 Click within your future table header cell.

No Wrap ☐

Header ☐

Figure 12.69 In Standard View, tick the Header checkbox in the Property inspector.

Number of Days in Each Month	
January	31
February	28 (29)
March	31
April	30
May	31
June	30
July	31
August	31
September	30
October	31
November	30
December	31

Figure 12.70 The text in the new table header cell is now bold and centered in the cell.

Figure 12.71 Use the Align drop-down menu in the Property inspector to choose the alignment setting.

Figure 12.72 A right-aligned table, complete with placeholder icon.

Figure 12.73 Horizontal alignment (Horz) options include Default, Left, Center, and Right.

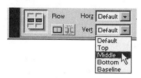
Figure 12.74 Vertical alignment options (Vert) include Default, Top, Middle, Bottom, and Baseline.

H=Default, V=Default	H=Left, V=Top	H=Center, V=Middle
H=Right, V=Bottom	H=Right, V=Top	H=Right, V=Middle
H=Default, V=Baseline	H=Center, V=Baseline	H=Right, V=Baseline

Figure 12.75 This table runs the gamut of content alignment options. The position of the Baseline vertical alignment is based on the imaginary lines that the characters rest on, and it generally follows the baseline of the bordering cells.

Terms of Alignment

If you align a table to the right, a small placeholder icon will appear in the left margin to mark the beginning of the table on the page. This icon may disappear if you change the alignment back to left. You can place the insertion point near this icon to put text to the left of the table, as seen in **Figure 12.72**.

Choosing the default setting will make the table follow the default browser settings.

Aligning Tables and Content

You can set the alignment for a table on a page or within another table, just as if it were text.

To set table alignment:

1. Select the table in Standard View.

2. In the Property inspector, click on the Align drop-down menu, and select Default, Left, Center, or Right (**Figure 12.71**).

Your table will change alignment (hopefully for the forces of good) (**Figure 12.72**).

Content alignment

In addition to table spacing, you can adjust how the content in your table's cells is aligned:

◆ In both horizontal and vertical alignment, choosing Default sets the alignment to the browser's default—usually left (horizontal) and middle (vertical). Therefore, you won't need to set alignment specifications for left or middle unless you're "changing it back."

◆ Cell alignment properties override column specs, and columns override row specs.

To change content alignment:

1. Select the column, row, or cell for which you want to specify the content alignment. In Layout View, take care that you've selected a cell instead of a table. You may have to click the edge of the cell again; check the Property inspector to see what you've selected.

2. Click on the Horz drop-down menu, and select an alignment option: Default, Left, Center, or Right (**Figure 12.73**).

3. Click on the Vert drop-down menu and select an option: Default, Top, Middle, Bottom, or Baseline (**Figure 12.74**).

Your changes will be apparent when you place content in that area of the table (**Figure 12.75**).

Adjusting Table Spacing

When you're using a table as a page layout tool, it's important to be able to control the space between elements in a table. We've already talked about table borders, which in part control the space between the table and the rest of the page.

Cell spacing is the amount of space between cells—sort of like table borders, but between the cells in a table rather than around the outside of the table. Cell padding is the amount of space between the walls of the cells and the content within them.

To adjust cell spacing (either view):

1. Select the table.

2. In the CellSpace text box, type a number (in pixels) (**Figure 12.76**).

Your changes will be visible in the width of the table's borders (**Figure 12.77**).

To adjust cell padding (either view):

1. Select the table to display table properties in the Property inspector.

2. In the CellPad text box, type a number (in pixels).

You'll notice a difference in the spacing between the content (or the cursor) and the borders (**Figure 12.78**).

✔ Tip

■ You can make these changes only to tables, not to individual cells. In Layout View, you can draw a table around a group of cells, and then adjust spacing properties for the new table. Cell spacing may not be immediately visible on tables with borders set to 0.

Figure 12.76 Type values for cell padding and cell spacing in the Property inspector.

Figure 12.77 I made the cell spacing 10 pixels wide. If I make the border width 0, the cell spacing will be invisible.

Figure 12.78 This is the same table shown in **Figure 12.77**, but I added 10 pixels of cell padding. Notice the space between the characters and the walls of the cells.

Using Vspace and Hspace

You can surround a table with extra space called Vspace and Hspace (above and below the table and to the left and right of the table, respectively), just as you can with images. Macromedia removed this feature from the both the Property inspector and from the WYSIWYG in Dreamweaver 4 because it doesn't work gracefully with Layout View.

To add Vspace or Hspace around a table, add it to the opening table tag, using the Code inspector or the Quick Tag editor:

```
<table vspace="4" hspace="10">
```

Preview the page in a browser to see what your changes look like.

ADJUSTING TABLE SPACING

Figure 12.79 I gave my table a border width of 10. Borders larger than 1 pixel affect only the outside edge of the table, whereas border widths of zero render all borders invisible.

Month	Birthstone
January	Garnet
February	Amethyst
March	Aquamarine
April	Diamond
May	Emerald
June	Pearl
July	Ruby
August	Peridot
September	Sapphire
October	Opal
November	Yellow Topaz
December	Blue Topaz

Figure 12.80 Dreamweaver displays a table with a border width of zero with light, dashed lines in the Document window.

Month	Birthstone
January	Garnet
February	Amethyst
March	Aquamarine
April	Diamond
May	Emerald
June	Pearl
July	Ruby
August	Peridot
September	Sapphire
October	Opal
November	Yellow Topaz
December	Blue Topaz

Figure 12.81 This is the same table we saw in **Figure 12.80,** as viewed in the browser window. The borders are invisible if their width is zero. You can also see your table without dashed lines by toggling off the table borders. From the Document window menu bar, select View > Visual Aids > Table Borders to uncheck that option.

Working with Table Borders

By default, when you insert a table in Standard View, a 1-pixel line, called a border, delineates the edges of the cells and the table. In Layout View, the border is set to 0 and marked with a dashed line. In either view, you can easily change the width and visibility of this border. (See the previous section on cell padding and cell spacing for more about table spacing.)

To adjust border size:

1. Select the table.

2. In the Border text box, type a number and press Enter (Return), or click on the Apply button.

You'll see your border adjustments immediately (**Figure 12.79**); if you set the border width to 0, you'll see a light, dashed line (**Figure 12.80**). No worries: it won't show up in your browser (**Figure 12.81**).

✔ Tips

- You can change the border width to whatever you want, including 0.

- Setting the border width to 0 is also known as turning off table borders.

- You can also set a border color for a table. Select the table and use the color picker, as described in the next section.

- You can toggle off the dashed lines, too, for a quick preview. With table borders set to 0, select View > Visual Aids > Table Borders from the Document window menu bar and they'll disappear.

WORKING WITH TABLE BORDERS

297

Coloring Tables

You can give a table a background color or background image that differs from the background of the overall page. You can also use different backgrounds in rows, columns, or individual table cells, as well as on borders.

To set a table background color:

1. Select the table, cell, column, or row (in either view) for which you want to change the background color (**Figure 12.82**).

2. On the Property inspector, locate the Bgcolor text box for your selection (rather than for text; **Figure 12.83**). Then:

   Type or paste a hex value for the background color in the Bgcolor text box.

   or

   Click on the gray Color selector button to pop up the color picker (**Figure 12.84**), and select a color.

   or

   On the color picker, click on the System Color button  to open up the Color dialog box (**Figure 12.85**). For more on using the Color dialog box, see Chapter 3.

When you're finished making your selection, click on OK to close the Color dialog box, if required. The color change should be apparent immediately.

✔ Tips

- You can also follow these steps for a single cell, a selection of cells, a column (**Figure 12.86**), or a row.

- To close the palette without choosing a color, press the Esc key (Windows only), or click on the Default Color button ▨. Chapter 3 includes more color tips and instructions for using the dialog boxes.

Figure 12.82 Select the table or other element for which you want to set the background.

Text color box

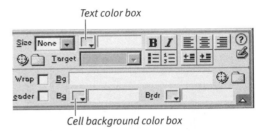

Cell background color box

Figure 12.83 Find the Bg button on the Property inspector. If you've selected a cell, column, or row, there will also be a color box for text properties; it's easy to get them confused.

Figure 12.84 Click on the color box to pop up the color picker, and then choose a color by clicking on it.

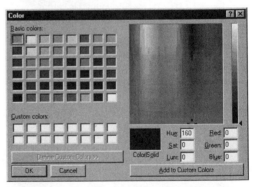

Figure 12.85 The Color dialog box offers additional color selection options. The Color dialog box for the Macintosh is substantively different, as discussed in Chapter 3.

Figure 12.86 I colored one column in this table. Notice that the table, the page, and the column use three different colors.

Figure 12.87 Type the pathname of the background image in the Bg text box on the Property inspector, or click on the Browse or Point to File buttons to use those options.

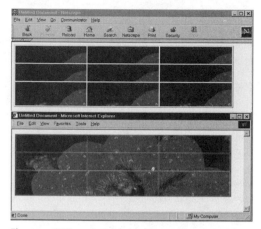

Figure 12.88 I used a table background image in this table. Navigator 4 (top) tiles the image in each cell, whereas IE 5 (bottom) uses the image as a background for the entire table.

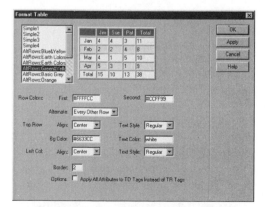

Figure 12.89 Use the Format Table dialog box to choose from predetermined color schemes. Any color choices you make for columns or individual cells will override these default schemes.

Setting a Background Image

You can set a background image for an entire table, a table cell, a column, or a row.

To use a table background image:

1. In Standard View in the Document window, select the table or table element you want to supply with a background image.

2. In the Property inspector, type the URL of the image you want to use in the Bg text box (the larger of the two identically named text boxes) (**Figure 12.87**).

   or

   Click on the Browse button to open the Select Image Source dialog box and select the image from your local machine.

   or

   If you're using a local Site, drag the Point to File icon onto the image file in the Sites window.

Either way, the image path will appear in the Bg text box, and the image will load in the table in the Document window

Figure 12.88 shows a table that uses a background image.

✔ Tip

■ A convenient shortcut for coloring tables is the Format Table dialog box (**Figure 12.89**), which allows you to choose from predetermined background color schemes. To use the dialog box, select the table in Standard View, and then select Commands > Format Table from the Document window menu bar. You can set border width, content alignment, and text options for rows and columns, too. **Figure 12.81** shows a table formatted this way.

Inserting Tabular Data

Using Dreamweaver, you can import complex sets of data from database or spreadsheet files into an HTML table. Theoretically, any program that can save content as a delimited data file (particularly comma- and tab-delimited) can be imported. Specific examples are Microsoft Excel, Microsoft Access, 4D, Emacs, and Oracle (**Figure 12.90**).

Before beginning, you (or your database expert) need to export the information from the database or spreadsheet program into a data file. You must know what character the file uses as a delimiter. If you don't know, get it from your database engineer.

✔ Tip

■ Nearly any database, spreadsheet, or even address book program can save data as comma-delimited or tab-delimited data files. Two notable exceptions are Lotus Notes and FileMaker. You may need to save out data and format it in another application to use data from these applications in a Dreamweaver table.

To import table data:

1. You can use either of two menu commands that work exactly the same:

   From the Document window menu bar, select Insert > Tabular Data.

   or

   File > Import > Import Tabular Data.

   Either way, the Insert Tabular Data (or Import Table Data) dialog box will appear (**Figure 12.91**). The dialog boxes are identical aside from their names.

2. To select the data file containing the data to be inserted into your table, click Browse. The Open dialog box will appear (**Figure 12.92**).

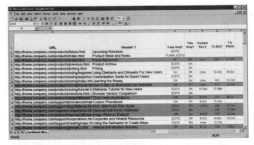

Figure 12.90 I want to put this Excel production worksheet on the corporate intranet. I want to convert it to HTML so that anyone in the office can access it without needing Excel in order to open it. Before I can import this file into Dreamweaver, I will need to save it as a CSV file.

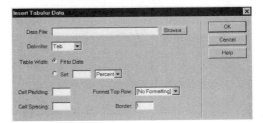

Figure 12.91 The Insert Tabular Data (or Import Table Data) dialog box allows you to choose a database or spreadsheet file to import as an HTML table, and to set parameters for how that table will look.

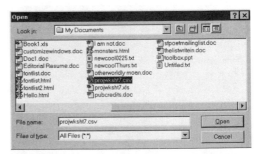

Figure 12.92 In choosing the file to import, note that I chose the CSV file (comma-separated values, in Microsoft terms) rather than the XLS (Excel Spreadsheet file) just below it.

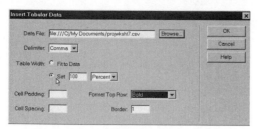

Figure 12.93 I have selected a file to import (the path is shown in the Data File text box); I have selected Comma as the delimiter; I have set the width of the table to 100 Percent of the page; and I have chosen Bold as the top-row formatting.

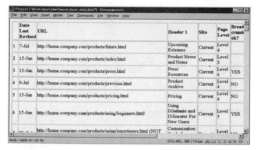

Figure 12.94 After importing the file, Dreamweaver drew this (rather plain) table. I will need to make some changes to make it look better. Also, any columns or fields that were hidden in the Excel file are still imported into the Dreamweaver table.

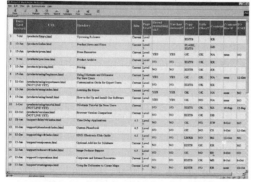

Figure 12.95 I applied Dreamweaver's autoformatting (Commands > Format Table). I also shortened the URLs to site-root relative paths to make the table easier to navigate, and applied some font formatting to the header cell.

3. Select the file and click on Open. You will return to the Insert Tabular Data (or Import Table Data) dialog box (**Figure 12.93**).

4. Your data file uses punctuation to mark the spaces between table cells. Usually, the file is comma-delimited or tab-delimited; it may also use semicolons or colons. Choose the proper mark from the Delimiter drop-down menu.

   or

   If the file uses another delimiter, select Other, and then type the name of the delimiter in the text box that appears.

5. You and Dreamweaver will allocate the width of the table in the Table Width area of the dialog box (**Figure 12.93**).

   To base the table width on whatever space the data takes up, click the Fit to Data radio button. (You can reformat the table later.)

   or

   To set the width—for example, at 100 percent—type an amount in the Set text box, and then choose Pixels or Percent from the Set drop-down menu.

6. To preset Cell Padding and Cell Spacing, type a number in those text boxes. (See the earlier section, *Adjusting Table Spacing*, to find out how this works.)

7. Presumably, the top row will consist of column headings; Mailing Address, for example. To format the top row, select Bold, Italic, or Bold Italic from the Format Top Row drop-down menu (**Figure 12.93**).

8. To set a border (1, 0, or other), type a number in the Border text box.

9. When you're done, click on OK, and Dreamweaver will import the data and create the table in the Document window (**Figures 12.94** and **12.95**).

Exporting Tables

You can also export table data from Dreamweaver into a data file. For instance, if you import data into Dreamweaver and then update the information in Dreamweaver, you may want to open the updated data in your database or spreadsheet program.

Before you begin, you need to have a page containing a table with data in it open in the Document window.

To export table data:

1. From the Document window menu bar, select File > Export > Export Table. The Export Table dialog box will appear (**Figure 12.96**).

2. From the Delimiter drop-down menu, select the delimiter you wish to use. This should be the default delimiter of the program you'll be importing the data into. If you're not sure, Comma and Tab are safe bets.

3. In data files, line breaks are actually characters. From the Line Breaks drop-down menu, select the platform your data file will be opened on. If you're not sure, check with your database guru; if you have to guess, pick Windows.

4. Click on Export and the Export Table As dialog box will appear. You will need to supply a file extension with your filename. If you're not sure what extension to use, you can add it later by changing the name of the file.

5. Click on Save. The Export Table As dialog box will close and the file will be saved on your computer.

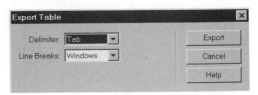

Figure 12.96 You can use the Export Table dialog box to save an HTML table as a data file.

Saving Excel Spreadsheets and Word Tables as HTML Tables

Although you can't paste spreadsheet data into Dreamweaver as you can into FrontPage, you can still convert your Excel spreadsheets into tables. Dreamweaver's features can also help. For Word, see *Cleaning Up Word HTML* in Chapter 4. For Excel, see *Inserting Tabular Data*, in this chapter. For basic advice on converting tables into HTML, read on.

Excel 95-2000 has utilities to save a spreadsheet as HTML. In Excel 95, choose Tools > Internet Assistant Wizard from the menu. For Excel 97 and later, the command is File > Save as HTML. Both of these programs use Wizards to guide you.

You can also save Microsoft Word table data as HTML. In Word 95, you select File > Save As from the menu bar, and choose HTML (*.htm) as the file type. In Word 97 and later, the command is File > Save as HTML.

Once you have one of these Office-created documents saved, you can open it in Dreamweaver and edit the page or cut and paste the table onto an existing page.

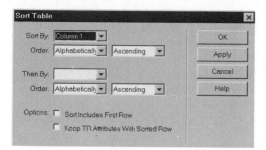

Figure 12.97 Use the Sort Table dialog box to specify criteria by which to sort the contents of a table.

Sorting Table Contents

Typing stuff into a table can be a pain in the butt if you need the contents to be in order. In Microsoft Word and Microsoft Excel, you can type the stuff in any order you like and then sort table contents alphabetically or numerically. In Dreamweaver, you can do the same thing. No, really!

To sort table contents:

1. Click within the table you want to sort.

2. From the Document window menu bar, select Commands > Sort Table. The Sort Table dialog box will appear (**Figure 12.97**).

3. From the Sort By drop-down menu, select the column (by number) to sort by first.

4. From the Order drop-down menu, select Alphabetically or Numerically.

5. From the next drop-down menu, select Ascending (A–Z, 1–9) or Descending (Z–A, 9–1).

6. To sort by a secondary column next, repeat steps 3-5 for the Then By section of the dialog box.

7. To include the first row in your sort, check the Sort Includes First Row checkbox.

8. To have any row formatting travel with the sort, check the Keep TR Attributes With Sorted Row checkbox.

9. Click on OK to close the Sort Table dialog box. The table will be sorted according to the criteria you specified.

FRAMING PAGES

Figure 13.1 Each frame is a distinct document with its own content—including different link and background colors and background images. When you click a link in one frame, the content appears in another window.

Figure 13.2 Designer Derek Powazek uses unusual frames layouts such as this one in his storytelling site The Fray (www.fray.com). The picture on the left stays visible while you scroll through the story on the right.

Web pages that use frames can be extremely versatile, because they allow you to keep parts of your Web site stationary—such as a logo or some navigation bars—while allowing others to change their content. Using frames, you don't have to place the same elements onto every Web page that you build, and the viewer won't have to reload them each time in the browser. A frames-based page is divided into several windows within windows, like the panes in an old-fashioned window (**Figure 13.1**). Frames pages can also blur obvious borders (**Figure 13.2**).

Although a frames-based page acts like a single Web page, each frame contains a single HTML document that can include completely separate contents and independent scrollbars.

The glue that holds together these documents is called the frameset definition document, or the frameset page; a frameset is a set of frames, and the frameset page is what defines them as a set.

Frames and Navigation

You can use frames to create some nifty layouts. Because each page is a discrete HTML document, it can contain any HTML element except the `<frameset>` tag—although we'll find out how to embed frames within frames in the section called *Nested Framesets*.

As I mentioned earlier, frames are best used when you want part of your page, such as a toolbar or a table of contents, to be visible the entire time the page is in the window—regardless of what kind of scrolling or clicking your visitors do.

Each document in a frameset is an individual HTML document. In the background, the frameset page acts as mission control, holding together all the documents. Each frame has a default document anchored to it so that something will load when the frames page is loaded. **Figure 13.3** presents a diagram of the frame structure. You can see the code for a frameset page in **Figure 13.4**—the frameset page is holding together the twelve frames pictured.

✔ Tip

■ The frameset page is called that because it includes the `<frameset>` tag, which defines the layout of the frames-based page, the location and names of the initial pages that occupy each frame, and details about the appearance and actions of the frames.

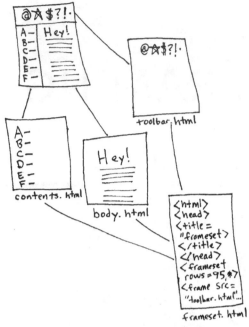

Figure 13.3 An infinite number of pages can be associated with a frames page via links so that your main design remains, while any number of pages can open in different frames within your main page.

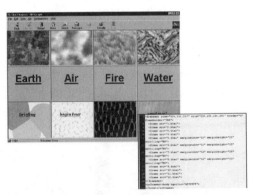

Figure 13.4 A frames-based page is held together behind the scenes by a frameset page, which keeps track of what belongs where. This page has twelve individual frames. The code is for the frameset page that holds these frames together.

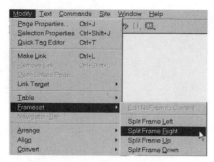

Figure 13.5 Choose Modify > Frameset from the Document window menu bar.

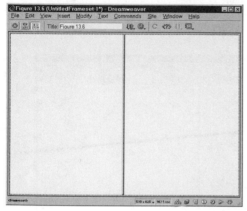

Figure 13.6 The Split Frame Left and Split Frame Right commands both split the current frame in half with a vertical frame border.

Figure 13.7 The Split Frame Up and Split Frame Down commands both split the current frame in half with a horizontal frame border.

Setting Up a Frames Page

Dreamweaver will automatically create a frameset when you divide a page into more than one frame.

To create frames by splitting the page:

1. Start Dreamweaver, and open a blank window, if necessary.

2. From the Document Window menu bar, select Modify > Frameset > (**Figure 13.5**). From there, choose one of the following options:

   ◆ Split Frame Left (**Figure 13.6**)
   ◆ Split Frame Right (**Figure 13.6**)
   ◆ Split Frame Up (**Figure 13.7**)
   ◆ Split Frame Down (**Figure 13.7**)

The window will split to display two frames.

You'll see new borders around each of the frames, as well as the entire page. The frame border outlines each frame. Around the outside of the page, the frame border appears dashed, indicating that the entire frameset page is selected.

Wherefore Untitled Frame 6?

Occasionally, you'll close a document on which you've created no frames, and Dreamweaver will ask you if you want to save an untitled frameset page. Why? Who knows. Just go ahead and click on No, you don't want to save the changes. You won't be losing any data.

Creating Frames by Dragging

You can also create a frame border and drag it to create multiple frames on a page.

To create a frame by dragging:

1. Create a new window, if you like, by pressing Ctrl+N (Command+N).

2. From the Document window menu bar, select View > Visual Aids > Frame Borders. A heavy outline will appear around the blank space in the window (**Figure 13.8**).

3. Mouse over one of the outside borders, and the mouse pointer will turn into a double-headed arrow.

4. Drag it to a new location (**Figure 13.9**), and release the mouse button when you've positioned the border where you choose (**Figure 13.10**).

You now have two frames in the window.

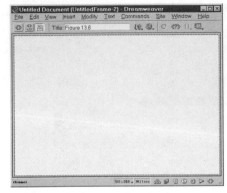

Figure 13.8 The heavy outline that appears should resemble the frame borders you've seen on pages around the Web.

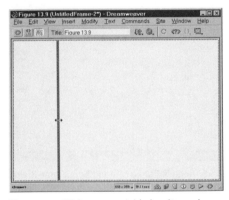

Figure 13.9 Click on an outside border, and you can create a new frame by splitting the original page.

Figure 13.10 Let go of the mouse button when the frame border is where you want. Ta-da! You now have two frames.

CREATING FRAMES BY DRAGGING

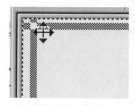

Figure 13.11 If you grab the corner of the page, the pointer will turn into a four-headed arrow, or a grabbing hand on the Mac. Drag the cursor to the middle of the page and let go to create four frames at once.

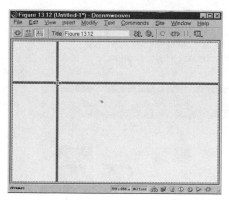

Figure 13.12 Here, I grabbed the top-left corner border, and I'm splitting the page into four frames.

✔ Tips

■ If you mouse over one of the corners of the page, the mouse pointer will turn into a four-headed arrow (**Figure 13.11**), or a grabbing hand on the Mac. You can drag the corner into the page and release the mouse button to create four new frames at once.

■ To split existing frame borders, hold down the Alt (Option) key while dragging a border or a corner border. (**Figure 13.12**).

Quick and Dirty Frames

Dreamweaver features two methods for getting prefab frames layouts: the menu command Insert > Frames and the Frames panel on the Objects panel. Both of these allow you to choose a basic, preset frames page layout without having to figure out what to split.

If you create a frames page using one of these methods, you can skip the next couple of sections about how to add frames to a page, but be sure to read the section called *Targeting Links,* later in this chapter.

To use the Insert Frames menu:

1. Create a new, blank page.

2. From the Document window menu bar, select Insert > Frames (**Figure 13.13**), and then choose one of the following options, as mocked up in **Figure 13.14**:
   ◆ Left
   ◆ Right
   ◆ Top
   ◆ Bottom
   ◆ Left and Top
   ◆ Left Top
   ◆ Top Left
   ◆ Split (Split Frame Center)

   The Document window will create the frameset design you selected (**Figure 13.15**). *Split* splits either the page or the selected frame into four equal squares.

✔ Tip

■ Frames pages created using the Frames menu or Objects panel shortcuts do not have frame borders, and they may have preset resize and scrollbar settings. (See *Frameset Options,* later in this chapter for more about these features). The frames on these pages are also prenamed; see *Naming Frames,* later in this chapter, for more about using frame names.

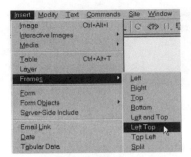

Figure 13.13 Select Insert > Frames from the Document window menu bar, and then choose a layout option.

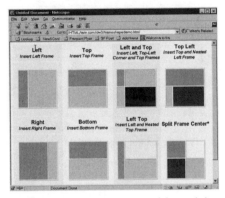

Figure 13.14 The heading over each layout is its name in the Insert > Frames menu, and the subhead is the name of the layout in the Frames panel of the Objects panel. Split Frame Center is available only in the Objects panel.

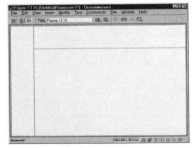

Figure 13.15 I selected Left Top from the Insert > Frames menu, and the layout appeared in the Document window. Note that the frame borders are not heavy; this is how Dreamweaver displays borders that have been turned off (or set to zero width)—in this case, in the preset attributes of the layout.

Figure 13.16 Click on the menu button on top of the Objects panel to display various flavors of objects, including Frames.

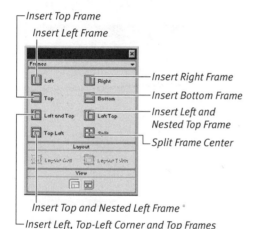

Insert Top Frame
Insert Left Frame
Insert Right Frame
Insert Bottom Frame
Insert Left and Nested Top Frame
Split Frame Center
Insert Top and Nested Left Frame
Insert Left, Top-Left Corner and Top Frames

Figure 13.17 Frames objects are actually layouts that you can apply to your page with the click of a button. I resized the panel (by dragging the lower-right corner) after selecting Frames objects.

Prefab Frames with the Objects panel

The Objects panel also offers similar options for adding frames-based layouts with the click of a button, as seen previously in **Figure 13.14**.

To create frames using the Objects panel:

1. Display the Objects panel, if necessary, by selecting Window > Objects from the Document window menu bar. The Objects panel will appear.

2. Click the menu button at the top of the Objects panel, and from the menu that appears, select Frames (**Figure 13.16**). The Objects panel will display Frame objects (**Figure 13.17**).

3. On Windows, if you mouse over the objects displayed, you'll see Tool tips describing various options. Click on any button to draw that layout, or drag the button to an existing frame to split a single frame in the manner pictured.

continued on next page

QUICK AND DIRTY FRAMES

✔ Tips

■ As with the Insert > Frames menu command, the frames created using the Object panel may have preset values for borders, the names of the frames, and other options such as scrollbars. These options, and how to change them, are described later in this chapter.

■ You may create more than one frameset when you use one of these layouts. If you click within an existing frame and then select one of the preset frames layouts (**Figure 13.18**), the frame you selected will be divided into that frames layout, just as if it were an entire page in the Document window (**Figure 13.19**). This is one way to create *nested framesets,* which are described in detail in the section with that name.

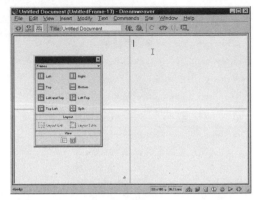

Figure 13.18 First, I used Split Frame Center on a blank page to create four square frames. Then, I selected the top, right frame page by clicking in it.

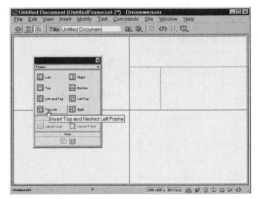

Figure 13.19 I applied the "Insert Top and Nested Left Frame" to the selected, top-right frame, and that frame page divided further into three more frames..

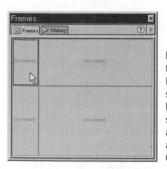

Figure 13.20 In this figure, the Frames panel stands alone. In **Figure 13.21**, I've stacked it with another panel, as described in Chapter 1.

Stacked panel tab

Figure 13.21 When you select a frame, a heavy line appears around the frame in the Frames inspector, and a dashed line appears around it in the Document window. Additionally, the Property inspector displays Frame properties for the frame you selected.

Figure 13.22 When you select an entire frameset by clicking on the frame border in the Document window or Property inspector, the Property inspector displays properties for the frameset.

The Frames Panel

The Frames panel is what you use to select individual frames or entire framesets. To view the Frames panel, select Window > Frames from the Document window menu bar or press Shift+F2. The Frames panel will appear (**Figure 13.20**).

You will need to select each individual frame or frameset in order to modify its properties.

To select a frame:

◆ Hold down the Alt (Shift+Option) key and click on the frame in the Document window.

or

In the Frames panel, click on the frame you want to select (**Figure 13.20**).

In either case, a dashed line will appear in the Document window around the frame you selected, and the Property inspector will display the frame's properties (**Figure 13.21**).

Selecting a Frameset

You can select an entire frameset in one of two ways:

◆ Click on any of the frame borders in the Document window.

◆ In the Frames panel, click on the border around the outside edge of the frames.

Either way, the Property inspector will display properties for the frameset, and a dashed line will appear around all the frames in the frameset (**Figure 13.22**).

Note that the Property inspector displays the layout of columns and rows in a frameset, but all frames are shown with the same dimensions.

THE FRAMES PANEL

Modifying the Frame Page Layout

You have limitless options when it comes to laying out pages with frames. You can divide frames the same way you created them initially: by splitting or by dragging. You'll probably do some experimenting before you achieve the layout you want.

To split frames:

1. In the Document window, click within the frame you want to split.

2. From the Document window menu bar, select Modify > Frameset > (as shown earlier in **Figure 13.5**), and then choose one of the following options: Split Frame Left, Split Frame Right, Split Frame Up, or Split Frame Down.

Splitting left or right, up or down may look exactly the same unless there is already content in the frame. For example, the left window in **Figure 13.23** shows a frame that was split left, and the right window shows the same frame split right instead.

To drag and reposition frame borders:

1. Mouse over the border between two frames, and the pointer will turn into a double-headed arrow (**Figure 13.24**).

2. Click on the border, and drag it to a new location. When the border appears where you want it to, release the mouse button.

✔ Tip

■ To split a frame while dragging it, hold down the Alt (Option) key while you click the mouse button (**Figure 13.25**).

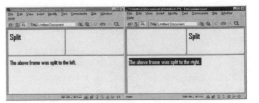

Figure 13.23 These two frames pages are pretty much the same. In the one on the left, the top frame was split left, whereas in the right-hand window, the same frame was split right. Which option you choose depends on where you want any content in the frame to land.

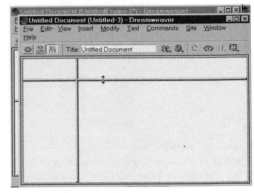

Figure 13.24 When you mouse over a border between frames, the pointer becomes a double-headed arrow that you can use to drag the border.

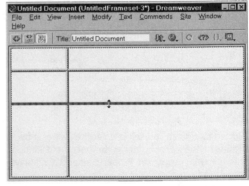

Figure 13.25 If you hold down the Alt (Option) key while clicking on the frame border, you can split a frame by dragging the border.

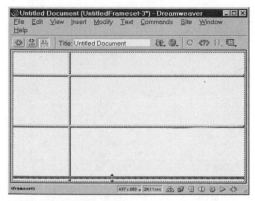

Figure 13.26 Click on the border of the unwanted frame, and drag it off the page. You'll get rid of both the frame and the border.

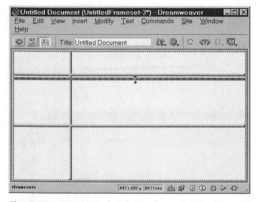

Figure 13.27 You can also drag a frame border into another frame border to get rid of it.

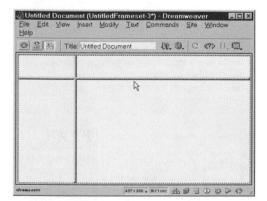

Figure 13.28 Either way, you'll be free of the unwanted frame.

Deleting a Frame

You can keep splitting frames until you achieve the layout you want, but if you create a few frames too many, getting rid of them is easy.

To delete a frame:

1. Click on the frame border, and drag it off the page (**Figure 13.26**).

   or

   Click on the frame border, and drag it until it meets another border (**Figure 13.27**).

2. Let go of the mouse button. The frame will disappear (**Figure 13.28**).

Moving Content Between Frames

Before you delete that frame, you can drag its content into another frame on the page. This works for all sorts of objects, including text, images, multimedia objects, and form fields. Click on the object to select it, or highlight the text you wish to move. Click and hold down the mouse button while you drag the object to a new frame. When the stuff is where you want it, let go of the mouse button, and it will reappear in the new location.

You can also select content and use key combinations to move it.

- To move the selection to an adjacent frame, hold down the Alt (Command) key and press the Left or Right arrow key.

- To move the selection to the parent frameset, press Alt+Up arrow (Command+Up arrow).

- To move the selection into the child frame, press Alt+Down arrow (Command+Down arrow).

Nested Framesets

Once your initial frame page layout is created, you can divide the space within any individual frame by inserting another frameset that is nested within the original frameset. Dreamweaver creates nested framesets automatically when you split a frame. The original frameset is called the parent, and the frameset within the parent set is called the child. You can theoretically keep nesting framesets until the cows come home, and the hierarchy will always have the child frameset reporting to its immediate parent.

An original frameset is shown in **Figures 13.29** and **13.30**. In framesets with no nested framesets inside them, all frame borders go from one edge of the browser or document window to the other. In **Figures 13.31** and **13.32**, the first frameset includes one frame of its own (the left-hand frame), plus the nested frameset. The second, nested frameset includes the two frames in the right-hand column.

Creating a nested frameset involves the same tasks as any other frameset. You can watch how Dreamweaver modifies the code by keeping the Code inspector open while you follow these steps.

To create a nested frameset:

1. Open (or create) a frameset page in the Dreamweaver window (**Figure 13.29**).

2. Click in one of the frames, and then split it by selecting, from the Document window menu bar, Modify > Frameset > and then Split Frame Left, Right, Up, or Down. In **Figure 13.31**, I selected Split Frame Up for the right-hand frame in **Figure 13.29**.

Dreamweaver has created a second frameset nested within the original frameset. You can examine the structure of the document by using the Frames panel.

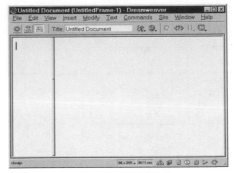

Figure 13.29 Here's a page that contains one frameset that is comprised of two frames.

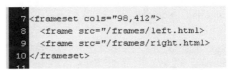

Figure 13.30 In the Code inspector, you can see the highlighted code for the frameset, which includes the locations of the documents within it. Two frames, one frameset.

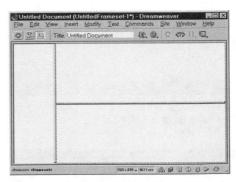

Figure 13.31 I split the right-hand frame in two; in order for one frame to contain two more frames (whose borders don't go across the whole frame), the original frameset must be subdivided to include a new frameset.

Figure 13.32 Now, in the Code inspector, you can see a new frameset tag nested within the original frameset tag.

Nested frameset (child) code selected
Child frameset selected

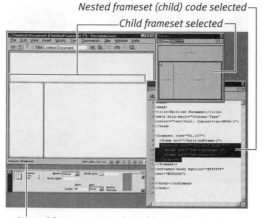

Nested frameset tag selected in tag selector

Figure 13.33 Dreamweaver automatically nests a new frameset inside the original, and you can select the child frameset with the Frames inspector. In the Code inspector, you can see that only the nested frameset code is selected. And in the tag selector, you can see two <frameset> tags, the second of which is selected.

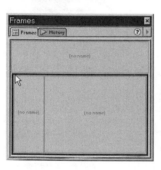

Figure 13.34 Click on the nested frameset border in either the Frames panel or the Document window.

Figure 13.35 In the tag selector, select either the parent or the child frameset (the latter is selected here).

✔ Tips

■ Remember that you may have already created nested framesets by splitting frames or by using one of Dreamweaver's preset layouts.

■ The main reason you need to be aware of nested framesets is so that you can select and modify them separately. I bet you're glad you don't have to hand-code this stuff.

Selecting nested framesets

It can be difficult to tell which frame belongs to which frameset; you can tell by selecting the frame and then the frameset around it (**Figure 13.33**). Additionally, you'll often want to modify the properties of framesets separately.

To select any frameset:

1. Display the Frames panel, if necessary, by selecting Window > Frames from the Document window menu bar.

2. As you click on each frame in the Frames panel, it becomes highlighted. Additionally, a dashed line appears around the frame in the Document window.

3. To select an embedded frameset, click on the heavy border around the frameset in the Frames panel (**Figure 13.34**). A dashed line will appear around each frame in the embedded frameset in the Document window.

✔ Tip

■ You can also select an embedded frameset by clicking on the nested frameset tag in the tag selector (**Figure 13.35**).

NESTED FRAMESETS

317

Setting Column and Row Sizes

Frames, just like tables, are divided into columns and rows. You could think of the individual frames as cells, each of which occupies a certain number of columns and rows. (See Chapter 12 for more on cells, columns, and rows).

When you split a frame or drag a frame border, Dreamweaver translates the information about the position of the frame border into a height or width amount for each frame, in pixels or percent of the window. To adjust the height or width of a frame, you can adjust the row height or column width.

The page in **Figure 13.36** is comprised of two framesets (you can tell because the vertical border doesn't span the entire window). The first frameset is made up of two rows. The top frame, or row, is 112 pixels high. The bottom row is set relative to that height; it will take up the rest of the browser window, however small or large (**Figure 13.37**).

The embedded frameset is made up of two columns. The left column occupies 25 percent of the available space—in this case, it's both 25 percent of the parent frame and 25 percent of the window. The right column, then, can be set to either 75 percent or to *relative* (to the parent frameset's width).

✔ Tips

■ Because the dimensions of any column or row affect the dimensions of the entire frameset, row height and column width are frameset properties, rather than frame properties.

■ It makes sense to set the height and width for one column or row in particular, and to set all other heights and widths as relative to that area of the page.

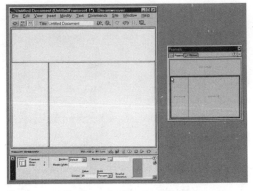

Figure 13.36 The frameset is made up of two rows (across the window), and a nested frameset that has two columns (vertical divisions of the lower frame). In this figure, the Property inspector is displaying Frameset properties for the child (nested) frameset.

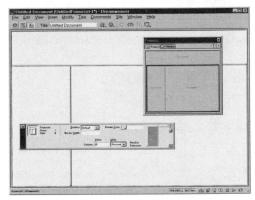

Figure 13.37 Here, you see the same frameset, in a resized (larger) window. Notice how the top frame retains the same, exact size (112 pixels) whereas the bottom frames retain their proportional settings. The left frame still occupies 25 percent of the window.

■ You must set a height or width for each frame in a document in order to guarantee that pixel or percentage widths will be followed when the window is resized.

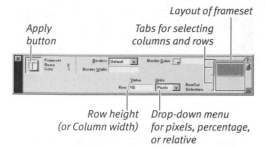

Apply button

Layout of frameset

Tabs for selecting columns and rows

Row height (or Column width)

Drop-down menu for pixels, percentage, or relative

Figure 13.38 The Property inspector displays frameset options when you click on a frame border in the Document window.

Figure 13.39 Click on a tab in the frameset preview of the Property inspector to adjust settings for that column or row.

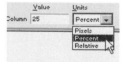

Figure 13.40 Select either Pixels, Percent, or Relative as the units for the height or width measurement.

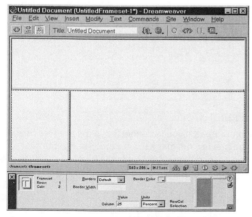

Figure 13.41 On this page, I first selected the parent, or whole-page, frameset and set the top row to 114 pixels and the bottom row to relative. Next, I selected the nested frameset and set the left-hand column to 25 percent and the right-hand column to relative. Always set the most-exact measurements you need first.

To adjust row height and column width:

1. Select the frameset by clicking on a frame border. The frameset properties will appear in the Property inspector (**Figure 13.38**).

2. Click on the Expander arrow in the bottom-right corner of the inspector to display column or row values.

3. Select the column or row whose area you wish to define by clicking on the associated tab, above the column or to the left of the row, in the Property inspector (**Figure 13.39**).

4. Type a value for the column or row in the associated text box and select one of the following units from the drop-down menu (**Figure 13.40**):

   ◆ *Pixels* sets an exact height or width. When the frameset is loaded in the browser, pixel measurements are followed exactly.

   ◆ *Percent* refers to a percentage of window (or frameset) size.

   ◆ *Relative* means that the height or width will be flexible in the frameset, compared to other elements that were given specific pixel or percent measurements.

5. Click on the Apply button to apply the height or width changes to the frameset.

6. Repeat these steps for the remainder of the elements in the frameset, or for additional framesets (**Figure 13.41**).

✔ Tip

■ When a browser is loading a frameset page, it draws the layout in the following order:

   ◆ Pixel measurements are given their space allotment first.

   ◆ Columns or rows with Percentage measurements are drawn next.

   ◆ Frames with Relative settings are drawn to fill the rest of the available space.

SETTING COLUMN AND ROW SIZES

Setting Content Pages

There are two ways you can go about putting content into those pretty, blank frames. One way is to open an existing page in one of the frames of the frameset; the other way is to create your new page right now in one of the frames in the Dreamweaver Document window.

In either case, to determine what your frames page will display when it's loaded into a Web browser, you'll attach a URL to each of the frames in the set.

To attach a page to a frame:

1. Select the frame you want to put some content in. The Property inspector will display the properties of that frame (**Figure 13.42**).

2. The SRC text box currently displays the pathname of the blank, untitled, unsaved page that's in it now. You can:

   ◆ Type (or paste) a location of an existing page—on the Web or on your computer—into the text box.

   ◆ Click on the Property inspector's Browse button  to open up the Select HTML File dialog box (**Figure 13.43**).

   ◆ From the Document window menu bar, select File > Open in Frame to display the Select HTML File dialog box.

If you use one of the two latter options, locate the file on your computer, and then click on Open (Choose) to attach the file to the frame you selected.

If the file you selected is on your local machine, it will appear in the frame within the Document window.

If you type a full Internet URL in the Frame Properties SRC text box, the Document window will display the "Remote File" message (**Figure 13.44**).

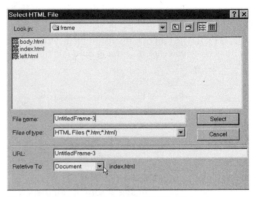

Figure 13.42 When the Property inspector displays frame properties, you can set the location for the default frame document in the SRC text box.

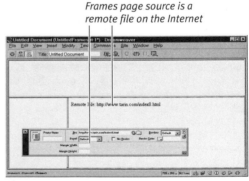

Figure 13.43 Use the Select HTML File dialog box to choose a file to load in the frame. Be sure to select Document from the Relative To drop-down menu.

Frames page source is a remote file on the Internet

Figure 13.44 If you're connected to the Internet when you preview this page in your browser, the browser should load the remote file in the frame.

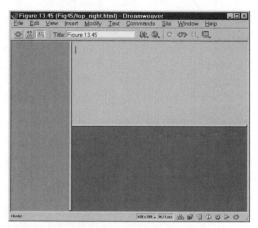

Figure 13.45 This page has three frames, each of which uses a different background color. Back in **Figure 13.4,** eight of the 12 frames used different background images.

Relativity Theory

In my experience most browsers prefer that frames documents be linked to one another using *document-relative links* rather than *site-root relative links*. The frameset document contains the links, and the initial frames pages within the frameset should be given paths relative to that page.

As you can see in **Figure 13.43**, when you select a file to use in a frame, you can use the drop-down menu at the bottom of the Select HTML File dialog box to choose that the files be Relative To the Document or to the Site Root. Choose Document, and Dreamweaver will automatically choose the Frameset page as the relative one.

After you save a page, you can check to see if it has a Document Relative relationship by attaching it to a frame, as described in *Setting Content Pages,* earlier in this chapter, and then making sure that the Relative To drop-down menu says Document instead of Site Root.

Creating Content within a Frame

Creating and editing content within one of the frames in a frameset is the same as doing so in a blank Dreamweaver window, only with less screen real estate.

On frames pages you can put text, images, multimedia objects, and tables—anything that you can use on a non-frames page.

Setting the background color for a frame is just like setting the background color for a stand-alone page. Each frame, remember, is a single HTML document, or page, and each page in the frameset has its own page properties. **Figure 13.45** shows a frames page in which every frame has a different background.

To set a frame background:

1. Display the page properties for the frame in one of two ways:

   Right-click (Control+click) on the frame and select Page Properties from the pop-up menu.

   or

   From the Document window menu bar, select Modify > Page Properties.

   Either way, the Page Properties dialog box will appear.

2. From here, you can adjust page properties for that frame, including background color, background image, page margins, text colors, and link colors.

For more on working with Page Properties, see Chapter 3.

✔ Tip

- Of course, you can create a page in Dreamweaver, save it, and then attach it to a frameset (as described in the preceding section), but if you're creating simple content, you can work easily in the frameset.

Saving Your Work

Because frames pages are made up of multiple documents, saving them is a multi-step process. If you just press Ctrl+S (Command+S), you might not be quite sure of which page you're saving, because Dreamweaver's Save dialog box doesn't offer any distinguishing marks. You need to save each frame separately because they are distinct documents.

You can skip these steps for any previously completed pages you attached to the frameset, as described in *Setting Content Pages*, earlier in this chapter.

To save each frame:

1. Select the frame you want to save by clicking in it in the Document window.

2. From the Document window menu bar, select File > Save, or press Ctrl+S (Command+S). The Save As dialog box will appear (**Figures 13.46** and **13.47**).

3. Type a meaningful filename in the File Name text box. You'll want to be able to distinguish one frame file from another when dealing with these documents later, so choose a name such as left.html or main_body.html rather than frame1.html.

4. Make sure that the Save In list box displays the folder you want to save the files in; otherwise, browse through the folders on your computer and select one.

5. Click on Save to close the Save As dialog box and return to the Document window.

6. Repeat these steps for each frame.

✔ Tip

■ If you create work within a frame in the Document window, you can save your work, and Dreamweaver will automatically set the URL for that page as the default page for that frame.

Figure 13.46 This Save As dialog box is no different from any other one in Dreamweaver. Some other Web page programs, such as Microsoft FrontPage, have distinct Save As dialog boxes for the different parts of a frameset.

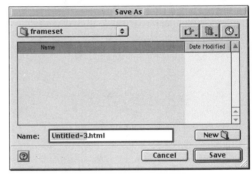

Figure 13.47 The Save As dialog box on the Mac.

Saving All Your Work at Once

After you've saved all the pages in your frameset once, you can periodically save all of them at the same time.

From the Document window menu bar, select File > Save All Frames. Changes to any frames currently open in any Dreamweaver window will be saved. A Save As dialog box will appear for any previously unsaved documents that you have open in Dreamweaver.

Figure 13.48 The URL for this page will end up being something like `http://www.yoursite.com/frameset/frames.html`. If you want your frameset to appear as the default page in a directory, name the frameset document `index.html`, or whatever your house convention is for a default page.

Titling the Frameset Page

Because the frameset page is the one whose URL you'll point to, and because it's the page in charge, you need to give it a title:

1. Select the frameset by clicking on the outermost frame border in the Document window or in the Frames panel. You can double-check that you've selected the frameset instead of a frame, because the filename (or "Untitled Frameset") will appear in the Document window title bar.

2. Type the title in the toolbar's Title text box, and press Enter (Return).

You can also set the page title for the frameset page

You'll see the title in the title bar when you preview the page in the browser window.

Saving the Frameset Page

The frameset page, which contains all the behind-the-scenes data that makes the page function as a frames page, needs to be saved separately as well.

To save the frameset page:

1. With your frames page visible in the Document window, choose File > Save Frameset from the Document window menu bar. The Save As dialog box will appear.

2. Type a meaningful filename in the File Name text box. This filename will be part of the URL, or pathname, for the entire frames-based page (**Figure 13.48**).

3. Make sure that the Save In list box displays the folder you want to save the files in; otherwise, browse through the folders on your computer until you find the one you want.

4. Click on Save to close the Save As dialog box and return to the Document window.

✔ Tips

- It's helpful to save all the files in a frameset in the same folder in order to keep those files separate from the rest of the HTML files on your computer. That way, not only will you be able to locate the files easily and distinguish them from your other projects, you'll have them tidily in their own folder when you get ready to upload them all to the Web.

- Of course, if you also place frameset files in their own directory on your Web site, you should use document-relative filenames, which work in all browsers.

- When you post your site on the Web or open it in the browser window, it's the frameset document that you will be using as the URL.

Frame Page Options

There are several options you can set for the frames in your page, including options for scrollbars and borders, whether the frames can be resized, and margin settings for each frame.

Using scrollbar settings

You can set scrollbar options for each frame on a page. **Figure 13.49** demonstrates the options.

To set scrollbar options:

1. Select the frame whose scrollbar settings you want to change.

2. In the Property inspector, choose a scroll-bar option from the Scroll drop-down menu (**Figure 13.50**):

   ◆ Yes (the frame will always have scroll-bars, whether they're needed or not)

   ◆ No (the frame will never have scroll-bars, whether they're needed or not)

   ◆ Auto (the frame will display scrollbars when they are needed)

   ◆ Default (uses browser default settings, which are usually Auto)

Note that these scrollbar settings affect both horizontal and vertical scrollbars. The Yes and No settings should be used with discretion.

Generally, when a frames page is loaded into a browser window, the user can resize the frames to personal taste or viewing convenience. If you want some or all of the frames in your page not to be resized, you can set the No Resize option.

To use the No Resize option:

1. Select the frame whose size you want to control. The Property inspector will display settings for that frame.

2. Place a check mark in the No Resize checkbox.

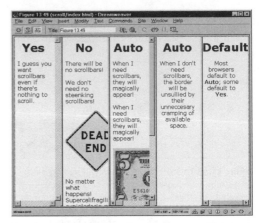

Figure 13.49 Scrollbar options demonstrated here are, from left to right, Yes, No, Auto (with scrollbars), Auto (without scrollbars), and Default. Obviously, Auto makes the most sense most of the time.

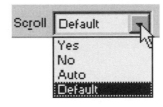

Figure 13.50 Choose one of the scrollbar options from the drop-down menu on the Property inspector.

✔ Tip

■ Obviously, all frames adjacent to frames with the No Resize option selected will not be able to be resized on that border. In **Figure 13.41**, it sure would be nice to be able to resize some of those frames.

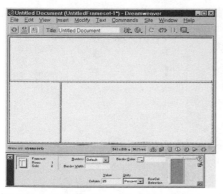

Figure 13.51 Here's the same page we saw in Figure 13.41, with a normal, default frame border. To change back to this setting after a departure, use a frame border of 5.

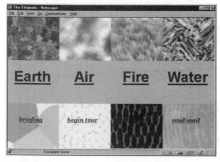

Figure 13.52 Here's the page with a border width of zero. You can also turn off the borders by selecting No from the Borders drop-down menu with an entire frameset selected.

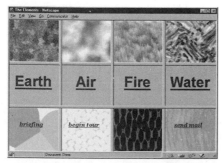

Figure 13.53 Same thing, with a rather thick border of 10. Play around with it; the most interesting effects are between 0 and 10. You can experiment with using different widths for nested framesets or different settings for frames within different framesets.

Using frame borders

You can turn off borders for the frames on a page, and you can set the width of all the borders on a page. You can set these options for a frameset or a single frame.

Figures 13.52 and 13.53 show the same page, with frame borders turned off in Figure 13.52, and a border width of 10 in Figure 13.53.

To turn borders off or on and set widths:

1. Select the frameset or the single frame to which you want to apply border settings. The Property inspector will display options for the frameset or the frame.

2. From the Property inspector's Borders drop-down menu, choose one of the following options:
   - Yes (displays all frame borders)
   - No (hides all frame borders)
   - Default (uses browser default settings, usually displaying borders)

3. To change the border width, select the entire frameset and type a number, in pixels, in the Property inspector's Border Width text box.

✔ Tips

- If adjacent frames have different border settings, No often overrides Yes.

- The default border width is 5.

- You can display or hide borders while you're working in Dreamweaver, regardless of what your final browser settings are. Just select View > Visual Aids > Frame Borders to toggle the borders on and off.

- Border width affects the spacing between the frames on a page whether or not the borders themselves are displayed. In other words, you can set a frame border of 10 and also turn off borders.

Using frame border colors

If you don't turn off frame borders or set their width to zero, you can set a border color.

To choose a border color:

1. Select the frameset, and the frameset properties will appear in the Property inspector.

2. Choose a border color by:

   Typing or pasting a hex code in the Border Color text box.

   or

   Clicking on the Border Color button to display the Colors panel, and then clicking on a color in the Colors panel.

   or

   Displaying the Colors panel, clicking on the Color Wheel button 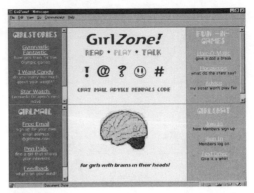, and using the Colors dialog box to select a specific color (see Chapter 3).

The color you selected will be displayed on the frame borders (**Figure 13.54**); the appearance will differ depending on border width.

✔ Tips

■ You can set border colors for individual frames, which will override any border color settings you made for the entire frameset, although your mileage may vary (**Figure 13.55**).

■ Border colors will not display if the borders are turned off or set to 0 width.

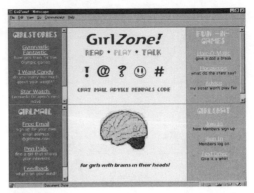

Figure 13.54 This frameset has colored borders and a border width of 3.

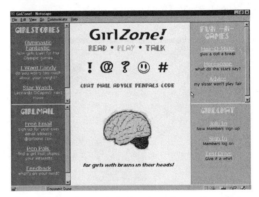

Figure 13.55 I changed the border color setting only for the top-left frame, and all the borders were affected except the border between the middle and right frames.

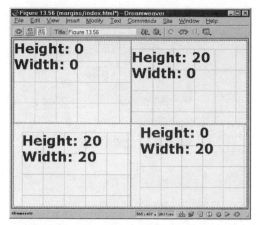

Figure 13.56 I turned on the grid in this view (View > Grid > Show) so that you could see the difference that margin settings make. Each of these four frames has different margin settings. Experiment with different settings for pages that use images or different sizes of text.

Setting Margins

Before Dynamic HTML, the only way to set page margins was by using frames. You can set two border values for each frame in a set: Margin Width (left and right margins) and Margin Height (top and bottom margins).

To set margins:

1. In the Frames panel, select the frame for which you'd like to set margins.

2. In the Property inspector, type a number (in pixels) in the Margin Width and/or Margin Height text boxes.

3. Press Enter (Return), or click on the Apply button to see your changes take effect.

Figure 13.56 demonstrates the effect that margins can have. In Dreamweaver, the upper-left corner of the grid, also called the zero point, actually moves in relation to the upper-left corner of the frame. This is a more accurate and useful depiction of the placement of the content of a frame than in earlier editions of the program. For more about the grid, see Chapter 1. See Chapter 11 to use style sheets to set other kinds of margins.

Targeting Links

Now you have a frames page that looks exactly like you want it to, and you have a default document attached to all the frames in your page. Before you can call your page finished, you need to set targets for the links in your pages (**Figures 13.57** and **13.58**).

When you click on a link in a regular Web page, it generally opens in the same window as the last document you were viewing. In a frames page, however, in which several documents occupy the same window, you don't always want the result of the user's next click—the target page—to appear in the same frame as the link they clicked on. A target tells the link in which frame it should open.

You can set targets so that when you click on a link in a frame, the link opens either in a particular frame in the frameset, or in a specialized target option such as a new window.

♦ If you don't declare any targets for a particular frame, the target page will open in the same frame as the link.

♦ You can set targets so that clicking on a link in one frame opens the page in another frame. Or, you can use one of the special targets (see the sidebar on this page) to control where a document opens.

♦ You can set a default, or base target, for all your frames; then you only need to set individual targets for links that differ from the frame's default target.

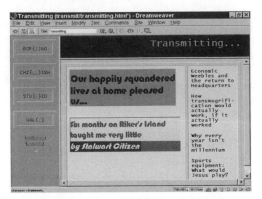

Figure 13.57 This page has an obvious navigation scheme: Click on one of the links in the left frame, and it should appear in the large frame at right. This is only possible using targets.

Figure 13.58 Two versions of the page in **Figure 13.57**. On the left, the targets haven't been set, and the navigation links open in the narrow frame at left. On the right, the left-hand frame was given a default target so the links would open properly in the right-hand frame.

Specialized Targets

In addition to targeting links to open in a specific frame, you can set targets that will control which window the pages will appear in.

♦ `target=_blank` makes the link open in a new, blank browser window.

♦ `target=_top` makes the link replace the content of the current window.

♦ `target=_parent` makes the link open in the parent frame, in cases where you're using nested framesets.

♦ `target=_self` makes the link open in the same frame as the link.

Figure 13.59 Name each frame by selecting it and then typing a meaningful word in the Frame Name text box.

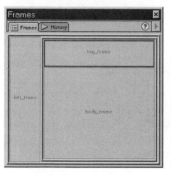

Figure 13.60 After you've named your frames, the Frames inspector will display the name of each frame.

✔ Tips

■ After you name your frames, their names will appear in the Property inspector's Target drop-down menu. In the upcoming section, *Setting Individual Targets,* you'll choose a target from that menu.

■ As is the case with most HTML entities, no spaces are allowed in frame names. Underscores are okay, but hyphens are not. Try to restrict yourself to lowercase letters and numbers.

■ Another great Dreamweaver advantage: You don't have to remember, memorize, write down, or tattoo the names of your frames on your forehead; just refer to the Frames panel.

Naming frames

Before you can set targets, you need to name each frame. A frame name is different from a filename or a page title. The frameset page needs to know both the filename and the frame name of each page in order to be able to load the pages in the proper position and order.

✔ Tip

■ The page title, in cases of frames pages, is unnecessary for all but the frameset page. The page title, as you'll recall, appears in the title bar of the Web browser; it's the frameset page's title that shows up when the frameset page is loaded. See the sidebar *Titling the Frameset Page,* earlier in this chapter.

To name a frame:

1. Select the frame you want to name by clicking on it in the Frames panel. The Frame properties will appear in the Property inspector.

2. Type a meaningful name in the Frame Name text box (**Figure 13.59**). You should be able to distinguish one frame from another by their names; for example, upper_left, main, or toolbar.

3. Press Enter (Return), or click on the Apply button. The name will remain in the Frame text box.

4. Repeat these steps for all the frames in the window.

When you open the Frames panel, the names of the frames will be displayed there (**Figure 13.60**).

Setting Targets

Once you name your frames, you can set a target for an entire frame or for individual links.

Setting a base target for a frame

By default, the target for each link in a frame is the frame itself. To set a different default target, also known as a base target, you need to specify the name of the target in the code. If you know that you'll want every link in your frame to open in a particular target frame, this could save you a lot of time, so you don't have to set each target individually.

To set a base target:

1. Click in the frame for which you want to set the base target.

2. Open the Code inspector for that frame by pressing F10, or by selecting Window > Code inspector from the Document window menu bar.

3. Locate the <head> tag, near the top of the Code inspector. It should look something like this: ─────────────▶

4. Within the <head> tag, but after the <title> tag, type the following line of code

   <base target="name">

   where "name" is replaced by the name of the frame you want to make the default target, or one of the special targeting instructions, such as "_top" (quotation marks included).

5. Your code should now look something like this: ─────────────▶

6. Press Ctrl+S (Command+S) to save the changes to your code. You can close the Code inspector, if you like.

```
<head>
<title>Untitled Document</title>
<meta http-equiv="Content-Type"
content="text/html; charset=
iso-8859-1">
</head>
```

```
<head>
<title>Untitled Document</title>
<base target="main_frame">
<meta http-equiv="Content-Type"
content="text/html; charset=
iso-8859-1">
</head>
```

Figure 13.61 Select the desired target from the Target drop-down menu.

Figure 13.62 Here's what you'll see when you first visit numbers.html: two frames introducing you to the site.

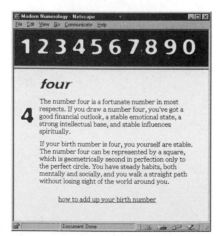

Figure 13.63 Click on one of the numbers in the top frame, and a new page opens in the bottom frame. The top frame has a base target of body, which is the name of the bottom frame.

Although behind-the-scenes changes like this one won't show up visibly in the Dreamweaver window, you can preview your frames pages in the browser window and test them to make sure they work.

Setting Individual Targets

When you want to set a target for a link that differs from the default, or base target, use the Property inspector to select a target for the link.

To target individual links:

1. Select the text or image that you want to target. The Property inspector will display properties for that object.

2. If there's not a link specified for that object as yet, type or paste the URL for the link in the Link text box.

3. From the Target drop-down menu (**Figure 13.61**), select a target. This can be either the name of one of the other frames on the page, or one of the special targets discussed in *Specialized Targets*, earlier in this chapter.

You're all set.

Figures 13.62 and **13.63** demonstrate a simple, common use of targeting: Click on a link in the top frame, and it opens in the bottom frame.

Testing Your Targets

It's vitally important, more so than with almost any other kind of Web page, that you test every link on your frames-based pages. You need to make sure that the links open where you think you told them to open. Targets can be tricky—they don't need to be difficult, but they absolutely must be done correctly if you don't want to drive your visitors away for good. **Figure 13.64** shows the evil recursive frame problem: A link to the entire frameset was accidentally targeted to open in one of the frames.

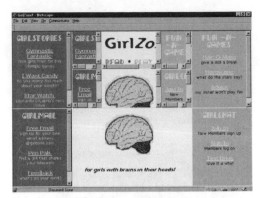

Figure 13.64 A misplaced target can be ugly, at best. Here, we see a recursive frameset—a link to the entire frameset was accidentally targeted to open in the top, center frame.

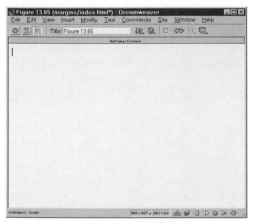

Figure 13.65 From the Document window menu bar, select Modify > Frameset > Edit No Frames Content, and the Document window will display the blank no-frames page.

Figure 13.66 With very little effort, I created a no-frames page that includes all the same links as the frameset page. To appease very old browsers, I also avoided frills like tables, background images, and image maps. See Appendix C on the book's Web site for more details.

Creating No-Frames Content

Not everyone who visits your site will have a frames-capable browser. Although most people are using some version or other of Netscape Navigator or Internet Explorer, not everyone is. See Appendix C on the Web site for the details. The point is that if you don't offer your non-frames visitors something, they won't see anything at all.

At the very least, you need to leave a message that says something like, "This site requires a frames-capable browser, such as Netscape Navigator 2 or later, or Internet Explorer 3 or later." Providing links to a site where they can download this software is also a good idea.

But even that is shortchanging your guests, in a way. Without much work at all, you can give them a fully functional page that will connect them with much of the same information.

To create a no-frames page from scratch:

1. To view the no-frames page, from the Document window menu bar, select Modify > Frameset > Edit No Frames Content. The Document window will display the blank no-frames page (**Figure 13.65**).

2. You can edit this page, including page properties such as background color, the same way you would when creating a page from scratch.

   or

   Select the contents of an existing page, and copy and paste into the no-frames page.

Figure 13.66 shows the no-frames page we created as the alternative to the frames-based page shown in **Figures 13.62** and **13.63**.

To return to the frames view, just select Modify > Frameset > Edit No Frames Content again.

To use existing code in a no-frames page:

1. In the HTML inspector or your favorite code editor, open the HTML or text for the page you want to use.

2. Select all the code between (and including) the <body> and </body> tags, and copy it to the clipboard.

3. In the Dreamweaver Document window, view the no-frames page by selecting Modify > Frameset > Edit No Frames Content from the menu bar. The Document window will display the no-frames page.

4. View the HTML for this page—which is really just part of the frameset document. The empty no-frames code should look like this:

   ```
   <noframes><body bgcolor="#FFFFFF">
   </body></noframes>
   ```

5. Select everything between the <noframes> and </noframes> tags, and delete it.

6. Paste in the HTML from the code you copied in step 2. You should get something like this:

   ```
   <noframes>
   <body bgcolor="#000000">

   This is all the neat content that's
   on my frames page, including <A
   HREF="links.html">links</A> and
   everything!

   </body>
   </noframes>
   ```

7. Save the changes to your HTML, and close the HTML inspector. The page you pasted in will show up in the No Frames Content window.

No-Frames Tips

Check to make sure that:

◆ You don't include any <html> or </html> tags within the <noframes> tags.

◆ You include one, and only one set of <body> and </body> tags between the <noframes> tags.

When you preview no-frames content in your regular browser, it won't show up. Why? Because your regular browser is probably frames-capable, and it will load the frames-based page instead—they are the same document, after all.

See Appendix C, on the Web site, for information about getting and using a non-frames browser for previewing your documents.

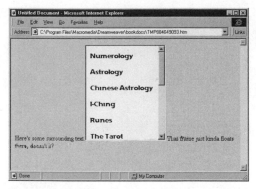

Figure 13.67 The inline frame is a particular feature of Internet Explorer—you'll need to experiment with the IFRAME attributes quite a bit to figure out how they work.

Inline Frames

Internet Explorer (IE) has introduced a proprietary tag called <IFRAME> to make frames appear within a page (**Figure 13.67**). This technique, called inline frames or floating frames, only works with Internet Explorer version 3 or later.

To use inline frames:

1. With the appropriate page open in the Document window, view the HTML code by selecting Window > HTML from the Document window menu bar.

2. Insert the following code

   ```
   <IFRAME SRC="float.html">
   </IFRAME>
   ```

   where "float.html" is replaced by the URL for the content you want to appear in the floating frame.

3. Type or paste some no-iframes content between the two tags, such as "To view this page, you need IE 3 or later."

4. Press Ctrl+S (Command+S) to save the changes to the code.

You'll need to view this page in IE to see the iframe.

This is the code for the iframe in **Figure 13.67**:

```
<IFRAME name="toc" src="toctoc.html"
frameborder=1 height="80%" width=200
scrolling=yes align=center, bottom>
You must use Internet Explorer to view
the inline frames on this page, but you
can get the same content <a
href="toctoc.html">here</a>.
</IFRAME>
```

✔ Tip

■ You can create the same visual effect by using borderless frames in combination with scrollbar options, and the page will be viewable by many more visitors.

Other IFRAME Attributes

You can adjust the appearance and behavior of an IFRAME by using these other attributes within an IFRAME tag. You should recognize most of these attributes from this and other chapters. As always, the pipe (|) means "or."

```
name="name"
align=top|middle|bottom|left|right|
   center
```

(Pick two, as in align="top, center".)

This has more to do with the relationship between the frame and the other content than with the position of the frame.

```
frameborder=1|0 (1=yes, 0=no)
height=x|"x%"
width=x|"x%"
marginheight=x
marginwidth=x
scrolling=yes|no|auto
```

LAYERS AND POSITIONING

Figure 14.1 This little collage is made with three layers, positioned so that they overlap in the browser window. Can't do that with tables!

Layers enable you to control the exact position of your elements on a Web page. A layer is basically a container for HTML content, delineated by the <div> or <span> tag, that you can position anywhere on a page. Unlike table cells, you can make layers overlap, or stack on top of one another. You can also use separate layers to make objects appear, disappear, or even move across your page.

Layers are called layers because they can be positioned in three dimensions. You can set an absolute or relative location for a layer along the page's X and Y axes. The third dimension is called the Z-index, which allows layers to overlap one another (**Figure 14.1**).

Designers really love layers for their versatility: they make Web pages more dynamic. For example, you can hide layers (through visibility), or even parts of layers (with the Z-index or with clipping areas) when a page initially loads. Then you can write a script that will cause the hidden areas to appear after a certain amount of time or when a certain user event happens (see Chapters 16 and 17 for information on Behaviors and Timelines).

✔ Tip

■ Browsers prior to IE or Netscape 4.0 will display the content of a layer. However, they ignore most layer properties, including positioning. See Appendix C on the Web site to find out how to accommodate older browsers.

CSS Positioning

Layers are part of the world of Cascading Style Sheets and Dynamic HTML. Cascading Style Sheets Positioning, or CSS-P, allows the most specific positioning in HTML to date. Earlier methods, using tables, frames, and frame margins, don't approach the specificity you can reach with CSS-P. Layout tables (see Chapter 12) give you some of the design flexibility, but they don't let you overlap elements, or animate parts of your page with timelines and behaviors.

You can apply CSS Positioning to a block of text, a block-type element, an image, or a layer. There are two ways to apply positioning: One is to create a style class and apply it to the selections or text blocks you want to position on the page (at which point, the object becomes a layer, for all practical purposes). The other is to create a layer in the Document window that you can modify independently of creating a style.

X and Y coordinates

A layer or other positioned element is positioned using X and Y coordinates. X and Y correspond to Left and Top. This can be the left and top of the page itself or of another parent container, such as another layer or a text block (**Figure 14.2**).

The Z-index

The third property of a layer aside from positioning on the X and Y axes is the *Z-index,* or stacking order. This property is used when there are two or more layers on a page that overlap, and it indicates the order in which the layers stack on top of one another (**Figure 14.3**). The higher a layer's Z-index, the closer it is to the top of the stack.

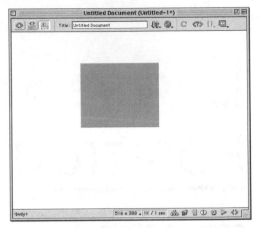

Figure 14.2 This layer is positioned 150 pixels from the left side of the window, and 70 pixels from the top of the window.

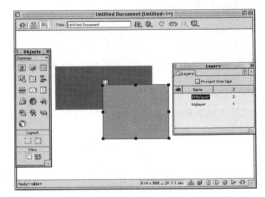

Figure 14.3 The smaller layer is positioned over the top of the bigger one. That means it has a bigger Z-index.

Layers and Animation

Dynamic HTML means that you can make layers change or move after the page is finished loading. Timelines, discussed in Chapter 17, are used to animate layers over time. The Show Layer Behavior and the Drag Layer Behavior both allow layers to change when the user performs an action. I describe both these behaviors in Chapter 16.

Figure 14.4 In static positioning, the layer is simply treated as a text block and thrown into the normal flow of text.

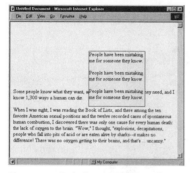

Figure 14.5 Relative positioning places the layer according to the specified X and Y coordinates, but it still affects the flow of text. The <div> tag, for instance, causes a paragraph break after the layer. Compare to **Figure 14.6**.

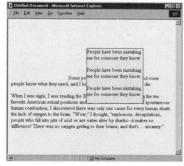

Figure 14.6 This code is exactly the same as in **Figure 14.5** except it uses a <span> instead of a <div> tag.

Absolute vs. Relative Positioning

The position of an element in an HTML document can be either absolute, relative, or static.

Normal positioning is called *static,* and causes the element to be positioned within the normal flow of text. Specifying coordinates for static positioning does you no good, as they will be ignored (**Figure 14.4**).

Relative positioning means that a layer or other element is given a position relative to the top-left corner of the parent container. However, the relative element is included in the flow of the page, and is also inline—it does not automatically cause any line breaks (**Figure 14.5**). To guarantee the inline properties, a <span> tag should be used instead of a <div> tag (**Figure 14.6**).

An element such as a layer that is positioned *absolutely* is completely outside the flow of the document. The regular flow of the material on the page neither contains the layer, nor is it interrupted by the layer (**Figure 14.7**).

Figure 14.7 The layer is back to being a <div> now, and it's positioned absolutely. That means that the regular text flow once again starts at the top of the page, and the layer simply overlaps it.

Positioning Properties

Positioning properties can be applied to any object, but when you set these properties, the behavior of the object becomes similar to layer behavior. Dreamweaver then treats it as a layer, although the browsers may respond differently to positioned elements that are not enclosed in <div> or <span> tags.

To apply positioning to objects other than layers, create and apply a style, as described in Chapter 11, using the Positioning properties in the Style Definition dialog box (**Figure 14.8**). In general, it's easier to create layers individually using the steps detailed in this chapter. Once you have the hang of both layers and style sheets, you can create a style that you can use to create batches of layers.

The following properties are discussed more fully throughout this chapter in terms of layers.

Type lets you designate the positioning as *absolute, relative,* or *static.*

Visibility determines whether the element will be visible when the page loads. You can declare an element as visible or hidden, or you can allow it to inherit its properties from the parent element. Using behaviors (Chapter 16), you can make a layer's visibility change over time or when the user performs an action.

Z-Index (**Figure 14.9**) determines the stacking order of overlapping elements; the Z-index is the third coordinate, combined with X and Y, that determines the location of the layer on the page in three dimensions. The higher the number, the higher priority the element is given (a layer with a Z-index of 3 will be stacked on top of elements with a Z-index of 1 and 2).

If the layers have no background colors, and the images within the layers use transparency, you can stack layers so that images appear to overlap one another (**Figure 14.10**).

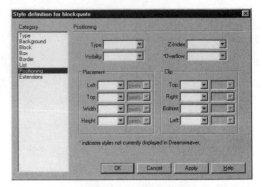

Figure 14.8 The Positioning panel of the Style Definition dialog box. I describe everything else to do with styles in Chapter 11; positioning is discussed in this chapter in terms of layers.

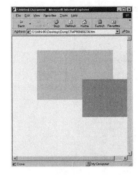

Figure 14.9 Two simple, rectangular layers. One is stacked on top of the other.

Figure 14.10 Each of these images is in a layer, and both images are transparent, so that each appears to float on the page.

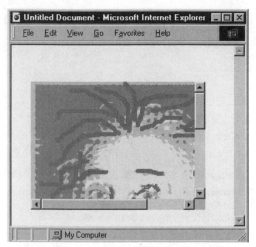

Figure 14.11 Internet Explorer will provide scrollbars for content that exceeds the dimensions of the layer. You can also designate this content as visible or hidden.

Figure 14.12 The clipping region allows you to define which areas of the layer are visible or hidden when the page loads. In this instance, only the top half of the image is being displayed on load.

Overflow determines the behavior of the layer when the content exceeds the borders of the layer. You can designate the out-of-bounds content as visible or hidden; or the layer can be given scrollbars to make the rest of the content accessible (generally, auto also provides scrollbars) (**Figure 14.11**).

✔ Tip

■ Overflow treatment is not displayed properly in Dreamweaver or supported by Navigator 4.x, but it is supported by Netscape 6. In Navigator 4, overflow content is visible, even if another option is set.

Placement (Figures 14.9 and **14.10**) of a layer is determined by its distance from the *Left* and *Top* of the parent unit. The *Width* and *Height* measurements are related to placement in that they determine the position of the lower-right corner of the layer.

Clip refers to the clipping area of the layer: the area of the layer in which content shows through (**Figure 14.12**). You could give a layer an area of 200 pixels by 200 pixels, and then allow only a 100x100 pixel area to show through. You set a clipping area as a rectangular area comprised of four measurements (Top, Right, Bottom, and Left).

✔ Tip

■ The clipping area is unrelated to overflow. Overflow is simply related to the layer's dimensions, regardless of whether a clipping region is defined.

POSITIONING PROPERTIES

Other Positioning CSS Attributes

Some other style-sheet attributes are somewhat related to positioning, although they position text rather than other objects. Still, here's a list for reference: All Block attributes position text (**Figure 14.13**), and you can use Text Align (**Figure 14.14**) to control the spacing of text within a layer. Miscellaneous others that you can use include Line Height, which is a Text attribute; the Position List attribute, which relates to indents; and most Box attributes, particularly Float, Clear, Margins, and Padding. You can also use Border attributes to place borders around a layer. These are all covered in Chapter 11.

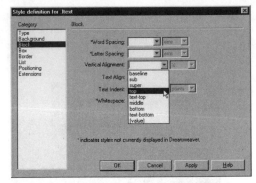

Figure 14.13 The Block panel of the Style Definition dialog box is where you apply vertical alignment attributes to text blocks or selections.

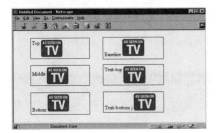

Figure 14.14 Vertical alignment options using styles.

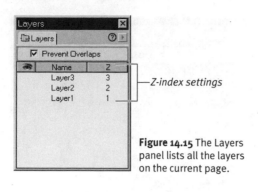

—*Z-index settings*

Figure 14.15 The Layers panel lists all the layers on the current page.

About the Layers Panel

The Layers panel (**Figure 14.15**) lists all the layers on the current page. When you create a new layer, its name will appear in the Layers panel.

To view the Layers panel:

◆ From the Document window menu bar, select Window > Layers.

   or

   Press F2.

Either way, the Layers panel will appear.

About the Grid

The grid displays an incremental series of boxes that look like graph paper. You can use grid lines to guide you in positioning or resizing layers.

To view the grid:

◆ From the Document window menu bar, select View > Grid > Show Grid.

The grid will appear (**Figure 14.16**).

About the Rulers

The rulers can be displayed along the top and left of the Document window to guide you in positioning and resizing layers.

To view the rulers:

◆ From the Document window menu bar, select View > Rulers > Show.

The rulers will appear (**Figure 14.17**).

✔ Tip

■ I discuss changing the preferences, snap-to settings, and units of the grid and rulers in *Customizing the Document Window* in Chapter 1.

Figure 14.16 Viewing the grid can give you a better idea of the position of things.

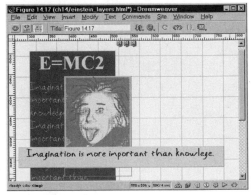

Figure 14.17 View the rulers, with or without the grid, when you want to measure exactly where things are.

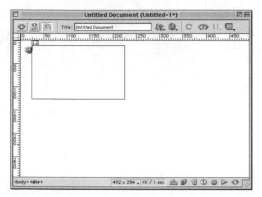

Figure 14.18 When you place a layer using the Insert menu, a default layer appears. You can change the properties of this layer after placing it.

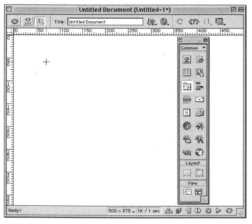

Figure 14.19 After you click on the Draw Layer button, the pointer will turn into crosshairs you can use to draw the layer.

Creating Layers

Before you can dig your fingers into all the nifty layer features, you need to put a layer on the page. You can insert a layer using the Objects panel, in which case you draw the layer on the page; or you can use the Insert menu, which places a default layer. In either case, you can modify the layer's size and location after placing it.

✔ Tip

■ You can modify the default layer properties. See *Layer Preferences*, near the end of this chapter.

To place a layer using the Insert menu:

◆ From the Document window menu bar, select Insert > Layer.

A default layer will appear at the top-left corner of the Document window (**Figure 14.18**).

To place a layer using the Objects panel:

1. View the Objects panel, if necessary, by selecting Window > Objects from the Document window menu bar.

2. Click on the Draw Layer button: 📑. The cursor will appear as crosshairs in the Document window (**Figure 14.19**).

3. Click the cursor at the point where you want the top-left corner of the layer to begin, and drag the cursor to where you want the bottom-right corner to be.

continued on next page

4. Let go of the mouse button, and a layer will appear in the Document window (**Figure 14.20**).

Along with the layer, a layer marker will appear that shows where the layer's code appears within the code of the page.

✔ Tip

■ If the layer markers aren't visible, view them by selecting View > Visual Aids > Invisible Elements. You can toggle the markers on and off this way as often as you choose.

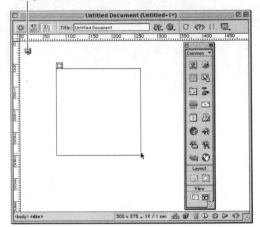

Layer marker

Figure 14.20 After you draw a layer, it appears exactly where you positioned it. A layer marker also appears in the window, indicating the layer's location in the code.

Layer button on Objects panel
Layer marker
Layer selection handle

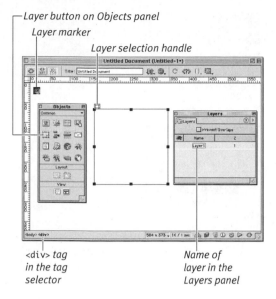

<div> tag
in the tag
selector

Name of
layer in the
Layers panel

Figure 14.21 To select a layer, you can click on the layer's selection handle; the layer marker in the Document window; the <div> or <span> tag in the tag selector; or the layer's name in the Layers panel.

Figure 14.22 When a layer is selected, eight handles will appear around the borders of the layer, and its name will appear highlighted in the Layers panel.

Figure 14.23 The Property inspector, displaying Layer properties.

Selecting Layers

In order to delete, move, or resize a layer, you need to select it. Clicking within a layer does not select it. There are several ways you can select a layer.

To select a layer:

1. Click on the layer.

2. Click on the layer's selection handle at the top-left corner of the layer (**Figure 14.21**).

   or

   Click on the name of the layer in the Layers panel.

   or

   Click on the layer's border.

   or

   Click on the layer's marker in the Document window.

   or

   Click on the layer's tag (<span>, <div>, <layer>, or <ilayer>) in the tag selector at the left of the Document window's status bar (**Figure 14.21**).

Eight points, called handles, will appear on the edges of the layer (**Figure 14.22**), and the name of the layer will become selected in the Layers panel. And, of course, our good old friend the Property inspector will display Layer properties (**Figure 14.23**).

When a layer is selected, you can delete it if you choose.

To delete a layer:

1. Select the layer.

2. Press the Delete or Backspace key.

The layer will go away.

Renaming a Layer

Layer names are used by the browser and by any scripts that treat the layer as a script object. By default, Dreamweaver names each successive layer "Layer1," Layer2," and so on.

You may want to give your layers more meaningful names.

To rename a layer:

1. Select the layer.

2. In the Property inspector, select the old layer name and delete it (**Figure 14.24**).

   or

   In the Layers panel, click on the name of the layer and hold down the mouse button (Windows) or double-click on the layer name (Macintosh). The row holding the name of the layer will become highlighted, and the name of the layer will appear in a text box.

3. Type the new name of the layer in the text box (**Figure 14.25**).

The layer will be renamed.

Figure 14.24 Type a new name for your layer in the Property inspector's Layer text box.

Figure 14.25 Type a new name for your layer in the Layers panel.

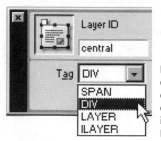

Figure 14.26 You can change tags by clicking on the Tag drop-down menu in the expanded Property inspector.

Choosing Tags

There are four tags used in creating layers. The <div> and <span> tags create what is called a CSS layer. The <div> tag uses absolute positioning; a paragraph break surrounds the <div> tag. If you prefer to create a layer that's inline with the rest of the page, without paragraph breaks, then you want to use the <span> tag, which uses relative positioning.

To change tags:

1. Select the layer.

2. In the Property inspector, choose either <div> or <span> from the Tag drop-down menu (**Figure 14.26**).

The tag will change to reflect your choice.

✔ Tip

■ The other available tags, <layer> and <ilayer>, are Netscape tags. I discuss the special properties of those tags in *Netscape's Layer Tags,* near the end of this chapter.

Moving Layers

The location of a layer on the page is measured by the distance from the top-left corner of the page (or the parent layer) to the top-left corner of the layer itself. You can change the location of a layer at any point—before or after you put content in it.

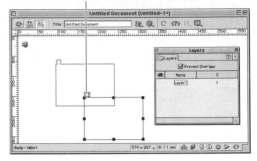

Figure 14.27 Click on the layer's selection handle and drag it to a new location.

To change the layer's location by dragging:

1. Select the layer.

2. Click on the layer's selection handle (**Figure 14.27**) and drag it to its new location (**Figure 14.28**). ·

   or

   Use the arrow keys to move the layer in one-pixel increments.

✔ Tip

■ To move the layer using the grid's snapping increment, select the layer and hold down the Shift key while using the arrow keys to move the layer.

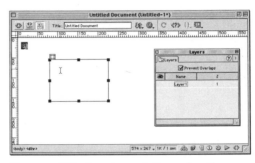

Figure 14.28 The layer is now in its new location.

To change a layer's location using exact measurements:

1. Select the layer.

2. In the Property inspector, type the distance of the layer from the left margin in the L (Left) text box, and the distance of the layer from the top margin in the T (Top) text box (**Figure 14.29**).

3. Press Enter (Return), or click on the Apply button.

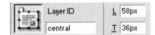

Figure 14.29 Type the X and Y (Left and Top) coordinates in the Property inspector's L and T text boxes.

The layer will change position on the page.

✔ Tip

■ The default units for positioning are pixels, but you can use cm, in, and other units. See the sidebar *Units*, in Chapter 11.

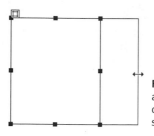

Figure 14.30 Click on the corner handle and drag it to resize two sides of a layer at once.

Figure 14.31 Click on a side handle and drag it to move one side of a layer.

Resizing Layers

You can change the height and width of a layer at any time, before or after you add content to the layer. You can resize a layer by clicking and dragging, by using the keyboard, or by typing exact measurements in the Property inspector.

To resize a layer by dragging:

1. Select the layer. The handles will appear.

2. To change both the height and width of the layer, click on one of the corner handles and drag it (**Figure 14.30**).

3. To change only one of the dimensions, click on one of the side handles and drag it (**Figure 14.31**).

When you let go of the mouse button, the layer will be resized.

To resize a layer using the keyboard:

1. Select the layer.

2. To resize by eyeballing it, press Ctrl+arrow (Option+arrow).

To resize using the grid's snapping increment, press Shift+Ctrl+arrow (Shift+Option+arrow).

✔ Tip

■ To find out how to change the grid settings, refer to *Measuring in the Document Window* in Chapter 1.

To resize a layer using exact measurements:

1. View the Property inspector, if you haven't already.

2. Select the layer.

3. In the Property inspector, type the width of the layer in the W (Width) text box, and the height of the layer in the H (Height) text box (**Figure 14.32**).

4. Press Enter (Return), or click on the Apply button.

✔ Tip

■ If you resize a layer with content already inside it, such as an image or a piece of text, you cannot make the layer visibly smaller than the content it contains. You can still resize the layer's measurements (as displayed by the Property inspector), but the layer will expand, or rather, not shrink, to fit the content. See *The Clipping Area* and *Content Overflow* to find out how to manage content size.

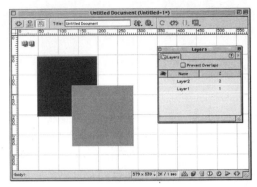

Figure 14.32 You can type new dimensions for your layer in the W(idth) and H(eight) text boxes in the Property inspector.

Prevent Overlaps checkbox unchecked

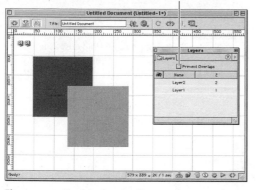

Figure 14.33 Two overlapping layers.

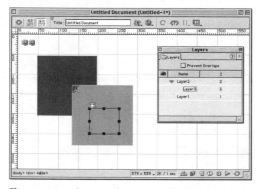

Figure 14.34 I drew one layer nested inside the other.

Figure 14.35 The Layers panel displays nested layers indented beneath their parent layer.

- To prevent layers from overlapping or nesting at all, check the Prevent Overlaps checkbox on the Layers panel. If you have already overlapped some layers when you check this option, and you want to un-overlap them, you'll need to do it manually, by dragging.

Nesting and Overlapping Layers

One neato thing about layers is that you can put a layer within a layer, or you can create two layers that overlap.

To overlap two or more layers:

All you need to do is move two layers so that they overlap, or create a layer that shares page area with another layer (**Figure 14.33**).

You can also nest two layers, which may or may not also overlap. Nested layers are placed on the page in relative position to the top, left corner of another layer rather than to the top, left corner of the page.

To nest a layer within a layer:

1. Create the first layer.

2. If you want the layers to overlap, make sure the Prevent Overlaps checkbox is unchecked on the Layers panel.

3. Click to place the insertion point within the existing layer.

4. Create a second layer inside the first (**Figure 14.34**).

The Layers panel will display nested layers indented beneath the name of the layer that contains them (**Figure 14.35**). The parent layer is the one that holds the child layer nested beneath it.

✔ Tips

- If you draw the layer, you may have to hold down the Ctrl (Option) key while you're drawing in order for the layers to be nested. See *Layer Preferences* for more details.

To nest two existing layers:

1. In the Layers panel, click on the name of the layer you wish to nest inside another layer (the child layer). A layer icon will appear (**Figure 14.36**).

2. Hold down the Ctrl (Command) key and drag the name of the layer on top of the name of the parent layer. A box will appear around the name of the new parent (**Figure 14.37**).

3. Let go of the mouse button. The name of the child layer you dragged will appear indented beneath the name of the new parent (**Figure 14.38**).

You may decide that you don't want one layer to be nested inside the other.

To un-nest a layer:

◆ Click on the layer's name (**Figure 14.39**) and drag it so that it's no longer indented beneath the parent layer's name.

✔ Tips

■ When you nest or un-nest a layer, its position may change (in other words, it may move; see **Figure 14.40**), because nested layers' positions (on the X-Y axis) are based on the parent layer's position. Just drag it back to where you want it.

■ In the Layers panel, you can collapse or expand the list of layers that are nested within the layer. Just click on the + sign next to the parent layer's name to expand the list, or the – sign to collapse the list.

■ When you're working with nested layers, the easiest way to select a layer is by clicking on its name.

■ You can also determine the stacking order of layers by dragging their names around. To find out about stacking order, refer to *Stacking Order,* later in this chapter.

NESTING AND OVERLAPPING LAYERS

Figure 14.36 Hold down the Ctrl (Command) key and click on the name of the to-be-nested layer in the Layers panel.

Figure 14.37 Drag the layer onto its parent layer's name.

Figure 14.38 Let go of the child layer, and it will become nested, and its name will be indented under its parent.

Figure 14.39 Click on the child layer that you want to un-nest.

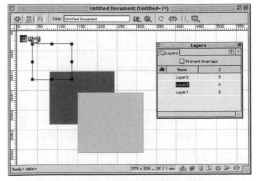

Figure 14.40 Drag the child away from its parent, and it will no longer be nested. Note that the new layer moved from its position in **Figure 14.34** because its position is now relative to the upper-left corner of the page, not of its parent.

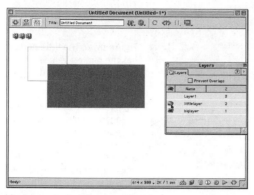

Figure 14.41 The layer that was on top and visible in **Figure 14.40** has been hidden.

Figure 14.42 You can set the visibility of each layer individually by changing the status of the eyeball in the visibility column.

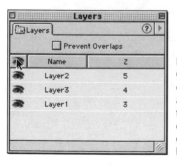

Figure 14.43 Click on the eyeball button at the top of the visibility column to show or hide all layers at once.

■ You can use hidden layers with Timelines or Behaviors (see Chapters 16 and 17), so that layers become visible over time, or when certain actions are performed.

Changing Layer Visibility

When you're working on a page with lots of layers, you may want to show or hide various layers depending on what area of the page you're working with. This is especially convenient when you're working with overlapping or nested layers.

Layer visibility also determines whether a layer will be visible when a page loads.

The layer's visibility is determined by its "eyeball status" in the Layers panel. The eyeball is a three-way toggle switch:

◆ A closed eye ![closed eye] means the layer is hidden.

◆ An open eye ![open eye] means the layer is visible.

◆ No eyeball means that the layer's visibility is determined by the status of the parent layer, if any.

To show or hide a layer:

1. In the Layers panel, click on the name of the layer you wish to view or hide.

2. Click within the leftmost column until you change to the desired eyeball status: closed, open, or none.

The layers will appear or disappear (**Figure 14.41**), as indicated by the eyeball (**Figure 14.42**).

To show or hide all layers:

◆ Click on the eyeball button at the top of the leftmost column in the Layers panel (**Figure 14.43**).

All the layers will appear with an open eyeball, or disappear with a closed eyeball.

✔ Tips

■ Layer visibility goes beyond working with Dreamweaver; hidden layers will not appear on the page when viewed in the browser window.

Stacking Order

The stacking order, or Z-index, of layers, determines the order in which the browser will draw them, as well as their stacking priority (**Figures 14.44** through **14.46**).

✔ Tips

■ Although Dreamweaver uses the term "stacking order" to describe the Z-index, that doesn't mean that it's an exclusive scale. If you have three non-overlapping layers on different parts of the page, you can make the Z-index 1 for all of them.

■ If two layers with the same Z-index (or with no Z-index specified) overlap, the first layer listed in the code will be placed on the top of the heap.

You can change each layer's Z-index individually, or you can determine the stacking order of all the layers in the Layers panel.

To change the Z-index of a single layer:

1. Display the Property inspector, if necessary, by selecting Window > Properties from the Document window menu bar.

2. Select the layer.

3. In the Property inspector (**Figure 14.47**), type a Z-index for the layer: the bigger the number, the higher the priority (a Z-index of 2 goes on top of a Z-index of 1).

Figure 14.44 The little person has the highest Z-index in this cheesy little montage.

Figure 14.45 In this version, I changed the overlap so that the gun has the highest Z-index, the sign is second, and the person is third. The money remains on the bottom.

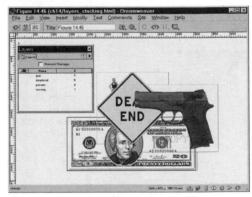

Figure 14.46 This is what the carnage looks like in Dreamweaver.

Figure 14.47 You can set the Z-index by typing a number in the properties inspector's Z-index text box.

Figure 14.48 You can move the order of the layers in the Z-index by dragging their names in the Layers panel.

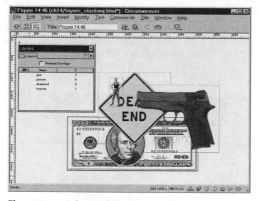

Figure 14.49 I dragged the "person" layer up through the stacking order. Its Z-index is now 6 (Dreamweaver gets sloppy with the numbering), and it's visible above the "deadend" layer.

To rearrange the stacking order in the Layers panel:

◆ Click on the name of a layer in the Layers panel, and drag it up or down to change its position (**Figure 14.48**).

The first layer listed in the Layers panel (and therefore, listed first in the code) has the highest priority in the stacking order, and so on down the line (**Figure 14.49**).

✔ Tips

■ Take care not to drag the layer's name onto the name of another layer; this will indent one layer beneath the other and thereby nest the layers (see *Nesting and Overlapping Layers,* earlier in this chapter).

■ The Layers panel may renumber the Z-index strangely when you drag layers; you might start out with index numbers of 3, 2, and 1 and end up with 6, 4, and 1. You can reset these in the Property inspector, if you like.

STACKING ORDER

Content and Layers

A layer can hold nearly any other kind of
HTML content: text, images, tables, forms,
multimedia content, and, as discussed previously, other layers.

To add content to a layer, click on the layer so
that the insertion point appears within it,
and then add content as you would to any
other part of a Web page (**Figure 14.50**).

✔ Tips

- You can drag content from outside a layer
to within the layer's borders. Just select
the object you wish to move, hold down
the mouse button, and drag it within the
borders of the layer.

- You can put nearly anything in a layer,
except a frame. You can put a form in a
layer, but you cannot spread out form
content over more than one layer.

- If a layer contains less content than the
layer's borders would indicate, Navigator
4.0 displays only the content (not the
entire layer)—although the layer's dimensions will still be considered in the layout.
Explorer 4.0 or later and Netscape 4.5 or
later display the entire layer dimensions,
regardless of the content (**Figure 14.51**).

- Pre-4.0 browsers will display the content
of layers, but will ignore the positioning,
overlap, and visibility attributes. The <div>
tag acts like a <p> tag, and the <span> tag
acts like a <br> tag (**Figure 14.52**).

- When drawing layers, Netscape has a
resize bug for which Dreamweaver offers
a JavaScript fix. See the sidebar, *Netscape
Resize Fix*, later in this chapter.

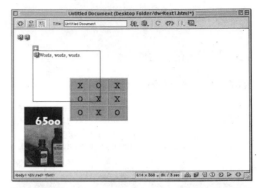

Figure 14.50 You can add any kind of content you want
to a layer. Here we've added a table, some text, and an
image to the various layers on this page. Just about
the only thing you can't put in a layer is a frame.

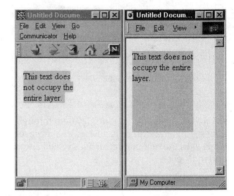

Figure 14.51 Navigator (on the left) displays
only the part of the layer that contains content,
not the entire layer.

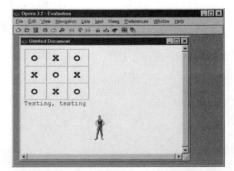

Figure 14.52 Pre-4.0 browsers such as Opera
3.2 display the content of layers, but ignore the
positioning attributes. The person image was
centered within the layer and is now centered
on the page.

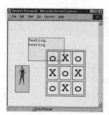

Figure 14.53 On this page, I redefined the `<div>` tag using style sheets so that all layers made with the `<div>` tag would have a one-pixel-wide black border.

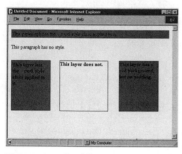

Figure 14.54 On this page, I assigned the .red class to the first paragraph and to the first of the three boxes. The third box has a red background color, but it is not modified by the .red class.

Layers and Styles

All the versatile style sheet attributes that I discussed in Chapter 11—not just positioning—can be applied to layers.

When you create a layer in Dreamweaver, the style attributes that guide the layer's behavior generally appear as the ID attribute directly within the `<div>` tag (rather than as a class or tag redefinition, in which case the attributes would appear in the `<style>` area of the `<head>` tag).

You can, as I discussed in Chapter 11, redefine the `<div>` or `<span>` tag so that it attains new properties that will be applied to every layer you create using those tags (**Figure 14.53**). For instance, you could redefine the `<div>` tag so that it always has a solid, 1-pixel border.

You can also create a style class that you can apply to a layer by selecting the `<div>` or `<span>` tag and then applying the class to the tag (**Figure 14.54**). For example, you could create a style called `.box` that would include a solid, 1-pixel border and use it on selected layers.

Or, let's say you were playing along at home by following up your experiments with styles in Chapter 11 by viewing the source code and learning how to write style sheets on your own. You can type additional styles into the code for your layers.

Layer code—pre-content—might look something like this:

```
<div id="Layer2"
style="position:absolute; left:23px;
top:155px; width:358px; height:33px;
z-index:2; background-color: #FFCC33">

</div>
```

All that stuff in the `<div>` tag is style sheet code. You can apply as many additional style attributes to a layer as you want. You can apply them by hand, by using the Property inspector on a layer, by creating a style class, or by redefining the tag. See Chapter 11 for more on CSS.

359

The Clipping Area

Layers are somewhat like table cells in that they expand to fit the content you put in them. Although you can specify an exact size for a layer, it will expand beyond those dimensions if you place larger content in it.

A layer is unlike a table cell, however, in that you can specify a clipping area for it. As I mentioned earlier, the clipping area is the part of the layer that is visible; it's somewhat like cropping an image, only the rest of the content remains hidden rather than being deleted out of the file. (The file size of clipped content remains the same as if you hadn't clipped it.)

You can make your clipping area the same size as the layer's area, or smaller than those dimensions (**Figures 14.55** and **14.56**). (You could make it larger, but that kind of defeats the purpose of having a layer of that size.)

To define the clipping area:

1. Display the Property inspector and expand it so that all the properties are displayed, if necessary.

2. Select the layer.

3. Define the clipping area by typing the numbers that define the region in the Top, Left, Right, and Bottom text boxes of the Property inspector (**Figure 14.57**).

4. Press Enter (Return), or click on the Apply button to apply the changes to the layer.

The area defined by the clipping area will be visible, and the rest will be hidden.

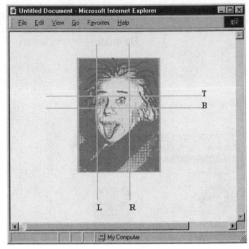

Figure 14.55 Clipping explained: The layer is the same size as the image. Lines T and B are measured from the top of the layer. T is 70 pixels from the top, and B is 96 pixels from the top. Lines L and R are measured from the left of the layer. Line L is 20 pixels from the left, and Line R is 101 pixels from the left. The rectangular area framed by these lines is what will be left visible. (I drew these lines; you're not going to see them when you clip a layer.)

Figure 14.56 The layer as it looks post-clip (in Dreamweaver, so you can see the outlines of the layer).

Figure 14.57 Define your clipping area using the Property inspector.

✔ Tips

■ The L and R measurements are from the left edge of the layer, and the T and B measurements are from the top edge of the layer (**Figure 14.55**).

■ The clipping occurs as follows: The area from the left margin of the layer to the L measurement is clipped out, and the area from the R measurement to the right margin is also clipped out. The area between L and R, therefore, is visible. The same goes for T and B, respectively (**Figure 14.56**).

■ Unspecified units are in pixels; you may define other units in the following format: 1.5cm (no space between the number and the unit).

■ To find how to manage content that exceeds a layer's dimensions, see *Content Overflow* on the following page.

■ For Navigator, you can define all four of these areas, or you can define only the bottom and right (the top and left will be set to zero, which is the top-left margin of the layer.)

■ For Explorer, however, you *must* indicate a measurement of zero for the top and left, if that's what you want.

Content Overflow

When the content of a layer is larger than the layer's dimensions (independent of the layer's clipping area), you have what is called *content overflow*.

You can let the browser defaults take care of content overflow in their own ways, or you can set one of three properties for content overflow: hidden, visible, or scroll. The last option adds scrollbars to the layer so users can scroll to see the rest of the layer's content (**Figure 14.58**).

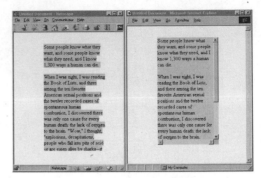

Figure 14.58 Navigator (left) displaying the hidden setting, and Explorer displaying the scroll setting for the same layer.

To control content overflow:

1. Select the layer.

2. In the expanded Property inspector, choose *hidden, visible,* or *scroll* from the Overflow drop-down menu (**Figure 14.59**).

3. Click on the Apply button.

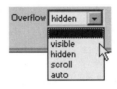

Figure 14.59 Select a content overflow setting from the Overflow drop-down menu on the Property inspector.

Dreamweaver doesn't display content overflow—it always displays all the contents of the layer, regardless of whether they exceed the layer's dimensions.

✔ Tips

- If you don't choose a setting (if you leave the drop-down menu blank), the browser will display all the contents of the layer, regardless of the layer's dimensions.

- The auto setting translates as hidden in Navigator and scroll in Explorer.

- Navigator 4 does not support the scroll setting.

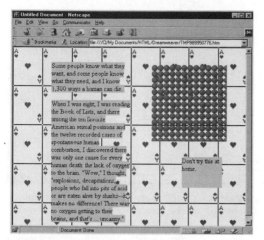

Figure 14.60 This self-consciously ugly page has a background image, over which the three layers are superimposed. In the layer at the upper right, the background image is a transparent GIF through which the background of the page shows.

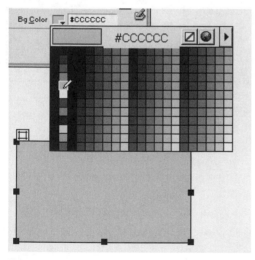

Figure 14.61 You can set a layer background color by clicking on the color box and choosing a browser-safe color from the color picker.

Setting a Background

Layers, like tables, table cells, and CSS text blocks, can have their own background colors or background images. Layer backgrounds will be layered over other background colors or images on the page (**Figure 14.60**).

To set a layer background color:

1. Select the layer.

2. In the Property inspector, type a hex code or color name in the Color text box.

   or

   Click on the color box to pop open the color picker, and choose a color by clicking on it (**Figure 14.61**).

   or

   In the Color selection menu, click on the Color Wheel button 🎨 to open the Color dialog box.

✔ Tip

■ For information about using the Color dialog box, see Chapter 3.

To set a layer background image:

1. Select the layer.

2. In the Property inspector, type the URL of the background image in the Bg image text box.

   or

   Click on the folder icon to open the Select Image File dialog box. Browse through the files and folders on your computer until you find the image file you want to use; then click on Open to select the file.

✔ Tip

■ You can apply additional attributes to a background image using style sheets. See the section of Chapter 11 called *Background Attributes*.

Layer Preferences

When you insert a layer using the Insert menu, Dreamweaver plunks down a default layer, and you can then adjust those properties (**Figure 14.62**). Of course, Dreamweaver being so clever, you can adjust the properties for those default layers, too. All the default properties except size properties will also be applied to layers you draw using the Draw Layer button on the Objects panel.

To set default layer properties:

1. From the Document window menu bar, select Edit > Preferences. The Preferences dialog box will appear.

2. In the Category list box at the left of the dialog box, click on Layers. The Layers panel of the dialog box will appear (**Figure 14.63**).

3. You can decide whether to use a <div>, <span>, <layer>, or <ilayer> tag for your layers by default. To change the default, choose one of these options from the Tag drop-down menu.

4. By default, visibility of the layers is controlled by the activity on the page. To make all layers visible or hidden by default, choose one of those options from the Visibility drop-down menu. You can also choose Inherit to have nested layers inherit their visibility from their parents.

5. The dimensions of a default layer are 200x115 pixels. To change these, type new dimensions in the Width and Height text boxes.

6. You can set a default background color or image for all new layers. Set these attributes as described in *Setting a Background*, earlier in this chapter.

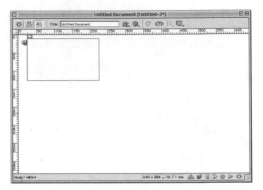

Figure 14.62 A default layer placed using the menu command Insert > Layer.

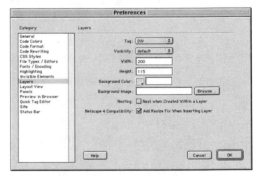

Figure 14.63 The Layers panel of the Preferences dialog box.

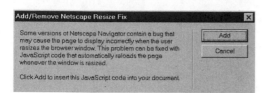

Figure 14.64 Click on Add to add the resize script to your page.

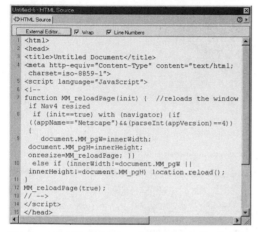

Figure 14.65 This is the complete script, in the Code inspector.

7. The Nesting option, when checked, makes all overlapping layers nested by default.

8. The Netscape 4 Compatibility option automatically adds JavaScript to each page that features one or more layers. The script fixes a resize bug; to use it, check the Add Resize Fix when Inserting Layer checkbox. See the sidebar, this page, for more details.

9. When you're all hunky-dory with your choices, click on OK to close the Preferences dialog box. Your choices will be applied to your next new layer.

✔ Tip

- You can toggle the automatic nesting of layers on and off by holding down the Ctrl (Option) key.

Netscape Resize Fix

Netscape Navigator version 4 and later display layers, but when you resize a Navigator window, any layers on the page may move around or scale improperly. Sometimes they disappear entirely.

Dreamweaver offers a small bit of JavaScript that detects whether the browser is Navigator 4, and if so, forces Navigator to reload the page when the window is resized, and therefore to redraw the layers properly.

To add this fix automatically to each and every page that uses layers, use the Netscape 4 Compatibility option as described in step 8 in *Layer Preferences* (this page).

You can also add this fix to a single page, even if it doesn't use layers.

1. From the Document window menu bar, select Commands > Add/Remove Netscape Resize Fix. The dialog box in **Figure 14.64** will appear.

2. Click on Add to add the fix. The code is shown in **Figure 14.65**.

To remove the resize fix—for instance, if the page no longer uses layers or if you're saving a 3.0 version of the page—repeat these steps and click on Remove.

Netscape's Layer Tags

Although layers are normally created by applying positioning attributes to <div> and <span> tags, the concept of layers is named after two proprietary tags introduced by Netscape with its first beta release of Navigator 4.

The <layer> and <ilayer> tags act similarly to CSS-P layers, in that you can control placement and overlap, but they also possess a few additional properties. The <ilayer> tag is for inline layers, which are embedded in the parent layer (**Figure 14.66**). You can also nest two layer tags; nesting behavior is somewhat different with Netscape layers (**Figure 14.67**).

Neither the <layer> nor <ilayer> tag is supported by Explorer or by Netscape 6. Their behavior in Dreamweaver is vaguely related to the way they appear in Navigator.

To create a layer or ilayer:

1. Create a layer as you normally would.

2. With the layer selected, choose Layer or Ilayer from the Tag drop-down menu in the Property inspector.

The CSS layer will become a layer or ilayer, and the Property inspector will display additional properties for the layer (**Figure 14.68**).

Figure 14.66 An ilayer (inline layer) nested within a layer.

Figure 14.67 A layer nested within a layer.

Figure 14.68 The Property inspector displays additional options for <layer> and <ilayer> tags.

Additional Netscape Layer Properties

The additional properties of Netscape's `<layer>` and `<ilayer>` tags are as follows:

When you're nesting two Netscape layers, you can choose between two X-Y relationships for the two layers. Top, Left refers to the regular relationship a nested layer's position has to the top-left corner of its parent layer. Choosing PageX, PageY instead changes a nested layer's location so that it relates to the top-left corner of the page rather than to the parent layer. (Your mileage may vary.)

Netscape layers can also have a relative Z-index relationship. You can position a layer as appearing Above or Below a "sibling" layer—that is, a layer that shares a parent container, whether that's a parent layer or the page itself. Both layers must already exist when you create Above and Below settings.

✔ Tips

- When working with nested layers, parents automatically appear below children in the Z-index.

- Netscape Layers and `<div>` tag layers don't nest together very nicely.

Setting Netscape Layer Properties

You can set the relationships between Netscape layers. You can also display an entirely other HTML document as the content of the layer by specifying the URL of the document in the Layer Source text box.

To set Netscape layer properties:

1. Create the <layer> or <ilayer> and select it.

2. To set either the Top, Left or PageX, PageY relationship, click on the associated radio button in the Property inspector.

3. To set the Above/Below relationship, choose Above or Below from the A/B drop-down menu, and then choose the name of the associated sibling layer from the drop-down menu to the right of the A/B menu.

4. To choose a source page for layer content, type the URL of the page in the Src text box.

   or

   Click on the folder icon to pop open the Choose HTML File dialog box, and browse through the files and folders on your computer to locate the file. When you find the file, click on Open to select it.

The <nolayer> Tag

Layers are proprietary, and importing layer source code is really, really proprietary.

Browsers that don't support the <layer> and <ilayer> tags, including Explorer 4, will display the content of a Netscape layer, completely devoid of positioning and of any scripting effects applied to it.

You can use a <nolayer> tag to either insult or "enlighten" users with browsers that don't support the <layer> and <ilayer> tags. Just add some code similar to the examples below.

For instance:

```
<LAYER SRC=monkey.html></LAYER>
<NOLAYER> You could see my dancing
monkey if you had Netscape 4 or later,
but you don't. Neener neener. </NOLAYER>
```

Or you could be a bit nicer:

```
<LAYER SRC=monkey.html></LAYER>
<NOLAYER> <img
src=/images/monkey.gif> This monkey
would really put on a show if you
downloaded <a href="home.netscape.com/">
Netscape</a>. </NOLAYER>
```

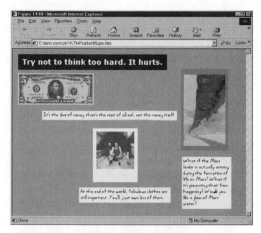

Figure 14.69 It would be a pain in the butt to write the code for tables that would replicate this layers-based layout. I'm showing this page in the browser window.

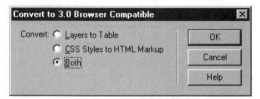

Figure 14.70 The Convert to 3.0 Browser Compatible dialog box lets you save layers as tables, style sheets as font tags, or both.

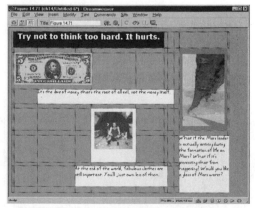

Figure 14.71 After converting the layers in **Figure 14.69** into tables, this is what the page looks like in Dreamweaver.

Converting Layers to Tables (and Vice Versa)

As versatile a layout tool as layers are, it's still the case that only version 4 and later browsers display them properly—although the content may be visible in earlier browsers, the positioning and Z-index properties will be ignored, which render the layers useless.

You can, however, export a layer-designed page into table format and then use a browser-detection behavior (see Chapter 16) to send the browser to the layered or non-layered page. You can also use layers to create a mockup for a complex layout and then convert your design into a table-based layout—although the Layout Tables feature of Dreamweaver 4 will do the job, too (see Chapter 12).

To convert layers to tables, in three steps:

1. Open the page that contains the layers you want to save as a table (**Figure 14.69**). Save the page if you haven't done so.

2. From the Document window menu bar, select File > Convert > 3.0 Browser Compatible. The Convert to 3.0 Browser Compatible dialog box will appear (**Figure 14.70**).

3. Select the Layers to Table radio button, and click on OK. A new, unnamed window will appear, containing a table that reproduces your layers layout (**Figure 14.71**).

Don't forget to save the new page.

✔ Tip

■ Dreamweaver cannot convert overlapping or nested layers. To prevent layers from overlapping before you begin designing, select the Prevent Overlaps checkbox on the Layers panel. If you have overlapping or nested layers on your page, you must manually un-nest the layers and readjust their positions so they do not overlap.

To convert layers to tables, with more options:

1. Open the file with the layers (**Figure 14.72**) and save it under a new name (File > Save As). If you don't do this, you'll lose your original layers design when you save your document.

2. From the Document window menu bar, select Modify > Convert > Convert Layers to Table. The Convert Layers to Table dialog box will appear (**Figure 14.73**).

3. In the Table Layout area of the dialog box, click on either Most Accurate or Smallest. Most accurate will perfectly replicate the placement on the page, but it may create an ungodly number of tiny cells in order to do so. The Smallest: Collapse Empty Cells setting will eliminate small gaps between layers and create a more stream-lined layout using a simpler table.

   If you choose Smallest, you can set the minimum number of pixels a column or row can be before it's included in the layout of the table.

4. Check the Use Transparent GIFs check-box, to insert transparent spacer images in the bottom row of your table to guar-antee exact widths for your columns. For more about controlling column widths, see Chapter 12.

5. To center your table on the page, select the Center on Page checkbox. Otherwise, your table will be left-aligned.

6. The other options—Prevent Layer Overlaps, Show Layer Palette, Show Grid, and Snap to Grid—control the visibility of your layout tools; these are really more useful when converting tables to layers.

7. Click on OK. Dreamweaver will convert your layers to a table (**Figure 14.74**).

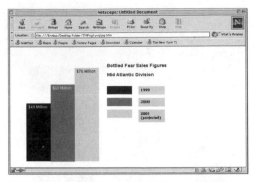

Figure 14.72 This page—bar chart, key, and all—was designed using layers and style sheets. Although it's convenient to be able to use HTML to present graphs, the design won't display in pre-4.0 browsers.

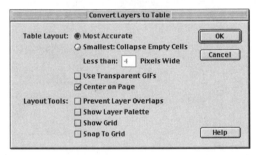

Figure 14.73 The Convert Layers to Table dialog box lets you set options for controlling the layout of the new table.

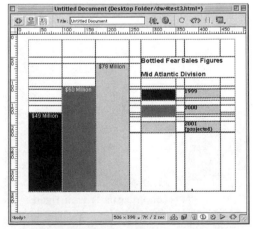

Figure 14.74 Dreamweaver automatically converted the layers-based design into a tables-based page. Each layer is a table cell; transparent GIFs also space the content.

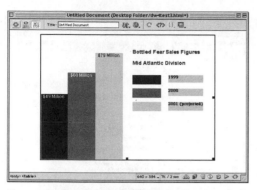

Figure 14.75 You can temporarily turn off table borders to see what the page will look like by selecting View > Visual Aids > Table Borders.

Figure 14.76 Tables-based layout.

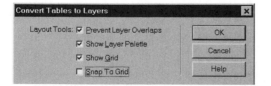

Figure 14.77 The Convert Tables to Layers dialog box offers options for creating and viewing your new layers page.

✔ Tips

- You can temporarily toggle off table borders to see the layout more clearly. From the Document window menu bar, select View > Visual Aids > Table borders (**Figure 14.75**).

- Any layers already on the tables-based page will be left untouched when you convert tables to layers.

- For more details on saving CSS pages as backwards-compatible pages, see the sidebar, *Saving CSS as Plain HTML*, in Chapter 11.

Converting tables to layers

You can also convert tables to layers in order to manipulate the cells on the page for a more precise layout. You can later convert those layers back to tables, if you like.

To convert tables to layers:

1. If you have not done so, save (File > Save As) your tables-based page (**Figure 14.76**) under a new name. If you're using a local site, save the page to the site in which the page will appear.

   The tables-based layout in **Figure 14.73** is okay—but if I convert each cell into layers, I could use Behaviors (Chapter 16) or Timelines (Chapter 17) to animate or otherwise control individual layers.

2. From the Document window menu bar, select Modify > Convert > Tables to Layers. The Convert Tables to Layers dialog box will appear (**Figure 14.77**).

continued on next page

3. The options in the dialog box let you preset options for the new window that will open.

- ◆ To automatically guard against overlaps, check the Prevent Layer Overlaps checkbox.
- ◆ Check the Show Layer Palette checkbox to make sure the Layers panel is open when the page opens.
- ◆ Check the Show Grid checkbox to view the grid when the page opens.
- ◆ The last item, Snap To Grid, you may actually want to uncheck. This will make all the layers on the page align with the grid, in the set increment (the default is 50 pixels).

4. When you've made your selections, click on OK to convert your tables into a layers-based page. Each table cell becomes a unique, individual layer positioned where the cell was in the original layout (**Figure 14.78**).

Now, if you like, you can reposition the layers at will. Following your design tweaks, you can follow the steps in the previous section to convert the layers back into a table (**Figure 14.79**).

✔ Tip

- ■ You'll get a new page if you convert by using File > Convert to 3.0, but not if you use Modify > Layout > Convert Layers to Table (or Tables to Layers). Make sure you save copies of what you need to save copies of.

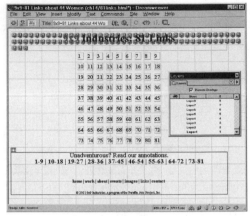

Figure 14.78 Each table cell in the original layout is now a layer, for a grand total of 83 layers (you can deselect View > Invisible Elements to hide the layer markers). Again, I wouldn't have wanted to position all those layers by hand.

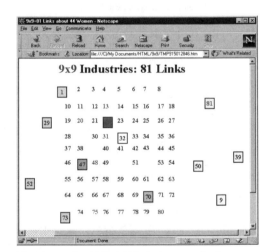

Figure 14.79 I twiddled with the layout using layers, and then converted the page back to tables and previewed it in Navigator 4.5. Using the same design in layers mode, I could create some interesting visual effects using the Drag and Drop Layers Behavior (Chapter 16) or Timelines (Chapter 17). I made the boxes using the Box and Border style sheet attributes (Chapter 11).

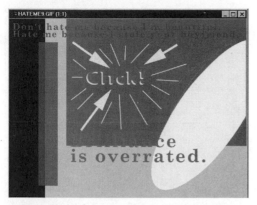

Figure 14.80 Here's an example of an image you can cut up and place as slices on a Web page. You can use the entire, un-sliced image as the tracing image on the background of the page.

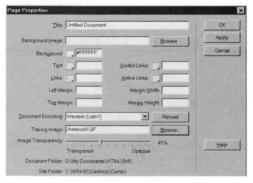

Figure 14.81 In the Page Properties dialog box, you can select an image file to use as a tracing image, and then set the opacity of that image. Tracing images will not show up in browser previews or on the Web.

Figure 14.82 This tracing image is displayed at 40 percent opacity in the Document window.

Using a Tracing Image

Some designers like to create page mockups in Photoshop (or another image editor) before production starts in on the HTML page itself. Wouldn't it be nice if the page hackers could view the mockup image behind the page and just drag and drop elements onto it?

Using Dreamweaver, you can do just that. You can display your mockup image (**Figure 14.80**) in the degree of transparency you prefer and then position layers on top of the image so that they line up exactly where God (or the designer) intended.

Then, of course, you can convert the exacting layers-based design into a tables-based page that the non-4.0 world can ooh and aah over.

To set a tracing image:

1. From the Document window menu bar, select Modify > Page Properties. The Page Properties dialog box will appear (**Figure 14.81**).

2. In the Tracing Image area of the dialog box, type the location of the image or click on the Browse button to pop open the Select Image Source dialog box and locate the image file (.jpg, .gif, or .png) on your hard drive.

3. Drag the Image Transparency bar to set the transparency/opacity of your image so that you can work with it.

4. Click on Apply to preview your tracing image (so you can adjust transparency).
   or
   Click on OK to close the Page Properties dialog box.

Either way, the tracing image will appear in the Document window, behind any content already in the window (**Figure 14.82**).

continued on next page

Now you can slice up an image in Fireworks or another editor, and then you can create a layer for each slice and drag each one onto the tracing image, replicating the image's layout (**Figure 14.83**).

To toggle the tracing image on and off:

◆ From the Document window menu bar, select View > Tracing Image > Show.

To move the tracing image:

1. From the Document window menu bar, select View > Tracing Image > Adjust Position. The Adjust Tracing Image Position dialog box will appear (**Figure 14.84**).

2. Type the X (top) and Y (left) coordinates for your tracing image in the text boxes.

   or

   With the Adjust Tracing Image Position dialog box open, use the arrow keys on your keyboard to move the tracing image in one-pixel increments.

3. When you're done, click on OK to close the dialog box and return to the Document window.

To reset the tracing image:

◆ From the Document window menu bar, select View > Tracing Image > Reset Position. The tracing image will resume its default coordinates.

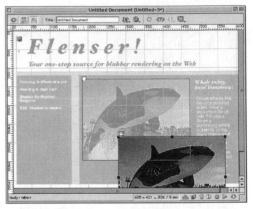

Figure 14.83 Using the tracing image as a guide, I'm placing GIF slices of the original image on the page, using layers to place them exactly. If I want to, I can replicate the tracing image and then convert the layers into tables.

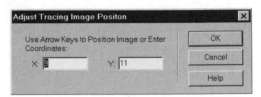

Figure 14.84 With this dialog box open, you can move the tracing image's position in the Document window using the text boxes or the arrow keys on your keyboard.

To align the tracing image with an object:

1. Select the object, such as a layer, table cell, or image, in the Document window.

2. From the Document window menu bar, select View > Tracing Image > Align With Selection. The tracing image and the selected layer or image will line up by their upper-left corners.

✔ Tips

- Because 0 percent opacity is invisible, and 100 percent is completely opaque, you'll probably find that between 40 and 60 percent works best for most images.

- Fireworks, Macromedia's image editor for the Web, lets you create a page mockup and then carve it up into smaller images that you can export into GIFs. You can then use Dreamweaver to position the images on your HTML page using layers, and line up the images so that they correspond exactly to their original locations on the mockup.

FILLING OUT FORMS

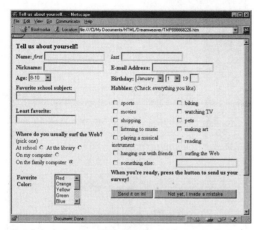

Figure 15.1 This feedback form includes most of the different kinds of fields that you can have in a form. I laid out the form using tables.

Figure 15.2 Not all forms have to be complicated, though. Some have only a few fields.

You fill out forms routinely when you apply for a driver's license or pay taxes or change addresses. Forms are getting to be more and more routine on the Web, too.

You'll want your visitors to fill out forms because it's the most efficient way for them to give you feedback about your site or about their identities (**Figure 15.1**), or just log in (**Figure 15.2**).

Online shopping sites, visitor surveys, and guestbooks use forms to collect data (called input) from your users. This data is then sent to a form handler—usually a CGI script, although other custom scripts can be used—which does something with this data. In some cases, such as surveys, the script simply saves the input for the site management to look at later. In other cases, such as search engines, the script takes the input and immediately uses it to provide some response or results for the user's edification. Typically, some form of interaction—even a simple thank-you page—assures the user that the information wasn't sent into a vacuum.

Dreamweaver simplifies the process of creating forms for your site. In this chapter, you'll learn the basics of how to create and name form objects such as checkboxes, radio buttons, drop-down menus, and text fields.

Creating a Form

The first step in creating a form is to put the form itself, represented by the <form></form> tags, on your page. It will be delineated in the Document window by a dashed red line that will be invisible when the page is loaded in the browser window (**Figure 15.3**).

Dreamweaver's Objects panel is especially handy for automating the process.

To display form objects on the Objects panel:

1. On the Objects panel, click on the menu button at the top.

2. From the pop-up menu that appears, choose Forms (**Figure 15.4**).

The Objects panel will display form objects (**Figure 15.5**).

Figure 15.3 In the Document window, forms are outlined by a red, dashed border.

Figure 15.4 Click on the menu button on the Objects panel and choose Forms from the pop-up menu.

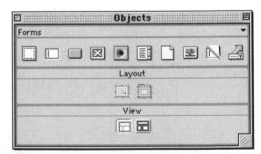

Figure 15.5 The Objects panel with form objects displayed. Note that I resized the panel—you can do that by clicking and dragging its lower-right corner.

Figure 15.6 A new, blank form.

To create a form:

1. You must have invisible element viewing turned on to view Form borders. To turn it on, select View > Visual Aids > Invisible Elements from the Document window menu bar.

2. From the Document window menu bar, select Insert > Form.

   or

   On the Objects panel, click on the Insert Form button [ ].

The form will appear (**Figure 15.6**). By default, your form will occupy 100 percent of the page width. The height is determined by the content you place within the form borders. You cannot resize forms with Dreamweaver, although you can format their content using tables (see Chapter 12 to find out how to use tables).

Forms Are Content

Although Dreamweaver enables you to create the interface for Web forms—all the buttons and menus that you need to make the form itself—it does not include the back-end tools that make the form operable. Before your visitors will be able to click the Submit button and whisk their data to you, you need to install a form handler on your server. Some free scripts are listed on the Web site for this book; for more complex functions, you may need an engineer.

Formatting Forms

It's essential to label each field in a form; otherwise, the users won't know what the heck they're supposed to do (**Figure 15.7**). I don't specify this in the steps for adding each field because it's pretty unlikely that you're going to forget.

You can use line breaks, paragraph breaks, preformatted text, or tables to format the stuff in your forms (**Figure 15.8**). A form can include nearly any HTML entity—text, images, tables—except another form. You can put a form in a table, or a table in a form, but you can't put a form within a form. You can, however, include more than one form on a page—just don't try to overlap them.

✔ Tip

- You can find out about working with tables in Chapter 12. I discussed text formatting in Chapters 8 and 9.

Figure 15.7 What is this form for? Without labels, it's impossible to tell.

Figure 15.8 An expanded version of the form we saw in **Figure 15.2** with the table, form borders, and labels revealed in the Document window.

Figure 15.9 The Objects panel, displaying form objects

Figure 15.10 A single-line text box

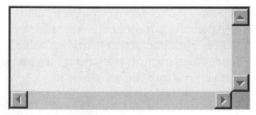

Figure 15.11 A multi-line text box

Figure 15.12 A flock of checkboxes

Figure 15.13 A gaggle of radio buttons

Figure 15.14 A drop-down menu and a list box

Figure 15.15 Submit and reset buttons

Adding Form Objects

Form objects, commonly referred to as form fields, are the nuts and bolts of a form. They're the boxes and buttons that people click on or type in to make their mark (technically called their *input*) on a form.

There are five different common flavors of form objects, each of which has its own button on the Objects panel (**Figure 15.9**), as well as its own entry in the Insert > Form Objects menu. Some of the less common ones do as well.

Text fields (also called text boxes) come in two flavors: single-line and multi-line. If a form were a test, a single-line field would be a short answer question (**Figure 15.10**), and a multi-line would be an essay question (**Figure 15.11**).

Checkboxes can be used singly or in groups of two or more (**Figure 15.12**). Checkboxes allow the user to specify yes or no answers.

Radio buttons, named after the buttons on old-fashioned console radios, always come in groups of two or more (**Figure 15.13**). They allow you to choose only one of a set of options—when you push in one button on a radio, the other buttons pop out.

Lists and *menus* (**Figure 15.14**) allow the user to choose from a long list of options that don't take up too much space on the page. What Dreamweaver calls a *menu* is also called a *drop-down menu*; it drops down when you click on it to reveal the full set of options. A list box offers several choices at once; in some cases, the user can choose more than one item from a list box.

Buttons are what make the form do something. A *submit button* sends the form off over the wires to its final destination. A *reset button* clears all the values entered in a form and resets the form to its default, or starting, values (**Figure 15.15**).

Names and Values

Each gadget, or form field, in a form is also known as an *input item* (the HTML tag is often <input>). That means it's used to collect input from the people who use it.

Each input item is represented in the form results by a name and a value. The name is a unique signifier that tells you (or the script handling the form) which field is which. The value is the content of the field.

Names and values are required for form fields; if you forget them, Dreamweaver will provide sequential names and values, such as radiobutton, radiobutton2, radiobutton3, and so on. Those sorts of names aren't very useful; for more about choosing a name and where values come in, read the sidebar, this page.

It's always useful, but the Property inspector will come in particularly handy for formatting just about everything—both the text of the labels and the form fields themselves. The Property inspector will display unique properties for each form field—and it's what you'll use to specify names and values.

To display the Property inspector:

◆ From the Document window menu bar, select Modify > Selection Properties.

 or

 From the Document window menu bar, select Window > Properties.

 or

 Press Ctrl+F3 (Command+F3).

Either way, the Property inspector will appear (**Figure 15.16**).

Figure 15.16 The Property inspector

Name That Value

When you name a form field, you may never need to personally read the form input but if you did, you'd see results in this format:

name=value   name=value
name=value   name=value
name=value

The name is the name you give the field, and the value is the input the user fills the field with. One argument for recognizable names for form fields is so that if there's a problem, it's with "the address field," not with "field six."

In a text box, the value of the input is equal to what the users type. Input for a text field might look like this:

address="675 Onionskin Road"

For a checkbox or a radio button, you really need to specify what value the field has by providing unique text that signifies what specific input means.

This is particularly important if you're using several checkboxes; a value of "checkbox5" won't tell you anything.

Checkbox input in form results could look like any of the four examples below:

carowner=yes   carowner=checked
carowner=carowner

I know, I said four examples—if it isn't checked, it doesn't get sent with the form results at all.

Apply button

Figure 15.17 The Property inspector, displaying properties for a single-line text field

Figure 15.18 To change the width of a text field, enter a value in the Char Width text box of the Property Inspector.

Displaying Properties

You can display properties for any form field by double-clicking it. The Property inspector will appear, displaying form object properties.

Text Boxes

Text fields are used to collect data that you can't predict. You can't offer a multiple-choice menu for every possible name or e-mail address, for instance.

Single-line text boxes

For short answers, such as address information or favorite TV show, you'll use a single-line text field.

To create a single-line text field:

1. In the Document window, click within the form boundaries.

2. From the Document window menu bar, select Insert > Form Objects > Text Field.
   or
   On the Objects panel, click on the Text Field button 🔲, or drag the button to the page.
   A single-line text field will appear [   ] .
   You can resize it, if you like.

3. To resize the text field, type a number, in characters, in the Char Width text box of the Property inspector (**Figures 15.17** and **15.18**).

4. Click on the Apply button or press Enter (Return), and your text field will resize.

TEXT BOXES

Password boxes

You can use a single-line text box to collect password information, in which case the stuff they type in the box will appear on screen as *** or ⋯ .

To create a password box:

1. Click on the text field to select it, and make sure the Property inspector is open (**Figure 15.17**).

2. In the Type area of the Property inspector, click on the Password radio button (**Figure 15.19**).

There won't be any visible change, but when your page is on the Web, the stuff the user types in it will be replaced by asterisks or bullets to prevent accidents and deviousness (**Figure 15.20**).

Big text boxes

A multi-line text field will create a "feedback box" that you can use to elicit longer responses from your users. Multi-line text boxes are commonly used for guestbooks, e-mail forms, and any other case in which you want more than a few words from your visitors.

To create a multi-line text field:

1. Create a single-line text field, as described on the previous page.

2. Double-click the text field, and the Property inspector will appear, if it isn't already showing.

3. In the Type area of the Property inspector, click on the Multi-line radio button. The text field will change appearance (**Figure 15.21**).

Figure 15.19 To make a text field into a password field, click on the Password radio button.

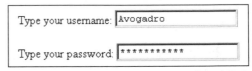

Figure 15.20 The first text box is a normal single-line text box, whereas the second one is a password box that masks the secret identities of its characters.

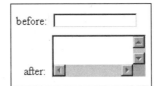

Figure 15.21 Change a single-line text field into a multi-line field by clicking on the Multi-line radio button in the Property inspector.

Figure 15.22 A default multi-line text box

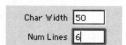

Figure 15.23 .To change the dimensions of a multi-line text box, type a character width and a line height in the Property inspector.

Figure 15.24 The new, improved text box

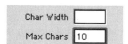

Figure 15.25 Restrict the number of characters allowed in a text box by typing a value in the Max Chars field.

To resize a multi-line text field:

1. Select the multi-line text field (**Figure 15.22**).

2. In the Property inspector, type a number (in characters) in the Char Width text box (**Figure 15.23**).

3. Type a number of lines in the Num Lines text box (**Figure 15.23**).

4. Click on the Apply button. The text box will resize to your specifications (**Figure 15.24**).

✔ Tip

■ Unfortunately, you can't resize a multi- or single-line text field by clicking and dragging.

Character Limits

You can set a character limit for a single-line text field; for example, credit cards generally have only 16 digits, or 19 with dashes. Other fields you may want to limit include pass-word, phone number, ZIP code, or state abbreviation.

To restrict the number of characters allowed:

1. Click on a single-line text field to select it, or double-click it to display the Property inspector.

2. In the Max Chars text box, type the maximum number of characters you'll allow in this field, and press Enter (Return) (**Figure 15.25**).

In a Web browser, the user will not be able to type more than the number of characters you specified. (Generally, they'll hear beeping when they try to type past the limit.)

TEXT BOXES

385

Default text values

If you want to give your visitors an example of what kind of input you're expecting, you can set an initial value for either kind of text box.

To set an initial value:

1. Select the text box (either single- or multi-line), and view the Property inspector.

2. In the Init Val text box, type the text you want to have displayed in the text box, and click on the Apply button.

The text will show up in the text box in the Document window (**Figure 15.26**) and in the Web browser.

✔ Tip

- ■ Beware of using the initial value. Although it might seem like a great idea at the time, a lot of wise guys (or dumb guys) won't bother to change something that's already filled in. It might be better, in some cases, to use example text outside the box, as shown in **Figure 15.27**.

Figure 15.26 The text you type in the Property inspector's Init Val text box will be included in the form field.

Figure 15.27 In the first text box, the user may neglect to replace the supplied text with his or her real e-mail address. In the second instance, the user is given a visual example, but the text box is left blank.

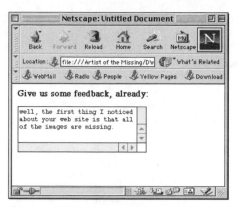

Figure 15.28 Netscape 4 wraps text by default in a multi-line text box.

Figure 15.29 The Property inspector for a File field allows you to set the character width, maximum number of characters, and initial value for the file's location.

File Fields

One kind of form field you may have reason to use, albeit rarely, is the file field. The file field consists of a text box and a button marked Browse. This field is used when you want your visitors to be able to upload files from their local computer to your remote server. The Browse button will open the Open File dialog box in their Web browser, which they will use to select the file; then they will use the form's submit button to send you the file.

To insert a file field, click on the Insert File Field button [icon] on the Forms panel of the Objects panel, or select Insert > Form Objects > File Field. The file field will appear: [field]

You can set a maximum character width, a maximum number of characters, and an initial value for this field in the Property inspector just as you can for normal text fields. See **Figure 15.29**.

Text wrapping

When users type in a multi-line text field, scrollbars appear when the user types text that's longer than the field. However, the text won't wrap in a multi-line text field unless you turn that option on.

To wrap text in a multi-line text field:

1. Select the multi-line text field.

2. Display the full Property inspector by clicking on the Expander arrow in the lower-right corner.

3. From the Wrap drop-down menu, select one of the following:

   Default (the browser default, which sometimes wraps and sometimes doesn't; see **Figure 15.28**).

   Off (turns off wrapping, in some browsers at least).

   Virtual (the text will wrap onscreen, but no line breaks will be inserted in the form input).

   Physical (the browser will insert line breaks into the form input where they occur onscreen).

Naming text fields

As with all form fields, it's a good idea to name your text fields so you can tell them apart.

To name a text field:

1. Select the text box and view the Property inspector.

2. In the TextField text box, highlight the text field text and type over it, replacing it with a meaningful word that will indicate the purpose of the field.

3. Press Enter (Return) on the keyboard.

Your text field will be named in the code, as well as in the form results that your users will submit.

Checkboxes

Checkboxes, which often appear in groups, allow users to make one or more selections from a set of options.

To create a checkbox:

1. Click to place the insertion point within the form in the Document window.

2. From the Document window menu bar, select Insert > Form Objects > Check Box.

   or

   On the Objects panel, click on the Insert Checkbox button , or drag the button to the form in the Document window. The checkbox will appear 🗔.

3. Repeat step 2 for each checkbox.

Remember to give each checkbox a uniquely useful name and value.

To specify name and value:

1. Select the checkbox by clicking on it, and double-click if you need to display the Property inspector (**Figure 15.30**).

2. In the Checked Value text box, type the text you want to see if the user checks the box. Good examples include send_info or owns_dog (**Figure 15.31**).

3. Name the checkbox by typing a name for it in the CheckBox text box. For example, the name could be mail or dog.

4. Press Enter (Return) to apply your changes.

✔ Tips

■ If the user does not check off the checkbox, there will be no indication of the checkbox data at all in the form results.

■ If you want the checkbox to appear checked when the page is loaded, click on the Checked radio button in the Initial State area of the Property inspector (**Figure 15.32**).

Apply button

Figure 15.30 The Property inspector, displaying checkbox properties.

Figure 15.31 Be sure to give each checkbox an appropriate name and value, using the Property inspector.

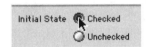

Figure 15.32 Set a checkbox to appear checked when the page is loaded by clicking on the Checked radio button.

■ If the user does put a check mark in a checkbox, the results will say something like NAME=VALUE. In our example above, the results would be mail=send_info or dog=owns_dog.

■ Names and values are case-sensitive.

Figure 15.33 The Property inspector, displaying radio button properties.

Figure 15.34 Use radio buttons to create multiple-choice questions. Be sure to give each button the same name and a different value.

Radio Buttons

Although checkboxes can appear either singly or in groups, radio buttons always appear in groups. You can use radio buttons for yes/no, true/false, or multiple-choice questions where only one answer can be selected.

To insert a radio button:

1. Click to place the insertion point within the form in the Document window.

2. From the Document window menu bar, select Insert > Form Objects > Radio Button.

   or

   On the Objects panel, click on the Insert Radio Button button 🔘, or drag the radio button to the form in the Document window.

   A radio button will appear 🔘.

3. Repeat step 2 for each radio button in the set.

You must name each radio button in a group with the same name, and you must give each radio button in a group a different value.

To specify names and values:

1. Select a radio button, and display the Property inspector, if necessary (**Figure 15.33**).

2. Type a name for the group of radio buttons in the RadioButton text box.

3. Type a value for that particular radio button in the Checked Value text box (**Figure 15.34**).

4. Repeat steps 1–3 for each radio button in the set. Be sure to spell the name exactly the same, and to give each button a different value, such as "male," "female," or "other."

continued on next page

5. Select one of the buttons to be initially selected when the page is loaded. Click on that button and, in the Property inspector, click on the Checked radio button.

6. Press Enter (Return) to apply your changes to the form.

✔ Tips

■ A group of radio buttons as described on this page is a set wherein only one button can be clicked at a time (**Figure 15.35**). The only way to create a group of radio buttons, and to give them group properties, is to give each button in the group the same exact name (in the Property inspector).

■ You can check to make sure you've grouped your radio buttons properly by previewing the page in a browser and making sure that, when you click on each button in turn, the other buttons in the set become deselected.

■ If you use more than one group of radio buttons in a single form, be sure to give each group a unique name.

■ To ensure the name is exactly the same for a group of buttons, you can name one button, then copy and paste it as many times as you want. Dreamweaver will give each copy the same name. (You'll have to set the value of each button by hand, though.)

■ Names and values are case-sensitive.

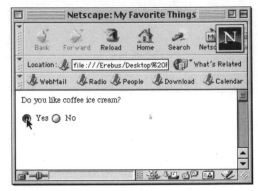

Figure 15.35 Give users a binary choice with radio buttons. Only one option can be clicked at a time.

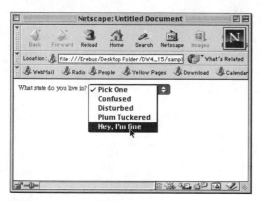

Figure 15.36 A menu in action.

Figure 15.37 The Property inspector, displaying menu properties.

Figure 15.38 The Initial List Values dialog box is where you add menu items to your menus and lists.

Figure 15.39 Press the Tab key to move to the next column and type the value for the menu item.

Menus and Lists

You can offer a range of choices by using drop-down menus, also called pull-down menus or pop-up menus (**Figure 15.36**).

To create a menu:

1. Click to place the insertion point within the form in the Document window.

2. From the Document window menu bar, select Insert > Form Objects > List/Menu.

   or

   On the Objects panel, click on the Insert List/Menu button ▦, or drag the button to the form in the Document window.

An itty-bitty drop-down menu will appear ▦.

To fill the menu with menu items:

1. Click on the list to select it, and display the Property inspector (**Figure 15.37**).

2. Click on the List Values button. The Initial List Values dialog box will appear (**Figure 15.38**).

3. Click below the Item Label menu button, and a text field will appear beneath it.

4. Type a menu item (what you want to appear in the menu) in the Item Label text field.

   If you want the values (the information that will appear in the form results) to be the same as the item labels, you can skip steps 5 and 6.

5. Press the Tab key or click on the Value menu button, and a text field will become visible (**Figure 15.39**).

continued on next page

6. Type the value of the menu item in the Value text field.

7. Repeat steps 2–6 for each menu item you want to include. (Press the Tab key or click on the + button to create a field for each new menu item.)

Menu Design

Normally, form objects, when viewed in the browser window, are displayed in the system font: Arial size 2 for menus, (the Mac uses Chicago or Charcoal, depending on the system version) and Courier size 3 for text boxes (Courier New on the Mac).

You can change the look of a drop-down menu or a text box by changing its font face and size. Be sure to test these effects in your favorite browser. The trick here is that if you select just the form field in the Dreamweaver window, you'll see menu object properties in the Property inspector, rather than text properties. To select a form object and change its font face, follow these steps:

1. Select, by clicking and dragging or by Shift-clicking, more than one form object (a menu and a checkbox, for instance), or a form object and some text. The Property inspector will display text properties.

2. Change the font face of the selected items by selecting it from the Font Face drop-down menu.

3. Change the font size of the selected objects by selecting size from the Size drop-down menu.

4. Preview the form in the browser window to see what your changes look like.

You can also wrap the `<font>` tag around the `<select>` tag using the Code inspector or the Quick Tag editor.

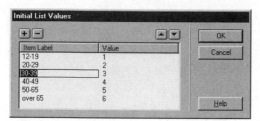

Figure 15.40 Use the + and – buttons to add and delete items—and the Up and Down arrow buttons to rearrange the order of the list.

Figure 15.41 When you load the page in the browser window, you can click on the menu to make sure it looks the way you want it to.

Editing Menu Items

You can edit this list before you close the dialog box (**Figure 15.40**).

To edit the menu items:

1. You can rearrange the menu items by moving them up and down through the list.
   - ◆ To move an item up through the list, click on the Up arrow button.
   - ◆ To move an item down through the list, click on the Down arrow button.

2. You can add or delete items as necessary.
   - ◆ To delete an item, click on it, and then click on the – (minus) button.
   - ◆ To add an item, click on the + button, and then move the item to a new location in the list, if desired.

3. And of course, you can edit the text of the menu items themselves. Just click on the item, and type your changes in the text field.

When you're all done with the Initial List Values dialog box, click on OK to close it. You'll return to the Document window. The menu will appear larger than it was before, which indicates that it contains multitudes, but Dreamweaver doesn't display the menu as active—you won't see the menu items themselves.

✔ Tips

- ■ To proofread your menu, you need to preview it in the browser window (**Figure 15.41**). Once there, you can click on it to drop-down the menu and scroll through the list of items.

- ■ Don't forget to name your menu by typing a name in the List/Menu text box on the Property inspector.

Creating a List Box

The drop-down menu is one kind of list-type form field you can create; the other kind is the list box. List boxes can be several items high and can offer multiple selections.

To create a list box:

1. Create a menu, as described in the preceding sections. (You can input the menu items at any point.)

2. Display the Property inspector by double-clicking the menu object (**Figure 15.42**).

3. In the Property inspector, click on the List radio button (**Figure 15.43**).

4. To adjust the height of the list, type a number of lines in the Height text box . The menu will change appearance in the Document window (**Figure 15.44**).

5. To allow multiple selections, make sure the Selections checkbox is checked. To disallow multiple selections, deselect the Selections checkbox (**Figure 15.45**).

6. Name your list by typing a name in the List/Menu text box and pressing Enter (Return).

✔ Tips

- To add menu items to a list box, follow the steps in the section *To fill the menu with menu items,* earlier in this chapter. The dialog boxes are identical.

- To specify the initial selection in a menu or list, select a menu item from the Initially Selected list box in the Property inspector (**Figure 15.46**). If no selection is made, the first item in the list will be the initial selection.

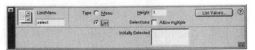

Figure 15.42 The Property inspector, displaying list properties.

Figure 15.43 To make a list, choose the List radio button in the Property inspector.

Figure 15.44 I gave the list a line height of 5. Because I have more than five items, scrollbars appear in the list box.

Figure 15.45 Check the Selections checkbox and users will be able to make multiple selections.

Figure 15.46 To specify a menu item other than the first as the initial selection, select the menu item from the Initially Selected list box in the expanded Property inspector.

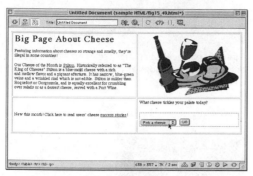

Figure 15.47 The only object in the form in the lower-right corner is a jump menu. The menu must appear in a form to work properly in the widest range of browsers, but you can make it the only object in the form.

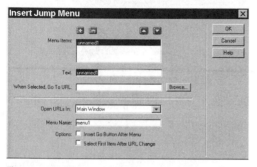

Figure 15.48 The Insert Jump Menu dialog box allows you to specify a list of pages the user can visit by choosing from a menu or list.

Figure 15.49 If you select a page from your local site as a list option, Dreamweaver will guess the text you want to use based on the filename of the page. You can edit this text later.

Jump Menus

A jump menu is a specialized kind of list or menu; when visitors select an option from a jump menu, their browsers take them to a URL associated with that option (**Figure 15.47**). Dreamweaver jump menus use JavaScript to do their magic, but it's all written behind the scenes and affixed to a regular list or menu without your having to worry about it.

Keep in mind, though, that not all browsers support JavaScript. See Chapter 16 for more about JavaScript, and be sure to offer alternate options for visiting all the pages in the menu.

To create a jump menu:

1. Save your page, if you haven't done so, to make any relative URLs work properly.

2. Insert a form and click within its borders.

3. On the Objects panel, click on the Insert Jump Menu button ![icon], or drag the button to the page. The Insert Jump Menu dialog box will appear (**Figure 15.48**).

4. First, we'll specify the URL. To select a page from your local site, click Browse, and locate the document on your computer.
   or
   Type (or paste) the URL (either a full path or a relative URL) of the page in the When Selected, Go to URL text box.

5. If you selected a document from your local site, the Text and Menu Items fields will be filled in (**Figure 15.49**).

   To edit or add the text that will appear in the menu, type the text in the Text text box. The Menu Items field will display both the text and the URL for your selection.

6. Repeat steps 4 and 5 for each additional menu item.

continued on next page

7. Type a name for the menu in the Menu Name text box.

8. To include a Go Button (**Figure 15.47**), check the Insert Go Button After Menu checkbox. Go ahead and do this; if you change your mind, you can delete the button, but for some reason you cannot add one after you close the Insert Jump Menu dialog.

9. From the Open URLs in the drop-down menu, choose where you want the selections to open:

   ◆ To open URLs in the main window, select Main Window.

   ◆ To open URLs in a frame, select the frame name.

   ◆ To open URLs in a new window, select the window name. (To do this, you must create the window first. See the next page.)

10. When you're finished, click on OK to close the Insert Jump Menu text box.

Editing a jump menu

The jump menu uses the same form-field code as does a regular list or menu. After you close the Insert Jump Menu dialog box, you can edit your choices by selecting the menu and then clicking on the List Values button on the Property inspector (**Figure 15.50**). To edit your jump menu, follow the instructions in the preceding sections, *To fill the menu with menu items* and *To edit the menu items*.

✔ Tip

■ More editing options for Jump Menus using behaviors are described in Chapter 16.

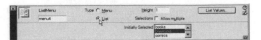

Figure 15.50 The Property inspector for a jump menu offers the same options as it does for a regular list or menu.

Figure 15.51 You can make selections from a jump menu appear in a new window, which may be a smaller, "remote" or "channel" style window, or a regular browser window whose size you specify.

No Script Required

I've already mentioned that you don't have to worry about the JavaScript involved in creating a jump menu. Even better, the actions involved in this widget are all client side; that is, the action of selecting the page to visit is performed by the browser, not by a remote script. This means that you don't need to add a submit button or set up a form handler, as you do to make regular forms work.

I recommend creating a separate form for a jump or go menu. If you place this form inside a table, it can take up as little space as possible on your page (**Figure 15.47**).

Figure 15.52 You can add a Go button, pictured here, by checking the Go Button checkbox in the Insert Jump Menu dialog box, which we saw previously in **Figure 15.48**.

To Go Button or Not to Go Button?

In the Insert Jump Menu dialog box, there's a checkbox marked Go Button. If this box is unchecked *and* the jump menu is a drop-down menu, the browser will jump to the page as soon as the visitor has made a selection from the menu.

If you check the Go Button checkbox (which you must do if you're using a list box), the automatic action will be replaced by a button the user can click on when he or she is done choosing (**Figure 15.52**).

Unfortunately, unless you use behaviors, you can't add a Go button after you close the Insert Jump Menu dialog box, but you can delete it if you don't want it anymore.

One rule of thumb is this: If your jump menu lists many, many options, you may want to include a Go button, because it's very easily to accidentally select an item from a long menu—and without a Go button, they'd get whisked away to a page they didn't choose on purpose. You can omit the Go button for menus with just a few items, say five or fewer.

Changing a jump menu's appearance

You can make your jump menu either a drop-down menu or a list box by selecting either the Menu or the List radio button on the Property inspector (**Figure 15.50**). For details about additional options for list boxes, see the section *To create a list box,* earlier in this chapter.

You can also choose which item to select initially by choosing an item from the Initially Selected list box. To have the menu return to this initially selected item after the user has used the menu to visit a new page, check the Select First Item After URL Change checkbox in the Insert Jump Menu dialog box.

To use a selection prompt, such as "Choose a Page," add the text in the Text box, and don't specify any URL. Move the selection prompt so that it's the first item in the list (by using the Up arrow button).

You can make the selections in a jump menu open in a new window (**Figure 15.51**). First, you have to create the window. It's best if you create the code for the new window before you add the jump menu, so that the window name will appear in the Open URLs In drop-down menu in the Insert Jump Menu dialog box.

✔ Tips

- To create an additional window for the jump menu URLs to open in, see *Opening a New Browser Window* in Chapter 16.

- To change the text on a Go button, see *To rename your button,* later in this chapter.

Hidden Form Fields

Besides the regular widgets you can use on a form, you can place hidden form fields in the code so that some fixed information is passed along with the rest of the data. This information might include the URL of the form, the version of the form, or any other information you want to receive with the form results.

To create a hidden form field:

1. Click to place the insertion point at the place on the form where you want the invisible field to be inserted.

2. From the Document window menu bar, select Insert > Form Objects > Hidden Field.

   or

   Click on the Insert Hidden Field button ![icon] on the Forms panel of the Objects panel, or drag the button to the page.

   If you have Invisible Element viewing turned on, a Hidden Field icon will appear ![icon].

3. Type the value of the hidden field in the Value text box in the Property inspector.

4. Type a name for the hidden field in the Name (unlabeled) text box.

You won't see the hidden fields on the Web page (duh!), but the value will be sent with the rest of the data when the user submits the form.

✔ Tips

■ If you use more than one hidden field, be sure to give each one a different name.

■ To view invisible elements, select View > Invisible Elements from the Document window menu bar.

Tweaking Your Menus and Boxes

Dreamweaver doesn't support the rather handy disabled attribute for menu items, but you can easily add the disabled attribute in the code. The disabled attribute allows you to prevent a user from selecting a particular menu item. If the first item in your drop-down menu is something like "Pick your favorite color," you want to make sure they can't submit that item, because it won't give you any data. You don't want to get 1,000 eager responses that say "Please select an item."

To add this attribute to a list or menu item, follow these steps:

1. Click on the list or menu in the Document window.

2. View the code for your page by selecting Window > Code Inspector from the Document window menu bar, or clicking on the Show Code View button (or the Show Code and Design Views button) in the document window toolbar. The code for the list or menu will be highlighted in the code.

The code for the menu or list should look something like this:

```
<select name="menu">
<option value="">red</option>
<option value="">white</option>
<option value="">blue</option>
</select>
```

Each option is a list item.

3. To prevent users from submitting a particular selection, add the disabled attribute to the option tag:

```
<option disabled value=""> Select a
Color</option>
```

Save your changes to the HTML, and be sure to test the form to make sure these changes work the way you want them to.

Figure 15.53 The Property inspector, displaying button properties.

Submit and Reset Buttons

There are three kinds of buttons you can put at the bottom of a form for your visitors to make use of.

Submit buttons are what you push to send the form off to the form handler, which compiles all the input and then does something with it.

Reset buttons clear the form of any new input and reset the form to its initial state.

The last kind of button (a "nothing" button) has no action; that is, it will neither reset nor submit the form, but it can be used with JavaScript or other active content to do something.

To create a button:

1. Click to place the insertion point within the form in the Document window.

2. From the Document window menu bar, select Insert > Form Objects > Button.

   or

   On the Objects panel, click on the Insert Button button 🔲 , or drag the Insert Button button to the form in the Document window.

3. A Submit button will appear.

4. Display the Property inspector, if it's not open, by choosing Modify > Selection Properties (**Figure 15.53**) from the Document window menu bar.

continued on next page

Covering Your Assets

Although most browsers these days support forms, some browsers can't deal with them—they display them improperly or not at all. Even some versions of Internet Explorer have bugs that prevent proper handling of forms, as well as of `mailto:` addresses. If getting input (or orders!) from your visitors is important to you, be sure to visibly include an e-mail address on your site—not just a hidden `mailto:` link.

5. In the Property inspector, choose the type of button you want:

- ◆ If you want a Submit button, click on the Submit radio button.

- ◆ If you want a Reset button, click on the Reset radio button.

- ◆ If you want a nothing button, click on the None radio button.

6. Click on the Apply button to apply your changes to the button.

✔ Tips

■ It's a convention on most Web pages that the Submit button appears to the left of the Reset button at the bottom of the form.

■ Dreamweaver displays push buttons with a smaller font face than either Navigator or IE uses.

■ You can change the size of the push button, too. See the instructions in the sidebar called *Menu Design* on page 392.

You can call your buttons whatever you want. By default, the Submit button will say Submit and the Reset button will say Reset, but that's an option, not an imperative. I've seen Reset buttons named Gorilla and Submit buttons named Fish.

To rename your button:

1. Click on the button to select it, and display the Property inspector, if necessary.

2. In the Button Label text box, type the text you want to appear on the button, and press Enter (Return).

Your button will be renamed (**Figure 15.54**).

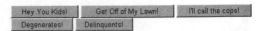

Figure 15.54 Your buttons can say anything you want.

Figure 15.55 The dialog box for inserting an image field is exactly like the generic Select Image Source dialog box.

Figure 15.56 The Property inspector, displaying Image Field properties. The dashed border around the image indicates that it's an image field rather than a plain old image.

Image Fields

Instead of the standard gray push buttons that usually appear in forms, you can use images as buttons. This method only works for Submit buttons.

To create an image field:

1. Click to place the insertion point at the place on the form where you want the image button to appear.

2. From the Document window menu bar, select Insert > Form Objects > Image Field.

   or

   Click on the Insert Image Field button on the Forms panel of the Objects panel, or drag the button to the page.

   The Select Image Source dialog box will appear (**Figure 15.55**).

3. This dialog box is just like the Insert Image dialog box. Type the pathname of the image in the Image File text box, or select the image from your hard drive.

4. Click on OK to close the Select Image Source dialog box. The image will appear in the Document window with a dashed line around it.

5. Display the Property inspector, if it's not open (**Figure 15.56**). The Src text box will display the path and filename of the image.

6. Type a name in the Name text box.

7. Type the alternate text for the image in the Alt text box.

continued on next page

✔ Tips

- Along with form object properties, Image field properties include characteristics such as image height (H), image width (W), alt text (Alt), and image alignment (Align). If you need information on using these attributes, consult Chapter 5.

- Along with the results of your form, you'll get coordinates that say *where* on the image the user clicked, appended to the name text (name.x and name.y). You can see whether they clicked on an apple or an orange, for instance.

The Button Tag

Another way to use images as buttons is by using the button tag instead of the input tag. The button tag allows images to be used as reset and nothing buttons, too.

1. Follow steps 1–4, in *To create an image field* (on previous page).

2. Select the image field in the Document window.

3. View the Code inspector by pressing F10. The code for the button will be highlighted in the inspector.

4. Replace the button code with this code:

   ```
   <button type=submit name="name"
   'value="value">

   <img src="button.gif"> </button>
   ```
   The button type can be Submit, Reset, or button (for forms that call a script—the "nothing button"). The name is the name of your button image; the value can reflect the value you want to be transmitted; and the src is the source of your image.

5. Save the changes to the code, and preview the page in a browser to make sure it works.

Figure 15.57 When the Property inspector displays Form properties, you can choose the method and action of the form handler.

Making It Go

In order to make a form actually do something, you have to set it up to work with a CGI script or other custom script, called a form handler. Dreamweaver can't write the script for you—you have to take care of this part on the server end. Many Internet service providers make available standard scripts for common forms such as mail forms and guestbooks, and they may offer other scripts as well. If you're working on a larger project, you may need to consult with a programmer, your systems administrator, or both.

Forms are sent by one of two methods: GET, which sends the results of the form in the URL submitted to the script; and POST, which encodes the material sent to the script. Check with your sysadmin to see which method you should use. Where does the stuff go? The script includes instructions on whether to store it in a database, e-mail it to someone, or save it as a data file.

Remember, you do not need to set up a form handler to run a Jump menu. Those use client-side JavaScript that Dreamweaver writes for you.

To set up the form handler:

1. In the Document window, select your form by clicking on the dashed border around it.

2. Choose the method and action of the form handler in the Property inspector (**Figure 15.57**).
   ◆ Click on the Method drop-down menu, and choose either GET or POST.
   ◆ In the Action text box, type the URL of the CGI or other script that will be processing the form.

3. Click on the Apply button to apply these changes to the form.

You won't see any changes in the Document window, but you can examine the HTML to make sure they're there.

✔ Tip

■ Even if you want results e-mailed to you, you must use a form handler. Many Web sites offer free form-handling scripts that are easy to set up. See the Web site for this book, or search for "free form handler."

BEHAVIOR
MODIFICATION

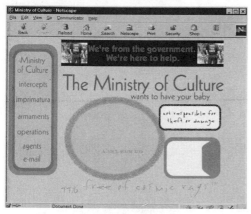

Figure 16.1 This page incorporates several behaviors, although you can't see them yet. In the background, the browser is pre-loading hidden layers and images.

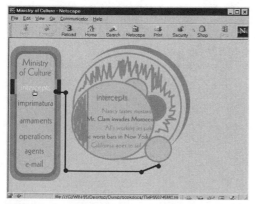

Figure 16.2 When I mouse over the button, the layers in **Figure 16.1** disappear and a new layer appears.

JavaScript behaviors can be used to make both flashy and actually useful gadgets, such as popup messages and complex rollovers. When used in conjunction with CSS styles (Chapter 11) and layers (Chapter 14), these tools are called Dynamic HTML, in which the page can change after it loads (**Figures 16.1** through **16.3**).

You can make things happen on a page when a user loads the page, clicks an object, or moves the mouse around. Obviously, I'm simplifying—there are a lot of fancy things you can do with JavaScript (see the sidebar, *Learning JavaScript*). In this chapter I discuss the stock behaviors that Dreamweaver lets you apply—all without writing a line of code by hand.

You've already used some preset behavior tools if you've inserted an image rollover or a navigation bar (Chapter 7) or a jump menu (Chapter 15). In Chapter 17, you can get even fancier with Timelines.

✔ Tips

- All the actions that Dreamweaver provides work with version 4.0 and later browsers, and many also work with earlier browsers (as I note when explaining each action).

- Not all events are available to all browsers, and not all actions work in all browsers, so choosing which behaviors to use depends on which browsers you want to target.

JavaScript Concepts

A JavaScript behavior is sort of like an equation:

Event + Object = Action.

or

If this event happens to this object, this behavior will happen.

You can see a simple example of this relationship in **Figure 16.4**.

An *object* is an HTML element on a Web page, such as an image, a link, a layer, or the body of the page itself.

An *event* is shorthand for both user event and event handler. A *user event* is what happens when the user, or the user's browser, performs a common task, such as loading a page, clicking on a link, or pointing the mouse at an image. An *event handler* is the JavaScript shorthand that designates a particular user event, such as onMouseOver or onLoad.

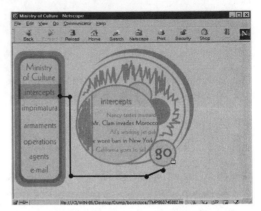

Figure 16.3 When I mouse over the image, a sound plays and another image appears (see the word "go"?).

Pointer is "mousing over" the image   Linked image

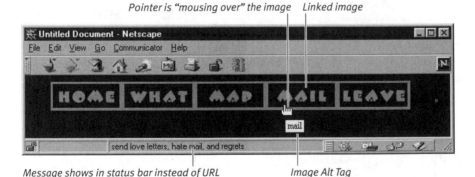

Message shows in status bar instead of URL   Image Alt Tag

Figure 16.4 This button bar, shown in Navigator, is made up of five linked images (with image borders set to 0). The object is the link around the image. The event is onMouseOver, and the action is Show Status Message.

An action is where the JavaScript comes in. Normally, when you click on a link, you go to the page that's that link's target. That's a normal browser action that has nothing to do with a script. A JavaScript action might start with the click and then play a sound or pop open a dialog box.

In Dreamweaver, to add behaviors to a page, you choose an object and an event, based on which browsers you want to make the script available to. Then you choose an action that the object + event combination will trigger.

In this chapter, I'm first going to describe how to add a behavior to a page, which is a pretty darn simple process. The rest of the chapter will be dedicated to listing and describing the objects, events, and actions you can combine in Dreamweaver behaviors.

Learning JavaScript

You've probably gotten the idea by now that if you're not used to coding HTML by hand, Dreamweaver is a great way to learn how to do so. You just highlight the objects you're curious about in the Document window, open the Code inspector, and, voilà, you can see what the code behind the page is.

You can do the same thing with JavaScript by creating Dreamweaver behaviors and viewing the code for them in the Code inspector. If you feel lost looking at Java-Script, you might refer to one of the Web sites I link to in the supporting site for this book.

If you want a handy-dandy JavaScript reference, try *JavaScript for the World Wide Web: Visual QuickStart Guide, Third Edition,* by Tom Negrino and Dori Smith, also from Peachpit Press.

Making Scripts Go

Dreamweaver doesn't actually run any JavaScript behaviors. You need to preview your page in a browser to test your behaviors. You can preview in your default browser by pressing F12, or you can choose a browser from the preview list by selecting File > Preview in Browser > [Browser Name] from the Document window menu bar.

Appendix C on this book's Web site includes instructions on adding browsers to the Preview list.

JAVASCRIPT CONCEPTS

Adding Behaviors

Adding a behavior to a page is incredibly simple—the devil is in the details. All Dreamweaver behaviors are added and edited with the Behaviors panel.

To view the Behaviors panel:

◆ From the Document window menu bar, select Window > Behaviors.

or

Click on the Behaviors button (**Figure 16.5**) on the Launcher or the Document window Launcher bar.

or

Press Shift+F3.

The Behaviors panel will appear (**Figure 16.6**).

To add a behavior:

1. In the Document window, click on the object you want the behavior to act on, or choose an entire tag (such as <body>) by clicking on the tag selector at the bottom-left of the Document window (**Figure 16.7**).

2. At the left of the Behaviors panel, click on the Add Action button ⊞ to pop up a menu which includes both a list of actions that are available and a way to select your target browser. Select the Show Events For submenu and choose your target browser (**Figure 16.8**). If you don't select a browser, the list of events will be limited to those available for both 3.0 and 4.0 browsers.

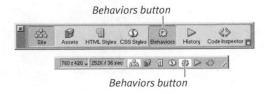

Behaviors button

Behaviors button

Figure 16.5 View the Behaviors panel by clicking on the Behaviors button on the Launcher or the Launcher bar.

Up and Down arrow buttons for changing actions' priorities

Add Event button

Selected object (tag)

Figure 16.6 The Behaviors panel is what you use to add JavaScript behaviors.

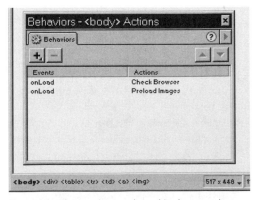

Figure 16.7 The tag that's selected in the tag selector is the one that will be affected by the behaviors you apply in the Behaviors panel.

ADDING BEHAVIORS

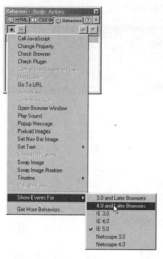

Figure 16.8 To limit the events shown to the ones appropriate to your target browser, select it from the submenu.

Figure 16.9 Click on the Add Action (+) button to pop up a menu and add an action to the selected event. The actions available depend on the selected browser + object combination.

Figure 16.10 Click on the Add Event (+) button to pop up a menu and add or change an event for the selected object. The events available depend on the selected browser + object + action combination.

3. Click on the Add Action button again to pop up a menu of actions that are available for that particular browser + object combination (**Figure 16.9**).

4. Choose your action from the menu (they're described later in this chapter). In most cases, a dialog box will appear.

5. Fill out the dialog box (guess what? I explain each of them later in this chapter), and click on OK. The name of the action will appear in the Actions list box.

6. Click on the arrow to the left of the Action name to drop down a list of available user events (**Figure 16.10**). The available events will depend on the object + browser + action combination you chose. More events are available if you choose 4.0 or later browsers, but remember that only the users with those browsers will be able to use them.

7. Choose your event from the menu (they're described later in this chapter). Its name will appear in the Events list box.

    To see only events for a specific browser, select the browser from the Show Events For submenu.

✔ Tips

- You can add more than one event to a single object. You might have different actions for onMouseOver and onClick. Just repeat steps 3–7 for each additional event.

- You can also attach more than one action to a single event. Just repeat steps 6–7 to add additional actions to an event (each action will be listed separately). For instance, you might have onMouseOver trigger both a sound and a status message.

Deleting and Editing Behaviors

After you create a behavior, you can remove it or edit it. To attach a behavior to a different object, you must delete it and re-create it (unless you want to edit the JavaScript).

To delete a behavior:

1. In the Document window (or the tag selector), click on the object to which you applied the behavior. The name of the event(s) associated with that object will appear in the Behaviors panel (**Figure 16.11**).

2. In the Behaviors panel, click on the behavior you want to delete.

3. Click on the Delete Action button ☐ or press the Delete key. The name of the behavior will disappear (**Figure 16.12**).

Editing Behaviors

You can edit the browsers, and events used in a behavior, as well as the data used by the actions (which you supply in those dialog boxes).

To edit a behavior:

1. In the Document window, click on the object to which you applied the behavior. The name of the events associated with that object will appear in the Behaviors panel (as we saw in **Figure 16.11**).

2. In the Behaviors panel's Actions list box, click on the action you want to change.

3. To edit the action, double-click on its name. The associated dialog box will appear (**Figure 16.13**). (Dialog boxes for each of the actions are explained later in this chapter.) Make your changes and then click on OK to close the dialog box.

Selected object

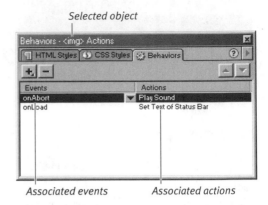

Associated events   *Associated actions*

Figure 16.11 When an object is selected, its associated events appear in the Behaviors panel.

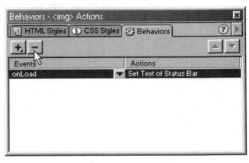

Figure 16.12 When I clicked on the Delete Action (-) button, the unwanted action disappeared.

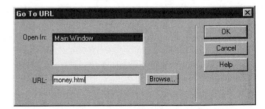

Figure 16.13 When you add a new action or double-click on the name of an existing action, a dialog box will appear in which you add or edit the variables for the action. This is the dialog box for the Go To URL action.

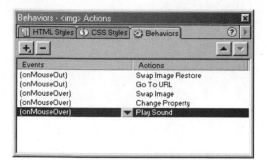

Figure 16.14 Select the proper object and then select the action whose position you wish to change.

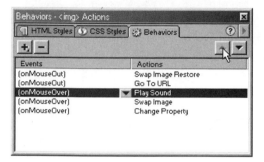

Figure 16.15 I moved the actions around by clicking on the Up and Down arrow buttons.

Reordering Actions

You can edit actions as often as you want. If you have an event that triggers more than one action, you may want to set the order in which the actions occur.

To change the order in which actions occur:

1. Select the object in the Document window or the tag selector.

2. Select the behavior in the Behaviors panel (**Figure 16.14**).

3. Change the order of the action by clicking on the arrow buttons:
   - Click on the Up arrow ▲ to move the action up in the list.
   - Click on the Down arrow ▼ to move the action down in the list.

The order of the actions will change immediately (**Figure 16.15**), and the browser will perform the actions in order from the top down.

That's about it for adding and editing behaviors. The rest of the chapter is dedicated to the details.

✔ Tip

■ Behaviors are arranged in groups in the Behaviors panel according to the user event they rely on. In **Figure 16.14**, the behaviors are grouped by onMouseOut and onMouseOver events. You can only move a behavior up and down within its group of like events. In **Figure 16.15**, I moved Play Sound as far up in the list as it would go.

DELETING AND EDITING BEHAVIORS

Common Objects

You can attach a behavior to nearly any HTML element, although some are more versatile than others. I'm going to describe some of the more common objects here.

Anchors <a>

Many events are only available to the <a> tag that is usually used for links. Other objects can be attached to these events by surrounding the object with the <a> tag, which can be a null link that doesn't go anywhere.

For images that require a link tag, Dreamweaver will automatically supply an <a> tag for the object.

The anchor code for a null link will look like this:

```
<a href="javascript:;">foo</a>
```

The link destination "javascript:;" basically means that the link doesn't go anywhere. You can also use a pound sign (#) for a null link. If you want to use a destination link later, you can replace either the "javascript:;" or the "#" with an actual link.

✔ Tips

- In the Behaviors panel's Events pop-up menu, events that can be activated by applying the <a> tag appear (in parentheses).

- You can use style sheets to remove the underlining or color changes from the added links on your page. See Chapter 11, and set text-decoration to "none."

Body <body>

If you want to apply behaviors to an entire page, the <body> tag is what you select.

If you select text that is not linked, Dreamweaver may apply the behavior to the <body> tag. Check the tag selector. Add a null link to your text if you want to apply a behavior to it.

Images <img>

Images have some nifty properties, one of which is that they load. A popular trick the kids are playing with these days is the rollover, in which mousing over an image causes another image to load in its place. You can also make a simple rollover using the instructions in Chapter 7.

Forms <form>

You can use special form behaviors with a form. The events available to a form include onSubmit and onReset.

Form Fields

You can attach behaviors to individual fields in a form, too, such as <option> (for items in a menu or list), <textfield>, and <checkbox>. One example is the Go to URL action, which can be applied to the <option> items in a drop-down menu, so that when you select an item from the menu, a new page loads.

Event Handlers

There are many different event handlers you can use in Dreamweaver behaviors. These events are detailed in **Table 16.1**.

✔ Tips

- Different events may appear in the Add Event menu in the Behaviors panel depending on the browser and object you've selected.

- Events surrounded (by parentheses) in the Add Event menu will become activated by adding an anchor tag to the selected object. Dreamweaver does this for you automatically. If you don't specify a link, Dreamweaver uses the "blank" link, which in Dreamweaver 4 is `"javascript:;"`. You can also use a pound sign "#" for a null link.

- Internet Explorer 4 and 5 include the most available events, but it's important to remember that only a fraction of your audience uses Explorer exclusively.

Table 16.1 Events are arranged in logical sets rather than alphabetically. This table does not include all event handlers available to JavaScript, only those that Dreamweaver utilizes for behaviors.

User Events available in Dreamweaver			
EVENT HANDLER NAME	**DESCRIPTION OF THE USER EVENT** *(The event handler may call any number of actions, including dialog boxes.)*	**BROWSERS** *(According to Dreamweaver.)*	**ASSOCIATED TAGS** *(Other tags may be used; these are the most common associated objects.)*
PAGE LOADING EVENTS			
onAbort	When the user presses the Stop button or Esc key before successful page or image loading	NN3, NN4, NS6, IE4, IE5	body, img
onLoad	When a page, frameset, or image has finished loading	NN3, NN4, NS6, IE3, IE4, IE5	body, img
onUnload	When the user leaves the page (clicks on a link, presses the back button)	NN3, NN4, NS6, IE3, IE4, IE5	body
onResize	When the user resizes the browser window	NN3, NN4, NS6, IE4, IE5	body
onError	When a JavaScript error occurs	NN3, NN4, NS6, IE4, IE5	a, body, img

(continues)

User Events available in Dreamweaver *(continued)*

EVENT HANDLER NAME	DESCRIPTION OF THE USER EVENT *(The event handler may call any number of actions, including dialog boxes.)*	BROWSERS *(According to Dreamweaver.)*	ASSOCIATED TAGS *(Other tags may be used; these are the most common associated objects.)*
FORM AND FORM FIELD EVENTS			
onBlur	When a form field "loses the focus" of its intended use	NN3, NN4, NS6, IE3, IE4, IE5	form fields: text, textarea, select
onFocus	When a form field receives the user's focus by being selected by the Tab key	NN3, NN4, NS6, IE3, IE4, IE5	form fields: text, textarea, select
onChange	When the user changes the default selection in a form field	NN3, NN4, NS6, IE3, IE4, IE5	most form fields
onSelect	When the user selects text within a form field	NN3, NN4, NS6, IE3, IE4, IE5	form fields: text, textarea
onSubmit	When a user clicks on the form's Submit button	NN3, NN4, NS6, IE3, IE4, IE5	form
onReset	When a user clicks on the form's Reset button	NN3, NN4, NS6, IE3, IE4, IE5	form
MOUSE EVENTS			
onClick	When the user clicks on the object	NN3, NN4, NS6, IE3, IE4, IE5 (IE3 uses this handler only for form fields)	a; form fields: button, checkbox, radio, reset, submit
onDblClick	When the user double-clicks on the object	NN4, NS6, IE4, IE5	a, img
onMouseMove	When the user moves the mouse	NS6, IE3, IE4, IE5	a, img
onMouseDown	When the mouse button is depressed	NN4, NS6, IE4, IE5	a, img
onMouseUp	When the mouse button is released	NN4, NS6, IE4, IE5	a, img
onMouseOver	When the user points the mouse pointer at an object	NN3, IE3, NN4, NS6, IE4, IE5	a, img
onMouseOut	When the user moves the mouse off an object they moused over	NN3, NN4, NS6, IE4, IE5	a, img
KEYBOARD EVENTS			
onKeyDown	When a key on the keyboard is depressed	NN3, NN4, NS6, IE3, IE4, IE5	form fields: text, textarea
onKeyPress	When the user presses any key	NN3, NN4, NS6, IE3, IE4, IE5	form fields: text, textarea
onKeyUp	When a key on the keyboard is released	NN3, NN4, NS6, IE3, IE4, IE5	form fields: text, textarea
INTERNET EXPLORER 4 EVENTS			
onHelp	When the user presses F1 or selects a link labeled "help"	IE4, IE5	a, img
onReadyStateChange	Page is loading	IE4, IE5	img
onAfterUpdate	After the content of a form field changes	IE4, IE5	a, body, img
onBeforeUpdate	After form field item changes, before content loses focus	IE4, IE5	a, body, img
onScroll	When the user uses the page scrollbars	IE4, IE5	body

EVENT HANDLERS

Common Actions

In this section of the chapter I describe how to set up some common JavaScript actions in Dreamweaver. This is not meant to be an all-encompassing JavaScript reference; the language is capable of much more than I'm able to sum up in a single chapter.

Setting up behaviors in JavaScript is very much like ordering Chinese food: you take one from Column A (objects), one from Column B (events), and one from Column C (actions).

Because it would be redundant for me to repeat every detail of how to set up a behavior for each of these actions, I'm going to skip some of the basic steps, like showing the Behaviors panel. You can review the details in *Adding Behaviors,* earlier in this chapter.

✔ Tips

■ The objects and events that I name in the instructions for these events are suggestions; many other combinations are possible.

■ Don't forget that JavaScript can crash older browsers. Heck, my computer crashed a half-dozen times just writing about it. Refer to Appendix C on the Web site for tips on writing pages for the masses.

Figure 16.16 Type your status bar message in the Message text box.

Status bar message

Figure 16.17 When the user mouses over the link, a message appears in the status bar.

Setting Status Bar Message

A status bar message is a little bit of text that appears in the status bar of the browser.

Usage Example: Combine <a> and onMouseOver with Display Status Message. When the user mouses over a link, they'll see a message in the status bar such as "Explore the Invisible Cities." This is also a great trick for hiding the target URL.

To add a status bar message:

1. In the Behaviors panel, select a browser (3.0 and later, or 4.0 and later if you want more event options).

2. In the Document window, select an object (a, body, img).

3. In the Behaviors panel, add the action Set Text of Status Bar (Set Text > Set Text of Status Bar). The Set Text of Status Bar dialog box will appear (**Figure 16.16**).

4. Type your message in the Message text box. Use a space to leave the status bar blank at all times.

5. Click on OK. The Set Text of Status Bar dialog box will close.

6. In the Behaviors panel, choose an event (onMouseOver, onMouseOut, onLoad, onClick).

When you load the page in a browser, the message will appear in the status bar when you perform the user event you specified (**Figure 16.17**).

✔ Tip

■ If you specify a status message for onMouseOver, you may also want to specify a status message for onMouseOut. This can be a blank message. Just type a space in the Message text box.

417

Going to a New URL

You can open URLs with actions other than a click.

Usage Example: Have a link open two windows at once or open a document in each of two frames. You can also specify URLs in this way using JavaScript; older browsers get the regular old link, while the JavaScript user goes to the JavaScript page.

To add a URL:

1. In the Behaviors panel, select a browser (3.0 and later).

2. In the Document window, select an object (a, img, body).

3. In the Behaviors panel, add the action Go to URL. The Go To URL dialog box will appear (**Figure 16.18**).

4. Add your URLs as follows:
   - ◆ To load a new URL in a single, non-frames window, type it in the URL text box.
   - ◆ To load a single URL on a page with more than one frame and URL, select the name of the single frame from the Open In list box and type the URL in the URL text box.
   - ◆ To load more than one URL on a page with more than one frame and more than one URL, repeat the preceding instruction for each single frame.

5. Click OK. The dialog box will close.

6. In the Behaviors panel, specify the event (onClick, onLoad, onMouseOver, onMouseOut). The URL(s) will open when the user performs the event (**Figure 16.19**).

✔ Tip

- ■ Be sure to test, test, and retest these links once they're on the server, particularly if you're targeting multiple frames.

Figure 16.18 Select the windows (or frames) and type in the corresponding URLs that will load when the event happens.

Figure 16.19 When you click on many different links on the Dreamweaver help page, frames on both the left and right load new images.

Window Dressing

In the example in **Figure 16.18**, I can choose between opening my URL in the main page body or in any frame on the page. If you want the page to open in a new window, you can do that, too. One way is to set a target. Type this code in the URL text box, where path/file.html is the URL of your page:

```
path/file.html target="_blank"
```

Additionally, you can have the URL open in a custom-sized window, with or without toolbars. See *Opening a New Browser Window*, later in this chapter. After you create a window, its name will appear in the Open In list box.

Figure 16.20 Type the message you want to appear in the dialog box in the Message text box.

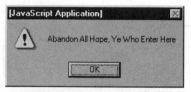

Figure 16.21 A popup message created with Dreamweaver. This message appears when the user clicks on a link. I used this in combination with the Go To URL action; when the user clicks on OK, the browser will open a new page.

Popup Message

In the Popup Message action, when the user performs an action, a pop-up message (or dialog box) will appear. In Dreamweaver, the only choice in this dialog box is OK.

Usage Example: Combine this action with the result of another action, such as form validation ("You forgot to type your e-mail address") or plug-in detection ("You need Shockwave to properly appreciate this page").

To add a pop-up message:

1. In the Behaviors panel, select a browser (3.0 and later).

2. In the Document window, select an object (a, body).

3. In the Behaviors panel, add the action Pop-Up Message. The Popup Message dialog box will appear (**Figure 16.20**).

4. Type your message in the Message text box.

5. Click on OK. The Popup Message dialog box will close.

6. In the Behaviors panel, specify the event (onClick, onMouseOver).

When you load the page in a browser, the pop-up message or dialog box will open when the user performs the event, such as a click (**Figure 16.21**).

✔ Tip

■ Don't overuse this one. I've seen pages where the slightest mouse movement would open a dialog box, and it was truly annoying.

Opening a New Browser Window

You know those little bitty JavaScript windows? You can pop one open using the Open Browser Window action—or you can pop open a regular-sized window. Incidentally, each of these pop-up windows has a unique URL that belongs to a distinct HTML document that you must create separately.

Usage Example: Pop open a floating toolbar, "control panel," or a window set to the exact size of a Shockwave applet or streaming video (**Figure 16.22**).

To add the Open Browser Window action:

1. In the Behaviors panel, select a browser (3.0 and later).

2. In the Document window, select an object (a, img, body).

3. In the Behaviors panel, add the Action Open Browser Window. The Open Browser Window dialog box will appear (**Figure 16.23**).

4. Type the URL of the content for the new window in the URL text box, or click Browse to select a local file. If you haven't created the content for the new window you can type a filename or URL in the URL to Display text box anyway.

5. If you want to specify a window width and window height, type these dimensions (in pixels) in the appropriate text boxes. If you don't specify these dimensions, a default-sized browser window will open.

6. The checkboxes allow you to display regular browser features such as navigation and location toolbars, the status bar, the menu bar, scrollbars, and resize handles. Leave all the boxes unchecked if you want a "featureless" window.

Figure 16.22 This sound control panel is set to pop open when a link in the parent window is clicked.

Figure 16.23 The open Browser Window dialog box. These are the attributes I set for the control panel in **Figure 16.22**.

Figure 16.24 Another floating toolbar. Note the extra space below the buttons—the window must be a minimum of 100 pixels high. If I were getting this control panel ready for prime time, I'd center the buttons within the window using a table, or I'd make bigger buttons.

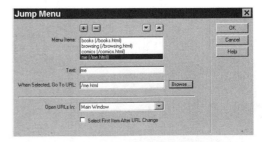

Figure 16.25 You can edit a jump menu after you insert it using the Jump Menu dialog box. See Chapter 15 for details.

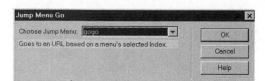

Figure 16.26 If you have more than one jump menu on your page, select the correct one from the drop-down menu. You can apply this action to an existing menu or to a form button.

Jump Menu Behaviors

Two actions listed in the Behaviors panel, Jump Menu and Jump Menu Go, apply to jump menus. Jump menus, discussed in Chapter 15, are small drop-down menus from which the user can select a page to visit. A jump menu can operate with a Go button or without a button, in which case the browser activates the link in the menu as soon as the user selects it.

To insert a jump menu, see Chapter 15.

To edit a jump menu, select it, and then in the Behaviors panel, double-click the action Jump Menu. The Jump Menu dialog box will appear (**Figure 16.25**).

To add a Go button to a jump menu after you've inserted the menu, you must add a form button (Insert > Form Object > Button). In the Property inspector, set the Action to Nothing, then label the button "Go," or whatever you like.

Then, in the Behaviors panel, select the button, and give it the event onClick and the action Jump Menu Go. The Jump Menu Go dialog box will appear (**Figure 16.26**). Keep in mind that the menu may still operate onSelect rather than by clicking the button. Unfortunately, the only reliable way to use a Go button is to add it while you're inserting the menu in the first place.

7. To specify a window name, type the title in the Window Name text box. (You can use these window names in other behaviors, such as Go to URL.)

8. Click on OK. The Open Browser Window dialog box will close.

9. In the Behaviors panel, specify the event (onClick, onLoad, onMouseOver).

In the browser window, when the action (page loading, link clicking) occurs, the new window will open (**Figure 16.24**).

✔ Tips

- By trial and error, I've found that Java-Script windows must be at least 100 pixels high. The window in **Figure 16.22** is 115 pixels wide and 150 pixels high, and the window in **Figure 16.24** is 100 pixels high, although I'd like it to be about 50 pixels high.

- If you want links on your page to be able to load into this window, use the Go to URL Behavior, and from the Open In list box, select the window name you specified in step 7 as if it were a target frame name.

- To set a page title for this window, open the separate HTML document in Dreamweaver (File > Open), and use the Page Properties dialog box (under the Modify menu).

- Once you add the code for opening a new window to a page, you can use it as a target for any link using the Go to URL behavior or the Jump Menu (see Chapter 15 and the sidebar, this page)

Checking Browser for Plugin

The Check Plugin action checks the user's browser to see if they have a particular plug-in installed. After the check, the action can load one of two URLs: one for Yes, and an alternate for No.

Usage Example: If the user has Shockwave installed, they will proceed to the Shockwave-enhanced version of the page. If not, they will be sent to a page that's designed to present the same information without Shockwave.

To add the Check Plugin action:

1. In the Behaviors panel, select a browser (3.0 and later).

2. In the Document window, select the <body> tag by clicking on it in the tag selector at the bottom left of the status bar, or select an <a> tag.

3. In the Behaviors panel, add the action Check Plugin. The Check Plugin dialog box will appear (**Figure 16.27**).

4. Choose a plug-in from the drop-down menu.

   or

   If the desired plug-in is not available from the drop-down menu, type the name of the plug-in, exactly as it appears in bold on Netscape's About Plug-ins page. For example, to look for the latest version of the RealPlayer, you'd type RealPlayer(tm) G2 LiveConnect-Enabled Plug-In (32-bit) (yes, the whole thing).

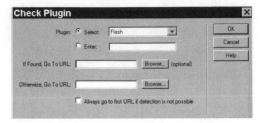

Figure 16.27 Choose your plug-in from the drop-down menu.

5. Type the URL for the Yes page in the URL text box (for example: shock_index.html).

6. Type the alternate URL for the No page in the Alt URL text box (for example: noshock_index.html).

7. Click on OK to close the Check Plugin dialog box.

8. In the Behaviors panel, specify the event (onLoad, onClick).

When the page loads or the link is clicked, the user will automatically be forwarded to the proper page.

✔ Tips

■ To view Netscape's About:Plug-ins page, select Help > About Plug-ins from Navigator's menu bar, or type about: plugins in the address bar and press Enter (Return). In Netscape 6, type about:plugins (no spaces).

■ Many Netscape plug-ins have ActiveX counterparts for Internet Explorer; check the documentation for the plug-in to find out whether Explorer supports it as ActiveX or as a plug-in. See Chapter 7 on using both the OBJECT and EMBED tags to work with both browsers.

■ I discuss plug-ins and ActiveX in Chapter 7. Appendix C on the Web site discusses making sites available to browsers other than the latest versions of Navigator and Explorer.

CHECKING BROWSER FOR PLUGIN

Checking Browser Version

The Check Browser action checks the brand and version of the user's browser; different browsers do have different capabilities. After the check, the action can load one of two URLs: one for Yes, and an alternate for No.

Usage Example: If the user has a 4.0 browser, they can proceed to the layers-intensive version of the page. If they have a 3.0 browser, they will be sent to a page that's designed to present the same information using tables.

✔ Tips

■ Browsers before Netscape 2 or Explorer 3 will not run this behavior, because they don't support JavaScript. The steps on the following page tell how to work around older browsers.

■ It's a good idea to have the page on which this behavior appears contain the equivalent information for users with older browsers, and to use the Stay on this Page option for them.

To add the Check Browser action:

1. In the Behaviors panel, select a browser (3.0 and later).

2. In the Document window, select the <body> tag by clicking on it in the Tag Selector at the bottom left of the status bar, or select an <a> tag.

3. In the Behaviors panel, add the action Check Browser. The Check Browser dialog box will appear (**Figure 16.28**).

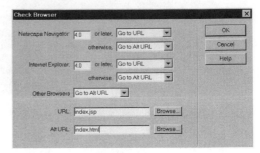

Figure 16.28 Specify different actions for different browsers using the Check Browser dialog box.

4. For each of the three options, Netscape Navigator, Internet Explorer, or Other Browsers, choose an option from the drop-down menu: Go to URL, Go to Alt URL, or Stay on this Page. (Browsers that don't support JavaScript will use the last option by default.)

5. In the Netscape Navigator and/or Internet Explorer text boxes, type the earliest version number that supports the feature you're working around. If the feature is, say, layers, type 4.0 in both text boxes; for frames, type 2.0 in the Navigator text box and 3.0 in the Explorer text box.

6. Type the URL for the main page in the URL text box (for example, `layers_index.html`).

7. Optionally, type an alternate URL, for the alternate page, in the Alt URL text box (for example: `nolayers_index.html`). (If you don't specify an alternate URL, the user will stay on the current page or will use the non-JavaScript link.)

8. Click on OK to close the dialog box.

9. In the Behaviors panel, specify the event (`onLoad`, `onClick`).

When the page loads or the link is clicked, the user will automatically be forwarded to the proper page.

Complex Rollovers

Swapping images is the same as performing the famous rollovers I talked about earlier.

Usage Example: When the user mouses over the image, it's replaced with a "lit up" image (**Figure 16.29**) or another image entirely.

✔ Tip

- You don't need to set up the Swap Image action in order to set up image rollovers. See the first section of Chapter 7 to find out how to use the Insert > Interactive Images > Rollover Image object. This option inserts an image, pre-loads the secondary image, and automatically restores the original image onMouseOut.

Images must be named in order for image swapping to work properly.

To name your images:

1. Select the image.

2. In the Property inspector, name the image by typing a name for it in the Image text box and pressing Enter (Return).

To add the Swap Image action:

1. In the Behaviors panel, select a browser (Netscape 3.0 and later).

2. In the Document window, select an image (img; Dreamweaver will add the anchor tag if needed).

3. In the Behaviors panel, add the action Swap Image. The Swap Image dialog box will appear (**Figure 16.30**).

Figure 16.29 The Dreamweaver help page uses image rollovers to make the buttons "light up" when you mouse over them.

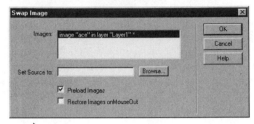

Figure 16.30 This is the Swap Image dialog box I used to set rollovers.

Figure 16.31 A popular way to implement image swapping is to use an image that's the reverse of the original. When the user mouses over the image on the bottom, it's swapped with an image that's the same size and shape, with reversed colors.

Figure 16.32 You can set the Swap Image action to swap several images at once. In this example, when the user mouses over the image on the bottom, all three images are swapped simultaneously.

4. The Images list box will display all the named images on your page. Click on the name of the image you want to swap.

   ◆ To swap the image you selected as an object in step 2, be sure to select the name of that image.

   ◆ To swap a different image when the user event occurs, select a different image.

5. Type the source for the new image (the one that will replace the named image when the action occurs) in the Set Source To text box, or click on Browse.

6. To have the images loaded with the page, select the Preload Images checkbox.

7. To automatically have the image revert to its original appearance when the user mouses out, select the Restore Images onMouseOut checkbox.

8. In the Behaviors panel, specify the event (onClick, onLoad, onMouseOver, onMouseOut).When you view this page in a 3.0 or later browser, the images you selected will be swapped (**Figure 16.31**).

✔ Tips

■ If you select more than one image in a single action, all selected images will roll over when you mouse over the single image you selected in step 2 (**Figure 16.32**).

■ To set rollovers for individual images, you need to follow steps 2–7 for each consecutive image.

■ Image swapping onMouseOver is often combined with image restoring onMouseOut. You can set this up automatically, but you can also decide not to do so.

■ This action will not work in Netscape 6 if you target an image in a different frame.

Preload Images

You can set up the Swap Image behavior to automatically preload images, but there are other instances in which you may want to preload images as well.

Usage Example: Preload a large image that appears in a DHTML/JavaScript window before the user ever gets there by adding this behavior to the home page.

To add the Preload Image action:

1. In the Behaviors panel, select 4.0 and later browsers.

2. In the Document window, select the body of the page by clicking on the <body> tag in the tag selector.

3. In the Behaviors panel, add the action Preload Images. The Preload Images dialog box will appear (**Figure 16.33**).

4. Type the pathname of the image you want to preload in the Image Source File text box, or click on Browse to choose the image from your computer.

5. For every image you want to preload, click on the Plus button ⊞, and then repeat step 4.

6. To delete an image, select it and click on the Minus button ⊟.

7. Click on OK to close the Preload Images dialog box.

8. In the Behaviors panel, make sure the onLoad event is selected.

Dreamweaver will write what's called an array in the head of the document. All image filenames that appear in this array will be preloaded when the browser loads the page.

Figure 16.33 Set the source for all the images you want cached and ready in the Preload Images dialog box.

Set Navbar Image

The behavior Set Navbar Image is used in conjunction with Navigation bars, described in Chapter 7. The behavior uses the same dialog box to change the image source for the navigation bar. You can also create additional user events using the Behaviors panel for a navbar; for instance, you could add button images for onMouseDown or onAbort.

Figure 16.34 There's no good way to demonstrate rollovers in print, so let's pretend that the window on the left and the window on the right are the same window. On the left, we're mousing over the image. On the right, we've just moused out, and the image is restored.

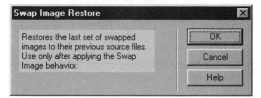

Figure 16.35 All you need to do with the Swap Image Restore dialog box is click on OK.

Restoring Swapped Images

When you set up an image rollover using either the Insert Rollover Image function or the Swap Image Behavior, you can select an option that automatically swaps the image back to its original source when the user mouses out (**Figure 16.34**). By checking the Restore Images onMouseOut check box in the Swap Image dialog box, your images will automatically restore themselves when the user mouses away from them.

Maybe, however, you have a different user event call the Swap Image behavior, or if you'd like not to turn on automatically restored images. If so, you can set a different event, perhaps on a different link, image, or button, to swap the images back by setting up the Swap Image Restore Behavior.

This is simple: Just select the image for which you've previously set up a Swap Image or Rollover Image Behavior, and then add the action Swap Image Restore. The Swap Image Restore dialog box will appear (**Figure 16.35**). Just click on OK, and that's it. Then, specify a different event, if necessary.

Play Sound

You can use the Play Sound action to play a sound when a user performs an action such as a mouseover or a click.

Usage Example: Combine a small (~20KB) sound with image rollovers so that a beep (or a ding, or a shriek) occurs.

To add a sound:

1. In the Behaviors panel, select a browser (Netscape 3, 4.0 and later).

2. In the Document window, select an object (a, body, img).

3. In the Behaviors panel, add the action Play Sound. The Play Sound dialog box will appear (**Figure 16.36**).

4. To play a sound onEvent, type the URL of the sound clip in the Play Sound text box.
   or
   Click on Browse. The Select File dialog box will appear. Choose the file from a folder in your local site.

5. Click on OK. The Play Sound dialog box will close.

6. In the Behaviors panel, specify the event (onClick, onLoad, onMouseOver).

When you load this page in the browser you can play a sound clip (**Figure 16.37**).

Figure 16.36 Using the Play Sound dialog box, you can add a sound to an event.

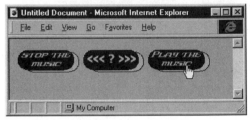

Figure 16.37 Using these images as the objects for the Play Sound behavior, you can let the user play a sound embedded using JavaScript.

The Fury of Sound

In past versions of Dreamweaver, you could purportedly use this behavior not only to play a sound but to stop one. You still can, if you're sneaky, since browsers will only play one sound at a time. For example, you may have a theme song set to play onLoad or onMouseOver. You can then attach a small (one second, even) sound to a button called, for example, Stop the Music (**Figure 16.37**). When the user mouses over the button, the sound that is currently playing will stop, and the short beep will play.

I cover plug-ins and sound files in Chapter 7. You can refer to that chapter for information on changing HTML or JavaScript code for hidden/visible sound controls, sound loops, and the like.

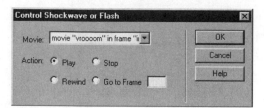

Figure 16.38 Using the Control Shockwave or Flash dialog box, you can provide controls to play, stop, rewind, or jump to a frame in a Shockwave movie.

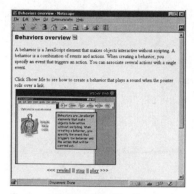

Figure 16.39 I modified the About Behaviors page from the Dreamweaver help files to add Shockwave controls that rewind, play, or stop the movie.

Control Shockwave or Flash

You can use the Control Shockwave or Flash action to play, stop, rewind, or jump to a particular frame in a Shockwave or Flash movie.

Usage Examples: Provide buttons or links marked Stop and Play. For a Shockwave game, provide a Play Again link that jumps back to the particular frame in which the game starts.

✔ Tip

- To use the Control Shockwave or Flash action, you must first embed a Shockwave or Flash object in the page using the <embed> or <object> tags. I discuss Shockwave and Flash in Chapter 7.

To add Shockwave or Flash controls:

1. In the Behaviors panel, select a browser (3.0 and later).

2. In the Document window, select an object (a, img, input).

3. In the Behaviors panel, add the action Control Shockwave or Flash. The Control Shockwave or Flash dialog box will appear (**Figure 16.38**).

4. If there is more than one Shockwave or Flash movie on your page, select the correct object from the Movie drop-down menu.

5. Click on the radio button for the control you want to add: Play, Stop, Rewind, or Go to Frame. For this last option, type the number of the frame in the Frame text box.

6. Click on OK. The Control Shockwave or Flash dialog box will close.

7. In the Behaviors panel, specify the event (onClick, onLoad, onMouseOver).

When you load this page in the browser, you can control the Shockwave movie (**Figure 16.39**).

Show or Hide Layers

The Show-Hide Layers action can make certain layers appear or disappear. You must already have the layers on your page to set up this behavior. The effectiveness of this behavior depends on the initial visibility setting you give your layers.

Usage Example: When a user mouses over an image or clicks on a link, one layer will disappear and another will appear; we saw this in **Figures 16.1** through **16.3**. Because layers are loaded with a page, you can make several sets of content available on a single page and hidden in different layers.

To add the Show-Hide Layers action:

1. In the Behaviors panel, select a browser (4.0 and later).

2. In the Document window that contains the layers, select an object (a, body, img).

3. In the Behaviors panel, add the action Show-Hide Layers. The Show-Hide Layers dialog box will appear (**Figure 16.40**).

   Dreamweaver may take a moment or two to detect all the layers on the page, at which point their names (id="" or name="") will appear in the Layers list box.

Figure 16.40 Set the (onEvent) visibility of your layers in the Show-Hide Layers dialog box.

Why Default?

The *Default* setting is most useful for a second Show-Hide Layers behavior.

For instance: Let's imagine a page with two layers. When the page loads, Layer Apple is showing, and Layer Banana is hidden—those are their default settings.

First behavior: When an onClick happens to a link called "Turn the Page" in Layer Apple, Apple hides and Banana appears.

Second behavior: When an onClick happens to a link called "Back to the Beginning" in Layer Banana, the Default settings of both layers are restored, and thus Apple appears and Banana hides.

Experiment with this; I got mixed results.

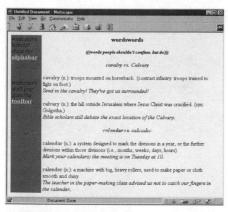

Figure 16.41 This page has two hidden layers. The links to them are in the table cell at the left.

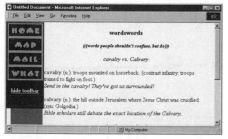

Figure 16.42 Click on the link that says Show Toolbar, and it calls a behavior that shows the Toolbar layer. Notice that that layer has a link called Hide Toolbar.

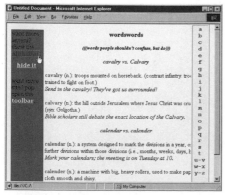

Figure 16.43 Here, we've hidden the toolbar again and are showing the layer called Alphabar. Notice the additional text in the left margin: that's yet another layer that has a link that will hide the Alphabar layer.

4. Click on the name of the layer whose visibility you want the event to change, and then click on one of the three buttons: Show, Hide, or Default. Default will restore the layer's original visibility setting.

5. Repeat step 4 for all the layers you want this behavior to affect.

6. Click on OK to close the Show-Hide Layers dialog box.

7. In the Behaviors panel, specify the event (onLoad, onClick, onMouseOver).

The page must be loaded in a 4.0 or later browser for this action to work, because earlier browsers don't show layers at all. **Figure 16.41** shows a page with all layers hidden. Figures **16.42** and **16.43** show the same page with the layers showing.

✔ Tips

- Another layer animation behavior, Drag Layer, is described later in this chapter.

- This action will not work in Netscape 6 if you are targeting a layer in another frame.

Validate Form Data

Form validation is useful—you can have JavaScript validate a form before it's even sent to the form-handling script.

Usage Example: You can require that certain fields be filled out, or require that data be in a certain format; for instance, a full e-mail address or only numbers instead of letters.

✔ Tip

■ You must already have the completed form on your page, with all fields named, before you can apply this behavior.

To add the Form Validation action:

1. In the Behaviors panel, select a browser (3.0 and later).

2. In the Document window that contains the form, select the form (click on <form> in the tag selector).

3. In the Behaviors panel, add the action Validate Form. The Validate Form dialog box will appear (**Figure 16.44**).

4. Dreamweaver may take a moment or two to detect all the named text form fields on the page, at which point their names will appear in the Named Fields list box.

5. Click on the name of the form field you want to validate.

Figure 16.44 In the Validate Form dialog box you can restrict the input into text or text-area form fields.

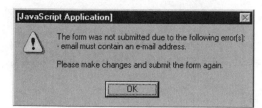

Figure 16.45 On my form, I required that the text in the e-mail field be in standard e-mail address format. If a user submits a form that doesn't conform to this validation requirement, they'll get a message telling them so.

6. To make the form field required, in which case the form will not be accepted unless this field is filled out, place a checkmark in the Required checkbox.

7. To restrict the content you'll accept, choose one of the following options:

    ◆ Number (content must be numbers)

    ◆ Number from n to n (range of numbers; type the range in the text boxes)

    ◆ E-mail address (text must be in the name@address.domain format)

8. Click on OK to close the Validate Form dialog box.

9. In the Behaviors panel, make sure the onSubmit event is specified.

When users submit the form, they'll see a dialog box informing them if they failed to meet your validation standards (**Figure 16.45**).

✔ Tip

■ Before you unleash the form-validation script on your users, test it to make sure it does what you want it to.

The onBlur Event

The onBlur event is kind of confusing at best, but it makes a cute party trick. To "blur" a form field means that it "loses the focus" of its intent. To this end, you can mini-validate a single form field. Follow the instructions above, substituting the following variables:

In step 2, select a <text> or <textarea> tag as the object, instead of the <form> tag.

In step 9, use the onBlur event instead of the onSubmit event.

The easiest way to test out the onBlur event is to use numbers; in step 7, require a number between 1 and 10.

Now load the page in a browser, and try typing a number less than 1 or greater than 10 in the form field, and press Enter (Return). Your input will disappear.

VALIDATE FORM DATA

Changing the Content of Frames and Layers

Dreamweaver offers a set of behaviors that allow you to change the text or HTML in a frame or a layer. Any HTML content may be inserted dynamically, that is, after the page loads initially.

Usage Examples: When the user clicks on a link, selects an option from a menu, or mouses over a button, the new text appears.

Changing Text in a Frame

Normally, when you click on a link in a frame, a new page can appear in that frame or another frame. So what's the advantage of using a behavior? For one thing, you can specify a user event other than onClick—for example, onMouseOver. For another, the code for the new page is pre-loaded by the browser and therefore will appear faster than if the browser had to fetch a new page. The behavior is illustrated in **Figures 16.46** through **16.48**.

To set the text of a frame:

1. Create and save a frames-based page, as described in Chapter 13. Be sure to name each frame, or Dreamweaver will refer to them by arbitrary numbers.

2. In the Behaviors panel, select a browser (3.0 and later).

3. In the Document window, select an object (a, body, img, select).

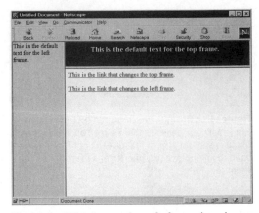

Figure 16.46 This is a mockup of a frames-based page that uses the Set Text of Frame behavior.

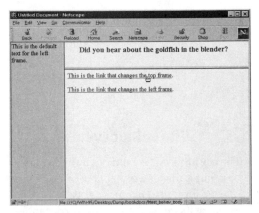

Figure 16.47 When the user clicks the link for the top frame, a simple text change occurs, and the background reverts to white.

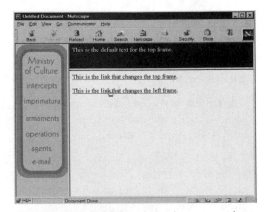

Figure 16.48 The left frame change is more complex, and includes a table, images, and links.

Figure 16.49 Choose the frame you want to edit, and then supply the new text or HTML. The easiest way to do it is to paste it in.

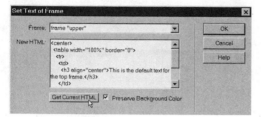

Figure 16.50 Here, I clicked on Get Current HTML for the "upper" frame; it includes the header formatting and the table.

4. In the Behaviors panel, add the action Set Text > Set Text of Frame. The Set Text of Frame dialog box will appear (**Figure 16.49**).

5. In the Set Text of Frame dialog box, you can edit the existing frame content, paste in text from another page, or write the page from scratch.

   To get the text of the current frame, click the Get Current HTML button. The text will appear in the New HTML text box, where you can edit it (**Figure 16.50**).

6. Otherwise, type or paste in the code.

7. Dreamweaver will entirely replace the code for the frame. If you want to preserve the current frame's background color, leave that box checked.

8. When you're finished, click on OK to close the Set Text of Frame dialog box.

9. In the Behaviors panel, specify the event (onLoad, onClick, onMouseOver).

10. Preview your page in a browser and check to make sure your changes work properly.

✔ Tip

■ This action does not work in Netscape 6.

Changing Text in a Layer

Setting the text and HTML of a layer allows you to make a layer useful by filling it with different things when different links are moused over or clicked. A layer can even be transparent and invisible on the page until this behavior acts on it (**Figures 16.51** and **16.52**).

To set the text of a layer:

1. Insert a layer on your page and name it, as described in Chapter 14.

2. In the Behaviors panel, select a browser (4.0 and later).

3. In the Document window, select an object (a, body, img, select).

4. In the Behaviors panel, add the action Set Text > Set Text of Layer. The Set Text of Layer dialog box will appear (**Figure 16.53**).

5. In the New HTML text box, type or paste in the code for the new content (**Figure 16.54**). This can include image pathnames.

6. When you're finished, click on OK to close the Set Text of Layer dialog box.

7. In the Behaviors panel, specify the event (onLoad, onClick, onMouseOver).

8. Preview your page in a browser and check to make sure your changes work properly.

✔ Tip

■ This action does not work in Netscape 6.

Figure 16.51 This is a layers-based page.

Figure 16.52 Mousing over the person layer pops up text and a link within a layer that wasn't even visible before.

Figure 16.53 Choose the layer you want to edit, and then supply the new text or HTML. The easiest way to do it is to paste it in.

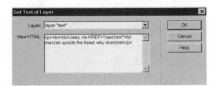

Figure 16.54 My new text for the layer includes a link.

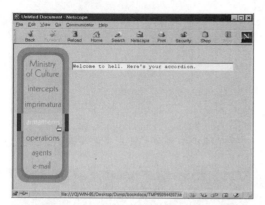

Figure 16.55 A single-line text box, displaying text during a mouseover.

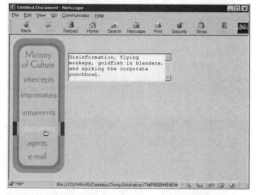

Figure 16.56 A multi-line text box, displaying text during a mouseover.

Figure 16.57 Type the text for the field in this dialog box.

Setting Text in a Form Field

You can use a text field in a form to display messages, almost like a frame within a page. You can also change a text field in an actual, working form when a user clicks on a link or a button. You can use a single-line (**Figure 16.55**) or multi-line (**Figure 16.56**) text field.

To set text field text:

1. Insert a form and a text field on your page, as described in Chapter 15.

2. In the Behaviors panel, select a browser (3.0 and later).

3. In the Document window, select an object (a, body, img, select).

4. In the Behaviors panel, add the action Set Text > Set Text of Text Field. The Set Text of Text Field dialog box will appear (**Figure 16.57**).

5. In the New Text text box, type or paste in the new text. When you're finished, click on OK to close the Set Text of Text Field dialog box.

6. In the Behaviors panel, specify the event (onLoad, onClick, onMouseOver).

7. Preview your page in a browser and check to make sure your changes work properly.

SETTING TEXT IN A FORM FIELD

Change Property

This action has more variables than any other. You can have an event that's associated with one object change the properties of that object or a different object. See **Table 16.2** to find out the objects available to this Dreamweaver behavior, and their associated properties.

Usage Examples: Provide a drop-down menu from which the user can pick a layer background color. Change the dimensions or Z-index of a layer when the user clicks on a button image. Change the destination of a form if the user checks a particular checkbox.

To set up the Change Property behavior:

1. In the Behaviors panel, select a browser (layer properties won't work in 4.0 or earlier browsers).

2. In the Document window that contains the layers, select an object (a, body, img, a form field, etc.).

3. In the Behaviors panel, add the action Change Property. The Change Property dialog box will appear (**Figure 16.58**).

4. In the Change Property dialog box, choose the kind of object whose action you wish to change from the Type of Object drop-down menu (see **Table 16.2** and **Figures 16.59** and **16.60**).

5. Dreamweaver may take a moment or two to detect all the named objects on the page, at which point their names (id="" or name="") will appear in the Named Object list box. Choose an object by selecting it from the list.

6. The properties you can change will be available from the Property drop-down menu (see **Table 16.2**). You may get additional properties by selecting a different browser from the Browser drop-down menu.

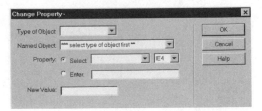

Figure 16.58 You can change several properties at once using the Change Property dialog box.

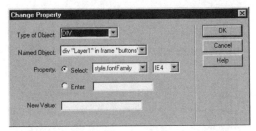

Figure 16.59 By selecting DIV, you can modify any named layer on the page, or a text block modified by a custom style. Modifiable properties include size, background color, and various style sheet attributes.

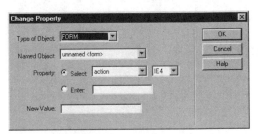

Figure 16.60 By selecting a form or a form field, you can change the functions of the buttons, the text fields, or the form itself.

✔ Tips

- In order to change an object's properties with this behavior, you must name the object. You can name any object by selecting it and typing a name for it in the Property inspector. The Name text box is always at the top and left of the Property inspector.

- You can also change additional properties by clicking on the Enter radio button and typing the property in the text box. There are too many variables for me to describe them all.

- If the object you're working with is a form field, you can provide a new value for the changed form field by typing it in the New Value text box. You can also type new values for layer attributes, etc. A little source-viewing should help you find the right format for things like stylesheet attributes.

7. Repeat steps 4–6 for all the objects you want this behavior to affect.

8. Click on OK to close the Change Property dialog box.

9. In the Behaviors panel, specify the event (onClick, onMouseOver, onBlur).

Table 16.2

Objects and Properties for Change Property action

OBJECT AND TAG	PROPERTIES
Layer `<div>`, `<span>`, `<layer>`, `<ilayer>` (provided those tags have positioning and Z-index elements)	Position (top, left), Z-index, Clipping area, Background color, Background image (4.0 and later); Width and height (IE4 and later only)
Div `<div>`	Styles, including font family, font size, border width and color, background color and image, and text within the `<div>` tag (all IE4 and later only; use layer or span for NN4, NS6)
Span `<span>`	Styles, including font family, font size, border width and color, background color and image, and text within the `<div>` tag (all IE4 and later only; use layer or span for NN4, NS6)
Image `<img>`	Source (NN3, NN4, NS6, IE4, IE5)
Form `<form>`	Action (3.0 and 4.0 browsers)
Checkbox `<input type=checkbox>`	Status (checked/unchecked) (3.0 and later)
Radio button `<input type=radio>`	Status (checked/unchecked) (3.0 and later)
Text box `<input type=text>`	Value (will appear in text box) (3.0 and later)
Text field `<textarea>`	Value (will appear in text field) (3.0 and later)
Password text box `<input type=password>`	Value (will appear in text box) (3.0 and later)
Menu or List `<select>`	selectedIndex (changes selection within menu, using index numbers for each `<option>` (3.0 and later)

Making Layers Draggable

You can make layers on your page draggable by applying the Drag Layer action to the body of the page.

Usage Examples: Create a toy such as a paper doll, a jigsaw puzzle in which the pieces snap into place, a design in which users must drag layers in order to read them, or a slide control.

✔ Tip

■ Because each layer has its own coordinates, you need to add this behavior once for each layer you want to make draggable.

To add the Drag Layer action:

1. In the Behaviors panel, select 4.0 and later Browsers.

2. In the Document window's tag selector, click <body> to select the entire page.

3. In the Behaviors panel, add the action Drag Layer. The Drag Layer dialog box will appear (**Figure 16.61**).

4. From the Layer drop-down menu, select the layer you want to make draggable.

5. To allow the user to drag the layer anywhere in the window, leave the Unconstrained option selected.

   or

   To restrict movement of the layer within a specific area (**Figure 16.62**), select Constrained. A series of text boxes will appear (**Figure 16.63**).

Figure 16.61 The Drag Layer dialog box allows you to make a layer draggable and to specify how and where a user can drag a layer.

Figure 16.62 On this page, the user cannot drag the layer outside the box, which is another layer. I set a constrained area of 100x100x100x100.

Figure 16.63 When you select the Constrained option, text boxes appear that allow you to set a draggable area based on the layer's original top-left coordinates.

6. The constrained movement values are relative to the top-left corner of the layer's original position and are in pixels.

- ◆ To restrict movement within a rectangular region, type values in all four text boxes.

- ◆ To restrict movement within a square, type the same value in all four text boxes.

- ◆ To allow only vertical movement, type 0 in the Left and Right text boxes and a value in the Up and Down text boxes.

- ◆ To allow only horizontal movement, type 0 in the Up and Down text boxes and a value in the Left and Right text boxes.

7. If you would like the user to drag the layer to a particular spot, you must declare a drop target. The drop target coordinates are applied to the top-left corner of the layer and are measured from the left and top of the window.

To declare a drop target, type a pixel value in the Top and Left text boxes. To set the layer's current position as the drop target, click the Get Current Position button, and Dreamweaver will fill in those text boxes.

8. The layer can snap to the drop target if the user lets go of the mouse button when the top-left corner of the layer comes within a certain number of pixels of the drop target. Type a number of pixels in the Snap if Within text box, or clear this field if you don't want to snap to the drop target.

9. To modify only these options, click OK to return to the Document window. Otherwise, keep reading.

Setting More Drag Layer Options

The following section assumes you have read the preceding one, *To add the Drag Layer action*. These instructions begin where the last set left off, in the Drag Layer dialog box.

✔ Tip

■ The easiest way to set the options for a puzzle-type game is to begin with all the pieces in their final resting places (**Figure 16.64**). Use the Get Current Position option to set the drop target for the layer, and then when you're done with the behavior, move the layer to its starting position on the page (**Figure 16.65**).

To set more Drag Layer options:

1. To select further options, click on the Advanced tab on the Drag Layer dialog box. A second panel of the dialog box will appear (**Figure 16.66**).

2. To allow the user to drag the layer by clicking on any part of it, set the Drag Handle option to Entire Layer.

   or

   To allow the user to drag the layer only if they click on a specific part of the layer (part of an image such as a button or a "window" title bar), select Area Within Layer from the Drag Handle drop-down menu. A series of text boxes will appear.

3. Type the area of the drag handle, in pixels, in the text boxes. This area will be a rectangle, measured from the top and left of the layer.

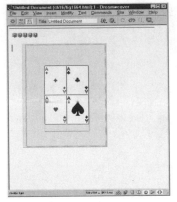

Figure 16.64 This is where I'd like the pieces to end up at the end of the puzzle. I put all the layers in place before I start setting up the Drag Layer behaviors, so I can use the Get Current Position feature to set drop targets.

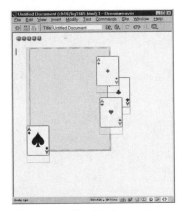

Figure 16.65 After I'm done setting up the behaviors, I put the layers where I'd like them to go when the page loads.

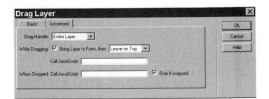

Figure 16.66 The second panel allows you to set selection handles for your layers; to specify the Z-index of the layer while dragging and after dropping; and call a JavaScript based on the user's drag-and-drop actions.

4. To change the Z-index of the layer so that it's on top while the user drags it, check the Bring Layer to Front checkbox.

   ◆ To leave the layer on top after dragging, select the Leave on Top option from the drop-down menu.

   ◆ To restore the layer's original Z-index after the user drops it, select Restore Z-Index from the drop-down menu.

5. To have the user's drag-and-drop actions call a JavaScript, see the *Calling Scripts by Dragging* sidebar.

6. When you're all set, click on OK to return to the Document window. Otherwise, keep reading.

✔ Tips

■ You must repeat these steps for each layer that you wish to make draggable.

■ This behavior does not work in Netscape 6.

Calling Scripts by Dragging

You can use the Drag Layer behavior to call a JavaScript that performs additional actions when the layer is dragged to a certain location. This script would use the layer coordinates provided by the values of MM_UPDOWN, MM_LEFTRIGHT, or MM_SNAPPED.

For example, the script could be called when the value of MM_SNAPPED is true, or, for multiple layers, when a certain number of the layers reach a MM_SNAPPED value of true.

Or, for a slide control, the location of the dragged layer could determine speaker volume, background color, or font size.

Another option is for the coordinates of a dragged layer to appear in form fields displayed on the page.

To call a JavaScript using this behavior, go to the second panel of the Drag Layer dialog box (**Figure 16.66**). Type the name of a JavaScript function in the Call JavaScript text box.

To call a script when the layer is dropped, type the name of a JavaScript function (such as, youWin()) in the When Dropped: Call JavaScript text box. Check the Only if Snapped checkbox if you want this script activated only if the layer has snapped to the drop target.

Adding New Scripts and Behaviors

If you're a veteran JavaScripter, and you want to set up your own scripts in Dreamweaver, you're more than welcome to. You can type or paste in a script using the Insert Script object, or you can set up your own actions to use in Dreamweaver behaviors.

To type in a script:

1. On the Objects panel, display the Invisibles panel by selecting it from the drop-down menu (**Figure 16.67**). then click on the Insert Script button 🦬. Or, from the Document window menu bar, select Insert > Invisible Tags > Script. The Insert Script dialog box will appear (**Figure 16.68**).

2. Type your script in the Insert Script dialog box, and click on OK. The Insert Script dialog box will close, and the Script icon 🦬 will appear in the Document window.

3. Select the Script marker, if it isn't already selected, and display the Property inspector, if necessary (**Figure 16.69**).

4. Select the type of script (JavaScript or VBScript) from the Language drop-down menu. If your script is in another scripting language, type the language's name in the Language text box.

You can also insert a script from a file on your hard drive.

Figure 16.67 To add a new script, you need to show Invisibles in the Objects panel.

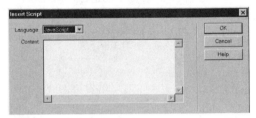

Figure 16.68 You can type a little script in the Insert Script dialog box.

Figure 16.69 The Property inspector, displaying Script properties.

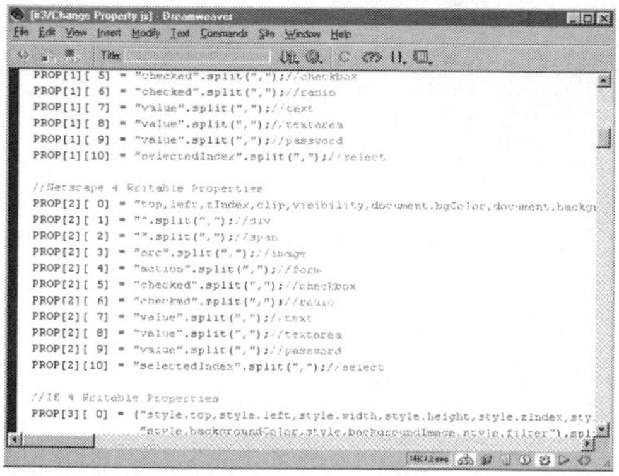

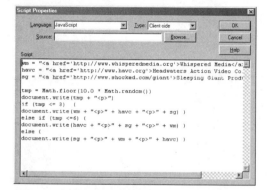

Figure 16.70 You edit external JavaScript files using the Code inspector.

Figure 16.71 The Script Properties dialog box is like a script-editing window, except that it's a dialog box. In other words, you can't switch back and forth between the Script Properties dialog box and, say, the Code inspector.

To insert a script from a text file:

1. Follow steps 1–3, above, but leave the Insert Script dialog box blank.

2. In the Property inspector, type the source of your script in the Source text box, or click on the folder icon to browse your hard drive for the file.

You can type or edit longer scripts in the Script Properties dialog box.

To edit a script:

1. View the script properties in the Property inspector.

2. Click on Edit. If you are editing a script contained in an external file, a new code window will open (**Figure 16.70**). Otherwise, the Script Properties dialog box will appear (**Figure 16.71**).

When you're finished typing or editing your script, click on OK to return to the Document window.

ADDING NEW SCRIPTS AND BEHAVIORS

Adding More Actions

You can add actions to the Behaviors panel that were written by other Dreamweaver developers. See the sidebar, this page, to find out how to add your own behaviors.

To add third-party actions:

1. In the Behaviors panel, click on the Add Action button, and select Get More Behaviors. Dreamweaver will launch your browser and open the Dreamweaver Exchange on the Web.

2. Download the behavior that interests you, and unzip it.

3. Quit Dreamweaver.

4. Drop the new file into the Actions folder:
   * On the PC: `C:\Program Files\ Macromedia\Dreamweaver 4\ Configuration\Behaviors\Actions`
   * On the Mac: `file:///Dreamweaver 4/ Configuration/Behaviors/Actions`

5. Launch Dreamweaver. The action will appear on the Add Action menu in the Behaviors panel.

✔ Tip

■ New in Dreamweaver 4, you can add and manage third-party extensions with the Extensions Manager. Since this chapter is quite long enough already, I cover the Extensions Manager in Appendix M on the Web site for this book.

Adding Your Own Actions

If you write JavaScript, you can write your own actions and add them to the Behaviors panel. However, this isn't quite as easy as just writing the HTML and JS files (as if that weren't hard enough!) and dropping them into the Actions folder. You need to format them and add some specific functions so Dreamweaver knows what to make of them.

To find out how to do the mysterious stuff that will make your JavaScript code work with Dreamweaver and show up in the Behaviors panel, consult the Extending Dreamweaver help files (Help > Extending Dreamweaver). These files include a sample behavior to get you started.

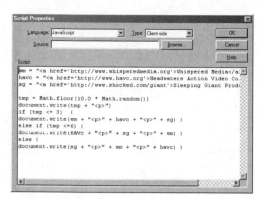

Figure 16.72 Type the JavaScript function, or the script itself, in the text box.

■ The Macromedia Dreamweaver Exchange offers a free script repository of behaviors written by Macromedia developers and Dreamweaver users. The site includes information on the version number of the script, the developer name, user ratings, and number of downloads. To get behaviors from the Web, click on the Add Action button in the Behaviors panel, and select Get More Behaviors. This will bring you to the main page for the exchange, where you can browse the behaviors by category.

To Call a Script

Something tells me that if you can write JavaScript, you can tell the script when to happen. Nevertheless, Dreamweaver covers all the bases with the Call JavaScript behavior.

To add the Call JavaScript behavior to the page:

1. In the Behaviors panel, select the browser you want to target.

2. In the Document window, select the object associated with the event.

3. Click the Add Action button, and from the pop-up menu, select Call JavaScript. The Call JavaScript dialog box will appear (**Figure 16.71**).

4. Type the name of a function, or a string of JavaScript in the text box.

5. Click on OK to return to the Document window.

6. In the Behaviors panel, specify the user event that you want to trigger the action.

Saves you a few lines of coding, anyway.

Debugging Your JavaScript

New in Dreamweaver 4 is a JavaScript Debugger, which allows you to find problems in your JavaScript code. Even if you are just using the built-in behaviors, there are times when they don't do exactly what you expect, and the debugger can be a valuable tool to find the problem.

Using the JavaScript Debugger

1. Open the page with the JavaScript you want to debug.

2. Select File > Debug in Browser > Netscape (or Internet Explorer), or select an option from the Code Navigation menu on the Code inspector toolbar. A browser window will open, and a Java Security window will open as well.

3. If you are debugging in Netscape Navigator, click on OK in the debugger warning box that appears, then click on Grant in the Java Security dialog box. If you are using Internet Explorer, click on Yes in the Java Security dialog box, then on OK in the debugger warning box that appears (Windows only; the debugger does not work on Internet Explorer for Macintosh).

   The Debugger window will appear (**Figure 16.73**), and the browser will stop at the first line of JavaScript code.

4. If you think you've identified where something is going wrong, click on the line of code preceding that area and add a breakpoint by clicking the Set/Remove Breakpoint button ⬤ or by pressing F7.

5. You can also set a breakpoint in the Code inspector by selecting Set Breakpoint from the {} Code Navigation menu.

Figure 16.73 The Debugger window allows you to follow along in your code as it runs.

Figure 16.74 Setting a breakpoint allows you to stop your code to take a look at what's happening.

Figure 16.75 The bottom pane of the debugger window is for watching and setting the values of variables. Until the script starts running, the variable's value will be undefined.

6. Click on the Run button ![Run button icon]. The code will start executing, and then stop at the point at which you set the breakpoint.

7. Click the Step Into button ![Step Into icon] (or press F10). This will step through one line of your code at a time (**Figure 16.74**). You can watch what happens in the browser window with each step.

8. Repeat step 7 until you find your error or pass the problem area.

Sometimes simply stepping through your code is not enough to figure out what's wrong. You can also watch the values of variables (and even set them) in the Debugger window as well.

To watch a variable's value:

Follow steps 1–5, above.

1. Highlight the variable that you want to watch.

2. Click on the Plus button in the bottom half of the Debugger window. The variable will appear in the bottom half of the window. Press Return.

or

Without highlighting a variable, click on the Plus button and type the variable name. Press Return.

3. Click on the Run button. The variable's value will be updated in the bottom half of the Debugger window (**Figure 16.75**).

One of the most useful ways to test any code —including JavaScript—is to set variables to really absurd values. What happens to your zodiac sign calculator, for example, when someone claims to have been born in 1865? Or clicks on a button 100 times? One way to test these unlikely possibilities is to set the variables in your code directly. The Dreamweaver debugger allows you to do just that.

To set a variable's value:

Follow steps 1–3, above.

1. Click on the line in the code right after the variable gets its initial value.

2. Click on the Set/Remove Breakpoint button.

3. Click on the Run button. This will run the code to the point where the variable has a value already set.

4. In the right pane of the variable watch section of the debugger window, click on the variable's value. Type in the desired value.

5. Click on the Run button or the Step Into button. This will show you what happens to your page when the variable is given the specified value.

✔ Tips

- The JavaScript Debugger window does not work with Netscape 6 or the Macintosh version of Internet Explorer.

- If you use only the built-in behaviors, after you click on Run, the debugger won't kick in until you actually trigger one of those behaviors with a user event.

DRAWING TIMELINES

Figure 17.1 The magic bus at futurefarmers.com uses a timeline in a JavaScript pop-up window.

Figure 17.2 It moves!

Figure 17.3 It keeps moving until it's off the screen, and then it starts over.

Figure 17.4 One click opens a new little window with a new timeline.

Timelines let you create animations on a Web page without having to use Flash or write the Dynamic HTML code yourself. Timelines can animate any object that's in a layer on the page. They use no ActiveX, Java, or plug-ins.

Timelines use JavaScript to control layers (**Figures 17.1** through **17.4**). A layer can move, resize, appear, or disappear—and these actions are controlled by a sequence of frames.

These frames are not the same as the frames I discussed in Chapter 13. These are *animation frames*. Just like the frames of footage in a movie, each frame can be slightly different from the last, which creates the illusion of movement over time on a 2-D surface. In this case, of course, the 2-D surface is a Web page projected on a computer screen rather than a film projected on a movie screen.

✔ Tips

- Because timelines rely on layers in order to work their magic, they can only be viewed in 4.0 and later browsers.

- If you need information on layers, refer to Chapter 14. For information about behaviors, turn to Chapter 16.

What Timelines Can Do

Timelines can incorporate three types of objects: layers, images, and behaviors.

In this chapter, I'm going to rely on a few modules to try to illustrate motion on the page. The layers on this page include a bordered one with an image of a little person in it, and a map.

Layer properties that a timeline can change include the following:

- **Moving a layer** by changing its X+Y coordinates (on the page or within the parent layer) (**Figure 17.5**).

- **Showing or hiding a layer** by changing its visibility. You can switch between the three optional states: visible, hidden, or default (**Figure 17.6**).

- **Changing the stacking order**, or Z-index (**Figure 17.7**).

- **Resizing a layer** by adjusting its dimensions (**Figure 17.8**).

✔ Tip

- Navigator 4 does not support resizing layers during a timeline.

The only image property that a timeline can change directly is the **image source**. This way, you can perform image rollovers during a timeline without using additional JavaScript.

Timelines can also **call a behavior** from a particular frame. You can also use a behavior to start, stop, or skip to a particular frame within a timeline.

Figure 17.5 The timeline moves the layer from left to right. You can use more complex movements, too.

Figure 17.6 You can use a timeline to show or hide layers. In this case, three layers appear over the background image. You can have this happen over time or you can have a user event trigger the action. The layers can appear all at once or in sequence.

Figure 17.7 The timeline changes the Z-index of the layers. In the first screen, the layers "person" and "deadend" are stacked behind "map." In the second screen, the map layer has the lowest z-index and is thus stacked behind the other two.

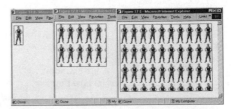

Figure 17.8 The timeline increases the size of the layer. This layer uses a background image that is tiled as the layer expands.

The Timelines Panel

The Timelines panel (**Figure 17.9**) is the tool you use to create and modify timelines in Dreamweaver.

To view the Timelines panel:

◆ From the Document window menu bar, select Window > Timelines.

or

Press Shift+F9.

Either way, the Timelines panel will appear.

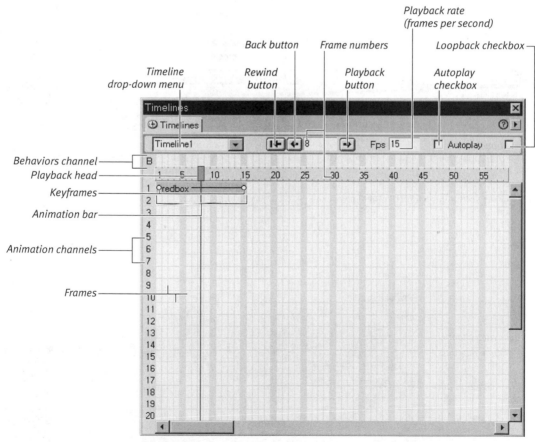

Figure 17.9 The Timelines panel

Dissecting the Timelines Panel

Each part of the Timelines panel controls a different aspect of a timeline. Some of these elements won't really make much cognitive sense until you see them in operation, but you can use this page as a reference for what things do. Let's start at the top (**Figure 17.10**).

If you include more than one timeline on a page, you can switch between timelines by choosing the timeline name from the **Timeline drop-down menu**.

You can play timelines in the Document window using the Timelines panel's playback controls. The **Rewind button** rewinds the timeline back to the beginning. The **Back button** rewinds one frame at a time; hold it down to play the timeline backwards. The **Playback button** advances one frame at a time; hold it down to play the entire timeline. The current frame is indicated in the **Frame number** text box.

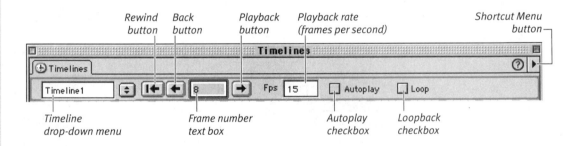

Figure 17.10 The Toolbar on the Timelines panel

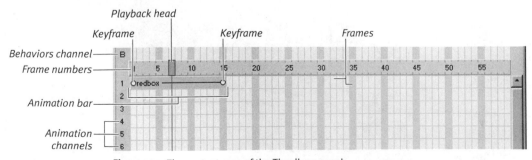

Figure 17.11 The content area of the Timelines panel

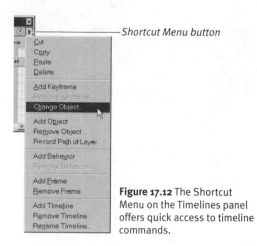

Shortcut Menu button

Figure 17.12 The Shortcut Menu on the Timelines panel offers quick access to timeline commands.

The **playback rate** is in frames per second (fps). The default is 15 fps; you can set it higher or lower depending on your content.

You can add behaviors that will control how the document plays. The **Autoplay checkbox** adds a behavior that will make the Timeline start as soon as the page finishes loading. The **Loopback checkbox** adds a behavior that will make the timeline play continuously while the page is in the browser.

Now we move to the part of the timelines panel that controls the content (**Figure 17.11**).

Use the **Behaviors channel** to add behaviors that will be called from a certain frame in the timeline.

Each numbered column in the Timelines panel is a frame. Each frame is numbered. The **playback head** (the red bar) shows the advance of the playback. As the playback head passes over each frame, the frame number will appear next to the Playback button.

Each numbered row in the Timelines panel is an **animation channel**. Different objects usually use different animation channels.

When an object is added to a timeline, the Timelines panel displays an **animation bar** in that object's animation channel. The little bullets at the beginning and end of the animation bar are **keyframes**. You can add other keyframes in the middle of an animation bar to add actions to the timeline.

✔ Tip

- In **Figures 17.10** and **17.12**, at the right side of the Timelines panel, you can see a Shortcut Menu button. This button pops up a menu of commands (**Figure 17.12**) you can use when editing a timeline.

DISSECTING THE TIMELINES PANEL

Adding a Layer to a Timeline

You create a timeline by adding a layer to the Timelines panel. Once you drag or add the layer, Dreamweaver creates a timeline for it and adds the code to the page automatically.

To add a layer to a Timeline:

1. Make sure the object you want to animate is in a layer, and that the layer has the size and position that you want it to start with. See Chapter 14 for help with layers.

2. Select the layer in the Document window (**Figure 17.13**) by selecting its handle or tag.

3. From the Document window menu bar, select Modify > Timeline > Add Object to Timeline.

   or

   Right-click (hold down the mouse button on a Mac) on an animation bar in the Timelines panel, and select Add Object from the pop-up menu.

A new, named animation bar will appear in the Timelines panel (**Figure 17.14**).

✔ Tips

- Before you add a layer to a timeline, be sure that you name it in the Property inspector. Named layers are easier to manage than numbered ones.

- You can also add image rollovers and behaviors to your timeline. See *Adding an Image Rollover to a Timeline* and *Adding a Behavior to a Timeline*.

- You can also drag a layer onto the Timelines panel to add it to the timeline. Click on the layer and drag it to the location (channel and frame) where you want it to appear (**Figure 17.15**).

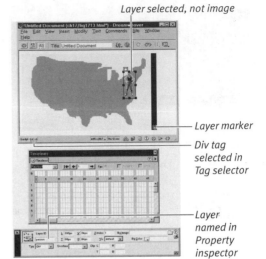

Layer selected, not image

Layer marker

Div tag selected in Tag selector

Layer named in Property inspector

Figure 17.13 Select the layer in the Document window. Notice that the Timelines panel doesn't have any objects in it yet.

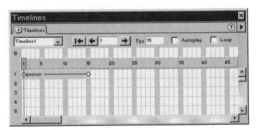

Figure 17.14 When you add the layer to the timeline, an animation bar appears in the first available animation channel.

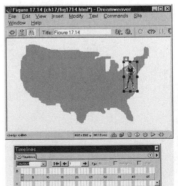

Figure 17.15 Dragging and dropping a layer into the Timelines panel—it lands in the channel and starts at the frame where you drop it.

Figure 17.16
Click on the last keyframe bullet in the layer's animation bar to select that frame as well as the layer.

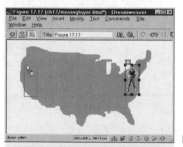

Figure 17.17
With the end keyframe selected, drag the layer to a new location and let go.

Figure 17.18 The Timelines panel will record the new position and draw a line from position 1 (where the layer used to be) to position 2 (where you dropped the layer).

Timeline Actions

Timeline actions were briefly described in *What Timelines Can Do* earlier in this chapter. In the next few sections, I'm going to go over each action, step by step, starting with moving a layer. As I go through each action a layer can perform, I'll describe the various modifications you can make to a timeline.

Moving a Layer

The easiest way to start learning about timelines is to move a layer on the page.

To move a layer using a timeline:

1. Add the layer to the timeline.

2. In the Timelines panel, click on the keyframe bullet at the end of the layer's animation bar (**Figure 17.16**). The playback head (the red bar) will move to that frame.

   The layer will automatically be selected in the Document window.

3. Click on the layer's selection handle and drag it to the position on the page where you want it to end up (**Figure 17.17**).

You'll see a line drawn from the layer's old position to its new position (**Figure 17.18**). The line connects the top-left corners of the layer in each position. This is the path that the timeline will follow.

✔ Tip

■ Notice on this page that I've stacked the Layers panel with the Timelines panel. I can flip back and forth between them easily and save desktop space. To move a panel onto or off of another one, click on its tab and drag it onto or away from the other.

TIMELINE ACTIONS

Recording Movement

If you want your layer to travel in a line that isn't straight, you can record its movement.

To record a layer's path:

1. Select the layer by its handle and move it to its starting position.

2. In the Timelines panel, click within the animation frame where you want movement to begin.

3. From the Document window menu bar, select Modify > Timeline > Record Path of Layer.

4. Drag the layer's selection handle along the path you want to use. Loop-de-loops are allowed (**Figure 17.19**). As you drag, dots will mark the path you're drawing.

5. When you let go of the mouse button, the layer's path will be translated into an animation channel (**Figure 17.20**), with keyframes marking specific spots between which the layer travels along its path.

Occasionally, you may get an error message stating that a layer with the same name is already in the timeline. Click within a different frame and draw your movement again.

✔ Tip

■ Recording the path of a layer will add the layer to the timeline, even it it already appears there. To rearrange animation bars, see the next section.

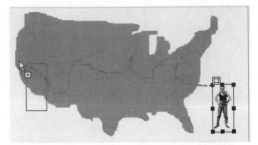

Figure 17.19 Using the Record Path of Layer option, I can drag a layer all over the place and the timeline will follow. The little dots represent points that the top-left corner of the layer has graced.

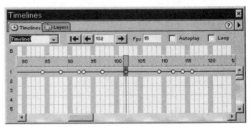

Figure 17.20 After I recorded the path of the layer, the layer appeared as an object in the Timelines panel—with over 100 frames.

Setting the Playback Rate

The default playback rate for Dreamweaver timelines is 15 frames per second. Macromedia advises not to set this rate much faster; the 15 fps rate is based on optimal performance on the average machine. Setting a faster playback rate might not actually make the animation go faster; while it might do so on your local machine, all the images and layers that you're playing with are stored in your memory cache. You can, however, set a lower rate for slower speeds.

Figure 17.21 If you've already added this layer to the timeline, Dreamweaver will add a separate animation sequence (with its own beginning and ending keyframes) after the initial sequence.

Figure 17.22 In this case, I haven't added any actions to the initial animation sequence. I can select it and delete it. I can also cut, copy, and paste it, as long as it doesn't overlap another sequence with the same object in it.

Figure 17.23 After deleting the sequence that didn't have any actions in it, I select the sequence that includes the recorded path by clicking on a non-key (unmarked) frame.

Figure 17.24 I drag the sequence to Frame 1 of the timeline. You can also drag sequences to later in the timeline or to other animation channels.

Deleting and Moving Animation Sequences

Recording the path of a layer adds that layer to the timeline. If the layer already appears in the timeline, Dreamweaver will add the layer again later in the same animation channel (**Figure 17.21**). Animation bars cannot overlap.

You can delete or move animation bars. For example, in **Figure 17.21**, the initial, blank bar remains. I select the bar (**Figure 17.22**) and press Delete to remove it. Then, I select the bar that includes the recorded path (**Figure 17.23**) and drag it to the beginning of the timeline (**Figure 17.24**).

Playing It Back

You can watch the movements you've recorded by playing back the timeline.

To play back a timeline:

1. In the Timelines panel, click on the Rewind button  to move the playback head back to the beginning of the timeline.

    or

    Click on Frame 1 in the Timelines panel to move it back (**Figure 17.25**).

2. Move the Timelines panel out of the way in the Document window.

3. In the Timelines panel, click on and hold down the Play button .

You'll see the layer move across the page (**Figure 17.26**).

✔ Tips

- You can click within any frame to see what the page looks like at that point in the timeline.

- You can play and rewind little bits of the timeline with the Rewind, Back, and Play buttons (**Figure 17.27**).

- To fine-tune a point within a timeline, see *About Keyframes*, on the next page.

Previewing in a Browser

A timeline won't play when previewed in a browser unless you instruct it to do so. If you add the Autoplay behavior, the timeline will play as soon as the page finishes loading.

Just check the Autoplay checkbox on the Timelines panel (**Figure 17.28**), and then preview the page (**Figure 17.29**). For more on controlling timelines, see *Making Timelines Go,* later in this chapter. For more on previewing, see Chapter 1.

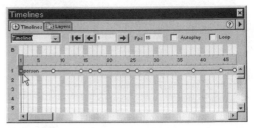

Figure 17.25 Click on Frame 1, or click on the Rewind button to return the timeline to its beginning.

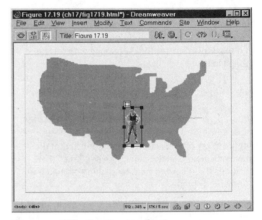

Figure 17.26 The timeline in mid-play.

Figure 17.27 Rewind, Back, and Play.

Figure 17.28 Click on the Autoplay checkbox to make the timeline play in the browser window.

Preview button

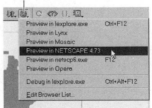

Figure 17.29 Preview your timeline in a 4.0 or later browser.

Playback head

Current frame number

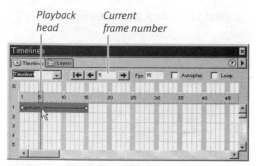

Figure 17.30 Click at the point on the animation bar where you want to add the new keyframe. The playback head will move, you'll see the frame number in its text box.

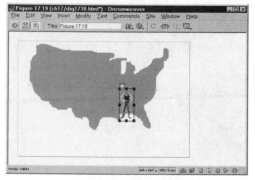

Figure 17.31 My person goes from Maryland straight to California. I want her to pay a visit to New York City first. I play the timeline and stop at a fairly early point, where I'll add a keyframe.

Figure 17.32 Select Add Keyframe from the pop-up menu.

Figure 17.33 A keyframe bullet will appear on the animation bar.

About Keyframes

The Timelines panel tracks the movement of a layer from one point to another, frame by frame, and it paces the movement of an object so that the frame-to-frame transitions are smooth.

If there are only two points in a timeline, the line in which the layer moves must be a straight one. You can add a third point to a timeline to make a layer move in an arc, or you can add points for multiple positions or actions.

You do this by adding keyframes. A *keyframe* is a point on a timeline where something happens. Each animation bar in a timeline includes at least two keyframes: the beginning frame and the end frame.

To add a keyframe:

1. In the Timelines panel, click on the place on the animation bar where you want the new action to happen (**Figure 17.30**), or press the Play button until you reach it (**Figure 17.31**). The playback head will move to the new frame.

2. From the Document window menu bar, select Modify > Timeline > Add Keyframe.

   or

   Right-click (hold down the mouse button on a Mac) on the object's animation bar in the Timelines panel, and select Add Keyframe from the pop-up menu that appears (**Figure 17.32**).

   or

   Press F6.

The Timelines panel will add a keyframe bullet to the animation bar (**Figure 17.33**).

Now you can attach a new position to that keyframe.

To add a new layer position to a keyframe:

1. In the Timelines panel, click on the new keyframe. The layer will become selected automatically (**Figure 17.34**).

2. Move the layer to the position on the page where you want it to be when that keyframe is played (**Figure 17.35**).

The line drawn between the beginning position on the page and the end position on the page will now arc to fit the third point into the movement line (**Figure 17.36**).

Play back the timeline now to see how this movement looks.

Now you know how to change a layer's position, play back a timeline, and add keyframes (and therefore, additional actions) to a timeline. Let's look at some of the other things timelines can do.

✔ Tips

■ You can add keyframes and then attach other actions to them, too. We'll do this throughout this chapter.

■ How do you detach movements from a layer? What if you make a layer move and then change your mind? First, click on the frame in which the layer is where you want it to be. Then, open the Property inspector and take note of the L(eft) and T(op) measurements. In the Timelines panel, move to the keyframe where the movement changes. In the Property inspector, type the numbers you jotted down in the L and T text boxes. Repeat for any additional keyframes where the layer's position attributes have changed.

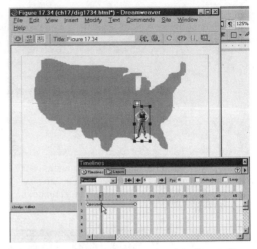

Figure 17.34 Select the keyframe, and the layer will automatically become selected.

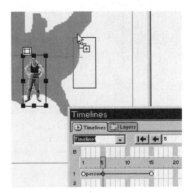

Figure 17.35 With the keyframe selected in the Timelines panel, move the layer to its new location.

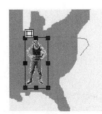

Figure 17.36 I fast-forwarded to later in the timeline so you could see the arc drawn by Dreamweaver between the three keyframes.

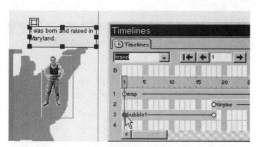

Figure 17.37 First, I add the new layer to the timeline, and put text in it.

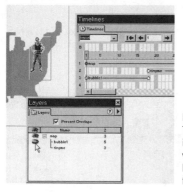

Figure 17.38 Then, I set its initial visibility to hidden on the first keyframe.

Keyframe 5 is selected for "bubble1" layer

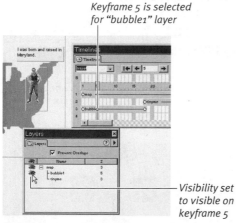

Visibility set to visible on keyframe 5

Figure 17.39 Finally, I added a new keyframe and set the layer's visibility to visible on the fifth keyframe. When the timeline plays, the second layer will appear on keyframe 5 after the first layer starts moving.

Showing and Hiding Layers

You can show or hide a layer in a timeline by changing its visibility to visible, hidden, or default.

To show or hide a layer:

1. If the layer is not already added to the timeline, add it.

2. Click on the first keyframe on the layer's animation bar (**Figure 17.37**).

3. Using the Layers panel or the Property inspector, set the layer's visibility to the state you want it to be in when the timeline begins playing (**Figure 17.38**).

4. On the layer's animation bar, add the keyframe where you want the visibility change to occur.

5. With the proper keyframe selected, change the visibility of the layer (**Figure 17.39**).

6. If you want the layer to change visibility again at the end of the timeline, click on the keyframe at the end of the layer's animation bar, and change the layer's visibility.

To change the location of a keyframe:

1. In the Timelines panel, click on the keyframe you want to move.

2. Hold down the mouse button and drag the keyframe bullet to a different frame.

3. Let go of the mouse button.

Voilà! The keyframe has moved.

✔ Tip

■ Images that are in hidden layers are automatically downloaded with the page. This is a good way to preload images for swapping image source. Or skip the source swapping altogether and just show or hide the layers that the new images are in.

Changing the Overlaps

As you know, a layer's Z-index, or stacking order, is what makes layers so layer-like. You can change the way layers overlap during a timeline (**Figure 17.40**) so that layers appear stacked in a different order. If you want Pop on top, you can make him hop.

✔ Tips

- Make sure all the layers have the Z-index you want them to have at their beginning keyframe(s) in the timeline (**Figure 17.40**).

- Z-index numbers affect the overlap of only those objects that are inside a layer; you can't make a layer hide under an image that isn't in a layer itself.

To change the Z-index of a layer during a timeline:

1. In the Timelines panel, add any keyframes you need to the layer's animation bar.

2. Click on the keyframe that marks the point at which the Z-index will change. The layer will be selected automatically.

3. Using the Layers panel or the Property inspector, change the Z-index number of the layer (**Figure 17.41**).

4. Play back the timeline to watch the layer move over or under another layer on the page (**Figure 17.42**).

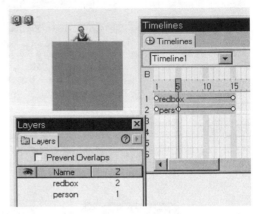

Figure 17.40. You can change the Z-index of a layer in the timeline. I set the Z-index in the first frame so that the box overlaps the person.

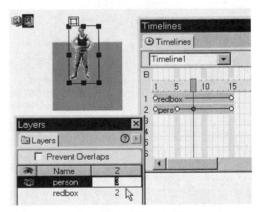

Figure 17.41 At frame 8, I added a keyframe and changed the Z-index of the person layer so that it will surface over the top square.

Figure 17.42 Three frames from a timeline. In frame 1, the square is visible. In frame 5, the person appears, and the box is stacked on top of the person. In frame 8, the person's Z-index changes so that it's on top of the square.

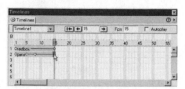

Figure 17.43 Click on the end keyframe and drag it to a new location.

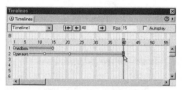

Figure 17.44 I lengthened the animation bar I selected in **Figure 17.43**. Notice how the keyframes in the middle of the animation bar are spaced out over the new length of the animation bar.

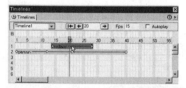

Figure 17.45 I moved the animation bar with the box in it. It will both start and end later in the timeline now.

Figure 17.46 You can also type a different playback rate in frames per second (FPS) in the FPS text box. Keep in mind that many computers can't process a faster playback rate than 15 FPS.

Changing the Timing

You can change the length and duration of an animation bar if you want an action to start sooner or end later within the timeline.

To move the beginning or end of an animation bar:

1. In the Timelines panel, click on the beginning or ending keyframe on the layer's animation bar (**Figure 17.43**).

2. Drag the keyframe to a new frame number within the animation channel (**Figure 17.44**). You may notice the other elements in the timeline moving around as you drag the keyframe.

3. Play the timeline to see how it looks.

4. Repeat steps 1 and 2 as needed.

Longer timelines allow for more actions and more gradual movement.

✔ Tips

- If you drag the end keyframe to lengthen the timeline, any keyframes within the timeline will be spaced out in proportion to their original position, to preserve the gradual arc of the timeline (**Figure 17.44**).

- You can also move an entire animation bar to make the action for that layer start at a different time. Click on the middle of the bar (not on a keyframe) to select the whole thing, and drag it to a new location (**Figure 17.45**).

- To find out how to move an individual keyframe, see *To change the location of a keyframe*, earlier in the chapter.

- You can also change the frames per second (FPS) of a timeline. Type a number *less than* 15 in the FPS text box (**Figure 17.46**). Remember that most computers can't process faster playback speeds.

Changing Layer Dimensions

Besides changing the visibility and Z-index of a layer, you can also use a timeline to change the dimensions of the layer.

✔ Tips

■ Layer size changes only work in Netscape 6 and Internet Explorer 4 and later, but not in Netscape 4.

■ If you want to make a layer shrink in size, remember to change the layer's overflow setting to *hidden* or *scroll* in the Property inspector; otherwise, the shrinking won't have any effect.

To change the dimensions of a layer using a timeline:

1. In the Timelines panel, click on the keyframe where you want the size change to occur. The layer will become selected automatically (**Figure 17.47**).

2. Change the size of the layer by dragging its handles, or by changing the W(idth) and H(eight) settings in the Property inspector (**Figure 17.48**).

3. Play back the timeline to see how the settings affect the size change.

Because the timeline code makes layer properties change gradually rather than abruptly, the size change will begin a few frames before the set keyframe (**Figure 17.49**).

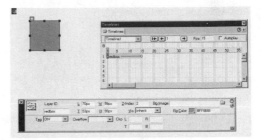

Figure 17.47 I added the layer to the timeline.

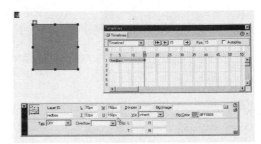

Figure 17.48 I selected the end keyframe and changed the size of the layer. If I click on each individual frame on the animation bar, the Property inspector will display the layer's size in each succeeding frame, leading up to the end frame's dimensions.

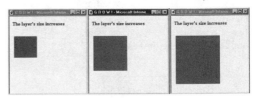

Figure 17.49 Three browser windows showing the progression in size from frame 1 to frame 8 to frame 15. I set two sizes: one in frame 1, and one in frame 15. With Dreamweaver Timelines, these changes happen gradually; for an abrupt change, make the size change happen in two adjacent keyframes.

Figure 17.50 In my map timeline, I use two different map images: a green one and a pink speckled one. I use a rollover to make the images switch at a certain point in the timeline.

Figure 17.51 In the example on the next page, these are the two images I'll be using.

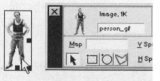

Figure 17.52 Name your image before you add it to the timeline.

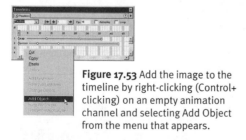

Figure 17.53 Add the image to the timeline by right-clicking (Control+clicking) on an empty animation channel and selecting Add Object from the menu that appears.

Figure 17.54 Here I am in the Document window. I've just added the image of the person—this time independent of any layers—to the timeline.

Adding an Image Rollover to a Timeline

You can also add an image rollover to a timeline (**Figures 17.50** and **17.51**). The only available action for images that are *not* in layers is swap source: That is, you can make an image roll over, but you can't make it hide or disappear unless it's in a layer.

To add the image rollover to a timeline:

1. Place (or select) the initial, pre-roll image in the Document window.

2. Name the initial image, using the Property inspector (**Figure 17.52**).

3. From the Document window menu bar, select Modify > Add Object to Timeline.

   or

   Right-click (Control+click on a Mac) on an empty animation bar in the Timelines panel, and select Add Object from the pop-up menu that appears (**Figure 17.53**).

A new animation bar will appear in the Timelines panel (**Figure 17.54**).

On the next page, we'll add the rollover.

✔ Tip

■ One way to preload images for source swapping is to place them in a hidden layer on the page. Another is to use the Preload Images Behavior described in Chapter 16.

Making the Rollover Work

Changing an image source with a Timeline is similar to using the Swap Image Behavior to create image rollovers, except the rollover will occur as time elapses rather than when triggered by a user event.

To change image source using a timeline:

1. Add the image to the timeline, as described on the previous page.

2. Add any keyframes you need to the image's animation bar (**Figure 17.55**).

3. Click on the keyframe in which you the image to roll over.

4. In the Property inspector, change the source of the image to the source of the new image (**Figures 17.56** and **17.57**) by editing the filename in the Src text box, or by clicking on Browse and selecting a new image.

5. To make the image stay in its second state for the rest of the timeline, select the end keyframe and set the source to be that of Image 2.

   or

   To make the image revert to its original state, add two keyframes, first the end-stop for the source for Image 2, and second, the resetting of the source for Image 1.

Play back the timeline to watch the effect (**Figure 17.58**).

✔ Tips

■ Sometimes, when you change the source of the image, Dreamweaver discards height and width information for both the original and the preloaded image. If you want the images to conform to a certain size, jot down the height and width before you create the rollover, and go back and fix them afterwards.

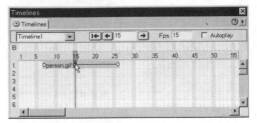

Figure 17.55 I added a keyframe to the image's animation bar; that's the point at which the source will change.

Figure 17.56 The two images, side by side for comparison. With the keyframe selected, change the source in the Property inspector. The image, which I selected with the mouse, shows the rectangular borders of the transparent image.

Figure 17.57 Edit the filename in the Src text box (for example, type person2.gif instead of person.gif), or click on Browse to open the Select Image File dialog box and choose a different image.

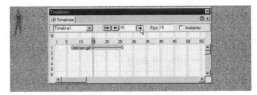

Figure 17.58 When the timeline plays the keyframe, the source changes to the second image. In this case, it's a subtle change of colors from one image to the next so that the person fades more into the background. You can use whatever images you like for the rollover, as long as they're the same size.

■ In previous versions of Dreamweaver, the image's animation bar had to be extended to the end of the timeline to make the source stay swapped. This has been fixed in Dreamweaver 4.

ADDING AN IMAGE ROLLOVER TO A TIMELINE

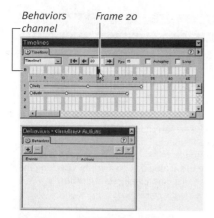

Behaviors channel   *Frame 20*

Figure 17.59 I double-clicked on the intersection of the Behaviors channel and frame 20, and the Behaviors panel appeared. It's empty until you add an action.

Figure 17.60 On the Behaviors panel, click on the Add Action button, and choose an action from the pop-up menu.

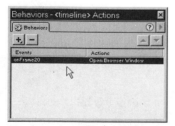

Figure 17.61 I added the Open Browser Window action to frame 20 of the timeline; when the timeline is played, the window will launch on frame 20. The event will be added automatically after you finish selecting the action.

Adding a Behavior to a Timeline

All the clever behaviors I discussed in Chapter 16 can be added to a timeline. For instance, you can make the timeline execute an animation and then load a new page; you can play a sound at a certain frame in a timeline; or you can use a timeline to start playing a Shockwave movie at a certain frame.

To add a behavior to a timeline frame:

1. In the Timelines panel, click on the frame that will launch the behavior to move the playback head to it.

2. Double-click on the frame number within the Behaviors channel (**Figure 17.59**). The Behaviors panel will appear. The browser version (4.0 and later browsers) will be preset.

3. In the Actions area of the Behaviors panel, click on the Add Action button to pop up the menu of available actions (**Figure 17.60**).

4. Choose the action you want to add. The associated dialog box will appear.

5. Fill out the dialog box and click on OK. The name of the action will appear in the Actions list box (**Figure 17.61**). The event, onFrameNumber, will be added to the Behaviors panel automatically.

The behavior will be added to the timeline. You'll see a little marker at that particular frame in the Behaviors channel.

✔ Tips

■ For details about individual JavaScript behaviors in Dreamweaver, see Chapter 16.

■ Add a behavior to a frame by moving the playback head to that frame and selecting Modify > Add Behavior to Timeline from the Document window menu bar.

ADDING A BEHAVIOR TO A TIMELINE

471

Making Timelines Go

Timelines won't start playing in a browser unless another piece of JavaScript tells them to. There are two ways you can make a timeline start playing, both of which use JavaScript behaviors.

One way is to make the timeline play automatically when the page is finished loading. The other way is to use a behavior, so that a user event such as a click or a mouseover triggers the timeline.

The Autoplay behavior is an onLoad behavior; once the page loads, the animation will begin.

To make a Timeline play automatically:

◆ In the Behaviors panel, place a checkmark in the Autoplay checkbox. A dialog box will appear (**Figure 17.62**) letting you know that Dreamweaver will add the Autoplay code.

Simple, yes?

Figure 17.62 When you check the Autoplay checkbox, a dialog box will appear informing you that it's going to add the Autoplay behavior. Once you get the point, you can make this dialog box go away by checking the Don't show me this message again checkbox.

Behavior Modification

What sort of behaviors could you add to a timeline? The timeline itself offers actions similar to Show/Hide Layer and Rollover Image. Here are some ideas to get you started.

◆ Set Text of Layer, Set Text of Status Bar, Set Text of Text Field, Popup Message: The user sees a message when a certain frame in the timeline passes.

◆ Open Browser Window, Popup Message: During or at the end of the timeline, a window or dialog box opens.

◆ Drag Layer: An animation plays in the timeline, and after it's over, all the layers become draggable.

◆ Play Sound: On a certain frame, a sound plays. For example, when the mouse hits the cat in the head with a hammer, the user hears "Doink!"

◆ Check Browser: When the page loads (onLoad), the user is sent to a page with a timeline if the browser is 4.0 or later, and to a page without the timeline if the browser is 3.0 or earlier. (It would be a nice idea to detect the browser with a timeline frame, but 3.0 browsers may or may not play the timeline properly. If you want to try this, you should test it in the browsers you're targeting.)

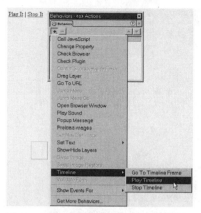

Figure 17.63 I selected the link called Play It and added the Play Timeline action.

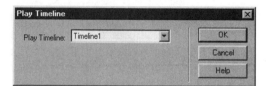

Figure 17.64 I chose Timeline > Play Timeline from the Add Action menu, and now I can select my timeline in the Play Timeline dialog box.

Figure 17.65 After you select the Play Timeline (or other) action, specify the user event by choosing it from the drop-down list.

Making a Behavior Play a Timeline

You can also make a behavior call a timeline so that when the user clicks on or mouses over a link or image, the timeline will play.

To make a behavior play a timeline:

1. In the Document window, click on the object you want to use to make the timeline play (a, img, form button). Make sure you do not have a behavior selected in the Timelines panel, or the behavior will be added to the timeline instead of the link.

2. If a timeline is on your page, the browser version will be preset to 4.0 and Later browsers. To check this, click the Add Action button, and then select Show Events For > 4.0 and Later Browsers.

3. In the Actions area of the Behaviors panel, click on the Add Action button 📷.

4. From the pop-up menu that appears (**Figure 17.63**), select Timeline > Play Timeline. The Play Timeline dialog box will appear (**Figure 17.64**).

5. If there is more than one timeline on your page, select the timeline you want to use from the Play Timeline drop-down menu.

6. Click on OK to close the Play Timeline dialog box.

7. To specify the user event that triggers the action, click on the arrow button and choose the event (onClick, onMouseOver) from the pop-up menu (**Figure 17.65**).

The event will call the timeline when the page is loaded in a browser.

✔ Tip

■ To make a link that can play a timeline and doesn't open a page, the content of the link should be "#".

Stopping a Timeline

You can also make a behavior stop a timeline.
This is a quite smart thing to do, especially if
you're using the Loop function (I'll get to
that in a minute). The browser's Stop button
will not stop an in-progress timeline.

To make a behavior stop a timeline:

1. In the Document window, click on the
   object you want to use to make the timeline stop (a, img, form button).

2. On the Behaviors panel, click on the Add
   Action button , and from the pop-up
   menu that appears, select Timeline >
   Stop Timeline (**Figure 17.66**). The
   Stop Timeline dialog box will appear
   (**Figure 17.67**).

3. If there is more than one timeline on your
   page, select the timeline you want to use
   from the Stop Timeline drop-down menu.

   or

   Select ALL TIMELINES from the drop-
   down menu.

4. Click on OK to close the Stop Timeline
   dialog box.

5. Click on the arrow button and select the
   user event from the drop-down menu
   (onClick, onMouseOver, and so on).

✔ Tip

- You cannot make the same link (or
  image) both play and stop a timeline. An
  event that signals both a Play and a Stop
  event will only advance the timeline one
  frame at a time. (If the order is Stop and
  then Play, it won't stop at all.) I have to
  admit, though, that this was a great way
  to get screen captures for this chapter.

Figure 17.66 Having selected the Stop It
link, I chose Timeline> Stop Timeline
from the Add action menu.

Figure 17.67 In the Stop Timeline dialog box, I can
choose to stop all timelines or one selected timeline.

MAKING A BEHAVIOR PLAY A TIMELINE

Figure 17.68 Click on the Loop checkbox, and this friendly dialog box will appear to tell you what's up and to which frame number it's adding the behavior. To make it go away, click on the Don't show me this message again checkbox.

Last keyframe ⎯⎤ ⎡⎯ Loop behavior

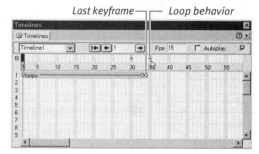

Figure 17.69 The Behaviors channel in this timeline has two behavior markers. The one that follows the last frame is the one to double-click if you want to edit the Loop behavior.

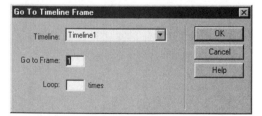

Figure 17.70 The Go To Timeline Frame dialog box controls the Loop behavior.

✔ Tip

■ You can move a behavior to a different frame if you want. Just click on the associated keyframe, if any, and move it to a different frame, and then click on the behavior (as in **Figure 17.69**) and move it to that same frame.

Loop and Rewind

Some timelines are so beautiful, you wish they'd go on forever. (Actually, the first 10 or so timelines you make will automatically be that beautiful.) You can make a timeline repeat either indefinitely or a certain number of times by using the Loop feature.

To add the Loop:

◆ In the Timelines panel, place a check-mark in the Loop checkbox. A dialog box will appear, letting you know that Dream-weaver will add the Go To Frame behavior code (**Figure 17.68**).

The Loop behavior uses the Go to Frame action. In case of automatic loop, the time-line reaches the end and returns to frame 1.

To modify the Loop:

1. In the Timelines panel, locate the last frame in the timeline. You'll see a marker in the Behaviors channel in the frame after that.

2. Double-click on the last Behaviors marker (**Figure 17.69**). The Behaviors panel will appear.

3. Double-click on the action Go To Timeline Frame listed in the Actions list box. The Go To Timeline Frame dialog box will appear (**Figure 17.70**).

4. To make the loop pick up at a frame other than frame 1, type the frame number in the Go to Frame text box.

5. To make the loop continue for a number of times less than infinity, type a number in the Loop text box.

6. Click on OK to close the Go to Timeline Frame text box.

Preview the timeline in a 4.0 or later browser to see if it does what you think it will.

Jumping to or starting with a specific frame

You can also use the Go to Frame behavior with an object outside the timeline. For instance, you can have a "Play Animation" button, a "Stop Animation" button, and a "Go Back to the Part with the Pie" button. You can use a link or button to begin playing the timeline at any frame.

To add a Go to Frame behavior:

1. In the Document window, click on the object you want to use to make the Timeline jump to a particular frame (a, img, form button).

2. Be sure that you don't have a behavior selected in the Timeline panel; click on any frame without a behavior marked in the Behaviors channel.

3. On the Behaviors panel, click on the Add Action button , and from the pop-up menu that appears, select Timeline > Go to Timeline Frame (**Figure 17.71**). The Go To Timeline Frame dialog box will appear (**Figure 17.72**).

4. If there is more than one timeline on your page, select the timeline you want to use from the Timeline drop-down menu.

5. To choose the frame to go to (the frame to rewind or fast forward to), type its number in the Go to Frame text box.

   You cannot set a loop from outside the timeline.

6. Click on OK to close the dialog box.

7. Click on the arrow button and select the user event from the drop-down menu (onClick, onMouseOver, and so on) (**Figure 17.73**).

When the user commits the event, the action will cause the timeline to jump forward or backward to a particular frame.

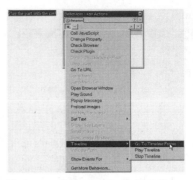

Figure 17.71 First, select your object. Then, click on the Add Action button on the Behaviors panel, and select Timeline > Go to Timeline Frame from the menu.

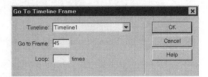

Figure 17.72 In the Go To Timeline Frame dialog box, I specified frame 45.

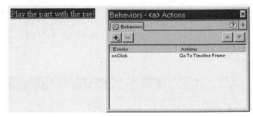

Figure 17.73 I added the onClick event and the Go to Timeline Frame action to the "Play the part with the pie" link.

✔ Tip

■ You can add a Go to Timeline Frame behavior within a timeline, too—not just at the end. Just add the behavior to the Behaviors channel within your timeline. Imagine this: On Frame 8, an image appears in a layer. On Frame 14, the Go to Timeline action makes the timeline jump back to Frame 7. With the number of loops set to 3, the timeline would go back to Frame 7 three times to make the image pop up three times before the animation continued to the end.

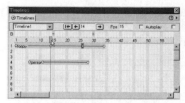

Figure 17.74 I placed the playback head one frame before a behavior on my Timeline.

Figure 17.75 Right-click on the frame, and select Add Frame from the pop-up menu.

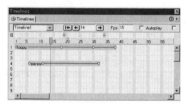

Figure 17.76 I added five new frames between the playback head and the behavior. If I want, I can move the keyframe back five frames by dragging it.

✔ Tips

- Tinkering with the middle of the timeline by changing the number of frames is easier than moving around all the keyframes, behaviors, and objects.

- Adding and removing frames from the middle of a timeline will remove any keyframes or behaviors that reside in those frames.

Adding and Removing Frames

I've already told you how to move the beginning and end of an animation bar, as well as the keyframes. You can also add or remove frames from the middle of a timeline.

To add frames to a Timeline:

1. In the Timelines panel, click on a frame to move the playback head to the place in the Timeline where you want to add a frame (**Figure 17.74**).

2. From the Document window menu bar, select Modify > Timeline > Add Frame.

   or

   Right-click (Control+click on a Mac) on the object's animation bar in the Timelines panel, and select Add Frame from the pop-up menu that appears (**Figure 17.75**).

The frame will be added to the right of the playback head (**Figure 17.76**).

You can also remove frames from a timeline if you want to shorten the duration of the animation or the space between keyframes.

To remove frames from a Timeline:

1. In the Timelines panel, move the playback head to the place in the timeline from which you want to remove a frame.

2. From the Document window menu bar, select Modify > Timeline > Remove Frame.

   or

   Right-click (Control+click on a Mac) on the object's animation bar in the Timelines panel, and select Remove Frame from the pop-up menu that appears.

The frame that the playback head is resting on will be removed.

Using Multiple Timelines

You may want to use more than one timeline if you want more than one animation to be available on the page. You can use the same objects in different timelines, which could then be called by behaviors attached to different links or buttons.

To add a Timeline:

◆ From the Document window menu bar, select Modify > Timeline > Add Timeline.

The Timelines panel will reset, hiding the animation bars for the original timeline; additionally, all the indicators of the timeline will disappear from the Document window (**Figures 17.77** and **17.78**).

To toggle between Timelines:

◆ In the Timelines panel, select the name of the timeline you want to work with from the Timeline drop-down menu (**Figure 17.79**).

You can have as many Timelines as you want.

✔ Tips

■ Each timeline should be fairly simple, or your page will take several days to load and will offer more opportunities to crash browsers around the world.

■ You can have both timelines play simultaneously, or you can have a behavior in a keyframe in the middle or at the end of one timeline call another timeline and have it start playing. Use the Play Timeline behavior, and add it to the first timeline.

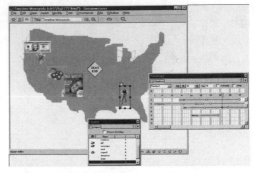

Figure 17.77 The Before Picture: Here's Timeline 1, in mid-play.

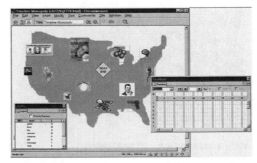

Figure 17.78 The After Picture: I just added Timeline 2. All traces of Timeline 1 are hidden—all the pictures are placed in their original positions, they're all visible, and they've got their original overlap settings.

Figure 17.79 Choose which timeline to work with from the drop-down menu on the Timelines panel.

Figure 17.80 Type a new name for the timeline in the Timeline Name text box.

Figure 17.81 Select Remove Timeline from the shortcut menu to remove the timeline code from the page.

✔ Tips

- If you have a timeline with objects and behaviors already added to it, it is a good idea to save a version of the document (File > Save As) before deleting so that you don't lose the entire thing. You might decide that you want to use a version of it later on.

- If you accidentally remove a Timeline, remember the magic word: Undo. Select Edit > Undo from the Document window menu bar, or press Ctrl+Z (Command+Z).

Renaming and Deleting Timelines

Tired of flipping between "Timeline 1" and Timeline 2"? Rename them.

To rename a Timeline:

1. View the timeline you want to rename.

2. From the Document window menu bar, select Modify > Timeline > Rename Timeline. The Rename Timeline dialog box will appear (**Figure 17.80**).

3. Type the new name for your timeline in the Timeline Name text box.

4. Click on OK. The Rename Timeline dialog box will close.

The new name for your timeline will appear in the Timeline drop-down menu in the Timelines panel.

Removing a timeline from a page is easy. Make sure you select the proper timeline—and if you want no timelines, delete each one.

To remove a timeline:

1. In the Property inspector, select the name of the timeline you want to remove.

2. Click on the Shortcut Menu button on the side of the Timelines panel, and select Remove Timeline from the menu (**Figure 17.81**).

Poof! It's gone.

Removing or Changing Objects

You can remove an object from a timeline if you no longer want to include it in the animation, or you might decide that the actions you've set up for a layer are dandy, but that they'd work better for a different layer.

To remove an object from a timeline:

1. In the Timelines panel, click on the animation bar for the object you want to remove from the timeline.

2. Press Backspace (Delete). The object will be removed from the timeline, but it will remain on the page.

✔ Tips

■ You can also select the object in the Document window and then use a menu command to remove it. Select Modify > Timeline > Remove Object from the Document window menu bar (**Figure 17.82**) or from a context menu.

■ To remove a behavior from a Timeline, select Modify > Timeline > Remove Behavior from the menu.

To change objects:

1. In the Timelines panel, select the animation bar for the object you want to switch with another object.

2. From the Document window menu bar, select Modify > Timeline > Change Object. The Change Object dialog box will appear (**Figure 17.83**).

3. From the Object to Animate drop-down menu, select an object (**Figure 17.84**).

4. Click on OK to close the Change Object dialog box. The animation bar will now describe the object you selected.

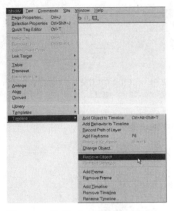

Figure 17.82 To remove an object, select Modify > Timeline > Remove Object. The Timelines panel doesn't even need to be open for this.

Figure 17.83 The Change Object dialog box allows you to transfer an animation channel from one object to another.

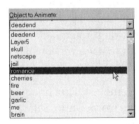

Figure 17.84 To switch which object is animated, select the name of an object from the Object to Animate drop-down menu.

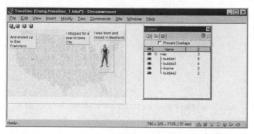

Figure 17.85 The raw materials. The page contains five layers: the map, the person, and three "bubbles." The other layers need to be positioned relative to the map, so they're all nested within the map.

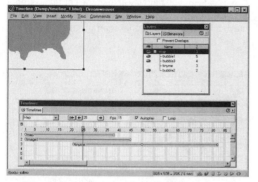

Figure 17.86 Frame 25 of the first timeline, called Map. I want the window to be blank to start. Then the first map is brought in from off screen.

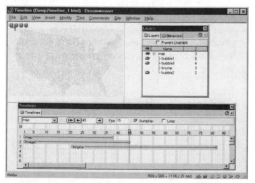

Figure 17.87 Frame 45 of the Map timeline. A few frames after the map layer arrives, the image source changes into a different map (on frame 45, I changed the source in the Property inspector). This map has a larger file size, but the image had been preloaded in a layer.

Bringing It All Together

Timelines are quite versatile, although moving objects are difficult to illustrate in print. To wrap up this chapter, I'm going to visually dissect a quasi-useful timeline I constructed using almost all timeline capabilities. Follow the figure captions for **Figures 17.85** through **17.93**.

One note about **Figures 17.90** through **17.92**: the Map layer doesn't do anything in the second timeline, but I added it so it would be visible while working. Dreamweaver displays the default image rather than the one that's been swapped in.

continued on next page

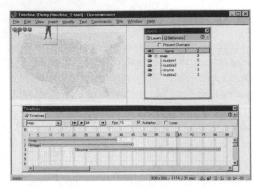

Figure 17.88 Frame 64 of the Map timeline. The person layer ("tinyme") begins to arrive from off screen. Like the map layer, the person was given negative coordinates (L –400px,T –300px) at the start of the timeline.

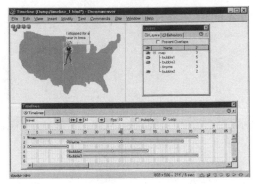

Figure 17.91 Frame 41 of the Travel timeline. The person has moved halfway across the country. Bubble 1 is hidden and Bubble 2 appears. Note that the playback rate is 10 fps rather than 15; this timeline moves more slowly.

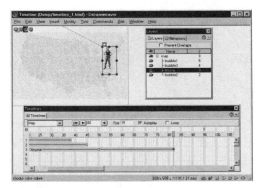

Figure 17.89 Frame 82 of the Map timeline. The person has arrived. A few frames later, in frame 95, a behavior will play the second timeline, called Travel.

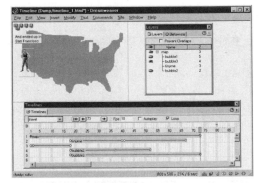

Figure 17.92 Frame 73 of the Travel timeline. At the end of the timeline, the person is all the way across the map. Bubble 2 is hidden, and Bubble 3 appears. I also added a Loop behavior in frame 80; after a pause, the second timeline will replay.

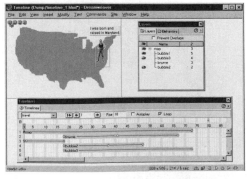

Figure 17.90 In frame 1 of the Travel timeline, the layer "Bubble 1" appears above the person's head.

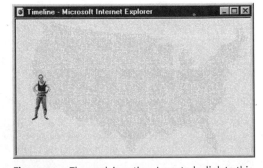

Figure 17.93 The work in action. I created a link to this timeline in a JavaScript window the same size as the map images.

Automating Dreamweaver

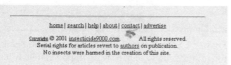

Figure 18.1 This page footer, including text, links, and the image and horizontal rule, is perfect fodder for a Dreamweaver library item. You can insert it onto any new or existing Web page in a matter of seconds. If one of the links changes or the information changes, you can automatically update all pages that use this footer.

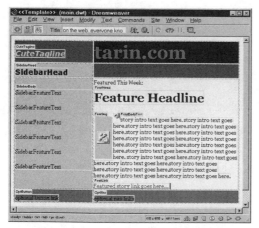

Figure 18.2 Dreamweaver templates allow you to create a basic shell page on which some areas are editable and some are read-only. The editable regions appear in highlighted boxes with tabs that show the name of the region.

Dreamweaver helps you save time by creating elements that you can reuse and update easily across an entire site. Library items are reusable chunks of code, and templates are page designs.

The Dreamweaver library is a storehouse of frequently used items (**Figure 18.1**) that are linked to the site cache. If you're familiar with server-side includes, library items work the same way: the HTML for the item is inserted into the page, along with a reference to the library item's URL. If you change a library item, you can then update the pages that use it. You can also insert actual server-side include tokens in Dreamweaver and view them inline.

Dreamweaver also lets you update pages by building templates (**Figure 18.2**); you can base pages on a template file that you can then update. And speaking of templates, you can export editable regions of templates as XML and import XML into templates.

One more way you can automate Dreamweaver is with the History panel (**Figure 18.3**), which lets you repeat actions you've performed during a session. You can even save sets of actions as macros to reuse later.

About Libraries

The library is a collection of HTML files with the extension .lbi. These files, called *library items*, are stored in a specifically designated Library folder in a local site on your computer (**Figure 18.4**). As part of Dreamweaver's site management tools, the Library folder is stored in the site root folder of each site you use with Dreamweaver.

If you have more than one local site on your computer, each will use its own Library folder.

✔ Tip

■ In Dreamweaver, a *local site* is the same as a folder or set of folders. If you designate a folder on your hard drive as a local site, Dreamweaver will then know how to keep track of locally linked files. For more on local sites, see Chapter 2.

You must set up, or define, a local site in Dreamweaver before you can use library items. Dreamweaver will create the Library folder for you.

You create, edit, and place library items using the Library category on the Assets panel. If you're upgrading to Dreamweaver 4, rest assured this panel works the same way as the old Library palette.

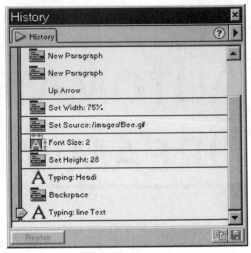

Figure 18.3 The History panel lets you redo and undo nearly any action you perform in the Document window. You can also save sets of actions as commands.

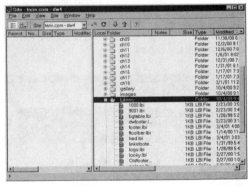

Figure 18.4 A local site on my hard drive. The Library folder is highlighted.

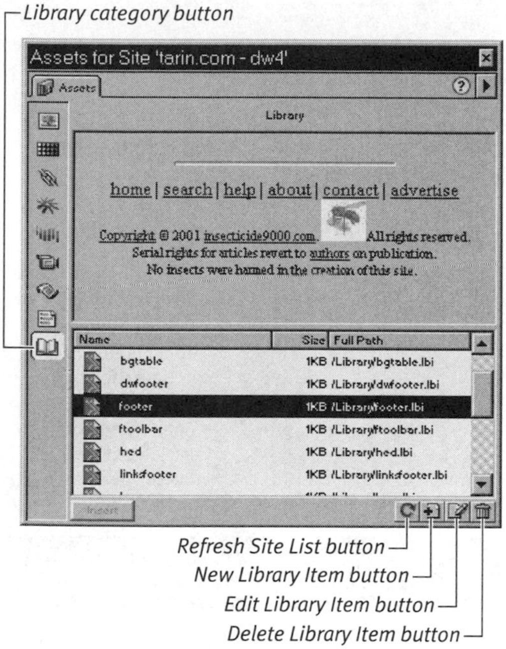

Library category button

Assets for Site 'tarin.com - dw4'

Library

home | search | help | about | contact | advertise

Copyright © 2001 insecticide9000.com. All rights reserved.
Serial rights for articles revert to authors on publication.
No insects were harmed in the creation of this site.

Name	Size	Full Path
bgtable	1KB	/Library/bgtable.lbi
dwfooter	1KB	/Library/dwfooter.lbi
footer	1KB	/Library/footer.lbi
ftoolbar	1KB	/Library/ftoolbar.lbi
hed	1KB	/Library/hed.lbi
linkfooter	1KB	/Library/linkfooter.lbi

Refresh Site List button —
New Library Item button —
Edit Library Item button —
Delete Library Item button —

Figure 18.5 Use the Library category on the Assets panel to create and insert library items.

So Which Is Which?

Libraries and objects (described in Chapter 19) do similar things, so which one do you use for your purposes? Think of it in terms of form and content: libraries are the content, and objects are the form.

Objects are good for inserting standard containers (like tables or layers) that you'll put content in later, or commonly used gizmos like JavaScript buttons or special-sized horizontal rules. However, they don't update automatically (as do libraries), and they aren't site-specific.

The superpower of libraries is that you can spread them over an entire site and still update them as often as you like. Libraries are best used for inserting content that may change over time. See the sidebar, *Bitchin' Examples,* on the next page.

To display the Library:

◆ From the Document window menu bar, select Window > Library.

or

On the Launcher or Launcher bar, click on the Assets button, and then click on the Library button on the Assets panel:

Either way, the Library category of the Assets panel will appear (**Figure 18.5**).

ABOUT LIBRARIES

What Library Items Do

Library items are little pieces of Web pages—pieces that you want to reuse on many pages, and pieces that you want to be able to update on every one of those pages.

Library items can contain HTML and JavaScript. Any objects (that is, images, plug-ins, and applets) will not be duplicated in a library item; just as on a Web page, the library items link to those objects.

Many big sites use CGI scripts to automatically replace text on page after page of a site, but library items can accomplish the same thing. They also act very much like server-side includes, described later in this chapter.

Unlike with server-side includes, when you use library items, the HTML code itself is stored locally in each page, and you must update your files locally and then re-upload them in order for your changes to go live. However, library items are a user-friendly substitute if you fear UNIX and know nothing about setting the environment on your Web server so that server-side includes execute properly.

If you move files around, this might affect the links to your library items. You can automatically update library references when files are moved; see *Updating Your Site,* later in this chapter.

✔ Tip

- In Dreamweaver 4, the Library is now a category on the Assets panel. To save words, I sometimes refer to "the Library category on the Assets panel" as "the Library." If you haven't yet played with the Assets panel, see Chapter 2.

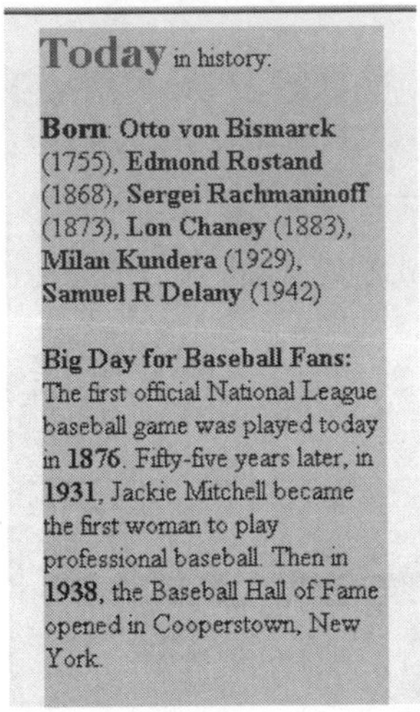

Today in history:

Born: Otto von Bismarck (1755), Edmond Rostand (1868), Sergei Rachmaninoff (1873), Lon Chaney (1883), Milan Kundera (1929), Samuel R Delany (1942)

Big Day for Baseball Fans: The first official National League baseball game was played today in 1876. Fifty-five years later, in 1931, Jackie Mitchell became the first woman to play professional baseball. Then in 1938, the Baseball Hall of Fame opened in Cooperstown, New York.

Figure 18.6 This "Today in History" sidebar gets updated daily. Making the whole chunk, including the layer containing the text, into a library item means you just update the library item to update the page—you don't even need to *open* the page.

Figure 18.7 If this navigation bar appeared on every page in your site, it would be a pain to replace every instance of it if you added a search function (and thus, a new toolbar button). Make it a library item, add a new image, and update the site automatically.

Bitchin' Examples

- ◆ The footer with copyright info at the bottom of every page in your site (like the one I showed you in **Figure 18.1**)

- ◆ Daily updates on pages that aren't otherwise updated (**Figure 18.6**)

- ◆ Navigation bars on sites that are still growing (**Figure 18.7**)

- ◆ Frequently used logo images, contact e-mail addresses, or mastheads

Tag selector

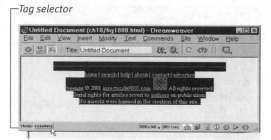

Figure 18.8 Select all the text, images, and other code you want to include in your library item. Here, I'm selecting the <center> tag in the tag selector, which includes all the tags and text I want to use.

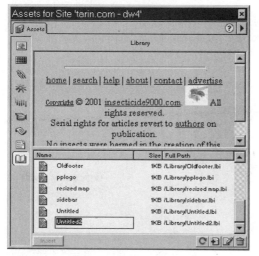

Figure 18.9 The Library, more wordily known as the Library category on the Assets panel. To just display the Library without adding a new item to it, select Window > Library from the Document window menu bar.

Figure 18.10 The elements you've added to the Library will be highlighted in yellow, and the entire chunk of stuff will be one object—click anywhere within the yellow area to select the item.

Creating a Library Item

You create a library item by copying a piece of existing HTML into the Library. You can select part of any existing page, or you can create a dummy page for the sole purpose of adding items from it to the Library.

To create a new library item:

1. Open the page that contains the stuff you want to add to the Library.

   If you are working with a new page, save the page in a folder on your local site.

2. Select the desired objects (**Figure 18.8**). (You may want to use Code View or the tag selector to select all the tags you need.)

3. From the Document window menu bar, select Modify > Library> Add Object to Library. The Library will appear (**Figure 18.9**).

   or

   Drag the selection into the list box on the Library category of the Assets panel.

   or

   On the Library category of the Assets panel, click on the New button 🔁.

4. Type a name for the library item in the text box, replacing the word Untitled.

Your new item will be highlighted in yellow in the Document window (**Figure 18.10**).

✔ Tips

- Once you designate a selection on a page as a library item, you will not be able to edit it freely. See *Editing Library Items,* later in this chapter, for more on this.

- To add the content of a selection to a library item without replacing the selection with the new uneditable library item, hold down the Ctrl (Command) key while creating the library item.

Inserting and Removing Library Items

Now that you've created a library item, you can add it to other new or existing pages in the site.

To insert a library item by dragging:

◆ The easiest way to add a library item to a page is to drag the library item icon from the Library category of the Assets panel to the Document window (**Figure 18.11**).

To add a library item at the insertion point:

1. Click to place the insertion point at the place in the Document window (such as a table cell) where you want the library item to appear.

2. In the Library, click on the icon for the library item you want to add.

3. Click on the Insert button. The library item will appear at the insertion point (**Figure 18.12**).

To remove a library item from a page:

1. Click anywhere within the highlighted library item to select the entire thing (**Figure 18.13**).

2. Press Backspace or Delete. The library item will disappear.

✔ Tip

■ To add the contents of a library item—the code and links—without linking it to the library, hold down the Ctrl (Command) button and drag the library item onto the page. You won't be able to update it.

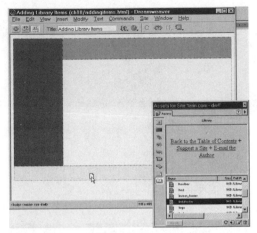

Figure 18.11 Drag a library item icon from the Library panel right onto the page. The library item will be inserted where you drop it.

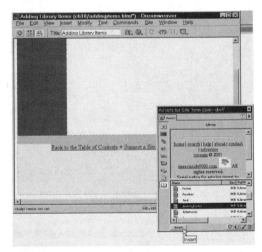

Figure 18.12 Click on the Insert button, and the library item will appear on the page at the insertion point.

Figure 18.13 Click anywhere on a library item to select the whole thing. Then you can delete it, or cut and paste it anywhere.

Figure 18.14 The Property inspector, displaying library item properties.

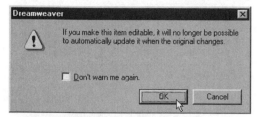

Figure 18.15 Dreamweaver warns you that the item will no longer be linked to the Library. To keep this dialog box from appearing, check the Don't warn me again checkbox.

First item still highlighted

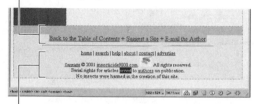

Second item detached from Library

Figure 18.16 After making the item editable, the yellow highlighting is removed and the item is no longer linked to the Library.

Creative Renaming Tricks

You can rename a library item if you want to divorce it on purpose from the pages that reference the item. Then, you can create a new item with the old name, and old references will point to the new item.

For example, say I have a library item called Toolbar. I want to completely change the toolbar, but I don't want to get rid of the library item entirely. I rename the old Toolbar OldToolbar, without updating. Then I create a new library item called Toolbar. The old references will point to the new item.

Editing Library Items

There are two ways to edit a library item:

◆ Make the library item editable on just one page by disconnecting it from the Library and then editing it on that page (change is local).

◆ Edit the library item in its own window (change is global).

Changing a single instance of a library item

Making an item editable, or detaching it from the Library, means that it has the same content as the library item had, but it is no longer linked to the Library. This means that if you automatically update the entire site from the Library, the ex-library item on the page you edited will not be updated.

To make a library item editable:

1. In any document that contains the library item you wish to edit, select the library item by clicking on it (as we saw in **Figure 18.13**).

2. View the Property inspector, if it isn't open (**Figure 18.14**), by selecting Window > Properties from the Document window menu bar or by double-clicking on the library item.

3. On the Property inspector, click on Detach from Original. A dialog box will warn you that this will prevent the library item from being affected by future Library updates (**Figure 18.15**).

4. Click on OK to close the dialog box. The item will be de-linked from the Site Library, and you can go ahead and edit it on that one page (**Figure 18.16**).

Changing a library item site-wide

If you want to edit all instances of a library item so that you can update it on all the pages that use it, you need to edit the item in its own window.

To edit a library item globally:

1. In the Library, click on the icon for the item you want to edit. The current version will be displayed in the preview area on the Assets panel (**Figure 18.17**).

2. Click on the Edit button .

   or

   Double-click either the name of the library item or the preview frame. Either way, a new document window will appear that contains only the HTML included in the library item (**Figure 18.18**).

3. Make your changes to the library item.

4. Save the changes to the library item using File > Save or Ctrl+S (Command+S). A dialog box will ask if you want to update all documents in your local site that contain the library item (**Figure 18.19**).

   ◆ To update now, click on Update.

   ◆ To update later, click on Don't Update. (You may want to postpone this until you're finished editing and then update everything at once.)

5. Close the library item Document window.

✔ Tips

■ To find out more about updating pages that use library items, see *Updating Your Site*, later in this chapter.

■ You can make the preview area larger or smaller by dragging the border between the two frames in the Assets panel (**Figure 18.20**).

Figure 18.17 When you select an item in the Library, it is displayed in the frame at the top of the Assets panel.

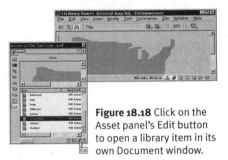

Figure 18.18 Click on the Asset panel's Edit button to open a library item in its own Document window.

Figure 18.19 When you save the changes to the library item, a dialog box will appear asking you if you want to update the entire site.

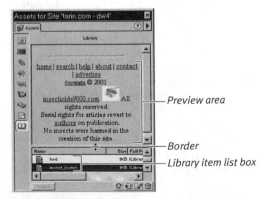

Preview area

Border

Library item list box

Figure 18.20 Drag the border between the two frames to change the size of the preview area.

—Delete button

Figure 18.21 Click on the name of the item you want to remove from the library.

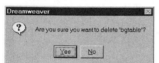

Figure 18.22 To commence deleting the item from the Library, click Yes.

Deleting a Library Item

Deleting a library item removes the file from the Library. However, the pages that use the library item will still include the code that links the page to the Library.

To delete a library item:

1. In the Library, select the item you want to delete (**Figure 18.21**).

2. Click on the Delete button: 🗑. A dialog box will ask you if you really want to delete the library item (**Figure 18.22**).

3. Click Yes. Poof! It's gone.

✔ Tip

■ Probably the easiest way to remove references to deleted library items is to select them and then make them editable. That removes references to the .lbi file, but leaves the content intact.

Library Code

The code for a library item consists of two things: The code for the item itself, such as table tags, image paths, anchors, text, and font formatting; and the code that links the item to the Library.

Code for a standard footer might look like this:

```
<!- #BeginLibraryItem "/Library/tabletalk.lbi" ->
<center>
<font size="-1">Copyright &copy; 2001, Animalogic. All rights reserved.
<a href="/legal/">Legal Notices</a>.</font>
</center>
<!- #EndLibraryItem ->
```

Dreamweaver keeps track of library-linked pages using the site cache (discussed in Chapters 2 and 20). When a library item is moved or renamed within the Library panel or the Site window, Dreamweaver looks in the cache for the #BeginLibraryItem marker in pages within your site.

If you want to remove all library item markers from a site, you can use Dreamweaver's Replace feature (Edit > Replace), discussed in Chapter 8, or the Clean Up HTML feature (Commands > Clean Up HTML; select Dreamweaver Comments), discussed in Chapter 4.

Re-creating a Library Item

If you delete an item from the Library, but it still exists on any page, you can re-create it.

Besides reinstating deleted library items, you can use the Recreate function to replace the contents of a library item with the contents of an edited library item (or vice versa). This is useful for renamed or mistakenly edited items.

To re-create a library item:

1. In the Document window, select an edited library item or an item that was deleted from the Library palette (**Figure 18.23**).

2. On the Property inspector, click on the Recreate button (**Figure 18.24**). If you're overwriting an existing library item, a dialog box will appear (**Figure 18.25**).

3. Click on OK. The contents of the selected library item will overwrite the contents of the existing library item (**Figure 18.26**). (In the case of deleted items, the original name will be re-added to the Library).

✔ Tips

■ You cannot overwrite a library item with the contents of another library item. In other words, you can't select the item July and overwrite it with the contents of June.

■ The ability to re-create library items is one reason not to update your site immediately after you edit a library item. As long as the old library item content exists on a page somewhere, you can re-create the original. I like to update my library items just before I upload pages. See *Updating Your Site,* later in this chapter. I cover updating Libraries and templates at the same time.

Figure 18.23 I accidentally edited the "Looky" library item so that it consisted of the text link on the bottom instead of the selected images. I still have a copy of the old library item on my page, so I select it.

Figure 18.24 I click on the Recreate button on the Property inspector.

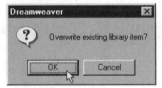

Figure 18.25 A dialog box warns me that I'm about to overwrite the contents of the library item.

Figure 18.26 I have successfully rewritten the Looky library item with the old contents.

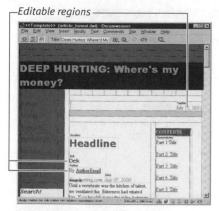

Editable regions

Figure 18.27 This template page has areas that are marked as editable. Other areas are not editable in Dreamweaver. If I change the design—fonts, colors, whatever—I can then update all the pages based on this template.

Figure 18.28 Templates are stored in the templates folder in your local site.

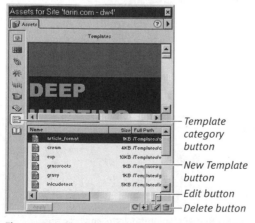

Template category button

New Template button

Edit button

Delete button

Figure 18.29 The Templates category on the Assets Manager shows all the templates available in the current site.

Dreamweaver Templates

In Dreamweaver templates, you design a page and then designate certain portions of the page as editable. The rest is locked to the user. So as a designer, you can give anyone a template-based page to edit, and they won't be able to mess up your precious page design.

If you update the template design after it's been used on any number of pages, you can painlessly update all pages on your local site that use that template. Then you just re-upload the affected pages, and they'll have the changed template content.

For instance, if you suddenly want to change the page background of your site from blue to orange, or the copyright date from 2000 to 2001, you change a single file—the template—and then update all pages that use that template (**Figure 18.27**). After you update the pages, you need to re-upload them to the Web server before your changes will be live.

Template Tools

As with library items, templates are stored in a local site folder called Templates (**Figure 18.28**). Each site uses a different Templates folder. For more about managing local sites, see Chapter 2.

The tool you use to work with templates is the Templates category on the Assets panel (**Figure 18.29**). To display Templates, select Window > Assets from the Document window menu bar, and then click on the Templates button [⊞]. (See Chapter 2 for more on Assets.)

The top half displays a preview of the template's content, and the bottom half lists the templates available to your local site.

Creating Templates

The first step is creating the template file itself.

To base a template on an existing file:

1. Open the file you'd like to use as the template for other pages on your site.

2. From the Document window menu bar, select File > Save as Template. The Save As Template dialog box will appear (**Figure 18.30**). Any existing templates will be listed in the Existing Templates list box.

3. If you have more than one local site, select the site the template will reside in from the Site drop-down menu.

4. Type a filename for the template in the Save As dialog box. The .dwt extension will automatically be appended to the file.

5. Click on Save to save the file as a template.

6. If you're overwriting an existing template, a dialog box will ask you to confirm this choice. Click on Yes to overwrite the old file.

The template will now be displayed in the Document window instead of the original HTML file. You can tell a template by the title bar—it says <<Template>> (**Figure18.31**).

To create a template from scratch:

1. On the Templates category of the Assets panel, click on the New Template button: ⊞. A new Template icon will appear in the Assets panel (**Figure 18.32**).

2. Type a name for the new template in place of "Untitled," and press Return.

3. On the Assets panel, double-click the name of the template, or click on the Edit button ⧉. A blank Document window will appear. You'll see the name of the template file (nn.dwt) displayed in the Document window title bar.

Figure 18.30 In the Save As Template dialog box, type the name of the new template, or choose a template to overwrite.

Title bar indicates template file

Figure 18.31 You can tell you have a template file open instead of a regular page—even if you haven't yet marked any editable regions—by looking at the title bar.

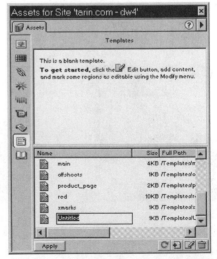

Figure 18.32 Click on the New Template button in the Templates palette, and type the name of your template in place of "Untitled."

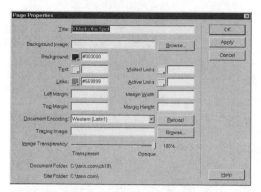

Figure 18.33 Remember to set any page properties for your template (Modify > Page Properties), such as the page background or text and link colors. The only page property that can be edited for a page based on a template is the page title.

Figure 18.34 On this page, which is based on the template I created in **Figure 18.31**, the title can be edited, but the background, text, and link colors cannot.

✔ Tips

■ To add dynamic content to a page based on a template, see *Detaching a Page from a Template,* later in this chapter.

■ To add a style sheet to pages that use a template, you must return to the template itself and link to the style sheet from there.

Setting Page Properties on Template-Based Pages

When users work with a page based on a template, they cannot edit any page properties other than the page title (**Figure 18.33**).

✔ Tip

■ When a user tries to change page properties for pages based on a template, the locked properties are not grayed out, and there is no error message. The user will simply hear a beep upon closing the Page Properties dialog box, and the properties will remain unchanged.

You should set page properties, such as the page background and text and link colors, in the template file itself (**Figure 18.34**). If you want some of your pages to have different page properties, then save the template with a different name and base the blue pages on the blue template and the orange pages on the orange template.

See Chapter 3 to find out more about page properties.

Using Styles and JavaScript in Templates

Because you cannot edit the <head> of a document that is based on a Dream Template, you cannot add or edit CSS styles, behaviors, or timelines in these pages. It's certainly convenient to be able to create style sheets in a template and have them apply to all pages based on that template, but less convenient not to be able to use scripts.

An exception to the styles rule: you can create layers (which use unique instances of CSS) in pages based on templates.

Setting Editable Regions

Everything you place on a template will be locked—that is, you or your staff will not be able to edit that part of the page—unless you mark it as a named editable region.

To create a new editable region:

1. Click to place the insertion point where you want the new editable region to appear.

2. From the Document window menu bar, select Modify > Templates > New Editable Region. The New Editable Region dialog box will appear (**Figure 18.35**).

3. Type a name for the editable region in the text box. Avoid funky characters, and don't use quotation marks or <angle brackets>.

4. Click on OK to close the New Editable Region dialog box and return to the Document window. The name of the editable region will appear highlighted in the Document window (**Figure 18.36**) in a little box with the name of the editable region on top. You can edit this text, if you like.

You can also create a page element and then mark it as editable.

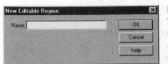

Figure 18.35
Type the name of the new region in the Name text box.

Name of new editable region

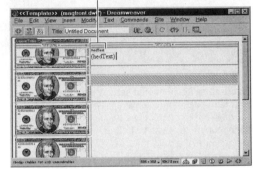

Figure 18.36 The text you typed as the name of the new editable region will appear in the Document window at the insertion point, and its name will appear inside {curly brackets}. The text will also appear inside a box with a tab marking the name of the region.

Name of new editable region

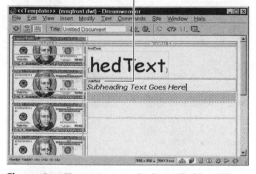

Figure 18.37 The text you marked as editable will be highlighted in a in the Document window with the name of the region on its tab. Note that I edited both regions for font size and such.

To set an editable region:

1. Type and select some placeholder text, such as "Headline or Image Goes Here."

2. From the Document window menu bar, select Modify > Templates > Mark Selection As Editable Region. The New Editable Region dialog box will appear (**Figure 18.35**).

3. Type a name for the editable region in the text box. Avoid funky characters, and don't use quotation marks or <angle brackets>.

4. Click on OK. The editable region will be boxed in the template's Document window with the name of the editable region on its tab (**Figure 18.37**).

Unmarking Editable Regions

To unmark an editable region, you remove it from the document. From the Document window menu bar, select Modify > Templates > Remove Editable Regions. The Remove Editable Regions dialog box will appear, listing all the regions you've created thus far. Select the region from the list, and click on OK to remove your selection and unmark it.

SETTING EDITABLE REGIONS

Creating Pages Based on a Template

Once you've got your template set up, you can create pages based on that template.

To create a template page:

1. From the Document window menu bar, select File > New From Template. The Select Template dialog box will appear (**Figure 18.38**).

2. Select the name of the template on which you want to base your page.

3. Click Select. The Select Template dialog box will close, and a new document window will appear (**Figure 18.39**), including:

   ◆ The formatting of your template, along with any HTML elements or page properties

   ◆ The editable regions of your template, marked in blue boxes with the name of each region on its tab (**Figure 18.40**)

   ◆ Locked regions are not marked but are untouchable. On Windows, this is indicated by a "Don't" sign (**Figure 18.41**)

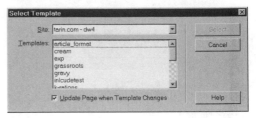

Figure 18.38 Select the template on which you want to base your page from the Select Template dialog box. You can also change sites by selecting a site from the drop-down menu.

New page is not saved

Figure 18.39 A blank page based on the main.dwt template. The locked regions are marked in yellow, and the rest of the text is editable.

Figure 18.40 The editable regions of your template are marked in blue boxes with the name of each region on its tab.

Figure 18.41 Can't touch this! Non-editable regions are locked and the cursor tells you so.

Figure 18.42 The whole page is now editable. No more locked or unlocked regions—just a page.

Detaching a Page from a Template

If you'd like to remove the link between a page and a template, you can detach the page from the template. This is what you need to do if you'd rather attach a page to a different template or if you want to make exceptions to your design rules.

To detach a template:

◆ From the Document window menu bar, select Modify > Templates > Detach from [Template name].

The editable regions will disappear (**Figure 18.42**), and nothing will be locked.

After you detach a page from a template, you can add scripts and such to the page.

Once you detach a template from a page, it will no longer be updated automatically when you edit the template file.

Deleting a Template

If you're utterly done with a template, you may delete it.

To delete a template:

1. In the Templates category of the Assets panel, select the template you wish to delete.

2. Click on the Delete button 🗑. A dialog box will appear asking you if you're sure you want to delete the template (**Figure 18.43**).

3. Click on Yes. The template will be deleted.

4. References to the deleted template will not be discarded; you'll need to attach affected pages to a new template.

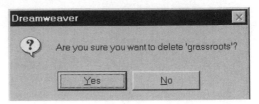

Figure 18.43 If you really want to delete that template, click on Yes.

DELETING A TEMPLATE

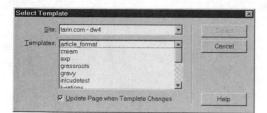

Figure 18.44 Select the template to which you want to attach the page.

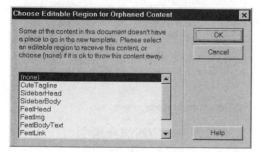

Figure 18.45 In the Choose Editable Region for Orphaned Content dialog box, pick an editable region to receive your content. If many different types of content are on the existing page, you can move the content from region to region after you convert the page. If this page already uses similar marked regions as the template, you can select None.

✔ Tip

- If a piece of placeholder text, for example, "HeadingA," matches the name of a template region (in our example, it would also be called "HeadingA"), Dreamweaver will automatically match the placeholder text with the editable region. If the blue template and the orange template use the same region names, you can detach a page from one template and then attach it to the other. Leave "None" selected, and the content will go where it's supposed to.

Attaching an Existing Page to a Template

You can attach existing pages to a new template, too. You have to choose a single region to dump all the content into, though, unless the page has similar marked regions.

To attach a page to a template:

1. From the Document window menu bar, select Modify > Templates > Apply Template to Page. The Select Template dialog box will appear (**Figure 18.44**).

2. Select the name of the template that you want, and click on OK. The Choose Editable Region for Orphaned Content dialog box will appear (**Figure 18.45**).

3. Because templates only allow new content to appear in editable regions, you need to select an editable region in which to stick your content. You'll be able to move it from region to region once the page is reopened, but for now, you have to pick one. Do so, and click on OK. (Clicking on None will throw away your content.)

4. To automatically have this page updated when you edit the template, leave the checkbox checked. For more on updating, see *Updating Your Site*, later on.

5. When the dialog box closes, your content will appear in the region you selected. You can edit your page now.

Using Editable Regions

If you're working with a page with a number of editable regions and you want to make sure you put the right stuff in the right slots, Dreamweaver can help you locate them.

To find an editable region:

1. From the Document window menu bar, select Modify > Templates > [region name]. All editable regions appear at the bottom of the menu (**Figure 18.46**).

2. The editable region will become highlighted (**Figure 18.47**), and you can type away.

✔ Tips

- Images and other objects can be marked as editable regions, too. The page in **Figure 18.47** uses an image as a drop cap, and this image needs to be replaced with every story update. **Figure 18.48** shows the highlighted editable region, called FeatImg, in which the letter I has been replaced with the letter F. If the image were not an editable region of the document, it would be locked and permanent.

- If you're giving a batch of blank template pages to a Webmonkey for filling in the blanks, you should point out this helpful feature so that your minions know for sure which content goes in which region. A printout of a mocked-up page with the region names clearly marked and labeled couldn't hurt, either, although now in Dreamweaver 4, region names are marked in the Document window.

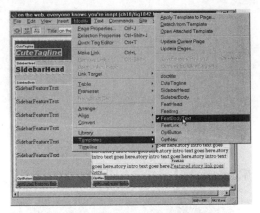

Figure 18.46 All editable regions available to the current page are listed at the bottom of the Modify > Templates menu.

Figure 18.47 After you select an editable region from the menu, it will become highlighted in the Document window so that you can type over it.

Figure 18.48 The image selected on this page is an editable region. If an image on a page will be changing, you can mark it as editable. You can also insert images into editable regions (such as the highlighted body text in **Figure 18.47**) so they can be deleted or replaced.

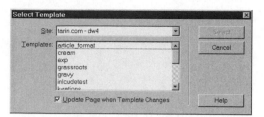

Figure 18.49 The Update Page When Template Changes checkbox does not do what it says it does. Dreamweaver still, as always, asks you whether you want to update your pages when you save changes to a template file.

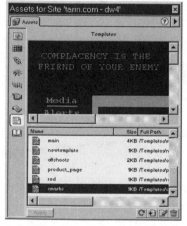

Figure 18.50 Select the name of the template to edit. (You can always do a File > Open, but using the Assets panel is expedient when working with multiple templates and opening pages based on them.)

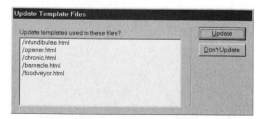

Figure 18.51 When you save changes to a template file, a dialog box will appear asking if you want to update your site.

Editing Templates

You can edit templates at any time, even after you've attached pages to them. Once you've edited a template, you can then perform an update to reflect your recent edits. For example, if you change the background color on your template from orange to blue, you can automatically change the background on all the pages based on that template, too.

There's a new checkbox in Dreamweaver 4. When you create a new page based on a template or when you attach a page to a template, you use the Select Template dialog box (**Figure 18.49**). This new checkbox, Update Page When Template Changes, purports to update pages based on this template automatically. In actuality, Dreamweaver still asks you, when you save your changes, whether you want to update the pages.

To edit a template:

1. In the Templates category of the Assets panel, select the name of the template to edit (**Figure 18.50**).

2. Click on the Edit button. The template will appear in a new Document window.

3. Make any changes you like, taking care to mark editable areas as such.

4. Save your changes. A dialog box will appear asking if you wish to update the pages that use this template (**Figure 18.51**).

   To update now, click Yes, and skip to the section on updating your site if you need more details. To update later, click No.

Highlights for Templates

Highlighting on templates works like this:

Code View: In template files, no code is highlighted in the Code inspector or Code View.

Code View: In pages based on templates, all non-editable code is highlighted in yellow in the Code inspector or Code View. Therefore, the only code that *isn't* highlighted is the code for editable regions.

Design View: In both template files and pages based on templates, editable regions are outlined by a blue border with the region's name on its tab in the Document window.

The best way to show you these distinctions is a page with very little code in it, in Split View (**Figures 18.52** and **18.53**).

You can also change library item colors.

To set the highlight colors:

1. From the Document window menu bar, select Edit > Preferences. The Preferences dialog box will appear.

2. In the Category box at the left, select Highlighting. The Highlighting panel of the dialog box will appear (**Figure 18.54**).

3. To select a color, click on the Color box next to the item's name. The color picker will appear. Select a color by clicking on it.

4. Click on OK to save your changes and return to the Document window.

✔ Tip

■ To turn off highlighting for a library or template entity, uncheck the Show checkbox for that item.

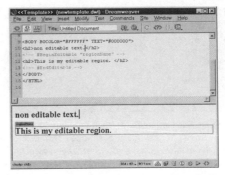

Figure 18.52 A template file displayed in Split View. In Design View, editable regions are outlined in a blue box with the name of the region on its tab, and nothing is highlighted in Code View.

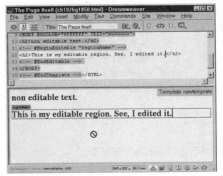

Figure 18.53 A page based on a template. In Code View, uneditable regions are highlighted in Library Item Yellow. Uneditable regions aren't marked at all in Design View, but the editable ones look the same as they do on template files.

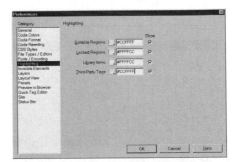

Figure 18.54 In the Highlighting panel of the Preferences dialog box, you can adjust the default highlight colors for editable and locked regions, as well as for library items and for third-party tags (such as new proprietary browser tags, tags introduced by other WYSIWYG editors, or RDF or XML tags).

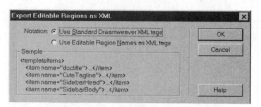

Figure 18.55 In the Export Editable Regions as XML dialog box, you may choose to save the editable regions of your template as Dreamweaver <item> tags or as self referential XML tags.

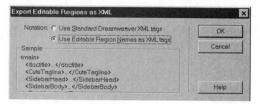

Figure 18.56 In the second option in this dialog box, the tags themselves—true to XML's custom nature—are named for the editable regions.

Exporting as XML

XML stands for eXtensible Markup Language, which basically means you can create your own tags as you see fit for your own back-end scripts and database hooks to interpret. XML tags do not modify the behavior of what they contain in the browser setting. Rather, they're used as containers to mark content. An XML tag may be something like <Headline></Headline>, and the tag may be used as a container into which to import content on dynamic pages; as a marker to export content out of a database; or as a marker for a search robot to find particular types of content.

Because the editable regions of a Dreamweaver template are all named, you may name them the same things as XML tags you're using (or vice versa—name the tags for the regions). You may then export the content of a template-based file as an XML file, with the editable region names converted into XML tags.

To export editable regions as XML:

1. Open a page based on a template.

2. From the Document window menu bar, select File > Export > Export Editable Regions as XML. The Export Editable Regions as XML dialog box will appear.

3. You may use one of two formats for the exported XML tags:

   ◆ The Dreamweaver format (**Figure 18.55**):

   <item name="RegionName"></item>

   ◆ The editable region = tag name format (**Figure 18.56**):

   <RegionName></RegionName>

   continued on next page

EXPORTING AS XML

Select the radio button for the format you wish to use, then click on OK. Another Export Editable Regions as XML dialog box will appear, this one looking like a Save As dialog box (**Figure 18.57**).

4. Select the directory in which to save the XML file, and type a name for the file in the File name text box.

5. Click on Save.

You now have an XML file containing the contents of your page, including both XML and HTML tags (**Figure 18.58**). You may edit this file in Dreamweaver's Code inspector, or in another text editor.

Importing XML

You may also take an XML file you've previously created and import it to use with a Dreamweaver template. The XML or item tags will become the names of editable regions. You may then add other elements such as page properties, tables, and so on to the file.

To import XML into a template:

1. From the Document window menu bar, select File > Import > Import XML Into Template. The Import XML dialog box will appear (**Figure 18.59**).

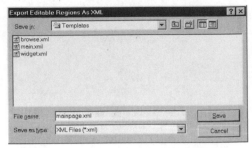

Figure 18.57 Type a filename for your new XML file in the second Export Editable Regions as XML dialog box.

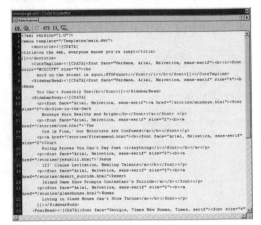

Figure 18.58 Here's the source of the XML file I just created, using the names of the editable regions as the names of the XML tags.

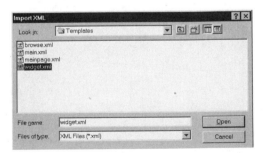

Figure 18.59 The Import XML dialog box. XML files must end in .xml.

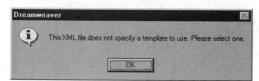

Figure 18.60 If the XML file does not include a line of code specifying the template, you'll be prompted to choose one. The code looks like this: <TmpName template="Templates/TmpNamc.dwt">

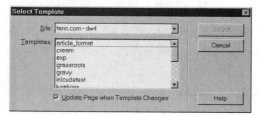

Figure 18.61 In the Select Template dialog box, choose the template into which to import the XML.

Figure 18.62 The Document window, displaying the "blank" page created by merging an XML file with a Dreamweaver template.

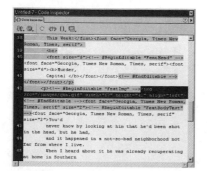

Figure 18.63 If you export a template as XML, then modify it and import it back into a template, the result will look much as it did before you exported it in the first place. I couldn't get any other sort of XML import to work.

2. Select an XML file to use, and click Open. If the XML file does not specify a base Dreamweaver template, a warning dialog box will appear (**Figure 18.60**).

3. Click on OK. The Select Template dialog box will appear (**Figure 18.61**).

4. Select a template into which you wish to import the XML tags, and click on Select.

5. A new, blank HTML window will appear. Dreamweaver will merge the XML file with the template regions, and you can view the result in the Document window (**Figure 18.62**) and the Code inspector (**Figure 18.63**).

✔ Attention!

■ This method of importing works best if you first create a Dreamweaver template and export it as XML, using your desired XML tags as the names of editable regions.

What Good Is It?

If you look at it from just a Dreamweaver standpoint, it might seem kind of silly to go through these steps:

1. Create a page based on a Dreamweaver template.

2. Update the editable regions with actual content.

3. Export the content and the region names as XML.

4. Import the content and the region names, merge them with the structure of a Dreamweaver template, and create the same page you started with in step 1.

The more innovative use, of course, is to set database exports to create XML files that use those region names.

That way, you can do one of two things: First, you can use Dreamweaver to create templates for pages that will be served dynamically based on search results, customer profiles, cookies, and the like.

Second, you can use XML database exports for static pages when building a large site. For example, suppose you're building an enormous catalog. You can create a page like the one in **Figure 18.62** that has slots for item names and images rather than headlines and stories. Then you can create XML files for the feature pages from your database, and use Dreamweaver to import the XML onto the static pages.

To be sure the import-export process works properly, make sure the files use Dreamweaver's flavor of XML, especially including the name of the template to base the pages on.

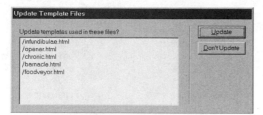

Figure 18.64 Whenever you save changes to a library item or template, Dreamweaver will ask you if you want to update the pages that link to that item.

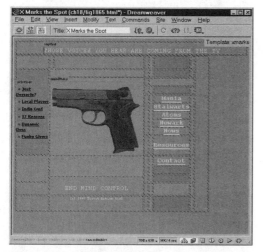

Figure 18.65 I redesigned the template you saw earlier in this chapter, and then updated all the pages that use that template as a format. Works for library items, too.

Figure 18.66 When you update a site that uses Libraries, this dialog box appears if you've deleted a library item referenced on an updated page.

Updating Your Site

After you edit a library item or a Dreamweaver template, you can update single pages, selected pages, or entire sites that use that item. You'll still have to upload the updated pages to your live Web site so they'll reflect your changes.

Updating when you edit

After you save changes to a template or library item, a dialog box will ask you if you want to update your site (**Figure 18.64**). This dialog box lists pages that link to the template or library item you just edited. You can click on Update, or you can postpone your edits.

Updating after you edit

You can update a single page at any time.

To update a single page:

1. Open the page you want to update in the Document window.

2. From the Document window menu bar, select Modify > Library > Update Current Page *or* Modify > Templates > Update Current Page.

3. If everything's all in order, no dialog box will appear, but the current page will be updated to reflect the newest version of the library or template (**Figure 18.65**).

✔ Tips

- If the page links to any library items that no longer exist, a dialog box will appear to tell you (**Figure 18.66**). Click on OK.

- If you want to add a previously deleted item to the library, you can re-create it. See the earlier section on re-creating library items. You don't need to re-create a library item unless you need it to be updatable.

Updating sets of pages

You can use the Update dialog box to update both library items and templates. You can update pages that use a particular library item or template, or you can update an entire site.

To update more than one page:

1. You don't need to have any particular page open to update your site. From the Document window menu bar, select Modify > Library > Update Pages *or* Modify > Templates > Update Pages. Either way, the Update Pages dialog box will appear (**Figure 18.67**).

2. The Update Pages window lets you update all library items and templates in a local site, or only those pages that reference a specific library item or template.

3. If you're going to search for a specific item, check the box for either library items or for templates (**Figure 18.68**). To update each of these in your site, check both boxes.

   To update an entire local site, select Local Site from the Look In drop-down menu. A menu of your local sites will appear; select the site you want to update (**Figure 18.69**).

   or

   To single out one library item or template and update pages that use it, select Files That Use from the Look In drop-down menu. A menu of your library items and/or templates will appear (**Figure 18.70**).

4. Click on Start. Dreamweaver will scan the cache, or site index, for the selected site for references to library items and/or templates.

5. When the update process is complete, a log file will appear, detailing how many files were scanned, which files were updated, and which files, if any, are missing from the Library or Templates folder (**Figure 18.71**).

6. When you're finished perusing this information, you can close the dialog box.

Figure 18.67 The Update Pages dialog box. You don't need to have any pages open to update your site.

Figure 18.68 Select either library items, templates, or both.

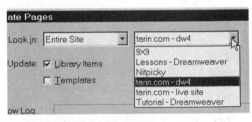

Figure 18.69 When you're updating an entire site, you can select your site from the drop-down menu.

Figure 18.70 If you want to update everything that's linked to a particular template or library item, choose Files That Use from the menu, and then select the item. In this case, I've checked off both library items and templates, and I can read through a big alphabetical list of all of them.

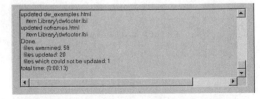

Figure 18.71 When you've finished updating the site or the selection of pages, a log file will appear telling you about pages updated, pages that couldn't be updated because they referred to deleted templates, and total pages reviewed.

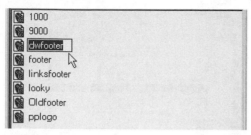

Figure 18.72 Click and hold on the name of a template or library item in the Assets panel, and when the little box appears around the name, type over it.

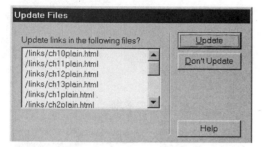

Figure 18.73 Dreamweaver can update all pages that link to a template or library item so that they link to its new name.

Renaming Templates and Library Items

Renaming templates and library items is easy, but there are a few things to keep in mind, considering that you must update your site if you rename one of these items.

You can rename a template and then update all pages in your site so that they refer to the new name. Or, you could skip the update and create a new template with the old name, and then the pages would refer to it.

When you rename a library item, Dreamweaver will ask you if you want to update files that link to it. If you don't, references to the item with its original name will not link to the newly renamed one. It will retain its HTML content, but it will no longer be updatable. You can then create a new item with the old name, or delete references to the old item.

To rename a template or library item:

1. In the Assets panel, click on either the Templates or Library button.

2. Select the name of the item so that a box appears around its name (**Figure 18.72**).

3. Type the new name and press Enter (Return). The Update Files dialog box will appear (**Figure 18.73**). Click on Update to update references to this item, or Don't Update to skip it.

4. Click OK. The template or library item will be renamed.

✔ Tip

- You can also rename a template or library item in the Site window. Right-click on the file, and from the pop-up menu that appears, select Rename. When you rename the file, the Update Files dialog box will appear. This is an excellent way to rename any file.

Using Server-Side Includes

Server-side includes (SSIs for short), much like library items, are pieces of HTML that can be reused on any number of pages. Also like library items, any time the included file is edited, the changes will be reflected in the documents that reference the include.

Unlike library items, however, there is no additional update process necessary. The files are stored and processed by the Web server, so changes are automatic as soon as you upload the edited SSI file to your site.

The Web document itself contains instructions for processing the included HTML files. These instructions, called tokens, include the location of the SSI file on the server.

What happens is, the server looks at the file, and sees that it contains an include. It then goes and gets the include and recreates the file with the include's contents on the page in the right location, and then it serves the new file to the browser. This is called *parsing* the file.

When you use Code view or the Code inspector to view the source of a page that uses a server-side include, you'll see the token (**Figure 18.74**), but not the HTML of the include itself. However, when you view the file in Dreamweaver, or if you use Dreamweaver to preview the file in a browser, the include (if it's stored locally) will be displayed inline in the page (**Figure 18.75**).

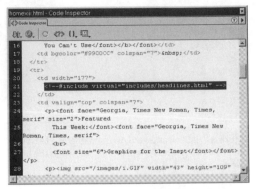

Figure 18.74 The Code inspector, displaying the code for a server-side include token. Note that the instructions are commented out so that they won't be displayed in the browser as is; also note that whatever content is in the file headlines.html is not displayed by the Code inspector.

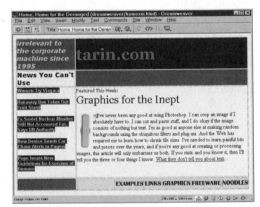

Figure 18.75 This is the Document window view of the same page seen in **Figure 18.74**. Again, the include is highlighted. As long as the included file is stored locally, Dreamweaver can process it and display it inline.

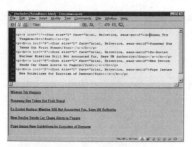

Figure 18.76 You can create or edit an include file in Dreamweaver. Here, in Split View, you can see that the only code in this file is the code that'll be displayed. There are no page-level tags here (like <html>, <head>, or <body>).

Why Won't It Go?

If you upload both the file that contains the include token and the include file itself, and the contents don't show up on the live site, then you need to contact the Web server administrator. A change to the Unix environment may need to be made before your server will process virtual or File includes. Check with your admin.

File includes must be stored in the same folder as the referencing page in order for Dreamweaver or a server to process them. I can tell you that Microsoft IIS servers prefer File includes and that Apache servers prefer Virtual includes. Otherwise, check with your sysadmin to see which format to use.

Instead of <!-include virtual, the code says <!-include file, and the file is imported into the document. When you use an include on a Web page and load the live file, you'll see the include on the page. When you View Source from the browser window on that same page, you'll see the HTML source of the included file as well as the token; it'll look like the include's code is just part of the page.

✔ Tips

- Before you get all excited about using server-side includes, make sure you *can* use them. If you use a free Web page service such as Yahoo, or a super-duper-easy template type page like those AOL offers, you may not have this option. Check your help files, or call tech support.

- Under most circumstances, a server-side include is like a library item in that it uses only enough HTML for the include, and not for an entire page (**Figure 18.76**). You may use any HTML tags except <html>, <head>, <title>, or </body>. You also want to avoid <frameset> and other associated tags, and embed frame instructions in the document rather than in the include.

- If you use Dreamweaver to create HTML files for server-side includes, be sure to delete the aforementioned tags.

- If your include file has HTML errors such as misordered or orphaned tags, these will show up as errors in the file that references the include; however, you should fix the errors in the include file instead.

- Opening a local page in your browser (File > Open) will not display the include contents. A server must process the file, include the new data, recreate the file, and send it to the browser. Since your browser can't do this on its own, the only way to view a server-side include inline in the browser window on a local page is to Preview (File > Preview > Browser Name) in the page with Dreamweaver. Dreamweaver simulates the action of the server and loads the file with the include contents.

Inserting SSIs

Inserting a server-side include is a gloriously simple process. First, however, let me review how to create the file to include.

To create a file to include:

1. Using Dreamweaver or another editor, create the file you wish to display in your document(s). Be sure to delete any *verboten* tags, as described on the previous page (**Figure 18.77**).

2. Save the file on your local site, in a location mirroring where it will be stored on the server.

To insert an SSI token:

1. Click to place the insertion point where you want the include to appear.

2. From the Document window menu bar, select Insert > Server-Side Include.

   or

   On the Objects panel's Common panel, click on the Server-Side Include button . Either way, the Select File dialog box will appear (**Figure 18.78**).

3. Select the file you wish to include.

4. In most cases, you'll want to use a document-relative path. If so, select Document from the Relative To drop-down menu.

5. Click on Select to select the file and close the Select File dialog box.

In the Document window, the contents of the include file will be displayed.

✔ Tip

■ If the include file is not stored locally, or if it does not yet exist, a Comment icon will be displayed instead of the contents of the file.

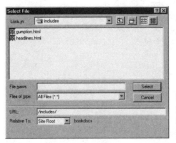

Figure 18.77
The Code inspector, displaying the contents of my include file.

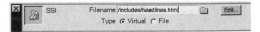

Figure 18.78
Select the file you wish to include.

Figure 18.79 Server Side Include properties.

Editing Server-Side Includes

In the Document window, select the server-side include by clicking anywhere on the text. (As with library items, select one part of an include, and you select the whole thing.)

Display the Property inspector, if necessary, by double-clicking the include. In the Property inspector (**Figure 18.79**), click on Edit. Dreamweaver will open the file in a Document window. If this does not open the file, use the File > Open command to open and edit the SSI file in the Document window. Select All File Types to be sure you can select the file. Make your changes and save the file. Any changes will be reflected on the pages that reference the file. Don't forget to upload the file to the server after you change it locally!

INSERTING SSIS

Figure 18.80 Click on the History button on the Launcher or Launcher bar to open the History panel.

Figure 18.81 The History panel, for a new document. No actions are listed because I haven't done anything on this new page.

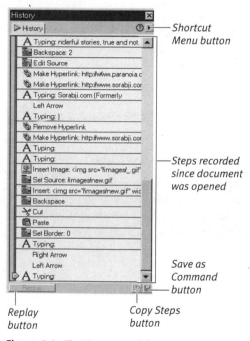

Shortcut Menu button

Steps recorded since document was opened

Save as Command button

Replay button

Copy Steps button

Figure 18.82 The History panel, for a page in progress.

Using the History Panel

Just as a Web browser keeps track of the sites you've visited, Dreamweaver keeps track of the actions you've performed and lists them in the History panel.

You can repeat or undo single or multiple actions using the History panel. You can also copy and paste actions or groups of actions. You can even save or record actions as commands to reuse later. If you've heard of macros, these are those.

To view the History panel:

◆ From the Document window menu bar, select Window > History.

or

On the Launcher or Launcher bar, click on the History button (**Figure 18.80**)

or

Press Shift+F10.

In any case, the History panel will appear (**Figure 18.81**).

When you open the History panel for a new document, it will appear blank (**Figure 18.81**). As you perform actions in Design View in Document window (not in Code view or the Code inspector), they appear listed as actions in the History panel. If you open the History panel after you've done some work, you'll see your previous actions listed (**Figure 18.82**).

What the History panel saves

What actions get stored, and for how long?

◆ Each Document window (and thus, each open document) has its own history list (**Figure 18.82**).

◆ On frames pages, each frame is a discrete document and has its own history list.

ccontinued on next page

- When you close a Document window, the history list is cleared for that page.

- When you quit Dreamweaver, all history lists are cleared.

- The Site window has no history list.

- Actions marked with a red X cannot be replayed or saved (See *What Can You Replay*, the sidebar on this page.)

Setting the Number of Stored Steps

The History panel stores all your actions up to a pre-set limit of 50 steps. As you perform more than this maximum number of steps, the oldest steps are erased. You can raise this limit, but the more steps you store, the more memory Dreamweaver requires. Therefore, if you need to free up memory, you can lower the limit.

To change the number of steps:

1. From the Document window menu bar, select Edit > Preferences. The Preferences dialog box will appear (**Figure 18.83**).

2. Click on General in the Category box at the left to display those preferences.

3. Type a new number in the Maximum Number of History Steps text box (**Figure 18.84**).

4. Click on OK to close the Preferences dialog box.

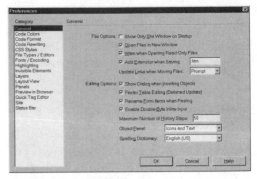

Figure 18.83 You can change the maximum number of stored steps in the General panel of the Preferences dialog box.

Figure 18.84 Type a number in the Maximum Number of History Steps text box.

What Can You Replay?

Most actions can be replayed, including inserting objects such as tables and images; resizing and adjusting other object properties; typing text; modifying text; and copying, cutting, pasting, and deleting text or objects.

Sometimes an action will show up in the History panel with a red X over its icon. That means you can't replay, copy, or save it. These actions include dragging objects such as layers in the Document window, or selecting objects with the mouse.

You can repeat a selection action if you use your keyboard's arrow keys to select an object or some text. When you repeat several steps, if you include an arrow-key selection as the last repeated step, Dreamweaver will select the adjacent object as the last action in the series.

Figure 18.85 I selected some text in the Document window.

Figure 18.86 I made the text bold, and the action Apply Bold appeared in the History panel.

Figure 18.87 I selected a second piece of text.

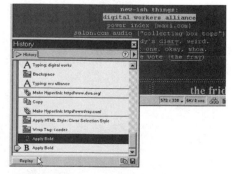

Figure 18.88 I clicked on Replay. The action was repeated on the new selection, and Apply Bold appeared listed again in the History panel.

Repeating and Undoing Actions

The History panel can repeat or undo single or multiple actions. Of course, you can undo and redo steps (singly or sequentially) in the Document window using keyboard shortcuts: Ctrl+Z (Command+Z) to Undo, Ctrl+Y (Command+Y) to Redo. These are also menu commands: Edit > Undo and Edit > Repeat. Dreamweaver saves the last 50 actions you perform, however, and gives you some leeway about when you can repeat them. The History panel is a visual representation of Dreamweaver's memory of your actions.

Let's look at an example.

Repeating Your Last Action

You can redo the last step you took in the Document window by replaying it with the History panel.

To repeat your last action:

1. In the Document window, select an object (**Figure 18.85**) and perform an action, such as making text bold (Ctrl+B or Command+B).

   The action will be listed in the History panel (**Figure 18.86**).

2. Now, select a different object on which you want to repeat the action. For example, select another piece of text (**Figure 18.87**).

3. In the History panel, click on the name of the action you want to repeat.

4. Click on Replay. In our example, the second piece of text would become bold. The action will also be listed again in the History panel (**Figure 18.88**).

Redoing Actions from the Distant Past

You can also redo any action you performed earlier, not just the last action you performed.

To redo any past action:

1. Select an object in the Document window. Or, if you want to repeat text that you typed or pasted, click where you want the text to appear.

2. Click on the action's name in the History panel (**Figure 18.89**).

3. Click Replay. The action will be repeated (**Figure 18.90**).

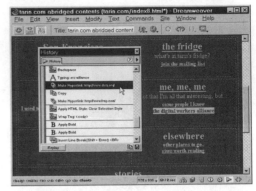

Figure 18.89 I selected some text, and then I selected the "Make Hyperlink" step (for the correct URL) way back in the History panel.

Step reappears — in History panel   Link is — applied

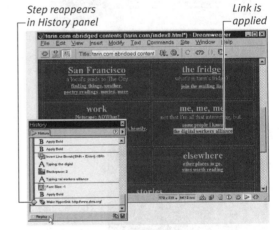

Figure 18.90 I clicked on Replay, and the link was made. The step also reappears as the last step in the History panel.

Figure 18.91
I selected three sequential steps in the History panel, and I can replay them all at once.

Figure 18.92
I selected three nonadjacent steps in the History panel by holding down the Ctrl (Command) key while I selected. I can play these back as a group, too.

—Replay Steps action

—Selected steps that were repeated

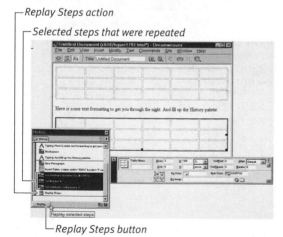

—Replay Steps button

Figure 18.93 I selected the second table and replayed the selected steps. The "Replay Steps" action appeared in the History panel.

Redoing a Series of Actions

The best part is, you can repeat an entire series of steps on the next object you select.

To redo a series of steps:

1. Select the object to which you want to apply the actions. In this example, I'm going to select a table.

2. In the History panel, select the steps you want to repeat. To select sequential steps, click and drag or Shift+click to select them (**Figure 18.91**). To select nonadjacent steps, hold down the Ctrl (Command) key while you select the steps (**Figure 18.92**). For my table, I'm going to repeat the steps Set Border: 1, Insert Table, and Set Attribute: cellpadding: 3.

3. Click Replay. The steps will be repeated on the selected object, and "Replay Steps" will appear as the last action in the History panel (**Figure 18.93**).

✔ Tip

■ To undo a set of actions like the one we just performed, you can undo the "Replay Steps" step. Just click on that step and roll back the slidebar one notch.

Undoing Actions

As I keep reminding you, when you screw up by deleting an entire chunk of important code, you can undo it by pressing Ctrl+Z (Command+Z). You can press Ctrl+Z repeatedly to undo action after action, or you can undo your last step, and your last several steps, with the History panel. Unfortunately, this is true only in Dreamweaver. I often wish that *life* had Ctrl+Z, and if you could see me on my bicycle swerving around double-parked cars, you'd hear me shouting "Control Zee! Control Zee!"

To undo your last action:

1. In the History panel, click on the slidebar on the left side.

2. Scroll up one notch, and the action you just performed will become undone, and its name will be grayed out in the History panel (**Figure 18.94**).

To undo your last several actions:

◆ In the History panel, click on the slidebar on the left side, and scroll up several notches (**Figure 18.95**). As you scroll, the actions you just performed will become undone in reverse order, and their names will be grayed out in the History panel.

✔ Tip

■ You cannot undo nonsequential steps in the History panel. They are arranged in reverse chronological order.

Figure 18.94 I scrolled back one notch in the History panel. My action was reversed, and its name is grayed out in the History panel.

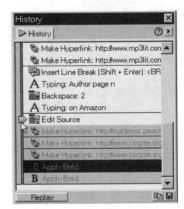

Figure 18.95 If I scroll back several notches, all those actions will be undone. To redo them, scroll back toward the bottom.

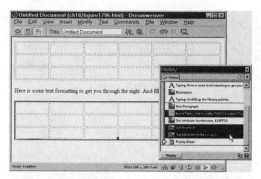

Figure 18.96 I selected three steps: inserting a table, setting the table border, and setting the cellspacing.

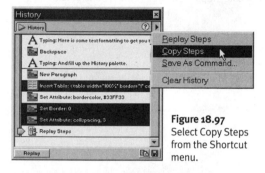

Figure 18.97 Select Copy Steps from the Shortcut menu.

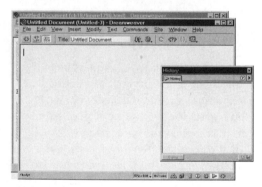

Figure 18.98 In this example, I'm opening a new, blank document in which to insert the table, but you can open an existing document or display one that's already open.

Copying and Pasting Steps

Dreamweaver keeps a separate history list for each open Document window. If you want to share steps between documents, you can copy and paste steps.

To share steps between windows:

1. Display the Document window that includes the steps you want to share, and select the steps (**Figure 18.96**).

2. In the History panel, click on the Shortcut Menu button, and select Copy Steps from the menu (**Figure 18.97**).

   or

   Click on the Copy Steps button ⬚.

3. Display the Document window (or open the document) that includes the objects you want to modify using the steps you copied.

4. Select the object you want to modify, or click to place the insertion point where you want to insert an object (**Figure 18.98**).

5. From the Document window menu bar, select Edit > Paste.

   or

   Press Ctrl+V (Command+V).

continued on next page

The steps will be replayed in the second window, and "Paste Steps" will appear in the History panel (**Figure 18.99**).

✔ Tips

- If you want to save steps permanently, see the section, *Saving Steps as Commands*.

- Do not attempt to copy and paste steps that include Copy or Paste as commands. You don't want to try to Paste a Copy, and you can't Paste a Paste that doesn't include a Copy, so just forget about it.

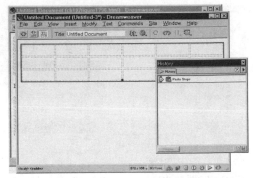

Figure 18.99 I pasted the steps. The table appeared with the other modifications, and the single step "Paste Steps" appeared in the History panel.

Pasting Steps into a File

Dreamweaver uses JavaScript as its native language for performing most actions. The steps stored in the History panel are little JavaScript widgets, not so different from the behaviors described in Chapter 16. If you copy a step or steps using the instructions on this page and then paste them into a text editor (or into the Code inspector), they will appear as JavaScript. You can save them to reuse later or to rewrite if you're learning JavaScript.

To save steps as a command to reuse later, see the next section, Saving Steps as Commands.

For more about JavaScript and editing Dreamweaver commands, see Chapter 19.

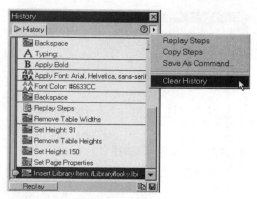

Figure 18.100 Select Clear History from the Shortcut menu.

Figure 18.101 The History panel was cleared of all its steps, but nothing was undone.

Clearing the History List

If you want to start fresh after stacking up a lot of steps in the History panel, you can clear the history list. This doesn't undo any steps, but it erases all the steps from the History panel and from Dreamweaver's memory.

To clear the history list:

◆ On the History panel, click on the Shortcut Menu button, and select Clear History from the menu (**Figure 18.100**).

The history list will be cleared (**Figure 18.101**).

✔ Tip

■ After you clear the history list, you won't be able to Undo previous steps by pressing Ctrl+Z (Command+Z), either.

Saving Steps as Commands

If you come up with some handy multi-step tricks you want to use again and again, you can save them as commands. That way, they'll be accessible—even after you quit and restart Dreamweaver—from the Commands menu. Saved commands are available as part of the Dreamweaver interface, regardless of which local site you're using.

To save steps as a command:

1. In the History panel, select the step(s) you want to save (**Figure 18.102**).

2. On the History panel, click on the Shortcut Menu button and select Save As Command (**Figure 18.103**)

   or

   Click on the Save As Command button 🖫.

   The Save As Command dialog box will appear (**Figure 18.104**).

3. Type a name for your command in the Command Name text box. Spaces and capital letters are okay.

4. Click on OK. The Command dialog box will close, and your command will be added to the Commands menu.

To play back your command, see *Replaying Commands,* later in this chapter.

Figure 18.102 Select the steps you want to save as a command. They can be adjacent or nonadjacent.

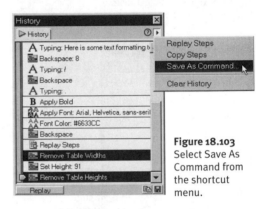

Figure 18.103 Select Save As Command from the shortcut menu.

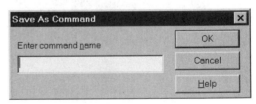

Figure 18.104 Type the name for your command in the Save As Command dialog box.

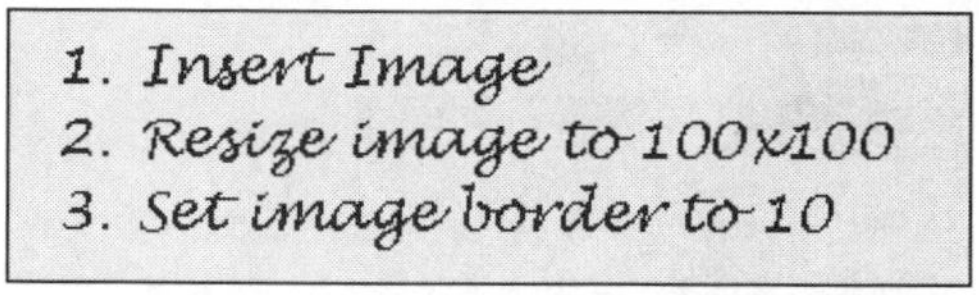

1. Insert Image
2. Resize image to 100x100
3. Set image border to 10

Figure 18.105 Figure out what you're doing before you do it.

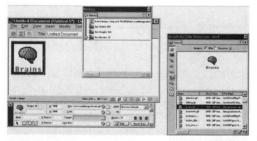

Figure 18.106 The mouse pointer, looking like a little cassette, awaits your next move.

Figure 18.107 I inserted an image, resized it using the Properties inspector, and changed the border to 10.

Figure 18.108 You can't record mouse movements. You can, however, drag the mouse to get this dialog box, and then click on Yes to stop recording.

Recording a Command

New in Dreamweaver 4, you can record a set of steps as a command as you perform them, without having to copy them from the History panel. You may have used Microsoft Word or BBEdit to record and save macros. That's exactly what you'll be doing here. A *macro* is a single, named computer command that contains many different actions. In order to perform the whole group of actions at once, you *play* the macro, just as you play back recorded music more than one note at a time.

To record a command:

1. Make a mental list (or jot it down) of the steps you want to perform (**Figure 18.105**). Sometimes once you start recording, you can forget what it is you wanted to save in your macro.

2. From the Document window menu bar, select Commands > Start Recording. The mouse pointer will turn into a little cassette tape icon (**Figure 18.106**).

3. Perform the steps you want to save (**Figure 18.107**). You can record menu commands, keyboard shortcuts, and changes made in the Property inspector or in dialog boxes. You cannot record mouse actions such as resizing a table with the mouse or dragging a layer (for either action, type values in the Property inspector instead of dragging). If you attempt to use the mouse, you'll get an error message (**Figure 18.108**).

4. From the Document window menu bar, select Commands > Stop Recording.

Your steps will appear in the Command menu as "Play Recorded Command."

Replaying Commands

If you use the Start Recording command to record your own macro, you can play it back using the Commands menu until you record another command.

To play back recorded steps now:

1. Make any selections or insertions you need to prepare to run the command.

2. From the Document window menu bar, select Commands > Play Recorded Command (**Figures 18.109–18.110**)

   or

   If you've played the steps back once already, select Run Command on the History panel.

To save recorded steps as a command:

1. On the History panel, select Run Command.

2. Follow the steps in the section *Saving Steps as Commands,* earlier in this chapter.

Playing back any command

After you record and save a command, whether by copying it from the History panel or using the Start Recording command, you can use it whenever you want

To use a recorded and saved command:

1. Select the object to modify, or click to place the insertion point where you want to insert an object or text.

2. From the Document window menu bar, select Commands > [Your Command Name] (**Figure 18.111**). The steps will be repeated.

✔ Tip

■ Commands are HTML files containing JavaScript, and Dreamweaver stores them in your Configuration folder.

Figure 18.109
Select Play Recorded Command to replay the macro you just recorded.

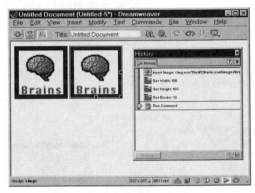

Figure 18.110 I replayed my command, and the image was reinserted with all its formatting intact. The command Run Command now appears in the Properties inspector. If I want to save it to the Commands menu, I can.

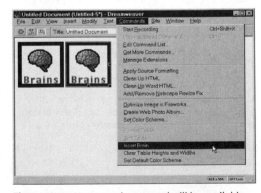

Figure 18.111 Your saved command will be available from the Commands menu—as soon as you save it.

Figure 18.112 In the Edit Commands List dialog box, you can rename or delete commands you added.

Figure 18.113 Type a new name for the command, or edit the existing name.

Renaming and Removing Commands

You can also edit the names of commands or delete commands you added.

To rename a command you created:

1. From the Document window menu bar, select Commands > Edit Command List. The Edit Command List dialog box will appear (**Figure 18.112**).

2. Click on the name of the command you want to rename so that a box appears around the name (**Figure 18.113**).

3. Edit the existing name, or type a new name for the command.

4. Click on Close to close the dialog box and save your changes.

Command Alternatives

What sorts of things make good commands? Well, the flip answer is, "Anything you do over and over again." But there's more than one way to skin a football.

Of course, it would be silly to save something like "Apply Bold" as a command, because there are already many ways to apply bold to text in the existing Dreamweaver interface.

But as we've seen in this chapter, Dreamweaver offers other automation tools you can use instead of commands. For instance, bits of text, images, and other page components that you reuse can be stored as updatable library items. And if you're setting the look of an entire page, you may want to use an updatable template.

Text formatting that you use a lot, such as Bold + Courier + Size +1, can be saved as an HTML Style, described in Chapter 10.

In Chapter 19 I discuss custom objects, which allow you to add widgets you use a lot to the Objects panel and the Insert menu. Good examples of custom objects include tables, layers, horizontal rules, form fields, logos, and so on—with all the formatting intact.

To remove a command you added:

1. From the Document window menu bar, select Commands > Edit Command List. The Edit Command List dialog box will appear.

2. Click on the name of the command you want to remove.

3. Click on Delete. A dialog box will appear asking if you're sure you want to delete it. Click on Yes.

   The command will be removed.

4. Click on Close to close the dialog box.

✔ Tip

■ To find out about editing, renaming, and rearranging menu items, including items in the Commands menu, see Chapter 19.

Commanding Ideas

Here are some starter ideas for commands I've found useful:

◆ Clear Row Heights and Clear Column Widths (for tables).

◆ Set Vspace and Set Hspace (for images or tables).

◆ Set Page Properties (for a color scheme you use frequently).

◆ Insert Library Item [Name] (for frequently used library items—you don't even have to open the Library!).

◆ Insert Copyright Mark.

◆ Adjust Cellpadding to n, Set Table Width to n, and so on (for adjusting tables to standard settings for your site).

◆ Set Bgcolor to [Teal] (for setting background colors of tables, cells, columns, and rows).

CUSTOMIZING DREAMWEAVER

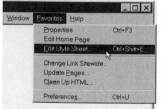

Figure 19.1 You can create a custom category in the Objects panel for storing custom objects.

Figure 19.2 I added a custom menu (called Favorites) to the Document window that includes all my most-used commands.

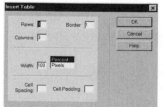

Figure 19.3 I changed the appearance of the Insert Table dialog box.

For all practical purposes, the entire Dreamweaver interface—that is, the back-end of the program itself—is written in JavaScript, HTML, and XML. That means you can customize the interface using a simple text editor.

If you know JavaScript, you can create your own dialog boxes, properties inspectors, panels, menu commands, and so on. Unfortunately, that's beyond the scope of this book, but I'll point you toward some resources if you want to learn more.

Some Dreamweaver customization is simple and easy, however. You can add objects to the Objects panel and the Insert menu (**Figure 19.1**). You can edit Dreamweaver's menus and keyboard shortcuts (**Figure 19.2**). And you can edit the appearance of many of Dreamweaver's dialog boxes (**Figure 19.3**).

You can also create *custom objects*—little widgets that let you insert chunks of code, with or without a dialog box. A line break, a comment, and a table are all objects, and you can add all sorts of HTML entities that you use over and over. You can also move, modify, or delete existing objects, and you can create your own panels in the Objects panel.

You can create custom menus, rename, move, or delete menu items, and change keyboard shortcuts by editing a single XML file. Working with existing XML isn't difficult if you're used to working with HTML, and most of it involves simple cutting and pasting.

And finally, you can edit many of the dialog boxes that Dreamweaver uses to insert and modify objects.

Other Customization Features

Other customizable features of Dreamweaver are discussed in the following chapters:

◆ Chapter 1: Stacking panels

◆ Chapter 2: Customizing the Site window

◆ Chapter 3: Using the grid, using the rulers, setting page properties, and using the color dialog boxes

◆ Chapter 4: Setting HTML formatting preferences

◆ Chapter 18: Using custom templates and library items, and adding to the Commands menu using the History panel

◆ The Web site for this book: Customizing the Launcher, customizing the Document window

Many other chapters discuss modifying various preferences in Dreamweaver.

CUSTOMIZING DREAMWEAVER

Figure 19.4 Our old friend the Objects panel. In this part of the chapter, we'll find out how to add objects to it.

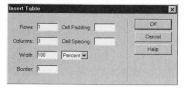

Figure 19.5 The Insert Table dialog box is called by a Dreamweaver object file. The dialog box takes user input before inserting the object.

Modifying Dreamweaver Objects

Besides creating new custom objects, you can modify existing Dreamweaver objects. This involves modifying the HTML and/or the JavaScript that controls the insertion of each object—yet another good way to pick up some JavaScript fluency. (In particular, check out the JavaScript form tools used to create dialog boxes like the one in **Figure 19.5**.)

In some instances, this is simple; for instance, you could make the <br> object always have the "clear" attribute by editing the object so that it always read <br="clear"> on insertion.

Before you start fooling around with the JavaScript, though, I recommend that you save a copy of the original object in a different folder, so you can restore it if you need to.

Custom Objects

Object files, which appear in the Objects panel and the Insert menu, are simple HTML files that contain just snippets of code (without any document formatting such as <html>, <head>, and <body> tags).

Once you create an object file, you add it to the Dreamweaver interface by adding an image to the Objects panel (**Figure 19.4**). Dreamweaver adds entries to the Insert Menu on your behalf.

Dreamweaver's pre-installed objects all use JavaScript to insert objects. Some objects, such as images and tables, use dialog boxes that you use to define the object before it's inserted (**Figure 19.5**), and these dialog boxes are also written in JavaScript. Other objects, such as horizontal rules and line breaks, include a single function, called the objectTag() function, that inserts the code onto the page.

For instance, the code for the Line Break object is as follows:

```
function objectTag() {
return "<br>";
}
```

You could also accomplish this with an HTML document that consisted of a single <br> tag.

Creating the object file

The first, and most important part of creating a custom object is creating the object file itself.

To create an object file:

1. Using Dreamweaver, another HTML editor, or a text editor, create a new, blank file.

2. Type or paste in the code for the object you want to create.

3. If the program automatically includes tags such as <html> and <body>, be sure to delete them (**Figure 19.6**).

4. Save the file as an HTML file (.htm or .html) in the Dreamweaver Objects directory:

   ◆ **Windows:**
   C:\Program Files\Macromedia\ Dreamweaver 4\Configuration\Objects\ [Object Folder Name]

   ◆ **Macintosh:**
   Hard Drive/Dreamweaver 4/Configuration/ Objects/[folder name]

You can also save the file in any of the folders within the Objects folder, including a new one (see the sidebar, facing page). The folder names correspond to the categories in the Objects panel, so if you create a new folder, you create a new display category.

Before you can use your new object, you need to add it to Dreamweaver. After you add both the file and the image to an Objects folder, you need to restart Dreamweaver. Once you do this, the object will appear in both the Objects panel and the Insert menu.

✔ Tip

- To download object files that other Dreamweaver users have made, select Insert > Get More Objects. Your Web browser will take you to an objects clearinghouse on Macromedia's site.

Figure 19.6 A normal HTML file (left) includes <html>, <head>, <title>, and <body> tags. I deleted them in order to save the code as an object file, which in this case includes only the tags for the layer.

Figure 19.7 I created a custom category (called Custom) in the Objects panel.

CUSTOM OBJECTS

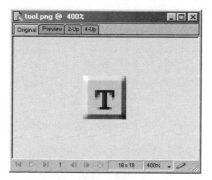

Figure 19.8 I created an 18x18-pixel image.

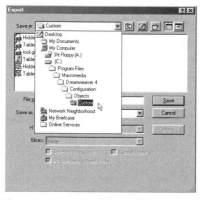

Figure 19.9 I saved the image in my Custom folder within the Objects folder. This is the same folder in which I saved the object file.

Adding the object to the Objects Panel and the menu bar

Now you need to add the object to the Insert menu and the Objects panel.

You add the new object to the Objects panel by creating a 18-pixel by 18-pixel image with the same name as the object file. For instance, if the object file is named GrayLayer.html, the GIF should be named GrayLayer.gif.

You save this image in the same Objects folder as your file. If the object file is in the Forms folder, the image goes in the Forms folder, too.

To add the new object to Dreamweaver:

1. Create an 18-pixel by 18-pixel GIF image (**Figure 19.8**).

2. Name it the same thing as the object file, and save it in the proper Objects folder (**Figure 19.9**).

   For example, if your HTML file is named OrangeTable.htm, you'd name the image OrangeTable.gif.

3. Quit and restart Dreamweaver.

CUSTOM OBJECTS

Custom Object Categories

The Objects panel contains seven categories: Characters, Common, Forms, Frames, Head, Invisibles, and Special. These categories correspond to folders within the Dreamweaver Objects folder. To create your own custom category in the Objects panel, just create a new folder within the Objects folder. **Figure 19.7** shows the Custom category of the Objects panel, which I added by creating a folder called Custom in the Objects folder to hold my custom objects.

You can rename any of these folders, and the category will be renamed. You can also move objects from folder to folder; just be sure to move both the image and the file.

You can create a new folder using Windows Explorer, the Finder in the Mac, or the Site window on either platform. The command is generally File > New Folder. To use the Site window to create an Objects folder, you have to designate the Configuration folder as a local site. See Chapter 2 if you need help.

Using your new custom object

Now that you've created the object file and its image button, you can insert the object.

To insert your object:

1. View the Objects panel (Window > Objects), and display the category that contains your new object (**Figure 19.10**).

2. Click on the image to make sure it does what you want it to.

   or

   On the Document window menu bar, open the Insert menu, and select your object from the menu (**Figure 19.11**).

✔ Tips

- You'll find a starter image, called generic.gif, in the Objects folder. This image has the size specifications for an object image, as do the images in the different panel folders (Common, Forms, and so on.).

- If you create an image larger than 18x18, Dreamweaver will scale it down to that size.

- If you don't create an image file, Dreamweaver will use generic.gif as the button image on the Objects panel (**Figure 19.10**).

- To find out more about editing menus, see the next section in this chapter, *Editing Dreamweaver Menus.*

Figure 19.10 Now the image is on the Objects panel. Dreamweaver automatically shows the file's filename as a tool tip (Windows only).

Figure 19.11 The object I added is now available from the Insert menu. Later in this chapter, we'll find out how to edit the display names and rearrange the menu.

Don't Do Images?

Not a big image person? Try creating a 18-pixel by 18-pixel GIF that consists of a color and a letter: W.

Another solution is to take an existing image from the Objects folder and invert or colorize it using an image editor: ▦.

If you're frightened by image editors, I recommend using Jasc Paint Shop Pro or Macromedia Fireworks.

Editing Dreamweaver Menus

You can edit any menu in Dreamweaver. You can rename, move, or delete items, and you can add or change a keyboard shortcut for any item. You can also add items, but that requires firm knowledge of JavaScript.

The Dreamweaver menu commands are all stored in a file called menus.xml, which is stored in the Menus folder, inside the Configuration folder. The location of this file is

- **Windows:**
  C:\Program Files\Macromedia\ Dreamweaver 4\Configuration\Menus\ menus.xml

- **Macintosh:**
  Hard Drive/Dreamweaver 4/Configuration/Menus/ menus.xml

Before you do anything to this file, make a backup copy of it. The file menus.bak is a pre-installed backup copy, as well, but one can never be too cautious when it involves editing application code.

✔ Tip

- To add items to the Commands menu using the History panel, see the sections about History in Chapter 18.

About XML

The eXtensible Markup Language, affectionately known as XML, is a markup language based on SGML, just as HTML is.

XML uses tags as containers to mark up text, just as HTML does. Most tags have an opener and a closer. For instance, in HTML, the <i> tag opens and closes like so:

```
<i>italic text</i>
```

The extensibility of XML means that developers can create new tags for specific purposes. So, in the Dreamweaver menus.xml file, you'll see tags called <MENU>, <MENUITEM>, <SEPARATOR>, and <MENUBAR>.

In HTML, if you use a tag that doesn't have a closer, you simply don't close it:

```
<img src="/images/image.gif">
```

In XML, if you use a tag that doesn't have a closer, you need to add a closing slash to the end of the tag:

```
<menuitem attributes="" />
```

Notice that there's a space before the closing slash.

✔ Tip

- Now in Dreamweaver 4, you can open XML files (as well as script files) in the Document window and edit them there. It's still a good idea, though, to edit application files in a text editor instead of trying to edit the program *with* the program.

Figure 19.12 The help files called Extending Dreamweaver cover basic concepts behind adding inspectors, palettes, objects, commands, and so on.

Extending Dreamweaver with the JavaScript API

If you have a firm grasp of JavaScript, you can do much more than rearrange menu items. You can add panels and inspectors, you can add and customize dialog boxes, and you can add translators for XML (like the one that translates server-side includes into inline HTML) or other content. You can modify the way the Site window works, the way code is written, the function of design notes, and more. Dreamweaver uses an extensible application programming interface (API) and allows modification of its Document Object Model (DOM).

Dreamweaver includes a second set of help files, called Extending Dreamweaver, which consists of instructions for people who want to add their own elements to the interface (**Figure 19.12**). This involves editing the source code, which means that commands must be written with JavaScript or C++ and then added to the interface using the JavaScript API. The location of the Extending Dreamweaver help files is:

◆ **Windows:**
   C:\Program Files\Macromedia\Dreamweaver 4\Help\Extending\ContextHelp.htm

◆ **Mac:**
   Hard Drive/Macromedia/Dreamweaver 4/Help/Extending/ContextHelp.html

If you're learning how to write JavaScript, one way to begin extending the code is by starting with elements other people have written. You can find a repository of code additions on Macromedia's Web site at:

http://www.macromedia.com/exchange/
dreamweaver/

Be sure you keep plenty of backup copies of any files you modify.

About the Menus.xml File

The menus.xml file (**Figure 19.13**) contains several sections. First is the list of keyboard shortcuts, for the Document window as well as for the shortcut menus found on some of the inspectors and panels. Second, for Windows users only, is the menu bar for the Site window (the Mac version uses the same menu bar for both). This is followed by the shortcut menus for the panels and inspectors that use them.

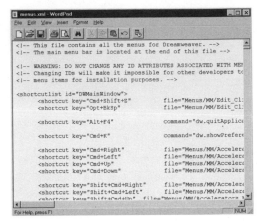

Figure 19.13 The menus.xml file is a behemoth.

✔ Attention!

- Do not use Dreamweaver to open or edit the menus.xml file. Use another text editor to open it. On Windows, you can use WordPad or HomeSite, for example. (I found that the file is too large to open with NotePad). On the Mac, you can use SimpleText or BBEdit. (BBEdit's versatile Find feature may help you out.)

- If you haven't created a backup copy yet, be sure to do a File > Save As when you open the file, so you don't accidentally delete anything vital.

- The menus.xml file ends with the menu bar for the Document window. You can scroll to the near the end of the document and look for this line of starting code:

```
<menubar name="Main Window"
id="DWMainWindow">
```

Or, you can do a Find (Edit > Find in your text editor) for this code or for part of it, such as id="DWMainWindow".

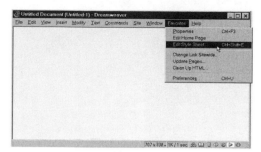

Figure 19.14 I added a menu called Favorites to the Document window menu bar.

Tags in the menus.xml file are nested, just as they are in HTML. So the outline of the code looks something like this:

```
<menubar>
  <menu name="Menu Name">
    <menuitem name="Menu Item" />
    <menuitem name="Menu Item 2" />
  </menu>
</menubar>
```

Menus that are nested within menus, such as the Table menu within the Modify menu, are similarly nested in the code:

```
<menu name="Menu Name">
  <menuitem name="Menu Item" />
  <menuitem name="Menu Item 2" />
  <menu name="Nested Menu Name">
    <menuitem name="Nested Menu Item" />
  </menu>
</menu>
```

You can add a new menu to the interface, within another menu or on a menu bar. Make sure to use both opening and closing <menu> tags; give the menu a unique name; and give the menu a unique ID. For the Favorites menu I added in **Figure 19.14**, I used the following code:

```
<menu name="_Favorites"
id="DWMenu_Favorites"> <menuitem name=""
/>
</menu>
```

Of course, in my menu, I used actual menu items.

About Menu Items

Each menu item is represented by an individual tag within the menus.xml file. The command Insert > Table is within the menu named "Insert," and it looks like this:

```
<menuitem name="_Table"
key="Command+Opt+T" file="Table.htm"
id="DWMenu_Insert_Table" />
```

Attributes for each item include name, key, file, and ID. The *name* is the name of the item, as it appears in the menu, and preceded by an underscore. *Key* is the keyboard shortcut, if any. *File* is the name of the file that contains the HTML and/or JavaScript for performing the menu command. And *ID* is the attribute that Dreamweaver uses to identify the menu item.

✔ Attention!

■ Do not change the ID attribute of any menu item, or Dreamweaver may not be able to perform the menu command.

Renaming menus and menu items

You can rename any menu or menu item. Let's look at the Text menu for examples (**Figures 19.15** and **19.16**). You might want to rename the Font menu Font Face, or the Size menu Font Size. Or you might want to rename Outdent "Unindent" instead.

Figure 19.15 The Text menu, in its original state.

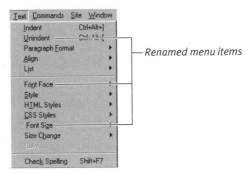

— Renamed menu items

Figure 19.16 The Text menu, after I edited some of the menu and menu item names.

Figure 19.17 I located the menu name I wanted to change.

Figure 19.18 I typed a new name for the menu.

To rename a menu or menu item:

1. Quit Dreamweaver.

2. Open your working copy (not the pristine backup) of menus.xml in your favorite non-Dreamweaver text editor.

3. Locate the menu or menu item you want to rename, and make sure it's within the correct menu bar (**Figure 19.17**).

4. Type a new name for the menu or menu item (**Figure 19.18**).

5. Don't touch the ID attribute.

6. Save your file as menus.xml in the Menus folder.

Launch Dreamweaver and look for the new name.

✔ Tip

- Many menu item names have underscore characters placed in what seem like random places. On Windows, the underscore indicates that the following character is the hot key equivalent for the menu item. For example, you will notice that the name of the close item in the File menu is "_Close". This allows you to press Alt + F to open the file menu, and then press C to close a file. The underscore has no use on the Macintosh.

ABOUT MENU ITEMS

Rearranging Menu Items

If you want, you can move a menu item from one menu to another, or you can rearrange the order of items within a single menu. For instance, you might want to move a frequently used item to the top of a menu; you could move Properties to the top of the Window menu, or Launcher to the bottom.

Or, you might want to create a new menu and move or copy your favorite menu items there (**Figures 19.19** and **19.20**).

To move a menu or menu item:

1. Quit Dreamweaver.

2. Open your working copy (not the pristine backup) of menus.xml in your favorite non-Dreamweaver text editor.

3. Locate the menu or menu item you want to move or duplicate, and select it (**Figure 19.21**). When selecting an entire menu, make sure to include both its opening and closing tags.

   ◆ To move the menu item, cut it (Ctrl+X/Command+X).

   ◆ To duplicate the menu item elsewhere, copy it (Ctrl+C/Command+C).

4. Place the insertion point where you want the selection to appear, whether it's in the same menu or a different one.

5. Paste the menu item (Ctrl+V/Command+V) into its new location (**Figure 19.22**).

6. Don't touch the ID attribute.

7. Save your file as menus.xml in the Menus folder.

8. Launch Dreamweaver and look for the new arrangement (**Figure 19.23**).

Figure 19.19 I created a custom menu called Favorites simply by adding a menu tag and copying and pasting my most-frequently used menu items into it.

Figure 19.20 This is the XML code for my custom menu in the menus.xml file.

Figure 19.21 Select the menu item you want to move.

Figure 19.22 I moved the Property inspector line above the Objects panel line in the Window menu.

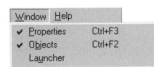

Figure 19.23 Now my Window menu on the Document window menu bar lists the Property inspector first.

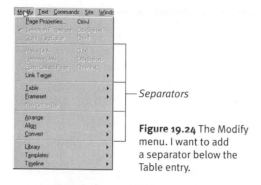

Separators

Figure 19.24 The Modify menu. I want to add a separator below the Table entry.

Figure 19.25 This is where I want the separator to go.

Figure 19.26 I added the separator tag.

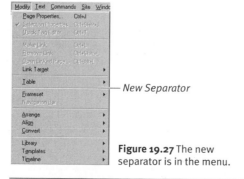

New Separator

Figure 19.27 The new separator is in the menu.

Deleting a Menu Item

You can remove a menu item entirely if you never use it. Or, for example, suppose you find yourself using the Insert > Layer command when you'd rather draw layers only with the Objects panel. You can remove the option.

To delete a menu item:

1. Follow steps 1–3, above, and cut the menu item.

2. Follow steps 7 and 8, above.

Remember that your backup copy retains the old menu item, should you want to restore it.

Adding a Separator

Separators, similar to horizontal rules, divide areas on a menu (**Figure 19.24**).

To add a separator:

1. Quit Dreamweaver.

2. Open your working copy (not the pristine backup) of menus.xml in your favorite non-Dreamweaver text editor.

3. Locate the place where you want your separator to appear (**Figure 19.25**).

4. On a new line, insert the following code (**Figure 19.26**):

   ```
   <SEPARATOR />
   ```

5. Save your file as menus.xml in the Menus folder.

6. Launch Dreamweaver and look for the separator (**Figure 19.27**).

✔ Tip

■ To remove a separator, simply remove the appropriate <SEPARATOR/> line from the menus.xml file.

Changing Keyboard Shortcuts

You can change keyboard shortcuts in Dreamweaver either by using a previously unused shortcut or by reassigning an existing shortcut to a different menu item.

✔ Tip

■ The Dreamweaver help files include a Keyboard Shortcut Matrix (**Figure 19.28**) that displays standard key combinations and the command attached, if any. The location on your computer is something like this:

- ◆ **Windows:**
  C:\Progam Files\Macromedia\ Dreamweaver 4\Help\UsingDreamweaver\ html\23AppAShortcuts26.html

- ◆ **Mac:**
  Hard Drive/Macromedia/ Dreamweaver 4/Help/ UsingDreamweaver/html/ 23AppAShortcuts26.html

You can also open the file called 23AppAShortcuts1.html, in the same folder, to browse through a list of shortcuts by category. Click the arrows to move through the pages.

Dreamweaver 4 includes a new Keyboard Shortcut editor, which not only makes editing keyboard shortcuts much easier, but allows you to have multiple sets of shortcuts.

To change a keyboard shortcut:

1. From the Document window bar, select Edit > Keyboard Shortcuts to display the Keyboard Shortcut editor (**Figure 19.29**).

2. Click on the Duplicate Set button ⊞ to duplicate the current set of shortcuts, so you can edit them. The Duplicate Set dialog box will appear (**Figure 19.30**).

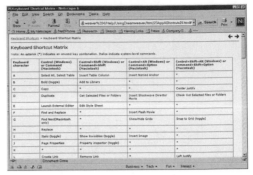

Figure 19.28 The Keyboard Shortcut Matrix lists all existing and empty keyboard shortcuts in Dreamweaver.

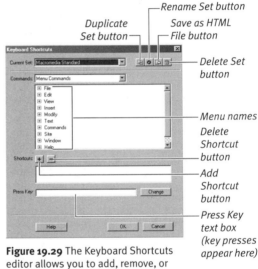

Figure 19.29 The Keyboard Shortcuts editor allows you to add, remove, or change keyboard shortcuts.

Figure 19.30 Type a name for your modified keyboard shortcuts file in the Duplicate Set dialog box.

Figure 19.31 To add a shortcut for Open Linked Page, I first expanded the Modify menu.

Figure 19.32 The first shortcut I tried (Ctrl + Shift + L) is already assigned to Remove Link. Fortunately, the editor warned me of that.

Figure 19.33 When I finally hit upon an unassigned key combination, I assigned it to the command by clicking the Change button.

Figure 19.34 If I decide to overtake a pre-existing shortcut, Dreamweaver will ask me to confirm my decision. Remember, you can keep different sets of shortcuts for different projects.

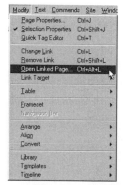

Figure 19.35 My new shortcut appears in the menu.

3. Type a name for your set in the Name of Duplicate Set text box.

4. Click on the icon next to the name of the menu that contains the command for which you want to change the shortcut. This will expand the menu (**Figure 19.31**), showing all the commands and submenu names it contains.

5. Click on the name of the menu item whose shortcut you want to change.

6. Click in the Press Key text box.

7. On the keyboard, type the key combination you want to assign to the selected menu item. If the key combination is already assigned to a menu item, a warning will appear just below the Press Key box (**Figure 19.32**).

8. Click on the Change button to assign the key command (**Figure 19.33**). If the key combination is already assigned to something, a dialog will appear asking you to confirm the shortcut's reassignment (**Figure 19.34**).

9. Click on OK. Your new shortcut should work just fine, and the new shortcut will appear in the menu (**Figure 19.35**).

Deleting a keyboard shortcut

Occasionally, you will want to remove a shortcut key combination from a command without assigning it to a new command.

To delete a keyboard shortcut:

Follow steps 1–5 of the previous task.

◆ Click on the delete shortcut button [−]. There is no warning dialog; the shortcut is simply removed (**Figure 19.36**).

◆ Click on OK to close the editor and save your changes.

Using multiple shortcuts

For actions you perform frequently, you might want to assign multiple key combinations to the same command. Fortunately, Dreamweaver's Keyboard Shortcut editor makes this easy.

To assign multiple shortcuts to a command:

Follow steps 1–5 under *Changing a Keyboard Shortcut,* above.

◆ Click on the Add Shortcut button [+].

◆ Click in the Press Key box.

◆ Type the key combination you want to add as a shortcut. The editor will display both combinations (**Figure 19.37**).

◆ Click on OK to close the editor and save your changes.

Now, both combinations will accomplish the same command.

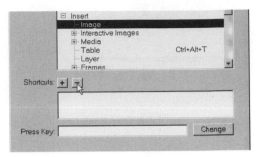

Figure 19.36 I removed the keyboard shortcut from the Insert > Image command. I can assign a new shortcut or I can leave the command without one.

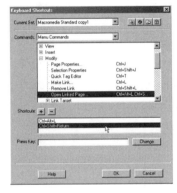

Figure 19.37 I assigned two shortcuts to the command. They both show up in the editor.

Mama's Little Baby Likes Shortcuts

Some people like clicking on buttons, some people prefer to do their selecting with menus, and others like the quick convenience of keyboard shortcuts.

Why would you want to be able to edit these shortcuts in Dreamweaver? I don't know about you, but I have a lot of standard keyboard shortcuts memorized, and not so many nonstandard ones. I remember that F10 opens the HTML inspector, but if I want to open any other palette or inspector, I'm pretty much wedded to the Window menu.

You can, however, change keyboard shortcuts so that they work for you.

For instance, the Property inspector didn't even get a keyboard shortcut in Dreamweaver 1.2, and I can't seem to remember Ctrl+F3. So I decided to make it more like P, for Properties. Ctrl+P is paste, and I don't want to change that. So I open the Keyboard Shortcuts editor, select Window > Properties, and then press Ctrl+Shift+P. It looks like Ctrl+Shift+P is Format: Paragraph. I don't use that shortcut, anyway. So I can go ahead and change it.

If you'd rather edit a text file than use a dialog box, see the section called *Modifying the Shortcut File* on the Web site for this book.

Customizing Dialog Boxes

You can customize the appearance of dialog boxes in Dreamweaver, too. These include the dialog boxes you use to insert objects and modify behaviors, as well as other commands. You can rearrange menu items, change the size of text boxes, relabel form fields, and remove unused items.

To customize a dialog box:

1. Locate the .htm or .html file for the dialog box you want to modify. It will be found in the Configuration folder, and then in either the Commands, Behaviors, or Objects folder (**Figure 19.38**).

2. Make a backup copy of the file in a different folder. I keep a Backups folder in the Configuration folder.

3. Open the file in Dreamweaver (**Figure 19.39**).

4. Use Dreamweaver's form tools to modify the file (**Figure 19.40**).

5. Save the file with its original name in its original folder. Make sure you're keeping a pristine backup, too.

6. Quit and relaunch Dreamweaver, then open the dialog box to test it (**Figure 19.41**).

✔ Tips

- To find out about modifying forms-based interfaces, see Chapter 15.

- You cannot add an item to a dialog box unless you also add the name of the object in the JavaScript API. See *Extending Dreamweaver with the JavaScript API*.

- In Chapter 15, the first thing we did when we added a form field was to name it. The names of form fields in Dreamweaver dialog boxes are linked to their functionality, so don't change them.

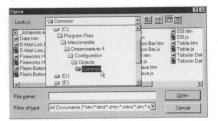

Figure 19.38 Open the file you want to modify. Its name will be similar to its menu command name.

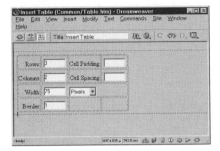

Figure 19.39 Doesn't look much like a dialog box, does it? Notice that a form border surrounds the contents of the dialog box.

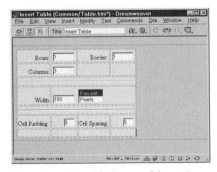

Figure 19.40 I modified some of the options in the Insert Table dialog box.

Figure 19.41 This is what the modified dialog box looks like after you quit and restart Dreamweaver.

MANAGING
YOUR WEB SITES

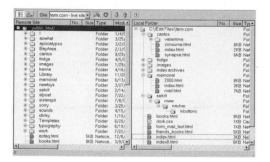

Figure 20.1 The Site window is not only a file management tool, but also a full-fledged FTP client.

File Management menu button

Figure 20.2 The new toolbar on the Document window includes a File Management menu that lets you put stuff on the Web while you're working on it and testing it.

Once you're ready to put a page—or an entire site—up on the Web for the whole world to see, you don't have to leave Dreamweaver. The Site window (**Figure 20.1**) is a full-fledged, handy-dandy FTP client—a built-in tool for *putting* files on the Web, or *uploading* them. You can also use Dreamweaver to *get* files from the Web, or *download* them.

Now in Dreamweaver 4, you can also put files up on the Web without leaving the Document window. The new toolbar includes a file management menu (**Figure 20.2**) that lets you upload saved files while you're working and download files into the Document window.

Also in this chapter, you'll find out about other site management tools, such as the site map (**Figure 20.3**) and file synchronization.

✔ Tips

- If you skipped Chapter 2, go back and use it to help you set up a local site. You can't manage a site without doing this.

- Chapter 21, *Workflow & Collaboration*, covers tools for workgroups, such as tracking changes using checkout names, design notes, and site reports that tell you who's working on which file.

Getting Ready to Put Your Site Online

In Chapter 2, you learned how to set up your site in the Site window by setting up the same folders on your local computer that will appear on the remote Web server. A *Web server*, once again, is a computer that does two things: It stores the files that make up a Web site, and it delivers files when Web browsers request them.

In this chapter, we'll take the files in that local site and put them up online. We'll also learn how to use site maps to examine your site for broken links, and how to use Dreamweaver to manage link updates.

Before you can put your site up on the Web, you need to have a Web account; you need to know the server information for that account, and you need to have a computer that can connect to the Internet. You can create a great site without even owning a modem, but before you put it online you need to get set up.

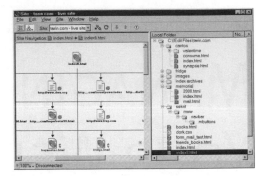

Figure 20.3 The site map lets you see the link relationships in your site at a glance.

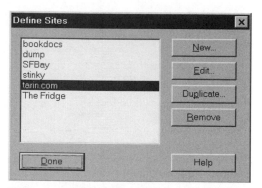

Figure 20.4 Choose which local site to set up for prime time in the Define Sites dialog box. You may have only one local site, but you need to have at least one to start. See Chapter 2.

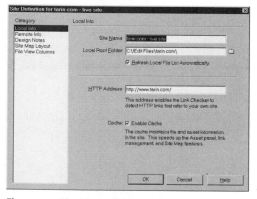

Figure 20.5 The Site Definition dialog box is where you set up and edit both local and remote site management information.

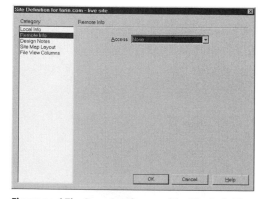

Figure 20.6 The Remote Info area of the Site Definition dialog box starts out blank.

Setting Up Remote Info

Remote site information allows you to connect to an existing Web site. You will be connecting either to an FTP site or to a local network. If you're not sure which, ask your network administrator.

If you're on a dialup account, it's likely you'll use an FTP (file transfer protocol) site. Even if you're on a local network, you may be using FTP. Check with tech support or with your Web site administrator if you're not sure.

✔ Tip

- In Dreamweaver 4 you can also work with WebDAV and VSS environments. See Chapter 21 to find out how.

Setting up remote info for FTP

If you're using a dial-up Internet account or an account on a Web-based hosting service, use this section to set up your account information. If your local network uses FTP, here you go.

To set up remote site info (FTP):

1. From the Site window menu bar or the Document window menu bar, select Site > Define Sites. The Define Sites dialog box will appear (**Figure 20.4**).

2. Select the local site you want to set up, and click on Edit. The Site Definition dialog box will appear (**Figure 20.5**).

3. In the Category box at the left, click on Remote Info. That panel of the dialog box will come to the front (**Figure 20.6**).

continued on next page

4. From the Access drop-down menu, select FTP. The dialog box will display FTP information (**Figure 20.7**).

5. In the FTP Host text box, type the alpha-numeric address for the Web server (for example, ftp.site.com or www.site.com). Do not include folders.

6. In the Host Directory text box, type the name of the initial root directory for the site (e.g., public_html or html/public/ personal).

7. In the Login text box, type the username for the ftp or www account. In the Password text box, type the password for the ftp or www account.

8. To save the username and password, place a checkmark in the Save checkbox.

9. When both the local and remote site information are filled out, click on OK to close the Site Definition dialog box. You'll return to the Site window, where you'll see your local site displayed.

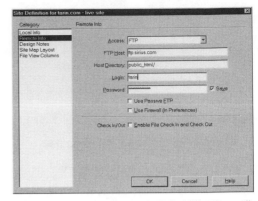

Figure 20.7 If your server access is through FTP, you'll enter all your account information here.

✔ Tip

■ If you use the same FTP host for several different sites, you can avoid having to repeat these steps again and again. In the Site Definition dialog box, you can select a site with remote information already set up, and then click on Duplicate to make a copy of it. Then, rename the site and edit the local root folder information.

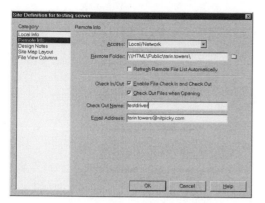

Figure 20.8 If you're using a local network via the Windows Network Neighborhood or Macintosh AppleTalk, you can choose your local machine here.

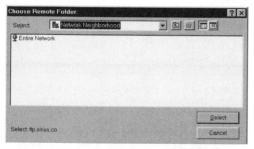

Figure 20.9 The Choose Remote Folder dialog box. It's just like selecting a folder, only it happens to be on a different computer.

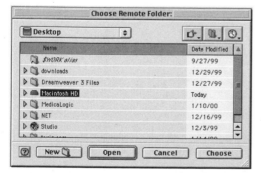

Figure 20.10 The Mac's Choose Remote Folder dialog box. By default, it starts you out on the Desktop, which is where your remote computer is after you connect with the Chooser.

Setting up for a local network

If you're on a local network at work, or a DSL (Digital Subscriber Line), or cable modem at home, you may connect to your Web server via a local network. Even if you use a local network, you may still use FTP to put files on the external or internal Web servers. If that's the case, use the previous section on FTP servers. In the case of a truly local intranet Web server, you connect using the Network Neighborhood (Windows) or AppleTalk (Macintosh) to choose a machine to put files onto.

To set up remote site info (local):

1. **Windows**: Log into your Network Neighborhood as yourself.

   Mac: Use the Chooser to connect to the local server using AppleTalk.

2. Follow steps 1–3 in the previous section.

3. From the Site Definition dialog box, with Remote Info chosen, select Local/Network from the Access drop-down menu. The dialog box will change appearance (**Figure 20.8**).

4. In the Remote Folder text box, click on the Folder icon, and the Choose Remote Folder dialog box will appear (**Figures 20.9** and **20.10**).

5. **Windows:** Choose Network Neighborhood from the Select drop-down menu, and then browse through the computers on the network as if they were regular folders. When you find the right machine and folder, click on Select.

   Mac: Select Desktop from the drop-down menu, then select the server from the ones displayed. When you find the right machine and folder, click on Choose.

6. Click on OK. You'll return to the Site window, where you'll see your local site displayed.

Connecting to Your Server

Before you can download an existing remote site or upload to it, you need to connect to it. Remember that you need to set up your remote info in the Site Definition dialog box first.

To connect to a remote site:

1. In the Site window, select the site you want to connect to from the Site drop-down menu (**Figure 20.11**).

2. Click on the Connect button . Dreamweaver will use your remote host information to connect to the Web server.

3. A Connecting to [host name] dialog box will appear while Dreamweaver contacts the Web server (**Figure 20.12**).

4. When you've successfully connected to the remote server, the Connect button will change to a Disconnect button, and the remote file list will appear (**Figure 20.13**).

After you've finished getting and putting files, you can disconnect from the remote site.

To disconnect from a remote site:

1. In the Site window, check in the status bar to make sure there aren't any files being transferred. If the window is idle, the status line should read "Connected to [site name]."

2. Click on Disconnect. The status line will read Disconnected.

✔ Tip

■ If you don't move a file for a period of 30 minutes, Dreamweaver will disconnect for you. To change this, see *Site FTP Preferences,* later in this chapter.

Figure 20.11 Choose the site you want to connect to from the Remote Site drop-down menu.

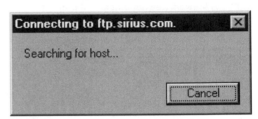

Figure 20.12 A series of dialog boxes will briefly appear while Dreamweaver connects you to the remote site.

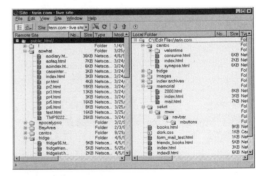

Figure 20.13 You'll know you're connected when Dreamweaver says so. The Connect button will become a Disconnect button. Oh, yeah, and the files will be displayed in the Remote Site pane of the Site window. (They do stay in view after you've disconnected, however.)

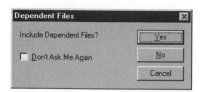

Figure 20.14 The Dependent Files dialog box can automatically get or put images or other files attached to the page.

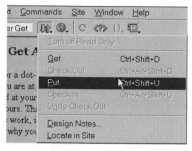

Figure 20.15 Select Get or Put to transfer the current file that's in the Document window. If you Put the file, Dreamweaver will save it for you. If you Get it, it will overwrite what's in view.

About Dependent Files

Dependent files include images, sound files, plug-ins, and other objects the page links to. Dependent files also include all the files in a frameset.

This feature can be really convenient; you can click on the frameset document and then click on Yes in the Dependent Files dialog box, and all the files and images in the frameset will be uploaded to the site.

On the other hand, if you do most of your dealing in single documents, you may find this feature annoying. Just place a checkmark in the Don't Ask Me Again checkbox and you won't see the dialog box any more.

You can show and hide dependent files in the Site Map view, which is described later in this chapter.

Getting and Putting Files

Now you're ready to download (get) stuff from and upload (put) stuff to your local and remote sites. If the files you download are in a directory on the remote site that doesn't yet exist on the local site, the directory will be created on the local site, and vice versa.

To download files from a remote site:

1. In the Site window, select the remote file(s) or folder(s) you want to download.

2. Click on the Get button ⬇. The Dependent Files dialog box will appear (**Figure 20.14**). This will include any other files needed to display the pages that you're downloading. Click on Yes or No (see the sidebar on this page).

3. The progress of the download will appear in the status bar of the Site window while the files are being retrieved.

To upload files to a remote site:

1. In the Site window, select the file(s) or folder(s) you want to upload. Or, you can upload the current saved page directly from the Document window.

2. Click on the Put button ⬆, or, if you're in the Document window, select Put from the File Management menu on the toolbar (**Figure 20.15**). The Dependent Files dialog box will appear (**Figure 20.14**). Click on Yes or No (see the sidebar on this page).

3. The progress of the upload will appear in the status bar of the Site window while the files are being sent to the remote server.

✔ Tip

- To stop the current transfer, click on the Stop Current Task button, or press Esc (Command+. (period) on the Mac).

Synchronizing Modified Files

Dreamweaver can automatically select a batch of newer files in a directory or entire site, so that you can be sure you're not overwriting the latest version of a file during a transfer.

To select newer files:

1. Select the proper local site and connect to the associated remote site.

2. From the Site window menu bar, select Edit > Select Newer Local or Edit > Select Newer Remote, depending on the pane in which you want the newest files to be highlighted. Dreamweaver will compare the dates of the local and remote files.

3. When the comparison is complete, the files that are newer than the ones on the other site will be highlighted (**Figure 20.16**). After double-checking, you can get, put, or synchronize the selected files.

The Synchronize feature selects newer files and then gets or puts them automatically, as a batch. You may want to make backups first.

To synchronize files:

1. From the Site window menu bar, select Site > Synchronize. The Synchronize Files dialog box will appear (**Figure 20.17**).

2. From the Synchronize drop-down menu, choose whether to sync the entire site or just a selection. From the Direction drop-down menu, choose whether to Get, Put, or Both.

3. Click on Preview to prepare to sync up. The Site dialog box will appear (**Figure 20.18**). Uncheck any files you don't want to include.

4. When you're ready, click on OK. The specified, newer files will upload or download, and the progress of the transfers will appear in the Site window status bar.

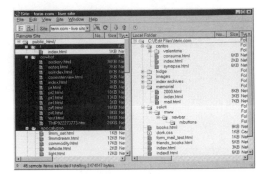

Figure 20.16 The newer files are automatically highlighted in the Site window.

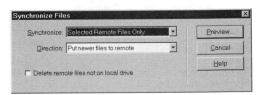

Figure 20.17 The Synchronize Files dialog box lets you select batches of newer files to get, put, or both.

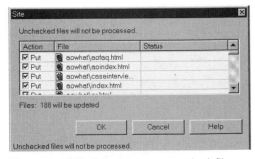

Figure 20.18 This dialog box lets you uncheck files out of a big batch to be left alone.

✔ Tip

■ I strongly discourage checking the Delete remote files not on local drive checkbox. If you get files, any ones on your local site that don't exist on the remote site will be deleted from your computer. If you put files, any ones on the remote site that are not on your local site will be deleted from the Web server. Yes, that goes both ways, even though the Synchronize Files dialog box doesn't show it.

Expander arrow

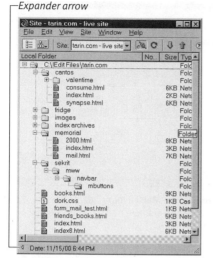

Figure 20.19 Conserve your desktop: Show only one view at a time in the Site window by clicking the Expander arrow. This is the Local view—you can choose which view always to show in Site Preferences.

More Site View Tips

◆ The fourth possible view is the Site Map, which I describe in the next section.

◆ To change which view is always showing, Local or Remote, see *Site FTP Preferences,* at the end of this chapter.

◆ Drag the lower-right corner of the Site window to change the window size. Drag the frame border between the two window panes to adjust the space given to each.

◆ To hide floating windows that may cover the Site window, press F4. Press F4 again to show only the windows that were open before.

◆ You can add columns to the Site window to view information that's associated with design notes. Both design notes and file view columns are described in Chapter 21.

Refreshing and Switching Views

If you move files around on your local site using a local file management program, or if you move them around on the remote site using a different FTP program, the Site window might not accurately reflect what's where. You can refresh the view—just like reloading a page in a browser window.

You also use the refresh command to view remote files when you're using a local network.

To refresh the Site window:

◆ On the Site window toolbar, click on the Refresh button **C**.

To refresh a particular view:

◆ From the Site window menu bar, select View > Refresh Local or View > Refresh Remote. On the Mac, the command is Site > Site Files View > Refresh Local or Refresh Remote.

Dreamweaver will check the displayed directory info against the actual directory info and display the latest file and folder paths.

Changing site views

There are three different site views you can use when working with site files: Local, Remote, or Both. The default view is Both.

To change the site view:

◆ Show the Show Always portion of the site, Local or Remote, by clicking on the Expander arrow (**Figure 20.19**). (You set which view you want always to show in the Site Preferences.)

Using the Site Map

Dreamweaver offers visual site maps for use in viewing the relationships of files, not only in the sense of what's in what directory but also regarding what links to what.

To use a visual site map, you must first select a file to be the home page file. This can be the default index page of a particular site. You may also decide to display a site map for a subsection of a site, in which case you would change the home page view to make that page the focal point of the site map.

To set the home page:

1. In the Site window, select Define Sites from the Sites drop-down menu. The Define Sites dialog box will appear.

2. Choose the site you want to edit, and click on Edit. The Site Definition dialog box will appear.

3. In the Category box at the left, click on Site Map Layout. That panel of the dialog box will come to the front (**Figure 20.20**). If your site root has a file called index.html, Dreamweaver will assume it's the home page and fill in the Home Page text box.

   If you want to change the selected home page, type the path of the file to set as the home page, or click on the Browse button to open the Choose Home Page dialog box (**Figures 20.21** and **20.22**).

4. Select the file, and click on Open to close the Choose Home Page dialog box and return to the Site Definition dialog box.

5. Click on OK to close the Site Definition dialog box and return to the Site window.

Now you can view the site map.

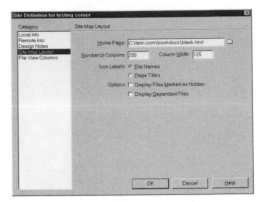

Figure 20.20 The Site Map Layout panel of the Site Definition dialog box. Go here first to set up a home page for your site map.

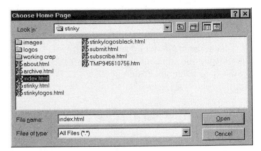

Figure 20.21 Choose your home page. This is just like an Open dialog box in Windows.

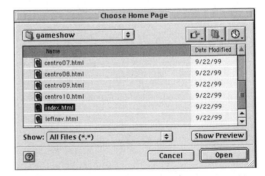

Figure 20.22 Choose your home page. This is just like an Open dialog box on the Mac.

USING THE SITE MAP

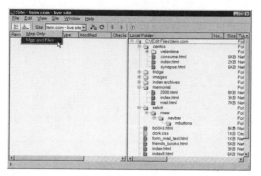

Figure 20.23 Click on the Site Map View button to view the site pane of the Site window. To view only the site map in the Site window, click and hold down the button, and from the pop-up menu that appears, select Map Only.

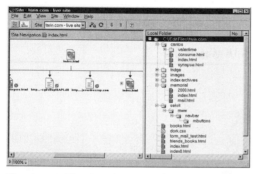

Figure 20.24 The site map. Ta-da! You can examine, visually, the relationships between pages on your site.

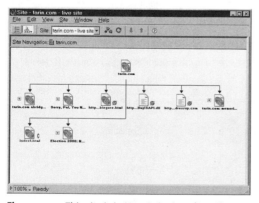

Figure 20.25 This site is in Map Only view. (See **Figure 20.23**) I adjusted the site map layout so that page titles instead of filenames are visible. I also changed the number of columns to 6 and the column width to 100.

To view the site map:

◆ On the Site window, click on the Site Map View button (**Figure 20.23**) ![icon]. The Site window will display the site map (**Figure 20.24**).

You can drag the lower-right corner of the window to enlarge it, and you can drag the border between the two frames.

To adjust the site map layout:

1. Follow steps 1–3 on the previous page to bring up the Site Map Layout panel of the Site Definition dialog box (**Figure 20.20**, previous page).

2. Set the maximum number of columns by typing a number in the Number of Columns text box.

3. Set the column width in pixels by typing a number in the Column Width text box.

4. You can use either filenames or page titles as the labels for each page icon.
   ◆ To view file names, select the File Names radio button.
   ◆ To view page titles, select the Page Titles radio button.

5. To display all files, including those that would normally be hidden (such as .LCK files and FTP logs), check the Display Files Marked as Hidden checkbox.

6. To display all dependent files, such as all files in a frame family, check the Display Dependent Files checkbox.

7. Click on OK to close the Site Definition dialog box and return to the Site window (**Figure 20.25**).

✔ Tip

■ You can toggle the last three options on and off by selecting them from the View menu on the Site window menu bar.

USING THE SITE MAP

Site Map Icons and Tips

In Site Map view, various icons are used to represent different types of pages or links. These icons are described in **Table 20.1**. Lower levels of the site use smaller versions of the same icons.

To view more levels:

◆ In the site map window, pages with more levels are marked by a + (plus) sign. Click on the plus sign to view the subsidiary links for that file (**Figure 20.26**).

To view the map from a branch:

◆ From the Site window menu bar, select View > View as Root (Macintosh: Site > Site Map View > View as Root). The map will rearrange as if the selected page were the site root (**Figure 20.28**, next page).

To temporarily hide a link:

◆ From the Site window menu bar, select View > Show/Hide Link. The link and the levels below it will disappear from view. Select this again to make the link reappear.

To save the site map as an image:

1. From the Document window menu bar, select File > Save Site Map As. The Save Site Map dialog box will appear (**Figure 20.27**, next page).

2. Type a filename for the graphic in the File Name text box.

3. From the Save as Type drop-down menu, select Bitmap (BMP), Ping (PNG), or PICT (on Mac).

✔ Tip

■ If you want to put this graphic up on a Web page, you must first use an image editor to convert it into a GIF. You can then create an image map so that it's clickable (see Appendix A on the Web site).

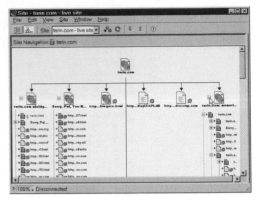

Figure 20.26 Click on the plus signs (+) to expand the links for each document in your local site. I'm using page titles here instead of file names for viewing, but full URLs that link out of my site are still printed as URLs.

Table 20.1

Site Map Icons	
ICON	**WHAT IT MEANS**
fridge.html	A page icon.
index.html	Green checkmarks indicate files you have checked out (see Chapter 21).
stinkylogos.html	Red checkmarks indicate files someone else has checked out (see Chapter 21).
about.html	Padlocks indicate locked or read-only files.
index.html	The broken icon indicates a broken link—that is, a link to a local file that there is no copy of on the local site.
http....com/index8.html	A blue globe indicates a file with a full, remote address (such as those starting with http://).
stinky.gif	An image icon.
mailto...mckinley.com	A mailto link icon.
http://www.tarin.com	A Web URL icon.
stuff.wav	A media or text file icon.

Figure 20.27 Save your site-map data as an image, a bitmap, ping or PICT graphic file.

Site Home Page   Currently Viewed Home Page (Branch)   Linking from

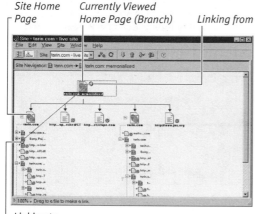

Linking to

Figure 20.28 From the link icon next to any page, draw a line to another page to make a link. Notice that I'm viewing the map from a branch here and that I'm viewing fewer columns.

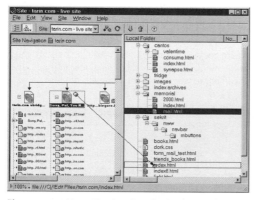

Figure 20.29 Here, I'm drawing the line to a page in the Local Sites pane.

Drawing Links in the Site Map

If you view the site map and select a page in it, the Link Tool icon appears next to the page: ⊕.

To use the Link tool:

1. Click and drag this icon to any page in the Site Map pane (**Figure 20.28**) or the Local Sites pane (**Figure 20.29**) to put a link onto the page you're drawing from, which links to the page you're pointing to.

2. You'll see a straight line while you're drawing. If you draw to a page in the Local pane, the page will appear in its new location in the site map. Additionally, a link to the page's title or the media file will appear at the bottom of the page.

To edit the new link:

1. Double-click the page you drew the arrow from. It will open in the Document window.

2. Locate the link at the bottom of the page (**Figure 20.30**). You can drag it anywhere you want, edit its text, or copy the location and link it to existing objects.

Figure 20.30 The link I drew appears in the Document window on the bottom of the page I drew the link from. The text is either the filename or page title of the page I drew the link to.

Managing Links

Dreamweaver can help you keep track of links, check them, and update them. In this section, we'll discuss how to link to files from the Site window, as well as how to check, fix, and change links over your entire site.

Linking in the Site window

You can select a file and create links to existing or new files.

To link to an existing file:

1. Select the file you want the link to appear on, in either site map view or the local pane (**Figure 20.31**).

2. From the Site window menu bar, select Site > Link to Existing File. The Select HTML File dialog box will appear.

3. Click on the file you want to link to, and click on Select to close the dialog box.

4. The link will appear at the bottom of the page (**Figure 20.32**). You can double-click the file you selected in Step 1 to edit and move the link in the Document window.

To link to a new file:

1. Select the file you want the link to appear on, in either the site map view or the local pane (**Figure 20.31**).

2. From the Site window menu bar, select Site > Link to New File. The Link to New File dialog box will appear (**Figure 20.33**).

3. Type the filename of the new file in the File Name text box, the title of the page in the Title text box, and the link text in the Link Text text box (**Figure 20.34**).

4. Click on OK. Dreamweaver will insert the link at the bottom of the page you selected in Step 1 (**Figure 20.32**), and it will create a new, blank document. Double-click either page to edit it in the Document window.

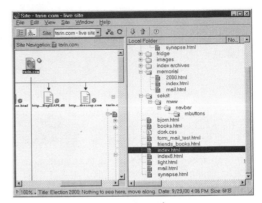

Figure 20.31 Select the file within which you want to create a new link. Notice the same file is selected in the Site Map and the Local Site panes.

Figure 20.32 The new link will appear at the bottom of the page. Here, I've added three new links. You can copy and paste this text or select and drag it to a new location. You can, of course, edit the text.

Figure 20.33 The Link to New File dialog box lets you simultaneously link to and create a new, blank document to which you can add content later.

Figure 20.34 Here's an example of how to fill out the Link to New File dialog box. The filename you use will appear in the Local Site window, where you can double-click it to edit it.

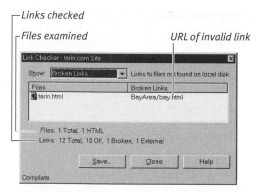

Links checked

Files examined   URL of invalid link

Figure 20.35 The Broken Links panel of the Link Checker dialog box displays relative links that do not exist on your local site.

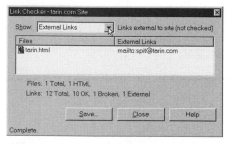

Figure 20.36 The external links summary for the same page indicates that an e-mail address is an external link and should be checked.

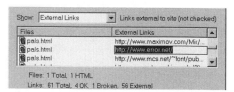

Figure 20.37 This page has a lot more external links. You can preview the page and check the links in the browser, or you can work with the URL list directly.

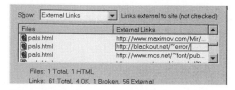

Figure 20.38 Here, I'm pasting in a new URL for a page that moved. Changes I make in this dialog box are saved even if I don't open the page in the Document window.

Checking Links

Dreamweaver can check all the relative links on a page or in a local site and see if any are broken. This does not check external links.

To check links on one page:

1. Open the page you want to check in the Document window.

2. From the Document window menu bar, select File > Check Links.

3. The Link Checker dialog box will appear (**Figure 20.35**). The Broken Links panel displays any links on your page that are not intact. This may include links to pages that exist but for which there is no copy on your local site.

To check external links:

1. Follow steps 1 and 2, above.

2. To see a list of external links on the current page, select External Links from the Show drop-down menu (**Figure 20.36**).

3. In the Link Checker, double-click on an external URL to select it (**Figure 20.37**).

4. Copy the URL (Ctrl+C or Command+C).

5. Open your browser, paste the link into the browser's location bar, and check the page.

6. You can change an external link by pasting the URL in the Link Checker (**Figure 20.38**).

To check links over a local site:

1. From the Document window menu bar, select Site > Open Site > Site name. The Site window will appear and display the contents of the selected site (**Figure 20.39**).

2. From the Site window menu bar, select Site > Check Links Sitewide. The Link Checker dialog box will appear (**Figure 20.40**) and begin scanning your local site.

3. This'll take a few seconds or so, depending on the size of your site. When it's done, the summary will display how many files were checked, how many links were checked, how many links are broken, and how many external links it found.

4. The Link Checker will also count any orphaned files; that is, files that are present in your local site, but are not linked to from any other page. To view a list of orphaned files, select Orphaned Files from the Show drop-down menu (**Figure 20.41**).

✔ Tip

- You can check links within a folder or a few files, too. Select the group of files in the Site window. Then select File > Check links from the Site window menu bar.

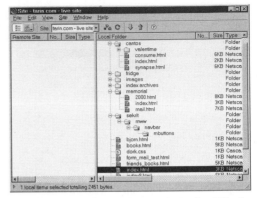

Figure 20.39 The Site window, displaying local files in the site I want to check.

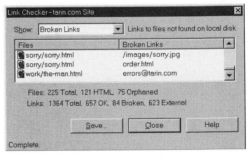

Figure 20.40 If I connect to my remote site, I'll be able to find out which of these listed pages are truly missing and which aren't copied to my local site.

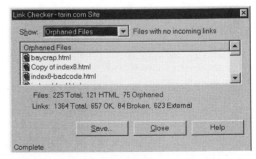

Figure 20.41 These orphaned files, mostly tests and backups, can be safely moved to a folder outside my local site, or they can be deleted.

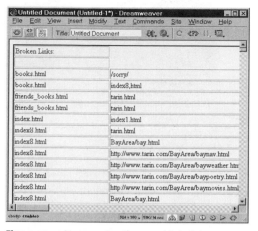

Figure 20.42 You can view the saved link data as a table. Keep in mind that these links may not be broken on the remote site; Dreamweaver is finding links that are not in the specified location on the *local* site.

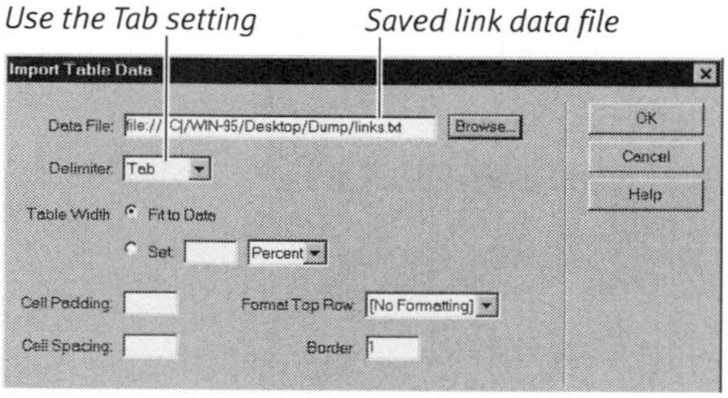

Use the Tab setting   *Saved link data file*

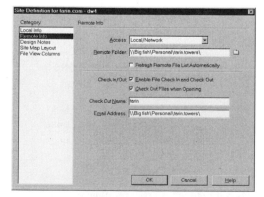

Figure 20.43 Chapter 12 explains what all this stuff means, but you can use this dialog box now to import your saved link data file onto a page as a perfectly readable table.

Figure 20.44 Chapter 21 describes how you can use file Check In and Check Out to keep track of group projects.

Saving link checker results

You can save your results so you can come back to them later. That way, you don't have to keep the dialog box open, and you can deal with the links later on wthout having to run Dreamweaver again.

You can also import the saved results as a table that you can edit, publish, or print.

To save the results as a file:

1. In the Link Checker dialog box, click on Save. The Save As dialog box will appear.

2. Select the correct folder, type a name for your file, and click Save. Use the extension .txt; the file format is tab-delimited text.

✔ Tip

■ You can insert the results onto a Web page as a table (**Figure 20.42**). From the Document window menu bar, select File > Import > Import Table Data, and in the dialog box (**Figure 20.43**), set the Delimiter to Tab, click the Browse button, and select the file you just saved. See Chapter 12 for explicit instructions on using this dialog box.

Fixing Links

You can use the Link Checker to help you fix links on a single page or over an entire site.

✔ Tip

■ If File Check In/Check Out is enabled, Dreamweaver will check out any file you need to fix. See Chapter 21 for more on checking in and checking out, including how to turn it on and off (**Figure 20.44**).

continued on next page

To open a listed page:

1. Double-click on any page in the list to open it. The link or image reference you clicked on will automatically be highlighted in the Document window (**Figure 20.45**).

2. You can fix the highlighted link in the Property inspector (**Figure 20.46**). Type the new link, or use the Browse For File button.

To fix broken links:

1. Use the Link Checker on a page, a group of pages, or a local site, as described earlier in *To check links on one page* or *To check links over a local site*.

2. In the Link Checker dialog box, click on the URL of a broken link from the list in the right-hand column. A browse button will appear (**Figure 20.47**).

3. Type the correct URL (external or relative) over the old URL.

   or

   Click on the browse button to open the Select HTML File dialog box. Choose the correct file from your local site and click on Select.

4. If the link occurs more than once, Dreamweaver will ask you if you want to fix all occurrences. Click on Yes to fix all links to that URL or click on No to change just this one link.

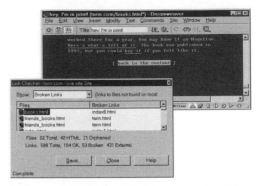

Figure 20.45 When I double-click on the broken link, the page opens in the Document window with the link conveniently highlighted.

Figure 20.46 I can fix the link in the Property inspector. This was a simple typo.

Browse button

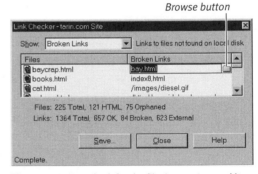

Figure 20.47 I can look for the file, in case I moved it or renamed it, using the Link Checker's Browse button.

Let the Circle Be Unbroken

When a link is fixed, it will disappear from the Link Checker's list of broken links. On the other hand, if the page doesn't exist on your local site, the Link Checker will still consider it broken.

The Link Checker checks image paths, and it also will mark an image path as broken if the image isn't on the local site.

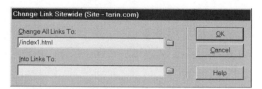

Figure 20.48 Find all links to any address, including an e-mail address or image path, and change them in a snap.

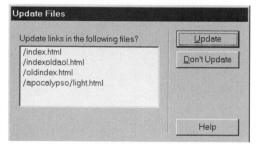

Figure 20.49 The Update Files dialog box lists everything that links to the given URL.

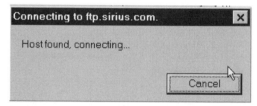

Figure 20.50 If you don't want to check out the files, click Cancel. Your changes will be saved locally, but nothing will happen yet on the remote site.

Changing a Link Sitewide

If you know that the location of a file to which you link often has changed, you can edit all occurrences of that link easily.

To change a link sitewide:

1. From the Site window menu bar, select Site > Change Link Sitewide. The Change Link Sitewide dialog box will appear (**Figure 20.48**).

2. Type the old URL in the Change All Links To text box, or click the browse icon to choose the file.

3. Type the new URL in the Into Links To text box, or click the browse icon to choose the file.

4. Click on OK to start scanning for links to that file.

5. If any links are found, the Update Files dialog box will appear and list them (**Figure 20.49**).

6. To proceed with the changes, click Update.

7. If File Check In/Check Out is enabled, Dreamweaver will attempt to check out the files. See Chapter 21 for details. You can Cancel the FTP dialog box (**Figure 20.50**) and the files will still be updated locally.

✔ Tip

■ Dreamweaver can automatically check links and change them over an entire site when you move a file or rename it. You can use the Site window as a file management tool, and it'll even warn you if you're about to delete a file that other pages link to. When you rename a file in the Site window, the Update Files dialog box will appear, and you can go from there.

Sharing Assets Between Local Sites

In order for Dreamweaver to manage your files, each of your local sites should refer to a different set of folders. Otherwise, you might get this scary dialog box (**Figure 20.51**).

Of course, you may have pages, images, scripts, style sheet files, or other assets you want to use in more than one local site. You can't copy them around using the Site window; use your computer's file management instead.

To copy files from one site to another:

1. On your computer, locate the local site folder for the site containing the file that you want to copy.

   Windows: Open Windows Explorer, and locate the local site folder (**Figure 20.52**).

   Mac: Open your hard drive window, and locate the local site folder (**Figure 20.53**).

2. Select the file in the window.

   Windows: From the Windows Explorer menu bar, select Edit > Copy.

   Mac: From the Finder menu bar, select Edit > Duplicate.

3. Open the folder for the second site, or choose a temporary location to store your copied file, such as the Desktop.

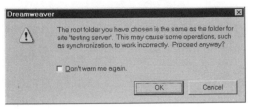

Figure 20.51 If you use overlapping folders for two different local sites, Dreamweaver won't like you very much.

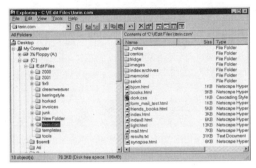

Figure 20.52 In Windows Explorer, I opened the folders for my local site.

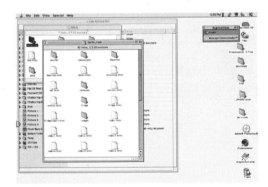

Figure 20.53 On my Mac, I clicked open each window in turn to locate the folders for my local site.

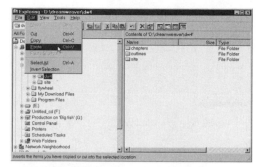

Figure 20.54 I'm pasting a file I copied from one site into a folder on another local site.

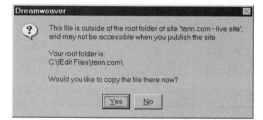

Figure 20.55 Unless you have crisis-level disk space issues, go ahead and copy the image when Dreamweaver asks you about it.

4. Paste (Ctrl+V) or drag (on a Mac) the copy of the file into its new location (**Figure 20.54**).

✔ Tips

- You can back up files the same way.

- If you attempt to insert an image or other asset onto a page, and the image isn't in your local site, a dialog box will appear asking you if you want to copy the file there (**Figure 20.55**). Unless disk space is a huge concern, go ahead and copy the file.

- Chapter 2 includes instructions on using the Assets panel to copy an asset, such as an image, Flash file, or library item from one local site to another.

SHARING ASSETS BETWEEN LOCAL SITES

Site FTP Preferences

You can change a variety of preferences for the Site window, including the appearance, timeout limit, and dependent file settings.

To change Site preferences:

1. From the Site window menu bar, select Edit > Preferences. The Preferences dialog box will appear.

2. In the Category box at left, select Site to display that panel (**Figure 20.56**).

3. By default, remote files appear on the left, and local files appear on the right in the Site window. If you'd prefer a different setup, select Local Files or Remote Files from the Always Show drop-down menu, and select Right or Left from the second drop-down menu. This setting will also affect the position of the site map in the Site window.

4. The Dependent Files dialog box (**Figure 20.57**) will appear whenever you get, put, check in, or check out a file. You can turn off the dialog by checking the Don't Ask Me Again box. To turn off the dialog, or to reinstate it, select or deselect the Dependent Files checkboxes.

5. By default, your connection terminates after 30 minutes of idling. To change this, type it in the Minutes Idle text box. To turn off automatic timeouts (for instance, if you have a direct network connection), deselect the Disconnect After checkbox.

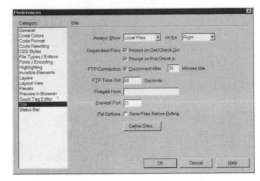

Figure 20.56 The Site FTP panel of the Preferences dialog box.

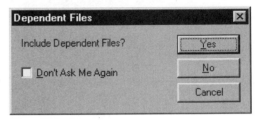

Figure 20.57 Our old pal, the Dependent Files dialog box.

6. If the server is not responding, processes such as connecting, viewing the file list, getting, and putting will expire. The default timeout period is 60 seconds (and it's a good rule of thumb). You can set a different limit by typing it in the FTP Time Out text box.

7. To save files when you upload them, check the Save Files Before Putting checkbox.

8. When you're satisfied, click on OK to save the changes to the preferences and close the Preferences dialog box. You'll return to the Site window.

Burn, Burn, Burn—A Wall of Fire

A firewall is a piece of security software that sits on the server and prevents outsiders and people without privileges from so much as viewing the stuff on all or part of a server. If your server uses a firewall, you need to set up your remote site information in Dreamweaver to get around the firewall. You set this up in the Preferences for Dreamweaver. Press Ctrl+J to view the Preferences dialog box, and click on Site to view that panel of the dialog box. Enter the hostname of the proxy server in the Host text box, and if the server uses an FTP port other than 21, enter that in the Port text box.

For any sites that use this proxy server, uncheck the Use Firewall checkbox in the Site Definition dialog box.

SITE FTP PREFERENCES

Making a Mirror Site

A mirror site is a more-or-less exact copy of an existing site that resides on a different server. Mirror sites are used for three main reasons:

◆ Testing

◆ Providing faster access to different physical locations

◆ Spreading the pain of downloads around to more than one site.

For instance, big, popular sites like TUCOWS, WebMuseum, and the Internet Movie Database have mirror sites positioned around the world so that everyone who uses the site can have speedier access.

Setting up a mirror site is easy using the Site window.

1. If you don't have a local copy of the original site, Site 1, create one. You can download an entire site by selecting everything in the remote Site window and "get"ting it into the local site folder.

2. Disconnect from the remote site.

3. Change the site information for the local site so that the Web server and username correspond to the Web server at Site 2.

4. Connect to Site 2.

5. Put the contents of the local site onto the Site 2 Web server.

Now you have three copies of the site: one local, one on Site 1, and one on Site 2.

WORKFLOW & COLLABORATION

File has associated design notes

New file view columns

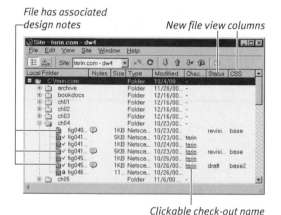

Clickable check-out name

Figure 21.1 The Site window, in local view only. I've created two new columns, Status and CSS. Also note that Design Notes now show up with a little icon, and that the checkout name is a clickable e-mail address.

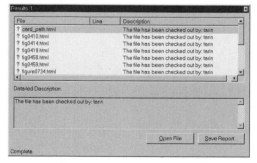

Figure 21.2 Site reports allow you to see who's checked out what file, among other things.

Macromedia introduced design notes in a nascent form in Dreamweaver 3. These are small text files that store information about a file in conjunction with that file. Instead of leaving comments about version numbers, due dates, and other tracking information in comments within the file, you can store an associated design note with the file—and it's not public information.

Now, in Dreamweaver 4, design notes have moved up in the world. Rather than just sitting there with the file, sans icons or searchability, these are great workflow tools you can use yourself or with your team to keep track of what folks are up to when they're working.

You can create custom columns in the site window that correspond to fields in design notes (**Figure 21.1**), and you can even share these columns with colleagues working on the site. You can also create site reports (**Figure 21.2**) that track specific fields in design notes. You can use reports, also new in Dreamweaver 4, to find other details such as untitled pages or redundant tags.

File check-in and check-out has also improved in Dreamweaver 4. Check-out names are now clickable e-mail links you can use to contact other users of a file on a remote site (**Figure 21.1**). You can also use site reports to search for all files checked out by a certain user (including yourself). You can manage content on small sites using these tools.

Also in this chapter, I cover how to share the HTML Styles file between sites or between users. And now you can hitch up your site tools in Dreamweaver to some popular content management systems, Visual Source Safe and WebDAV.

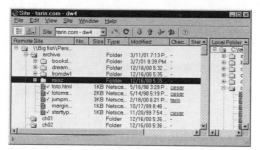

Figure 21.3 The files with checkmarks have been checked out; you can see the check-out names in the Checked Out By column.

Checking In and Checking Out

If several people are collaborating on a site, it might be helpful to know who put which file where, and when they did it. (If there are only one or two of you, you should already know the answer.)

Checking out a file locks it on the remote server and allows you to edit it locally, while a flag appears on it (a red checkmark) that says to others, "Can't Touch This." Checking in a file unlocks it on the remote server, but makes it read-only on your local site so that you don't accidentally edit a file that is not checked out.

Think of it like a library book: When you check out a book, no one else can borrow it until you return it. When you check it back in, anyone can access it but you.

Checking out a file marks the file with a green checkmark, assigns your username to that file, and locks it in the Dreamweaver Site window. Other team members who use Dreamweaver will not be able to overwrite locked files (files checked out by another person). These files can be overwritten by any other FTP client, however. This is a simpler, user-based, and less secure approximation of CVS checkout, a Unix-based tool used in production groups.

Files other people have checked out are marked in the Site window with a red checkmark and the person's check-out name appears in the Checked Out By column in both the local and remote panes (**Figure 21.3**).

Setting up file check-in

Before you can check files in or out, you must enable that option in the site's definition.

To enable check-in and check-out:

1. From the Site window menu bar, select Site > Define Sites. The Define Sites dialog box will appear (**Figure 21.4**).

2. Select the site for which you want to set check-in and check-out options, and click on Edit. The Site Definition dialog box will appear.

3. In the Category box at the left, select Remote Info. That panel will move to the front of the dialog box (**Figure 21.5**).

4. To enable check-in and check-out, click that checkbox. More options for file check-in will appear (**Figure 21.6**).

5. If you want to mark files as checked out when you open them in the Document window, check the Check Out Files When Opening checkbox.

6. Type the name you want others to see when you check out files in the Check Out Name text box. This can be your full name or your username.

7. If you want colleagues to be able to contact you about checked-out files, type your full e-mail address in the Email Address text box. (See Tips, below.)

8. Click on OK. Now, each time you get a file from the remote server, it will be marked as checked out, and each time you put a file, it will be marked as checked in.

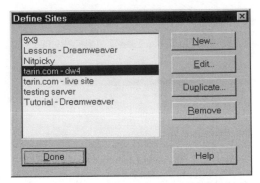

Figure 21.4 Choose which site's check-in preferences to modify in the Define Sites dialog box.

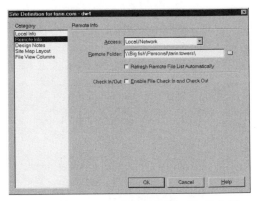

Figure 21.5 The Remote Info panel of the Site Definition dialog box, before file check-in is enabled.

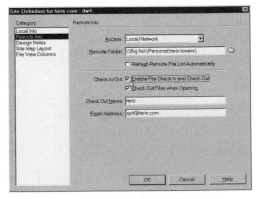

Figure 21.6 Enable file check-outs and set your check-out name in the Check In/Out panel of the Site Definition dialog box.

CHECKING IN AND CHECKING OUT

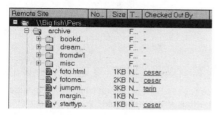

Figure 21.7 Check-out names, if they've been entered with e-mail addresses, appear as clickable links in the Site window.

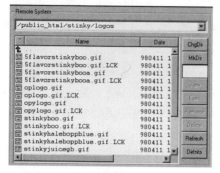

Figure 21.8 You can see the .LCK files if you examine the site with an FTP client other than Dreamweaver's.

About .LCK Files

When you check out a file using Dreamweaver, a lock is placed on the file in the Dreamweaver Site window. This lock is a text file with the .LCK extension. .LCK files are invisible in the Dreamweaver Site window, but you can see them in a different FTP client (**Figure 21.8**).

An .LCK file contains the username of the person who checked it out. This file also shows the date and time of the checkout in the time stamp.

You can see the date and time of a .LCK file in most FTP clients in the date and time column. The .LCK files I examined were only 7 bytes each (there are 1000 bytes in 1 kilobyte), so they aren't going to make you run out of server space any time soon.

✔ Tips

■ If you access your files from a different computer and cannot perform an upload because the files are checked out, you can still upload or download them by using a different FTP client, such as Telnet/CVS, WS_FTP, Fetch, or Cute FTP.

■ Even if you work alone, you might want to use these features. For instance, if you work on two different machines, you can use check-out names such as PC and Mac, or Home and Work, so you'll know where the latest version is hiding.

■ If you're using the Check In/Out feature to prevent others on your team from overwriting each other's work, make sure they are using Dreamweaver to manage their FTP sessions. If they work with another FTP program, however, they will see Dreamweaver's .LCK file listed after the checked-out file. If you let them know what this means, they can open the .LCK file, see your name, and contact you to find out whether they can use it.

■ If you use a valid e-mail address in the Site Definition dialog box, your name will appear as a link in the Checked Out By column in the Site window (**Figure 21.7**). Just like with a mailto: link in the browser window, other users will be able to click the link and pop open an e-mail message window. Your email address will be supplied, and the name of the file will appear in the subject line.

Checking Out Files

When file check-in is enabled, you'll see two new buttons on the Site window (**Figure 21.9**), one for checking in and one for checking out. You can use these just as you do the Get and Put buttons described in Chapter 20—although if you use the same old buttons, files will still be checked in and out with your name.

To check-out one remote file:

1. Connect to the appropriate site in the Site window.

2. Select the file in the Remote Site panel (**Figure 21.10**).

3. Click on the Check Out button ⬇️.

4. Respond to the Dependent Files dialog box (see Chapter 20 for details on this).

The file (and its folder, if necessary) will be copied to the local site (**Figure 21.11**), but it won't open.

You may have to refresh the Local site view to see the file (or its folder, if that was freshly created, too).

✔ Tip

■ You can double-click on a remote file in the Site window to open the file at the same time that you check it out.

Check Out Files button   Check In button

Figure 21.9 The toolbar on the Site window will include two new buttons after you enable file check-out.

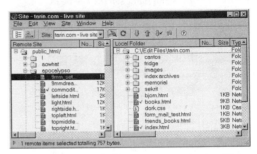

Figure 21.10 Select the file you want to check out in the Remote Site pane.

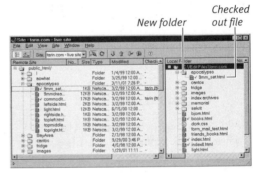

New folder   Checked out file

Figure 21.11 The file and its folder were both copied to the local site, and the file appears checked out in the remote site pane.

CHECKING OUT FILES

Red checkmarks   Files selected for check-out

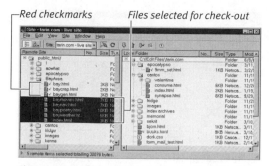

Figure 21.12 This time, I'm selecting multiple files. The other files in this folder have been checked out by someone else—if this were color, you'd see that the checkmarks are red.

Checked out files   Refresh button   New folder

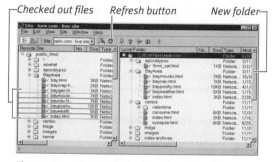

Figure 21.13 After I refreshed my site view, the new folder and the files I checked out appeared in the local site pane.

To check out more than one file:

1. Select the files or folders you want to check out in the remote site (**Figure 21.12**).

2. From the Document window menu bar, select File > Check Out (Site > Site Files View > Check Out on the Mac), or click on the Check Out button.

3. Respond to the Dependent Files dialog box.

The files will be transferred to the local site (**Figure 21.13**). The files will get a green checkmark and a .LCK file on the remote server. Your check-out name will appear in the Checked Out By column.

To undo a file check-out:

◆ After checking out the files, select File > Undo Check Out (Site > Site Files View > Undo Check Out) from the Site window menu bar.

Checking In Files

After you've finished working on a file, you can check it back in. That means two things: you're uploading the current version back up to the live site (or the staging server), and you're freeing up the file so others can work on it.

To check in files:

1. In the local site, click to select the files or folders you want to check-in (**Figure 21.14**)

2. From the Document window menu bar, select File > Check In (Site > Site Files View > Check In on the Mac). Or, click on the Check In button 🗂.

3. Respond to the Dependent Files dialog, as well as the Overwrite dialog box in **Figure 21.15** or **21.16**, if one appears.

The file will appear with a locked icon on the local site. The Checked Out status will be removed from the remote server and your name will disappear from the Checked Out By column (**Figure 21.17**).

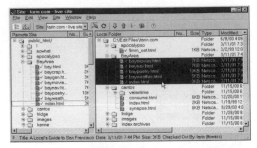

Figure 21.14 I updated the files that I checked out earlier, and now I'm going to check them back in.

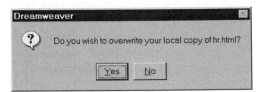

Figure 21.15 You may get a dialog box like this if you try to overwrite a newer, single file, either when checking in or checking out.

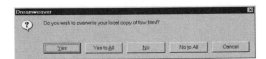

Figure 21.16 You may get a dialog box like this if you try to overwrite a batch of files.

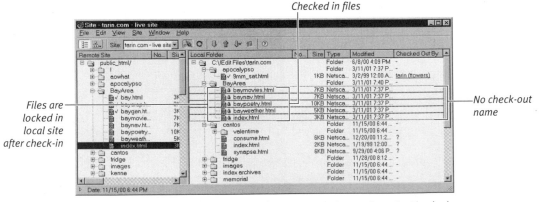

Checked in files

Files are locked in local site after check-in

No check-out name

Figure 21.17 I checked the files back in, and now my name is gone from the Checked Out By Column. When files have been checked into the site, they appear locked in the Local pane of the Site window. That's because you're supposed to check out a file before you edit it locally.

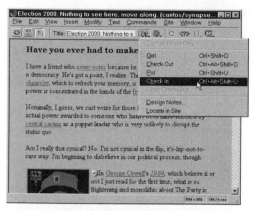

Figure 21.18 You can check in a file while you're working on it, but then it'll lock. You can always select Turn Off Read Only from the same menu to keep working on it.

✔ Tips

■ When you check a file back in, it gets locked on your local machine. That's because Dreamweaver safeguards the file so that you can't work on it unless you check it out first. If you need to work on a file you've checked in, and it hasn't changed, and you don't want to bother checking it out again, just unlock it. From the Document window menu bar, select File > Turn Off Read Only (Macintosh: Sites > Site Files View > Turn Off Read only). You can also select Turn Off Read Only from the File Management menu on either window's toolbar.

■ You can also check files in and out while you're working on them, if need be. On the Document window's toolbar, select Check In or Check Out from the File Management menu (**Figure 21.18**). Files that you check out will *overwrite* your work in the Document window. Files that you check in will be saved automatically before they're put up on the remote site.

CHECKING IN FILES

Setting Up Design Notes

Design notes (**Figure 21.19**) allow you to save workflow information about a file in an attached file—they're individual documents. That means you can save non-public information along with a file, rather than saving it as a comment *inside* a file. Using design notes, you can flag files that need attention, keep track of who's worked on a file, and store notes regarding just about anything.

In order to use design notes, you need to enable the use of them with your local site.

To enable design notes:

1. From the Site window menu bar, select Sites > Define Sites. The Define Sites dialog box will appear (**Figure 21.20**).

2. Click on the name of the site for which you want to enable design notes.

3. Click on Edit. The Site Definition dialog box will appear.

4. In the Category box at the left, click on Design Notes. That panel of the dialog box will appear (**Figure 21.21**).

5. If the Maintain Design Notes checkbox is checked, leave it alone. If it's unchecked, check the box to enable design notes.

6. If everyone in your workgroup is using Dreamweaver to produce a site, you may want to upload design notes along with their files. To enable automatic uploading of design notes, check the Upload Design Notes for Sharing checkbox.

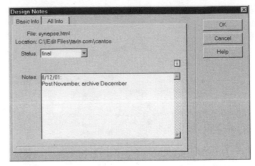

Figure 21.19 Design notes let you leave love notes for your Web design team. These files are managed each in their own dialog box, where you can enter status, dates, comments, and other data about a file.

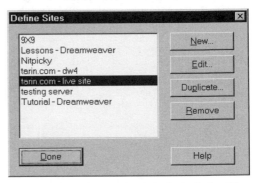

Figure 21.20 Choose your local site in the Define Sites dialog box. If you haven't set up a local site yet, turn to Chapter 2 for instructions on how to do so.

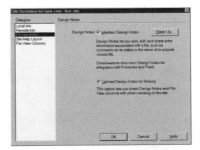

Figure 21.21 Enable design notes by checking the first box in the Design Notes. If you want to share design notes and File View Columns, select the Upload Design Notes for Sharing checkbox.

✔ Tips

- If you're working alone on a project or if your group isn't using Dreamweaver as a team, you should make sure to uncheck the Upload Design Notes for Sharing checkbox, or the server will be cluttered with files useless to everyone but you.

- On the other hand, if you want to keep notes on more than one machine, by all means, share them with yourself.

- To disable design notes, follow the steps above and then uncheck the Maintain Design Notes checkbox. See *Turning Off Design Notes,* later in this chapter, for details on what this does.

Using Design Notes

A design note is basically a hidden text file that stores information about another file. You can use design notes not only with Web pages, but also with images, multimedia files, CSS or HTML style sheets, library items, templates, and any other file in your local site.

Figure 21.22
Access design notes for the current page by selecting Design Notes from the File Management menu on the toolbar.

To create a design note:

1. Select the file you want to notate in the Site window, or open it in the Document window. Then, select File > Design Notes from the Site window menu bar or the Document window menu bar.

   You can also select Design Notes from the File Management menu on the toolbar (**Figure 21.22**).

   Either way, the Design Notes dialog box will appear (**Figure 21.23**), displaying the name of the file and its site path/location.

2. The Status drop-down menu allows you to flag a file with the following labels: draft; revision 1, 2, or 3; alpha, beta, or final; or needs attention (**Figure 21.24**). You may select any or none of these.

3. To stamp the current date in the design note, click on the Date button above the vertical scrollbar in the Notes text box. The date will appear in the Notes text box.

4. Type additional notes in the Notes text box.

5. To have Dreamweaver pop open the design notes whenever the file is opened, check the Show When File Is Opened box.

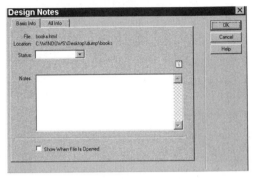

Figure 21.23 Leave notes for yourself or your coworkers in the Design Notes dialog box.

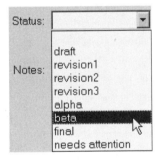

Figure 21.24 Select an option from the status menu. To add a status value that doesn't appear on this menu, see Step 7 and use Status as the Name.

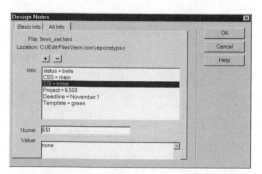

Figure 21.25 Add formatted notes (name=value) in the All Info tab of the Design Notes dialog box. These are some examples of names and values you might find useful.

Extending Design Notes

As I said at the beginning of this chapter, design notes have improved greatly since their initial implementation in Dreamweaver 3.

Although you can't use Find and Replace with design notes or export only those files that use them, you can run a site report that lists design note properties. Site reports are covered later in this chapter.

Fireworks, Macromedia's image editing program, also uses design notes. The source files in Fireworks are PNG files; when you export a PNG as a GIF, for example, Fireworks creates a design note lists that the name and location of the original PNG file.

If you're a developer, you can use XML and JavaScript to extend Dreamweaver to include a Design Notes inspector or to use a status flag in a design note to change tags within a file. You can also write extensions to site reports that search on specific HTML tags as well as on design notes. If you're not a developer, check the Macromedia Exchange (Help >Macromedia Exchange) to see if other users have implemented design note extensions.

6. To add specific notes to be used consistently from file to file, click on the All Info tab to make that panel of the dialog box visible (**Figure 21.25**).

7. To add a note, click on the + button. In the Name and Value text boxes, type the information, such as "Project" and "Intranet," "Due" and "[Date]," or "Author" and "ttowers" (**Figure 21.25**).

8. When you're done, click on OK to close the dialog box and save your design notes.

✔ Tip

■ You can create file view columns to use with the custom fields you create in Step 7. See *Adding File View Columns,* later in this chapter.

Accessing Design Notes

Opening a design note for a Web page or other file is similar to creating one. You open the same Design Notes dialog box, and then you can read and edit the design notes.

To open a design note:

1. In the Site window, select the file whose design notes you want to read.

2. From the Site window menu bar, select File > Design Notes.

   or

   Double-click the Notes icon next to the filename in the Site window 💬.

   Either way, the Design Notes dialog box will appear (**Figure 21.26**).

You can also select Design Notes from the File Management menu on the toolbar in the Document window (see **Figure 21.22**).

Now you can read, update, or edit the notes.

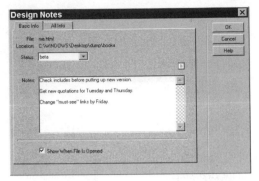

Figure 21.26 The Design Notes dialog box displays information I saved earlier about the progress of the page.

Where Are The Files?

The first time you create a design note, Dreamweaver creates a folder called _notes. Unfortunately, there isn't one central folder—Dreamweaver creates a _notes folder for each separate location of each separate file. For instance, if you create a design note for a page in the site root folder, and then another note for an image in the /images folder, Dreamweaver creates a _notes folder in each place.

What's more, the _notes folders are not visible using the Site window; to open the folder, you need to use your regular file manager (Windows Explorer or the Finder).

Inside the _notes folder, each design note is named for its file, plus an additional extension, .MNO (Macromedia Notes). So if your file is called calendar.html, the design note is called calendar.html.mno.

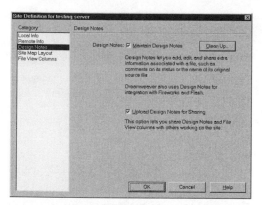

Figure 21.27 The Design Notes panel of the Site Definition dialog box.

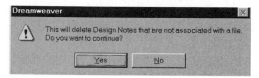

Figure 21.28 After I clicked on Clean Up, the dialog box asked me if I was really sure I wanted to clean up.

Cleaning Up Design Notes

After you delete a file, Dreamweaver does not automatically delete its associated design notes. You can clean up orphaned design notes easily.

To clean up design notes:

1. From the Site window menu bar, Sites > Define Sites. The Define Sites dialog box will appear.

2. Click on the name of the site for which you want to clean up design notes.

3. Click on Edit. The Site Definition dialog box will appear.

4. In the Category box at the left, click on Design Notes. That panel of the dialog box will appear (**Figure 21.27**).

5. Click on the Clean Up button. A dialog box will appear (**Figure 21.28**) asking you if you really want to do that. Click on Yes.

6. Dreamweaver will remove all orphaned design notes from the selected site.

Turning Off Design Notes

Before you disable design notes, keep in mind:

◆ If you disable design notes, Dreamweaver can remove notes and _notes folders from your site.

◆ When design notes are disabled, you cannot use Personal or Shared File View Columns, and you cannot use any Site Reporting features that include design note properties. I cover using both these functions in detail later in this chapter.

To disable and delete all design notes:

1. Follow steps 1–4, above.

2. Uncheck the Maintain Design Notes checkbox. If you have File View Column Sharing enabled, a dialog box will appear (**Figure 21.29**). Click on OK.

3. Click on OK to close the Site Definition dialog box and save your changes. Another dialog box will appear, asking you if you want to delete Design Notes (**Figure 21.30**). Click on Yes to delete them or No if you want to keep them around.

Figure 21.29 If you have File View Column sharing enabled, Dreamweaver will warn you that turning off design notes will turn off the columns.

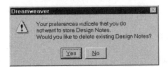

Figure 21.30 You can now choose whether or not to delete all design notes after you disable maintaining them.

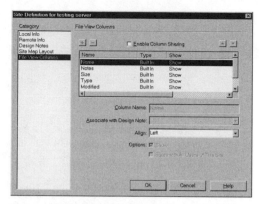

Figure 21.31 The File View Columns panel of the Site Definition dialog box allows you to rearrange and hide columns, as well as add new ones.

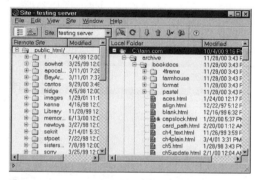

Figure 21.32 Here, I've hidden all but the Name and Modified columns.

Modifying Columns in the Site Window

New in Dreamweaver 4, you can add or remove columns, called *File View Columns*, from the Site window. You can hide columns you don't use, and you can also create columns that are associated with particular design notes attributes.

To show or hide an existing column:

1. From the Site window menu bar, select Define Sites. The Define Sites dialog box will appear.

2. Select the site for which you want to define new columns, and click on Edit. The Site Definition dialog box will appear.

3. In the Category box at left, select File View Columns. That panel of the dialog box will appear (**Figure 21.31**).

4. Six built-in columns are displayed by default. These are: Name (filename), Notes (a note icon appears for pages with design notes; only shown when design notes are enabled), Size (file size), Type (file type, such as HTML or GIF), Modified (date last changes were saved), and Checked Out By (check-out name; only shown when file check-in is enabled).

   To show or hide any of these columns (except Name) or a column you create yourself, check or uncheck the Show checkbox in the options area of the dialog box. **Figure 21.32** shows the Site window with all but the Name and Modified fields hidden.

continued on next page

5. You can also change the alignment of the text in a column. **Figure 21.33** uses default alignment settings. The Name column is set to Left, so that the beginning of the filename shows; the Notes column is set to Center, so that Notes icons are centered in that column; and the File Size column is set to Right, so that the numbers line up with the file size. You can change any of these.

To reorder columns in the Site window:

1. In the File View Columns panel of the Site Definition dialog box, select the name of the column you want to move to the right or left in the Site window.

2. To move the column, click on the Up arrow to move it to the left or the Down arrow to move it to the right (**Figure 21.34**).

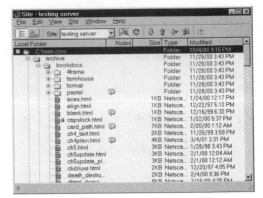

Figure 21.33 This is standard text alignment in the Sites window (local view only, in this figure). To see more or less of what's in a column, you can experiment with rearranging alignment options. Note that the Notes column has Center alignment set, but it still looks like left alignment.

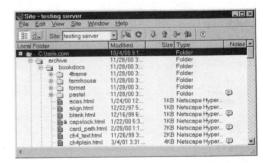

Figure 21.34 Here, I've rearranged the standard columns.

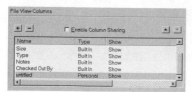

Figure 21.35
Click on the
Plus button
to create a
new column
in the Sites
window.

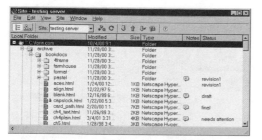

Figure 21.36 I've added a Status column, the labels in which correspond to status settings in design notes on this site.

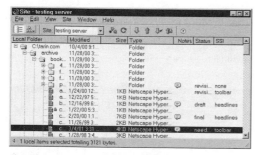

Figure 21.37 Here I've added a brand-new column called SSI, which corresponds to custom settings I added in the All Info section of design notes. SSI, in case you're wondering, refers to server-side includes, and these settings are the name of the include the file uses.

✔ Tip

- You can associate a field with the Status field on design notes. The other fields supplied, such as Due and Priority, are suggestions. You can set those to any field you create in Design notes. Other ideas for columns include author names, include or template names, style sheet version names, and weekly or daily site sections. See *Using Design Notes,* earlier in this chapter, to find out how to set these fields.

Adding File View Columns

Not only can you show or reorder existing columns, you can add your own columns to the Site window. These columns can display design note details, such as the status of a file or other custom fields that you create.

To create a new column in the Site window:

1. Design notes must be enabled in order for you to add personal or shared columns. See the preceding sections on setting up and creating design notes.

2. Follow steps 1–3 under *To show or hide an existing column* on the previous page to display Site View Column details in the Site Definition dialog box.

3. Click on the Plus button. A new Personal column called Untitled will appear (**Figure 21.35**).

4. Type the display name for the column as you want it to appear in the Site window in the Column Name text box.

5. To associate the column with a design note field, select it from the Associate With Design Note menu. Not all these fields are already in the design notes; see Tip, below. If you have not yet created the field in your design notes, you can go ahead and type it in the text box and create it later.

6. To set alignment of the text in the column, select Left, Center, or Right from the Alignment menu.

7. Click on OK to close the Site Definition dialog box and add the column to the Site window.

In **Figure 21.36**, I've added the Status column, which will now display the status I've set for files with design notes. In **Figure 21.37**, I've created a new design note category called SSIs and added a column for it.

Sharing Columns

If you've created a handy column and you want your coworkers or your other machines to be able to use it, you can share the column information.

To share column information:

1. Create a new column, as described above.

2. At the top of the File View Column panel of the Site Definition dialog box, check the Enable Column Sharing dialog box. If you have not enabled design note sharing, a dialog box will appear asking if you wish to do so (**Figure 21.38**). Click on OK.

3. In the File View Columns panel of the Site Definition dialog box, select the column you created.

4. Check the Share With All Users of This Site checkbox. The column Type will change to Shared (**Figure 21.39**).

5. Click on OK to close the Site Definition dialog box and share the column with other users.

The next time your colleagues connect to or refresh their view of the Site window for the selected site, they'll see the new column and the new data (**Figure 21.40**). They can hide this column if they don't want to use it. Keep in mind that anyone can edit or add columns—they can't rearrange the columns in your window, but they can add and rename any Shared column on this site.

Figure 21.38 If you haven't yet enabled uploading of design notes and you want to share columns, this dialog box will ask you to turn on that option.

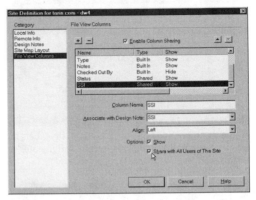

Figure 21.39 When you select the Share With All Users of This Site checkbox, the column type will turn from Personal to Shared.

Figure 21.40 Users who share access to this site will see the columns I added, Status and SSI, on both their local and remote site. They can hide the columns if they want to.

Editing Personal or Shared Columns

You can delete a column, rename one, or associate it with a different design note field at any time. If this is a shared column, the change will affect all users who share design notes on your site.

To edit a column:

1. In the File View Columns panel of the Site Definition dialog box, select the name of the column to edit. You cannot rename or delete a Built In column.

2. To delete the column, click on the Minus button.

3. To rename the column, type a new name in the Column Name text box.

4. To associate the column with a different Design Note, select a new note from the Associate With Design Note menu, or type a new name.

Site Reporting

You can have site reports created on various file attributes in your local site, a new feature in Dreamweaver 4. These include who's checked out which file, what the design notes have to say, and a few specific HTML attributes.

Running a site report

You can run a site report on any local site, a folder, a page, or on a batch of pages. Details on what reports can do are covered on the next page.

To run and use a site report:

1. From the Site window menu bar, select Site > Reports. The Site Reports dialog box will appear (**Figure 21.41**).

2. From the Report On menu, select what pages you want the report to cover:
   - ◆ To report on a page open in the Document window, select Current Page.
   - ◆ To report on a few pages select Selected Files in site, and then Shift+Click or Ctrl+Click to select files in the Site window before you run the report.
   - ◆ To report on a specific folder, select Folder. A text box and a browse button will appear; click the button to select the folder in your site.
   - ◆ To report on the entire site, select Entire Local Site. Make sure the proper local site is open in the Site window.

3. Select the items you wish Dreamweaver to report on (see *What Site Reports Can Tell You).*

4. Click on Run. The Results dialog box will appear (**Figure 21.42**). The dialog box will summarize the results, such as what line the code is on or what the design notes say.

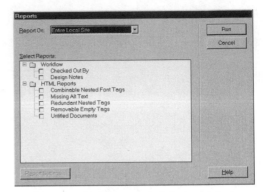

Figure 21.41 In the Site Reports dialog box, select which options you want to hear back about.

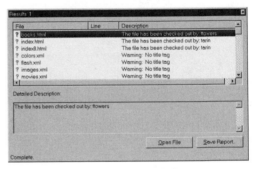

Figure 21.42 I ran a report on Untitled Documents and Checked Out By. Here are my results.

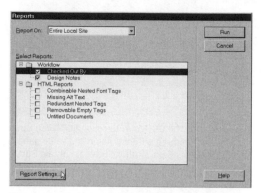

Figure 21.43 Select Checked Out By or Design Notes, and the Report Settings button will become visible.

Figure 21.44 In the Checked Out By dialog box, type the check-out name of the person you want to search for.

5. To open a file referenced in the results, select the file name and click on Open File.

6. To save the results to deal with later, click on Save Report. This will save the report as an XML file. See the sidebar later in this chapter for details about using this file.

What site reports can tell you

Site reports can provide information about the HTML in the files themselves and about design notes that you and your team have created and saved.

Workflow Reports

Workflow Data includes Checked Out By and Design Notes. Checked Out By reports, obviously, tell you which files have been checked out by which users. Design Notes reports, run without any additional details, bring back details on every page that uses design notes in your selected site or folder. Both of these categories can be refined even further.

To refine Checked Out By reports:

1. In the Reports window, select the checkbox for Checked Out By (**Figure 21.43**).

2. Click on Report Settings. The Checked Out By dialog box will appear (**Figure 21.44**).

3. In the Checked Out By text box, type the check-out name of the person whose pages you want to search on.

4. Click on OK. You'll return to the Reports window.

To refine Design Notes reports:

1. You need to know the names and values in your design notes in order to use this function. In **Figure 21.45**, the name I want to search on is SSI and the value is headlines.

2. In the Reports window, select the checkbox for Design Notes (see **Figure 21.43**).

3. Click on Report Settings. The Design Notes dialog box will appear (**Figure 21.45**).

4. Type the exact name you want to search on in the first blank text box. In my example, I'd type SSI.

5. Choose your search option from the menu. For a partial match, select "contains." For an exact match, select "is." To exclude data, select "does not contain" or "is not." In my example, I can search for such things as "SSI *is* headlines," "date *contains* 03," or "SSI *does not contain* gravy."

6. Click on OK. You'll return to the Reports window. These settings may be saved; review them next time.

✔ Tip

- Matches regex has to do with regular expressions, which are covered on the Web site for this book.

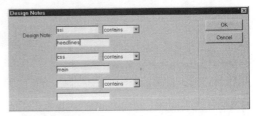

Figure 21.45 In the Design Notes dialog box, you can search on up to three different name and value pairs, such as Status is Beta, Author does not contain Bob, or Date contains 1999.

Figure 21.46 These are the available options for HTML reports.

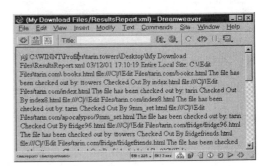

Figure 21.47 This is what the saved report looks like in the Document window.

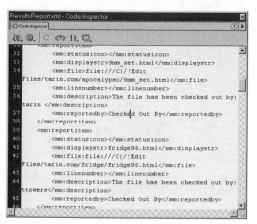

Figure 21.48 Open the file in Code View or the Code inspector to see the tag names Dreamweaver uses for coding report fields in XML.

Using Saved Reports

When you save a report using the Results window, you're saving an XML file. You can open this file in Dreamweaver, but it will look like the page in **Figure 21.47**. That might be good enough, but there are a couple other things you can do with it. If you have an intranet content management system, you can import the XML file into a database or into an existing template.

You can also create a Dreamweaver template in which to import the file. Dreamweaver templates, and importing XML into them, are covered in Chapter 18. A couple things to keep in mind:

You need to create editable regions with the same names as the XML fields, which are shown in **Figure 21.48** (code view). And you need to insert a line into the XML file that tells Dreamweaver which template to use. This line looks like this:

```
<templateItems template="/Templates/
report.dwt">
```

where `report.dwt` is the name of the template you created.

HTML Reports

HTML Reports (**Figure 21.46**) can search for specific concerns in HTML files.

◆ **Combined Nestable Font Tags** look like this:

```
<font size="+1"><font color="FFFFFF">
modified text</font></font>
```

Both Dreamweaver and other HTML programs can sometimes create redundant tags like this. You don't need both those tags, and reports can find them.

◆ **Missing Alt Text** will find every single image in your selected site or folder that does not use an alt tag to serve as a backup description of your image. Alt tags are important, although images such as spacer gifs or background images for table cells don't use these tags.

◆ **Redundant Nested Tags** look like this:
```
<b><b>bold text</b></b>
```
Often, though, the tags are further apart than this and harder to see.

◆ **Removable Empty Tags** look like this:
```
<p></p>
```
You can take them out.

◆ **Untitled Pages** include those that Dreamweaver has titled "Untitled Document" for you. It's a big help to be able to find and fix these.

Dreamweaver can find any and all of these things for you. In addition, Dreamweaver can clean up everything but the Alt tags and the untitled pages using the Commands > Clean Up HTML command. This process is covered in detail in Chapter 4, *Editing HTML*.

Sharing the Styles File

Chapter 10 covers using HTML Styles, which are named sets of font characteristics that you can reuse. You may want to copy your styles for use in different sites or by different users. The HTML Styles file is called styles.xml, and it's stored in the Library folder of each different local site.

The styles.xml file will not exist until you create at least one style other than those preset by Dreamweaver. And if you have more than one local site, remember that each site has a unique Library folder, and therefore, a unique styles.xml file. To share styles, you must copy the file into the Library of each local site.

For more about using local sites, see Chapter 2. For more about the Library, see Chapter 18.

To use the Styles file in more than one local site:

1. On your computer, locate the local site folder for the site containing the Styles file that you want to copy. This will vary based on where you set up your local site in Chapter 2.

   Windows: Open Windows Explorer, and locate the local site folder (**Figure 21.49**).

   Mac: Open your hard drive window, and locate the local site folder (**Figure 21.50**).

2. In the Local Site folder, open the Library folder and single-click on styles.xml.

   Windows: From the Windows Explorer menu bar, select Edit > Copy.

   Mac: From the Finder menu bar, select Edit > Duplicate.

3. Open the Library folder for the second site, or choose a temporary location to store your copied file, such as the Desktop.

4. Paste (Ctrl+V) or drag (on a Mac) the copy of the file into its new location (**Figure 21.51**).

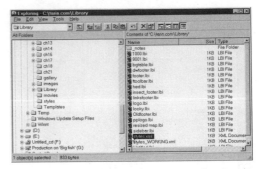

Figure 21.49 In Windows Explorer, I opened my Local Site root folder for one site, and then opened the Library folder within that folder.

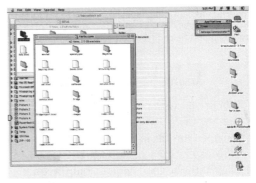

Figure 21.50 On my Mac, I clicked open each window in turn in order to get to the folder containing my Local Site and its Library folder.

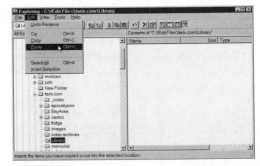

Figure 21.51 Then, I opened up the other Library folder in a different local site, and here I am pasting the styles.xml file into it.

✔ Tip

- You can make a back-up copy of the Styles file the same way.

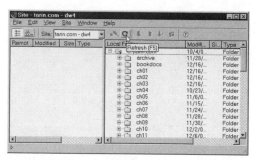

Figure 21.52 In the Site window, click on Connect or Refresh to connect to the remote site. Since I have local/network access for this site, I click on Refresh to display remote files.

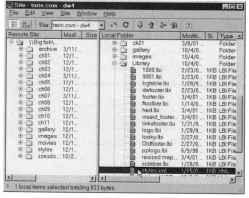

Figure 21.53 Open the Library folder and select the styles.xml file.

New folder   *New file*

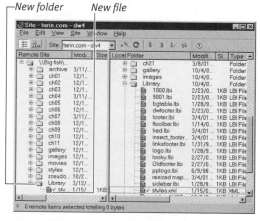

Figure 21.54 The styles.xml file was uploaded to the site, and the Library folder was created on the remote site.

Sharing styles with other users

If you want to share HTML styles with another computer or with a workgroup, you can do one of several things. You can e-mail the file to another user or you can put it on a disk; either way, you should instruct them to put it in the Library folder. Or, you can use the Site window to upload the file to a shared remote site.

To share an HTML style with other users on a remote site:

1. In the Site window, click on Connect or Refresh to connect to your remote site (**Figure 21.52**).

2. In the right pane, open the Library folder and single-click on the styles.xml file (**Figure 21.53**).

3. Click on Put to upload the file.

   or

   Click on Check In to upload the file and check it in with your username.

   Either way, the file will be uploaded to the remote site. If there is not yet a Library folder on the remote site, it will be created when the file is uploaded (**Figure 21.54**).

✔ Tips

- If you use Check In to upload the file, your copy of the file will become read-only. You can check out the styles.xml file again from the remote site to regain write access (so you can add and change styles), however, others won't be able to download the file.

- For more about uploading files, see Chapter 20. Earlier in this chapter, I cover design notes, which you can use to leave yourself or your team notes about the styles.xml file.

SHARING THE STYLES FILE

Using Dreamweaver with Content Management

Content management systems, affectionately known as CMS, can be a godsend to large workgroups that are trying to keep track of who touched what file when and whether it's ready for primetime. You must already have these tools installed in order to use them. (I bet you knew that.)

Using WebDav

WebDAV (pronounced Web Dave) stands for the Web-based Distributed Authoring and Versioning protocol. Two commercial examples include Apache and Microsoft IIS. When you work with WebDAV using Dreamweaver, you set up your remote site information so that WebDAV is your remote site, rather than your FTP or local network.

To set up your remote site info to work with WebDAV:

1. Open the Site Definition dialog box for the appropriate local site.

2. In the Category box at left, select Remote Info.

3. From the Access drop-down menu, select WebDAV. The dialog box will change appearance (**Figure 21.55**).

4. To set up automatic file check-out with Dave, select that checkbox.

5. Click on Settings. The WebDAV Connection dialog box will appear (**Figure 21.56**).

   The URL may use local server info, but it must include both the protocol and the port number for Dave. An example would be http://staging/WebDAV/home.

   Your username and password must be those you use with that server. Your email address will be attached to your check-out name.

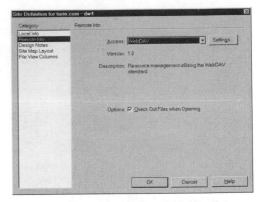

Figure 21.55 Select WebDAV from the Access drop-down menu in the Site Definition dialog box.

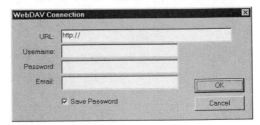

Figure 21.56 In the WebDAV Connection dialog box, specify the URL for the Web server that uses WebDAV.

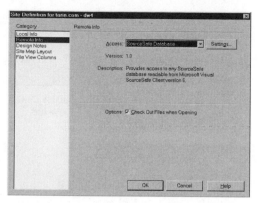

Figure 21.57 Select SourceSafe Database from the Access drop-down menu in the Site Definition dialog box.

6. Click on OK to save your settings, and OK again in the Site Definition dialog box. You're all ready to go. You can use Get, Put, and all the other features as usual, except you're using them with Dave's help.

Using Visual Source Safe Databases with Dreamweaver

Microsoft Visual Source Safe is a version control system for all sorts of code, including HTML, scripts, and images. It's a content-management database that supports file sharing, branching, and merging.

Dreamweaver 4 supports VSS client version 6. To use VSS with Dreamweaver on the Macintosh, you must have the MetroWerks SourceSafe version 1.1.0 client, and you can work with VSS version 5.0, but not 6.0.

When you work with VSS using Dreamweaver, you set up your remote site information so that VSS is your remote site, rather than your FTP or local network.

To set up your remote site info to work with VSS:

1. Open the Site Definition dialog box for the appropriate local site.

2. In the Category box at left, select Remote Info.

3. From the Access drop-down menu, select SourceSafe Database. The dialog box will change appearance (**Figure 21.57**).

4. To set up automatic file check-out with VSS, select that checkbox in the Options section.

continued on next page

5. Click on Settings. The Open SourceSafe Database dialog box will appear (**Figure 21.58**).

6. In the Database Path text box, type the address of the VSS database, or click Browse to select the database file. This file is the srcsafe.ini file used to initialize SourceSafe when you connect using the Site window.

7. In the Project text box, enter the name of the VSS Project that you want to use as the root folder for your remote site.

8. The username and password you enter should be those you use to log in to VSS. To save your password, select that checkbox.

9. Click on OK to save your settings, and OK again in the Site Definition dialog box. You're all ready to go. You can use Get, Put, and all the other features as usual, except you're using them on VSS.

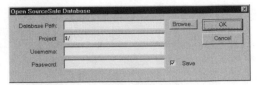

Figure 21.58 In the Open SourceSafe Database dialog box, specify the location of the VSS database file.

INDEX

INDEX

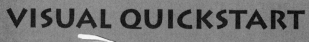